American Public Policy
Promise and Performance

Sixth Edition

B. Guy Peters
Maurice Falk Professor of American Government
University of Pittsburgh

CQ PRESS

A Division of Congressional Quarterly Inc.
Washington, D.C.

CQ Press
1255 22nd Street, N.W., Suite 400
Washington, D.C. 20037

202-729-1900; toll-free: 1-866-4CQ-PRESS (1-866-427-7737)

www.cqpress.com

Printed and bound in the United States of America

08   07   06   05   04   5   4   3   2   1

♾ The paper used in this publication exceeds the requirements of the American National Standard for Information Sciences—Permanence of Paper for Printed Library Materials, ANSI Z39.48-1992.

Cover design: Rachel Hegarty
Cover image: ©Bettmann/Corbis

Photo credits:
AP/Wide World Photos: 9, 58, 92, 132, 183, 213, 240, 277, 318, 341, 368, 415, 439, 451, 467
Reuters: 27, 100

Library of Congress Cataloging-in-Publication Data

Peters, B. Guy.
American public policy : promise and performance / B. Guy Peters.--
6th ed.
        p. cm.
Includes bibliographical references and index.
ISBN 1-56802-906-3 (alk. paper)
    1. United States--Politics and government. 2. Political
planning--United States. 3. Policy sciences. I. Title.
JK271 .P43 2004
320.6'0973--dc22
                                                        2003025300

Contents

PART TWO
The Making of Public Policy

PART THREE
Substantive Policy Issues

PART FOUR
Policy Analysis

Tables and Figures

Preface

PUBLIC POLICY IS THE FUNDAMENTAL reason that scholars and citizens should be concerned about government, whether in the United States or any other country. As much as we may find voting and elections entertaining, or are interested in the ways in which lobbyists cajole public officials, in the end the outcome of the political process is a set of policies that affects the lives of citizens, often in very profound ways. As Harold Lasswell argued almost seventy years ago, politics is about "who gets what." The policy choices of the United States are perhaps particularly important, given that the economic and military power of this single country establishes parameters within which many other political systems make their own policy choices.

At times public policies change rather rapidly and dramatically, and at times they persist for long periods with only incremental change. Likewise, the policy process itself may appear stable, yet it also undergoes slight changes in response to changing political ideas and the relative power of institutions and individuals within the process. Therefore, relatively frequent updates concerning both process and substance are required to capture the contemporary nature of the U.S. government and the dynamics of this extremely complex system for governing and making policy.

This book is an attempt to provide a rather comprehensive view of policy and policymaking in the United States. The first section describes the structure of the policymaking system and the process through which ideas and demands are converted into policy. While the "stages" model used in this analysis is generic, there are a number of important peculiarities in U.S. government that must be examined if we are to be able to understand how the system succeeds—and when it fails—in making choices. If nothing else, the multiple divisions caused by the separation of powers, federalism, and a decentralized bureaucracy tend to make the process more difficult than in other countries.

The second section examines a number of important policy areas. These policies are discussed primarily at the federal level, although state and local governments do have a significant impact in these areas as well. To do a detailed analysis of the role of each level of government would, however, require a much larger book. Likewise, although the policy areas included are important, there are others. Unfortunately I could not include everything in this one book.

The final section provides an introduction to two forms of policy analysis. One depends on economic assumptions and is an attempt to make government more efficient and cost effective. The other mode focuses on the normative element of public policy, an element of analysis often ignored when thinking about policy. Rather than asking questions of efficiency, normative analysis is concerned with equity and justice. Neither of these modes of analysis can provide a complete answer to the difficult question of what is good policy, but in combination they may begin to help readers develop an answer.

Although this is the sixth edition of *American Public Policy*, this is the first edition to be published with CQ Press. I appreciate their moving so quickly to publish this edition once the final arrangements were made with the previous publisher. I look forward to working with them in the future.

B. Guy Peters
Pittsburgh, Pa.
November 2003

PART ONE

The Nature of Public Policy

CHAPTER 1

What Is Public Policy?

GOVERNMENT IN THE UNITED STATES has grown from a small, simple "night watchman state" providing defense, police protection, tax collection, and some education into an immense network of organizations and institutions affecting the daily lives of all citizens in countless ways. The United States is not a welfare state in the sense of most European states, but there is now an extensive array of social and health programs that serve much of the population. The size and complexity of modern government make it necessary to understand what public policies are, how those policies are made and changed, and how to evaluate the effectiveness and morality of policies.

Government in the United States is large. Today its revenues account for one dollar in three of total national production. This money is rarely wasted; most of the money returns to citizens through a variety of cash-benefit programs or in the form of public services. Likewise, one working person in six is employed by government. But the range of activities of modern government in the United States is not confined to such simple measures as spending money or hiring workers. Governments also influence the economy and society through many less obvious instruments such as regulation, insurance, and loan guarantees.

Government in the United States today also is complex and is becoming more complex every day. The institutions of government are becoming more complicated and numerous. More public business is now conducted through public corporations and quasi-autonomous public bodies, and over 87,700 separate governments now exist in the United States, many of which provide a single service with little or no public oversight through elections.[1] There are also a number of increasingly complex relationships between the public and private sectors for the delivery of services, as the private and not-for-profit sectors are becoming heavily involved in delivering public services.[2] Also, the subject matter of government policy is more complex and technical than it was even a few years ago. Governments must make decisions about the risks of nuclear energy, the reliability of technologically sophisticated weapons systems, and the management of a huge economic system. Attempting to influence socioeconomic problems—poverty, homelessness, education—may be even more difficult than addressing problems arising in the physical and scientific world, given the absence of a proven method of solving social problems.[3] Even when the subject matter of policy is less complex, increasing requirements for participation and accountability make managing a public program a difficult undertaking—often more difficult than managing in the private sector.

This book is intended to help the reader understand the fundamental processes and content of public policy that underlie the size and complexity of American government. It is meant to increase knowledge about how public policies are made, what the policies of the United States are in certain areas, and what standards of evaluation should be applied to those policies. I begin with a discussion of the policy process in the United States—concentrating at the federal level—and the impact that the structures and procedures of that government have on the content of policies. I then discuss the means that professionals and citizens alike can use to evaluate the effects of public policies, and the methods that will enable them to decide what they want and can expect to receive from government.

Defining Public Policy

Mark Twain once commented that patriotism is the last refuge of fools and scoundrels. To some degree, "public policy" has become just such a refuge for some academic disciplines. As public policy studies are now popular, everything government does is labeled "policy." I adopt a somewhat more restrictive definition of public policy.

Stated most simply, public policy is the sum of government activities, whether pursued directly or through agents, as those activities have an influence on the lives of citizens. Operating within that definition, we can distinguish three separate levels of policy, defined by the degree to which they make real differences in the lives of citizens. At the first level, we have policy *choices*—decisions made by politicians, civil servants, or others granted authority and directed toward using public power to affect the lives of citizens. Congressmen, presidents, governors, administrators, and pressure groups, among others, make such policy choices. What emerges from all those choices is a policy that can be put into action. At the second level, we can speak of policy *outputs*—policy choices being put into action. Here the government is actually doing things: spending money, hiring people, or promulgating regulations that are designed to affect the economy and society. Outputs may be virtually synonymous with the term *program* as it is commonly used in government circles.[4]

Finally, at the third level, we have policy *impacts*—the effects that policy choices and policy outputs have on citizens, such as making them wealthier or healthier, or the air they breathe less polluted. These impacts may be influenced in part by other factors in the society—economic productivity, education, and the like—but they also reflect to some degree the success or failure of public policy choices and outputs. Also, these policy impacts may reflect the interaction of a number of different programs. Successful alleviation of poverty, for example, may depend upon a number of social programs, education, economic programs, and the tax system. If any of these programs does not perform well, it may be impossible for government, and the society that it represents, to reach its desired goals.

Several aspects of public policy require some explanation. First, although we are focusing on the central government in Washington, we must always remember that the United States is a federal system of government in which a large number of subnational governments also make decisions. Even when they attempt to cooperate, those levels of government often experience conflicts over policy. For example, attempts by the Clinton administration to enforce national standards for education encountered opposition from the states and from Congress, each with their own ideas about what those standards should be.[5] The same issues arose early in the George W. Bush administration, as there were continuing pressures for improving educational standards, resulting in the Educational Act of 2002 (No Child Left Behind) and a strong federal role in enforcing standards. Even within the federal government, the actions of one agency may conflict with those of another. The U.S. Department of Agriculture, for example, subsidizes the growing of tobacco, while the U.S. Office of the Surgeon General encourages citizens not to smoke.

Second, not all government policies are implemented by government employees. Many are actually implemented by private organizations or by individual citizens. We must understand this if we are to avoid an excessively narrow definition of public policy as concerning only those programs directly administered by a public agency. A number of agricultural, social, and health policies involve the use of private agencies operating with the sanction of, and in the name of, government. Even the cabin attendant on an airplane making an announcement to buckle seat belts and not to smoke is implementing a public policy. As government has begun to utilize an increasing number of alternative mechanisms, such as contracts, for implementation, these private-sector providers are becoming increasingly important actors in delivering public policy.

Even if a government is to implement a program through public employees, it may not act through its own employees. The federal government in particular depends on state and local governments to implement a large number of its programs, including major social programs such as Medicaid, the recent "workfare" reforms to the welfare system, and a good portion of environmental policy. The degree of control that the federal government can exercise in these instances may be as little, or even less, than when the program is delivered through private-sector actors, who often depend on government for contracts and loans and therefore may be very compliant with demands from Washington.

Third, and most important, we are concentrating on the effects of government choices on the lives of individuals within the society. The word *policy* is commonly used in a number of ways. In one usage it denotes a stated intent of government, as expressed in a piece of legislation or a presidential speech. Unfortunately, any number of steps are required to turn a piece of legislation into an operating program, and all too frequently significant changes in the intended effects of the program result from difficulties in translating ideas and intentions into actions. In this analysis we will place greater emphasis on the effects of policies than on the intentions of the individuals who formulated them. We must also have some degree of concern for the legislative process, which produces the good intentions that may or may not come to fruition.

Our definition recognizes the complexity and the interorganizational nature of public policy. Few policy choices are decided and executed by a single organization or even a single level of government. Instead, policies, in terms of their effects on the public, emerge from a large number of programs, legislative intentions, and organizational interactions that affect the daily lives of citizens. This conception of policy also points to the frequent failure of governments to coordinate programs, with the consequence that programs cancel out each other, or produce a costly duplication of effort.[6] The question about government posed many years ago by Harold Lasswell, "Who gets what?" is still central for understanding public policy.

The Instruments of Public Policy

Governments have a number of instruments through which they can influence society and the economy and can produce changes in the lives of citizens. For example, government can choose to provide education by directly supplying that service or by providing vouchers that parents can use to pay for their children's education (see Chapter 12). The choice of which instrument to employ in any particular instance may depend on the probable effectiveness of the instrument, its political palatability, the experiences of the policy designers, and national or organizational tradition. Further, some policy instruments may be effective in some circumstances but not in others. Unfortunately, governments do not yet have sufficient knowledge about the effects of their "tools," or the relationship of particular tools to particular policy instruments, to be able to make effective matches.[7] It appears that most choices are now made out of habit and familiarity, not out of certain knowledge of effectiveness.

Law

Law is a unique resource of government. It is not available to private actors who have access to the other instruments of policy discussed here.[8] Governments have the right to make authoritative decrees and to back up those decrees with the legitimate power of the state. In most instances, simply issuing a law is sufficient to produce compliance, but monitoring and enforcement are still crucial to the effectiveness of the instrument. Citizens may obey speeding laws most of the time, but the prospect of a policeman with a radar set makes compliance more probable. Citizens daily obey many laws without thinking about them, but police, tax collectors, and agencies monitoring environmental damage, occupational safety, and product safety (to name only a few) are also busy attempting to ensure compliance through their enforcement activities.

We should make several other points about the use of law as an instrument of public policy. First, laws are used as the means of producing the most important outputs of government: rights. Such laws are usually of a fundamental or constitutional nature and are central in defining the position of citizens in society. In the United States the fundamental rights of citizens are defined in the Constitution and its amendments, but rights also have been extended in a variety of other legislation. This extension has been most significant for the rights of nonwhites and women, as reflected in the passage of the Voting Rights Act of 1965, the Equal Employment Opportunity Act of 1972, and the Civil Rights Act of 1991. The Americans with Disabilities Act (1990) extended a variety of rights to people with various forms of disability and handicap, with the courts tending to expand the applicability of that law to groups, such as AIDS sufferers,[9] for whom it was perhaps not intended by the framers of the legislation.

Second, the United States uses laws to regulate economic and social conditions to a greater extent than most countries do. The United States is frequently cited as having a small public sector in comparison with other industrialized countries because of lower levels of taxing and spending. If, however, the effects of regulations are included, government in the United States approaches being as pervasive as European governments.[10] The costs of government's interventions in the United States tend to appear in the price of products, however, as much as in citizens' tax bills.[11] This indirect effect of intervention tends to be less visible to the average citizen than a tax and therefore is more palatable in a society that tends to be skeptical about government.

Third, law can be used to create burdens as well as benefits. This is certainly true for tax laws and is also true for legislation that mandates the recycling of metal or glass. Often a law that creates benefits for one group of citizens is perceived by others to be creating a burden; environmental laws satisfy conservationists but often impose costs on businesses. Any action of government requires some legal peg on which to hang, but the ability of a simple piece of paper to create both rights and obligations is one of the essential features of American public policy.

Services

Governments also provide a number of services directly to citizens, ranging from defense to education to recreation. In terms of employment, education is by far the largest directly provided public service, employing almost 9 million people. The Department of Defense employs just under another 3 million people, both military and civilian. Government tends to provide services when there is a need to ensure that the service is provided in a certain way (education) or where the authority of the state (policing) is involved. Further, services tend to be delivered directly to parts of the population that are less capable of making autonomous decisions on their own, such as children and the mentally impaired.

The direct provision of public services raises several questions, especially as there are continuing pressures for government to control expenditures and to "privatize."[12] An obvious question is whether the direct provision of services is the most efficient means of ensuring that a service is delivered to citizens. Could that service be contracted out instead? A number of public services have been contracted out to private corporations, including traditional government services such as firefighting, tax collection, and prisons.[13] Contracting out removes the problem of personnel management from government, a problem magnified by the tenure rights and pension costs of public employees under merit systems. Also, government tends to build a capacity to meet maximum demands for services such as fire protection and emergency medical care, resulting in an underutilization of expensive personnel and equipment. This over-capacity tendency can be corrected in part by contracting out.

Another interesting development in the direct provision of services is the use of quasi-governmental organizations to provide services.[14] There are some services that government does not want to undertake entirely but that require public involvement for financial or other reasons. The best example is Amtrak, a means of providing public subsidies for passenger train service in the face of declining rail service in the United States. Government may also choose quasi-governmental organizations for programs that require a great deal of coordination with private-sector providers of the same service, or when the service is in essence a marketable service. At an even greater degree of separation, governments also use not-for-profit organizations to provide public services, and the George W. Bush administration has pressed for wider use of such organizations, especially faith-based organizations.

Dwight Watson held Washington, D.C., police at bay for three days after driving his tractor into a pond on the National Mall in protest of dwindling tobacco subsidies. The North Carolina farmer blamed the federal government for the loss of the farm his family has owned for several generations.

Money

Governments also provide citizens, organizations, and other governments with money. Approximately 62 percent of all money collected in taxes by the federal government is returned to the economy as transfer payments to citizens. Transfers to citizens range from Social Security and unemployment benefits to payments to farmers to support commodity prices. Interest on the public debt is also a form of transfer payment. Another 12 percent of tax receipts is transferred to other levels of government to support their activities.

The use of money transfers to attempt to promote certain behaviors is in many ways an inefficient means for reaching policy goals. The money paid out in Social Security benefits, for example, is intended to provide the basics of life for the recipients, but nothing prevents those recipients from using it to buy food for their pets rather than for themselves. The claims about how Aid to Families with Dependent Children payments are used and abused are legion, if often inaccurate. Thus, while the direct provision of services is costly and requires hiring personnel and erecting buildings, many less expensive transfer programs are much less certain of reaching the individuals and achieving the goals for which they were intended.

Money dispersed to other levels of government can be restricted or unrestricted. Of the $120 billion given in 1999 to state and local governments, most was distributed as categorical grants, with an increasing proportion being given as block grants. Categorical grants channel resources more directly to the problems identified by the federal government as needing attention, but also they tend to centralize decision making about public policy in Washington.[15] Categorical grants also tend to encourage state and local spending through matching provisions and to create clienteles that governments may not be able to eliminate after the federal support has been exhausted. Although this pattern of funding was largely associated with social and economic programs, the Clinton administration's program for funding the hiring of additional policemen may create expectations among citizens that local governments will have to fulfill in the future.

The federal government has less control over the impact of block grants than over the effects of categorical grants.[16] Block grants allow greater latitude for state and local governments to determine their own priorities, but most still have some strings attached. Also, giving block grants to the states tends to concentrate power in state governments, rather than allowing local (especially city) governments to bargain with Washington directly. Given that state governments are, on average, more conservative than local governments—especially large city governments that need federal grant money the most—block grants have been a useful tool for Republican administrations, as well as for the Republican Congress.[17]

Taxes

The government giveth and the government taketh away. But the way in which it chooses to take away may be important in changing the distribution of burdens and benefits in society. In the United States we are familiar with tax "loopholes," or, more properly, *tax expenditures*.[18] The latter term is derived from the theory that granting tax relief for an activity is the same as subsidizing that activity directly through an expenditure program.[19] For example, in 1999 the federal government did not collect $54.5 billion in income tax payments because of mortgage-interest deductions, and another $18 billion because state and local property taxes were deductible. This is in many ways exactly the same as government subsidizing private housing in the same amounts, a sum far greater than the amount spent on public housing by all levels of government. The use of the tax system as a policy instrument as well as for revenue collection is perhaps even less certain in its effects than transfer payments, for the system is essentially providing incentives rather than mandating activities. Citizens have a strong incentive to buy a house, but there is no program to build houses directly. These instruments are, however, very cheap to administer, given that citizens make all the decisions and then file their own tax returns.

Taxes may also be used more directly to implement policy decisions. For example, there are proposals to substitute taxes on pollution for direct prohibitions and regulation of emissions. The logic is that such an action would establish a "market" in pollution; those firms willing to pay the price of polluting would be able to pollute, while those less willing (or, more importantly, less able) because of inefficient production means would have to alter their modes of production or go out of business. The use of market mechanisms is assumed to direct resources toward their most productive use, whereas regulations at times may inhibit production and economic growth. Critics argue that what is being created is a "market in death," when the only real solution to the problem is the prohibition or severe restriction of pollution.

Tax incentives are a subset of all incentives available to government to encourage or discourage activities. The argument for their use, as well expressed by Charles Schultze, is that private interests (e.g., avarice) can be used for public purposes.[20] If a system of incentives can be structured effectively, then demands on the public sector can be satisfied in a more efficient and inexpensive manner than through direct regulation. Clearly, this form of policy instrument is applicable to a rather narrow range of policies, mostly those now handled through regulation, but even in that limited range the savings in costs of government and in the costs imposed on society may be significant. The use of such incentives also conforms to traditional American ideas about limited government and the supremacy of individual choice.

Other Economic Instruments

Government has a number of other economic weapons at its disposal.[21] Governments supply credit for activities such as a farmer's purchase of land and supplies.[22] When it does not directly lend money, government may guarantee loans, thus making credit available (e.g., for student loans or FHA mortgages) where it might otherwise be denied. Governments can also insure certain activities and property. For example, federal flood insurance made possible the development of some lands along the coasts of the United States, thereby creating both wealth and environmental degradation. Almost all money in banks and thrift institutions is now protected by one of several insurance corporations within the federal government.

Although these instruments may be important to their beneficiaries and may influence the spending of large sums of money, they do not appear as large expenditures in most government accounting schemes. Thus, as with regulations and their costs, the true size of government in the United States may be understated by looking simply at expenditure and employment figures. In addition, the ability of these programs to operate "off budget" makes them not only less visible to voters but also more difficult for political leaders and citizens to control. Only when there are major problems, as in the savings-and-loan industry in the early 1990s, do government insurance or guarantee schemes make the news.

Suasion

When all other instruments of policy fail, governments can use moral suasion to attempt to influence society. Government as a whole or particular political officials are often in a good position to use such suasion because they can speak in the name of the public interest and make those who oppose them appear unpatriotic and selfish. As Theodore Roosevelt said, the presidency is a "bully pulpit." Suasion, however, is often the velvet glove disguising the mailed fist, for governments have formal and informal means of ensuring that their wishes are fulfilled. So when Lyndon Johnson "jawboned" steel industry officials to roll back a price increase, the patriotism of the steel officials was equaled by their fear of lost government contracts and Internal Revenue Service investigations of their corporate and personal accounts.

Suasion is an effective instrument as long as the people regard the government as a legitimate expression of their interests. There is evidence that the faith and trust of the American citizens in government is declining (see table 1.1) in response to the excesses of Vietnam, Watergate, the savings-and-loan crisis, Iran-*contra*, Whitewater, budget deficits, and so forth. As governments lose some of their legitimacy, their ability to use suasion naturally declines, pushing them toward more direct tools of intervention, which may lead to increases in government employment and taxation and perhaps to an accelerated downward spiral of government authority. One exception may be in times of war, as President George H.W. Bush showed during the Persian Gulf crisis. The second President Bush has also been able to use suasion and to manipulate powerful national symbols in the "war on terror."

The Effects of Tools

Governments have a number of instruments with which they attempt to influence the economy and society by distributing what burdens and benefits they have at their disposal. The most fundamental benefits governments have to confer are rights. These are largely legal and participatory, but with the growth of

TABLE 1.1 Public Perception of Honesty and Ethics of Various Professions
(percentages of "Very High" and "High" responses combined)

	1976	*1981*	*1985*	*1988*	*1990*	*1992*	*1995*
Pharmacists	n.a.	59	65	66	62	66	66
Clergy	n.a.	63	67	60	57	54	56
Medical doctors	56	51	50	53	52	52	54
College teachers	49	45	53	54	51	50	52
Engineers	49	48	53	48	50	48	53
Policemen	n.a.	44	47	47	49	42	41
Journalists	33	32	31	23	30	27	23
Bankers	n.a.	39	38	32	32	27	27
Lawyers	25	25	27	22	22	18	16
Business executives	20	19	23	16	25	18	16
Local officeholders	n.a.	14	18	14	21	15	21
Real estate agents	n.a.	14	15	13	16	14	15
Labor union leaders	12	14	13	14	15	14	14
U.S. senators	19	20	23	19	24	13	12
State officeholders	n.a.	12	15	11	17	11	15
Congressmen	14	15	20	16	20	11	10
Car salesmen	n.a.	6	5	6	6	5	5

Source: Gallup Poll Monthly, November 1995, 31.

large entitlement programs that distribute cash benefits to citizens, rights may now be said to include those programs as well.

Governments also distribute goods and services. They do this directly by giving money to people who fall into certain categories (e.g., unemployed) or by directly providing public services such as education. They also do this less directly by structuring incentives for individuals to behave in certain ways and to make one economic decision rather than another. Governments also distribute goods and services through private organizations and through other governments in an attempt to reach their policy goals. A huge amount of money flows through the public sector, where it is shuffled around and given to different people.[23] The net effect is not as great as might be expected, given the number of large expenditure and revenue programs in operation in the United States, but that effect is to make the distribution of income and wealth somewhat more equal than that produced through the market.[24]

Finally, governments distribute burdens as well as benefits. They do this through taxation and through programs such as conscription for military service.[25] Like expenditures, taxes are distributed broadly across the population, with state and local taxes tending to be collected from an especially broad spectrum of the population. Even the poorest citizens have to pay sales taxes on many things they purchase, and they must pay Social Security taxes as soon as they begin to work. In other words, everyone in society benefits from the activities of government, but everyone also pays the price.

The Environment of Public Policy

Several characteristics of the political and socioeconomic environment in the United States influence the nature of policies adopted and the effects of those policies on citizens. Policy is not constructed in a vacuum; it is the result of the interaction of all these background factors with the desires and decisions of those who make policies. Neither individual decision makers nor the nature of "the system" appears capable alone of explaining policy outcomes. Instead, policy emerges from the interaction of a large number of forces, many of which are beyond the control of decision makers.

Conservatism

American politics is relatively conservative in policy terms. The social and economic services usually associated with the mixed-economy welfare state are generally less developed in the United States than those in Europe, and to some extent they declined in the 1990s. This is especially true of government involvement in the management and ownership of economic enterprises such as public utilities and basic industries such as coal and steel. In general, this is the result of the continuing American belief in limited government. As Anthony King has said: "The State plays a more limited role in America than elsewhere because Americans, more than other people, want it to play a limited role."[26]

Several points should be brought out in opposition to the description of American government as a welfare state laggard. First, the government of the United States regulates and controls the economy in ways not common in Europe, and in some areas, such as consumer product safety, it appears to be ahead of European governments. If the effects of regulation are tabulated along with more direct public interventions into the economy, the U.S. government appears more similar to that of other industrialized countries. We also have a tendency to forget about the activities of state and local governments, which frequently provide gas, electricity, water, and even banking services to their citizens.

Also, it is easy to underestimate the extent of the changes in public expenditures and the public role in the economy that followed World War II. Let us take 1948 as the starting point. Even in that relatively peaceful year, defense expenditures were 29 percent of total public expenditures and 36 percent of federal expenditures. At the height of the Cold War in 1957, defense expenditures were 62 percent of federal expenditures and 37 percent of total public expenditures. In contrast, 1999 defense expenditures were 8 percent of total expenditures and 14 percent of federal expenditures. Spending on social services—including education, health, social welfare, and housing—increased from 7 percent of total spending in 1948 to over 21 percent in 1999. Even for the federal government, social spending now accounts for over 50 percent of total expenditures. American government and its policies may be conservative, but they are less so than commonly believed, and less so in the early twenty-first century than in the 1950s.

It is also easy to overestimate the conservatism of the American public because Americans are often very ambivalent about government.[27] Lloyd A. Free and Hadley Cantril described Americans as "ideological conservatives" and "operational liberals"[28] because they tend to respond negatively to the idea of a large and active government but positively to individual public programs (e.g., Social Security, police protection, and education). For example, a majority of voters leaving the polls in California after voting in favor of Proposition 13 to cut taxes severely in that state were in favor of reducing public expenditures for only one program—social welfare. For most programs mentioned by the researchers, larger percentages of respondents wanted to increase expenditures than wanted to reduce them.[29]

The huge federal deficit is to some degree a function of this set of mismatched ideas about government; politicians can win votes both by advocating reducing taxes and by advocating spending for almost any program. For example, surveys show that the majority of Americans believe that they pay too much tax and that the federal government wastes almost half of all the tax money it collects.[30] On the other hand, there are generally majorities in favor of a variety of social programs, especially those for the more "deserving poor"—the elderly, unemployed workers whose companies have closed, divorced and widowed mothers, and the like.

Participation

Another attitudinal characteristic that influences public policy in the United States is the citizen's desire to participate directly in government. A natural part of democratic politics, public participation has a long history in American politics—the cry of "No taxation without representation" was essentially a demand to participate. More recently, populist demands for participation and the rights of "the little man" to shape policy have been powerful political forces. In a large and decentralized political system that deals with complex issues, however, effective participation may be difficult to achieve. The low rate of participation in most elections appears to indicate that citizens do not consider the voting process a particularly efficacious means of affecting government. Further, many experts believe that citizens are not sufficiently informed to make decisions about such complex technical issues as nuclear power. Still, citizens argue that they should and must have a role in those decisions.

Government has increasingly fostered participation. The laws authorizing community action in 1964 were the first to mandate "maximum feasible participation" of the affected communities in renewal decisions. Similar language was then written into a number of other social and urban programs. Also, the regulatory process poses requirements for notification and participation that, in addition to their positive effects, have slowed the process considerably. Government also has been allowing more direct participation in making rules, with the affected interests allowed to negotiate among themselves the rules that will govern a policy area (see pp. 86–88).

The desire for effective participation has to some degree colored popular impressions of government. Citizens tend to demand local control of policy and to fear the "federal bulldozer." Although objective evidence may be to the contrary, citizens tend to regard the federal government as less benevolent and less efficient than local governments. The desire to participate and to exercise local control then produces a tendency toward decentralized decision making and a consequent absence of national integration. In many policy areas, such decentralization is benign or actually beneficial. In others, it may produce inequities and inefficiencies. But the ideological and cultural desires for local control may override practical arguments.

Ideas about participation in the United States also have at times had a strong strand of populism, meaning the belief that large institutions—whether in government, business, or even labor—are inimical to the interests of the people. Further, there is a belief that those institutions are structured to prevent effective participation. Those institutions have, however, themselves begun to respond to demands for effective participation, and *empowerment* has become one of the more commonly used words in government circles.[31] Balancing popular demands for greater direct democracy with the demands of governing an immense land mass with over 250 million citizens will continue to be a challenge for American democracy.

Pragmatism

The reference to ideological desires seemingly contradicts another cultural characteristic of American policymaking, pragmatism—the belief that one should do whatever works rather than follow a basic ideological or philosophical system. American political parties have tended to be centrist and nonideological; perhaps the surest way to lose an election in the United States is to discuss philosophies of government. Ronald Reagan to some degree questioned that characteristic of American politics, interjecting an ideology of government that was to some extent continued by George H.W. Bush. Bill Clinton's self-description as a "new Democrat," and George W. Bush's claim to be a "compassionate conservative" represented a return to greater pragmatism, which tends to make American politics a clash of platitudes and narrow programmatic issues rather than of ideas such as Marxism or fascism—probably mercifully.

One standard definition of what will work in government is "that which is already working," and so policies tend to change slowly and incrementally.[32] The basic centrist pattern of political parties tends to produce agreement on most basic policies, and each successive president tends to jiggle and poke policy but not to attempt significant change. A crisis such as the Great Depression or a natural political leader such as Reagan may introduce some radical changes, but stability and gradual evolution are the most acceptable patterns of policymaking. Indeed, American government is different after Reagan, but not as different as he had hoped or intended,[33] nor has President George W. Bush yet been able to change but so much of the system, This persistence of policies can be typified by the continuing battle over reform of Social Security (see Chapter 11)—there has been concern about the financial soundness of this crucial program for a number of years but no agreement on the direction or degree of change.

The pragmatism of American politics appears to be declining. Several issues over which there appears to be little room for compromise have split the American public. The obvious example is the abortion issue, which intruded into the debate over national health care reform, with some members of Congress refusing to support any bill that paid for abortions and another group opposing any bill that did not.[34] Other issues of a moral or religious or ethnic basis also have taken more prominent places in the political debate, leaving fewer possibilities for compromise or pragmatic resolution of disputes. The religious right has become especially important in the internal politics of the Republican Party, as groups such as the Christian Coalition and the Family Research Council have taken over at local and even state levels and attempted to shape national party policy.[35]

Wealth

Another feature of the environment of American public policy is the great wealth of the country. Although it is no longer the richest country in the world in per capita terms, the United States is the largest single economy in the world by a large margin. This wealth permits great latitude for action by American government, so even the massive deficits experienced in the 1980s and 1990s (and recurring) have not required government to alter its folkways. The federal government can continue funding a huge variety of programs and policy initiatives, despite its own efforts to control the size of the budget (see Chapter 6).

This great wealth is threatened by two factors. First, the U.S. economy is increasingly dependent on the rest of the world. This is apparent in financial and monetary policy as the United States becomes the world's largest debtor, but it is true especially in terms of dependence on raw materials from abroad. We are familiar with this nation's dependence on foreign oil, but the economy is also heavily dependent on other countries for a range of commodities necessary to maintain its high standard of living. The American economy historically has been relatively self-sufficient, but increasing globalization in recent decades has emphasized its relationship to the world economy.[36]

Wealth in the United States is also threatened by the relatively slow rate of productivity growth and capital investment. The average American worker is still productive but has lost some ground to workers in many other countries. Also, many U.S. factories are outmoded, so competition on the world market is difficult. These factors, combined with relatively high wages, mean that many manufacturing jobs have gone overseas, and more are likely to do so. The U.S. government has had to borrow abroad to fund its deficits, and we also have chronic balance-of-payments problems because of a relative inability to export. These international trade problems are not often direct domestic concerns of American politicians, other than a few such as Representative Richard Gephardt, D–Mo., but they do affect the ability of the nation to spend money for the programs that many politicians and citizens want.

Diversity

The American society and economy are also diverse, which provides a great deal of richness and strength to the country as well as real policy problems. One of the most obvious diversities is the uneven distribution of income and wealth in the society. Even with the significant social expenditures mentioned earlier, approximately 35 million people in the United States live below the poverty line (see Chapter 11). This persistence of poverty in the midst of plenty remains perhaps the most fundamental policy problem for the United States, if for no other reason than it affects so many other policy areas, including health care, housing, education, crime, and race relations. Even among those citizens who are not poor, there is a growing concentration of income and wealth in the very affluent stratum at the top of society that may undermine confidence in the economic and social justice of the political system.

Diversity of racial and linguistic backgrounds is another significant factor affecting policy in the United States. The underlying problems of social inequality and racism persist despite many attempts to correct them. The concentration of minority-group members in urban areas, the continuing influx of immigrants, and the unyielding economic distress of some cities all combine to exacerbate these underlying problems. Again, this diversity affects a variety of policy areas, especially education. Race in particular pervades policymaking and politics in the United States, and this fundamental fact conditions our understanding of education, poverty, and human rights.[37]

The social and economic characteristics of the country taken as a whole are also diverse. The United States is both urban and rural, both industrial and agricultural, both young and old. It is a highly educated society with several million illiterates; it is a rich country with millions of people living in poverty. In at least one state (California) there is already no majority ethnic group, and in a few generations that may be true for the country as a whole. American policymakers cannot concentrate on a single economic class or social group but must provide something for everyone if the interests of the society as a whole are to be served. But serving that whole range of social interests forces government to spend for other purposes the resources that would be required to rectify the worst inequalities of income and opportunity.

World Leadership

Finally, the United States is an economic, political, and military world leader. Since the collapse of the Soviet Union, it is the only remaining superpower. If America sneezes, the world still catches cold because the sheer volume of the American economy is so important in influencing world economic conditions. Also, despite the upheaval in global political alignments, the world still expects military leadership for the West to come from the United States. The initial failure of the world to make a systematic response to the war in former Yugoslavia was due in large part to American diffidence on the subject; the eventual American involvement produced an effective response. The United States also has become a leader in international bargaining and negotiation, as Camp David and the subsequent Middle East peace accords demonstrated, although the absence of an effective American role in the Palestinian intifada in 2001–2002 helped perpetuate that violence.

The position as world leader imposes burdens on American policymakers. This continues to be true of defense policy even after the end of the Cold War; the role of peacekeeper required a good deal of military might even before the "war on terror" escalated military spending. Burdens also arise from the need to provide diplomatic and political leadership. The U.S. dollar, despite some battering and significant competition, is still a major reserve currency in the world economy, and this status imposes additional economic demands on the country. The role of world leader is an exhilarating one, but it is also one filled with considerable responsibility and economic costs. Indeed, the globalization of the economic system is making many Americans rethink the desirability of playing such a major international role.

The policies that emerge from all these influences are filtered through a large and extremely complex political system. The characteristics of that government and the effects of those institutional characteristics on policies are the subject of the next chapter. Policy choices must be made, and thousands are made each day in government; the sum of those choices, rather than any one, will decide who gets what as a result of public policies. In the United States more than in most countries, there are a number of independent decision makers whose choices must be factored into the final determination of policy.

Summary

American public policy is the result of complex interactions among a number of complex institutions. It also involves a wide range of ideas and values about what the goals of policy should be and what are the best means of reaching desired goals. In addition to the interactions that occur within the public sector, there are a number of interactions with an equally complex society and economy. Indeed, society is playing an increasingly important role in policymaking and implementation, with reforms in the public sector placing increasing emphasis on the capacity of the private sector to implement, if not make, public policy.

Making policy requires obtaining some form of social and political consensus among all these forces. There does not have to be full agreement on all the values and all the points of policy, but enough common ground must be found to pass and implement legislation. Building those coalitions can extend beyond reaching ideological agreement to include bargaining and "horse-trading" that in turn assigns a central role to individual policy entrepreneurs and brokers. There is so much potential for blockage and delay in the American political system that some driving force may be needed to make the system function.

CHAPTER 2

The Structure of Policymaking in American Government

THE STRUCTURES THROUGH WHICH public policy is formulated, legitimated, and implemented in the United States are extremely complex. It could be argued that American government has a number of structures but no real organization, for the fundamental characteristic of these structures is the absence of effective coordination and control. This absence of central control is largely intentional. The framers of the Constitution were concerned about the potential for tyranny of a powerful central executive within the federal government; they also feared the control of the central government over the constituent states. The system of government the framers designed divides power among the three branches of the central government, and further between the central government and state and local governments. As the system of government has evolved, it has become divided even further, as individual policy domains have been able to gain substantial autonomy from central coordination. To understand American policymaking, therefore, we must understand the extent of fragmentation that exists in this political system and the (relatively few) mechanisms devised to control that fragmentation and enhance coordination.

The fragmentation of American government does present some advantages. First, having a number of decision makers involved in every decision should reduce errors, as all must agree before a proposal can become law or be implemented as an operating program, and there will be full deliberation. Also, the existence of multiple decision makers should permit greater innovation both in the federal government and in state and local governments. And, as the framers intended, policymaking power is diffused, reducing the capacity of one central government to run roughshod over the rights of citizens or the interests of socioeconomic groups. For citizens, the numerous points of access to policymaking permit losers at one level of government, or in one institution, to become winners at another point in the process.

Americans also pay a price for this lack of policy coherence and coordination. It is sometimes difficult to accomplish *anything*, and elected politicians with policy ideas find themselves thwarted by the large number of decision points in the policymaking system. The policymaking situation in the United States in the 1980s and 1990s was described as "gridlock," in which the different institutions blocked each other from developing and enforcing policies.[1] The crisis provoked by the events of 11 September 2001 eliminated this gridlock for a short period, but it soon returned—even in some aspects of national security. Likewise, programs may cancel each other out as, for example, progressive (if decreasingly so) federal taxes and regressive state and local taxes combine to produce a tax system in which most people pay about the same proportion of their income as tax, or as the surgeon general's antismoking policies and the Department of Agriculture's tobacco subsidies attempt to please both pro- and antitobacco advocates.[2] The apparent inability or unwillingness of policymakers to choose among options means that policies will be incoherent and the process seemingly without any closure, and that decisions may cancel each other out. It also means that because potential conflicts are resolved by offering every interest in society some support from the public sector, taxes and expenditures are higher than they might otherwise be.

I have already mentioned the divisions that exist in American government. I now look at the more important dimensions of that division and the ways in which they act and interact to affect policy decisions and real policy outcomes for citizens. "Divided government" and "gridlock" have become standard descriptions of American government, and the impact of these divisions, as well as that of federalism, must be considered in analyzing the way in which policy emerges from this political system. Further, we need to be careful to understand the extent to which gridlock really exists, as more than simply a convenient description of institutional conflict.

Federalism

The most fundamental division in American government traditionally has been federalism, or the constitutional allocation of governmental powers between the federal and state governments. This formal allocation at once reserves all powers not specially granted to the federal government to the states (Ninth and Tenth Amendments) and establishes the supremacy of federal law when there are conflicts with state and local law (Article 6). Innumerable court cases and, at least in part, one civil war have resulted from this somewhat ambiguous division of powers among levels of government.

By the first years of the twenty-first century American federalism has changed significantly from the federalism described in the Constitution. The original constitutional division of power assumed that certain functions of government would be performed entirely by the central government and that other functions would be carried out by state or local governments. In this "layer cake" federalism, or "separated powers model," the majority of public activities were to be performed by subnational governments, leaving a limited number of functions, such as national defense and minting money, as the responsibility of the federal government.[3]

As the activities of government at all levels expanded, the watertight separation of functions broke down, and federal, state, and local governments became involved in many of the same activities. The layer cake then was transformed into a "marble cake," with the several layers of government still distinct, although no longer horizontally separated from one another. This form of federalism, however, still involved intergovernmental contacts through central political officials. The principal actors were governors and mayors, and intergovernmental relations remained on the level of high politics, with the representatives of subnational governments acting almost as ambassadors from sovereign governments, and as supplicants for federal aid. Furthermore, in this form of federalism the state government retained its role as intermediary between the federal government and local governments.

Federalism evolved further from a horizontal division of activities into a set of vertical divisions. Whereas functions were once neatly compartmentalized by level of government, the major feature of "picket fence" federalism is the development of policy subsystems defined by policy rather than level of government.[4] Thus, major decisions about health policy are made by specialized networks involving actors from all levels of government and from the private sector. Those networks, however, may be relatively isolated from other subsystems making decisions about highways, education, or whatever. The principal actors in these subsystems frequently are not political leaders but administrators and substantive policy experts. Local health departments work with state health departments and with the Department of Health and Human Services (HHS) in Washington in making health policy, and these experts are not dependent on the intervention of political leaders to make the process function. This form of federalism is as much administrative as it is political, and it is driven by expertise as much as by political power.

In many ways, it makes little sense to discuss federalism in its original meaning; it has been argued that contemporary federalism is as much façade as picket fence. A term such as *intergovernmental relations* more accurately describes the complex crazy quilt of overlapping authority and interdependence among levels of government than does a more formal, constitutional term such as *federalism*.[5]

In addition to being more oriented toward administrative issues than high politics, contemporary intergovernmental relations is more functionally specific and lacks the coherence that might result if higher political officials were obliged to be involved in the principal decisions. Thus, like much of the rest of American politics, intergovernmental relations often now lacks the mechanisms that could generate effective policy control and coordination.

Despite the complexity, overlap, and incoherence that exist in intergovernmental relations, one can still argue that centralization of control in the federal system has increased.[6] The dependence of state and local governments on federal financial support for their services has been variable over the past several decades. The Reagan administration reduced federal support for state and local activities, especially social services, but the level of federal support has been creeping back upwards (see table 2.1). With financing has come increased federal control over local government activities. In some cases that control is absolute, as when the federal government mandates equal access to education for the handicapped or establishes water-quality standards for sewage treatment facilities. In other instances the controls on state and local governments are more conditional, based on the acceptance of a grant; if a government accepts the money, it must accept the controls accompanying that money.

In general, the number and importance of mandates on state and local governments, and the number of conditions attached to those grants, have been increasing. For example, the Department of Health and Human Services threatened to cut off funding for immunization and other public health programs in states that did not implement restrictions on procedures performed by doctors and dentists with AIDS. Even the existence of many federal grant programs may be indicative of a subtle control from the center, inasmuch as they direct the attention, and especially the money, of local governments in directions they might not otherwise have chosen.

In addition to controls exercised through the grant process, the federal government has increased its controls over subnational governments through intergovernmental regulation and mandating. These regulations require the subnational government to perform a function such as wastewater treatment, whether or not there is federal money available to subsidize the activity. These regulations are certainly intrusive and can be expensive for state and local governments. Even when the mandates are not expensive and are probably effective, such as the requirement that states raise the minimum drinking age to twenty-one or lose 5 percent of their federal highway money, they can still be perceived as "federal blackmail" of the states.[7] Even the Reagan and George H.W. Bush administrations, dedicated to restoring the balance in favor of the states in federalism, found mandates an almost irresistible means for implementing their policy goals.

Table 2.1 Changing Levels of Federal Grants-in-Aid to State and Local Governments

	1970	1980	1985	1990	1995	1998	2000
Total Amount ($ million)	24,065	91,385	105,852	135,325	224,991	246,128	284,659
Percentage of State and Local Expenditures	29.1	39.9	29.6	25.2	31.5	30.3	31.3

One part of the "Contract with America" promoted by the incoming Republican majority in Congress in 1994 was to end unfunded federal mandates, and this assault on mandates was the first section of the "contract" enacted into law. In particular, the Unfunded Mandates Reform Act of 1995 requires the Congressional Budget Office to estimate the mandated costs in legislation reported out of committee in Congress. This provision by no means outlaws federal mandates, but it does require that members of Congress at least know what they are doing to the states and localities if they pass the legislation. Also, this reform act did not in any way affect existing mandates, nor will the federal government have to pay the bill for those mandates. In practice conservatives believe that the legislation has been largely toothless,[8] while liberals believe that environmental and consumer standards are in danger of being undermined. The shift from mandates to suggestions to control drunk-driving in the 1998 highways bill may indicate something of the shift in attitudes about mandates— there is still some attempt to impose federal priorities, but mostly through suasion rather than through direct commands.

One complicating factor for intergovernmental relations has been the proliferation of local governments in the United States. As fiscal restrictions on local governments have caused problems for mayors and county commissioners, a number of new local governments have been created to circumvent those restrictions. States frequently restrict the level of taxation or bonded indebtedness of local governments, but when a local government reaches its legal limit, it may simply create a special authority to undertake some functions formerly performed by the general-purpose local authority. For example, as Cleveland faced severe fiscal problems in 1979 and 1980, it engaged in a "city garage sale" in which it sold its sewer system and transportation system to special-purpose local authorities. The fiscal crisis in New York in the early 1990s prompted the city, and even the state, to sell off facilities such as roads and prisons to special-purpose authorities.[9]

During the 1980s and 1990s, an average of almost 500 local governments were created every year, primarily special districts to provide services such as transportation, water, sewerage, fire protection, and other traditional local government services.[10] These new special-purpose governments multiply the problems of coordination and may frustrate citizens who want to control the level of taxation but find that every time they limit the power of one government, a new one is created with more fiscal powers. The new forms of local governments also present problems of democratic accountability. The leaders of special-purpose governments often are not elected, and the public can influence their actions only indirectly through the general-purpose local governments (cities and counties) that appoint the boards of the special-purpose authorities.[11]

The Reagan and George H.W. Bush administrations attempted to reverse some of the historic course of centralization in federalism. One approach was to reduce the amounts spent for intergovernmental grants, especially general-purpose subsidies for subnational governments. Their strategies also involved eliminating a number of categorical (program) grants and providing more federal grants to subnational governments as large block grants to the states. By providing for all programs in a broad policy area, such as maternal and child health or community development, these grants at once give state governments power over local (especially city) governments and provide the state governments with more capacity to make decisions about how the money will be spent.

The economic circumstances of the late 1980s and early 1990s—rapidly mounting federal deficits and the then-healthy state treasuries—tended to push power back toward the states.[12] The recession of the early 1990s ended public surpluses in almost all states and turned eyes in state capitols back toward Washington and the incoming Democratic administration. The Clinton administration, however, proved to be as decentralizing as most previous Republican administrations, and perhaps even more so. For example, the welfare reform passed in 1996 was a major decentralization of power to the states, and the general pattern of policy change was to increase the powers of states and localities vis-à-vis Washington. President Clinton's experience as a governor and his natural inclinations, in conjunction with those of the Republican Congress, pushed power to the states. President George W. Bush also had been a governor and brought a decentralizing agenda with him to the White House, but the events of September 11, 2001, tended to move power back toward Washington more clearly than at any time since the 1960s.

Despite those earlier trends, the American federal system still centralizes power more than was planned when the federal system was formed. The grant system has been purchasing a more centralized form of government, although the shift in power appears to have resulted less from power-hungry federal bureaucrats and politicians than from the need to standardize many basic public services, and the need to promote greater equality for minorities. Further, even if programs are intended to be managed with "no strings attached," there is a natural tendency, especially in Congress, to demand the right to monitor the expenditure of public funds to ensure that those funds are used to obtain desired goals. In an era in which the accountability of government is an increasingly important issue, monitoring is likely to increase in intensity, even when a Republican Congress is in place to stress the need to limit federal power.

Separation of Powers

The second division of American government exists within the federal government itself and, incidentally, within most state and local governments as well. The Constitution distributes the powers of the federal government among three branches, each capable of applying checks and balances to the other two. In addition to providing employment for constitutional lawyers, this division of power has a substantial impact on public policies. In particular, the number of "veto points" in the federal government alone makes initiating any policy difficult and preventing change relatively easy.[13] It also means, as I mentioned when discussing the incoherence of American public policy, that the major task in making public policy is forming a coalition across a number of different in-

President Bush's chosen envoy to Iraq, Paul Bremer (front left) greets (from left to right) Patrick Leahy, D-Vt.; Ted Stevens, R-Alaska; and Pete Domenici, R-N.M., prior to testifying before the Senate Appropriations Committee in support of Bush's request for $87 billion to maintain military and reconstruction efforts in Iraq and Afghanistan.

stitutions and levels of government. Without "legislating together" in such a coalition, either nothing will happen or the intentions of a policymaker will be modified substantially in the policy process.[14] The United States is not a tightly administered political system in which one actor makes a decision and all other actors must fall neatly into line. This country has an intensely political and highly complex policymaking system in which initiatives must be shepherded through the process step by step if anything positive is to occur.

The president, Congress, and the courts are constitutionally designated institutions that must agree to a policy before it can be fully legitimated. The bureaucracy, however, although it is only alluded to in the Constitution, is now certainly a force in the policy process with which elected politicians must contend. Despite its conservative and obstructionist image, the bureaucracy is frequently the institution most active in promoting policy change, given government workers' close connections with the individuals and interests to which they provide services.[15] Further, the bureaucracy is given the latitude to elaborate congressional legislation, as well as to adjudicate the application of laws within each policy area.[16]

The bureaucracy, or more properly the individual agencies of which it is composed, has interests that can be served through legislation. The desired legislation may only expand the budget of the agency, but it usually has a broader public policy purpose as well. Administrative agencies can, if they wish, also impede policy change or even block it entirely. Almost every elected or appointed politician has experienced delaying tactics by nominal subordinates who disagree with a policy choice and want to wait until the next election or cabinet change to see if someone with more compatible policy priorities will come into office. The permanence of the "bureaucrats," and their command of technical details and of the procedural machinery, provide bureaucratic agencies much more power over public policies than one would assume from reading formal descriptions of government institutions. It has become increasingly evident that agencies may drive the congressional agenda almost as much as Congress shapes the agenda of the agencies.[17]

The institutional separation in American government has led to a number of critiques based upon the concept of "divided government."[18] The argument is that American government is incapable of being the decisive governance system required in the twenty-first century, and that some means must be found of generating coherent decisions. This has been especially true when the two major institutions have been controlled by different political parties, as they were during the Reagan and George H.W. Bush presidencies. The early days of the Clinton presidency indicated that even when the same party controls both branches there are still enough differences within parties, and enough institutional rivalry, to make cooperation difficult.[19] After the defection of one Republican senator,

George W. Bush also faced one house of Congress controlled by the opposition party, although the events of September 11 created at least a short period of partisan cooperation. Despite the impacts of divided government, David Mayhew, Charles O. Jones, and other scholars have argued that the system is capable of making decisions and even of rapid policy innovation, and that it can govern effectively.[20]

Whether the policymaking system is efficient or not, one principal result of the necessity to form coalitions across a number of institutions is the tendency to produce small, incremental changes rather than a major revamping of policies.[21] This might be best described as policymaking by the lowest common denominator. The need to involve and placate all four institutions within the federal government—including the many component groups of individuals within each—and, perhaps, state and local governments as well, means that only rarely can there be more than minor changes in the established commitments to clients and producer groups if the policy change is to be successful.[22] The resulting pattern of incremental change has been both praised and damned. It has been praised for providing stability and limiting the errors that might result from more significant shifts in policy. If only small policy changes are made, and these changes do not stray far from previously established paths, it is unlikely that major mistakes will be made.

The jiggling and poking of policies characteristic of incremental change is perfectly acceptable if the basic patterns of policy are also acceptable, but in some areas of policy, such as health care and mass transportation, a majority of Americans have said (at least in polls) that they would like some significant changes from the status quo.[23] The existing system of policymaking appears to have great difficulty in producing the major changes desired; if anything the increasing partisanship in Congress has made making change even more difficult. In addition, the reversibility of small policy changes, assumed to be an advantage of incrementalism, is often overstated.[24] Once a program is implemented, a return to the conditions that existed before the policy choice is often difficult. Clients, employees, and organizations are created by any policy choice, and they usually will exert powerful pressures for the continuation of the program.

The division of American government by the constitutional separation-of-powers doctrine represents a major institutional confrontation at the center of the federal government. Conflicts between the president and Congress over such matters as war powers, executive privilege, and the budget represent conflicts over those manifest issues as well as a testing and redefinition of the relative powers of institutions. Is the modern presidency inherently imperial, or is it still subject to control by Congress and the courts? Does too much checking by each institution over the others generate gridlock and indecision? Likewise, can the unelected Supreme Court have as legitimate a role as a rule-making body in the political system, as do the elected Congress and president? Further, do the regulations made by the public bureaucracy really have the same standing in law as the legislation passed by Congress or decrees coming from the court system? These questions posed by the separation-of-powers doctrine influence substantive policy as well as relationships among the institutions.

Subgovernments

A third division within American government cuts across institutional lines within the federal government and links it directly to the "picket fence" of federalism. The results of this division have been described variously as "iron triangles," "cozy little triangles," "whirlpools," and "subgovernments."[25] The underlying phenomenon described by these terms is that the federal government rarely acts as a unified institution making integrated policy choices, but tends instead to endorse the decisions made by portions of the government. Each functional policy area tends to be governed as if it existed in splendid isolation from the remainder of government, and frequently the powers and legitimacy of government are used for the advancement of individual or group interests in society, rather than for a broader public interest.[26]

Three principal actors are involved in the iron triangles still so relevant for explaining policymaking in the United States. The first is the interest group, which wants something from government, usually a favorable policy decision, and must attempt to influence the institutions that can act in its favor. Fortunately for the interest group, it usually need not influence all of Congress or the entire executive branch, but only the relatively small portion concerned with its particular policy area. For example, tobacco growers who want continued or increased crop supports need not influence the entire Department of Agriculture but only those within the Agricultural Stabilization and Commodity Service who are directly concerned with their crop. Likewise, in Congress (although the heightened politicization of the smoking issue requires a somewhat different strategy) they need only influence the Tobacco Subcommittee of the House of Representatives Agriculture Committee, the Senate Subcommittee on Agricultural Production and Stabilization of Prices, and the Rural Development, Agriculture, and Related Agencies Subcommittees of the Appropriations Committees in the Senate and House. In addition to the usual tools of information and campaign funds, interest groups have an important weapon at their disposal: votes. They represent organizations of interested individuals and can influence, if not deliver, votes for a congressman. Interest groups also have research staffs, technical information, and other support services that, although their outputs must be regarded with some skepticism, may be valuable resources for congressmen or administrative agencies seeking to influence the policy process.

The second component of these triangular relationships is the congressional committee or subcommittee. These bodies are designated to review suggestions for legislation in a policy area and to make recommendations to the whole Senate or House of Representatives. An appropriations subcommittee's task is to review expenditure recommendations from the president, then to make its own recommendations on the appropriate level of expenditures to the entire committee and to the whole house. Several factors combine to give these subcommittees substantial power over legislation. First, subcommittee members develop expertise over time, and they are often regarded as more competent to make decisions concerning a policy than is the whole committee or the whole house.[27] Norms have also been developed that support subcommittee decisions for less rational, and more political, reasons.[28] If the entire committee or the entire house were to scrutinize any one subcommittee's decisions, it would have to scrutinize all such decisions and then each subcommittee would lose its powers. These powers are important to individual congressmen, because each congressman wants to develop his or her own power base in a subcommittee or perhaps even the entire committee.[29] Finally, the time limitations imposed by the huge volume of policy decisions being made by Congress each year mean that accepting a subcommittee's decision may be a rational means of reducing the workload of each individual legislator.

Congressional subcommittees are not unbiased; they tend to favor the very interests they are intended to oversee and control. This is largely because the congressmen serving on a subcommittee tend to represent constituencies whose interests are affected by the policy in question. As one analyst argued, "a concerted effort is made to insure that the membership of the subcommittee is supportive of the goals of the subgovernment."[30] For example, in 1996 the Energy and Mineral Resources Subcommittee of the House Resources Committee contained representatives from the energy producing states of Texas (2), California (2), Louisiana, West Virginia, Tennessee, Wyoming, and Ohio and from the mining states of Arizona, New Mexico, Idaho, and Colorado; there was also one representative from Hawaii. This pattern is not confined to natural resources. The Housing and Community Development Subcommittee of the House Banking, Finance, and Urban Affairs Committee has representatives from all the major urban areas of the United States.

These patterns of committee and subcommittee membership are hardly random; they enhance the ability of congressmen to deliver certain kinds of benefits to constituents, as well as their own familiarity with the substantive issues of concern to constituents. Subcommittee members also develop patterns of interaction with the administrative agencies over which they exercise oversight. The individual members of Congress and agency officials may discuss policy with one another and meet informally. As both parties in these interactions tend to remain in Washington for long periods of time, the same congressmen and officials may interact for many years. The trust, respect, or simple familiarity this interaction produces further cements the relationships between committee members and agency personnel, and it also tends to insulate each individual policy area from meddling by outside interests.

Obviously, the third component of the iron triangle is the administrative agency, which, like the pressure group, wants to promote its interests through the policymaking process. The principal interests of an agency are its survival and its budget. The agency need not be, as is often assumed, determined to expand its budget—it may wish merely to retain its "fair share" of the budget pie as it expands or contracts.[31] Agencies are not entirely self-interested; they also have policy ideas that they wish to see translated into operating programs, and they need the action of the congressional committee or subcommittee for that to happen. They also need the support of organized interests in that process.

Each actor in an iron triangle needs the other two in order to reach its goal, and the style that develops is symbiotic. The pressure group needs the agency to deliver services to its members and to provide a friendly point of access to government, while the agency needs the pressure group to mobilize political support for its programs among the affected clientele. Letters from constituents to influential congressmen must be mobilized to argue that the agency is doing a good job and could do an even better job, given more money or a certain policy change. The pressure group needs the congressional committee again as a point of access and as an internal advocate in Congress. And the committee needs the pressure group to mobilize votes for its congressmen and to explain to group members how and why they are doing a good job in Congress. The pressure group can also be a valuable source of policy ideas and research for busy politicians. Finally, the committee members need the agency as an instrument for producing services to their constituents and for developing new policy initiatives. The agency has the research and policy analytic capacity that congressmen often lack, so committees can profit from their association with the agencies. And the agency obviously needs the committee to legitimate its policy initiatives and provide it with funds.

All the actors involved in a triangle have similar interests. In many ways they all represent the same individuals, variously playing the roles of voter, client, and organization member. Much of the domestic policy of the United States can be explained by the existence of functionally specific policy subsystems, and by the absence of effective central coordination. This system of policymaking has been likened to feudalism, with the policies being determined not by any central authority but by aggressive subordinates—the bureaucratic agencies and their associated groups and committees.[32] Both the norms concerning policymaking and the time constraints of political leaders tend to make central coordination and policy choice difficult. The president and his staff (especially the Office of

Management and Budget) are in the best organizational position to exercise this control, but the president must serve political interests, just as Congress must, and he faces an even more extreme time constraint. Thus, decisions are rarely reversed once they have been made within the iron triangles, except in a time of crisis. For example, following the 2001 terrorist attacks there was pronounced movement toward greater presidential control over a range of organizations and less separation among the policy subsystems. That change was most pronounced in the area of "homeland defense," but to some degree all organizations in government became less particularistic.

One effect of this subdivision of government into a number of functionally specific subgovernments is the incoherence of public policy already mentioned. Virtually all societal interests are served through their own agencies, and there is little attempt to make overall policy choices for the nation. Further, these functional subgovernments at the federal level are linked with functional subsystems in intergovernmental relations—the picket fences described earlier. The result of this segmentation of decision making is that local governments and citizens alike may frequently receive contradictory directives from government and may become confused and cynical about the apparent inability of their government to make up its mind.

A second effect of the division of American government into a number of subgovernments is the involvement of a large number of official actors in any one policy area. This proliferation of actors is in part a recognition of the numerous interactions within the public sector, and between the public and private sectors, in the formulation and implementation of any public policy. For an issue area such as health care, the range of organizations involved cannot be confined to those labeled "health" but must inevitably expand to include consideration of the social welfare, nutrition, housing, education, and environmental policies that may have important implications for citizens' health.[33] But the involvement of an increasing number of public organizations in each issue area also reflects the lack of central coordination, which allows agencies to gain approval from friendly congressional committees for expansion of their range of programs and activities.

From time to time a president will attempt to streamline and rationalize the delivery of services in the executive branch, and in the process he generally will encounter massive resistance from agencies and their associated interest groups. For example, when creating the cabinet-level Department of Education, President Jimmy Carter sought to move the educational programs of the (then) Veterans Administration into the new department.[34] In this attempt he locked horns with one of the best organized and most powerful iron triangles in Washington—the Veterans Administration, veterans' organizations, and their associated congressional committees. The president lost. Subsequently the veterans' lobby was sufficiently powerful to have the VA elevated to a cabinet-level department. Presidents do not always lose: President Clinton was able to downsize or eliminate several organizations during implementation of his National Performance Review, including several that had substantial political clienteles.[35]

As easy as it is to become enamored of the idea of iron triangles in American government—they do help explain many of the apparent inconsistencies in policy when viewed broadly—there is some evidence that the iron in the triangles is becoming rusty.[36] More groups are now involved in making decisions, and it is more difficult to exclude interested parties from decisions, leading Charles O. Jones to describe the current pattern as "big sloppy hexagons," rather than "cozy little triangles."[37] For example, the health care reform debate in 1994 included not just representatives of the medical professions, the hospitals, and health insurers but a range of other interests such as small businessmen, organized religion, and organized labor. A simple Internet search on a policy issue will reveal a wide range of groups expressing their views and attempting to influence public—and congressional—opinion.[38]

The concepts of *issue networks* and *policy communities*, involving large numbers of interested parties, each with substantial expertise in the policy area, now appear more descriptive of policymaking in the United States, as well as other industrialized democracies.[39] These structures of interest groups surrounding an issue are less unified about policy than were the iron triangles, and they may contain competing ideas and types of interests to be served through public policy—the tobacco subsystem may even be invaded by health care advocates. There has been some rusting of the iron in the triangles, but the indeterminacy and lack of coherence of networks makes them less valuable in the day-to-day work of governing. As important as the network idea has been for explaining changes in federal policymaking, it does not detract from the basic idea that policymaking is very much an activity that occurs within subsystems.

American government, although originally conceptualized as divided horizontally by level of government, is now better understood as divided vertically into a number of expert and functional policy subsystems. These virtually feudal subsystems divide the authority of government and attempt to appropriate the mantle of the public interest for their own more private interests. Few if any of the actors making policy, however, have any interest in altering these stable and effective means of governing. The system of policymaking is effective politically because it results in the satisfaction of most interests in society. It also links particular politicians and agencies with the satisfaction of those interests, thereby ensuring their continued political success.

The basic patterns of decision making in American politics are *logrolling* and the *pork barrel*, through which, instead of clashing over the allocation of resources, actors minimize conflict by giving each other what they want. For example, instead of contending over which river and harbor improvements will be authorized in any year, Congress has tended to approve virtually all proposals so that all congressmen can claim to have produced something for the folks back

TABLE 2.2   Per Capita Appropriations in Highway Bill of 1998

No representatives	One representative	Multiple representatives
$29.70	$40.40	$43.20

home. Or congressmen from farming areas may trade positive votes on urban development legislation for support of farm legislation by inner-city congressmen. This pattern helps incumbents to be reelected, but it costs taxpayers a great deal more than would a more selective system.

Although logrolling does tend to spread benefits widely, being directly involved in the decision-making subsystem tends to produce more benefits for congressmen and their constituents. This could be seen easily in the distribution of funds from the 1998 highway bill. This was one of the largest public works bills ever passed by Congress, dispensing highway funding widely while still rewarding House Transportation Committee members more than others. As shown in table 2.2, states that had members on this committee received substantially more per capita than did states without such representatives. It could be argued that the states represented on the committee needed more highway repair and construction than the others, but the pattern does appear suspiciously political, especially given that states with multiple representatives on the committee did even better than those with a single representative.

These patterns of policymaking are very effective as long as there is sufficient wealth and economic growth to pay for the subsidization of large numbers of public programs.[40] Nevertheless, this pattern of policymaking was one (but by no means the sole) reason for massive deficits of the federal government in the 1980s and early 1990s, and it appears that the pattern can no longer be sustained comfortably. Various attempts at budget reform have attempted to make pork-barrel politics more difficult to pursue. In particular, the institutionalization of the PAYGO system in Washington, by requiring consideration of the alternative uses of the money or an alternative source of revenue, has made it more difficult for Congress to spend (see Chapter 6). Given the divisions within American government, however, it is difficult for the policymaking system as a whole to make the choices among competing goals and competing segments of society that would be necessary to stop the flow of red ink from Washington.

Public and Private

The final qualitative dimension of American government that is important in understanding the manner in which contemporary policy is made is the increasing confusion of public and private interests and organizations. These two sets of actors and actions have now become so intermingled that it is difficult to ascertain where the boundary line between the two sectors lies. The leakage across the boundary between the public and private sectors, as artificial as that boundary may be, has been occurring in both directions. Activities that once were almost entirely private now have a greater public-sector involvement, although frequently through quasi-public organizations that mask the real involvement of government. Also, functions that are nominally public have significantly greater private-sector involvement. The growth of institutions for formal representation and for implementation by interest groups has given those groups perhaps an even more powerful position in policymaking than that described in the discussion of iron triangles. Instead of vying for access, interest groups are accorded access formally and can exert a legitimate claim to their position in government.

The other major component of change in the relationship between public and private has been the push toward privatization of public activities.[41] This trend began to some degree in the 1970s with Presidents Ford and Carter, but was more pronounced during the 1980s under President Reagan. The United States traditionally has had an antigovernment ethos; that set of values was articulated strongly, and the positive role of the federal government minimized, during the 1980s.[42] For example, a large amount of federal land was sold by the Department of the Interior, and a number of public services were contracted out to the private sector. At one extreme, security checks for the Department of the Navy were being contracted out to a private security firm. It was not only at the federal level that privatization and contracting was popular. At the state and local levels, a large number of functions—hospitals, garbage collection, janitorial services, and even prisons—were contracted out or sold off as a means of reducing the costs of government.[43]

The blending of public and private is to some degree reflected in employment.[44] Table 2.3 demonstrates public and private employment in twelve policy areas, as well as changes that occurred from 1970 to 1997. By 1980, for example, only education retained more than 80 percent public employees, and that percentage was dropping. Even two presumed public monopolies—defense and police protection—had significant levels of private employment. These two policy areas differ, however, in the form of private employment. Defense employment in the private sector is in the production of goods and services used by the armed forces, whereas in police protection a number of private policemen actually provide the service.

The development of mechanisms for direct involvement of interest groups in public decision making is frequently referred to as *corporatism* or *neocorporatism*.[45] These terms refer to the representation in politics of members of the political community not as residents of a geographical area but as members of

TABLE 2.3   Percentages in Public Employment, Selected Policy Areas, 1970–1997

Policy area	1970	1980	1990	1997
Education	87	85	83	81
Post office[a]	92	73	70	64
Highways[b]	74	68	62	63
Tax administration[c]	90[d]	57	55	51
Police[e]	85	60	56	58
Defense[f]	63	59	62	60
Social services[g]	26	35	32	26
Transportation	33	31	34	31
Health	26	30	37	37
Gas/electricity/water	25	27	24	19
Banking	1	1	1	1
Telecommunications	<.5	1	1	1

Sources: Bureau of the Census, *Census of Governments,* quinquennial; Department of Defense, *Defense Manpower Statistics*, annual; Employment and Training Administration, *Annual Report.*

   a. Private-sector counterparts are employees of private services, couriers, etc.

   b. Private-sector counterparts are employed by highway construction contracting firms.

   c. Private-sector counterparts are tax accountants and staffs, H&R Block employees, etc., some only seasonally.

   d. Rough estimate.

   e. Private-sector counterparts are security guards, private policemen, etc.

   f. Private-sector counterparts are employed by military suppliers.

   g. Private-sector counterparts are employed in social work and philanthropy, many only part-time.

functionally defined interests in the society—labor, management, farmers, students, the elderly, and so forth. Associated with this concept of representation is the extensive of interest groups both as instruments of input to the policy process and as a means of implementing public policies. The United States is a less corporatist political system than most industrialized democracies, but there are still corporatist elements. Most urban programs mandate the participation of community residents and other interested parties in decision making for the program. Crop-allotment programs of the U.S. Department of Agriculture have used local farmers' organizations to monitor and implement the programs for some time. County medical societies have been used as professional service review organizations for Medicare and Medicaid, checking on quality and costs of services, and medical and legal associations license practitioners on behalf of government. In addition, as of the late 1990s there were approximately 6,000 advisory bodies in the federal government, many containing substantial interest-group representation.[46]

In addition to the utilization of interest groups to perform public functions, a number of other organizations in society implement public policy. For example, when cabin attendants in an airplane require passengers to fasten their seat belts, they are implementing Federal Aviation Administration policies. Also, universities are required to help implement federal drug policies (statements of nonuse by new employees) and federal immigration policies (certification of citizenship or immigration status of new employees). Manufacturers of numerous products must implement federal safety and environmental standards (e.g., seat belts and pollution-control devices in automobiles) or they cannot sell their products legally.

The increasing use of quasi-public organizations, changes in the direction of a limited corporatist approach to governance in the United States, and privatization (largely through contracting) raise several questions concerning responsibility and accountability in government. These changes involve the use of public money and, more important, the name of the public by groups and for groups that may not be entirely public. In an era in which citizens appear to be attempting to exercise greater control over their governments, the development of these forms of policymaking "at the margins of the state" may be understandable in terms of financial hardships but may only exacerbate the underlying problems of public loss of trust and confidence in government.

The Size and Shape of the Public Sector

We have looked at some qualitative aspects of the contemporary public sector in the United States. What we have yet to do is to examine the size of that public sector and the distribution of funds and personnel among the various purposes of government. As was pointed out, drawing any clear distinctions between public and private sectors in the mixed-economy welfare state is difficult, and growing more difficult, but we will concentrate on the expenditures and personnel that are clearly governmental. As these figures are only those that are clearly public, they inevitably understate the size and importance of government in the United States. This understatement is perhaps greater in the United States than in other countries, given the numerous attempts on the part of government to hide the extent of its involvement in the private sector.

Table 2.4 contains information about the changing size of the public sector in the United States since the post–World War II era and the changing distribution of the total levels of expenditures and employment.[47] Most obvious in this table is that the public sector in the United States has indeed grown, with expenditures increasing from less than one-quarter to more than one-third of

TABLE 2.4   Growth of Public Employment and Expeditures, 1950–1999

Year	Public employment, civilian (in thousands)			Public expenditures (in thousands)		
	Federal	State and local	Total	Federal[a]	State and local	Total
1950	2,117	4,285	6,402	$44,800	$25,534	$70,334
1960	2,421	6,387	8,808	97,280	54,008	151,288
1970	2,880	10,147	13,028	208,190	124,795	332,985
1975	2,890	12,083	14,973	341,517	218,612	560,129
1980	2,876	13,315	16,191	576,700	432,328	1,009,028
1990	3,105	14,976	18,081	1,243,125	976,311	2,219,436
1994	2,952	16,468	19,420	885,324	1,264,348	2,149,672
1999	2,799	17,506	20,305	893,900	1,720,899	2,624,800
	As percentage of total employment			As percentage of GNP		
1950	3.6	7.3	10.9	15.7	8.9	24.6
1960	3.7	9.7	13.4	19.2	10.7	29.9
1970	3.7	12.9	16.6	21.2	12.7	33.9
1975	3.4	14.2	17.6	22.5	14.4	36.9
1980	2.9	13.1	16.0	20.0	16.4	36.4
1990	2.6	12.5	15.1	23.2	18.2	41.4
1994	2.0	12.5	14.5	19.5	21.4	40.9
1999	2.1	12.8	14.9	16.7	24.1	40.8

Source: *Statistical Abstract of the United States,* annual

a. Does not include federal monies passed through grant programs to states and localities for final expenditure at state and local levels.

gross national product. Likewise, public employment has increased from 11 percent of total employment to almost 15 percent. The relative size of the public sector, however, has decreased from the mid-1970s, especially in terms of the percentage of employment. Although the number of public employees increased by over 2 million from 1990 to 1999, government's share of total employment dropped slightly. Government in the United States is large, but it does not appear to be the ever-increasing Leviathan that its critics portray it to be.[48]

It is also evident that growth levels of public expenditures are more than twice as large, relative to the rest of the economy, as public employment figures. Also, public expenditures as a share of gross national product have continued to increase slightly. The differences relative to the private sector and the differences in the patterns of change are largely the results of transfer programs, such as Social Security, which involve the expenditure of large amounts of money but require relatively few administrators. In addition, purchases of goods and services from the private sector (e.g., the Department of Defense's purchases of weapons from private firms) involve the expenditure of large amounts of money (over $200 billion in 2000) with little or no employment generated in the public sector. In 1988, however, those purchases did create approximately 2.1 million jobs in the private sector, a figure similar to the number of people then in the armed forces.[49] From these data it appears that some portions of "big government" in the United States are more controllable than others, even during the eight-year term of a popular president determined to reduce the size of the public sector.

The distribution of expenditures and employment among levels of government also has been changing. In 1950 the federal government spent 64 percent of all public money and employed 33 percent of all public employees. By 1997, the federal government spent approximately 60 percent of all public money but employed only 14 percent of all civilian public employees.[50] The remarkable shift in employment relative to a rather stable distribution of expenditures is again in part a function of the large federal transfer programs, such as Social Security. It also reflects the expansion of federal grants to state and local governments and the ability of the federal government to borrow money to meet expenditure needs, as contrasted to the requirement that state and local governments balance their current budgets.

In addition, the programs provided by state and local governments—education, social services, police and fire protection—are labor intensive. The major labor-intensive federal program, defense, had declining civilian and uniformed employment even before the apparent end of the Cold War in the late 1980s. These data appear to conflict somewhat with the popular characterization of the federal government as increasingly important, or intrusive, in American economic and social life. While certainly it is a large institution, employing over 4 million people when the armed forces are included, its level of employment actually has been declining—absolutely as well as relatively— with the major growth of government employment occurring at the state and local levels. The increased emphasis on security, at home and abroad, in response to the terrorist attacks of 2001 was expected to shift employment trends back toward the center and toward defense, but that would require a major reordering of priorities.

Another factor involved in the declining share of employment in the federal government is the shift from defense programs toward social programs. In 1952, national defense accounted for 46 percent of all public expenditures and for 49 percent of all public employment. By 1995, defense expenditures had been reduced to 13 percent of all expenditures and 5 percent of public employment. By contrast, a panoply of welfare-state services (health, education, and social services) accounted for 20 percent of public expenditures in 1952 and 24 percent of public employment. By 1995, these services accounted for 52 percent of expenditures and 53 percent of all public employment. Within the welfare-state services, education has been the biggest gainer in employment, involving over 6 million more employees in 1996 than in 1952. And Social Security programs alone increased their spending by well over $300 billion during that time period. The United States is often described as a "welfare state laggard," but the evidence is that although it is still behind most European nations in the range of social services, a marked increase has been occurring in the social component of American public expenditures and employment.

It was argued that the landslide victories of the Republican Party in the presidential elections from 1980 to 1988 were a repudiation of this pattern of change, and that they should have produced little increase, or actual decreases, in the level of public expenditures for social programs. There was a slight relative decrease in social spending from 1980 until 1992—in part a function of increasing expenditures for other purposes, such as interest on the public debt—but sustained decreases remain difficult to obtain. Most social programs are entitlement programs, and once a citizen has been made a recipient of benefits, or has made the insurance "contributions" for Social Security, future governments find it difficult to remove those benefits. This is especially true of programs for the retired elderly, as they cannot be expected to return to active employment to make up losses in benefits, and, unfortunately for budget cutters, public expenditures are increasingly directed toward the elderly. For example, in the early 1990s, almost 50 percent of the federal budget went to programs (Social Security, Medicare, housing programs, and so forth) for the elderly. As the American population continues to grow older, expenditures for this social group can only be expected to increase. What is true in particular for the elderly is true in general for all entitlement programs, and reducing the size of the government's social budget will be difficult indeed.

The 1990s were something of a surprise in other ways. The election of a moderate Democrat as president seemed likely to produce an upward shift in public expenditures, especially for social purposes. The election of an extremely conservative Republican Congress in 1994, and the fiscal conservatism of the Clinton administration, however, actually generated a relatively smaller increase in social spending than might have been expected. The politics of controlling the budgetary deficit, so central to the politics of the 1990s, was associated with slow growth in social spending, and indeed in public spending more generally. By the end of the 1990s the federal government was predicted to have huge surpluses, rather than the equally massive deficits with which it began the decade (see Chapter 8). That prediction came true, but the effect was only temporary, so that by late 2002 the federal government was sinking rapidly into deficit. The slow increase in spending in the 1990s was to some extent ideological, but it also reflected the relative economic success of that decade—fewer people were on social programs and hence there was less need for spending.

We have been concentrating attention on public employment and public expenditures as measures of the "size" of government, but we should remember that government influences the economy and society through a number of other mechanisms as well. For example, the federal government sponsors a much larger housing program through the tax system (deductibility of mortgage interest and property taxes) than it does through expenditures by the Department of Housing and Urban Development (see table 9.2, p. 225). Likewise, government provides a major education program of guaranteed and subsidized student loans that shows up only indirectly in public expenditures.

In the United States, because of the generally antistatist views of many citizens, regulation has been the major form of government intervention into the economy, rather than the more direct mechanisms used in other countries. The regulatory impact of government on the economy can be counted in the billions of dollars—one estimate was $542 billion in 1992.[51] Reliance on such indirect methods of influence has been heightened by the conservative administrations of the 1980s and early 1990s, and the conservative Congress since 1994. The conservatives in Congress have, however, been successful in creating requirements for government to report on the estimated size of the regulatory impact.[52] Therefore, we must be very careful in making assessments of the size, shape, and impact of government in the United States based solely upon figures about public expenditures and public employment.

Summary

American government at the outset of the new century is large, complex, and to some degree unorganized. Each individual section of government, be it a local government or an agency of the federal government, tends to know clearly what it wants, but the system as a whole lacks overall coordination, coherence, and control. Priority setting is not one of the strongest features of American government. An elected official coming to office with a commitment to give direction to the system of government will be disappointed by his or her ability to produce desired results, by the barriers to policy success, and by the relatively few ways in which the probability of success can be increased. These difficulties, however, may be compensated for by the flexibility and multiple opportunities for citizen inputs characteristic of American government.

Despite the problems of coordination and control, and the tradition of popular distrust of government, contemporary American government is active. It spends huge amounts of money and employs millions of people to perform a bewildering variety of tasks. These activities are not confined to a single level of government; instead, all three levels of government are involved in making policy, taxing, spending, and delivering services. This activity is why the study of public policy is so important. It is a means of understanding what goes on in the United States, and why government does the things it does. The emphasis on the next portion of the book is on the processes through which policy is made. All governments must follow many of the same procedures when they make policy: identify issues, formulate policy responses to problems, evaluate results, and change programs that are not producing desired results. American governments do all these things, but they do them in a distinctive way and produce distinctive results.

PART TWO

The Making of Public Policy

CHAPTER 3

Agenda Setting and Public Policy

THIS CHAPTER DISCUSSES two aspects of the policymaking process that occur rather early in the sequence of decisions leading to the actual delivery of services to citizens but are nonetheless crucial to the success of the entire process. These two stages of policymaking—agenda setting and policy formulation—are important because they establish the parameters within which any additional consideration of policies will occur. Agenda setting is crucial, given that if an issue cannot be placed on the agenda, it cannot be considered, and nothing can possibly happen in government. Policy formulation then begins to narrow and structure the consideration of the problems placed on the agenda and to prepare a plan of action intended to rectify the problem identified. These two stages are also linked because it is often necessary to have a solution before an issue can be accepted on the agenda. In addition, the manner in which an issue is defined as it is brought to the agenda determines the kinds of solutions that will be developed to solve the problem.

Agenda Setting

Before a policy choice can be made by government, a problem in the society must have been accepted as a part of the agenda for the policymaking system—that is, as one member of the set of problems deemed amenable to public action and worthy of the attention of policymakers. Many real problems are not given any consideration by government, largely because the relevant political actors are not convinced that government has any role in attempting to solve those problems. Although problems once accepted as a part of the general, systemic agenda tend to remain for long periods of time, problems do come on and go off the active policy agenda.

One of the best examples of a problem being accepted as part of the agenda after a long period of exclusion is that of poverty in the United States. Throughout most of this nation's history, poverty was perceived not as a public problem but as merely the result of the (proper) operation of the free market. The publication of Michael Harrington's *The Other America* and the growing mobilization of poor people brought the problem of poverty to the agenda and indirectly resulted in the launching of a war dedicated to its eradication.[1] Once placed on the agenda, poverty has remained an important public issue, although different administrations have given different amounts of attention to the problem.

Another obvious case of external events contributing to setting the policy agenda is that the perceived poor quality of American elementary and secondary education, especially in science and technology, did not become an issue at the federal level until the Soviet Union launched *Sputnik I*. Although now redefined to some extent in terms of economic competitiveness rather than the Cold War, educational quality has remained on the agenda and gained renewed importance as an issue in the 1990s (see Chapter 12). The case of O. J. Simpson also helped to place issues of domestic violence in a more prominent position on the agenda of American governments. In each of these examples, some dramatic public event awakened the populace to an existing social problem that needed to be addressed.[2]

The best example of an issue being removed from the policy agenda is the repeal of Prohibition, when the federal government said that preventing the production and distribution of alcoholic beverages was no longer its concern. Despite the end of Prohibition, all levels of government have nonetheless retained some regulatory and taxing authority over the production and consumption of alcohol. Likewise, the movement to privatize some public services (usually at the local level) also has removed some issues from direct concern in the public sector, although again a regulatory role usually continues.

What can cause an issue to be placed on the policy agenda? The most basic cause is a perception that something is wrong and that the problem can be ameliorated through public action. This answer in turn produces another question: What causes the change in perceptions of problems and issues? Why, for example, did Harrington's book have such far-reaching influence on the public when earlier books about social deprivation, such as James Agee's *Let Us Now Praise Famous Men,* had relatively little impact?[3] Did the timing of the "discovery" of poverty in the United States result from the election of a young, seemingly liberal president (John Kennedy) who was succeeded by an activist president (Lyndon Johnson) with considerable sway over Congress? When do problems cease to be invisible and become perceived as real problems for public consideration?

Issues also appear to pass through an "issue attention cycle," in which they are the objects of great public concern for a short period and generate some response from government.[4] The initial enthusiasm for the issue is generally followed by more sober realism about the costs of policy options available and the difficulties of making effective policy. This realism is, in turn, followed by a period of declining public interest as the public seizes on a new issue. The histories of environmental policy, drug enforcement, and, to some degree, the women's movement illustrate this cycle very well. More recently, the "discovery" of sexual harassment as a policy issue during the confirmation hearings of Clarence Thomas for the Supreme Court was followed relatively quickly by doubts about the possibility of effective enforcement of the laws and even the exact definition of the offense. Attention to the issue, and its possible ambiguity, was reinforced by allegations against Senator Robert Packwood, and later by the several claims against President Bill Clinton.

Just as individual issues go through an issue-attention cycle, the entire political system may also experience cycles of differential activity. One set of scholars has described this pattern as "routine punctuated by orgies."[5] A less colorful description developed by Frank Baumgartner and Bryan D. Jones is "punctuated equilibria."[6] Some time periods—because of energetic political leaders, large-scale mobilization of the public, or a host of other possible reasons—are characterized by greater policy activism than are others. Those periods of activism are followed by periods in which the programs adopted during the activist period are rationalized, consolidated, or perhaps terminated.[7]

This chapter discusses how to understand, and how to manipulate, the public agenda. How can a social problem be converted into an issue and brought into a public institution for formal consideration? In the role of policy analyst, one must understand not only the theoretical issues concerning agenda setting but also the points of leverage within the political system. Much of what happens in the policymaking system is difficult or impossible to control: the ages and health of the participants, their friendships, constitutional structures of institutions and their interactions and external events, to name but a few of the relevant variables. Some scholars have argued that agendas do not change unless there is an almost random confluence of events favoring the new policy initiative.[8] Such random factors may be important in explaining overall policy outcomes, but they are not the only pertinent factors to consider when one confronts the task of bringing about desired policy changes. Despite all the imponderables in a policymaking system, there is still room for initiative and for altering the political behavior of important actors in the system.

It is also important to remember that social problems do not come to government fully conceptualized with the labels already attached. Policy problems need to have names if government is to deal with them, and labeling is itself a political process.[9] For example, how do we conceptualize the problem of illegal drugs in the United States? Is it a problem of law enforcement, as it is commonly treated, or is it a public health problem, or a problem of education, or a reflection of poverty, despair, and social disorder? Perhaps drug use indicates something more about the society in which it occurs than it does about the individual consumers usually branded as criminals. There are a number of possible answers to such definitional questions, but the fundamental point is that the manner in which the problem is conceptualized and defined determines the remedies likely to be proposed, the organizations that will be given responsibility for the problem, and the final outcomes of the public intervention into the problem.

Kinds of Agendas

Until now we have been discussing "the agenda" in the singular and with the definite article. There are, however, different agendas for the various institutions of government, as well as a more general agenda for the political system as a whole. The existence of these agendas also is to some degree an abstraction. Most agendas do not exist in any concrete form; they exist only in a collective judgment of the nature of public problems or as fragments of written evidence such as legislation introduced, the State of the Union message of the president, or notice of intent to issue regulations appearing in the *Federal Register*. On the other hand, cases appealed—and especially cases accepted for appeal—do constitute a clear agenda for the Supreme Court.

Roger Cobb and Charles Elder, who produced some of the principal writing on agendas in American government, distinguished between the systemic and institutional agendas of government. The systemic agenda consists of "all issues that are commonly perceived by members of the political community as meriting public attention and as involving matters within the legitimate jurisdiction of existing governmental authority."[10] This is the broadest agenda of government, including all issues that might be subject to action or that are already being acted on by government. This definition implies a consensus on the systemic agenda—a consensus that may not exist. Some individuals may consider a problem—abortion, for example—as part of the agenda of the political system (whether to outlaw abortion or to provide public funding for it), while others regard the issue as entirely one of personal choice. The southern states' reluctance for years to include civil rights as part of their agendas indicated a disagreement over what fell within the "jurisdiction of existing governmental authority." Setting the systemic agenda is usually not consensual, as it is a crucial political and policy decision. If a problem can be excluded from consideration, then those individuals and organizations that benefit from the status quo are assured of victory.[11] It is only when a problem is placed on the agenda, and made available for active discussion, that the forces of change have some opportunity for success.

The second type of agenda that Cobb and Elder discuss is the institutional agenda: "that set of items explicitly up for active and serious consideration of authoritative decision-makers."[12] An institutional agenda is composed of the issues upon which the individuals in power within a particular institution actually are considering taking action. These issues may constitute a subset of all problems they will discuss, as the complete set will include "pseudo issues" discussed to placate clientele groups but included in the institution's deliberations without any serious intention to make policy.[13] Actors within institutions do run a risk, however, when they permit discussion of pseudo issues: once they appear on the docket, something may actually be done about the problem.

A number of institutional agendas exist—as many as there are institutions—and there is little reason to assume any agreement among institutions as to which problems are the most appropriate for consideration. As with the discussion of conflicts over placing issues on the systemic agenda, inter-institutional conflicts will arise in moving problems from one institutional agenda to another. The agendas of bureaucratic agencies are the narrowest, and a great deal of the political activity of those agencies is directed at placing their issues onto the agendas of other institutions. As an institution broadens in scope, the range of its agenda concerns also broadens, and supporters of any particular issue will have to fight to have it placed on a legislative or executive agenda. This is especially true of *new problems* seeking to be converted into active issues. Some older and more familiar issues will generally find a ready place on institutional agendas. Some older issues are *cyclical issues*: a new budget must be adopted each year, for example, and many other public programs are designed with periodic reviews—there is, for example, a quadrennial defense review for national security policy.[14] Other older agenda items may be *recurrent issues*, indicating primarily the failure of previous policy choices to produce the intended or desired impact on society. Even recurrent issues may not be returned easily to institutional agendas when existing programs are perceived to be "good enough," or when no new solutions are readily available. Indeed, the beneficiaries of a program may work hard to keep it off an active agenda, lest new legislation upset the existing policy.[15]

Jack Walker classes problems coming on the agenda in four groups.[16] He defines issues that are dealt with time and time again as either periodically recurring or sporadically recurring issues (similar to our cyclical and recurrent issues). He also examines the role of crises in placing issues on the agenda, as well as the difficulties of having new, or "chosen," problems selected for inclusion on agendas. Within each institution, the supporters of an issue must use their political power and skills to gain access to the agenda. The failure to be included on any one institutional agenda may be the end of an issue, at least for the time being.

Who Sets Agendas?

Establishing an agenda for society, or even for one institution, is a manifestly political activity, and control of the agenda gives substantial control over the ultimate policy choices. Therefore, to understand how agendas are determined requires some understanding of the manner in which political power is exercised in the United States. The idea of a punctuated equilibrium may be a good description of the process of change, but it does not explain how the punctuations come about. The most important answer to that question is that political power is used to alter the agenda.[17] As might be imagined, there are a number of different conceptualizations of just how power is exercised. To enable us to understand the dynamics of agenda setting better, I will discuss three important theoretical approaches to the exercise of political power, and the formation of policy agendas: pluralist, elitist, and state-centric.

Pluralist Approaches

The dominant, though far from undisputed, approach to policymaking in the United States is pluralism.[18] Stated briefly, the pluralist approach assumes that policymaking in government is divided into a number of separate arenas and that interests and individuals who have power in one arena do not necessarily have power in others. The American Medical Association, for example, may have a great deal of influence over health care legislation but little influence over education or defense policy. Furthermore, interests that are victorious at one time or in one arena will not necessarily win at another time or place. The pluralist approach to policymaking assumes that there is something of a marketplace in policies, with a number of interests competing for power and influence, even within a single arena. These competitors are conceived as interest groups competing for access to institutions for decision making and for the attention of central actors in the hope of producing their desired outcomes. These groups are assumed, much as in the market model of the economy, to be relatively equal in power, so on any one issue any interest might be victorious. Finally, the actors involved in the political process generally agree on the rules of the game, especially the rule that elections are the principal means of determining policy. The principal function of government is to serve as an umpire in this struggle among competing group interests, and to enforce the victories through public law.

The pluralist approach to agenda setting would lead the observer to expect a relatively open marketplace of ideas for new policies. Any or all interested groups, as a whole or within a particular public institution, should have the opportunity to influence the agenda. These interest groups may not win every time, but neither will they systematically be excluded from decisions, and the agendas will be amenable to adding new items as sufficient political mobilization is developed. This style of agenda setting may be particularly appropriate for the United States, given the multiple institutions and multiple points of access inherent in the structure of the system.[19] Even if an issue is blocked politically, the courts can enable otherwise disadvantaged groups to bring it into the policy process, as has happened with civil rights and later with some aspects of sexual harassment.

Elitist Approaches

The elitist approach to American policymaking seeks to contradict the dominant pluralist approach. It assumes the existence of a "power elite" who dominate public decision making and whose interests are served in the policymaking process. In the elitist analysis, the same interests in society consistently win, and these interests are primarily those of business, the upper and middle classes, and whites.[20] Analysts from an elitist perspective have pointed out that to produce the kind of equality assumed in the pluralist model would require relatively equal levels of organization by all interests in society. They then point out that relatively few interests of working- and lower-class individuals are effectively organized; when compared to its European counterparts, American labor is not particularly well-organized or powerful. While all individuals in a democracy certainly have the right to organize, elitist theorists point to the relative lack of resources (e.g., time, money, organizational ability, and communication skills) among members of the lower economic classes.[21] Thus, political organization for many poorer people, if it exists at all, may imply only token participation, and their voices will be drowned in the sea of middle-class voices described by E. E. Schattschneider.[22]

The implications of the elitist approach are rather obvious. If agenda formulation is crucial to the process of policymaking, then the ability of elites to keep certain issues off the agenda is crucial to their power. Adherents of this approach believe that the agenda in most democratic countries represents not the competitive struggle of relatively equal groups, as argued by the pluralist model, but the systematic use of elite power to decide which issues the political system will or will not consider. Jürgen Habermas, for example, argues that the elite uses its power systematically to exclude issues that would be a threat to its interests and that these "suppressed issues" represent a major threat to democracy.[23] If too many significant issues are kept off the agenda, the legitimacy of the political system can be threatened, along with its survival in the most extreme cases.

Peter Bachrach and Morton Baratz's concept of "nondecisions" is important here. They define a nondecision as a decision that results in suppression or thwarting of a latent or manifest challenge to the values or interests of the decision maker.[24] More explicitly, nondecision making is a means by which demands for change in the existing allocation of benefits and privileges in the community can be suffocated before they are even voiced; or kept covert; or killed off before they gain access to the relevant decision-making arena; or failing all else, maimed or destroyed in the decision-implementing stage of the policy process.[25] A decision not to alter the status quo is a decision, whether it is made overtly through the policymaking process or whether it is the result of the application of power to prevent the issue from ever being discussed.

State-Centric Approaches

Both the pluralist and elitist approaches to policymaking and agenda setting assume that the major source of policy ideas is the environment of the policymakers—primarily interest groups or other powerful interests in the society. It is, however, quite possible that the political system itself is responsible for its own agenda.[26] The environment, in a state-centric analysis, is not filled with pressure groups but with "pressured groups," activated by government. As governments become more interested in managing the media and in influencing public opinion, the state-centric view may be more viable.[27]

The state-centered concept of agenda setting conforms quite well to the iron-triangle conception of American government but would place the bureaucratic agency or the congressional committee, not the pressure group, in the center of the process.[28] This approach does emphasize the role of specialized elites within government but, unlike elitist theory, does not assume that these elites are pursuing policies for their own personal gain. Certainly their organizations may obtain larger budgets and greater prestige from the addition of new programs, but the individual administrators have little or no opportunity to appropriate any of that budgetary increase.

In addition, the state-centric approach places the major locus of competition over agenda setting within government itself, rather than in the constellation of interests in society. Agencies must compete for legislative time and for budgets, committees must compete for attention for their particular legislative concerns, and individual congressmen must compete for consideration of their own bills and their own constituency concerns. These actors within government are more relevant in pushing agenda items than are interests in the society.

One interesting question arises about agenda setting in the state-centric approach: what are the relative powers of bureaucratic and legislative actors in setting the agenda? An early study by the Advisory Commission on Intergovernmental Relations argued that the source of the continued expansion of the federal government was within Congress.[29] The authors of this study argued that congressmen, acting out of a desire to be reelected or from a sincere interest in solving certain policy problems, have been the major source of new items on the federal agenda. Other analyses have placed the source of most new policy ideas within the bureaucracy as much as or more than in Congress.[30] Also, the nature of American government requires that the president and Congress work together to set agendas and make policy.[31] Given the complexity of the chain of events leading to new policies, it may be difficult to determine exactly where ideas originated, but there is (at least in this model) no shortage of policy advocates.[32]

The agenda resulting from a state-centric process might be more conservative than one resulting from a pluralist process but less conservative than one from the elitist model. Government actors may be constrained in the amount of change they can advocate on their own initiative; they may instead have to wait for a time when their ideas will be more acceptable to the general public. Congressmen can adopt a crusading stance, but this is a choice usually denied to the typical bureaucratic agency. Except in rare instances—efforts by the surgeon general and the Food and Drug Administration concerning the regulation of cigarette smoking perhaps—a government-sponsored agency may be ahead of public opinion, but only slightly so.

Which approach to policymaking and agenda formation is most descriptive of the process in the United States? The answer is probably all of them, for the proponents of each can muster a great deal of evidence for their position. More important, policymaking for certain kinds of problems and issues can best be described by one approach rather than another. For example, we would expect policies that are very much the concern of government itself (e.g., civil service laws or perhaps even foreign affairs) to be more heavily influenced by state-centric policymaking than would other kinds of issues. Likewise, certain kinds of problems that directly affect powerful economic interests would be best understood through elite analysis. Energy policy and its relationship to the major oil companies might well fit into that category. Finally, policy areas with a great deal of interest-group activity and relatively high levels of group involvement, both by clients and producers—education is a good example—might be best understood through the pluralist approach. Unfortunately, these categorizations are largely speculative, for political scientists have only begun to produce the kind of detailed analysis required to track issues as they move on and off agendas.[33]

From Problem to Issue: How to Get Problems on the Agenda

Problems do not move themselves on and off agendas. Nevertheless, a number of their characteristics can affect their chances of becoming a part of an active, systemic, or institutional agenda. We should remember, however, that most problems do not come with these characteristics clearly visible to most citizens, or even to most political actors. Agendas must be constructed and the issues defined by a social and political process in a manner that will make them most amenable to political action.[34] Further, it usually requires an active policy entrepreneur to do the necessary political packaging that can make an issue appear on an agenda.[35]

The Effects of the Problem

The first aspect of a problem that can influence its placement on an agenda is whom it affects, and how much. We can think about the extremity, concentration, range, and visibility of problems as influencing their placement on agendas. First, the more extreme the effects of a problem, the more likely it is to be placed on an agenda. An outbreak of a disease causing mild discomfort, for example, is unlikely to produce public action, but the possibility of an epidemic life-threatening disease, such as AIDS, usually provokes some kind of public action.

Even if the problem is not life threatening, a concentration of victims in one area may produce public action. The unemployment of an additional 50,000 workers, while certainly deplorable, might not cause major public intervention if the workers were scattered around the country, but might well do so if the workers were concentrated in one geographical area. Most industries in the United States are concentrated geographically (automobiles in Michigan, aerospace in California, oil in Texas and Louisiana), and that makes it easier for advocates of assistance to any troubled industry to get the help they want from government. Even conservatives who tend to oppose government intervention in the economy appear happy to assist failing industries when it is clear that there will be major regional effects.

The range of persons affected by a problem may also influence the placement of the issue on an agenda. In general, the more people affected or potentially affected by a problem, the greater is the probability that the issue will be placed on the agenda. There are limits, however; a problem may be so general that no single individual believes that he or she has anything to gain by organizing political action to address it. An issue that has broad but only minor effects therefore may have less chance of being placed on the agenda than a problem that affects fewer people but affects them more severely.

The intensity of effects, and therefore of policy preferences of citizens, is a major problem for those who take the pluralist approach to agenda setting.[36] Many real or potential interests in society are not effectively organized because few individuals believe that they have enough to gain from establishing or joining an organization. For example, although every citizen is a consumer, few effective consumer organizations have been established, whereas producer groups are numerous and are effective politically. The specificity and intensity of producer interests, as contrasted to the diffuseness of consumer interests, creates a serious imbalance in the pattern of interest-group organization that favors producers. An analogous situation would be the relative ineffectiveness of taxpayers' organizations compared to clientele groups, such as defense industries and farmers, which are interested in greater federal spending. The organizational imbalance against consumers and taxpayers was mitigated somewhat during the 1980s, but it still exists.[37]

Finally, the visibility of a problem may affect its placement on an agenda as an active issue. This might be called "mountain climber syndrome." Society appears willing to spend almost any amount of money to rescue a single stranded mountain climber but will not spend the same amount of money to save many more lives by, for example, controlling automobile accidents or vaccinating children. Statistical lives are not nearly so visible and comprehensible as an identifiable individual stuck on the side of a mountain. Similarly, the issue of the risks of nuclear power plants have been highly dramatized in the media, while less visibly an average of 150 men die each year in mining accidents and many others die from black-lung disease contracted in coal mines. Likewise, the existing environmental effects of burning coal, although certainly recognized and important, appear to pale in the public mind when compared to the possible effects of a nuclear accident.

Analogous and Spillover Agenda Setting

Another important aspect of a problem that can affect its being placed on an agenda is the presence of an analogy to other public programs. The more a new issue can be made to look like an old issue, the more likely it is to be placed on the agenda. This is especially true in the United States because of the traditional reluctance of American government to expand the public sector, at least by conscious choice. For example, the federal government's intervention into medical-care financing for individuals with Medicare and Medicaid was dangerously close to the then-feared "socialized medicine."[38] It was made more palatable, at least in the case of Medicare, by making the program appear similar to Social Security, which was already highly legitimate. More recently, the Clinton administration attempted to make its plan for health care reform appear as much as possible like the existing health maintenance organizations (HMOs) that earlier had been sponsored by federal policy.[39] If a new agenda item can be made to appear as only an incremental departure from existing policies rather than an entirely new venture, its chances of being accepted are much improved.

Also, the existence of one government program may produce the need for additional programs. This spillover effect is important in bringing new programs onto the agenda and in explaining the expansion of the public sector. Even the best policy analysts in the world cannot anticipate the consequences of all the policy choices made by government. Thus, the adoption of one program may soon lead to the adoption of other programs directed at "solving" the problems created by the first program.[40] For example, the federal government's interstate highway program was designed to improve transportation and to serve domestic defense purposes. One effect of building superhighways, however, has been to make it easier for people to live in the suburbs and work in the city. Consequently, these roads assisted in the flight to the suburbs of those who could afford to move. This, in turn, contributed to the decline of central cities, which created a need for the federal government to pour billions of dollars into urban renewal, Urban Develop-

Children from a local Head Start program join parents and educators to rally in support of day-care legislation at the Illinois State Capitol.

ment Action Grants, and a host of other programs for the cities. Although the inner cities would probably have declined somewhat without the federal highway program, the program certainly accelerated the process.

Policies in modern societies are now tightly interconnected, and they may have so many secondary and tertiary effects on other programs that any new policy intervention is likely to have results that spread like ripples in a clear lake. To some degree the analyst should anticipate those effects and design programs to avoid negative interaction effects, but he or she can never be perfectly successful in doing so. Tax policies in particular tend to spawn unanticipated responses, as individuals and corporations seek creative ways of legally avoiding paying tax and the Internal Revenue Service tries to close unanticipated loopholes.[41] As a consequence, "policy is its own cause," and one policy choice may beget others.[42]

Relationship to Symbols

The more closely a problem can be linked to important national symbols, the greater is its probability of being placed on the agenda. Seemingly mundane programs may thus be wrapped up in rhetoric about freedom, justice, and traditional American values. Conversely, a problem will not be placed on the agenda if it is associated primarily with negative values. There are, of course, some exceptions—although the gay community is not a positive symbol for many Americans, the AIDS issue was placed on the agenda with relative alacrity, even before the possibilities of other sectors of the population becoming infected with the disease became widely known.[43]

There are several interesting examples of the use of positive symbols to market programs and issues that might not otherwise have been accepted on the agenda. The federal government traditionally eschewed most direct involvement with education, but the success of the Soviet Union in launching *Sputnik I* highlighted the weaknesses of American elementary and secondary education. This led to the National Defense Education Act, which associated the perceived problem of education with the positive symbol of defense, a long-term federal government concern. More recently, increased federal involvement in education has been associated at least in part with problems of global economic competitiveness.[44] In addition, although American government has generally been rather slow to adopt social programs, those associated with children and their families have been more favorably regarded. Therefore, if someone wants to initiate a social welfare program, it is well to associate it with children, or possibly with the elderly. It is perhaps no accident that the basic welfare program in the United States was long known as Aid to Families with Dependent Children. More recently, the 1994 crime bill contained a variety of social programs (the famous "midnight basketball" provisions) that might not have even made it to a vote if they were not attached to the symbolic issue of crime control.

Symbol manipulation is an extremely important skill for policy analysts. For example, creating the label "death tax" for the inheritance tax had no little effect on the attempts at repeal in 2001—the symbolism helped to obscure the extremely regressive nature of the change in tax policy.[45] In addition to being rational calculators of the costs and benefits of their programs, analysts must be capable of relating their programs and program goals to other programs and of justifying the importance of the problem and the program to actors who may be less committed to it and its goals. Placing a problem on the agenda of government means convincing powerful individuals that they should make the effort necessary to rectify the problem. The use of symbols may facilitate this process when the problem itself is not likely to gain wide public attention.

The Absence of Private Means

In general, governments avoid accepting new responsibilities, especially in the United States with its laissez-faire tradition, and especially in a climate of budgetary scarcity (even after a balanced budget has been attained). The market, rather than collective action, has become the standard against which to compare good policy.[46] There are, however, problems in society that cannot be solved by private market activities alone. Two classic examples are social problems that involve either "public goods" or "externalities."

Public goods are goods or services that, once produced, are consumed by a relatively large number of individuals, and whose consumption is difficult or impossible to control—they are not "excludable." This means that it is difficult or impossible for any individual or firm to produce public goods, for they cannot be effectively priced and sold.[47] If national defense were produced by paid mercenaries rather than by government, individual citizens would have little or no incentive to pay that group of fighters; citizens would be protected whether they paid or not. Indeed, citizens would have every incentive to be "free riders"—to enjoy the benefits of the service without paying the cost. In such a situation, government has a remedy for the problem: it can force citizens to pay for the service through its power of taxation.

Externalities are said to exist when the activities of one economic unit affect the well-being of another and no compensation is paid for benefits or costs created externally.[48] Pollution is a classic case: it is a by-product of the production process, but its social costs are excluded from the selling price of the products made by the manufacturer. Thus, social costs and production costs diverge, and government may have to impose regulations to prevent the private firm from imposing the costs of pollution—such as damage to health, property, and amenities—on the public. Alternatively, government may develop some means of pricing the effects of pollution and then imposing those costs on the polluter.

All externalities need not be negative, however; some activities create public benefits that are not included in the revenues of those producing them. If a dam is built to generate hydroelectric power, the recreational, flood-control, and economic development benefits cannot be included as part of the revenues of a private utility, although government can include those benefits in its calculations when considering undertaking a project with public money (see Chapter 16). Thus some projects that appear infeasible for the private sector may be feasible for government, even on strict economic criteria.

Public goods and externalities are two useful categories for consideration, but they do not exhaust the kinds of social and economic problems that have a peculiarly public nature.[49] Of course, the consideration of issues of rights and the application of law is considered peculiarly public. In addition, programs that involve a great deal of risk may require the socialization of that risk through the public sector. For example, lending to college students who have little credit record is backed by government as a means of making banks more willing to take the risk. These loans illustrate the general principle that the inability of other institutions in society to produce effective and equitable solutions may be sufficient to place an issue on the public agenda.

The Availability of Technology

Finally, a problem generally will not be placed on the public agenda unless there is a technology believed to be able to solve it. For most of the history of the industrialized nations, it was assumed that economic fluctuations were, like the weather, acts of God. Then the Keynesian revolution in economics produced what seemed to be the answer to these fluctuations, and governments soon placed economic management in a central position on their agendas. In the United States this new technology was reflected in the Employment Act of 1946, pledging the U.S. government to maintain full employment. The promise of "fine tuning" the economy through Keynesian means, which appeared possible in the 1960s, has since become increasingly elusive, but the issue of economic management remains on the public agenda.[50] Subsequent governments have provided new technologies (e.g., "supply-side economics" during the Reagan years), but they have not been able to evade responsibility for the economy.

Another way of regarding the role of technology in agenda setting is the "garbage-can model" of decision making, in which solutions find problems, rather than vice versa.[51] A problem may be excluded from the agenda simply because of the lack of an instrument to do the job, and the example of economic management points to the danger of the lack of an available instrument. If government announces that it is undertaking to solve a problem and then fails miserably, public confidence in the effectiveness of government will be shaken. Government must then take the blame for failures along with the credit for successes. The garbage-can model also illustrates the relationship between agenda setting and policy formulation, because an issue is not accepted as a part of the agenda unless it is known that a policy has been formulated, or is already on the shelf, to solve the problem. Solutions may beg for new problems, like a child with a hammer finding things that need hammering.[52]

As with all portions of the policymaking process, agenda setting is an intensely political activity. Indeed, it may well be the most political aspect of policymaking, because it involves bringing to the public consciousness an acceptance of a vague social problem as something government can, and should, attempt to solve. It may be quite easy for powerful actors who wish to do so to exclude unfamiliar issues from the agenda, making active political mobilization of the less powerful necessary for success. Rational policy analysis may play only a small role in setting the agenda for discussion; such analysis will be useful primarily after it is agreed that there is a problem and that the problem is public in nature. In agenda setting, the policy analyst is less a technician and more a politician, understanding the policymaking process and seeking to influence that process toward a desired end. This involves the manipulation of symbols and the definition of often vague social problems. Nevertheless, agenda setting should not be dismissed as simply political maneuvering; it is the crucial first step on the road to resolving any identified problem.

Policy Formulation

After the political system has accepted a problem as part of the agenda for policymaking, the logical question is what should be done about the problem. We call this stage of the process *policy formulation*, meaning the development of the mechanisms for solving the public problem. At this point, a policy analyst can begin to apply analytic techniques to attempt to justify one policy choice as superior to others. Economics and decision theory are both useful in assessing the risks of certain outcomes, or in predicting likely social costs and benefits of various alternatives. Rational choice, however, need not be dominant; the habits, traditions, and standard operating procedures of government may prevail over rational activity in making the policy choice. But even such seemingly irrational sets of choice factors may be, in their way, quite rational. This is simply because the actors involved have experience with the "formula" to be used, are comfortable with it, and consequently can begin to make it work much more readily than they could a newer instrument in which they may have no confidence, even if that instrument were technically superior.

The Clinton administration's formulation of its health care reform proposal demonstrates some of the potential pitfalls of rationalistic and expert policy formulation. Although the proposal may have been excellent technically, it simply did not correspond to the familiar political and administrative patterns of the United States. The plan was excessively complex and could easily be labeled "bureaucratic," whereas simpler insurance-based systems have been more successful. Further, the formulation was carried out largely behind closed doors, rather than permitting affected groups to help shape the proposal and perhaps forestall some of its more egregious errors.

The federal government has followed several basic formulas in attempting to solve public problems. In economic affairs, for example, the United States has relied on regulation more than on government ownership of business, which has been more common in Europe. In social policy, the standard formulas have been social insurance and the use of cash transfer programs rather than direct delivery of services. The major exception to the latter formula has been the reliance on education as a means of rectifying social and economic inequality. And finally there has been a formula involving the private sector as much as possible in public-sector activity through grants, contracts, and use of federal money as "leverage" for raising money from private sources and from state and local governments.

We should not, however, be too quick to criticize the federal government for its lack of innovation in dealing with public problems. Most governments do not use all the "tools" available to them in their tool kit.[53] Also, there is very little theory to guide government policymakers trying to decide what tools they should use.[54] In particular, there is very little theory, or practical advice, that links the nature of public problems with the most appropriate ways of solving them. As a consequence, a great deal of policy formulation is done by inertia, by analogy, or by intuition.

Who Formulates Policy?

Policy formulation is a difficult game to play because any number of people can and do play, and there are few rules. At one time or another, almost every kind of policy actor will be involved in formulating policy proposals, although several kinds of actors are especially important. Policy formulation is also very much a political activity but not always a partisan activity. Political parties and candidates, in fact, are not as good at promulgating solutions to problems as they are at identifying problems and presenting lofty ambitions for society to solve the problems. Expertise begins to play a large role here, given that the success or failure of a policy instrument will depend to some degree on its technical characteristics, as well as on its political acceptability.

The public bureaucracy.   This is the institution most involved in taking the lofty aspirations of political leaders and translating them into more concrete proposals. Whether one accepts the state-centric model of agenda setting or not, one must realize that government bureaucracies are central to policy formulation. Even if programs are formally introduced by congressmen or the president, it is quite possible that their original formulation and justification came from a friendly bureau.

Bureaucracies presumably are the masters of routine and procedure. This is at once their strength and their weakness. They know how to use procedures and how to develop programs and procedures to reach desired goals. Yet an agency that knows how to do these things too well may develop an excessively narrow vision of how to formulate answers for a particular set of problems. As noted earlier, certain formulas have been developed at the governmental level for responding to problems, and much the same is true of individual organizations that have standard operating procedures and thick rule books. Many of the administrative reforms undertaken during the 1990s sought to jog bureaucracies from these established routines, but old habits are difficult to break. Of course, some commitment to established programs and approaches may not be all bad, as it may serve to complicate the task of reformers who want to embark on untried programs.[55]

Certainly familiarity with an established mechanism can explain some of the conservatism of organizations in the choice of instruments to achieve their ends, and faith in the efficacy of the instrument also helps explain reliance on a limited range of policy tools. One important component of the restrictiveness of choice, however, appears to be self-protection. That is, neither administrators nor their agencies can go very wrong by selecting a solution that is only an incremental departure from an existing program. This is true for two reasons: (1) such a choice will not have as high a probability of failure as a more innovative program, and (2) an incremental choice will almost certainly keep the program in the hands of the existing agency. Hence, reliance on bureaucracy to formulate solutions may be a guarantee of stability, but it is unlikely to produce many successful policy innovations.

Also, agencies will usually choose to do *something* when given the opportunity or the challenge to do so. Making policy choices is their business, and it is certainly in their organizational self-interest to make a response to a problem. The agency personnel know that if they do not respond, some other agency soon will, and their agency will lose an opportunity to increase its budget, personnel, and clout. Agencies do not always act in the self-aggrandizing manner ascribed to them,[56] but when confronted directly with a problem already declared to need solving, they will usually respond with a solution—one that involves their own participation.

There is one final consideration about bureaucratic responses to policy problems: an agency often represents a concentration of a certain type of expertise. Increasingly this expertise is professional, and a growing percentage of the employees of the federal government have professional qualifications.[57] In addition to assisting an agency to formulate better solutions to policy problems, expertise narrows the vision of the agency and the range of solutions that may be considered. Professional training tends to be narrowing rather than broadening, and it tends to teach that the profession possesses *the* solution to a range of problems. Thus, with a concentration of professionals of a certain type, an agency will tend to produce only incremental departures from existing policies. For example, although the Federal Trade Commission and the Antitrust Division of the Department of Justice are both concerned with eliminating monopolistic practices in the economy, the concentration of economists in the former and lawyers in the latter may generate different priorities.[58]

The occupation of public manager itself is becoming more professionalized, so the major reference group for public managers will be other public managers, a factor that may further narrow the range of bureaucratic responses to policy problems. Much of the drive of the new public management,[59] however, has been to empower public managers to make more of their own decisions and to be more significant forces in implementing, if perhaps not making public policy. Thus, senior bureaucrats may be expected to employ their professional expertise, and that of their colleagues, to develop new programs and strategies, as well as simply to make programs perform well.

Think tanks and shadow cabinets.   Other sources of policy formulation are the "think tanks" that encircle Washington and the state capitals around the country. These are organizations of professional analysts and policy formulators who usually work on contract for a client in government—often an agency in the bureaucracy. We would expect much greater creativity and innovation from these organizations than from the public bureaucracy, but other problems arise in the types of policy options they may propose. First, an agency may be able virtually to guarantee the kind of answer it will receive by choosing a certain think tank. Some organizations are more conservative and will usually formulate solutions relying more on incentives and the private sector, while other consultants may recommend more direct government intervention. These reports are likely to have substantial impact, not only because they have been labeled as expert, but also because they have been paid for and therefore should be used.

Another problem that arises is more a problem for the consultants in think tanks than for the agencies, but it certainly affects the quality of the policies recommended. If the think tank is to get additional business from an agency, the consultants believe—perhaps rightly—that they have to tell the agency what it wants to hear. In other words, a consulting firm that says that the favorite approach of an agency is entirely wrong and needs to be completely revamped may be both technically correct and politically bankrupt. Hence, a problem of ethical judgment arises for the consulting firm, as it might for individual analysts working for an organization: what are the boundaries of loyalty to truth and loyalty to the organization?

Three particular think tanks have been of special importance in U.S. policy formulation. Traditionally, the two dominant organizations were the Brookings Institution and the American Enterprise Institute. During the Nixon, Ford, and Reagan administrations, the Brookings Institution was described as "the Democratic party in exile." The Carter and Clinton administrations did indeed tap a number of Brookings staff members for appointments, including Alice Rivlin (formerly at the Congressional Budget Office), who eventually became director of the Office of Management and Budget under Clinton. On the other side of the fence, the American Enterprise Institute (AEI) had housed a number of Nixon and Ford administration personnel, although relatively few were tapped by the more conservative Reagan administration. Both of these think tanks support wide-reaching publication programs to attempt to influence elite public opinion, in addition to their direct involvement in government.

The third major think tank is the Heritage Foundation, which came to prominence during the Reagan years as an advocate of a number of neoconservative policy positions, especially privatization and deregulation.[60] It was less prominent in the George H.W. Bush administration than it had been during the Reagan administration, when its proposals were central to policy formulation in some fields.[61] There has been an increase in the number of think tanks on the political right, funded largely by contributions from industry and wealthy individuals. Prominent among these are the Cato Institute, Citizens for Tax Justice, and the National Center for Policy Analysis. There also has been some resurgence of think tanks on the political left, such as the Center for Budget Priorities. Perhaps most important, these developments demonstrate the continuing polarization of political ideas in the United States.

Universities also serve as think tanks for government. This is true especially for the growing number of public policy schools and programs across the country that, in addition to training future practitioners of the art of government, provide a place where scholars and former practitioners can formulate new solutions to problems. Robert Reich, for example, developed some of the ideas he later attempted to implement as secretary of labor while at the Kennedy School of Government at Harvard.[62] In addition to the policy programs, specialized institutes such as the Institute for Research on Poverty at the University of Wisconsin and the Joint Center on Urban Studies at Harvard and MIT develop policy ideas concerning their specific policy areas.

It is sometimes difficult to determine where think tanks end and interest groups and lobbying organizations begin. The term *think tank* has a more positive connotation than does *interest group*, so the lobbying groups have gone to some lengths to appear as if they were doing objective public policy research. Again, if we go to the Internet and begin to look at the range of opinions that appear on any issue, we can find a number of "institutes," "centers," or "foundations" that are attempting to influence opinion; a careful analysis will reveal that these are really subsidiaries of interest groups.[63]

Interest groups.   Another important source of policy formulation are the interest groups, which must not only identify problems and apply pressure to have them placed on the agenda but also have to supply possible remedies for those problems. Those cures will almost certainly be directed at serving the interests of their group members, but that is only to be expected. It is the task of the authoritative decision makers to take those ideas about policy choices with as many grains of salt as necessary to develop workable plans for solving the problem. Given the continued existence of iron-triangle relationships in many policy areas, a close connection is likely to exist between the policy formulation ideas of an agency and those of the pressure group. The policy choices advocated by established pressure groups will again be rather conservative, and incremental, and they rarely produce sweeping changes from the status quo in which they and their associated agency have a decided interest.

Some interest groups that contradict the traditional model of policy formulation by interest groups are the public-interest groups, such as Common Cause, the Center for the Public Interest, and a variety of consumer and taxpayer organizations. Perhaps the major task of these groups is to break the stranglehold that the iron triangles have on policy and to attempt to broaden the range of interests represented in the policymaking process. These groups are oriented toward reform—some of the issues they have taken up are substantive, such as the strengthening of safety requirements for a variety of products sold in the marketplace. Other issues are procedural, such as campaign reform and opening the regulatory process to greater public input. In general, however, no matter what issue they decide to interest themselves in, these groups advocate sweeping reforms as opposed to incremental changes, and they are important in providing balance to the policy process and in providing a strong voice for reform and change.

Congressmen. Finally, although we have previously tended to denigrate the role of politicians in formulating policy, a number of congressmen do involve themselves in serious formulation activities instead of just accepting advice from friendly sources in the bureaucracy. Like the public-interest groups, these congressmen are generally interested in reform, for if they were primarily interested only in incremental change, there would be little need for their involvement. Some congressmen are also interested in using formulation and advocacy as means of furthering their careers, adopting roles as national policymakers as opposed to the more common pattern of emphasizing constituency service.

Congress as an institution in the early twenty-first century is better equipped to formulate policy than it has ever been, even given the nature of the policy challenges it faces. There has been a continuing growth in the size of congressional staffs, both the personal staffs of congressmen and the staffs of committees and subcommittees.[64] For example, in 1965 Congress employed just over 9,000 people; by 2000 the number of employees had increased to over 31,000. These employees are on the public payroll at least in part to assist members of Congress in doing the research and drafting necessary for active policy formulation, and they are quite important in rectifying what some consider a serious imbalance between the power of Congress and that of the executive branch. For example, the Congressional Budget Office now shadows the Office of Management and Budget, providing an independent source of advice on budgeting and a range of other issues. The Republicans who took control of Congress in 1994 reduced their staffing as a good example to the rest of government, but after those large initial reductions, staffing tended to creep back upward.

How to Formulate Policy

The task of formulating policy involves substantial sensitivity to the nuances of policy (and politics) and a potential for the creative application of the tools of policy analysis. In fact, many of the problems faced by government require substantial creativity because little is known about the problem areas. Nevertheless, governments may have to react to a problem whether or not they are sure of the best, or even a good, course of action. In many instances, the routine responses of a government agency to its environment will be sufficient to meet most problems that arise, but if the routine response is unsuccessful, the agency will have to search for a more innovative response and perhaps involve more actors in policy formulation. In other words, a routine or incremental response may be sufficient for most policy problems, but if it is not, the policymaking system must initiate some form of conscious search behavior. Making policy choices that depart radically from incremental responses will require methods of identifying and choosing among alternatives.

Two major barriers may block government's ability to understand the problems with which it is confronted. One is the lack of some basic factual information about the policy questions at hand. The most obvious example is defense policy, in which governments often lack information about the capabilities and intentions of the opposing side. Indeed, since the end of the Cold War it has become difficult even to identify the potential enemies, much less anticipate their actions. Similarly, in making risk assessments about dangers from various toxic substances or nuclear power plants, there may not be sufficient empirical evidence to determine the probabilities of undesirable events or the probable consequences of those events.[65] Even more difficult for government is that frequently there are no agreed-upon indicators of the nature of social conditions, and even widely accepted indicators for economic variables, such as gross national product and unemployment rates, are somewhat suspect.[66]

Perhaps more important, government decision makers often lack adequate information about the underlying processes that have created the problems they are attempting to solve. For example, in order to address the poverty problem one should understand how poverty comes about and how it is perpetuated. But despite the masses of data and information generated, there is no accepted model of causation for poverty. This dearth of a causal model may be contrasted with decisions about epidemic diseases made by public health agencies using well-developed and accepted theories about how diseases occur and spread. Clearly, different decision-making procedures should be used to attempt to solve different kinds of problems.

Figure 3.1 demonstrates possible combinations of the knowledge of causation and basic factual information about policy problems. The simplest type of policymaking involves *routine* policy, such as Social Security. Making policy in such areas, with adequate information and an accepted theory of causation, primarily requires routine adjustment of existing policies, and for the most part the changes made will be incremental.[67] This relative simplicity would be complicated, however, if the basic theories about creating a desirable retirement situa-

Knowledge of causation

		High	Low
Information	*High*	Routine	Conditional
	Low	Craftsman	Creative

FIGURE 3.1   Kinds of Policy Formulation

tion or the mechanism for financing such a system were seriously altered (see Chapter 11).

Creative policy formulation lies at the other extreme of information and knowledge held by decision makers. In this instance, they have neither an adequate information base nor an adequate theory of causation. Research and development operations, such as those in the National Institutes of Health or in numerous agencies within the Department of Defense, provide important examples of policy formulation of this type.[68] Another example may be the formulation of policies for personal social services, such as counseling. In these instances, a great deal of creativity and care must be exercised in matching the particular needs of the individual with the needs of the agency for efficient management and accountability. Such policies require building in reversibility of policy choices so that creative formulations that prove unworkable can be corrected.

In some situations there may be sufficient information but an inadequate understanding of the underlying processes of causation. These policymaking situations require the formulation of *conditional* policies, in which changes in certain indicators would trigger a policy response of some sort, even if only the reconsideration of the existing policy. It is possible that government can know that certain policies will produce desired results, even if the underlying processes are not fully understood. Following the general loss of faith in Keynesian theories of economic management, it may be that macroeconomic policy is made in this manner. There are several accepted indicators of the state of the economy—unemployment, inflation, and economic growth rates, for example—and changes in these indicators may trigger relatively standard reactions, even if the policymakers cannot always specify, or agree upon, the underlying logic behind those policy responses.[69] Also, it generally is advantageous to build a certain amount of automaticity into the policy response, or at least to provide some insulation against political delay or interference. In economic management, for example, countries with relatively independent central banks have been more successful than those with more politicized central banks.[70]

Finally, in some policy areas governments may have a model of causation for the problem but lack sufficient information to have confidence in any policy response they may formulate. Defense policies may fit this category of *craftsman* policies, for governments appear to understand quite well how to respond to threats and how to go to war, although they frequently have only limited, and possibly distorted, information about the capabilities and intentions of their adversaries. Formulating policies of this type depends on developing a number of contingencies and potential forms of response, as well as identifying means of assessing the risks of possible occurrences. The complex policy deliberations of the American government concerning the possible nuclear capabilities of North Korea and Iraq illustrate the "craftsman" nature of defense and foreign policy. In other words, formulating such policies involves building a probabilistic basis for response, instead of relying on the certainty that might be taken for granted in other policy areas.

These four categories of policymaking are important, but the definition of a policy is a political issue, and the clever policy formulator will attempt to define problems and issues so that they will fit into one category or another. For example, if a problem lies within an agency's range of action, it will attempt to keep it there by defining it as routine, while any agency or interest group that wants to shift the definition—whether to improve the policy or to increase its budget—will attempt to define it as requiring more of a craftsman or creative solution.

Aids for Policy Formulation

Given the difficulties of formulating effective policy responses to many problems, it is fortunate that some techniques have been developed to assist in that formulation. In general, these techniques serve to clarify the consequences of certain courses of action and to provide a summary measure of the probable effects of policy along a single scale of measurement, usually money, so that different policy alternatives can be more effectively compared with one another. I discuss two of these techniques only briefly here, reserving a more detailed exposition and discussion of cost-benefit analysis for Chapter 16. It is important, however, to understand at this point in the discussion something about the considerations that one might take into account when selecting a policy alternative.

Cost-benefit analysis.   The most frequently applied tool for policy analysis is cost-benefit analysis. The utilitarian assumptions and methodology underlying this technique reduce all the costs and benefits of proposed government programs to a quantitative, economic dimension and then compare available alternative policies using that standard. In this mode of policy analysis, economic considerations are almost always paramount. As the methodology has been developed, attempts have been made to place economic values on factors that might be primarily noneconomic, but the principal means of evaluating programs remains utilitarian.[71]

Cost-benefit analysis is in some ways deceptively simple. The total benefits created by the project are enumerated, including those that would be regarded as externalities in the private market (amenity values, recreation, and the like). The costs of the program are also enumerated, again including social costs (e.g., pollution or inequalities). Long-term costs and benefits are also taken into account, although they may be discounted or adjusted because they do occur in the future. Projects whose total benefits exceed their total costs are deemed acceptable, and then choices can be made among the acceptable projects. The general rule is to adopt the project with the greatest net total benefit for society (total benefits minus total costs), and then all others that fit within the total available budget.

Some of the more technical problems of cost-benefit analysis will be discussed later, but it is important to talk about some of the ethical underpinnings of the technique here, as they have a pronounced effect on the formulation of policy alternatives. The fundamental ethical difficulties arise from the assumptions that all values are reducible to monetary terms and that economic criteria are the most important ones for government when making policy. There may well be some values, such as civil liberties or human life or the environment, that many citizens would not want reduced to dollars and cents.[72] Even if such a reduction were possible, it is questionable whether the primary goal of government should be maximizing economic welfare in the society.

Decision analysis.   Cost-benefit analysis assumes that certain events will occur: a dam will be built; it will produce X kilowatts of electricity; Y people from a nearby city will spend Z hours boating and water-skiing on the newly created lake; farmers will save Q dollars in flood protection and irrigation but lose N acres of land for farming. Decision analysis, in contrast, is geared toward making policy choices under conditions of less certainty.[73] This method assumes that in many instances government, having inadequate information, is making probabilistic choices about what to do—that, in fact, government may be almost playing a game, with nature or other human beings as the opponent. As pointed out, governments often do not have a very good conception of the policy instruments they choose, and that lack of knowledge, combined with inadequate knowledge about patterns of causation within the policy area, can be a recipe for disaster. However, if we have some idea about the probabilities of certain outcomes (even without a model of causation), there is a better chance of making better decisions.

Take, for example, a situation in which a hurricane appears to be bearing down upon a major coastal city. On the one hand, the mayor of that city can order an evacuation and cause a great deal of lost production as well as a predictable number of deaths during the rush to escape the city. On the other hand, if he or she does not order the evacuation and the hurricane actually does strike the city, a far larger loss of life will occur. Of course, the hurricane is only forecast to be heading in the general direction of the city, and it may yet veer off. What should the mayor do? How should he or she assess the risks and the possible outcomes of the decision?[74]

This decision-making problem can be organized as a "decision tree," in which the mayor is essentially playing a game against nature (see figure 3.2). The mayor has two possible policy choices: evacuate or not evacuate. We can assign a probability of the two potential occurrences in nature—hit or miss the city—based on the best information available from the weather bureau, and we have estimates of the losses that would occur as a result of each outcome. In this analysis we assume that if the hurricane does strike, the loss of property will be approximately the same whether or not the city is evacuated. As the problem is set up, the mayor makes the smallest possible error by choosing to evacuate the city. By doing so, he or she may cause an expected unnecessary loss of $7 million ($10 million multiplied by the probability of the event of .70) if the hurricane does not hit, but there would be an expected unnecessary loss of $30 million if the evacuation were not ordered and the hurricane did actually strike. Such a simple decision will be easy to make if there is sufficient information available.

In more complex situations, when many facts need to be considered simultaneously, the decision-making process becomes more difficult, especially when one faces a human opponent, rather than nature. Even then, the technique, like cost-benefit analysis, is only an aid to decision making and policy formulation. Decisions still must be made by individuals who will consider ethical, economic, and political factors before making a judgment about what should be done. And as the results of policy formulation will be felt in the future, the exercise of judgment is especially important. When an issue is newly placed on the agenda, the first formulation of a solution will to some degree structure subsequent attempts at solution and therefore will have an enduring legacy that must be considered very carefully.

Policy Design

All the aids that government can utilize when formulating policy still do not generate an underlying approach to policy design. That is, no technical means of addressing public problems relates the characteristics of those problems to the

Decision	Probability	Nature	Expected loss

	−3 ——	Hurricane hits	$0
Evacuate			
	−7 ——	Hurricane misses (Loss = $10 million)	$7 million
	−3 ——	Hurricane hits (Loss = $100 million)	$30 million
Not evacuate			
	−7 ——	Hurricane misses	$0

FIGURE 3.2   A Decision Tree on Evacuation

instruments that might be used to solve them, or to the values that would be used to evaluate the success of the policy.[75] Without such a comprehensive approach to design, much policy formulation in government is accomplished by intuition or inertia, or by analogy with existing programs. This inertial pattern produces frequent mistakes and often much wasted time and effort. Thus, one of the many tasks of policy analysis is to develop a comprehensive approach to the problems of formulating effective policies—requiring not only some idea of what "good" policies are but also some strategies for developing policymaking processes that can produce desirable policies.

In the United States, any such comprehensive approach to policy design is likely to be resisted. In the first place, the generally antistatist values of American politics make a planned, rationalistic approach unacceptable to many politicians and citizens. Second, as was pointed out earlier, for institutional as well as ideological reasons American politics tends toward incremental solutions to problems rather than imposition of comprehensive frameworks or use of design concepts for policymaking.[76] Attempting to impose a design on a policy area may threaten the interests of agencies and committees that believe that they "own" the problem and have been responsible for the development of the existing policy over time. Third, for many of the most important policy problems that American government now faces, there is yet inadequate agreement on the nature of the problem, much less on the nature of the solution to the problem. Important policy problems such as poverty, crime, maleducation, and the like still lack clear definitions of causes, much less of solutions. These important political realities should not, however, prevent policy analysts from attempting to understand social problems in a less haphazard fashion than is sometimes encountered in government or from advocating innovative program designs for solving those problems.

Summary

This chapter has taken the policymaking process through its first stages: considering problems and then developing some mechanisms for solving them. Both activities—and indeed the entire activity of policymaking—are political exercises, but they also involve the application of techniques and tools for analysis. The tools for agenda setting are largely political, requiring the "selling" of agenda items to authorized decision makers who may believe that they already have enough to do. Agenda setting also requires a detailed knowledge of the issue in question so that it can be related first to the known preferences of decision makers and second to existing policies and programs. Agenda setting is in some ways the art of doing something new so that it appears old.

The techniques that can be applied to policy formulation are more sophisticated technically, but they also require sensitive political hands that can use them effectively. To a great extent, the use of old solutions for new problems applies in formulation as well as in agenda setting. For both agenda setting and policy formulation, incremental solutions are favored in the United States. This incrementalism produces a great deal of stability in the policy process, but it makes rapid response to major changes in the economy and society difficult.

The solutions that emerge from these first stages of the policy process, then, are designed to be readily accepted by legislators and administrators who must authorize and legitimate the policies selected. A more comprehensive approach to design might well produce better solutions to problems, but it would face the barrier of political feasibility. The task of the analyst and advocate then becomes stretching the boundaries of feasibility to produce better public policies.

CHAPTER 4
Legitimating Policy Choices

ONCE IT HAS BEEN DECIDED that a certain program is required, or is feasible, as a response to a policy problem, that choice must be defended as a legitimate one for government to make. No matter what course of action is decided on, it is almost certain that some citizens will believe themselves disadvantaged by the choice. At a minimum, any public program or project will cost money, and citizens who pay taxes and receive (or perceive) no direct benefits from the new program will frequently consider themselves to be harmed by the policy choice. Because policy choices inevitably benefit some citizens and disadvantage others, a great deal of attention must be given in a democratic government to the process by which decisions are made. It is by means of the official process of government that substantive policy decisions are legitimated; that is, the process attaches the legitimate authority of the state to the policy that is chosen.

Legitimacy is a fundamental concept in the discipline of political science, and it is important in understanding policymaking. Legitimacy is conventionally defined as a belief on the part of citizens that the current government represents a proper form of government, and a willingness on the part of those citizens to accept the decrees of the government as legal and authoritative.[1] The vast majority of Americans regard the government of the United States as the appropriate set of institutions to govern the country. And most Americans consequently accept the actions of that government as authoritative (as having the force of law) as long as the actions are carried out in accordance with the processes established in the Constitution, or by procedures derived from the processes described in the Constitution. It is understood that all policies adopted must be within the powers granted to the federal government by the Constitution. The boundaries of the policies considered "constitutional" have expanded during the history of the United States, but the limits current at the time establish the boundaries of legitimate action.

Several things should be understood about legitimacy as it affects contemporary policymaking in the United States. First, legitimacy is largely a psychological property. It depends on the majority's acceptance of the appropriateness of a government. A government may come to power by all the prescribed processes, but if the population does not willingly accept that government or the rules by which it gained power, then in practice it has no legitimacy. For example, many constitutions (including those of France and Britain) give governments the right to suspend civil liberties and declare martial law, but citizens accustomed to greater freedom may find it difficult to accept decrees such as that,[2] unless a crisis such as that of 11 September 2001, intervenes to expand the range of acceptable action. Further, changes in a government may cause some citizens to question the legitimacy of a new government's actions.

Legitimacy has substantive as well as procedural elements. It matters not only how issues are decided but also what is decided. The government of the United States might decide to nationalize all oil companies operating in the country. (It will not do this, but just imagine so for a moment.) The decision could be reached with all appropriate deliberation as prescribed by the Constitution, but it would still not be acceptable to the majority of citizens. A more realistic example was provided by the war in Vietnam, which was conducted according to the procedures of the Constitution but was nevertheless rejected as illegitimate by a significant proportion of the population. In consequence, that conflict evoked a response from Congress, in the form of the War Powers Act, that would change the procedures by which the United States could become involved in any future foreign conflicts.[3] The substantive question of legitimacy therefore produced a procedural response, although the debate in 2002 and 2003 over the ability of President George W. Bush to attack Iraq demonstrated that the procedures are themselves far from clear. At a somewhat less dramatic level, the attempts on the part of Congress to increase its own pay during 1989 and 1990 were procedurally correct but raised such an outcry from the public that they could not be implemented; the American public clearly regarded those actions as illegitimate.

Legitimacy is both a variable and a constant—it differs among individuals and across time. Some citizens of the United States may not accept the legitimacy of the current government. For example, some African-American leaders have rejected the legitimacy of the U.S. government and called for the formation of a separate African-American nation within the country. On the other side, white supremacists have organized settlements in parts of the West that reject the authority of all the constituted governments, and they even have engaged in armed conflict with federal agents. Citizens also appear more willing to accept the actions of state and local governments than those of the federal government.

A general decline in confidence in American institutions has been occurring, and that decline has been especially pronounced for government institutions other than the military (see table 4.1).[4] There was some upturn in confidence in

TABLE 4.1 Confidence in American Institutions, 1973–2002 (percentage saying "Great deal" or "Quite a lot")

	2002	1998	1996	1994	1993	1991	1990	1989	1988	1987	1985	1983	1979	1973
Military	71	64	66	64	68	85	68	63	58	61	61	53	54	n.a.
Organized religion	23	59	57	54	53	59	56	52	59	61	66	62	65	66
Supreme Court	41	42	45	42	44	48	47	46	56	52	56	42	45	44
Presidency	50	22	39	38	43	72	n.a.	n.a.	n.a.	n.a.	n.a.	n.a.	n.a.	n.a.
Public schools	n.a.	37	38	34	39	44	45	43	49	50	48	39	53	58
Newspapers	16	31	32	29	31	32	39	n.a.	36	31	35	38	51	39
Organized labor	11	26	25	26	26	25	27	n.a.	26	26	28	26	36	30
Big business	16	22	24	26	22	26	25	n.a.	25	n.a.	31	28	32	26
Congress	22	28	20	26	22	30	24	32	35	n.a.	39	28	34	42

Source: The Gallup Poll Monthly, April 1994, 6; CNN/Gallup Poll, May 1998; Harris Poll, January 2002.

the early 1980s, but that has decayed and Americans now have less confidence in government than they have had in the past. In particular, Congress now is one of the least respected institutions in the United States. The various scandals during the second Clinton administration had an impact on the confidence of citizens in the presidency, and the first year of the George W. Bush administration seemed to have restored legitimacy to the office, despite the extreme confusion of the 2000 election.[5] The ability of President Clinton to hold on to popularity and positive evaluations indicates in large part the role that economic performance has on the perceptions of citizens.[6]

In societies that are deeply divided ethnically or politically, the rejection of the sitting government by one side or another is a constant fact of life. Even a government that is widely accepted may lose legitimacy or strain its legitimate status through unpopular activities and leaders. The Vietnam War and the Watergate scandal illustrate the low points to which the legitimacy of even a widely accepted political regime may fall. Nevertheless, the American government was able to survive those problems, as well as such subsequent problems as the Iran-*contra* controversy and the several scandals during the Clinton administration, and continue to govern with legitimate authority.

Because of the variability of legitimacy, a fully legitimated government may gradually erode its legitimate status through time. A series of blatantly unpopular or illegal actions may reduce the authority of a government, making it open to challenge, whether of a revolutionary or more peaceable nature. Or a government may lose legitimacy through incompetence rather than unpopular activities. Citizens in most countries have a reservoir of respect for government, and governments can add to or subtract from that stock of authority. As a result, governments are engaged in a continuing process of legitimation for themselves and their successors.

Finally, government must somehow legitimate each individual policy choice. No matter how technically correct a policy choice may be, it is of little practical value if it cannot be justified to the public. For example, the decision to correct the over-indexing of Social Security pension benefits once the mistake was discovered was absolutely correct, but it created a huge political controversy and a sense of betrayal among some elderly citizens.[7] Policy analysts, in their pursuit of elegant solutions and innovative policies, frequently forget this mundane point, but their forgetfulness can present a real barrier to their success.[8] To design a policy that can be legitimated, a policy analyst must understand the political process, for that process will define the set of feasible policy alternatives in a more restrictive fashion than does the economic and social world—that is, more programs could work than could be adopted within the political values of the American system. Thus, the task of the policy analyst is to be able to "sell" his or her decisions to the individuals who are crucial to their being legitimated. This does not mean that the an-

Characteristics of decisions

		Majoritarian	Nonmajoritarian
Range of actors	*Mass*	Referendums	—
	Elite	Congress	Courts; administrative regulations

FIGURE 4.1 Modes of Legitimation

alyst must advocate only policies that fit the existing definitions of feasibility, but it does mean that the analyst must have a strategy for expanding that definition if a highly innovative program is to be proposed.[9]

In general, legitimation may be performed through the legislative process, through the administrative process designed for the issuing of regulations (secondary legislation), through the courts, or through mechanisms of direct democracy. As shown in figure 4.1, these modes of legitimation can be seen as combining characteristics of decisions—majoritarian and nonmajoritarian—and the range of actors involved. The nonmajoritarian mass cell is empty in this table, but it might be filled by revolutionary or extremely powerful interest-group activities. Indeed, the ongoing political controversy over abortion policy may fall into this cell, given that there is apparently no popular majority for the policies being pushed by an intense and active minority, although that minority has been successful in some states (see Chapter 15). We next discuss each type of legitimation and its implications for the policy choices that might be feasible as a result of each process.

Legislative Legitimation

In the United States we traditionally have equated lawmaking with Congress, the principal legislative body at the federal level, or with similar bodies at the state level. As this section points out, that notion is now excessively naive, for the workload and the technical content of many subjects on which decisions have to be made have overwhelmed Congress. This loss of capacity to legislate effectively is true despite the massive growth of legislative staffs and the increased availability of policy advice for congressmen. Governments are simply too large and involved in too many issues to permit a large legislative institution such as Congress, with all its intricate procedures, to make the full range of decisions required to keep the society functioning (from a public policy perspective).

Of course, Congress remains the crucial source for primary legislation. That is, although administrative bodies are responsible for writing regulations in large numbers, Congress must supply the basic legislative frameworks within which other bodies can operate. Congress tends to pass legislation written in relatively broad language, allowing administrators latitude for interpretation. Thus, despite the resurgence of congressional power in opposing the "imperial presidency" from the 1970s and the Reagan administration in the 1980s, it is best to think about the legitimating role of Congress as the authorizing of relatively diffuse statements of goals and structures. Those broad statements are then made operational by the executive branch, which fills in the details by writing regulations and by using the implementation process.

Congress also retains its supervisory powers—oversight—so that if the executive branch strays too far when writing regulations (see pp. 84–86), Congress can reassert its intentions in constructing the legislation.[10] Until 1983, Congress had virtually unlimited powers to pass "legislative vetoes," which required agencies issuing certain types of regulations to submit those regulations to Congress for approval. Although the Supreme Court has declared that the legislative veto is excessive meddling by one branch of government into the affairs of another and so is not constitutional,[11] Congress has continued to utilize similar instruments in other policy areas.[12] If nothing else, Congress can always pass amendments to a previous law to clarify its intentions, or if it must, even repeal the previous legislation.

Congress places a great deal of emphasis on procedural legitimation and has established elaborate sets of procedures for processing legislation.[13] In fact, its institutions and procedures have become so well developed that it is difficult for legislation to be passed. Typically, a bill must be passed by a subcommittee, by a full committee, and by floor action in each house. And because one house is unlikely to pass a bill in exactly the same form as the other house, conference committees are often necessary to reconcile the two versions. Given the possibility of using more arcane procedural mechanisms, such as filibusters, amendments, and recommitals, legislation can be slowed down or killed at a number of points by failure to attract the necessary majority at the proper time. Or, to put it the other way around, all that the opponents of a bill have to do is to muster a majority at one crucial point to prevent the passage of legislation.[14]

Legislative procedures are important as mechanisms to prevent unnecessary or poorly formulated legislation from becoming law, but they can also frustrate good and needed legislation. The ability of the opposition to postpone or block civil rights legislation during the 1950s and 1960s demonstrated clearly the capacity of legislative procedures to thwart the apparent majority will of Congress. More recently, the continuing inability to produce a national health insurance bill or to pass a strong bill to control tobacco, indicates the difficulties of passing legislation even when a significant portion of the population favors some change from the status quo.[15] A well-supported and committed minority is thus able to use legislative procedures to achieve its own ends.

Legitimation through the legislative process is majoritarian. It depends on building either simple or special majorities at each crucial point in the process. The task of the policy analyst or the legislative leader is to construct such majorities. In addition to appealing for support on the basis of the actual qualities of the proposed legislation, the analyst can form the needed majorities in several other ways. One method, which has been referred to as *partisan analysis*,[16] involves convincing members of Congress that the piece of legislation that the analyst wants is something that they want as well. The trick here is to design the legislation in such a way that it will appeal to a sufficient number of interests to create a winning coalition. For example, the National Defense Education Act of 1958 was passed by a coalition of congressmen interested in education and in defense. The title of the bill indicates that it was intended to serve those two purposes, and it affects those two areas. It brought together liberals favoring a stronger federal role in education with conservatives favoring a stronger defense posture. Likewise, many social and housing programs have been "sold" to conservatives as benefiting business—as urban renewal certainly did—or as providing employment.[17]

Another strategy for forming coalitions that is not dissimilar to partisan analysis is *logrolling*,[18] in which coalitions are formed not around a single piece of legislation but across a set of legislative initiatives. In the simplest example, Congressman A favors bill A but is indifferent toward bill B. Congressman B, on the other hand, favors bill B but is indifferent to bill A. The logical thing for these two congressmen to do is to trade their votes on the two pieces of legislation, with A voting for bill B and B voting for bill A. The real world may not be so convenient, however, and several bills may be involved in vote trading across time. In some ways, logrolling is a rational activity because it allows the passage of legislation that some congressmen—and presumably their constituencies—favor intensely but that might not otherwise be able to gain a majority. But logrolling also has the effect of approving a great deal more legislation than would otherwise be passed, thus boosting public expenditures and taxation. It enables relatively narrow interests in the nation to develop coalitions for their legislation that may not be justifiable in terms of the broader "public interest."

As well as being a majoritarian body, Congress has universalistic norms that promote the spreading of government expenditures very broadly.[19] This is commonly referred to as *pork-barrel legislation*, or as the parochial imperative in American politics. Pork-barrel legislation often concerns capital expenditures, for which the classic examples are river and harbor improvements. Obtaining such capital projects for their home districts has become a measure of congressmen's success; some argue that "bringing home the bacon," instead of policymaking on broad national issues, has become the dominant activity of

Congress.[20] Thus, the tendency in designing legislation of this kind is to spread benefits as broadly as possible geographically and to create a majority by benefiting virtually anyone who wants a piece of the "pork." As with logrolling, this pattern of decision making tends to increase the costs of government. Douglas Arnold is quite correct in pointing out that pork-barrel legislation costs very little when compared with national defense or Social Security,[21] but it stands as an example of the way in which government misuses money by funding projects with relatively low social benefit in order to ensure the reelection of incumbent congressmen. Politically, the importance of this style of decision making may outstrip the actual amount of money spent.

This description of legitimation through the legislative process does not give the most favorable impression of Congress. Actually, a good deal of congressional decision making is based on the merits of the legislation. To the extent that partisan analysis, logrolling, and pork-barrel legislation characterize the actions of Congress, however, the legislative process has certain effects on the kinds of rules that can be legitimated. It can be argued that the legislative process almost inevitably produces broad and rather diffuse legislation. The necessity of building a coalition requires that one take care not to offend potential members and that the proposed legislation does produce benefits for individual congressmen and their districts. As a consequence, the bill must be designed to be amenable to partisan analysis and must not be so clearly worded as to reduce the number of possible coalition members. This strategy of obfuscation allows administrators to make politically charged decisions on difficult issues by deflecting criticism from individual members of Congress.

Both logrolling and pork-barrel legislation are related to the expansion of government beyond the bounds that could be set if there were no possibility of vote trading. The possibility of trading votes and building coalitions across pieces of legislation fuels a tendency to adopt public projects that are marginal in terms of social productivity. It is obvious that the world of policymaking is not perfectly rational, but these patterns of institutional decision making seem to exacerbate the irrational character of much of politics, producing programs that benefit the few at the expense of the many.[22] Logrolling and the pork barrel also make reducing the size of unneeded programs difficult. For example, the only effective way for Congress to accomplish the closing of redundant military bases in the early 1990s was to specify in advance that an independent commission would recommend closings that would then be voted on as a group. Otherwise, logrolling might have prevented the closing of any bases at all. This self-denying restraint appeared to break down in 1998, when Congress demanded more influence in retaining bases that the Department of Defense itself wanted to close.[23]

These difficulties in congressional decision making suggest more general points concerning problems of social decision making. In its simplest terms, the problem is this: how can a set of social preferences best be expressed in a single decision? Congress faces this problem when it attempts to combine the preferences of its members and their constituents in a single decision whether or not to adopt a piece of legislation; the same general problem arises in club, committee, and college faculty meetings.

One underlying problem facing decision makers in legislatures and elsewhere is the varying intensity of preferences. We faced this problem when discussing the logic of logrolling—in a majoritarian system, it may be possible to construct a majority composed of individuals who are not much interested in a proposal or do not feel intensely about it. This decision-making problem is in part a function of each legislator's having only one vote, whereas individuals in the market setting have more than one dollar and can apply their resources differentially depending on their preferences and the intensity of those preferences. Logrolling is one means of attempting to overcome the intensity problem, but it can be successful only in a limited set of circumstances with a certain distribution of preferences.

In majoritarian institutions with one vote per member, it is difficult to reflect accurately the preferences of the participants in a manner that creates the greatest net satisfaction for the participants. Generating such an optimal decision is made more difficult if in a number of successive decisions (e.g., voting on amendments) the order in which options are eliminated affects the final preferences.[24] In examining problems about making choices of this type, the economist Kenneth Arrow argued that it is impossible to devise a social-choice mechanism that satisfies the logical conditions for rationality.[25] The only way in which such decisions can be arrived at, in Arrow's framework, is to impose them, which he rejects on philosophical grounds. But the imposition of administrative regulations as another means of legitimating decisions has some characteristics of imposed solutions, although the procedures for adopting regulations have been sanctioned legally.

Oversight

Once Congress has enacted legislation, it has played its major role in legitimating policy, but its involvement is not over. We have already pointed out that the administrative agencies perform a major role in translating legislation into specific regulations. Congress then exercises some degree of oversight over the actions of the agencies.[26] The committees that initially approved the legislation monitor the way in which the agencies implement it and then can act legislatively to correct anything the agencies may do incorrectly. Congress may not even have to do anything directly—often it can rely on its implicit authority over legislation and budgets to gain compliance from the agencies.

Oversight is in essence a second round of legitimation by Congress, which passes the initial legislation and then looks over the shoulders of the implementers to ensure that its intentions are followed. This oversight activity can be only so effective, however, because of the scarcity of time and the need of congressional actors to proceed with the next round of legislation. Furthermore, even the well-staffed U.S. Congress may lack the necessary expertise to judge the numerous, complex, and technical regulations issued by administrative agencies and the even more numerous administrative decisions taken by the agencies. This means that oversight tends to be more "fire alarm" (reaction to crises) than "police patrol" (routine scanning of the relevant environment).[27] The efforts of the Republican Congress in the 1990s to reduce the number of committees and subcommittees has therefore also reduced its capacity to exert oversight over agencies, given that there is less focused expertise.[28]

Regulations and the Administrative Process

Most rulemaking in the United States and other industrialized societies is now done through the regulatory process.[29] Here we are referring to the regulatory process in a rather broad context to include the rulemaking activities of executive branch agencies as well as those of independent regulatory commissions.[30] We will discuss the process by which administrative or independent regulatory bodies can issue binding regulations that are subsidiary to congressional legislation—these regulations are sometimes referred to as *secondary legislation*. Issuing such regulations is definitely a legislative or legitimating activity because it makes rules for the society, but those rules must be pursuant to primary legislation already adopted by Congress.

The volume of regulation-writing in the federal government is immense, as can be judged by the size of the *Federal Register*, a weekly publication containing all regulations and proposed regulations (approximately 70,000 pages per year), and by the size of the *Code of Federal Regulations* (*CFR*), which contains all the regulations currently in force. One example of the volume of regulatory activity is provided by the Occupational Safety and Health Administration (OSHA) in the Department of Labor. OSHA, which has been a frequent target of the critics of government regulation, issued 4,600 regulations during the first two years of its existence and continues to issue hundreds of new regulations each year. As of 1997 these regulations amounted to almost 4,000 pages of rather fine print in the *CFR*. Taken together, three areas of public policy—agriculture, labor, and the environment—account for rules requiring approximately 25,000 pages in the *Code of Federal Regulations*.[31]

Although conducted through a legal process, the decision making required for adopting regulations is not majoritarian. If it were, many of the regulations adopted by OSHA and other regulatory bodies might never be approved. Decision making in the regulatory process can be more technical and less tied to political considerations than is decision making in Congress, although political considerations cannot be neglected entirely, especially by agencies that are components of executive branch departments. Executive branch agencies are directly responsible to the president, and consequently they are under pressure to issue regulations that address the president's political priorities. Recent presidents have taken greater pains than their predecessors to know what regulations are being issued and to ensure that they match presidential priorities. Even the regulations issued by independent regulatory agencies cannot afford to stray too far from the basic political and ideological norms of the public; if they do, the agency threatens its own survival or at least its latitude to issue further regulations.

One of the ways in which government has attempted to keep regulatory activity in check is through regulatory analysis. President Carter, for example, required agencies to justify their choice of any one particular regulation against others, largely on economic grounds. President Reagan went further, requiring executive agencies to submit all new regulations for review by the Office of Management and Budget (OMB) and later to report their plans for regulatory activity for the subsequent year. These regulatory reviews were as much political as economic, and they resulted in critics referring to the OMB as the "regulatory KGB."[32] The Republican Congress first elected in 1994 took regulatory analysis even further by mandating, through a formal regulatory review statute (PL 104–208), that OMB submit to Congress an economic assessment of each new regulation so that the magnitude of the impact on the economy could be assessed.

Although the OMB review of regulations has been in many cases political and ideological, it also has served a legitimation function. In the first place, the elected presidency does have greater legitimacy than does the unelected bureaucracy, especially given the generally low opinion that Americans have of the bureaucracy. Further, it can be argued that because the techniques used in regulatory analysis are "rational," any regulations that survive it may be more likely to make a positive contribution to the well-being of society.[33]

Even by the time of the George H.W. Bush administration, some analysts were arguing that deregulation had gone too far. So, for example, during that administration the Environmental Protection Agency began to issue a number of important new regulations, including significant new air pollution standards for five northeastern states. The Clinton administration took a somewhat more positive view of regulation and its impact on the economy and society. Proclaiming themselves to be "new Democrats," members of this administration adopted a more activist position in environmental and economic regulation, but they attempted to write those regulations with greater amounts of consultation and negotiation—including substantially more public involvement and public disclosure—than had been common in the past, even though some of the tools of regulatory analysis remained in place.[34] Early in the George W. Bush administration, however, the more analytic regulatory review was replaced by a moratorium on regulation, and many of the regulations issued toward the end of the Clinton administration were suspended.

Public Access to the Regulatory Process

The process of making regulations is open to the public's influence, as well as that of the president and OMB. The procedures of the Administrative Procedures Act and several other laws affecting the issuing of regulations require that agencies accept advice and ideas from interested citizens as the process goes forward and that time be given at each stage for affected interests in the society to respond to the agency initiatives.[35] For some segments of the economy, in fact, the regulatory process may be more democratic than decision making in Congress. The regulatory process permits direct access of affected interests to decision makers, whereas in Congress those affected interests may be excluded from effective involvement, especially if they represent an interest not widely considered "legitimate" by congressmen. Furthermore, the regulatory outcomes may be more "in the public interest" than those devised by Congress, given that special-interest influences are funneled through an administrative process and frequently made subject to judicial review.[36]

Access to the regulation-writing process does not, of course, mean that the ideas of the affected interests, or "public-interest groups," will be dominant in the decisions finally made. Simply granting access does not protect the interests of segments of the society that are not sufficiently well organized, or sufficiently alert, to make their presentations to the agency. Maintaining access to agency decision making is by no means costfree, so many less-well-funded groups may be excluded. This has led some agencies, such as the Federal Trade Commission, to provide funding for interests that might not otherwise have the lawyers and other resources needed to participate effectively.[37] Again, there are no guarantees of success, but the procedures do indicate the openness of the regulatory process to a range of ideas and opinions.

The Processes of Writing Regulations

There are two principal ways in which regulation writers collect ideas and opinions. The first, *formal rulemaking,* has some of the appearance of a court proceeding, with a formal hearing, the taking of oral testimony from witnesses, and the use of counsel.[38] Formal rulemaking is a time-consuming and cumbersome process, but it is deemed necessary when the social and economic interests involved are considered sufficiently important. Examples of formal rulemaking are the approval of new medications by the Food and Drug Administration and the licensing of nuclear power plants by the Nuclear Regulatory Commission. The written records generated in such proceedings are important, given that these rulings are important to many elements in society and may be the subject of subsequent discussion and litigation.

The second method of collecting inputs is *informal rulemaking*, which proceeds through three basic steps. First, the agency is required to publish in the *Federal Register* a notice of its intent to issue a certain regulation. Then, a period of several months is specified, during which individuals and groups who believe themselves potentially affected by the rule can offer opinions and make suggestions about the content of the regulation. Finally, after the designated time has passed, the agency may issue a draft of the regulation that the agency would ultimately like to see put into effect. The draft may be based on the suggestions received from affected interests, or it may be what the agency had been planning all along. Then there is another waiting period for responses to the draft regulation, which may be made directly to the agency or submitted indirectly—by having a friendly congressman contact the agency with proposed alterations. Then, based on these responses, as well as its own beliefs about the appropriateness of the regulation, the agency issues the final regulation that will have the force of law.

In addition to the two principal forms of rulemaking, administrative law has developed two other ways of adopting regulations. *Hybrid rulemaking* represents an attempt at compromise between the thoroughness of the formal process and the relative ease of the informal process.[39] This form of rulemaking came about in part because of the courts[40] but also was required by some acts of Congress, especially for environmental policy.[41] Although full-scale judicial proceedings are not called for, there may be requirements for the opportunity to cross-examine witnesses in order to create a full judicial record, which can then be the basis for an appeal if further judicial proceedings are demanded.

The other emerging form of rulemaking is *negotiated rulemaking*. Given the complexity of many of the policy areas into which government must now venture, and the number of interests involved in each policy, it may be easier to negotiate rules than to attempt to make them administratively.[42] This process can save a great deal of future ill will among the affected interests, and it may actually create superior policies to those that might emerge from a more centrally directed process. Congress recognized the validity of this form of rulemaking by passing the Negotiated Rulemaking Act of 1990 to specify the conditions under which this procedure can be used and the procedures required. Language about negotiated rulemaking has also been included in the authorizing legislation for several executive agencies.[43]

While negotiated rulemaking is an attempt to open the process to a variety of actors and thus make it somewhat more democratic, there are also pressures to make the process more technocratic. In particular, there has been increasing interest in regulatory analysis, or the attempt to apply cost-benefit analysis and other forms of economic analysis to regulations before they are adopted. The legitimate force of a regulation is derived from passage of a statute by Congress and from then following correct procedures (as specified in the Administrative Procedures Act) in issuing the regulation. In general, issuing a regulation takes about eighteen months from beginning to end and allows for substantial representation of affected groups and individuals. Attempts to short-circuit the process will probably result in the regulation's being rejected, no matter how reasonable on its face, if appealed through the court system. The law does authorize, however, some provisions for emergency rulemaking for some agencies.

The role assigned to affected interests in responding to issues in the regulatory process brings up another point about social decision making. In part as a means of justifying slavery, John C. Calhoun argued that a proper democracy would take into account not only the majority of individuals but also a majority of interests in society. His idea of "concurrent majorities" would have assigned greater importance to the role of pressure groups than is true in most of American political thought and would have made the opinions of the groups more central in process of writing regulations. The fundamental point is that a decision should reflect not a simple majority but rather a more complex agreement upon a range of segments of society.

The role of interest groups in decision making about regulations is similar to the development of "neocorporatism" in Western Europe.[44] The principal difference is that interest groups in the United States usually are not granted the quasi-official status as representatives of the economic or social group that they have acquired in much of Europe. Further, the affected interest groups are rarely brought together to negotiate a compromise decision, as they might be in many European systems,[45] although the Clinton administration did so in organizing a conference between logging interests and conservationists in the Pacific Northwest to discuss their differences over protection of the spotted owl.[46] Decision making in the United States is still done largely within the agency itself, however, with interest groups involved primarily as sources of information. In addition to protecting the interests of their members, the interest groups frequently make substantive points about proposed regulations and can help prevent agencies from making serious substantive errors in their rules.

Finally, regulatory decision making is threatened by the classic problem of the "capture" of regulatory agencies by the very interests they were designed to regulate.[47] Agencies that regulate a single industry have tended to become advocates for their industries rather than impartial protectors of the public interest. Capture results from the agencies' need to maintain political support when, especially with independent regulatory commissions, the only logical source of such support is the regulated industry itself. The public is usually too amorphous a body to offer the specific support an agency requires to defend its budget, or even its very existence, before Congress. Thus, reforms intended to remove political pressures from regulatory decision making by making the agencies independent have succeeded only in making them independent of one source of political pressure but dependent on another. In Theodore J. Lowi's terminology, the public interest is appropriated for private gain.[48]

The capture argument is less applicable to newer regulatory agencies, which operate across a number of industries, than it is to single-industry regulatory bodies.[49] For example, both the Consumer Products Safety Commission (CPSC) and the Occupational Safety and Health Administration (OSHA) regulate virtually every industry in the country; their advocacy and protection of any one industry might only injure other industries. It is generally too difficult for an industry to capture these cross-cutting regulators, and they are therefore more likely to operate "in the public interest"—although the agency itself may be permitted to define the public interest. These organizations are not immune from political pressures, however. The George W. Bush administration quickly became embroiled in a conflict over appointments to the CPSC in an attempt to make the organization more friendly to business in general than it had been during the Clinton years.

Regulation is a central process in the legitimation of policies, although it is one that many citizens would challenge. Many critics, both popular writers and academics, comment negatively on the making of laws by bureaucrats without the direct congressional involvement that they consider the essential process for legitimation.[50] These regulatory procedures used are "due," however, and they have been ordained by several acts of Congress. Each regulation adopted must have a legislative peg to hang on, but unlike acts of Congress, these regulations tend to make specific judgments and decisions, and by so doing to affect individual interests more directly. Many regulations issued through this process have been criticized as impractical and unnecessary—everyone has his or her favorite silly regulation. Presidents have also been concerned about the effects of regulation on the economy and society and, beginning at least with President Ford, have sought to create more deregulation than regulation.[51] Although the regulatory process offers a possibility of greater objectivity and scientific "rationality" than does the more politicized arena of Congress, it may well be that the very attempt to apply such strict criteria for decisions is the source of many objections.

The Courts

Another nonmajoritarian means of legitimating policies is provided by the courts. Just as the administrative process has assumed an increasing role in legitimation, the courts have become increasingly involved in issuing authoritative policy statements. Some critics have argued that public policy in the United States is indeed dominated by the court system, and not to the benefit of the types of policies generated.[52] Further, along with complaints against the administrative process, there have been complaints about "judge-made law" as an illegitimate usurpation of congressional prerogatives. Of course, the courts have been involved in legitimating actions and issuing law-like statements in the United States for some time. However, perhaps because of the increasing litigation involving social issues (e.g., abortion) and the willingness of the courts to make declarations about remedies to remove violations of the Constitution from federal laws, popular awareness of the role of the courts in making rules for society has grown.

The constitutional basis for the courts to make legitimating decisions is the "supremacy clause," which says that all laws and treaties made in pursuance of the Constitution are the supreme law of the land. In *Marbury v. Madison*, Chief Justice John Marshall decided that it was incumbent on the courts to decide whether or not a law conformed to the Constitution and to declare, if it did not, that the law was void. Following from that basic declaration of judicial power, the courts have been able to make rules based on their interpretation of the Constitution. Particularly crucial to their role in legitimating actions is their ability to accept or reject the remedies proposed by parties to particular disputes. If an action is declared unconstitutional, the courts frequently become involved in determining the actions needed to correct that unconstitutionality.

The most obvious examples of courts prescribing remedies to situations they find unconstitutional have been in cases involving school desegregation and prison overcrowding. In several cases, for example, *Swann v. Charlotte-Mecklenburg Board of Education*, the courts declared that the existence of boundaries between school districts constituted an intent on the part of local governments to maintain or create racial segregation of the schools and then that cross-district busing was the logical remedy for the problem. In other cases, the courts declared that seriously overcrowded prisons constituted cruel and unusual punishment, violating the Eighth Amendment to the Constitution. Judges then decided that they would take over the prison systems and run them directly in order to correct the situation, or they would make very specific policies that state administrators were obliged to follow.[53] These decisions represent greater involvement of the courts in mandating state and local government actions than many citizens consider proper.

The role the courts have accepted for themselves in legitimating action is twofold. In its simplest sense, the courts may further legitimate the actions of other decision makers by declaring that their actions are acceptable under the Constitution. As mentioned above, American society appears to be becoming increasingly litigious, so more and more issues are not fully decided until they have been ruled on by the courts. Litigation presents an important means of protecting individual rights in the policymaking process, but it can also slow down greatly the implementation of policy. Putting an issue into the court system is sometimes a means of winning a conflict simply by delay, as in the largely successful attempts to block construction of nuclear power plants.

In a second sense, the courts take part in policy legitimation by deciding that certain conditions existing in the society are in contradiction of the Constitution and by then offering solutions to those problems. The role of the courts in school desegregation is an example of this kind of legitimation, having been manifested not only in busing cases but also in the entire process of desegregation beginning with *Brown v. Board of Education* (1954). The courts have acted relatively independently of other political institutions and have been active in making decisions and offering remedies that they believe are derived from sound constitutional principles. Just as administrative agencies need a legal peg to hang their rulemaking on, so too do the courts need a constitutional peg on which to hang their interventions. Such phrases as *due process* and *equal protection* are sufficiently broad, however, to permit a wide scope for judicial involvement in legitimation activity.

Because the role of the courts is to judge the constitutionality of particular actions and to protect individual liberties against possible incursions by government or other individuals, decision making in the courts can be expected to be different from decision making through a legislative body. In many ways, the decisions made by courts are more authoritative than are other legitimating decisions, both because of the courts' connection to constitutional authority and because of the absence of any ready avenue of appeal once appeals through the court system are exhausted. The courts leave less room for compromise and vote trading than does a legislative body, and they have a less clearly defined constituency, if they have any constituency at all. Finally, a court decision is narrower, generally speaking to the particular case in question rather than a general principle of policy to be implemented in other specific cases. Thus court decisions legitimate certain actions but leave future decisions somewhat ambiguous, whereas decisions taken by both legislatures and administrative agencies are attempts to develop more general principles to guide subsequent actions and decisions.

Popular Legitimation

The three methods of legitimation discussed so far share one common feature: they are all performed by elites through political institutions. A number of

Lawyers George E.C. Hayes, Thurgood Marshall, and James M. Nabrit leave the Supreme Court on 17 May 1954, after announcement of the court's decision declaring school segregation uncon- stitutional.

American states provide mechanisms for direct democracy that allow voters to legitimate policy decisions.[54] The referendum device is in part a way for state legislatures to "pass the buck" to the people on issues that the legislators fear might be too hot to handle for the good of their future political careers. In some instances, on the other hand, the public can use these mechanisms to bypass legislatures entirely or to prod them into action. Despite some agitation, these mechanisms for direct democracy have not been adopted at the federal level.

A *referendum* is a vote of the people on an issue put to them by the legislature or some other authoritative body. Approval by popular vote is required before the measure in question can become law. The majority of states in the United States employ referendums for some policy decisions—typically, to pass bond issues and to change the state constitution—but some states use them to enact other legislation as well. An issue thought by the legislature to be sufficiently important, or highly charged politically, may be put to the voters for a decision. This practice certainly satisfies the tenets of democracy, but it may lead to small numbers—turnout on referendums is low—of relatively uninformed voters deciding about issues of great importance that might be better decided by more deliberative bodies. Further, money for campaigning is at least as important in referendum campaigns as it is in campaigns for office, so more powerful and affluent interests may be able to influence these elections significantly.

An even more extreme means of involving the public in policymaking is the *initiative*, which permits voters not only to pass on an issue put to them by government but also to place an issue on the ballot themselves. If the requisite number of signatures on a petition is obtained, an item can be placed on the ballot at the next election and, if approved by the voters, will become law. A number of significant policy issues—most notably Proposition 13 limiting property taxes and several important environmental laws in California—have been adopted through the initiative process. The initiative poses many of the same problems as the referendum. One difficulty is that important policy disputes such as the use of nuclear power become embroiled in political campaigns, so that the complex issues involved become trivialized and converted into simple yes-no questions. The initiative does provide an avenue for the expression of popular opinion, however, and it gives real power to the voters, who often think of themselves as absent from representative policymaking institutions.

In addition to these established mechanisms for popular involvement, there is a continuing call for additional means of citizen involvement that would go beyond mere voting or public hearings. Such mechanisms are usually discussed under the term *deliberative democracy*, or sometimes *strong democracy*.[55] The basic idea is that in a true democracy the role of citizens would not be confined to selecting their leaders but would extend to the debate and selection of policies. This model has worked in the traditional New England town meeting, and the advocates of expanded participation would like to make it more general. The difficulty is in making it work in a country of 250 million people.

Even if it cannot work for such a large aggregation, deliberative democracy could perhaps be applied to smaller settings when making public policy. For example, there is a tradition of public hearings in the policy process at all levels of government in the United States. The typical pattern has been for citizens to make statements of their views to a decision-making body. In some areas, however, this basic pattern is being revised to allow citizens to discuss policy among themselves, and perhaps even to make the final decisions themselves. Ideas such as "citizens juries" and "deliberative elections" are providing opportunities for increased participation for ordinary citizens.

Summary

Legitimation is at once the most difficult and the simplest component of the policymaking process. It generally involves the least complex and technical forms of policy analysis, and the number of actors is relatively constrained, unless the initiative and referendum are used. On the other hand, the actors involved are relatively powerful and have well-defined agendas of their own. Consequently, the task of the policy analyst seeking to alter perceptions and create converts to new policies at this stage is difficult. The type of formal evidence used at other stages of the process may not carry much weight at this stage, while political factors become paramount.

The barriers that the policy analyst faces in attempting to push through his or her ideas are sometimes individual and political, as when congressmen must be convinced through partisan analysis or vote trading to accept the analyst's concept of the desirable policy alternative. Conversely, the task may be one of altering substantial organizational constraints, and mediating turf wars, on a decision that would facilitate the appropriate policy response to a particular problem or a whole set of problems. Alternatively, the problem may be a legal one of persuading the courts to respond in the desired fashion to a set of facts and to develop the desired remedy for the perceived problem. Or, finally, the problem may be political in the broadest sense of persuading the voters (through the political mastery of the analyst) to accept or reject a particular definition of an issue and its solution. This is a great range of problems for the analyst, and they demand an equally great range of skills.

No individual is likely to have all these skills, but someone must make strategic choices as to which skills are the most appropriate for a particular problem. If the problem is to get a dam built, then Congress is clearly the most appropriate arena; if the problem is a civil rights violation, the best place to begin is probably the court system; if the problem is a specialized environmental issue, then the regulatory process is the appropriate locus for intervention. Policies do not simply happen, they must be made to happen. This is especially true given the degree of inertia existing in American government and the number of points at which action can be blocked. As with so many problems, the major task of the policy analyst may be to define clearly the problem that must be solved. Once that is done, the solution may not be simple, but it is at least potentially analyzable, and a feasible course of action may become more apparent.

CHAPTER 5

Organizations and Implementation

ONCE A PIECE OF LEGISLATION or a regulation has been accepted as a legitimate public law, in some ways the easiest portion of the policymaking process has already transpired, for government must then put the legislation into effect. This action requires the development of organizations that will apply the principles of the legislation to specific cases, monitor the performance of the policies, and, perhaps, propose improvements in the content and administration of the policy. Even policies that are primarily self-administered, or that rely on incentives rather than formal regulations, require an organizational basis for administration, although these organizations can certainly be smaller than those needed for implementing programs that depend on direct administration and supervision. For example, the collection of the income tax, which is largely self-administered, requires many fewer persons for each dollar collected than does collecting revenues from customs duties, even leaving aside the role of customs agents in controlling smuggling.

American political thinkers have generally denigrated the roles of public administrators and bureaucrats in policymaking. The traditional attitude has been that policy is made by legislatures and then the administrators merely follow the guidelines set forth in the legislation. Such an attitude fails to take into account the important role of administrative decision making and especially the importance of decision makers at the bottom of the organization in determining the effective policies of government.[1] The "real" criminal justice policy of the nation or city is to a great extent determined by the way in which the police enforce the laws, just as the "real" social welfare policy is determined by decisions made by caseworkers or even by receptionists in social service agencies. We have noted that bureaucrats play an important role in interpreting legislation and in making regulations to put that legislation into effect; they also play an important role in making decisions while applying laws and regulations to individual cases.[2]

It is also customary to consider government as an undivided entity and to regard government organizations as monolithic. In fact, this is not the case at all. We have mentioned that American government is divided horizontally into a number of subgovernments and vertically into levels of government in a federal system. But within the federal bureaucracy, and even within single cabinet-level departments, there are a number of bureaus, offices, and sections, all competing for money, legislative time, and public attention. Each of these organizations has its own goals, ideas, and concepts about how to address the public problems it is charged with administering. As in the making of legislation, these ideas will influence the implementation of legislation. Implementation often involves conflicts and competition, rather than neat coordination and control, and struggles over policy content persist long after Congress and the president have enacted legislation. Policies, as operating instruments, commonly emerge from these conflicts as much as from the initial design of legislation. Policies should not necessarily be designed to be implemented easily, but anyone interested in policy outcomes must monitor implementation as well as formulation.

Dramatis Personae

The organization of the federal government is complicated not only because of the number of organizations but also because of the number of different kinds of organizations. There is no single organizational format for accomplishing the work of government, and the various organizations exist in different relationships to elective officials and even to government authority as a whole. In addition to the three constitutionally designated institutional actors—the president, Congress, and the courts—at least eight different organizational formats exist within the federal government (see table 5.1).[3] One of these is a catchall category containing organizations that are difficult to classify within the other major types.

The absence of a basic organizational format tends to weaken central coordination and thus contribute to the incoherence of the policy choices made by the federal government. Further, the eight forms of organizations themselves have a great deal of internal variation. As shown in table 5.1, the organizations differ greatly in size; they can also differ greatly in their internal organization. For example, the Department of Agriculture consists of almost fifty offices and bureaus, while the Department of Housing and Urban Development is structured more around several assistant secretaries and their staffs, with few operating agencies within the department.

The most familiar forms of organization are the fourteen *executive departments*, such as the Department of Defense and the Department of Health and Human Services. Each is headed by a secretary who is a member of the presi-

TABLE 5.1   Examples of Employment in Federal Organizations

Kind of organization	Employment
Executive departments	
Department of Defense (civilian)	795,813
Department of Education	4,721
Executive Office of the President	
Office of Management and Budget	518
Office of National Service	1
Legislative organizations	
General Accounting Office	4,342
Biomedical Ethics Board	1
Independent executive agencies	
Social Security Administration	64,095
Appalachian Regional Commission	29
Independent regulatory commissions	
Nuclear Regulatory Commission	3,148
Consumer Products Safety Commission	468
Public corporations	
U.S. Postal Service	852,208
Neighborhood Reinvestment Corporation	226
Foundations	
National Science Foundation	1,249
National Endowment for the Arts and Humanities (combined)	337
Other	
Smithsonian Institution	5,168
Office of Government Ethics	96

Source: Office of Management and Budget, *Budget of the United States, FY* 1998.

dent's cabinet and who is directly responsible to the president. These executive departments should not, however, be regarded as uniform wholes but as collections, or "holding companies," of relatively autonomous agencies and offices.[4] Departments vary in the extent to which their constituent agencies respond to central direction. Some, such as the Department of Defense, have relatively high degrees of internal coordination; others, such as the Department of Commerce, are extremely decentralized.[5]

Although the cabinet departments are important, in some instances the individual agency may have more political influence than does the department as a whole. One such agency is the FBI, which is part of the Department of Justice but often can operate as if it were independent. (Its "clout" diminished in the last days of the Clinton administration following a series of spectacular errors, but it soon was able to restore its position.) And in some instances it is not entirely clear why agencies are located in one department rather than another—for example, why the U.S. Forest Service is located in the Department of Agriculture rather than in Interior, or why the U.S. Coast Guard is now located in the Department of Homeland Security, rather than in Treasury, Defense, or Transportation.[6]

Although the executive departments are linked to constituencies and provide services directly to those constituencies, the organizations within the *Executive Office of the President* exist to assist the president in carrying out his tasks of control and coordination within the executive branch as a whole.[7] The most important units within the Executive Office of the President are the Office of Management and Budget (OMB), the Council of Economic Advisers, the National Security Council (NSC), the Domestic Policy Council, and the White House Office. The first two units assist the president in his role as economic manager and central figure in the budgetary process. The NSC provides advice and opinion on foreign and defense issues independent of that provided by the Departments of State and Defense, while the Domestic Policy Council performs a similar role for domestic policy. The White House Office manages the everyday complexities of serving as president of the United States and employs a number of personal advisers for the president. The units within the Executive Office of the President now employ almost 1,800 people—an insignificant number compared with a total federal civilian workforce of more than 2 million, but quite large when compared with the personal offices of the chief executives of other nations.[8]

Congress has also created organizations to assist it in its role in policymaking. The three most important *legislative organizations* are the General Accounting Office (GAO), the Congressional Budget Office (CBO), and the Congressional Research Service. Legislatures in democratic political systems generally audit the accounts of the executive to ensure that public money is being spent legally. The General Accounting Office, for most of its existence, had been strictly a financial accounting body, but in the 1970s the organization began to expand its concerns to the cost effectiveness of expenditures.[9] For example, in one report the GAO agreed that the Internal Revenue Service (IRS) had been acting perfectly legally in the ways it sought to detect income tax evaders but recommended changing the IRS program to one the GAO considered more efficient. Few organizations in the federal government have escaped similar advice.[10] The CBO has its major policy impact on the annual preparation of the budget; its role is discussed thoroughly in Chapter 6. The Congressional Research Service, located within the Library of Congress, assists Congress in policy research and prepares background material for individual congressmen and committees.

In addition to the executive departments responsible to the president, there are a number of *independent executive agencies*. These organizations perform executive functions, such as implementing a public program, but they are independent of the executive departments and generally report directly to the president. The independence of these agencies can be justified in several ways. Some, such as the National Aeronautics and Space Administration (NASA), are mission agencies created outside existing departmental frameworks so as to have enhanced flexibility in completing their mission. Others, such as the Environmental Protection Agency (EPA) and the Small Business Administration, are organized independently to highlight their importance, and in recognition of the political power of the interest groups supporting them. Moving the Social Security Administration out of the Department of Health and Human Services in March 1995 was a recognition of the importance and size of this organization, which spends close to one-quarter of the federal budget. Other organizations, such as the General Services Administration and the Office of Personnel Management, provide services to a number of government departments, so locating them in any one department might create management difficulties.

The fifth form of organization is the *independent regulatory commission*. Three such organizations are the Federal Trade Commission, the Federal Energy Regulatory Commission, and the Consumer Products Safety Commission.

The Columbia *disaster brought into sharp relief the budgetary and organizational problems plaguing NASA's space shuttle program. Here, technicians at the Kennedy Space Center use diagrams of the destroyed shuttle to aid in attempts to reconstruct* Columbia *from the remaining debris. The boxes contain tile material.*

These commissions are different from independent executive agencies in that they do not perform executive functions but act independently to regulate certain segments of the economy.[11] Once the president has appointed the members of a commission, the application and formulation of regulations are largely beyond his control. The absence of direct political support often results, however, in the "capture" of the regulatory commissions by the interests they were intended to regulate.[12] Over time, lacking ties to the president or Congress, the independent agencies may seek the political support of the regulated interests in order to obtain their budgets, personnel, or legislation from the other institutions in government. The tendency toward capture is not so evident in agencies that must deal with several industries—the Federal Trade Commission or Consumer Products Safety Commission, for example.[13] Also, not all economic regulation is conducted through the independent commissions, and some of the more important regulatory agencies, such as the Occupational Safety and Health Administration (OSHA) and the Food and Drug Administration (FDA), are in executive departments—OSHA is in the Department of Labor, and the FDA is part of Health and Human Services.

The government of the United States has generally avoided becoming directly involved in the economy other than through regulation, but there are a number of *public corporations* in the federal government.[14] For example, since 1970 the U.S. Postal Service has been a public corporation rather than part of an executive department, as it was before. This one public corporation employs over 800,000 people, or almost one-third of all federal civilian employees. Another public corporation, the Tennessee Valley Authority, has about 6 percent of the total electrical generating capacity of the United States. There are, however, some very small public corporations: the Overseas Private Investment Corporation, for instance, employs only 100 people.

A public corporation is organized much like a private corporation, with a board of directors and stock issued for capitalization. The principal difference is that the board members are all public appointees and the stock is generally held entirely by the Department of the Treasury or by another executive department. There are several reasons for choosing the corporate form of organization. One is that these organizations provide marketed goods and services to the population and hence can be better managed as commercial concerns.[15] Also, this is a means of keeping some government functions at arm's length so that the president and Congress are not held directly responsible for the actions of these organizations.

There are also several *foundations* within the federal government, the principal examples being the National Science Foundation, the National Endowment for the Humanities, and the National Endowment for the Arts. The foundation format is intended primarily to separate the organization from the remainder of government because of a justifiable fear of creating a national orthodoxy in the arts or in science and thereby stifling creativity. Again, the foundation's relative autonomy enables government to support the activities while being removed from the decisions. The independence of foundations is far from complete, however, for Congress has not been reluctant to intervene in their decisions, for example by criticizing projects supported by the National Endowment for the Arts that conservatives alleged supported "pornography."[16] The NEA responded with a "general standard of decency" standard for funding, a provision that has been upheld by the Supreme Court as not violating the First Amendment.[17] The president can also attempt to influence the foundations, primarily through the appointment of directors and board members.

In addition to the wholly owned government corporations described here, there is a group of organizations described as *quasi-governmental* or as being in the "twilight zone." Examples are the National Railroad Passenger Corporation (Amtrak), the Corporation for Public Broadcasting, and the Federal Reserve Board. These organizations have some attributes of public organizations—most important, access to public funding—but they also have some attributes of private organizations. They are similar to public corporations except that a portion of their boards of directors is appointed by private-sector organizations; the board of Amtrak is appointed in part by the member railroad corporations. Also, not all their stock may be owned by the public sector, as is true for wholly owned corporations; some may be owned by the cooperating private-sector organizations. For example, up to half the stock of Comsat (Communications Satellite Corporation) may be held by communication common carriers.[18] Finally, employees of these quasi-governmental organizations generally are not classified as public employees, and they generally are not subject to other public-sector regulations such as the Freedom of Information Act.

The justification for the formation of quasi-governmental organizations such as these is, again, to permit government to become involved in a policy area without assuming any real or apparent direct control. The federal government clearly subsidizes certain activities—passenger railroad service would almost certainly have vanished in the United States without the formation of Amtrak—but this intervention is not as obvious as other forms of public sector involvement in the economy. Further, intervention by a quasi-governmental organization gives the public a greater role in decision making and provides greater representation of private interests such as the affected corporations. And, as with the Corporation for Public Broadcasting, this form of organization permits the federal government to become involved in an area from which it has traditionally been excluded.

It is important to understand just how vital these quasi-governmental organizations are to the federal government. For example, the Federal Reserve Board fits comfortably into this twilight zone, given its isolation from executive authority and its relationship to its member banks. But the Federal Reserve Board is responsible for making monetary policy for the United States and thereby has a significant—probably now the most significant—influence on this nation's economic conditions. Similarly, Amtrak has received massive subsidies, and the public sector has no firm control over its policies, yet it is a significant element in national transportation. Similarly, the Corporation for Public Broadcasting is a significant complement to commercial radio and television broadcasting, although Congress often fails to support public broadcasting with anything like the funds available to the commercial channels.[19]

Finally, there is a catchall category of *other organizations*, which contains several regional commissions that coordinate economic or environmental policy in several parts of the country. Other organizations, including various claims commissions and the Administrative Conference of the United States Courts, operate on the fringes of the judicial process. Finally, organizations such as the Smithsonian Institution, the National Academy of Sciences, and the American Red Cross are mentioned in federal legislation and receive subsidies, but they are far removed from the mainstream of government action.

We should note several other points about the complexity of the organizational structure of the federal government. One is the redundancy that has been built into the system. First, both Congress (through the Congressional Budget Office) and the Executive Office of the President (through the Office of Management and Budget) have organizations to deal with budgeting and with many other economic aspects of government. Because of the doctrine of separation of powers, such duplication makes a great deal of sense, but this overlap still conflicts with conventional managerial thinking about eliminating duplicative organizations.

Second, within the federal executive branch itself, we have seen that some units within the Executive Office of the President duplicate activities of the executive departments. Most notably, presidents appear to demand foreign policy advice other than that provided by the Departments of State and Defense, and they get it from the National Security Council. This demand may be justified, as those executive departments have their own existing policy commitments and ideas that may limit their ability to respond to presidential initiatives in foreign policy. But during at least every administration since Richard Nixon, conflicts have arisen between the two sets of institutions, and the management of foreign policy may suffer as a result. In most instances, this conflict has been perceived as a conflict between the experienced professionals in the Department of State and committed amateurs in the National Security Council.

In other policy areas, more that one federal organization may exercise a regulatory function. For example, both the Federal Trade Commission and the Antitrust Division of the Department of Justice are concerned with antitrust policies and monopolies.[20] Some redundancy in this activity can be rationalized as a means of limiting error and providing alternative means for accomplishing the same tasks, and even alternative definitions of the issues.[21] But if the redundant institutions are occupied by ambitious men and women, the potential for conflict, "gridlock," or perhaps excessive regulation is substantial.[22]

It is also interesting to note that not all central fiscal and management functions of the federal government are located in the Executive Office of the President. Several important management functions—monetary policy, personnel policy, debt management, and taxation—are under the control of agencies outside the president's office, and in one instance an organization in the "twilight zone." This diffusion of duties and responsibilities is a definite limitation on the president's ability to implement his policy priorities and consequently to control the federal establishment for which he is held accountable politically and to some extent legally.

Third, we have mentioned the variations in the "publicness" of organizations in, or associated with, the federal government. Some organizations are clearly public: they receive their funds from allocations in the federal budget; their employees are hired through public personnel systems; and they are subject to legislation such as the Freedom of Information Act, which attempts to differentiate public from private programs.[23] Other organizations described appear tied to the private sector as much as to government: they receive some or all of their funds as fees for service or interest on loans; they have their own personnel policies; and they are only slightly more subject to normal restrictions on public organizations than is General Motors. Again, for a president—who will be held accountable to voters and to Congress for the performance of the federal government—this presents an immense and perhaps insoluble problem. How can the president really take responsibility when so many of the organizations charged with implementing his policies are beyond effective control? This is but one of many difficulties a president encounters when he attempts to put his policies into effect; it also serves as a bridge to our discussion of implementation.

The issue of the publicness of organizations has arisen in a particularly controversial form in President George W. Bush's proposal to use "faith-based organizations" to deliver a range of social services.[24] These organizations are primarily private, and the tradition of the separation of church and state in the United States makes their affiliation with government perhaps more suspect than would be true for other private organizations. Many citizens have expressed concern about the possibility that these organizations would proselytize recipients of their services or make religious adherence a criterion for receiving benefits. The organizations themselves have expressed some doubts about their closer involvement in the public sector, fearing that entanglement with government will reduce their capacity to maintain religious and programmatic freedom.

Implementation

All the organizations described earlier are established to assist in some way the execution of legislation or the monitoring of that execution. Once enacted, laws do not go into effect by themselves, as was assumed by those in the (presumed) tradition of Woodrow Wilson who discussed "mere administration."[25] In fact, one of the most important things to understand about government is that it is a minor miracle that implementation is ever accomplished.[26] There are so many more ways of blocking intended actions than there are of making results materialize that all legislators should be pleased if they live to see their pet projects not only passed into law but actually put into effect. Although this is perhaps an excessively negative characterization of the implementation process, it should underline the extreme difficulties of administering and implementing public programs.

Policies do not fail on their own, however, and a large number of factors may limit the ability of a political system to put policies into effect. Rarely will all these factors affect any single policy, but all must be considered when designing a policy and attempting to translate that policy choice into real services for citizens. Further, any one of these factors may be sufficient to cause failure, or suboptimal performance by a policy, while all may have to be in good order for the policy to work. In short, it is much easier to prevent a policy from working than it is to make the policy effective.

The Legislation

The first factor that affects the effective implementation of a policy is the nature of the legislation that establishes it. Laws vary according to their specificity, clarity, and the policy areas they attempt to influence, as well as in the extent to which they bind the individuals and organizations charged with implementing them to perform in the way the writers intended. Unfortunately, both legislators and analysts sometimes overlook the importance of the legislation. Also, laws that are easier to implement are, everything else being equal, more difficult to pass. Their specificity may make it clear who the winners and losers are and thus complicate the task of building the necessary political coalitions for passage.

Policy Issues

Legislators frequently choose to legislate in policy areas where they may not have sufficient information about the causal processes underlying policy problems to enable them to make good policy choices. Although they may have the best intentions, their efforts are unlikely to succeed if they make only stabs in the dark when attempting to solve difficult problems. If we refer to the four kinds of policy formulation discussed earlier (see figure 3.1, p. 69), we can estimate the likelihood of effective implementation of a policy. We anticipate that the highest probability of effective implementation will occur when we have both sufficient information about the policy area and an adequate knowledge of the causes of the problems. In such situations, governments can design legislation to solve, or at least ameliorate, the problem under attack. Likewise, we would expect little likelihood of effective implementation in policy areas where there is inadequate information and little knowledge of the causes of the problem.

The other two possible combinations of knowledge of causation and information may differ very little in their likelihood of effective implementation, although we would expect a somewhat better probability of implementation when there is a knowledge of the patterns of causation as opposed to more basic information. If the underlying process is understood, it would appear possible to formulate policy responses based on available information, however poor the information may be. When there is inadequate information, policy responses involve a certain amount of overkill and excessive reaction. If the underlying process is misunderstood, or is not understood at all, there is little hope of effectively implementing a policy choice, except by pure luck. In this instance, governments often wind up treating the symptoms, as they do with the problem of crime and delinquency, instead of dealing with the underlying social processes.

Perhaps the best example of a large-scale policy formulation and implementation in spite of inadequate knowledge of patterns of causation was the War on Poverty in the United States several decades ago. There were (and are) as many theories about the causes of poverty as there were theorists, but there was little real understanding even of the basics of the economic and social dynamics producing the problem.[27] Thus, war was declared on an enemy that was poorly understood. Daniel P. Moynihan put it this way:

> This is the essential fact: The Government did not know what it was doing. It had a theory. Or rather a set of theories. Nothing more. The U.S. Government at this time was no more in possession of a confident knowledge as to how to prevent delinquency, cure anomie, or overcome that midmorning sense of powerlessness than it was the possessor of a dependable formula for motivating Vietnamese villagers to fight Communism.[28]

Not only was it a war, but it was a war that appeared to be based on something approaching a dogma about the plan of attack—for example, the use of large-scale and rather expensive programs involving direct services to clients. Arguably, these programs were doomed to fail as soon as they were adopted because they were based on dubious assumptions about the operations of the society and the mechanisms for approaching such problems. But those interventions, if misguided, had the political appeal and visibility that smaller-scale efforts would have lacked.

An even more extreme example of a policy made without adequate knowledge was the Clean Air Act of 1970 (see Chapter 13). The sponsors of this legislation were, in fact, quite sure that they did not understand the processes and that the technology for producing the environmental cleanup they legislated did not exist. The legislation was in fact designed to force the development of the technology for improving the environment. To some extent, the same was true of the space program of the 1960s, which did not have a sure technology for accomplishing its goals when President John Kennedy pledged to place an American on the moon by the end of the decade. More recently, the Strategic Defense Initiative, and subsequent attempts to build an anti-missile defense under the George W. Bush administration, have required development of technologies that may be at least as important for domestic as defense purposes.[29]

Technology forcing is an interesting if somewhat novel approach to designing public programs, but it is not one that can be recommended as a strategy for policymaking. It has been successful in some policy areas, in part because the problems being dealt with were aspects of the physical world, rather than the more complex social and economic realities that governments often face.[30] These potential difficulties should not be taken to mean that governments should just keep to their well-worn paths and do what they have always done in the ways they have always done it. Instead, they should caution that if one expects significant results from programs based on insufficient understanding of the subject matter of the legislation, one's hopes are likely to be dashed.

Political Setting

Legislation is adopted through political action, and the political process may plant within the legislation the seeds of its own destruction. The very compromises and negotiations necessary to pass legislation may ultimately make it virtually impossible to implement. The implementation problem becomes especially evident when the construction of the necessary coalition requires logrolling and trade-offs among competing interests and competing purposes in the legislation.

The effects of the political process on legislation are manifested in different ways. One is the vagueness of the language in which the legislation is written: lack of clarity may be essential to develop a coalition for its passage, as every time a vague term is made specific, potential coalition members are lost. But by phrasing legislation in vague and inoffensive language, legislators risk leaving their intent unclear to those who must implement the laws, thus allowing the implementers to alter the entire meaning of the program substantially. Phrases such as "maximum feasible participation," "equality of educational opportunity," "special needs of educationally deprived students," and that favorite vague concept, "public interest," are all subject to a number of different interpretations, many of which could betray the true intent of the legislators. For example, the rather vague language of Social Security legislation from 1962 to 1972 provided for open-ended grants for "improved services" for citizens.[31] The assumption was that additional services would be provided with this money. Instead, quite contrary to the intent of the drafters of the legislation, the money was used to subsidize existing programs and provide fiscal relief for state budgets. These grants also grew much more rapidly than had been anticipated because states found new ways of using them to shift a substantial portion of the cost of their social service programs to the federal government. Even words about which most citizens can agree may be sufficiently vague to produce problems during implementation, as when the Reagan administration attempted to define ketchup as a "vegetable" under the School Lunch Program.[32]

In addition to coalitions formed for the passage of a single piece of legislation, other coalitions may have to be formed across several pieces of legislation—the classic approach to logrolling. In order to gain support for one favored piece of legislation, a coalition-building legislator may have to trade his or her support on other pieces of legislation. In some instances, this may simply increase the overall volume of legislation enacted. In others, it may involve the passage of legislation that negates or decreases the effects of desired legislation. Some coalitions that must be formed are regional, so it may become virtually impossible to give one region an advantage that may be justified by economic circumstances without making commensurate concessions to other regions, thereby nullifying the intended effect. It is also difficult to make decisions that are redistributive across economic classes—either the legislation will be watered down to be distributive (giving everyone a piece of the pie), or additional legislation will be passed to spread the benefits more broadly. The Elementary and Secondary Education Act and a good deal of the politics of taxation are examples of this tendency in writing legislation.[33]

Similar problems of vagueness and logrolling can occur when other institutions make rulings that must be implemented. In a number of instances, a judicial decision intended to mandate a certain action has been so vague as to be difficult or impossible to implement. One of the best examples of this lack of clarity is the famous decision in *Brown v. Board of Education*, which ordered schools to desegregate with "all deliberate speed." Two of those three words, *deliberate* and *speed*, appear somewhat contradictory, and the decision did not specify exactly what the phrase meant. Similarly, the police are prohibited from searching an individual, an automobile they stop, or a home without "probable cause," but that phrase was left largely undefined until a series of cases required the courts to be clearer. Further, the process of writing regulations in administrative agencies, intended to clarify and specify legislation, can itself create ambiguities that require more regulations to clarify and more delay in implementing the decisions.

In summary, politics is central to the formulation of legislation, but the results of the political process often are such that the resulting legislation cannot be implemented effectively. The compromises necessitated by political feasibility may result in just the reductions in clarity and purpose that make laws too diffuse to be implemented so as to have a real effect on society. The vagueness of legislation may make room for another type of politics dominated more by interest groups than by elected officials.

Interest-group Liberalism

Related to the problems of vagueness and the lack of knowledge of causation is Theodore J. Lowi's concern about government involvement in the more abstract aspects of human behavior.[34] Lowi's argument is that the United States has progressed from concerted and specific legislation such as the Interstate Commerce Act of 1887, which established clear standards of practice for the Interstate Commerce Commission, to abstract and general standards, such as "unfair competition" in the Clayton Act of 1914. This tendency has been extended through even more general and diffuse aspects of human behavior in the social legislation enacted after the 1960s to regulate what Lowi refers to as the "environment of conduct." It is simply more difficult to show that a person has discriminated against another person on the basis of race, color, or sex than it is to show that a railroad has violated prohibitions against discriminatory freight rates.

Lowi believes that the problems in these vague laws arise not from their commendable intentions but from the difficulties of implementing them. The diffuseness of the targets specified and the difficulty of defining standards subject policies for regulating those behaviors to errors in interpretation during implementation. Further, it becomes more difficult to hold government accountable when it administers ambiguous legislation. The interest-group liberalism inherent in American politics, in which the public interest tends to be defined in terms of many private interests, and especially the private interests of more well-organized groups, means that implementation of legislation will generally differ greatly from the intentions of those who framed the legislation. Implementation will be undertaken by agencies that are themselves tied to clients and to particular definitions of the public interest and that will not want to be swayed from their position by a piece of legislation. Problems of accountability created by the deviation of policies in practice from the intentions of their framers can only alienate the clients and frustrate the legislators, and perhaps the administrators as well.

The Organizational Setting

As noted earlier, most implementation is undertaken by organizations, especially organizations in the public bureaucracy. Given the nature of public organizations, and organizations in general, the probability that such an organization will effectively implement a program is not particularly high—not because of any venality on the part of the bureaucracy or the bureaucrats but simply because the internal dynamics of large organizations often limit their ability to respond to policy changes and implement new or altered programs.

To begin to understand what goes wrong when organizations attempt to implement programs, a model of "perfect" administration may be useful. Christopher Hood points to five characteristics "perfect" administration of public programs would have:

1. Administration would be unitary; it would be one vast army all marching to the same drummer.
2. The norms and rules of administration would be uniform throughout the organization.
3. There would be no resistance to commands.
4. There would be perfect information and communication within the organization.
5. There would be adequate time to implement the program.[35]

Clearly these conditions are often absent in organizations attempting to implement programs, and almost never are all of them present. Governments depend on large organizations to implement their policies, and consequently, difficulties arise in administration and implementation. These difficulties need not be insurmountable, but they do need to be understood and anticipated if possible, if successful implementation is to occur. Just what characteristics and difficulties in organizations lead to difficulties in implementation?

Organizational Disunity

Organizations are rarely unitary administrations—indeed, a number of points of disunity are almost inherent in organizational structures. One aspect of organizational disunity that affects implementation is the disjunction between central offices of organizations and their field staffs. Decisions may be made by politicians and administrators sitting in national capitals, but those decisions must be implemented by field staff members who may not share the same values and goals as the administrators in the home office.

This disjunction of values may take several forms. A change in central values and programs may occur, perhaps as a result of a change in presidents or in Congress, and the field staff may remain loyal to the older policies. For example, the field staff, and indeed much of the central staff, of the Department of Health, Education, and Welfare regarded the Nixon administration as a temporary phenomenon and remained loyal to the more liberal social values of previous Democratic presidents.[36] This was true despite pressures from above for changes in policies. Much the same was true of the staffs of the Environmental Protection Agency and the Department of the Interior under the Reagan and Bush administrations' apparent retreats on environmental issues.[37] The Clinton administration then inherited a government shaped in most other areas by twelve years of Republican presidents, and the George W. Bush administration, in turn, found itself forced to deal with the residual organizational values of the Clinton years.[38] Such problems with field staffs over policy changes produce frustration for politicians nominally in control of policymaking and make the implementation of policies that violate the norms of the existing field staffs extremely difficult.

A more common disparity between the goals of field staffs and those of the home office may occur as the field staff is "captured" by clients. Field staff members are frequently close to their clients, and they may adopt their clients' perspective in their own relationships with the remainder of the organization.[39] This is especially true when the clients are relatively disadvantaged and the organization is attempting either to assist them or to exercise some control over them. The identification of staff members with their clients is fostered by frequent contact, sympathy, empathy, and, quite commonly, by genuine devotion to a perceived mission that is in contrast to the mission fostered by the central office. This pattern of conflict between central and field staffs is emerging as welfare reform (see Chapter 11) begins to have negative impacts on recipients and social workers attempt to protect their clients.[40] For whatever reason, this identification does make implementation of centrally determined policy difficult.

In many ways, government has increased its own difficulties when using field staffs to implement policy. The requirement for community participation in decision making in many urban social service programs further lessens the control of central organizations over the implementation of the programs. Developing community organizations that fulfill the requirements for participation is a major focus for pressures to divert the program toward more locally determined priorities, including successful efforts to say "Not In My Backyard" (NIMBY).[41] Even when community organizations are not used to implement programs, requirements for local participation can make it more difficult for agencies to do what they had planned.[42] Further, the ethos of local control is being spread widely enough that even without formal requirements for participation there may be effective demands for involvement.[43] The concept of empowerment, as expressed, for instance, in the National Performance Review (the Gore Report), has helped fuel demands for greater involvement of clients and lower-echelon employees in policy implementation and administration.[44]

Arguably, community participation has been less effective than was intended, and at worst it has been a façade for control by bureaucracies, but to the extent that it has been successful, it may well have made implementation less successful. Even in policy areas where community participation has not been directly fostered by government, either the lessons learned from community participation elsewhere or the general climate favoring participation has provoked greater activity by individuals and communities affected by policies. A whole range of programs—including decisions by the Army Corps of Engineers about project siting, the construction of portions of the Interstate Highway System, and, most dramatically, the siting of nuclear waste facilities—have been seriously affected by local participation.[45]

Field staffs may also find that if they are to perform their tasks effectively, they cannot follow all the directives coming to them from the center of the organization. In such instances, in order to get substantive compliance the organization members may not comply with procedural directives. For example, in a classic study of the FBI, Peter M. Blau noted that field agents frequently did not comply with directives requiring them to report the offering of a bribe by a suspect.[46] The agents had found that they could gain greater cooperation from a subject by using the threat to have the person prosecuted for offering the bribe at any time. Their performance of the task of prosecuting criminals was probably enhanced, but it was done at the expense of the directive from the central office.

Eugene Bardach and Robert A. Kagan have argued that regulatory enforcement in the United States could be improved if field staffs were granted greater latitude for independent action.[47] They believe that rigidities resulting from strict central controls actually produce less compliance with the spirit of the regulations than would a more flexible approach. This interest in enhancing regulatory latitude can, however, be contrasted with the continuing (and strengthening) interest in control over bureaucracies, especially regulatory bureaucracies. Congress is concerned with efficient enforcement, but it is often more concerned with ensuring that what is being implemented corresponds with its intentions.[48] In attempting to design programs to ensure that compliance, lawmakers paradoxically may limit enforcement as a result.

Standard Operating Procedures

Organizations develop standard operating procedures (SOPs) to respond to policy problems. When a prospective client walks into a social service agency, the agency follows a standard pattern of response: certain forms must be filled out, designated personnel interview the prospective client, specific criteria are used to determine the person's eligibility for benefits. Likewise, if a "blip" appears on the radar screen of a defense installation, a certain set of procedures is followed to determine if the blip is real and, if so, whether it is friendly or hostile. If it should be hostile, further prespecified actions are taken.

Standard operating procedures are important for organizations because they reduce the amount of time spent processing each new situation and developing a response. The SOPs are the learned response of the organization to certain problems; they represent to some extent the organizational memory in action. SOPs may also be important for clients, as they are adopted at least in part to ensure equality and fairness for clients. Without SOPs, organizations might respond more slowly to each situation, they might respond less effectively, and they would probably respond more erratically.

Although SOPs are generally beneficial for organizations, they can also constitute barriers to good implementation. This is most obvious when a new policy or a new approach to an existing policy is being considered. Organizations are likely to persist in defining policies and problems in their standard manner, even when the old definition or procedure no longer helps fulfill the mission of the agency. For example, when the Medicare program was added to the responsibilities of the Social Security Administration, the agency was faced with an entirely new set of concerns in addition to its traditional task of making payments to individuals. In particular, it assumed responsibility for limiting the costs of medical care. It chose, however, to undertake this responsibility in much the same way that it would have attempted to manage problems arising from pensions—by examining individual claims and denying those that appeared to be unjustified. It took the Social Security Administration some time to focus attention on more fundamental and systemic problems of medical cost inflation and to develop programs such as Diagnostic Related Groupings (DRGs) (see Chapter 10). The agency took some time even to cope with adding the Supplemental Security Income program, which was much closer to its original portfolio of income-maintenance policies, but which was more similar to a means-tested program than to a social insurance program.[49]

Thus there is a need for designing programs and organizations that will consistently reassess their goals and the methods they use to reach those goals. In some instances—for example, correlating the number of births and the future need for schools—the response should be programmed to be almost automatic; other situations will require more thought and greater political involvement. Organizations do not like to perform these reassessments, which may threaten both the employees of the organizations and their clients. One reason for creating organizations with standard operating procedures is to ensure some stability and predictability, but that stability can become a barrier to success when problems and needs in the issue area change.

Standard operating procedures also tend to produce inappropriate or delayed responses to crises. The military, perhaps more than any other organization, tends to employ SOPs and to train its members to carry through with those procedures in the absence of commands to the contrary. In this way, the military can be sure of a certain reaction even when there is no direct link to the command structure. President Kennedy found that although he was nominally in charge of the armed forces of the United States, many things occurred that he had not ordered during events such as the Cuban missile crisis, and he realized that they were happening simply because they were standard procedures. The brief invasion of Grenada in 1983 encountered difficulties when the communication SOPs of the navy and army did not correspond, so that the soldiers on the island could not communicate with the ships providing them support. Soldiers found the best way to communicate was to use their telephone credit cards to call the Pentagon, which would then communicate with the navy. More recently, the predictability of the intelligence gathering activities of the CIA enabled India to prepare its nuclear tests without alerting the American government.[50] Like the military, fire and police units develop standard operating procedures, and some of these routines—and the consequent inability to recognize the novelty of new events—appear to have contributed to the huge loss of life by firemen during the World Trade Center collapse in 2001.

One standard means of avoiding the effects of SOPs in a new program is to create a new organization. When the Small Business Administration was created in 1953, it was purposely not placed in the Department of Commerce, whose SOPs tended to favor big business. The Office of National Drug Control Policy was established within the Executive Office of the President to ensure both its priority and its independence from other organizations, such as the Drug Enforcement Agency and the Customs Bureau. There are, of course, limits to the number of new organizations that can be set up, for the more that are created, the greater chance there will be of interorganizational barriers to implementation replacing the barriers internal to any one organization. Drug policy, for example, suffers from coordination problems among the numerous agencies—the three mentioned above as well as the Coast Guard, the Department of Defense, the FBI, and numerous state and local authorities, among others—all involved in the policy area.

Paradoxically, SOPs aid in the implementation of established programs, whereas they are likely to be barriers to change and to the implementation of new programs. Likewise, the procedures may be too standardized to permit effective responses to nonstandard situations or to nonstandard clients, thereby creating rigidity and extremely inappropriate responses to novel situations. The established procedures often prompt organizations to try to classify new problems as old ones as long as they can and to continue to use familiar responses even when the problems appear, to an outsider, demonstrably different.

Organizational Communication 4

Another barrier to effective implementation is the improper flow of information within organizations. Because government organizations depend heavily on the flow of information—just as manufacturers rely on the flow of raw materials—accurate information and the prevention of blockages of information are extremely important to the success of these public organizations. Unfortunately, organizations, and particularly public organizations, are subject to inaccurate and blocked communication.

In general, information in bureaucracies tends to be concentrated at the bottom of the hierarchy.[51] Field staffs are in closer contact with the environment of the organization, and technical experts tend to be clustered at the bottom of organizations, while more generalist managers are concentrated at the top. This concentration means that if the organization is to be steered by changes in its environment, and if it is to make appropriate technical decisions, the information at the bottom must be transmitted to the top and then directions must be passed back down to the bottom for implementation. Unfortunately, the more levels through which information has to be transmitted, the greater is the probability that the information will be distorted when it is finally acted upon.

This distortion in communications may result from random error or from *selective distortion*, which results when officials at each stage of message transmission attempt to transmit only the information that they believe their superiors wish to hear or that they think will make them look good to their superiors. And the superiors, in turn, may attempt to estimate what sort of distortion their subordinates may have passed on and then attempt to correct for that distortion.[52] The result of this transmitting of messages through a hierarchical organization frequently is rampant distortion and misinformation that limits the ability of the organization to take effective implementation decisions.

Certain characteristics of the organization may improve the transmission of information through its hierarchy. Clearly, if all members of an organization "speak the same language," less distortion of communication should occur. In other words, if organization members share common technical or professional backgrounds, their communication with one another should be less distorted. There is a danger, however, that the creation of a common language can prevent an organization from responding to new situations or producing innovative solutions. Its ability to communicate effectively with other organizations may also be diminished. In addition, attempts on the part of the organization to create internal unity through training and socialization should also improve internal patterns of communication.[53] Finally, the "flatter" the organization (i.e., the fewer levels through which communication must go before being acted on), the less distortion is likely to occur.[54]

Another way to improve communication in organizations is to create more, and redundant, channels. For example, President Franklin Roosevelt developed personal ties to lower-level members of federal organizations and placed his own people in organizations to be sure that he would receive direct and unvarnished reports from the operating levels of government.[55] Alternatively, a president or manager might build in several channels of communication in order to make them function as checks on one another. Again, Franklin Roosevelt's frequent development of parallel organizations (e.g., the Works Progress Administration and the Public Works Administration) provided him with alternative channels of information about the progress of his New Deal programs. In more contemporary times, the development of several channels of advice and communication to the president about national security policy and drug policy may be a way of ensuring that the information he receives is both accurate and complete.

One particularly interesting threat to effective organizational communication is secrecy.[56] While a certain level of secrecy is understood to be important for some government organizations, secrecy also may inhibit both communication and implementation. Secrecy frequently means that a communication may not be transmitted because it has been classified; other parts of the organization or other organizations are consequently denied needed information. Again, the Cuban missile crisis offered numerous examples of how the military's penchant for secrecy can prevent a rapid response to situations. Also, secrecy may produce inefficiency, as when FBI agents had to spend a great deal of time reporting on one another as they infiltrated subversive organizations such as the Ku Klux Klan. In order to make themselves more acceptable to the organizations they had infiltrated, the agents tended to be among the most vociferous members and consequently became the subjects of a disproportionate share of reports from other agents. More recently, the CIA's identification of spies within its midst was slowed because different parts of the organization were unwilling to share information with other parts. Finally, secrecy may be counterproductive even when it is justified. For example, one argument holds that the interests of military deterrence are best served by informing an adversary of the full extent of one's arsenal, instead of masking its strength—uncertainty may only create a willingness to gamble on the strength of the opponent, while openness may prevent war. This logic may be particularly applicable in a nuclear age, when every major power has the ability to destroy the world several times over.

In modern organizations knowledge is power, and the inability of an organization to gather and process information from its environment will certainly be a serious detriment to its performance. Clearly the management of communication flows within an organization is an important component of taking raw information and putting it into action. Most organizations, however, face massive problems in performing even this simple (or apparently simple) task and as a consequence do not implement their programs effectively. Their own internal hierarchical structures, the differential commitment to goals, and the differences in professional languages all conspire to make organizational communication more difficult than it may appear from the outside.

Time Problems 5

Related to the problem of information management in the implementation of policies is the problem of time. Christopher Hood points to two time problems that inhibit the ability of public organizations to respond to situations in their policy environments. One is a linear time problem in which the responses of implementing organizations tend to lag behind the need for the response.[57] This often happens in organizations that have learned their lessons too well and that base their responses on previous learning rather than on current conditions. This problem is somewhat similar to the problem of standard operating procedures, but it has less to do with processing individual cases than with designing the mechanisms for putting new programs into effect. Organizations frequently implement programs to deal with a crisis that has just passed, rather than with the crisis they currently face or might soon face. To some degree the American armed forces in Vietnam used the lessons they had learned, or thought they had learned, in World War II and the Korean conflict. Unfortunately for them, a highly mechanized, technologically sophisticated, and logistically dependent fighting force broke down in a tropical, guerrilla war.

Government also has at times failed to respond even to obvious social changes such as demography. The fact that newborn babies will five or six years later require places in public schools sometimes seems to amaze public officials. At the other end of the life cycle, governments have not prepared well for the aging "baby boomer" generation that will begin to reach retirement age around 2012. The public sector has allowed this large population to proceed through the life cycle without making adequate plans for the burdens it will surely impose on the Social Security retirement system and on health care (see Chapter 11 and Chapter 12).

Other time problems are cyclical, and delaying implementation, instead of solving them, may actually contribute to their persistence and severity. This is especially important in making and implementing macroeconomic policy—in which, even if the information available to a decision maker is timely and accurate, any delay in response may exaggerate economic fluctuations. If a decision maker responds to a threatened increase in inflation by reducing money supplies or reducing expenditures, and if that response is delayed for a year, or even for only a few months, it may only accelerate an economic slowdown that has emerged in the meantime, basically resulting from other causes. Thus, it is not sufficient merely to be right; an effective policy must be both correct and on time if it is to have the desired effect.

Horseshoe-Nail Problems and Public Planning

The final organizational problem in implementation arises when organizations plan their activities incompletely or inaccurately. Hood calls these "horseshoe-nail" problems because the failure to provide the nail results in the eventual loss of the horse and, eventually, the battle.[58] And because government organizations often must plan for implementation with limited access to information and no cues about the necessary choices, problems of this kind are likely to arise in the public sector. Examples of this problem abound: passing requirements to inspect coal mines but failing to hire inspectors; requiring clients to fill out certain forms but neglecting to have the forms printed; forgetting to stop construction of a $160 million highway tunnel leading to nowhere once the plan to build the rest of the highway is terminated. There are countless examples of this political and policy version of Murphy's law.[59]

To ensure effective management and implementation, planners must identify the crucial potential blockages, or "nails," in their organization and allow for them in their planning. Clearly, with a new program or policy, this planning may be extremely difficult, as the problems that will arise may be almost impossible to anticipate. Some planners use these difficulties to justify incremental or experimental approaches when introducing new policies. Instead of undertaking large projects with the possibility of equally large failures, they may substitute smaller projects for which any failures or unanticipated difficulties would impose minimal costs but would help prepare the organization to implement full-scale projects. The problem, of course, is that the programs often are not permitted to grow sufficiently to reach an effective level but may remain small and "experimental."

But some programs will be effective only if they are comprehensive and implemented on a large scale. Schulman's analysis of the National Aeronautics and Space Administration points out that a program like the space program—designed to reach a major goal within a limited amount of time and with an engineering as opposed to a pure research focus—must be large-scale in order to be effective.[60] Similarly, it has been argued that the War on Poverty, instead of being the failure portrayed in the conventional wisdom, actually was never tried on a scale that might have made it effective. In contrast, the so-called war on cancer was implemented as if it were a program that required a centralized mission format, whereas, in reality, it required a more decentralized structure to allow scientific research to pursue as many avenues as possible.[61] Those who design programs and organizations must be very careful to develop programs to match the characteristics of the problem and the state of knowledge concerning the subject. Even if perhaps objectively correct, a strategy may still provoke political criticism, as has the failure to launch a "war on AIDS" in many circles.[62] Even the "war on terrorism" may best be fought by a collection of largely autonomous and decentralized, albeit coordinated, organizations than by a comprehensive and hierarchically organized program.

Interorganizational Politics

Few if any policies are designed and implemented by a "single lonely organization."[63] Certainly individual organizations have their problems, but many more difficulties are encountered in the design of implementation structures—the pattern of interactions among organizations as they attempt to implement a policy. The problems of organizational disunity and communication become exaggerated when the individuals involved are not bound even by a presumed loyalty to a single organization but have competing loyalties to different organizations, not all of which may be interested in the effective implementation of a particular program.[64] This tendency may be exaggerated when a central element in implementation is private contractors, whose goals of profit and contract fulfillment conflict with goals of service delivery and accountability in the public sector.[65]

Jeffrey L. Pressman and Aaron Wildavsky, who popularized the concern for implementation several decades ago, speak of the problems of implementing policies through a number of organizations (or even within a single organization) as problems of "clearance points"—defined as the number of individual decision points that must be agreed to before any policy intentions can be translated into action.[66] Even if the decision makers at each "clearance point" are favorably disposed toward the program in question, there may still be impediments to reaching agreement for implementation. Some problems may be legal, some may be budgetary, and others may involve building coalitions with other organizations or interests in the society.

Statistically, one would expect that if each decision point is independent of the others and if the probability of any individual decision maker's agreeing to the program is 90 percent (.9), then the probability of any two agreeing is 81 percent (.9 x .9); and for three points, the probability would be 73 percent (.9 x .9 x .9); and so forth. Pressman and Wildavsky determined that there were at a minimum seventy clearance points in the implementation of the Economic Development Administration's decision to become involved in public works projects in Oakland, California.[67] With this number of clearance points, the probability of all of them agreeing, given an average probability of 90 percent for each clearance, would be less than one in a thousand. Only if there were a probability greater than 99 percent at each clearance point would the odds in favor of implementation be greater than 50–50. Of course, implementation is not just a problem in statistics, and the political and administrative leaders involved in the process can vastly alter the probabilities at each stage. With so many independent clearance points and limited political resources, however, a leader may well be tempted to succumb to the inertia inherent in the implementation system.

Judith Bowen has argued that the simple statistical model proposed by Pressman and Wildavsky may understate the probabilities of successful implementation.[68] She points out that if persistence is permitted, and each clearance point can be assaulted a number of times, the chances for a successful implementation increase significantly. She also explains that the clearance points may not be independent, as assumed, and that success at one clearance point may produce an increased probability of success at subsequent steps. Similarly, the clever implementer can make strategic choices about which clearance points to try first and how to package the points so that some success can be gained even if the whole campaign is not won. Thus, while successful implementation is still not perceived to be a simple task, it is subject to manipulation, as are other stages of the policy process. The clever policy analyst therefore can improve his or her probabilities of success by understanding how to intervene most effectively.

The administrative reforms of recent decades have tended to exacerbate these problems of implementation by building into the process more actors, and especially private-sector (both for-profit and not-for-profit) organizations. A common admonition now is that governments should "steer but not row"[69]— that is, governments should make policy but depend upon other organizations who may be more efficient in conducting the actual implementation. This strategy is presumed to both reduce cost (and public employment) and boost the quality of the services delivered to citizens. Whether those goals are achieved or not, it is clear that the new style of administration does build in more clearance points and hence more opportunities for policies to go astray in the implementation process.

Vertical Implementation Structures

One problem in implementation occurs vertically within the hierarchical structures of government. I have described some problems of intergovernmental relations in the United States associated with the several levels of governments. The impact of intergovernmental relations is especially evident for federal social and urban legislation, in which all three levels of government may be involved in putting a single piece of legislation into effect. For example, Title XX of the

Social Security Amendments of 1972 called for the availability of day-care services for poor working mothers. These services were to be funded through the Social Security Administration in Washington but implemented through state and
local governments. For the typical poor child to receive day care, supported by
the federal government, the Social Security Administration must agree to give a
grant for the proposed program to a local government. But this money would
be channeled through the state government, which would issue regulations to
carry out the intentions of the program within the structure of the particular
state government. The grant money was then transferred to the local government. But the local government could rarely provide the day care itself; instead,
it contracted with day-care providers (usually private) to provide the services.
The local government would have to monitor the standards and contract compliance of the private-service providers to ensure that no federal policy guidelines were violated—and even that regulation might differ substantially from
state to state or local government to local government.[70] More recently, the welfare reforms of the 1990s depended upon the same mixture of state governments,
local governments, and private contractors to move poorer citizens off public assistance and into productive work, and again that produced an immense implementation problem.[71]

Such a vertical implementation structure can give rise to several possibilities
for inadequate implementation or no implementation. One source of such
problems is simple partisan politics, when state or local governments and the
federal government are controlled by different political parties and consequently
have different policy priorities. Or localities may, for other reasons, have different policy priorities than does the federal government and may choose to implement programs differently than the federal government desires. Two good
examples of such differences can be seen in the resistance of local governments
to federally mandated scattering of public housing projects in middle-class
neighborhoods and in the resistance of most state and local governments to federal proposals to locate nuclear waste disposal facilities in their territory. The
state of Nevada, for example, has been fighting the federal government for more
than fifteen years over the proposed location of a repository for nuclear waste at
Yucca Mountain.

Even if local governments want to do what the federal government would
have them do, they sometimes lack the resources to do it. For example, local
governments have attempted to resist various federal mandates, such as the
Water Pollution Control Act of 1972 and day-care quality standards, claiming
they lacked the funds to meet the standards imposed.[72] Also, the states and localities may have few incentives to comply with federal directives. For example,
in the Elementary and Secondary Education Act of 1965 the states were to receive their grants merely for participating in the program, without having to do

anything in particular to improve education. When easy money is available, there is little or no reason, other than good faith and a desire to encourage good government, to comply with federal regulations.

The increasing emphasis on the use of the private sector to achieve public purposes means that implementation is increasingly being performed by private groups as well as by subnational governments. For example, tenants' organizations have begun to manage public housing projects, and churches and other charitable organizations became the contractors for services under the Americorps volunteer program in the Clinton administration. This pattern of implementation can easily create the problems of "capture" described earlier. For instance, some attempts to regulate the amount of fish that can be caught in the Atlantic have been implemented by the affected parties (fishermen and processors among others) through eight management councils, with the result that over-fishing has been permitted and fish stocks seriously depleted.[73]

Horizontal Implementation Structures

In addition to problems incurred in achieving compliance across several levels of government, difficulties may occur in coordinating activities and organizations horizontally. That is, the success of one agency's program may require the cooperation of other organizations, or at least the effective coordination of their activities. As one simple example, the Department of Agriculture has assisted the Department of Health and Human Services in implementing the Women, Infants and Children's (WIC) program, which provides nutritional support for the groups listed in the program's title. Agriculture has bargained to keep the price of infant formula lower so that the funds provided by WIC to women can go farther.

The breakdown of coordination can come about in several ways. One is through language and encoding difficulties. Individual agencies hire certain kinds of professionals and train all their employees in a certain manner. As a result, the Model Cities Program's housing experts decided that the problems of residents resulted from substandard housing, whereas employment experts thought that the problems arose from unemployment, and psychiatric social workers perceived the problems as resulting from personality problems. Each group of professionals, in other words, was oblivious to the perspectives of the other groups and consequently found it difficult to cooperate in treating the "whole client"—one of the stated objectives of the program. This was strongly demonstrated in the pattern of referrals among agencies. The vast majority of referrals of clients from one agency to another occurred within policy areas, rather than across policy areas.[74] A client who visited an agency seeking health care services would frequently be referred to another agency, most commonly another health care agency rather than a social welfare agency that might offer assistance in receiving funds to provide better nutrition, which might have been as effective as medical care in improving clients' health. Agencies tend to label and classify clients as belonging in their own policy areas; they often do not refer clients broadly or provide services for the client's whole range of needs. The perceptual blinders of organizations and their members prevent them from seeing all of a client's needs, and their training as professionals makes it difficult for service providers to shake off these blinders.

The lack of control among agencies and the consequent deficiencies in the implementation of programs may also occur because the objectives of one organization conflict with those of one or more other organizations. Agencies have to live, and to live they require money and personnel. Thus, at a basic level, an organization may be unwilling to cooperate in the implementation of a program simply because the success of another agency may threaten its own future prospects. On a somewhat higher plane, organizations may disagree about the purposes of government or about the best ways to achieve the goals about which they do agree. Or an agency may want to receive credit for providing a service that inevitably involves the cooperation of many organizations, and its insistence on receiving credit may prevent anything from happening. For example, several law enforcement agencies knew about a major drug shipment, but they allowed it to slip through their fingers simply because they could not agree on which of the "cooperating" agencies would make the actual arrest and receive the media attention.

Finally, a simple failure to think about coordination may prevent effective implementation. This is the result of oversight and failure to understand linkages among programs; it is not a result of language problems or an attempt to protect an organization's turf. Even if a program can be implemented without adequate coordination with other agencies, its effectiveness may be limited or substantial duplication of efforts may result. Most citizens have heard their share of horror stories about the same streets being dug up and repaired in successive weeks by different city departments and by private utilities. Equally horrific stories are told of reporting requirements issued by a variety of federal agencies that require contradictory definitions of terms or that involve excessive duplication of effort by citizens. Venality is rarely at the root of these problems, but that neither prevents the loss of efficiency nor makes citizens any happier about the problems of management in their government.

Coordination of programs appeared to become more difficult during the 1990s, and the problems appear to become more important every day. As the public sector began to rely more on the private sector to deliver public programs and also to use state and local governments to deliver these services, it became more difficult to provide integrated services. This remains true despite widespread pressure to make the public sector more "user friendly" and "customer oriented."[75] Further, effective coordination is increasingly important as the interactions between these various program providers become more evident. For example, social programs are becoming increasingly dependent on effective job training programs, and economic success is becoming increasingly dependent on educational policy. Also, the demands of homeland security are requiring a number of organizations to coordinate and cooperate in ways that previously have not been considered.

From the Bottom Up?

It has been argued that many of the problems encountered with implementation are a function of their being considered from a "top-down" perspective."[76] That is, the person providing evaluation looks at what happens to a law and considers that the bureaucracies have failed because they have not produced outcomes exactly like those intended by the framers of the legislation. The assumption here, rather like Hood's, is that bureaucracies should march to a single drummer—and that the drummer should be Congress or the president. Anticipating such an orderly approach to governance and implementation may be expecting too much from American government, given its complexity and the multiple and competing interests organized within the system. Indeed, the appropriate questions may be: in what policy areas can we accept the slippage between goals and outcomes, and what can be done to produce greater compliance in the most sensitive areas?[77]

An alternative to the "top-down" perspective is to think of implementation from the "bottom up," or through "backward mapping."[78] This approach holds that the people who design public programs should think about the ease, or even the possibility, of implementation during the development stage. Also, programs should take into account the interests of the lower echelons of the bureaucracy, their contacts with the program's clients, and indeed the values and desires of the clients themselves. With these factors in mind, policymakers should then design a set of policies that can be readily implemented. Such a program may not fulfill all the original goals of the policy formulators, but it will be able to gain a higher degree of compliance than a program based on strict legal norms of compliance and autonomy of policy formulators.

The "bottom-up" concept of implementation and program design is appealing, for it promises rather easy victories in the complicated wars involved in making programs work. Even if these promises could be fulfilled, however—and there must be some reasonable doubts—there are important problems with this approach. The most important is the normative problem that political leaders and their policy advisers have the responsibility (and usually the desire) to formulate programs that meet their political goals and fulfill the promises made in political campaigns.[79] Programs that are easily implementable may not meet those goals. This is perhaps especially true when conservative administrations attempt to make changes in social programs through field staffs committed to more liberal goals, or when liberals attempt to carry out expansionary economic policies through more conservative economic institutions inside and outside government. Governments may wind up doing what they can do, or what they have always done, rather than what they want to do.

In addition, the ability of agency field staffs to define what is "feasible" may allow them substantially greater control over policy than may be desirable within a democratic political system. Their definition of feasibility may be excessively conservative, limiting the options that might be available with proper design. Finally, there may be little reliable evidence about what really is feasible in implementation terms and what is really impossible.[80] Too-facile definitions of feasibility may undervalue the abilities and leadership of politicians and administrators alike.

The Third Generation?

After the original top-down and bottom-up implementation studies, and some attention to political factors in implementation, there might be said to be a third generation of thinking about the problem.[81] This generation attempts to replace these relatively simple models with more complex descriptions of the relationships that exist in the process of implementation. Much of the earlier literature on implementation tended to provide a single answer regardless of the question. The third wave, on the other hand, tends to answer most questions about implementation with the accurate, if somewhat unsatisfying, answer "it depends."

The real task for understanding implementation, then, is to identify what factors serve as contingencies for success or failure. Some such factors are expressly political, while others are a function of the type of policy being implemented. Still others may be a function of the organizations that are used as the agents of implementation. Specifying why a program succeeds or fails, therefore, involves the identification and interaction of all these factors. This is a complex research task, just as it is a complex practical task to design an implementation structure that can actually make the program function in something close to the manner intended by the people who designed it.

Summary

American government is a massive, complex, and often confusing set of institutions. It contains numerous organizations but lacks any central organizing principle. Much of the structure of American government was developed on an ad hoc basis to address particular problems at particular times. Even with a more coherent structure, many of the same problems might still arise in the attempt to implement a program. Many problems are inherent in any government, although they are certainly exacerbated by the complexity and diffuse structure of American government. For public policy, implementation is a vital step in the process of governing because it involves putting programs into action and producing effects for citizens. The difficulty in producing desired effects, or indeed any effects, then, means that policy is a much more difficult commodity to deliver to citizens than is commonly believed. The barriers to effective implementation often discourage individuals and organizations from engaging in the activities devised for their benefit. Public management then becomes a matter of threatening or cajoling organizations into complying with stated objectives, or of convincing those organizations that their goals can best be accomplished through the programs that have been authorized.

CHAPTER 6

Budgeting:
Allocation and Public Policy

To IMPLEMENT public policies, government requires money as well as institutional structures. The budgetary process provides the means of allocating the available resources of government among the competing purposes for which they could be used. In principle, all resources in the society are available to government, although in the United States a politician who openly expressed such a position probably would not last beyond the next election. Likewise, almost all the purposes for which politicians and administrators wish to spend public money have some merits. The question is whether those purposes are sufficiently meritorious to justify using the resources in the public sector, instead of putting those resources to use in the private sector. Finding answers to such questions requires economic and analytical judgment, as well as political estimates of the feasibility of the proposed policies.

Two different aspects of budgeting sometimes merge. One is the question of system-level allocation between the public and private sectors: How many activities or problems justify government intervention into the economy for the purpose of taxing and spending?[1] Could the best interest of society be served by keeping the money in the hands of businesses or individuals for investment decisions and thereby allowing some potentially beneficial programs in government to go unfunded? Or do the equity, equality, and economic growth potentially produced through a public project justify the expense of political capital by officials to pass and collect an additional tax or to increase an existing tax? These system-level questions also include the proportion of its expenditures government should finance through taxes and fees, or, in other words, how large a deficit could the United States afford to run?[2]

The second major budgeting question is this: How should available public-sector resources be allocated among competing programs? When they devise a budget, decision makers function within resource constraints—they must base their decisions on the assumption that no more revenue will come in (or that no larger deficit will be accepted). Decision makers must therefore attempt to allocate available money for the greatest social, economic, and political benefit. This is not an easy task, of course, because of differing opinions about what uses of the money would be best. In addition, decision makers are often constrained by commitments to fund existing entitlement programs, such as Social Security, before they can begin to allocate the rest of the funds to other worthy programs. Because money can be divided almost infinitely, however, it offers a medium for resolving social conflicts that indivisible forms of public benefit, such as rights, often do not. Therefore, although there are a number of possible justifications for budgetary decisions, we must be aware that political considerations tend to dominate and that many of the most effective arguments revolve around votes and coming elections.

Characteristics of the Federal Budget

Before discussing the budget cycle through which the federal budget is constructed each year, we should explain several fundamental features of that budget. These features offer some benefits for decision makers but also constrain them and at times help create undesirable outcomes; the format of the budget is not politically neutral but directly affects the outcomes of the process. There are, therefore, attempts at one time or another to reform almost all features of the budgetary process. Those reform efforts encounter resistance by the interests advantaged by the status quo, so that the process, as well as the content, of budgeting becomes part of the political debate.

An Executive Budget

The federal budget is an executive budget, prepared by the president and his staff, approved by Congress, and then executed by the president and the executive branch. This has not always been the case; before 1921, the federal budget was a legislative budget, prepared almost entirely by Congress and then executed by the president. One major tenet of the government reform movement in the early twentieth century was that an executive budget was a necessity for more effective management in government.[3] According to that doctrine, no executive should be required to manage a budget that he or she had no part in planning or preparing.

The Budget and Accounting Act of 1921 marked a new stage in the conflict between the executive and legislative branches over their respective powers in budgeting.[4] In general, budgetary power has accumulated in the executive branch and in the Executive Office of the President, in large part because of the analytical dominance of the Office of Management and Budget (OMB; it was called the Bureau of the Budget until 1971). The excesses of the Nixon administration—and to some degree those of the Johnson administration during the Vietnam War—led to the development of the Congressional Budget Office (CBO) as a part of the Congressional Budget and Impoundment Control Act of 1974. The CBO provides Congress with much of the analytical capability of the executive branch, just as the development of the budget committees in both houses gives Congress greater control over budgeting than before the passage of the act in 1974. The negotiations with President George H.W. Bush over the fiscal year 1991 budget appeared to give Congress much greater responsibility in framing budget options. Congress also played a major part in the 1997 budget settlement that contributed to attaining a balanced budget as early as fiscal year 1998.⁵ Nevertheless, Congress remains in the position of responding to budgetary initiatives from the White House.

Line Item

Despite several attempts at reform, the federal budget remains a line-item budget. That is, the final budget document appropriating funds allocates those funds into categories—wages and salaries, supplies, travel, equipment, and so forth. These traditional categories are extremely useful to Congress in that they give the legislature some degree of control over the executive branch. Moneys are appropriated for organizations and are also allocated for specific purposes within the agency budget. It is then rather easy for the legislature, through the General Accounting Office, to make sure that the money is spent under legal authority; it is more difficult to determine if it is being spent efficiently and effectively.⁶ The rigidities of the line-item budget may actually prevent good managers in government from managing effectively by limiting how they can spend the money—it may be that more equipment and less personnel could do the same job better and/or more cheaply, but managers generally are not given that option.

Input controls, such as line-item budgets, are now considered an inefficient means of control over public organizations and their managers. Critics have argued that it would be better to give a manager a relatively unrestricted budget and then judge him or her on the achievement of program goals with that money. Congress, however, tends to want to maximize its oversight over the executive instead of allowing managerial flexibility. Through the Government Performance and Results Act of 1993, Congress attempted to overlay the fundamental line-item nature of the budget with a more performance-based system of assessment and allocation—using output controls to replace the input controls. That system is now being implemented and there have been some early successes, but it may well be that the older patterns of emphasizing financial control, rather than performance, will come to dominate even a reformed budget process.

An Annual Budget

The federal budget is primarily an annual budget. Agencies are now required to submit five-year forecasts for each of their expenditure plans, but these are used primarily for management purposes within the Office of Management and Budget. The budget presented to Congress and the appropriations bills eventually adopted by Congress together constitute only a one-year expenditure plan. The absence of a more complete, multiyear budget makes planning difficult for federal managers, and it does little to alert Congress to the long-term implications of expenditure decisions made in any one year. A small expenditure in one year may result in much larger expenditures in subsequent years, and it may create clientele who cannot be eliminated without significant political repercussions. Conversely, a project that would have to run several years to be truly effective may be terminated after a single year. Many state and local governments in the United States now operate with multiyear budgets, but the federal government still does not. OMB's annual advice to the agencies serves as a guide for preparing budgets and provides some information about expectations for five years, but the information for the four "out years" is speculative at best.

One of the several recommendations of the Gore Commission (the National Performance Review) was to move the federal government toward a biennial budget, in order to enable organizations to plan more effectively and therefore to deliver services more efficiently.[7] In addition, this reform might allow Congress to reduce the amount of time that it must devote to the budget process and thus enable it to spend more time performing its other legislative duties. Again, however, Congress does not appear to favor this reform, largely because it might lessen congressional control over the organizations within the executive branch. Likewise, there has been little enthusiasm for capital budgeting or better identification of the investment aspects of federal expenditures.[8]

The Budget Cycle

Each year there must be a new budget, and an annual cycle has evolved for the appropriation and expenditure of public money. The repetitive nature of the budget cycle is important, for the agency officials involved might behave differently if they did not know that they have to come back year after year to obtain more money from the same OMB officials and from the same congressmen. In addition to the emphasis this repetition places on building trust and a reputation for dependability, it allows policy entrepreneurs multiple opportunities to build their cases for new programs and changes in budgetary allocations. If they fail one year, they can try the next; if they fail in one institutional setting, they can try at another. Preparing the budget is an extremely long, deliberative process, requiring about a year to complete, which allows for a great deal of analysis and political bargaining among the many parties involved.[9]

Setting the Parameters: The President and His Friends

Most of this chapter pertains to the micro-level allocation of resources among programs, rather than the setting of broad expenditure and economic management policy. It is necessary, however, to begin with a brief discussion of the initial decisions concerning overall levels of expenditure and revenue that will influence subsequent decisions about programs. Inevitably, changes in particular programs and in socioeconomic conditions (wars, recessions, and the like) will influence the total spending levels of government, so this stage mostly involves setting targets rather than making final decisions.

The first official act of the budget cycle is the development, each spring, of estimates of the total size of the federal budget to be prepared for the fiscal year. Although agencies and the OMB will already have begun to discuss and prepare expenditure plans, the letter from the president through the OMB (usually in June) is an important first step in the formal process, providing a statement of overall presidential budgetary strategy and of the financial limits within which agencies should begin to prepare their budgets. In addition to setting the overall parameters, this letter presents more detailed information on how those parameters apply to individual agencies. Naturally, the past experience of budgeting officials in each agency gives them some further sense of how to interpret the general parameters. Defense agencies, for example, knew during the Cold War era that they were not necessarily bound by those parameters, whereas planners of domestic programs with little client support and few friends on Capitol Hill could only hope to do as well as the letter had led them to believe they might.

The overall estimates for spending are prepared some sixteen months before the budget goes into effect. For example, the fiscal year 2001 budget went into effect on 1 October 2000, but the planning for that budget began in June 1999 or even earlier. For any budget, this means that the economic forecasts on which the expenditure estimates are based may be far from the prevailing economic reality when the budget is actually executed. Any deviations from those economic forecasts are important. The recession of 2000, for example, meant a reduction in revenues and an increase in expenditures—people who are out of work do not pay income or Social Security taxes and they demand unemployment insurance payments and perhaps welfare.

The fiscal downturn of the early twenty-first century has resulted in the loss of countless jobs nationwide. Budgetary constraints can affect state and federal unemployment benefits and become a bone of contention between unions and corporations.

Furthermore, these important economic forecasts are not entirely the product of technical considerations; they are also influenced by political and ideological considerations. For example, during the first years of the Reagan administration the belief that "supply-side" economics would produce larger revenues through increased economic activity led to a serious overestimation of the amount of revenue. This was the beginning of the large federal deficits that were a feature of American public finance for over fifteen years.[10] After the Clinton administration had succeeded in generating a balanced budget, and even a substantial budget surplus, the first year of the George W. Bush administration produced a return to something approaching the supply-side logic. President Bush and his advisers assumed that a substantial tax cut could be reconciled with maintaining a balanced budget, given their expectation that higher economic growth would result from lower taxes. In some way that assumption was never tested, given the immense budgetary impact of the September 11 terrorist attacks, but prior experience might produce some skepticism about that assumption.

The preparation of economic and expenditure estimates is the result of the interaction of three principal actors—the Council of Economic Advisers (CEA), the OMB, and the Treasury—which are collectively referred to as the "troika."[11] The CEA is, as the name implies, a group of economists who advise the president. Organizationally, they are located in the Executive Office of the President. The role of the CEA is largely technical, forecasting the state of the economy and advising the president on the basis of these forecasts. Its economists also mathematically model the probable effects of budgetary choices on the economy. Of course, the economics of the CEA must be tempered with political judgment, for mathematical models and economists do not run for office—but presidents must. One chairman of the Council of Economic Advisers in the Reagan administration said that he relied on his "visceral computer" for some of the more important predictions.[12]

The OMB, despite its image as a budget-controlling organization, comes as close to a representative of the expenditure community as exists within the troika. Even though the agencies whose budgets OMB supervises find it difficult to perceive the OMB as a benefactor, some of its personnel may be favorably disposed toward expenditures. They see the huge volume of agency requests coming forward and are aware of a large volume of "uncontrollable" expenditures (e.g., Social Security benefits) that will have to be funded regardless of changes in economic circumstances. These considerations of commitments and inertia were not as important under the Reagan and George H.W. Bush administrations as during previous administrations, in part because of the political commitment of several directors of the OMB to reducing federal expenditures. The Clinton administration also grappled with the problem of entitlement spending, reflecting in part the fear that these programs would swamp the entire budget process and thwart its desire to launch new programs.[13]

Finally, the Treasury represents the financial community, and historically it has been the major advocate of a balanced budget within the troika, for it must cover any debts created by a budget deficit by issuing government bonds. The principal interest of the Treasury in troika negotiations often is to preserve the confidence of the financial community at home and abroad in the soundness of the U.S. economy and the government's management of that economy. Some particular (and increasing) concerns of the Treasury may be relationships with international financial organizations, such as the International Monetary Fund, that are important for maintaining international economic confidence.

Even at this first step in the budgetary process, a great deal of hard political and economic bargaining occurs among participants. Each member of the troika must compete for the attention of the president as well as protect the interests of the particular professional, organizational, and political community it represents in budgeting. But this bargaining is just the beginning of a long series of political debates and bargains as agencies attempt to get the money they want and need from the budgetary process.

Agency Requests

As in so much American policymaking, the agency is a central actor in the budgetary process.[14] Whether working independently or within a cabinet-level department, the agency is responsible for the initial preparation of estimates and requests for funding. The agency makes these preparations in conjunction with the OMB and, if applicable, with the agency's executive department budgeting personnel. During the preparation of estimates, OMB provides guidance and advice about total levels of expenditure and particular aspects of the agency's budget. Likewise, the agency may have to coordinate its activities with those of other agencies within the executive department in which it is located. Accomplished through a departmental budget committee and the secretary's staff, this coordination is necessary to ensure that the agency is operating within presidential priorities and that the secretary will provide support in defending the budget to OMB and Congress.

The task of the agency in the budgetary process is to be aggressive in seeking to expand its own expenditure base while at the same time recognizing that it is only one part of a larger organization.[15] In other words, the agency must be aggressive but reasonable, seeking more money but realizing that it operates within the constraints of what the federal government as a whole can afford. Likewise, the executive department must recognize its responsibilities to the president and his program as well as to the agencies under its umbrella. The cabinet secretary must be a major spokesperson for his or her agencies at higher governmental levels, although agencies often have more direct support from interest groups and perhaps from Congress than does the department as a whole. Thus, a cabinet secretary may not be able to go far in following the president's program if that program seriously jeopardizes ongoing programs, and their clienteles, in his or her department. This problem reflects the general fragmentation of American government, which places much of the power and the operational connections between government and interest groups at the agency, rather than the department, level.

An agency may employ a number of strategies in seeking to expand its funding, but the use of these strategies is restrained by the knowledge that budgeting is an annual cycle. Any strategic choice in a single year may preclude the use of that strategy in later years and, perhaps more important, may destroy any confidence that OMB and Congress have had in the agency.[16] For example, an agency may employ the "camel's nose" or "thin wedge" strategy to get modest initial funding for a program, with the knowledge that the program will have rapidly increasing expenditure requirements. Even if that strategy is successful once, however, the agency may be assured that any future requests for new spending authority will be carefully scrutinized. Therefore, agencies may be well advised to pursue careful, long-term strategies and to develop trust among the political leaders who determine their budgets.

Executive Review

After the agency has decided on its requests, it passes them on to the OMB for review. The OMB is a presidential agency, one of whose principal tasks is to amass all the agency requests and conform them to presidential policy priorities and to the overall levels of expenditure desired. This may make for a tight fit, as some spending programs are difficult or impossible to control, leaving little space for any new programs the president may consider important. Even the more conservative presidents of the past two decades have found it difficult to make overall spending levels conform with their view that government should tax and spend less.

After OMB receives the estimates, it passes them on to its budget examiners for review. In the rare case in which an agency has actually requested the same amount, or less, than OMB had planned to give it, there is no problem. In most cases, however, the examiners must depend on their experience with the agency in question, as well as whatever information about programs and projected expenditures they can collect, to make a judgment concerning the necessity and priority of requested expenditure increases.

On the basis of agency requests and the information developed by the examiners, OMB holds hearings, usually in October or November, at which each agency must defend its requests before the examiner and other members of the OMB staff. Although OMB sometimes seems to be committed to cutting expenditures, several factors prevent it from wielding its axe with excessive vigor. First, it is frequently possible for an agency to pull an "end run" on the hearing board by appealing to the director of OMB, the president, or ultimately to its friends in Congress. Also, some budget examiners come, over time, to favor the agencies they are supposed to control, so they may become advocates of an agency's requests rather than the fiscal controllers and financial conservatives they are expected to be. This is a pattern not dissimilar to that of regulatory "capture."

The results of the hearing are forwarded to the director of OMB for the "director's review," which involves the top staff of the bureau. At this stage, through additional trimming and negotiation, the staff attempts to pare the final budget down to the amount desired by the president. After each portion of the budget has passed through the director's review, it is forwarded to the president for final review, and then for compilation into the final budget document. This stage necessarily involves final appeals from agency and department personnel to OMB and the president as well as last-minute adjustments to take into account unanticipated changes in economic forecasts and desired changes in the total size of the budget. The presidential budget is then prepared for delivery to Congress within fifteen days after it convenes in January each year. Presidents differ in the amount of time they devote to budgeting, but the budget is perceived as a statement of the priorities of the president and his administration, even if it is really prepared largely by the public servants at OMB.

In this way the presidential budget is made ready to be reviewed through the appropriations process in Congress, but the two branches of government will already have begun to communicate about the budget. By mid-November each year, the president must submit to Congress the "current services budget," which includes "proposed budget authority and estimated outlays that would be included in the budget for the ensuing fiscal year . . . if all programs and activities were carried on at the same level as the fiscal year in progress."[17] This is a form of "volume budgeting," for it posits a constant volume of public services and then determines the price.[18] During a period with a rapidly rising rate of inflation, such as the 1970s and early 1980s, this constant-service budget can give Congress an early warning of the anticipated size of current expenditure commitments if they are to be extended. But these estimates are subject to substantial inaccuracy, either purposive or accidental, so they provide a rough estimate for planning purposes, but only that.

Congressional Action

Although it is specifically granted the powers of the purse in the Constitution, by the 1960s and 1970s Congress had clearly ceased to be the dominant actor in making budgetary decisions. It then attempted a counterattack, largely through the Congressional Budget and Impoundment Control Act of 1974. Among other provisions, this act established in each house of Congress a budget committee to be responsible for developing two concurrent resolutions each year outlining fiscal policy constraints on expenditures, much as the troika does in the executive branch. The act also established the Congressional Budget Office to give the budget committees a staff capacity analogous to that which OMB provides for the president.[19] This enhanced analytic capacity is important for Congress in understanding its budgetary activity, but the need to implement somewhat more immediate and less analytic expenditure reforms has tended to make these changes less important than they might otherwise have been.

Decisions on how to allocate total spending among agencies and programs are made by the appropriations committees in both houses.[20] These committees are extremely prestigious and powerful, and those serving on them generally are veteran members of Congress. Members tend to remain on these committees for long periods, thereby developing not only budgetary expertise but also political ties with the agencies they supervise as well as with their own constituencies.[21] These two committees—and especially the House Appropriations Committee—do most of their work through subcommittees, which may cover one executive department, such as Defense, or a number of agencies, such as Housing and Urban Development and independent executive agencies, or a function, such as public works. Most important, the whole committee does not closely scrutinize the decisions of its subcommittees, nor does the House of Representatives as a whole frequently reverse the decisions of its appropriations committee.

Scrutiny by the whole House has increased, however, in large part because of the general opening of congressional deliberations to greater "sunshine," meaning greater public scrutiny. In addition, the politics of deficit reduction have tended to place greater restraints on committee and subcommittee autonomy. The committees must now submit appropriations levels that correspond to the total spending levels permitted under the previously enacted joint resolutions on taxing and spending. Provided that the committees can keep their appropriations within those predetermined levels, they can have substantial autonomy; once an agency's budget has been accepted by a subcommittee, that budget has, in all probability, been decided.[22]

Beginning with the presidential recommendations, each subcommittee develops an appropriations bill, or occasionally two, for a total of thirteen or fourteen bills each year. Hearings are held, and agency personnel are summoned to testify and to justify the size of their desired appropriations. After those hearings, the subcommittee will "mark up" the bill—make such changes as it feels are necessary from the original proposals—and then submit it, first to the entire committee and then to the House of Representatives. In accordance with the Congressional Budget Act, appropriations committees are expected to have completed mark-ups of all appropriations bills before submitting the first for final passage, so as to have a better idea of the overall level of expenditure that would be approved. The Senate follows a similar procedure, and differences between the two houses are resolved in a conference committee.

This procedure in Congress needs to be finished by 15 September in order for the budget to be ready to go into effect on 1 October, but the Congressional Budget Act also requires the passage of a second concurrent resolution setting forth the budget ceilings, revenue floors, and overall fiscal policy considerations governing the passage of the appropriations bills. Because there will undoubtedly be differences in the ways in which the two houses make their appropriations figures correspond with the figures in the concurrent resolution, the reconciliation bill, in which both houses agree on the spending totals, must be passed by 25 September.

While the reconciliation bill appears to be a technicality, the Reagan administration used this opportunity to impose its budgetary will when Reagan first entered office,[23] and the 1996 welfare reforms also technically came about as a part of the reconciliation bill. Further, the need to pass a single reconciliation bill tends to move power away from the appropriations committees and sub-committees and to centralize it in the leadership, especially in the House of Representatives.[24] After all these stages have been completed, the budget (in the form of the various appropriations bills) is then ready to go to the president for his signature and execution. Although this process has clear deadlines, they are often missed and, as in 2002, Congress frequently must pass continuing resolutions to maintain funding for programs until the appropriations bills are finally passed.[25]

Budget Execution

Once Congress has appropriated money for the executive branch, the agencies must develop mechanisms for spending that money. An appropriations warrant, drawn by the Treasury and countersigned by the General Accounting Office, is sent to each agency. The agency then makes plans for its expenditures for the year, on the basis of this warrant, and submits a plan to OMB for apportionment of the funds. The funds appropriated by Congress are usually made available to the agencies on a quarterly basis, but for some agencies there may be great differences in the amounts made available each quarter. For example, the National Park Service spends a very large proportion of its annual appropriation during the summer because of the demands on the national parks at that time. Two principal reasons for allowing agencies access to only a quarter of their funds at a time are to provide greater control over spending and to prevent an agency from spending everything early in the year and then requiring a supplemental appropriation. Such overspending may still happen, but apportionment helps to control any potential profligacy.

The procedures for executing the budget are relatively simple when the executive branch actually wants to spend the money appropriated; they become more complex when the president decides he does not want to spend the appropriated funds. Prior to the Congressional Budget Act of 1974, a president had at least a customary right to impound funds, that is, to refuse to spend them.[26] Numerous impoundments during the Nixon administration—as when half the money appropriated for implementing the Federal Water Pollution Control Act Amendments of 1972 was impounded from the 1973 to 1975 budgets—forced Congress to take action to control the executive and to reassert its customary powers over the purse.

The Congressional Budget and Impoundment Control Act of 1974 was designed to limit the ability of the president to use impoundment as an indirect means of overruling Congress, when he was not able to do so through the nor-

TABLE 6.1   Rescissions Proposed and Enacted, by President

President	Number proposed	Number accepted	Amount proposed (in millions)	Amount enacted (in millions)
Ford	152	52	$7,935.0	$1,252.2
Carter	89	50	4,608.5	2,116.1
Reagan	602	214	43,436.6	15,656.8
Clinton*a*	125	82	6,153.9	3,308.5

Source: General Accounting Office, *Frequency and Amount of Rescissions,* OGC–97–59 (Washington, D.C.: GAO, 26 September 1997).

a. Through 1996.

mal legislative process (the water-pollution control legislation had been passed over a presidential veto). The 1974 act defined two kinds of impoundment. The first, *rescissions,* are cancellations of budgetary authority to spend money. Deciding that a program could reach its goals with less money or simply that there are good reasons not to spend the money, the president must then send a message to Congress requesting the rescission. Congress must act positively on this request within forty-five days; if it does not, the money is made available to the agency for obligation (see table 6.1). Congress can, however, also rescind money on its own by passing a resolution in both houses withdrawing the agency's authority to spend.

Deferrals, on the other hand, are requests merely to delay making the obligational authority available to the agency. In this case, if either house of Congress does not exercise its veto power, the deferral is granted. The comptroller general (head of the General Accounting Office) is given the power to classify specific presidential actions, and at times the difference between a deferral and a rescission is not clear. For example, attempting to defer funds for programs scheduled to be phased out is, in practice, a rescission. These reforms in the impoundment powers of the president have substantially increased congressional leverage in determining how much money will indeed be spent by the federal government each year.

Budget Control

After the executive branch spends the money appropriated by Congress, Congress must check to be sure that the money was spent legally and properly. The General Accounting Office (GAO) and its head, the comptroller general, are responsible for a postexpenditure audit of federal spending. Each year the comptroller general's report to Congress outlines deviations from congressional intent in the way in which government agencies have spent their money. Requests from individual congressmen or committees may produce earlier, and perhaps more detailed, evaluations of agency spending or policies. Each year the GAO provides Congress and the interested public with hundreds of evaluations of expenditures, as well as general audit reports on federal expenditures.

The General Accounting Office has undergone a major transformation from a simple accounting organization into a policy-analytic organization for the legislative branch.[27] It has become concerned not only with the legality of expenditures but also with the efficiency with which the money is spent. Although GAO reports on the efficiency of their expenditures have no legal standing, any agencies wishing to maintain good relations with Congress are well advised to take those findings into account. Congress will certainly be cognizant of any adverse reports when it reviews agency budgets the following year and may expect to see some changes in the way in which the agency conducts its business. These GAO recommendations also form one part of the ongoing process of congressional oversight of administration. The problem with GAO controls—whether accounting or more policy-analytic—is that they are largely ex post facto, which means that the money will probably have been spent long before the conclusion is reached that it has been spent either illegally or unwisely.

Summary

A long and complex process, taking almost eighteen months to complete, is required to perform the difficult task of allocating federal budget money among competing agencies. The process involves much bargaining and analysis, from which emerges a plan for spending billions of dollars. But even this complex process, made more complex by numerous reforms of congressional budgeting procedures and deficit fighting procedures, cannot control all federal expenditures as completely as some would desire, nor can it provide the level of fiscal management that may be necessary for a smoothly functioning economic system. Let us now turn to a few problems that presidents and congressmen confront in making the budgetary process an effective allocative process. Because it is inherently political as well as economic, the process may never be as "rational" as some would like, but there are identifiable problems that cause particular difficulty.

Problems in the Budgetary Process

The major problems arising in the budgetary process of the federal government affect the fiscal management function of budgeting, as well as the allocation of resources among agencies. It is difficult, if not impossible, for any president or any session of Congress to make binding decisions as to how much money will be spent during any one year, or even as to who will spend it for what purposes, and this absence of basic controls makes the entire process subject to error. Those elected to make policy and control spending frequently find themselves incapable of producing the kinds of program or budgetary changes they campaigned for, and this can result in disillusionment for both leaders and citizens.

The Deficit

The existence or prospect of a deficit has been a major driving force for budget reform in the United States, for deficits and public debt are very negative symbols in American political discourse. As the substantial budget surplus of the early twenty-first century moves into deficit, politicians are again becoming concerned about claims of fiscal irresponsibility. Given the ideological baggage associated with deficit and debt, it has been difficult at times to discuss them rationally. The definition of a deficit at the federal level is itself something of an artifact of a number of decisions made about the nature of the public sector and its budget. The most obvious factor influencing the rather artificial nature of discourse about the budget is that we tend to discuss the federal budget in isolation from state and local government spending and revenues (see pp. 145–147). Given the ability of the federal government to shift some of its financial burdens to lower levels of government, however, looking at only one level of government may give a false impression of the state of public finance (see table 2.4, p. 39).

A less obvious problem in calculating the federal deficit is the role that Social Security funds play in reducing the deficit. At present the Social Security Trust Fund is receiving substantially more (roughly $40 billion per year) in tax income than it is having to pay out to retirees, but this situation will change around 2010 when large numbers of "baby boomers" will begin to retire. In the meantime, the extra income enabled the Clinton administration to balance the budget (see table 6.2).[28] This definition of the budget as including Social Security funds helps government leaders present balanced budgets in the short term, but presents immense long-term challenges to maintain the soundness not only of the retirement system (see chapter 11) but also of the budget system. The federal government also controls public employee retirement funds, which it has at times manipulated in order to keep the deficit lower than it would otherwise be.[29]

Another, less obvious definitional problem in the federal budget is the absence of a separate capital budget. All state governments in the United States save one (Vermont) must, according to their state constitutions, have balanced budgets. The states do, however, separate out their capital projects—roads, bridges, schools, and the like—into separate capital budgets, and they can borrow money, by issuing bonds, to build those projects. The federal budget does not separate capital from current expenditures, however, so a good deal of fed-

TABLE 6.2 Estimated Federal Budget Deficits with and without Social Security (in billions of dollars)

	With Social Security	*Without Social Security*
1997	−21.9	−103.3
1998	−10.0	−106.3
1999	9.5	−95.7
2000	8.5	−104.9
2001	28.2	−94.1
2002	89.7	−44.6
2003	82.8	−62.8

Source: Calculated from Office of Management and Budget, *Budget of the United States* (annual).

eral borrowing is for projects for which borrowing is reasonable—even good fiscal conservatives borrow money to buy a house or an automobile. With that in mind, the usual (if inaccurate) analogy between government and private household budgeting can be maintained even if government borrows extensively. If we take the amount of federal spending that reasonably could be labelled "capital" out of the total budget, a very different picture of that deficit emerges: the federal government could be seen to have been running a surplus, or at least a much smaller deficit, for a number of years.

This discussion of Social Security funds and capital budgeting should make it clear that many of the terms used in public policy have no single, accepted definitions. Instead, definitions, like all other parts of the process, are constructed politically. It pays for incumbent politicians to calculate the deficit with Social Security revenues counted in, although some fiscal conservatives argue that this is actually a misuse of these funds and that the entire system should be privatized to prevent just such "abuses." Likewise, it pays for conservatives to calculate the deficit with capital expenditures included, although liberals might like to exclude those figures from the totals to justify greater borrowing of funds, and therefore higher public expenditures.

Uncontrollable Expenditures

Much of the federal budget is uncontrollable in any one year (see table 6.3). Many expenditure programs in the federal government cannot be controlled systematically without making policy changes that would be politically unpalatable.[30] For example, a president or Congress can do very little to control the level of expenditure for Social Security in any one year without either changing the

TABLE 6.3 Changes in "Uncontrollable" Federal Expenditures (in percentages)

	1976	1980	1990	1991	1992	1993	1995
Controllable	63.7	46.8	40.0	40.4	38.7	37.2	34.6
Uncontrollable	36.3	53.2	60.0	59.6	61.3	62.8	65.4

Source: Office of Management and Budget, *Special Analyses of the FY 1995 U.S. Budget* (Washington, D.C.: Government Printing Office, annual).

criteria for eligibility or altering the formula for indexation (adjustment of the benefits for changes in consumer prices or workers' earnings). Either policy choice would produce a major political conflict that might well make it impossible. Some minor changes, such as changing the tax treatment of Social Security benefits for beneficiaries with other income, may be entertained, but the vast majority of expenditure for the program is essentially uncontrollable.

The most important uncontrollable expenditures are the large entitlement programs of social welfare spending such as Social Security, Medicare, and unemployment benefits.[31] These expenditures are uncontrollable both because they cannot be readily cut and because government cannot accurately estimate while planning the budget exactly how much money will be needed for them. The final expenditure levels will depend on levels of inflation, illness, and unemployment, as well as on the number of eligible citizens who actually take advantage of the programs. In addition, outstanding contracts and obligations constitute a significant share of the uncontrollable portion of the budget, although these can be altered over several years, if not in a single year. The major controllable component of the federal budget is the defense budget. The end of the Cold War made this a particularly attractive target for budget cutting, although the apparent shift from large strategic forces to tactical (personnel-intensive) forces reduced the overall savings, and the large-scale shift toward defense spending in the George W. Bush administration has instead increased this category of spending.

The uncontrollable element of the budget has meant that even a president committed to the goals of reducing federal expenditures and producing a balanced budget (without figuring in a short-term Social Security surplus) will find it difficult to determine where the expenditure reductions will come from. Congress has begun to grapple with controlling these expenditures but finds the political forces of entitlements difficult to overcome.[32] Some discretionary social expenditures have been reduced over the past decade, but the bulk of federal expenditures have continued to increase (see table 2.4, p. 39) and remain likely to continue to increase. Thus, any president coming into office with a desire to balance the budget or to reduce federal spending will soon find it difficult to do so.

Back-Door Spending

Linked to the problem of uncontrollable expenditures is "back-door spending"—expenditure decisions that are not actually made through the formal appropriations process. These expenditures to some degree reflect an institutional conflict within Congress, between the appropriations committees and the substantive policy committees. They also reflect the difficulties of making the huge number of spending decisions that must be made each year through formal, and somewhat recondite, procedures. There are three principal kinds of back-door spending.

Borrowing authority.   Agencies are sometimes allowed to spend public money not appropriated by Congress if they borrow that money from the Treasury—for student-loan guarantees, for instance.[33] It has been argued that these are not actually public expenditures because the money will presumably be repaid eventually. In many instances, however, federal loans have been written off, and, even if the loans are repaid, the government may not know when that repayment will occur—students do not begin paying off loans until they complete their education. Further, the ability of government to control expenditure levels for purposes of economic management is seriously impaired when the authority to make spending decisions is so widely diffused.

The presence of all these loans, loan guarantees, and other contingent obligations is becoming more evident to government, and it reduced some of the glee about the apparent end of the federal deficit during the last years of the Clinton administration.[34] The federal government has been able to reduce directly budgeted expenditures, but there are few effective controls over loans, loan guarantees, or insurance obligations. For example, there are a dozen major federal insurance programs with authority to borrow over $60 billion.[35] As much as some decision makers would like to move to firmer budget ceilings for these programs, finding the way to do so and preserve all their insurance coverage is difficult.

Contract authority.   Agencies also may enter into contracts that bind the federal government to pay a certain amount for specified goods and services without going through the appropriations process. Then, after the contract is let, the appropriations committees are placed in the awkward position of either appropriating the money to pay off the debt or forcing the agency to renege on its debts. While this kind of spending is uncontrollable in the short run, any agency attempting to engage in this circumvention of the appropriations committees probably will face the ire of those committees when attempting to have its next annual budget approved. Also, Congress has been developing rules that make spending of this type increasingly difficult for agencies. Still, the more general shift toward implementation of public programs through third parties makes contracting a more important part of the process of governing.

Permanent appropriations.   Certain public programs have authorizing legislation that requires the agencies responsible to spend money for designated purposes almost regardless of other conditions. The largest expenditure of this kind is payment of interest on the public debt; although it has been dropping slightly over the past several years, this expense is still a substantial part of the federal budget, constituting over 12 percent of total federal expenditures in 2003. Likewise, federal support of land-grant colleges is a permanent appropriation that began during the administration of Abraham Lincoln. In the case of a permanent appropriation, the appropriations committees have relatively little discretion (other than to add to the spending), unless they choose to renege on these standing commitments.

The Overhang

Money appropriated by Congress for a fiscal year need not actually be spent during that fiscal year; it must only be *obligated.* That is, the agency must contract to spend the money, or otherwise make commitments about how it will be spent, with the actual outlay of funds coming perhaps some years later. In 1997 there was a total budget authority of about $2.71 trillion (see figure 6.1, p. 146), with only $1.6 trillion being appropriated during that year.[36] Thus, the "overhang" was almost two-thirds as large as the amount of money appropriated by Congress during that fiscal year. The president and the executive agencies could not actually spend all that overhang in the single fiscal year—a good deal of it was in long-term contracts—but it represented a substantial amount in unspent obligations for the agencies and the government as a whole.

The major problem is that the overhang makes it difficult for a president to use the budget as an instrument of economic management. One principal component of economic management, even in a post-Keynesian era, is the amount of public expenditure; because of the overhang, the president and Congress cannot always control the actual outlay of funds. The agencies may have sufficient budget authority, convertible into actual outlays, to damage presidential forecasts of outlays. They might do this, not out of malice, but out of a perceived need to keep their programs operating as they thought best, especially if the president were seeking to restrict the creation of new obligational authority.

Intergovernmental Budget Control

Although it does not specifically affect the federal budgetary process, the lack of overall fiscal control in the public sector of the United States makes it impos-

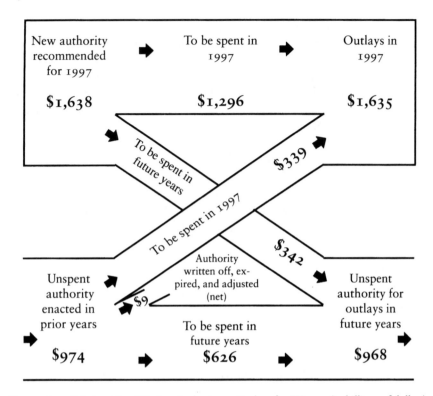

FIGURE 6.1　Relationship of Budget Authority to Outlays for FY 1997 (in billions of dollars)

sible for the federal government to control total public expenditures and hence to exercise the kind of fiscal management it might like. Just as a president cannot control the overhang within the federal government, he cannot control the taxing and spending decisions of thousands of state and local governments.

As of 2000, the federal government itself spent only about two-thirds of the total amount of money spent by governments in the United States. Although it has the capacity to stimulate state and local government expenditures through matching grants, encouraging reductions in subnational expenditures is more difficult. The federal government has even less control over revenue collection. For example, in 1963 the Kennedy administration pushed through a tax cut at the federal level, only to have nearly the entire effect of that cut negated by state and local tax increases. A federal tax cut in the 1980s was also offset (albeit somewhat more slowly) by increases in state and local taxation,[37] and the Bush tax cuts of 2001 and 2003 may yet suffer the same fate as state budgets begin to encounter major problems.

The principles of federalism would appear to reserve to state and local governments a perfect right to decide on their own levels of revenues and expenditures. However, in an era in which the public budget is important for economic management as well as for the distribution of funds among organizations, there may be a need for greater overall control of expenditures. This control need not be imposed unilaterally by the federal government but could perhaps be decided by "diplomacy" among representatives of the several levels of government, as it is in Germany and to some extent in Canada.[38] The potential effects on economic performance of uncoordinated fiscal policies were to some degree reflected by the presence of large state and local government surpluses in the mid-1980s, at the same time that the federal government was running large deficits.[39] Depending on one's point of view, this was either a good thing (helping to reduce total public borrowing) or a bad thing (counteracting the economic stimulus of the deficit). In either case, it represented the absence of an integrated fiscal policy within the United States.

Reprogramming and Transfers

The first four problems we have identified in the federal budgetary process primarily affect the total level of expenditures. The next two problems, reprogramming and transfers, affect levels of spending by individual agencies and the purposes for which the agencies spend their money.

Reprogramming refers to the shifting of funds within a specific appropriations account. A congressional appropriations bill contains a number of appropriations accounts, which in turn contain a number of program elements. For example, the appropriations bill for the Department of Agriculture contains an appropriations account for crop supports, which is subdivided into separate program elements for cotton, corn, wheat, and so on. Reprogramming involves shifting obligational authority from one program element to another. The procedures for making reprogramming decisions have been thoroughly developed only in the Department of Defense. In general, there is a threshold (variable by agency) below which agencies are relatively free to reprogram funds, but above which they require approval from appropriations committee or subcommittee personnel, although not from the entire Congress. There are also requirements for reporting reprogramming decisions to the appropriations committees.

Transfers are more serious actions, for they involve transferring funds from one appropriations account to another. In the Department of Agriculture bill described above, this might involve shifting funds from crop supports to the Farmers Home Administration or to rural electrification. Transfer funds have been subject to significant abuse and circumvention of congressional authority, especially during the Nixon administration and the Vietnam War. And, as with reprogramming—outside the Department of Defense—few established procedures exist for controlling the use of transfer funds other than those that specifically forbid the use of such funds for certain functions.

Both reprogramming and transfer funds are important in providing the executive branch with some flexibility in implementing its programs and in using public funds more effectively. These opportunities have been the subject of many abuses, however, and are ripe for reform and improvement. In particular, they frequently allow an agency to circumvent the judgment of the entire Congress through an appeal to the appropriations committee, or perhaps even to its chairman. In the institutional battles for control over the budget this represents one area where Congress may want to be more active.

Supplemental Appropriations

Even with the apportionment of funds mentioned earlier, agencies may require supplemental appropriations—those made outside the normal budget cycle—to cover shortfalls during the fiscal year. Agencies sometimes simply run out of money, either because of improper management or, more often, because of changes in the demand for services or poor estimates of demand for a new service. For example, during a recession, the demand for unemployment assistance will naturally increase, and supplemental funding will be required. Likewise, a year of poor weather may force additional funding for crop insurance in the Department of Agriculture. Or a new program, such as food stamps, may acquire more clients than anyone anticipated during the early years of its existence.

Supplemental appropriations are not insignificant amounts of money. In 1996 a net of some $3.52 billion was appropriated through supplementals, but this figure ballooned to over $5 billion in 2002 with the impact of terrorism. While a few supplemental actions were to reduce the amounts appropriated, the additions to agency obligational authority ranged from $1.8 million for land acquisition for the U.S. Fish and Wildlife Service to almost $500 million for the Department of Defense (for additional expenses incurred in operations in Somalia and Bosnia). There was also $225.5 million for the Soil Conservation Service to help recovery from disastrous floods in the Midwest. The changes in budget procedure required by deficit reduction strategies discussed later in this chapter have reduced the size of supplemental appropriations, but they still constitute a potential avenue for additional funding.

The request for supplemental appropriations may be a useful strategy for agencies attempting to expand their funding. An agency may be able to initiate a program with minimal appropriations through the usual budgetary process, anticipating a wide acceptance of its program by prospective clients, and then return to Congress for supplemental appropriations when clients do indeed materialize and demand benefits. Supplemental appropriations frequently are not scrutinized as carefully as are regular appropriations, and this relative invisibility may permit friendly congressmen to hide a rapidly expanding program. The scrutiny exercised over supplementals has increased because of the requirements for expenditure proposals to be "deficit neutral," but supplementals usually still are easier to push through Congress than are regular appropriations. Obvious and frequent abuse of the supplemental appropriations process will damage the relationship between the agency and Congress, however, and that may hurt more than help the agency in the long run, given the importance of trust in the politics of the budgetary process.

Assessing the Outcomes: Incrementalism or What?

One standard term used to describe changes in budgetary allocations in the United States is *incremental*. Any number of meanings are attached to this word.[40] Broadly, incrementalism means that changes in an agency's budget from year to year tend to be predictable, but the word has taken on several additional, more specific interpretations. First, incremental decision making is described as a process that is not "synoptic," or not fully "rational"[41]—that is, incremental decision making does not involve examining sweeping alternatives to the status quo and then making a decision about the optimal use of budgetary resources. Rather, incremental decision making involves "successive limited comparisons," or the sequential examination of marginal changes from the status quo and decisions about whether to make these marginal adjustments to current policies.[42] An incremental decision-making process tends to build on earlier decisions, seeking means to improve the existing situation rather than altering current policies or budgetary priorities completely. In budgetary terms this means that an agency can expect to receive in any year approximately what it received the previous year, plus a little more to adjust for inflation or expanded services.

Advocates of incremental decision making argue that this method of making policy choices is actually more rational than the synoptic method. Because it provides an experiential base from which to work, the incremental method offers a greater opportunity to make good policy choices than does the apparently more rational synoptic method. In addition, errors made in an incremental decision-making process can be more easily reversed than can major changes made in a synoptic process. In many ways, incremental decision making is a cost-minimizing form of rationality rather than a benefit-maximizing approach. Incrementalism reduces costs, first, by limiting the range of alternatives and thereby limiting the research and calculation costs for decision makers; and, second, by reducing the costs of change, particularly of error correction. Because in an incremental world few choices involve significant deviations from existing policies or appropriations, there is little need to make major adjustments either in the actual programs or in the thought patterns of decision makers about the policies. Given the limited calculative capacity of human beings—even with the aid of modern technology—and the resistance of most individuals and organizations to change, incrementalism can be argued to be a rational means for making choices.

Incrementalism also is used to describe the pattern of outcomes of the budgetary process. In particular, Otto A. Davis, M. A. H. Dempster, and Aaron Wildavsky demonstrated that there is a great deal of stability in the increase in agency appropriations from year to year.[43] The changes in budgets are not only small but also quite stable and predictable, so the best estimate of an agency's budget in one year is the previous year's budget plus a stable percentage increase. Some agencies grow more rapidly than others, but each exhibits a stable pattern of growth.

Several factors contribute to incremental budgeting in the United States. One is that such a large percentage of the budget is uncontrollable that few significant changes in appropriations can be made from year to year. Also, most empirical examinations of incremental budgeting have been made during periods of relative economic stability and high rates of economic growth; as less favorable economic conditions became more common in the United States, the incrementalism appropriate for rich and predictable budgeting systems diminished.[44] These changes in the economic climate of budgeting are to some degree reflected in the reform efforts described later.

Most important, the repetitive and sequential nature of budgeting tends to produce incremental budget outcomes. A budget must be passed each year, so minor adjustments can be made from year to year as the need arises, thus avoiding the need to attempt to correct all the problems of the policy area at once. Also, the annual cycle prevents an agency from trying to "shoot the moon" in any one year—to expand its budget base greatly, perhaps with flimsy evidence. Agency leaders know that they will have to return for more money next year, and any attempt to deceive only invites future punishment. The sequential nature of the process, in which several actors make their own decisions one after another, also tends to produce incremental outcomes. Many decisions have to be made, and many bargains must be struck. The incremental solution not only provides a "natural" choice but also helps minimize bargaining costs among institutions. Once a decision rule of a certain percentage increase for a particular agency each year has been established, it is far simpler to honor that rule than to seek a "better" decision for one year and then have to do the same hard bargaining and calculation in each subsequent year.

Critiques of Incrementalism

A number of criticisms have been leveled at incrementalism, both in its prescriptive capacity (decisions should be made incrementally) and in its descriptive capacity (decisions are made incrementally). The basic argument against incrementalism as a prescription for policymaking is that it is excessively conservative—the status quo is perpetuated long after better solutions are available. This is true for some program decisions as well as for expenditure decisions. Incrementalism may be a perfectly rational means of policymaking so long as all parties agree that a policy or program is functioning well and is well managed. But how many policies currently fall in that happy category in the United States? In addition, even the incrementalist might agree that at times (e.g., during periods of crisis) nonincremental decisions are required, but the approach provides no means of identifying when and how those nonincremental decisions should be made.[45] If one uses the incremental approach to provide a prescriptive model for governmental decision making, then one must be able to specify what a "big" change would be, when it would be appropriate, and how it might be made.

Several problems also relate to incrementalism as a description of budgetary decision making. In the first place, the majority of empirical examinations of incremental budgeting have been performed at the agency level. This is certainly justifiable, given the importance of those organizations in American public policy, but it is perhaps too high a level of aggregation for examining incremental budgeting.[46] When other researchers have disaggregated agency budgets into program-level budgets, they have found a great deal of nonincremental change, although, as pointed out, it is sometimes difficult to define just what is or is not an incremental change.[47] Thus, while public organizations may have a stable pattern of expenditure change, the managers of these organizations may drastically alter priorities among the operating programs within the agency and produce more rapidly shifting fortunes for the programs.

In addition, when the uncontrollable elements of public expenditures are removed from the analysis, the pattern of expenditure change for the controllable portion is anything but incremental.[48] As budgets have been squeezed by inflation, by citizen resistance to taxation, and by presidents committed to reducing the public sector, budgetary increments have not been granted as usual, and at times the base has also been cut—that is, there have been real reductions in the amount of new obligational authority for an agency as compared with the preceding year. Incrementalism may therefore now be descriptive only of certain kinds of expenditures, and not of the budget process as a whole. Of course, since uncontrollable expenditures accounted for approximately 80 percent of total federal expenditures in 2000, the incrementalist approach may still be a useful description.

Also, incrementalism may apply only to certain kinds of agencies and programs, such as those whose existence has been fully accepted as a part of the realm of government activity; it may not apply to newer or more marginal programs. For example, the budgets of programs such as food stamps are always more subject to change than are programs such as veterans' benefits or Social Security, although all would be broadly classified as social service expenditures. The food stamps program has been in existence for a number of years but still does not have the legitimacy that other programs have developed. In addition, incrementalist theory does not explain how and when programs make big gains—or big losses—in their appropriations. Even if the approach is successful in explaining a great deal of the variance in normal times, it seems incapable of explaining the most interesting and most important aspects of budgeting—who wins and who loses.

Finally, the prescriptive appeal of incrementalism is based in part on the reversibility of small changes, but in the real world of policymaking, many changes are not reversible.[49] Once a commitment is made to a client, or a benefit is indexed, it is difficult to go back and take away the benefit. This is especially true of programs that have a "stock" component, that is, involve the development of a capital infrastructure or the development of a financial base.[50] Once a program such as Social Security is introduced, individuals covered under the program take the benefits under the program into account when making their financial plans for retirement; any reduction or elimination of benefits may therefore create a hardship.

Whether *incrementalism* accurately describes the budget process in the United States or its results, it has certainly become the conventional wisdom to believe that it does. And, in turn, the presumed incrementalism of the process has prompted a number of proposals for reform of the budgetary process to make it more "rational" and to try to reduce the tendency for programs, once authorized, not only to remain in existence forever but to receive steadily increasing appropriations. It is to those attempts at reform that we now turn our attention.

Reforming Budgeting

Numerous criticisms have been directed at the budgetary process in the United States. For most of our contemporary history, these criticisms have focused on the incremental, "irrational," and fragmented nature of the process. More recently, however, the focus has shifted from imposing rationality toward finding somewhat simplistic means of correcting the negative results of the process, which reflect in part the incremental nature of the decisions, but more directly the huge federal deficits of the 1980s and early 1990s. During the first stage of reforms, several methods sought to make the consideration of expenditure priorities more comprehensive and to facilitate government's making the best possible use of its resources. The two most important budgeting reforms of that type were program budgeting and zero-base budgeting. We discuss those two reforms briefly, for even though they were implemented several decades ago, the ideas behind these reform movements remain important. After that, we turn to the less rational but perhaps more effective reforms of the 1980s and 1990s.

Program Budgeting

Program budgeting was largely a product of Lyndon Johnson's administration, although it had been tried previously in some agencies. Whereas traditional budgeting allocates personnel costs, supplies, equipment, and so forth among organizations, program budgeting allocates resources on the basis of the activities of government and the services that government supplies to society.[51] It also places a pronounced emphasis on the analysis of programmatic expenditures and the most efficient use of scarce resources.

Underlying program budgeting—or, more specifically, the planning, programming, budgeting system (PPBS)—is a systems concept. That is, it is assumed that the elements of government policy are closely intertwined, so that a change in one type of policy may affect all others. For example, if one wants to improve the quality of health for citizens in the United States, it may be more efficient to improve nutrition and housing than to invest money in medical care. Program budgeting was always looking for interactions among policy areas and for means of producing desired effects in the most efficient manner.

There were six basic characteristics of PPBS as practiced in the federal government. First, the major goals and objectives of government were to be identified; it was necessary to specify what government was attempting to do, but this identification was to be made high in the hierarchy of government, usually by the president and Congress. Whereas traditional line-item budgeting is initiated by the agencies, the concept of program budgeting began with a specification of the central goals and priorities of government, which could be supplied only by the principal political leaders.

Second, programs were to be developed according to the specified goals. How would government attempt to attain its goals? These programs were analytically defined and might not exist as organizational entities. For example, when Robert McNamara—who, with his "whiz kids," was largely responsible for introducing program budgeting into the Defense Department and thence into the federal government as a whole—developed the program structure for Defense, one of the programs developed was "strategic deterrence." This program was spread among three services: the air force had its manned bombers and some missiles, the navy had Polaris submarines, and the army had Intermediate Range Ballistic Missiles located in Europe. Strategic deterrence certainly described a set of activities of the defense establishment, but no organization was specifically responsible for that program.

Third, resources were to be allocated among programs. Although many traditional line items were used in developing the program budget, the final budget document was presented as overall costs for the achievement of certain objectives. These costs would then be justified as an efficient and effective means of reaching the desired goals. PPBS thus emphasized the costs of reaching certain objectives, whereas line-item budgeting emphasizes the costs of keeping organizations or programs in operation.

Fourth, organizations were not sacrosanct in program budgeting, and there was no assumption that each program would be housed within a single agency, or that each agency would provide only a single program. As in the defense example mentioned earlier, program budgeting attempted to expand the framework of budgeting to include all actors who contributed to the achievement of the goals. This was obviously a realistic attitude toward the interaction of activities and organizations in producing the final effects on the society, but it made budgeting more difficult in an environment composed of many organizations, each attempting to sustain its own interests.

Fifth, PPBS extended the time limit on expenditures found in line-item budgeting, attempting to answer questions about the medium- and long-term implications of programs. Programs that appeared efficient in the short run might actually be less desirable when their long-term implications were considered. For example, most publicly supported health care programs concentrate on curative medicine, while it may be more efficient in the long run to emphasize prevention.

Sixth, alternative program structures were systematically analyzed in an effort to find more effective and efficient programs. Agencies were expected to present their justifications for programs—to show, in other words, that the chosen program was superior to the alternatives investigated. This aspect of program budgeting relates to our previous discussion of policy formulation, for agencies were expected to develop alternatives and to examine their relative merits, using techniques such as cost-benefit analysis.

Criticism of program budgeting. Advocates of program budgeting pointed with pride to the enhanced rationality and analytic rigor associated with this form of budgeting and to the way that it could break down organizational control over budgetary outcomes. Despite these apparent advantages, PPBS was not especially successful in most of its applications. There were some technical reasons for these apparent failures, but the most severe problems in the implementation of program budgeting were political.

Technically, applying PPBS successfully required a great deal of time and effort, as well as an almost certain knowledge of unknown relationships of spending to program success. The systems concept inherent in the method implies that if one aspect of the system is altered, the entire system must be rethought. This in turn may mean that program budgeting actually institutionalizes the rigidity that it was designed to eliminate. Also, it is difficult if not impossible to define programs, measure their results, and evaluate the contributions of individual agencies and activities to the achievement of those results. One major problem in public policy analysis is the difficulty of measuring the effects of government, and such measurement occupies a central place in program budgeting.[52]

Program budgeting also had several political disadvantages. First, as mentioned, the method forced decisions to a higher level of government.[53] Agencies disliked this centralizing tendency, as did congressmen who had invested considerable effort in developing relationships with clientele groups supporting an agency. Likewise, the assumption that organizations are not the most appropriate objects of allocation ran counter to all the folkways of American government. Finally, the need to analyze systematically alternative strategies for achieving ends forced the agency to expose its program to possible attack, as it might develop and eliminate alternative programs that others might prefer, and the explicit nature of the process brought those alternatives up for active consideration. The discussion of alternative policies reduced the maneuverability of the agency, as it had to justify its policy choice in writing and consequently could not play games with OMB or with Congress if information developed from the program budgeting system was passed on to the legislative branch.

In short, PPBS was a dagger pointed at the central role of the agency in policymaking, and it should not have been expected to succeed, except perhaps in organizations such as the Department of Defense. That organization had a strong leader committed to the concept of program budgeting, and it produced extremely nebulous results that could be tested only against simulations or scenario-building exercises; it also had few potent political enemies. For other agencies, with much greater political opposition and with real clients demanding real services, PPBS was doomed to failure from the beginning.

The rebirth of program budgeting?   Although it has been declared dead as a formal device for allocating resources, the ideas of program budgeting continue to appear in thinking about the budgetary process, and especially in thinking about budget reforms. The basic idea of making the most efficient allocation of money among competing resources is an extremely alluring one, and politicians and analysts will attempt to pursue that rationalistic goal even in the face of massive evidence that it may not be attainable in the rough world of politics.

The latest rebirth of the basic idea of making the allocation of funds more rational is the Government Performance and Results Act of 1993 (GPRA).[54] The principal concept underlying this legislation was to shift the focus in assessing organizations in the budgetary process away from inputs and toward outcomes and "results." Thus each organization in the federal government has been required to develop a strategic plan and a set of operational indicators of attaining the goals specified in that plan. The degree of success or failure in attaining those goals then plays a significant role in determining the budgetary success of the organization. This process involves neither the direct linkage to expenditures nor the level of analysis inherent in program budgeting, but it does depend upon some of the same assumptions.

The early days of implementing GPRA have begun to demonstrate some of the consequences of this more rationalist style of budgeting.[55] The most obvious outcome of the adoption of performance-based budgeting is that there is much greater emphasis on identifying what government is attempting to do and then on assessing how well the goals are being achieved.[56] This style of budgeting can be done without tampering with the agency basis of budgeting or developing a systems framework for policy. However, even a decade after the adoption of this legislation, the difficulties of measurement and implementation are only beginning to be overcome.

Zero-Base Budgeting

If program budgeting required an almost superhuman analytical capability and rafts of data, the conceptual underpinnings of zero-base budgeting (ZBB) were extremely simple. The idea was that, whereas traditional incremental budgeting operates from the assumption that the previous year's budget (the "base") was justified and so increments are all that need examination, a more comprehensive examination of all expenditures should be made. That is, there should be no base, and the entire spending plan should be justified. It was assumed that weaker programs, which were being extended largely through inertia, would be terminated or at least severely cut, and more meritorious programs would be fully funded. This form of budgeting came to Washington with the Carter administration, after having been tried by President Carter when he was governor of Georgia.

Zero-base budgeting was carried out on the basis of decision units, which might be agencies but frequently were smaller components such as operating programs within an agency. Each budget manager was expected to prepare a number of decision packages to reflect his or her priorities for funding. These packages were to be presented in rank order, beginning with a "survival package" that represented the lowest level of funding on which the unit could continue to exist. On top of the survival package, additional decision packages were to reflect, first, the continuation of existing programs at existing levels of service and, then, expansions of service. Each decision package was to be justified in terms of the services it would provide at an acceptable cost.

Decision packages prepared by lower-level budget managers were then passed up the organizational hierarchy to higher-level managers who prepared consolidated decision packages that reflected ranking priorities among the several decision units that they might supervise. These rankings were then passed up and consolidated further, ending in the Office of Management and Budget. All the rankings from the lower levels were passed along with the consolidated packages so that higher levels could examine the preferences of lower-level managers and their justifications of those preferences. Like program budgeting, ZBB was geared toward multiyear budgeting to better understand the implications of budget choices made during any one budget cycle.

Zero-base budgeting, again like program budgeting, had several apparent advantages. Obviously, the method would eliminate incremental budgeting. The agency's base is no longer protected but must be defended—although in practice the survival level might function as a base. Also, ZBB focused on cost-effectiveness in the justification of the rankings of decision packages and even of the survival level of funding. One principal advantage of zero-base budgeting was the involvement of managers at relatively low levels of the organization in the consideration of priorities and goals for the organization. Also, this method considered the allocation of resources in package terms, whereas the incremental budget assumes that any additional money can be effectively used. It makes substantially greater sense to think of adding meaningful amounts of money that can produce additional services, rather than simply adding more money without regard for the threshold values for service provision and efficiency.

Nevertheless, there were a number of glaring difficulties with zero-base budgeting. For example, implementing this form of budgeting threatened the existence of some agencies. In practice, a number of factors, such as powerful clientele groups and uncontrollable expenditures, could negate the concern that many administrators might have had about the method, but it was nevertheless clear that the intent of the method was to bring the existence of each program into question each year.

To some degree the enormity of the task of examining each program carefully each year was a major weakness of this method. There was simply no means by which OMB, held to a reasonable size, or a Congress with its other commitments, could carefully consider the entire budget each year. Instead, there would be either a superficial analysis of each program under the guise of a zero-base review—probably with incremental results—or a selective review of a number of more controversial programs. Either would be an acceptable means of reducing the work load, but neither would constitute a significant departure from the incremental budget or justify the massive effort required to prepare the necessary documents.

In addition, ZBB threatened established programs by allowing the reopening of political conflicts during each budget cycle. One virtue of traditional incremental budgeting is that once a program has been agreed to, it is accepted and is not subject to significant scrutiny unless there are major changes in the environment or serious administrative problems in the agency. With zero-base budgeting, however, the existence of the program was subject to question each year, and the political fights that authorized the existence of the agency might have to be fought again and again. Of course, this presented no problem for well-established and popular programs, but it was certainly a problem for newer and more controversial programs. Also, ZBB tended to combine financial decisions with program decisions and to place perhaps an excessive burden on budgetary decision makers.

From Scalpels to Axes: Budget Reform in the 1980s and 1990s

The fundamental incrementalist patterns have been more seriously challenged by the continuing fiscal problems of government than by the analytic methodologies proposed in program budgeting and (to some extent) zero-base budgeting. These persistent fiscal problems have spawned a number of "solutions,"[57] some of which have been implemented, including the Gramm-Rudman-Hollings Act (technically the Balanced Budget and Emergency Deficit Control Act of 1985), the budget agreement between Congress and President George H.W. Bush in 1990, and the Balanced Budget Act of 1997. Other proposed reforms include the balanced-budget amendment and the partially implemented line-item veto. Most of these reforms are simply incrementalism turned around—they share incrementalism's tendency to substitute minimization of decision-making costs for maximization of benefits from expenditures. These are, for the most part, "no-think solutions," just as incrementalism has been a nonanalytic means for making budgetary decisions. But, while incrementalism has been successful and acceptable, these methods for dealing with complex problems have been proposed just because of their simplicity. Simple policies are perhaps only rarely the best solutions for complex problems, but they are often the most acceptable in the political world.

Gramm-Rudman-Hollings

As the deficits created by the Reagan tax cuts grew during the 1980s, Congress began to look for means to staunch the budgetary "hemorrhaging." This was difficult to do by traditional means because of the logrolling and pork-barrel legislative styles so typical of Congress. Instead, Congress adopted a method, commonly referred to as "Gramm-Rudman-Hollings" after its sponsors, that removed some of its discretion and forced spending cuts if Congress and the president could not reach agreement on how to do so. The initial idea was to reduce the federal deficit to zero within five years (fiscal year 1991). This target was indicative of the totemic status of a balanced budget in American thinking about public finance,[58] but it soon proved to be an unattainable and perhaps unwise target.

The basic idea behind Gramm-Rudman-Hollings was that in order to meet the declining deficit target in any year, Congress and the president could cut spending, raise taxes, or do some combination of the two. If no agreement could be reached on those actions, however, automatic cuts in spending (called sequestrations)—half taken from defense and half from domestic programs—would be imposed. Certain types of expenditures (interest on the federal debt, Social Security, veterans' benefits, and the like) were excluded, so the automatic reductions would have to come from only 30 percent of the budget. That, in turn, meant that those cuts would have to be severe.

The scorekeeper in the process was to be the General Accounting Office, and this feature proved to be the downfall of the initial version of the process. The Supreme Court ruled that the GAO as a legislative organization could not perform an executive act—ordering budget cuts for specific executive agencies.[59] After considerable discussion, the scorekeeper role was reassigned to the Office of Management and Budget in the Executive Office of the President. Although Congress feared that its interests might be slighted by this change, it appeared to be the only possible compromise if the original mechanisms of the act were to be maintained.

But the original intentions of the act proved to be extremely difficult and painful politically, so Congress agreed to several changes in 1987–1988. First, the time period for reducing the deficit to zero was extended to fiscal 1993. Second, most of the truly significant cuts were postponed until after the 1988 presidential and congressional elections, thereby confirming the adage that future budget cuts are always more acceptable than current ones, especially for incumbents. Congress attempted to restore deficit reduction to its original trajectory after the election but was deterred by economic and political circumstances.

The principal factor hampering the ability of the president and Congress to reach their targets was a sluggish, then decelerating, economy. President George

H.W. Bush proposed a budget that would meet the Gramm-Rudman-Hollings target of a $64 billion deficit for fiscal 1991, but as the budget process progressed in 1990 it became clear that the actual deficit would be closer to $300 billion because of the slowed economy. The sense of crisis emerging from these negotiations then produced a new program for deficit reduction, or at least deficit management. Adopted as the Budget Enforcement Act of 1990 (BEA), the legislation provided for the following measures:

1. Separation of mandatory spending from discretionary spending;
2. Differentiation of three types of discretionary spending: defense, international, and domestic, with separate spending targets for each;
3. A "pay as you go" plan for mandatory spending and revenues, so any increase in spending or reduction in revenue must have another spending reduction or tax increase associated with it to keep the package deficit-neutral;
4. Elimination of overly optimistic or unrealistic targets for deficit reduction;
5. Inclusion of loan programs in the budgetary calculations (they had been excluded previously), and;
6. The Office of Management and Budget as scorekeeper.[60]

Gramm-Rudman-Hollings, like all the other legislative manifestations of fiscal control, represents a major effort at reform of the budgetary process to eliminate the federal deficit and to force government to live within its revenues. It also points to the extreme difficulties of making and implementing such an agreement. Not only were unrealistic future targets set and then dismissed, but important segments of federal financial operations, such as credit (initially) and the savings-and-loan bailout, were ignored. Further, the automatic cuts were imposed on a relatively small proportion of the budget and therefore fell very heavily in those areas.

The other effect of Gramm-Rudman-Hollings and its sequels has been to add a new level of analysis to the budget process. One crucial element of budgeting introduced in the 1990s is "scorekeeping" in the PAYGO—pay as you go—system. Any spending bill now must be scored to determine whether it is revenue-neutral—that is, does it provide sufficient revenues or savings from other programs to cover the costs of the new program. If the legislation does not meet that fiscal neutrality criterion, it must be redesigned so that it will. Making the determination of neutrality is by no means simple, for it often involves a number of economic assumptions and a variety of ways to do the calculations; politics enters here as well as in the rest of the budget process.[61] In many ways, the Gramm-Rudman-Hollings and BEA enterprises helped add to the already high level of cynicism that the American people have about government.[62]

In early 1993 the incoming Clinton administration used the provisions of the Budget Enforcement Act to begin to implement its own budgetary and economic strategy. Changes in timing within the process contained in the Budget Enforcement Act allowed the new administration to submit that year's budget, rather than having to accept the budget prepared by the outgoing administration. The first proposed Clinton budget contained a very modest increase in expenditures over that previously projected but a much larger increase in revenues, thereby producing some reduction in the deficit.[63] Congress did change the budget but left intact much of the administration's plans for economic change and some reduction in the deficit. After the initial use of the act, the Clinton administration continued to reduce the deficit systematically, and the Budget Enforcement Act remains the basis of most of contemporary budgetary politics in Washington.

The Balanced-Budget Amendment

The size of the federal budget deficit has elicited a number of proposed solutions in addition to the Gramm-Rudman-Hollings machinery and its sequel. Among the most commonly discussed solutions has been the balanced-budget amendment to the Constitution, which would require Congress to pass a balanced budget each year unless an extraordinary majority of Congress declared that a sufficient economic emergency existed to justify running a deficit.[64] Somewhat like the PAYGO budgetary process, such an amendment would force a more explicit comparison of revenue and expenditure figures, and it would further require those involved in the budgetary process to be responsible for the amount of money that they appropriate. The difference, of course, is that this arrangement would be constitutional and therefore permanent.

The proposed balanced-budget amendment has had substantial political appeal and has gained some support. When it was voted on in 1993, it came close to receiving enough votes in Congress to send it to the states. Like many simple "solutions" to complex problems, however, it has some major difficulties. First, as already noted, the planning for a budget begins over a year before the start of its execution, and over two years before the completion of the budget year. Further, both the revenue and expenditure projections on which a budget is based are to some degree influenced by the condition of the economy and the projected state of the economy during the time the budget is to be executed.[65] It is easy to get the projections wrong—over the past twenty-five years, the official figures have overestimated revenues by an average of 3.5 percent and underestimated expenditures by an average of 3.9 percent.[66] Even if Congress acts in good faith and attempts to comply with the spirit of the amendment, it could easily miss the target of a balanced budget badly—by an average of almost 8 percent.

In addition to the potential economic problems caused by an unplanned deficit, such a deficit might appear to be a violation of the Constitution and thus further undermine already weakened public respect for Congress. A more cynical scenario would have Congress passing a budget that, although balanced on paper, would be known to have little chance of being balanced when executed. In either case, there could be substantial political damage to the legitimacy of Congress and to government as a whole. The difficulties already encountered in implementing Gramm-Rudman-Hollings to limit spending give some idea of how a balanced-budget agreement would, or would not, work.

In addition, deficits are not necessarily a public evil. When adopted for economic reasons, as opposed to those created by political unwillingness to impose the true costs of government on citizens, budget deficits can be an important tool for economic management, following the Keynesian tradition. Passing a balanced-budget amendment would only remove this management tool from the federal government, without any certainty of generating economic benefits sufficient to justify that loss.

The Line-Item Veto

In his 1985 budget submission, President Reagan proposed that a presidential line-item veto be adopted, especially for appropriations bills. He was not the first president to make this recommendation—Ulysses Grant had done so—nor was he the last. Similar to the powers already invested in governors in forty-three states, the line-item veto would allow the president to veto a portion of a bill while permitting the rest to be put into effect.[67] Bill Clinton also advocated this instrument of presidential power, and it had been one part of the Republicans' Contract With America. Congress, seemingly against its own institutional interests, then passed legislation in 1996 giving the president the line-item veto.[68]

This selective veto is seen as a weapon for dealing with the tendency of congressmen to add their pet projects to appropriations bills, placing the president in the awkward position of having to refuse money for a large segment of the federal government in order to prevent the funding of one or two small, and often wasteful, projects. The proliferation of these pork-barrel provisions in the early twenty-first century is making this instrument appear all the more desirable. Also, as noted earlier, the majority of appropriations for the federal government are contained in a dozen or so appropriations acts. In order to eliminate a few items, the president would have to veto the entire act and create disruption and hardships for citizens and federal employees.

One of the justifications for this change in the budgetary process is that it attacks the problem of growing federal deficits. This may be so, but the veto cannot be applied to many uncontrollable programs, such as debt interest and Social Security. Further, with the powers of rescission the president can achieve some of the same ends, although he does need the agreement of Congress. In 1992, for example, President George H.W. Bush attempted to rescind $7.9 billion, but by the time Congress had finished with the proposal, there was a rescission of $8.2 billion containing few of the items the president had proposed to cut.[69] Congress also has the option of overriding a presidential line-item veto, first by a simple majority and then by a two-thirds majority if the president maintains his convictions about eliminating the expenditure.

The line-item veto might actually encourage Congress to add more pet projects onto appropriations acts, placing the onus of removing them from the budget on the president. Indeed, in his first use of the veto (before the courts intervened) President Clinton singled out some spending items that were apparent "pork," concentrated in a few congressional districts.[70] The line-item veto might also give the president independent powers over public spending not intended by the framers of the Constitution nor desired by the public.

After the first use of the line-item veto, several lawsuits were brought by affected parties and by members of Congress. The courts then ruled that the act was indeed unconstitutional, that it violated the basic separation of powers provisions of the Constitution by conferring legislative powers on the president in enabling him to make selective decisions about what would be spent and what would not. The Constitution does give the president the veto, but over entire bills and not over the particular parts he dislikes. The line-item veto provision now appears to be dead, but the debate over its suitability, and its constitutionality, is likely to continue. As with the balanced-budget amendment, this episode shows that there are few magic solutions for solving budget problems, but there is a continuing need for political will and courage to solve them.

Decrementalism

The preceding discussion of the balanced-budget amendment and the line-item veto is indicative of the general problem facing American government and the governments of other industrialized countries: the control of public expenditures. While incrementalism has become the conventional wisdom for describing budgeting, many politicians are looking for means of enforcing decrementalism, or the gradual reduction of expenditures, on government.[71] The majority of these political leaders are from the political right—as exemplified by President George W. Bush—but even some on the political left are seeking to reduce expenditures while maintaining levels of service. The word *reform* has often been heard coming from national capitols, but there has been little agreement on how much reform is needed and whether simple procedural reforms will be sufficient to address the deep and abiding difficulties faced in budgeting.[72]

In addition to the rationalistic approaches to budgeting and the Gramm-Rudman-Hollings machinery discussed earlier, somewhat more blunt instruments have been employed to try to reduce federal expenditures. One of these was the president's Private Sector Survey on Cost Control (the Grace Commission) in the early 1980s. This survey, similar to ones that had been conducted in most state governments, brought to Washington some 2,000 volunteers from business and other private-sector organizations to examine the management of the federal government. The volunteers prepared 2,478 distinct recommendations, which were projected to save the government $424 billion a year if all were implemented.[73] Many of these proposals for cost reduction have since been criticized as being politically naive or simply impossible, given the political realities of Washington and the connection of the agencies with powerful clientele groups.[74] The survey did, however, give politicians and administrators in Washington something to think about.

Other efforts at controlling the costs of government have been even cruder, including across-the-board reductions in staffing levels and budgets and moratoria on the implementation of new programs and regulations. In addition, President Reagan and his advisers attempted to reduce the pay of public employees to 94 percent of that earned by comparable employees in the private sector—the 6-percent difference was to be offset by the greater job security and fringe benefits associated with federal employment.[75] The Clinton administration had few proposals for changing the mechanisms for budgeting, other than the familiar arguments for a line-item veto and the proposals for a biennial budget contained in the National Performance Review.[76] The George W. Bush administration has offered some ideas about cash management but little in the way of fundamental change in the budgeting process.

Reaction to these reform efforts has been almost opposite to that directed at proposals such as program budgeting and zero-base budgeting. The more recent across-the-board reform exercises have been criticized as mindless, and as simply attacking government without regard to the real benefits created through some agencies and the real waste created by others. This simplistic strategy contrasts with the large-scale analytic exercises that would have been required to implement PPBS or ZBB. Perhaps sadly, across-the-board exercises, such as those contained in the Gramm-Rudman-Hollings procedures, have a much greater chance of being implemented than do the more analytic methods.

Is Budget Change Its Own Reward?

All the attempts at budget reform described here have had some impact on the way in which the federal budget is constructed. Both program budgeting and zero-base budgeting were significant rationalistic efforts at reforming the budgetary process, but, although both methods had a great deal to commend them, neither was particularly successful in producing changes in the behavior of budgetary decision makers. The less rationalistic methods, such as Gramm-Rudman-Hollings, have had a somewhat greater impact on the budget, in part because they did not attempt to change the basic format of the process or the outcomes.

Why does the traditional line-item incremental budget persist despite the real problems in both the budget process and budget outcomes?[77] There appear to be several reasons. One is that the traditional budget gives the legislature an excellent means of controlling the executive branch. It allocates funds to identifiable organizations for identifiable purposes (personnel, equipment, etc.), not to nebulous "programs" or "decision units." The political and administrative leaders who manage the real organizations to which the funds are allocated can then be held accountable for the expenditure of the money appropriated to them. The blunt instruments now tacked onto the process, such as the Budget Enforcement Act, enhance the control elements of the budgetary process without altering its basic elements.

More important, while the benefits promised by both PPBS and ZBB were significant, so too were the costs, in terms both of the calculations required to reach decisions and of the political turmoil created by nonincremental changes. Incremental budgeting provides ready guidelines for those who must make budget decisions, minimizing the necessity for them to engage in costly analysis and calculation. In addition, as most political interests are manifested through organizations, the absence of threats to those organizations in incremental budgeting means that political conflicts can be confined to marginal matters instead of repeated battles over the very existence of those organizations.

In short, although incremental budgeting does nothing very well, neither does it do anything very poorly. Incrementalism is a convenient means of allocating resources for public purposes. It is not an optimal means of making policy, but it is a means that works. It is also a means of making policy in which policymakers themselves have great confidence. These factors are not in themselves sufficient to explain perpetuation of the incremental budgetary processes in the face of so many challenges by presumably superior systems of budgeting. There are always proposals for change, but there is rarely sufficiently agreement on which of the possible changes to make to move the system away from the status quo. There have been some successful reforms, but the system remains firmly incremental. The Government Performance and Results Act is yet another attempt to produce more rationalist outcomes in the budget process; although there have been some positive outcomes to date, it has a long history of incremental budgeting to overcome.

CHAPTER 7

Evaluation and Policy Change

THE FINAL STAGE of the policy process is to assess what has occurred as a result of the selection and implementation of public policy and, if necessary, to produce some change in the current policies of government. Critics of government tend to believe that these evaluative questions are extremely easy to answer, that the activities of government are rather simple, and that inefficiencies and maladministration could be corrected easily if only government really wanted to do so. As this chapter points out, however, producing a valid evaluation of government programs is a difficult and highly political process in itself. That evaluation is much more difficult than for most activities in the private sector.[1] Further, if the evaluation determines that change is necessary or desirable, the policymaking process involved in making the change is perhaps even more difficult to implement successfully than is the process of policy initiation—the first adoption of a policy. Government organizations have a number of weapons to protect themselves against change, so any attempts to alter existing policies and organizations are almost certain to engender conflict.

However, we should not be too quick to assume that government organizations are always wedded to the status quo. Change is threatening to any organization, public or private, but most organizations also know their own strengths and weaknesses and want to correct the weaknesses. The difficulties these organizations encounter in producing change arise as often from the rules imposed by Congress and from the demands of the organizations' clients as they do from internal conservatism. Most organizations, public as well as private, are engaged in continuous evaluation of their performance, and changes in public sector management implemented over the past several decades have made public organizations even more conscious of their performance.[2] What they must find is the means to bring about effective change in that performance when they detect any shortcomings.

Problems in Evaluating Public Programs

Evaluation is an important requirement for programs and organizations in government. Like other organizations, they need to know how they are performing. In its simplest form, evaluating a public program involves cataloging the goals of the program, measuring the degree to which these goals have been achieved, and, perhaps, suggesting changes that might bring the performance of the organization more in line with the stated purposes of the program. Although these appear to be simple things to do, it is actually very difficult to produce unambiguous measurements of the performance of a public organization.[3] Several barriers stand in the way of anyone who attempts to produce such valid evaluations.

Goal Specification and Goal Change

The first step in an evaluation is to identify the goals of the program, but even this seemingly simple task may be difficult, if not impossible.[4] The legislation that establishes programs or organizations should be the source of goal statements, but we have already seen (in Chapter 4) that legislation is frequently written in vague language in order to avoid offending potential members of the coalition necessary to pass it. As a result, it may be difficult to attach any readily quantifiable goals to programs or organizations. In addition, the goals specified in legislation may be impossible or even contradictory. For example, one program had as its goal to raise all students to the mean reading level (think about it), while the expressed aim of one foreign aid program was to assist those nations in greatest need, provided that they were the most likely to use the money to produce significant developmental effects. When an organization is faced with merely impossible goals, it can still do something positive, but when it is faced with contradictory goals, its own internal political dynamics become more important in determining ultimate policy choices than any legislative statement of purpose. Further, as organizations do not function alone in the world, the contradictions existing across organizations—as when the federal government subsidizes tobacco production and simultaneously discourages tobacco consumption—make identification of the goals of government as a whole that much more difficult.

Of course, internal political dynamics are still important in organizations with clear and unambiguous goals stated in their legislation. An initial statement of goals may be important in initiating a program, but once that program is in operation, its goals may be modified. The changes may be positive, as when programs adapt to changing environmental conditions in order to meet new societal needs. Positive changes in goals have been noted most often in the private sector, as when the March of Dimes shifted its goal from serving victims of polio to helping children with birth defects, but they also do occur in the public sector.[5] For example, the Bureau of Indian Affairs has been transformed from an organization that simply exercised control over Native Americans into one that now frequently serves as an advocate for the rights and interests of those people.[6] Also, the Army Corps of Engineers transformed its image from one of gross environmental disregard to one of environmental sensitivity and even environmental advocacy.[7]

Goal transformations may, of course, be negative at times. The capture of regulatory bodies by their regulated industries is a commonly cited example of negative goal change.[8] A more common example is the "displacement of goals" among the employees of an organization—although they may have been recruited on the basis of public service goals, over time those individuals' goals may become more focused on personal survival and aggrandizement.[9] Similarly, the goals of the organization as a whole may shift toward its own maintenance and survival. Anthony Downs describes organizations (as well as the individuals within them) as going through a life cycle, beginning as zealots or advocates of certain social causes but over time becoming more interested in surviving and maintaining their budgets than in doing anything for clients.[10] In these instances, the operating goals of a program deteriorate, even if the stated goals remain the same. The organization may not even realize that the change has occurred, but its clients almost certainly will.

We should be aware that organizational transformation of goals and individual transformations have very different implications for policy and for evaluation (see figure 7.1). If an individual member of the organization attempts to impose his or her own goals, whether in implementing policy or in attempting to protect his or her own position, the evaluative problem becomes that of identifying those personal deviations. The problem is in motivating or sanctioning individuals rather than in making an assessment of the performance of the or-

	Actors exhibiting transformation	
Modes of goal transformation	*Individuals*	*Organizations*
Reflexive	Displacement	Empire building
Operational	Street-level bureaucracy	Adaptation

FIGURE 7.1 Types of Goal Change

ganization (other than in its management). On the other hand, when the organization itself makes such deviations, there is more reason to evaluate the policies of the organization and the actual goals that undergird them.

Among the managerial changes in the public sector over the past several decades has been an attempt to develop ways to prevent goal displacement. One common change has been to make managers more directly responsible for the performance of their organizations, with rewards for those whose organizations perform well and possible dismissal for the managers of poorly performing organizations.[11] At lower levels, performance pay schemes are designed to produce the same results.[12] In addition, there have been attempts to make the public sector more "consumer driven," involving a variety of mechanisms developed to permit clients, and the general public, to know what is going on in an organization and to have some influence over the outcomes.[13]

Even when the goals are clearly expressed, they may not be practical. The Preamble to the Constitution, for instance, expresses a number of goals for the American government, but few, if any, are expressed in concrete language that would enable a researcher to verify that these lofty goals are or are not being achieved. Specifying such goals and putting them into operation would require further political action within the organization or the imposition of the values of the researcher in order to make it possible to compare performance with aspiration. For example, the Employment Act of 1946 pledged the government of the United States to maintain "full employment." At the time the act was passed, full employment was declared to be 4 percent unemployment. Over time, the official definition crept upward to 4.5 percent and then to 5 percent unemployed, and some economists have argued that 6 percent is an appropriate level. Obviously, political leaders want to declare that full employment has been achieved, and in order to justify the claim, they apply pressure to change the definition of "full employment." In this case, an admirable goal has been modified in practice, although the basic concept has remained a part of the policy statement. This is but one instance of government playing the "numbers game" to attempt to prove that goals have been reached.[14]

In addition, most public organizations serve multiple constituencies and therefore may have different goals for those different groups in society. For example, the Comprehensive Employment and Training Act (CETA) performed a number of different functions for different segments of society and was differentially successful at serving those constituencies. For people employed by the program, it was a source of employment and potentially of training for a better job. For individuals concerned about unemployment and those whose political careers may have depended on reducing unemployment, it was a means of reducing unemployment without undertaking a more difficult task such as stimulating the entire economy or altering the economic structure to supply more jobs for unskilled and semiskilled workers. Finally, for mayors and other local government officials, the program was a source of cheap labor that enabled them either to balance their city budgets or to prevent even more rapid tax increases than otherwise would have been necessary to maintain services. To the extent that the program pleased mayors by providing cheap labor in unskilled jobs such as garbage collection, however, it could never fulfill the goal of training the program participants for better private-sector jobs. Thus, when programs are being evaluated, it is important to ask whose goals, as well as what goals, are being achieved.

Finally, it should be noted that goals may be either straitjackets or opportunities for an organization. In addition to telling an organization what it should be doing, specific goal statements tell it what it is not supposed to be doing. This may limit the creativity of the organization and may serve as a powerful conservative force within the organization. Further, the specification of goals may limit the efficiency and effectiveness of government as a whole. Any one statement of goals may divide responsibilities in ways that are less meaningful, given an expansion of knowledge and information or a change in social values, for citizens and policymakers in general than alternative statements might do. So, for example, locating the U.S. Forest Service in the Department of Agriculture may mean that trees are treated more as a crop than as a natural resource, as they might be if the agency were located within the Department of the Interior. Giving any one program or organization a goal may mean that other, more efficient means of delivering the same service will not be explored or that existing duplication of services will not be eliminated. The ideals of program budgeting, which attempted to look at the full range of possible ways of providing services, were worthy, even if politically not acceptable.

Measurement

Once goals have been identified and expressed in clear, concrete language, the next task is to devise a means to measure the extent to which those goals have been attained. In the public sector, measuring results or production is frequently difficult. In fact, one fundamental problem that limits the efficiency and effectiveness of government is the absence of any ready means of judging the value of what is being produced.[15]

One of the best examples of this measurement problem occurs in one of government's oldest functions: national defense. The product called "defense" is, in many ways, the failure of real or potential enemies to take certain actions. Logically, the best defense force would never do anything, for there would be no enemy willing to risk taking offensive actions; in fact, to some degree, if a defense force is called into action, it has already failed. But measuring nonevents and counterfactual occurrences is difficult, so defense is frequently measured by surrogate measures. Thus, the mega-tonnage of nuclear weapons available and capable of being launched in fifteen minutes and the number of plane-hours of flight time logged by the Strategic Air Command have been used as measures of defense. In a post–Cold War era, the indicators of an effective defense policy are even less clear, involving as much the capacity to enforce peace settlements as the ability to wage war.[16]

The illustration from defense policy helps make the point that frequently activity measures are substituted for output measures when attempting to evaluate performance in the public sector. Some scholars, as well as some politicians and analysts, despair of finding more adequate means to measure the benefits of many public-sector programs. For example, I. C. R. Byatt argues that "it is not possible to measure benefits from defense by any known techniques, nor is it easy to even begin to see how one might be developed." He goes on to say that "it is quite impossible to allocate costs to the final objectives of education."[17] He might well have extended the list to include most of the functions of the public sector.[18]

Scholarly pessimism aside, the perpetuation of activity measures serves the interests of existing organizations. First, it can shield them from stringent evaluations on nonprocedural criteria. Perhaps more important, action becomes equated with success, and this will have a predictable effect of raising levels of government expenditure. It may also have the less obvious effect of giving incentives to program personnel to keep their clients on a program when its benefits are no longer needed. Despite skepticism and organizational politics, governments continue to express interest in measuring what their organizations actually deliver for the public, and reforms in recent years have attempted to focus more clearly on the impacts of government.

Several factors inhibit the adequate measurement of government performance. One is the time span over which the benefits of many programs are created. For example, although the short-term goal of education is to improve reading, writing, and computation, the ultimate and more important goals of education can only be realized in the future. They cannot be measured or even identified during the time in which a child is attending school. Among other things, education is supposed to increase the earning potential of individuals, make society more stable, and more generally improve the quality of life for the individuals who receive it. These are elusive qualities when an evaluation must be done quickly. The time problem in evaluation is also illustrated by Lester Salamon's analysis of the "sleeper" effects of the New Deal programs in the rural South, where it was widely believed these programs were failures while in operation, although significant results became apparent thirty years after the programs were terminated.[19]

The other side of the time problem is that any effects produced by a program should be durable.[20] Some programs may produce effects only after they have been in existence for years, whereas other programs produce demonstrable results in the short term but have no significant effects in the long run. It has been argued that the latter is true of the Head Start program. Participants in the program do tend to enter school with skills superior to those of non–Head Start children, but after several years no significant differences can be discerned—it seems that without reinforcement in later years, the effects of Head Start decay.[21] The program per se therefore may not be unsuccessful or ineffective; it may simply not have been carried through for a sufficient amount of time.[22]

The time element in program evaluation also produces significant political difficulties. The individuals responsible for making policy decisions are often short of time, and they must produce results quickly if their programs are to be successful. Congressmen, for example, have a tenure of only two years before facing reelection, making it necessary that any program they advocate show some "profit" before those two years have passed. Thus, the policy process tends to favor short-term gains, even if they are not durable, over long-term successes. Some actors in the policy process, notably the permanent public bureaucracy, can afford to take a longer perspective, but most politicians cannot. Thus, time itself is crucial in evaluation.[23] The policymaking cycle is largely determined by the political calendar, but the effects of policies have their own timetables. Part of the job of the analyst and evaluator is to attempt to make the two coincide.

The evaluation of public programs is also confounded by many other factors affecting the population. If we are to evaluate the effectiveness of a health program on a poor population, for example, we may find it difficult to isolate the effects of that program from those of a nutrition program or a housing program. All these programs may have the effect of improving the health of the population, and we may find it difficult to determine which program caused the observed changes. In fact, all the programs listed may be related to those changes, in which case it becomes difficult to determine which program is the most efficient means of affecting the health of that community. We may be able to isolate the effects of an individual program with a more controlled social experiment, but few people would want to be the subjects of such an experiment.[24] Further, it is difficult to hold constant all the social and economic factors that might affect the success of a public program independent of any policy; health may have improved because more people are employed and can afford more nutritious food for their families. All these problems illustrate that measurement in policy analysis is not as simple as the measurement that a scientist can make of a passive molecule or an amoeba.

In addition, measurement of the effects of a public program can be confounded by the history of the program and of the individuals involved.[25] Few truly new and innovative policies are initiated in industrialized countries such as the United States, and programs that have existed in the same policy area for some years may jeopardize the success of any new program. Clients may well become cynical when program after program promises to "solve" their problems. Likewise, administrators may become cynical and frustrated after changing the direction of their activities several times. Any number of policy areas have gone through cycles of change and contradiction, with inevitable effects on the morale and cooperation of clients and administrators alike. The numerous attempts to "solve" the problems of the poor offer the best example of endless change and confusion.[26] In addition to creating frustration over the inability of government to make up its collective mind, one policy may not be successful after another policy has been in place. For example, if a policy of lenient treatment and rehabilitation has been tried in a prison, it may be difficult for jailers to return to more punitive methods without disruption. Interestingly, the reverse may also be true.

Another problem in the measurement of policy effects is that the organizational basis of a good deal of evaluation limits excessively the scope of the inquiry, so that many unintended consequences of a program are not included in the evaluation. For example, highway engineers probably regard the interstate highway system as a great success. Many miles of highways have been built in a relatively short period, and these highways have saved many lives and many millions of gallons of gasoline—assuming that Americans would have driven the same number of miles if these superhighways had not been built. The mayor of a large city or members of the Department of Energy, however, may regard the program as a colossal failure. They realize that the building of highways in urban areas has facilitated urban sprawl and the flight of whites to the suburbs, which has in turn reduced the tax base of the cities and caused social and economic problems there (and raised the costs of urban programs), while the surrounding suburbs grew affluent. Likewise, the rapid automobile transportation promised by the highways encouraged people to move to the suburbs and consequently to consume millions of gallons of gasoline each year in commuting to their jobs. This one program and its widespread effects demonstrate that measures used by any single agency to evaluate its programs may be too narrow to detect many unintended social or economic consequences.

Finally, if experimentation is used as a means of attempting to ascertain the possible utility of a program, the danger that the "reactive effects of testing" will influence the results becomes an important consideration.[27] If citizens are aware that a certain policy is being tried "as an experiment," they may well behave differently than they would if it were declared to be a settled policy. In other words, those who favor the policy may work especially hard to make the program effective, whereas those who do not support the program may attempt to make it appear ineffective. Even those who have no definite opinions on the policy may not behave as they would if the policy were thought to be a true attempt at change instead of an experiment. For example, if a voucher plan for educational financing is being experimented with, neither parents nor educational providers are likely to behave as they would if a voucher plan were said to be fully in operation. Parents may be reluctant to place their children in private schools for fear the voucher program will be terminated, and providers are unlikely to enter the marketplace if the number of parents capable of paying for their services is apt to decrease soon.

The simple knowledge that a policy initiative is considered to be a test will alter the behavior of those involved and consequently influence the results of the experiment, or quasi-experiment. There have been some very successful experimental evaluations of programs, such as the New Jersey Income Maintenance Experiment, but most have required some strong incentives to gain the effective participation of the subjects.[28] Researchers then may have difficulty knowing if the participants are behaving "normally" or simply responding to the unusual, and often exciting, opportunity to be a guinea pig.

In evaluation research, problems are also encountered with research designs, experimental or not, that reduce the analysts' ability to make definitive statements about the real worth of policy. The importance and expense of public programs have led to more experimental evaluations of programs before they are implemented; nearly 100 were instituted from 1991 to 1993.[29] These experiments are concentrated very heavily in the area of social policy, in part because of the controversy surrounding many of those programs, and they are expensive, though not as expensive perhaps as implementing a poorly designed program. Conversely, not using an experimental method means that a large number of mainly unmeasured social and economic factors, not the program in question, may be the cause of any observed effects on the target population.

Targets

Related to the problem of goals is the question of identifying the targets of a program.[30] It is important for the evaluator to know not only what the program is intended to do but also whom it is intended to impact. Programs that have significant effects on the population as a whole may not have the desired effects on the more specific target population. For example, the Medicare program was intended, in part, to benefit less affluent older people, although all the elderly were declared eligible for the program. However, although the health of the elderly population in general has improved, probably at least in part as a result of Medicare, the health of the neediest portion of the elderly population has not improved commensurately.[31] And, as the program has been implemented, substantial coinsurance has been required, along with substantial deductibles if the insured enters a hospital. As a consequence, it is difficult for the neediest elderly citizens to participate in the Medicare program.

A similar problem has been developing with the Head Start program. Conceived as a component of the War on Poverty, Head Start was primarily intended to serve lower-income families and to enable their children to participate and learn effectively once they entered school. Head Start is, however, only a part-day program, whereas in most low-income families, all the adults who can do so will be working all day and therefore need day-care providers for the full day. The educational qualities of Head Start are largely absent from such day-care programs, but the parents must go to work. As a result, Head Start tends to be used by higher-income families, and the "target population" has been largely missed or, at a minimum, has been underserved.[32]

One problem in defining a target population and measuring a program's success in reaching that population is that participation in many programs is voluntary and depends on individuals who are potential beneficiaries "taking up" the benefit. Voluntary programs directed at the poor and the less educated members of society frequently face difficulties in making the program's availability widely known among the target population. Even if it is made widely known to potential beneficiaries, factors such as pride, real and perceived administrative barriers, and real difficulties in using the benefits offered may make the program less effective than intended. An extreme example may be taken from the United Kingdom's experience with its National Health Service (NHS). One ostensible purpose of the NHS was to equalize access to medical care among members of all social classes, but the evidence after more than four decades of its existence did not indicate that such equalization had taken place.[33] Instead, the disparities in health status that existed before the adoption of the NHS and that in fact existed in the early twentieth century had not been narrowed by an almost completely free system of medical care. Noneconomic barriers such as education, transportation, free time, and simple belief in the efficacy of medical care served to ensure that although there was a general improvement in health status among the British population, little or no narrowing of class differentials occurred. The less affluent simply were not availing themselves of the services offered to the extent that they might, especially given their relatively greater need for medical services. Although the evidence is less dramatic, it appears that social programs in the United States have suffered many of the same failures in equalizing access, and especially utilization, of some basic social services.

A program may create a false sense of success by "creaming" the segment of the population it serves.[34] Programs with limited capacities and stringent criteria for eligibility may select clients who actually need little help instead of those who have the greatest need. This can make the programs appear successful, although those being served did not need the program in the first place, while a large segment of the neediest go unserved. This pattern has been observed, for example, in many drug-treatment programs that take addicts who are already motivated to rid themselves of their habits. Likewise, some of the early successes of welfare reform in the United States may reflect the fact that clients with the greatest motivation entered training first and got jobs—but would they have done so anyway, without the program?[35] Such programs can show a high rate of success when they argue for additional public funding, but their success is of a limited nature. Further, it would be a mistake for policymakers to generalize from the "successes" of such programs and assume that similar programs would work if applied to a general population, whose level of motivation might be much lower. Of course, excessively negative results may be produced by including too many subjects, many of whom may be inappropriate, as members of the population selected for treatment.[36]

As with so much of policy evaluation, defining the target population is a political exercise as much as an exercise in rational policy analysis. As we noted when discussing legitimation, one tendency in formulating and adopting policies is to broaden the definition of the possible beneficiaries and loosen eligibility requirements for the program. Although it helps to build the political coalition necessary to adopt the program, this political broadening frequently makes the target population of the program more diffuse and consequently makes the program more difficult to evaluate. It is therefore often unfair to blame program managers for failing to serve the target population when those who constructed the legislation have provided broad and unworkable definitions of that target. Further, with the increasing strains on the public budget, it may become more politically feasible to target programs more tightly simply to reduce program costs.

Efficiency and Effectiveness

A related problem is the search for the philosopher's stone of efficiency in government, a search that often leads to a dead-end street. Measuring efficiency requires relating the costs of efforts to results and then assessing the ratio of the two. As noted, measuring results is difficult in many policy areas; it is often equally difficult to assign costs to particular results, even if those results were measurable. For much the same reasons, equal difficulties may arise in attempting to measure effectiveness. Surrogate measures of the intended results are frequently developed for public programs and policies, but all require the suspension of disbelief to be accepted as valid and reliable descriptions of what is occurring in the public sector.

As a consequence of these difficulties in measuring the substantive consequence of government actions, much of the assessment of performance in government depends on the evaluation of procedural efficiency. That is, what is assessed is not so much what is produced as how the agencies go about producing it. Some of this proceduralism depends on the legal requirements for personnel management, budgeting, and accounting, but attempts to assess procedural efficiency go beyond those formal requirements. The efficiency of public agencies may be assessed by determining the speed with which certain actions occur or by ensuring that every decision goes through all the appropriate procedural stages specified for a process. The important point here is that goals may be displaced when evaluations are made on such a basis, as the process itself, rather than the services that the process is intended to produce, becomes the measure of all things.[37] The concern with measuring efficiency through procedures may, in fact, actually reduce the efficiency of the process in producing results for citizens, because of the proliferation of procedural safeguards and their associated "red tape."

Values and Evaluation

Yet another problem is that the analyst who performs an evaluation requires a value system to enable him or her to assign valuations to outcomes. However, value systems are by no means constant across the population or across time, and the analyst who evaluates only a single program may perceive very different purposes and priorities within its policy area. Thus, there may be no simple means of determining the proper valuation and weighting of the outcomes of a program. This problem of assessment is especially true when the program has significant unintended effects (usually negative) that must be weighed against the intended consequences.[38] For instance, in the highways building program discussed earlier (p. 174), how do we compare the lives saved by the greater safety of interstate highways against the social and economic problems of center cities that this program may have exacerbated?

One point for consideration is that the analyst brings his or her own values to the evaluation process. Despite their rational and neutral stance, most analysts involved in policymaking have proceeded beyond the "baby analyst" stage to the point at which they have values they wish to see manifested through the policy process.[39] And as the analyst is in a central position in evaluation, he or she may have a substantial influence over the final evaluation of outcomes. However, the analyst's values will be but one of several sets of values involved in making that final assessment of a program or policy. The organizations involved will have their own collective values to guide them in evaluating outcomes, or at least their own activities. The professions with which members of the organization or external service providers identify will also provide sets of well-articulated values that may affect the assessment of policies. Frequently, all these different sets of values conflict with one another, or with the values of clients or of the general public. Thus, assessing a policy is not a simple matter of relating a set of known facts about outcomes to a given set of values. As in almost all aspects of the policy process, the values themselves may be the major source of conflict, while rational argumentation and policy analysis are merely the ammunition.

Politics

Finally, we must always remember that evaluations of public programs are performed in a political context. Therefore, there may well be a sharp difference between the interpretation that an analyst might make about the success or failure of a program and the conclusion that political officials might draw from the same data. Most evaluation schemes, for example, may be based on total benefits for the society, but political leaders may be interested only in the benefits created for their constituents; if that narrow range of benefits is significant, the overall inefficiency of a program may be irrelevant. The widespread use of pork-barrel legislation to fund projects in the constituencies of individual congressmen is a clear case in point. Political leaders may also be supportive of programs that their constituents like, whether or not the programs have any real impact on the social problems for which they were intended.

It is also important to remember that evaluations may be done not for the purpose of evaluating a program but in order to validate a decision that has already been made for very different reasons. Thus, evaluations are often performed on very short notice, and the evaluators may be given little time to do their work. The purpose then may be simply to produce some sort of a justification for public consumption, not to produce a "real" answer about the quality of the program. That is, in part, why institutionalized forms of evaluation, such as the General Accounting Office, are so important in the public sector.[40] Their stability and relative impartiality offer some guarantee of the quality of the assessment made. For example, the evaluations of the Missile Defense System made by the Department of Defense were quite positive, while the GAO found that the "successes" of the program were extremely questionable.

Increasing Requirements for Evaluation

One component of the wave of managerial change that has swept government over the past several decades[41] is a focus on the outputs of government as opposed to the inputs (budgets, personnel, etc.). The conventional means of controlling organizations in the public sector is to control their budgets and their personnel allocations stringently (see Chapter 6). Evaluations based on outputs, on the other hand, examine what government organizations do and the effects of their programs. This approach to evaluation is presumed to be a superior means of understanding the programs' real contribution to public welfare.

In 1993 Congress passed the Government Performance and Results Act (GPRA), the basic idea of which was to appraise government organizations on the basis of their strategic plans and on the quantitative indicators that were developed as components of those plans.[42] As noted earlier, this legislation was an attempt to make programs justify their existence on the basis of the outputs they produced and to use changes in these outputs as a means of judging the continuing performance of those organizations. This emphasis on outputs would, of course, enhance the need for evaluation within the federal government. The danger, as with many other exercises in evaluation, was that Congress would focus attentions on a few simple quantitative indicators and fail to understand the complexities of both the evaluation process and the programs that were being evaluated.

Other initiatives in the federal government also require greater emphasis on evaluation than was present during the Reagan and George H.W. Bush administrations.[43] The Gore Report contained some of the same emphasis on outputs as did the GPRA.[44] Also, regulatory review required the economic evaluation of all new regulatory initiatives, although this would only touch the surface of the kind of evaluation that would be required to understand fully the impact of these rules on the economy and society. The continuing debates over educational quality also appear to require an extensive effort at evaluation, although again the effort seems to be narrowing to simple standardized tests rather than a broader assessment of quality in education.[45] The moves by the George W. Bush administration to punish poorly performing schools are based on these rather simplistic measures of progress, creating the additional risk that all schools will focus on their children's ability to pass the tests rather than on learning at a more fundamental level.

Summary

Policy evaluation is a basic political process, and although it is also an analytic procedure, the central place of politics and value conflict cannot be ignored. As increasing pressures are brought to bear on the public sector to perform its role more effectively and efficiently, evaluation will probably become even more of a source of conflict. Negative evaluations of the effectiveness and efficiency of a program now will be more likely to lead to the termination of the program than would have been true in more affluent times. The content of an evaluation, the values that are contained in it, and even the organization performing the evaluation will all affect the final assessment. Evaluation research is now a major industry involving numerous consulting firms ("beltway bandits"), universities, and organizations within government itself. Even these evaluative organizations will have their own perspectives on what is right and wrong in policy and will bring those values with them when they perform an analysis.

The latter point is demonstrated clearly by the evaluation of a CETA program performed some years ago by both the John F. Kennedy School of Government at Harvard University and the School of Public Policy at the University of California, Berkeley. These two schools stressed different values and approaches in their evaluations of the program. The JFK School researchers concentrated on the costs and benefits of the program in strict economic terms, reflecting more utilitarian values. They found the program to be failing, with the costs surpassing the value of the benefits created. The Berkeley researchers, in contrast, stressed the political and participatory aspects of the program.[46] They found the program to be a great success, with the participants being pleased with the outcomes and more involved in society. The difficulty is, of course, that both sets of evaluators were correct.

Policy Change

After evaluation, the next stage of the policy process is policy change. Rarely are policies maintained in exactly the same form over time; instead, they are constantly evolving—sometimes as the direct result of an evaluation, but more often in response to changes in the socioeconomic or political environment, learning on the part of the personnel administering the program, or simple elaboration of existing structures and ideas. Further, a great deal of policymaking in industrialized countries such as the United States is the result of attempts at policy change rather than the result of new issues coming to the public sector for the first round of resolution.[47] Most policy areas in industrialized democracies are already populated by a number of programs and policies, so that what is usually required is change rather than creation of totally new policies. Policy succession, or the replacement of one policy by another, is therefore an important concept in examining the development of contemporary public policies.

When a policy or program is reconsidered or evaluated, three outcomes are possible: policy maintenance, policy termination, or policy succession.[48] *Policy maintenance* occurs rarely as a conscious choice but happens rather as a result of simple failure to make decisions. It is possible, but unlikely, that a policy will be considered seriously and then maintained in exactly the same form. In the first place, politicians make names for themselves by advocating new legislation, not by advocating the maintenance of existing programs. Less cynically, few policies or programs are so well designed initially that they require no changes after they are put into operation. The implementation of programs frequently demonstrates weaknesses in the original design that require modification. Through what might be considered almost continuous experimentation, programs can be made to match changes in society, in the economy, and in knowledge, and can thus be made to work more effectively.

It is also unlikely that many public programs will be *terminated*. Once begun, programs have a life of their own—they develop organizations, which hire personnel, and they develop a clientele, who come to depend on the program for certain services. Once clients use the services of a program, they may find it difficult ever to return to the market provision of goods or services, or to do without. This is especially true for programs that create a "stock" of benefits, as opposed to those that are merely a flow of resources. For example, Social Security created a stock of future benefits for its clientele, so once the program was initiated, future recipients began to plan differently for their retirement; any reduction in benefits would thus create severe hardships that the participants in the program could not have anticipated. Programs such as welfare or food stamps, which involve no planning by recipients, also create hardships if they are reduced, but the planning or "stock" element is not involved, and so it may be possible to move clients back into the market system. Public programs, policies, and organizations may not be immortal, but relatively few are ever fully terminated.[49] Even the Reagan administration, which came into office with promises to terminate organizations such as the Department of Education and the Small Business Administration, found those promises difficult to keep because the support for existing programs tends to keep them running.[50] The desire of the Republican Congress of the late 1990s to eliminate other federal organizations such as the Department of Commerce likewise ran afoul of strongly entrenched interests and was quickly forgotten.

Dismissing the other two options leaves *policy succession* as the most probable outcome for an existing policy or program. Policy succession may take several forms:

1. *Linear.* Linear succession involves the direct replacement of one program, policy, or organization by another, or the simple change of location of an existing program. For example, the replacement of the Aid to Families with Dependent Children welfare program by the Personal Responsibility and Work Opportunity Reconciliation Act of 1996 was an example of a linear succession.

2. *Consolidation.* Some successions involve placing several programs that have existed independently into a single program. The rolling together of a number of categorical health and welfare programs into a few block grants in the Reagan administration, as well as reflecting a change in the delivery system, was a consolidation.

On July 29, 1998, Bill Clinton appeared with cabinet members and task force representatives to celebrate the signing of an executive memorandum extending provisions of the Americans with Disabilities Act.

3. *Splitting.* Some programs are split into two or more individual components in a succession. For example, the Atomic Energy Commission was split in 1974 into the Nuclear Regulatory Agency and the Energy Research Development Agency, reflecting the contradictory goals of regulation and support of nuclear energy that had existed in the earlier organization.

4. *Nonlinear.* Some policy and organizational successions are complex and involve elements of other kinds of successions. The multiple changes involved in creating the Department of Energy from existing programs (including the two nuclear energy agencies mentioned above) are examples of nonlinear succession.

Although they entail much of the same process described for making policy (see Chapters 3–6), policy successions are processed in a distinctive manner. First, the agenda-setting stage is not so difficult for policy succession as it is for policy initiation. The broad issue at question has already been accepted as a component of the agenda and therefore needs only to be returned to a particular institutional agenda. Some issues, such as debt ceilings and annual reauthorizations of existing programs, automatically return to an agenda every year or even more frequently. More commonly, dissatisfaction with the existing programs returns an issue for further consideration, but returning the issue to the institutional agenda is easier than its initial introduction, because there are organizational manifestations of the program and identified clients who are in a better position to bring about the consideration. Furthermore, once organizations exist, it is more likely that program administrators will learn from other similar programs and will thus find opportunities for improving the program, or that they will simply think of better "solutions" to the problems.

The legitimation and formulation processes will also be different from those employed in policy initiation. But instead of fewer obstacles, as in agenda setting, there are likely to be more barriers. As noted, the existence of a program produces a set of client and producer interests that may be threatened by any proposed policy change. This is especially true if the proposed succession involves a "policy consolidation" (combining several programs) or a change in the policy instrument delivering the program in a direction that will demand less direct administration. For example, using policy consolidation to combine a number of categorical grants into block grants during the Reagan administration provoked outcries from both clients (primarily big-city mayors) and producers (administrators who had managed the categorical programs). And part of the conflict over the negative income tax proposed in President Nixon's Family Assistance Plan, as well as over some of President Carter's welfare reforms, concerned the changes in the instruments used to deliver the benefits, as well as ideological conflicts over the level of benefits.[51] Thus, once a policy change of whatever kind enters an institutional arena, it is quite likely to encounter severe resistance from the affected interests. This may be true even if the threat to those interests is not real—the mere prospect of upsetting established patterns of delivering services may be sufficient to provoke resistance.

Of course, some policy successions may be generated within the organization administering the program rather than imposed from the outside. An array of external political forces may be strong enough to effectuate the change, so that the organization and the clientele will "gladly" accede and possibly even publicly cosponsor the change. Also, unlike most public bureaucrats, who tend to be risk avoiders, some program managers may be risk takers, who are willing to gamble that the proposed change will produce greater benefits for the organization, so they need not attempt to hang on to what they have. Finally, some programs may have expanded too far; their personnel may wish to pare off some of the peripheral programs in order to target their clientele more clearly and protect the organizational "heartlands."[52] The pared-off programs will not necessarily be terminated; they may only change their organizational locations.

Clientele groups may seek to split a program from a larger organization in order to develop a clearer target for their political activities. Pressures from the National Educational Association and other educational groups to break up the Department of Health, Education, and Welfare (HEW) and establish an independent Department of Education illustrate this point. It was argued that HEW did not give educational interests the direct attention they deserved and that, because the education budget had the greatest flexibility of all the budgets in HEW (the remainder being primarily entitlement programs), any cutting that was done was likely to be in education.[53] Although there were pressures on the Reagan administration to eliminate the Department of Education, once established it has proven difficult to alter its independent status. To some degree the administration of George W. Bush, by virtue of its increased emphasis on education, placed the Department of Education in a more central position.

Forming a coalition for policy change requires careful attention to the commitments of individual congressmen to particular interests and to ongoing programs. As with the initial formulation and legitimation of a policy, an attempt at policy succession requires the use of the mechanisms of partisan analysis, logrolling, and the pork barrel, in order to deliver that change (see Chapter 4). Again, this stage of the policy process may be even more difficult than that of policy initiation. While the implications of a new policy are often vague, the probable effects of a change in an existing policy are likely to be more readily identifiable. It may be easy to persuade legislators of the benefits of a new policy on the basis of limited information, but once a program has been running for some time, information will become available to the legislators, making it much more difficult to persuade them to change a program that is "good enough."

There may, however, be many clients, administrators, and legislators who are dissatisfied with the program as it is being implemented, and those individuals can be mobilized to advocate change. A coalition of this kind may involve individuals from both the right and left who oppose the existing policy. The coalition built around the 1986 tax reform illustrates this type of process rather well—it combined liberals who wanted more equitable treatment of the working and middle classes and greater equity in the tax system with some conservatives who wanted greater fairness in the tax code for all types of businesses.[54] Managing a policy succession by organizing such a broad coalition runs the risk that termination of the policy may be the only alternative to the status quo on which the coalition can agree. Before beginning the process, therefore, it is crucial for the analyst to have in mind the particular policy succession that he or she would like to have implemented. Otherwise, allowing political forces to follow their own lead may threaten the existence of the program.

Implementing a policy succession may be the most difficult aspect of the process. That is also true for the initiation of a policy, because putting a policy into effect in the intended manner is problematic at best. But several features of policy succession as a process may make it even more difficult. First, it is important to remember that organizations exist in the field as well as at headquarters.[55] People working in the field may have policy preferences as strong as those of the home-office workers, but they may not be consulted about proposed changes. Yet it is the field workers who must put the policy change into effect and ultimately decide who will get what as a result of the change. Thus, if policy change does not involve significant and clear modification of the existing policies, the field staffs may well be able to continue doing what they were doing prior to the nominal change and so subvert the intention of the succession legislation. This subversion need not be intentional; it may be only the result of inertia or inadequate understanding of the intentions of headquarters or of the legislation.

In this context, it is important to remember that organizations do not exist alone in the world, nor do policies.[56] Instead, each organization exists within a complicated network of other organizations, all of which must cooperate if any of them are to be successful.[57] Any change in the policies of one organization may reduce the ability of other organizations to fulfill their own goals. Education and job-training may now be as important for economic performance, especially in the long run, as is formal economic policy. This interaction is perhaps especially evident in the field of social policy, where a variety of programs are necessary to meet the many and interrelated needs of poor families and in which changes in any one policy or program may influence the success of all the programs. Terminating food stamps, for example, would mean that welfare payments would not be sufficient for families to buy the amounts of food they used to buy. As a consequence, housing, education, and even employment programs would be adversely impacted by increasing demands. The reform of welfare during the Clinton administration changed eligibility for food stamps, but it did so in the context of a general weakening of the social safety net and a greater emphasis on employment.

As government shifts its focus of activities from direct provision of services to "new governance," in which it operates through a variety of third-party and indirect mechanisms, the capacity to associate particular outcomes with particular programs may become even more difficult. Further, generating change in this setting implies changing not only the public-sector programs and their intentions but also the network that will become responsible for delivering programs.[58] Dependence on a network for service will further complicate the process of policy change, given the resilience that appears to characterize the behavior of both public and private organizations.

Finally, implementing policy succession is almost certain to be disappointing. The massive political effort required to bring about a policy succession is unlikely to be rewarded the first month, or even the first year, after the change. This is likely to create disappointment in the new program and perhaps cynicism about the entire policy area. As a consequence, one policy succession may generate enough disruption to engender a rapid series of changes. Further, once a stable set of policies and organizations has been disturbed, there will no longer be a single set of entrenched interests with which to contend, so forming a new coalition in favor of policy change or termination may be easier. The advocate of policy change must be cognizant that he or she may produce more change than was intended once the possibility of reform becomes apparent to participants in the policy area.

Since we now understand that implementing policy succession will be difficult, we should address the problem of designing policy changes for easier implementation. The ease with which change can be brought about is a function at least in part of the design of previous organizations and programs. In an era of increased skepticism concerning government and bureaucracy, policies are being designed with built-in triggers for evaluation and termination.[59] The interest in "sunset laws" means that any administrator joining such an organization, or any client becoming dependent on its services, has reason to question the stability of those arrangements.[60] If the declining sense of entitlement to either employment or benefits from an organization can make future policy successions more palatable to those already connected with a program, then one major hurdle to policy change will have been overcome. However, this declining sense of entitlement may be related to a declining commitment of workers to the program, which can have negative consequences for the organization that exceed the costs of change.

It is not possible to reverse history and redesign programs and organizations that are already functioning without such built-in terminators. The analyst or practitioner of policy change must therefore be prepared to intervene in existing organizations in order to produce the smooth transition from one set of policies to another. One obvious trigger for such change would be a change in the party in office, especially in the presidency. Before the Reagan presidency, however, the alternation of parties in office had produced little significant policy change,[61] and the Clinton administration in many ways represented a return to that earlier pattern, for "New Democrats" seemed very similar to a moderate Republican like George H. W. Bush. The Clinton administration encountered substantial difficulties in asserting a more activist agenda for government, given the legitimation of the antigovernment perspective during twelve years of Republican presidents, the election of a Republican Congress, and the constraints imposed by attempting to balance the budget.[62] As the Clinton years have been followed by the "compassionate conservatism" of George W. Bush, the initial emphasis seemed to be more on the conservative element and the downsizing of programs. The need to pursue homeland security has, however, combined with the conservatism of the administration to produce efforts at greater policy change than might have been anticipated from the campaign rhetoric.

Rapid changes in demand and environmental conditions may also trigger attempts at policy succession, but organizations have proved to be remarkably effective in deflecting attempts at change and in using change for their own purposes. At present it is fair to say that there is no available technology for implementing policy succession, just as there is no reliable technology for implementation in general. A common finding is that organizations are able to interpret new policy initiatives in ways that fortify their current approaches. As with the discussion of the social construction of issues on the agenda (see pp. 55–56), organizations also socially construct the meaning of policy and law, and do so in ways that will benefit them.

Summary

Policies must be evaluated, and frequently policies must be changed. But neither task is as easy as some politicians, and even some academicians, make it appear. Identifying the goals of policies, determining the results of programs, and isolating the effects of policies compared with the effects of other social and economic forces all make evaluating public policies tricky, and at times impossible. The surrogate measures that must be used at times may be worse than no measures at all, for they emphasize activity of any sort rather than actions performed well and efficiently. The method of evaluation then places pressure on agencies merely to spend their money rather than always to spend it wisely.

Evaluation frequently leads to policy change, and the process of producing desired changes and of implementing those changes in a complex political environment will tax the abilities of the analyst as well as the politician. All the usual steps in policymaking must be gone through, but they must be gone through in the presence of established organizations and clients. The implications of the proposed policy changes may be all too obvious to those actors, and they may therefore strenuously oppose the changes. As often as not, these entrenched forces will be successful in deflecting pressures for change. Without the application of significant and skillful political force, then, American government often is a great machine that simply proceeds onward in its established direction. Those whose interests are already being served benefit from this inertia, but those on the outside may continue to be excluded.

PART THREE
Substantive Policy Issues

CHAPTER 8
Economic Policy

THE PERFORMANCE OF the economy in Western societies was once considered something like the weather: everyone talked about it, but no one was able to do anything about it. Economic cycles and fluctuation were considered natural acts of God, beyond the control of governments or human beings. That concept of the economy was altered during the Great Depression in the 1930s and during the postwar economic boom.[1] The magnitude and duration of the depression were such that even conservative governments were forced to pay some attention to its effects.[2] Perhaps more important, the work of John Maynard Keynes, Knut Wiksell, and other economists provided the economic tools, and the intellectual justification for using those tools, for government to control an economy.

The confidence of governments in their ability to manage economies is perhaps best exemplified in the postwar full-employment acts in both the United States and the United Kingdom, pledging that the governments of those two nations would never again permit mass unemployment to afflict their people. This confidence was bolstered during the economic miracles of the 1950s, 1960s, and early 1970s, in which most Western nations experienced rapid and consistent economic growth, very low levels of unemployment (the United States being a notable exception), and relatively stable price levels. In the early 1960s, advisers to President Kennedy spoke of the government's ability to "fine tune" the economy and to manipulate economic outcomes for the society, by pulling a few simple economic levers.[3]

During the 1980s and early 1990s anyone reading that account of economic policy would have considered it very curious,[4] for during the period following the "oil shocks" of the 1970s, the American economy was characterized instead by unreliable and usually slow growth, high unemployment, extremely high trade deficits, and relatively high (by American, if not international, standards) inflation (see table 8.1, p. 192). This "stagflation" resulted in diminished public faith in the capacity of governments effectively to manage their national economies; politi-

TABLE 8.1   Performance of the U.S. Economy, 1950–1999 (in percentages)

	1950–59	1960–69	1970–79	1980–89	1990–99
Average unemployment rate	4.5	4.8	6.2	7.2	5.6
Average GNP growth	4.0	4.1	2.8	2.7	2.4
Average price change	2.1	2.3	7.1	5.6	3.1
Average real wage growth	3.6	2.9	0.8	−0.2	0.4

Source: Organization for Economic Cooperation and Development, *Main Economic Indicators* (Paris: OECD, monthly).

cians who promised a bright economic future were regarded with substantial skepticism.[5] The Reagan administration was able to produce some economic growth during part of the 1980s with its "supply-side economics," but it did so at the cost of a much higher public deficit, increased income inequality, and increased unemployment.[6] Even with those social costs, the administration's efforts still produced an average annual rate of economic growth (3.2 percent) that was noticeably lower than the postwar average (3.6 percent). The economic growth rate during the first Bush administration (2.1 percent) was even lower, and that fact played a significant role in President Bush's defeat in the 1992 election.

The Clinton economic strategy was more expansionist, focusing on job creation and economic growth. Although he was more interested in using the power of government than his immediate predecessors, President Clinton's emphasis on growth and "growing down the deficit" did well politically in a country facing numerous uncertainties about its economic future. His proposals were not explicitly Keynesian, but they depended on somewhat increasing government activity to help move the economy forward and on microeconomic tools, such as industrial policies, job training, and the like, to achieve the desired results.[7] Despite these interventions, however, the "flexible labor market," argued to be so important for American economic success during the 1990s, at its heart implied a willingness to let the market function with minimal regulation. Finally, the Clinton economic strategy continued unabated from Republican administrations the free-trade strategy that included implementation of the North American Free Trade Agreement and continued advocacy of free trade in a variety of international forums.[8]

The economic indicators remained positive for most of the Clinton administration, and indeed the economy soared during the late 1990s, with the lowest level of unemployment for years and the stock market reaching new highs seemingly day after day. However, many underlying structural problems remained in the American economy, perhaps most important among them the continuing trade deficits and persistent, if not increasing, levels of economic inequality.[9] Thus, the economy that George W. Bush inherited was going well, but it was vulnerable and was already beginning to slow. The Bush administration attempted early in its time in office to stimulate the economy by means of a tax cut and an immediate tax rebate, but even before the events of 11 September 2001, there was little evidence that the economy was turning around quickly.[10] Although there was some positive news early in 2002, the confidence of the later Clinton years was gradually replaced by a return to deficits in the public budget.[11]

Economic policy is a central concern of government—as Bill Clinton was reminded during the 1992 campaign, "It's the economy, stupid"—but it is also a by-product of many other policy choices. One important step that a government must take is to form a more or less coherent set of policies intended to manage the economy. That overall policy is the result of many separate decisions about matters such as spending for public programs, patterns of taxation, and the interest rate charged by the central bank (the Federal Reserve System in the United States). Even if the federal government chooses to make relatively consistent decisions in these areas, a host of other governmental actors (50 states and over 85,000 local governments) are also making taxing and spending decisions that affect the overall economic performance of the country.

Economic policy also depends heavily on the actions of individual citizens over whom governments have little or no direct control. In the basic Keynesian paradigm of fiscal policy, an excess of public expenditures above revenues is supposed to stimulate the economy because citizens will spend the additional money, creating additional demand for goods and services. But if citizens do not spend the additional money, then the intended stimulation effect will not be created. Only when governments choose to regulate the economy directly through instruments such as wage-and-price controls can they be reasonably confident that their actions will generate desired behaviors. Even then, policing compliance with a wage-and-price policy presents severe administrative difficulties of its own, and individuals and firms have shown themselves to be extremely creative in avoiding attempts at control.

The Goals of Economic Policy

Economic policy has a number of goals, all of which are socially desirable, but some of which are not always mutually compatible. Political leaders frequently must make decisions that simultaneously benefit some citizens and impose burdens on others. For example, although it is by no means as clear as it once was, there is a trade-off between inflation and unemployment.[12] To the extent that governments attempt to reduce unemployment, they may increase the inflation rate. The results of such a decision may benefit the worker about to be laid off but will harm the senior citizen living on a fixed income, as well as all citizens who hold assets of fixed value (savings bonds, for example). In general, economic policy has four fundamental goals, which German political economists have labeled "the golden quadrangle": economic growth, full employment, stable prices, and a positive balance of payments from international trade. To these four may be added an additional intermediate policy goal: positive structural change in the economy.

Economic Growth

Economic growth has been a boon both to citizens and to governments. Although ecologically minded citizens may question the benefits of economic growth and praise smaller and less technologically complex economic systems, most American citizens still want more of everything.[13] They became accustomed to receiving more and more income each year during the postwar period up until at least the mid-1970s. All this economic growth translated into massive increases in the availability of consumer goods, making items such as television sets and automobiles, which were not widely available in 1950, almost universally obtainable today. In material terms, economic growth produced an average standard of living in 2002 that was much higher than that of 1950, or of 1980, or even of 1990, and almost all Americans were enjoying that affluence.[14]

Economic growth has also been important in the political history of the postwar era, acting as political "solvent" to ease the transition of the United States from a "warfare state" to more of a "welfare state." Economic growth was sufficiently great that virtually every segment of the society could be given its own government programs without exhausting all the newly created wealth. Public programs grew along with private affluence, so individuals did not feel particularly disadvantaged by their taxes or by government benefits granted to others.[15] Further, economic growth aided the redistribution of income to the less advantaged—one calculation is that 90 percent of the postwar improvement in the economic status of African Americans has been the result of economic growth rather than of redistributive public programs. The best welfare program is still a good job with a good salary, a fact emphasized by the 1996 welfare reforms that stressed work rather than direct cash benefits as the best solution to poverty and inequality (see pp. 309–311).

Yet American economic growth did not compare well with that of the majority of our major trading partners during most of the postwar period. Average annual growth in per capita GNP for the United States from 1960 to 1980 was

2.2 percent, while it was 3.1 percent for Germany, 3.8 percent for Italy, and over 6.3 percent for Japan. In addition, the American economic growth rate was falling (although not as rapidly as growth in most other industrialized countries); average economic growth in the 1980s was less than half what it was during the 1950s and became even slower, or negative, in the early 1990s.

After the first few years of the 1990s, however, American economic performance improved significantly, outstripping most of our trading partners. For example, in the period from 1990 to 2000 per capita income in the United States increased by over 8 percent in real terms, while that of most of its trading partners was growing by 4 percent or less. The U.S. economy was particularly productive toward the end of that time period, as growth in major economies such as Germany, and particularly Japan, slackened. These positive results led many observers to extol the virtues of the "flexible" model of the U.S. economy, in contrast to the more regulated economies of Europe.

Despite this success of the American economic model during much of the 1990s, the United States may still be confronting the problems of a "zero-sum society," in which the gains achieved by one segment of the society come at the expense of some other segment.[16] To some degree that has already happened. During the economic growth of the Reagan years, the middle and upper classes gained at the expense (relatively and in some cases absolutely) of the poor and working classes. The relatively slow rate of growth was highlighted by the real (adjusted for price changes) income of the average American worker from 1970 to 1990. This important indicator of economic well-being for individuals hardly changed at all over these two decades, but it did begin to move upward again significantly in 1994 and continued upward, albeit slowly, for most of the rest of that decade.

The situation worsened significantly during the first years of the twenty-first century, however, as the economic success of the 1990s gave way to a mild recession (although for anyone who became unemployed during that time, the recession was anything but mild). There was little economic growth during most of 2001, and for the last three quarters of that year there was a decline in real GDP. This drop in economic performance—the first recession for almost a decade—reminded many people in and out of government of the realities of economic scarcity and made the economic future appear cloudy.

Whereas previous generations could expect to do better than their parents economically, the economic future for young people entering the labor market in the near future seems uncertain, despite the good times of the late 1990s. Increasing benefits for the elderly through Social Security also may put a greater drain on the income of working-age citizens, and programs for the poor may increase the tax burden on the income of the middle and upper classes. Even in times of economic growth and a balanced budget, there are vigorous conflicts between advocates of tax cuts and advocates of public programs, and the continuing uncertainty about economic growth, combined with more ideological politics, may well make policymaking more contentious and more difficult in the early years of the new century.

Full Employment

The benefits of full employment are obvious. Most adults want to work and utilize their talents. The welfare state has provided a floor for those who become unemployed so that they and their families are unlikely to starve or do without medical care. These social benefits, however, cannot match the income that could be earned by working, nor can social programs replace the pride and psychological satisfaction that comes from earning one's own living. These psychological advantages are perhaps especially pronounced in the United States, where the social and political culture attaches great importance to individualism and self-reliance—which explains, in turn, the significantly higher rates of family problems, suicides, and alcoholism among the unemployed than among the employed. Further, changes in social policy are now making working almost mandatory, and the relevant question now is whether the economy can provide enough jobs for all the people who want and need them.

In addition to its negative effects on individuals, unemployment has some influence on government budgets. When individuals are not working, they do not contribute to Social Security or pay income tax. Also, they cost the government money in unemployment benefits, Medicaid payments, food stamps, and the services of other social programs. Thus, increasing unemployment may upset the government's best plans to produce a balanced budget or a deficit of a certain size. Even if the higher level of unemployment is accurately anticipated, revenues are still lost and more expenditures required. Also, other important public programs may be funded inadequately because of the need to assist the unemployed.

The good news is that, compared to many of its major trading partners, the United States has achieved relatively low rates of unemployment. Beginning during the late 1980s and early 1990s, American unemployment rates began to fall lower than those in other industrialized democracies, and in the late 1990s were at the lowest levels in decades. Although unemployment has crept up in the first years of the twenty-first century, it remains lower than in most other industrial economies. Critics argued that many of the jobs being created were for "hamburger flippers" (i.e., low-paid workers in the service sector), but while there certainly were a number of such new jobs, there was also evidence that more highly paid jobs—many also in service industries (finance, computers, etc.)—were being created as well. Indeed, in some urban areas the demand for labor in the late 1990s was so great that even hamburger flippers were earning well above the minimum wage. That level of demand dropped in 2001 and early

2002, but even so, unemployment in the United States remained lower than in most industrialized countries.

What is perhaps more important than the aggregate performance of the United States on this indicator is the concentration of unemployment by race and age. Blacks and young Americans bear by far the highest rates of unemployment; among young blacks, the rate of unemployment still approaches 25 percent. And although aggregate employment figures appear very good, there has been a shift in the types of jobs being created in the economy. There were over 29 million more nonfarm jobs in the United States in 1996 than in 1980, and 10 million more than in 1990. Between 1990 and 2002 the number of goods-producing jobs declined by 680,000, while the number of service-producing jobs increased by almost 11 million. Of the new service jobs created, at least one-third were in restaurants, hotels, and other relatively low-wage environments, while the other two-thirds were in a variety of more lucrative service occupations, such as financial services, computer firms, and the like.[17]

The same pattern of employment change is projected to continue for at least the next decade.[18] In the first months of the twenty-first century, the number of service jobs continued to increase, while the number of goods-producing jobs remained stagnant and then began to drop off significantly. There were 1.3 million fewer manufacturing jobs in January 2002 than there had been in January 2001. Some of that change was cyclical, reflecting the slowdown of the economy, but some of it indicated the shifting nature of the workplace. The good news was that despite the economic slowdown, there were over 100,000 more new jobs in service industries at the beginning of 2002 than there had been at the beginning of 2001.[19]

The changing pattern of job creation to some degree reflects changes in the structure of the U.S. economy, which, as a whole, has been shifting away from manufacturing and toward a service base.[20] Further, in the post–Cold War period, manufacturing industries such as aerospace have not been employing as many people as they once did. Also, in the late 1990s the oil industry was hit by very low prices and little need for domestic exploitation. These shifts pose problems for some regions of the country (e.g., Louisiana and Alaska) as well as for the traditional industrial labor force (see table 8.2, p. 198). Even with the return to high oil prices, domestic oil production has not rebounded significantly. Many dozens of new jobs are created in the United States every day, but these jobs tend either to be suited for individuals with strong technical skills (computer programming) or to pay relatively little (clerking in fast-food restaurants).

Industrial workers accustomed to earning high wages in unskilled or semiskilled occupations have found the structural shift in the economy very disturbing, but they have been almost powerless to change it. Labor unions (outside government and some service industries) have been losing large numbers of

TABLE 8.2   Unemployment in the United States, 1970–2001

				Across Time					
1970	*1980*	*1985*	*1990*	*1992*	*1995*	*1998*	*1999*	*2000*	*2001*
4.4	7.0	7.2	5.6	7.5	5.6	4.5	4.2	4.0	4.8

By State (April 2002)			
High		*Low*	
Oregon	7.5	South Dakota	3.4
Washington	7.1	Iowa	3.6
Mississippi	7.0	North Dakota	3.6
North Carolina	6.9	Nebraska	3.8
Alaska	6.6	Connecticut	3.8

Source: U.S. Bureau of Labor Statistics, *Bulletin of Labor Statistics*

members, and employees know that business can simply move jobs to lower-wage economies if there is too much pressure on them in the United States. The increased prevalence of low-wage jobs often makes two incomes necessary to maintain a reasonable family lifestyle, even after the economic growth of the Clinton years. This economic shift in turn increases demands for improved social (family leave) and educational (early childhood) programs from the public sector. In this instance, as in almost any area of social or economic life, it is impossible to contain the effects of change within a single policy area.

Stable Prices

Unlike unemployment, inflation affects all citizens through increases in the prices they pay for goods and services.[21] Increased rates of interest are also a form of inflation because they increase the costs of borrowing money for business, a cost that is then passed on in higher prices. Inflation affects different portions of the community differently, however, and it may even benefit some people. On the one hand, inflation particularly hurts those living on fixed incomes, such as the elderly who live on fixed pensions, and those (such as college professors) who are not sufficiently well organized to gain wage increases equal to increases in price levels.

On the other hand, inflation benefits individuals and institutions that owe money, because the significance of a debt is reduced as inflation eats away at the real value of currency. As the biggest debtor in the society, government is perhaps particularly benefited by inflation. The amount governments owe, relative to the total production of their economies, can diminish if inflation makes everything cost more and each unit of currency worth less. Governments with progressive tax structures also benefit from inflation, as people whose real incomes (i.e., incomes adjusted for changes in purchasing power) have not increased see their money incomes increase. They are then moved into higher tax brackets and pay a larger portion of their income in taxes; as a consequence, government receives a relatively painless (politically) increase in its revenues. Many tax reforms adopted during the 1980s were aimed in part at reducing the progressivity of taxation, or requiring governments to relate the thresholds of tax brackets to inflation so that government would not receive this automatic "fiscal dividend" from inflation.

Inflation is by no means an unqualified boon for governments, however. Many benefits paid out by governments now are *indexed*, or adjusted for changes in the price level.[22] As a consequence, much of any increase in revenues from inflation must be paid out directly as increased benefits. The things that a government must buy, most notably the labor of its employees, also increase in price during inflationary periods. This is especially important since government has been more labor intensive than the private economy, so that its costs increase more rapidly than do labor costs for other "industries" in the society.[23] As information technology advances, however, governments have tended to be major beneficiaries. More than anything else, governments process information—so computers, e-mail, and the Internet have tended to boost productivity in government.[24]

The performance of the American economy in maintaining a stable price level during the postwar period has been better than that of most of its major trading partners (see table 8.3, p. 200). Only Germany and Japan have been more successful in holding down price increases, while countries such as Italy have had more than double the rate of inflation of the United States over this period. The relatively superior performance of the U.S. economy in this area can be explained by several factors, including its relatively low unemployment over the same period. It is also argued that the Federal Reserve Board's independence from political interference has allowed it to use monetary policy to regulate the price level effectively.[25] Also, the relative weakness of the labor movement in the United States has meant fewer strong pressures to push wages upward than have been brought to bear in most other Western countries, although the power of large corporations might also have been expected to be related to increasing prices.[26]

For whatever reason, in comparison with other nations the United States maintained a low-inflation economy during most of the postwar period, although many Americans may be far from pleased with the price increases that have occurred. That record began to weaken relative to the rest of the industrialized world during the late 1980s, in part because of the inflationary effects of large-scale budget deficits. The recession of the early 1990s helped keep prices virtually stable for the first years of that decade, however, and even with the re-

TABLE 8.3   Inflation Rate of United States and Major Trading Partners, 1988–2000

	1988	1990	1993	1995	1997	1998	1999	2000
United States	4.0	5.3	3.0	2.6	2.6	2.3	2.2	3.4
Canada	4.0	4.8	1.5	2.2	1.6	1.0	1.7	2.7
Japan	0.6	3.1	1.7	0.6	1.7	0.6	-0.1	-0.6
France	2.6	3.4	2.4	1.8	1.2	0.7	0.5	1.7
Germany	1.3	2.7	4.0	1.8	1.9	0.9	0.6	1.9
Italy	5.1	6.5	5.4	5.2	2.0	2.0	1.7	2.5
Sweden	6.8	6.9	2.2	2.5	0.5	-0.1	0.5	1.0
United Kingdom	4.9	9.4	3.7	3.4	3.1	3.4	1.6	2.9

Source: International Monetary Fund, *International Financial Statistics,* monthly.

turn to economic growth in the mid-1990s, inflation remained very low, in part because of the active intervention of the Federal Reserve. Indeed, one of the astounding features of the economic system in the late 1990s was that there was relatively high growth, low unemployment, and an inflation rate of almost zero; this was not supposed to happen.

By the beginning of the twenty-first century it was becoming apparent that inflation may no longer be the threat that it once was, although central banks, politicians, and businessmen continue to run the risk of overreacting to that threat by too tightly restricting the money supply and thus endangering both economic growth and employment. A number of economic factors appear to be interacting to make inflation a less significant economic threat than it was in the past. One factor is the increased number of energy sources, with greater access to oil in the former Soviet Union and a number of new sources, which should stabilize or lower energy prices, a major component of costs in industrialized economies (especially the United States). Further, the prices for other raw materials (including agricultural products) are stable or decreasing, as many Third World countries stress export of primary commodities rather than rapid industrialization. Also, wage rates in the United States dropped (in real terms) from the late 1980s and into the 1990s, so that a major cost of production was also decreasing. Even with some growth in average real wages during the late 1990s, however, productivity was higher and labor costs lower than in most competitor countries. In short, continued price stability—and even deflation—seemed possible.

A Positive Balance of Payments

The economy of the United States is relatively autarkic and relatively less involved in international trade than are the economies of most other industrialized countries.[27] It is, however, still important for the United States to manage its balance of payments from trade—the net result of the cost of imports and the income from exports. If a country spends more money abroad than it receives from abroad, it has a negative balance of payments, while a country that spends less overseas than it receives has a positive balance. The final figure for the balance of payments is composed of the balance of trade (payment for real goods traded) and the balance on "invisibles"—services such as insurance, banking, and shipping fees.

Over the past several decades, the United States has generally had a very large negative balance of trade but a positive balance on invisibles, and these have added up to a negative balance of payments. A number of factors have contributed to the large negative balance of payments. During much of the 1980s world oil prices were low, but they began to increase in the early 1990s. The United States had learned little from earlier oil crises and had again become heavily dependent on foreign oil (see Chapter 13), while its demand for other foreign products, such as automobiles and electronics from Asian countries, continued to increase. By the mid-1990s, the relatively rapid recovery of the American economy (as compared to the rest of the industrialized world) meant that U.S. demand for foreign goods tended to increase more rapidly than did foreign demand for American goods. This latter factor was exacerbated in 1997 and 1998, when many Asian economies suffered massive downturns and stopped buying almost all foreign goods, while dropping prices on their own goods in an attempt to sell more.[28]

The effects of a net negative balance of payments are generally detrimental to a country's economy. In the first place, a negative balance of payments indicates that the country's products are not competitive with those from other countries. This may be because of price, because of quality, or because a country cannot produce a commodity, such as oil. More important, a negative balance of payments tends to reduce the value of the country's currency in relation to that of other nations. If a country continues to trade its money for commodities overseas, the laws of supply and demand dictate that the value of the country's currency eventually will decline, as more money goes abroad than is returned. This effect has been especially difficult for the United States, because the dollar has been the "top currency" in international trade for some years and because so many dollars are held overseas and used in international transactions.[29] Finally, as in the case of trading for raw materials, a negative balance of payments may indicate a country's dependence on the products of other nations, which introduces the potential for international "blackmail." And holding a great deal of a country's currency abroad may mean that the value of that currency is especially vulnerable to the actions of others—governments and individuals.

For the United States in recent years, international flows of capital have also posed difficulties, for several reasons. First, money has flowed into the United States since the early 1990s, in part because of political stability and high interest rates, but this has meant that a number of businesses and a large amount of property are now owned outside the country.[30] These capital flows are in part offset by the property and industries overseas owned by American firms and individuals. The dependency on foreign capital makes some important industries seemingly difficult to steer toward national policy goals, although firms totally owned domestically are not always amenable to national goals either. Further, as money began to exit in 2002 (in part as a result of increased tensions in the Middle East) the American economy began to look more vulnerable to the international market.

Further, as the world economy becomes more internationalized, large capital flows across borders are becoming increasingly a fact of economic life.[31] The ease with which capital now moves places restraints on the ability of national governments to make domestic economic policy as they might like, and it also strengthens international businesses that bargain with governments over where to locate.[32] Nevertheless, there is some evidence that capital flows do not totally obviate the capacity of countries to influence the behavior of businesses and individuals. For example, there appears to be more variance in both tax policy[33] and economic regulations[34] than might be expected if governments had wholly lost the ability to control their economies. The United States, given the huge size of its domestic economy and its central position in the world economy, has more capacity than most countries to exercise that control.

The absence of a clear connection between the flow of capital and economic indicators in the United States is rather pronounced. Despite the continuing outflow of money through a negative balance of payments, the U.S. dollar has remained strong in the international currency market. Indeed, the strength of the dollar plays some role in the balance of payment difficulties: American products are more expensive abroad than are products made elsewhere, even with equal levels of productivity, because the dollar is strong, and that naturally makes those products more difficult to sell. The dollar remains the principal currency for international commerce; some countries in Latin America have even abandoned their own currencies in favor of the dollar.

Structural Change

The final goal of economic policy is structural change, or changing the industrial and regional composition of production. Some regions of a country may be less developed than others; the South traditionally was the least developed section of the United States, but it is now relatively prosperous compared to some of the Great Lakes states. In addition, the composition of production makes some regions extremely vulnerable to economic fluctuations. The experience of Michigan during the continuing slump in automobile production and that of Louisiana and Alaska during periods of declining oil prices are graphic evidence of the danger of relying too heavily on a single product. In addition, government may want to alter the structure of the entire economy—as in the efforts of Third World countries to industrialize their agricultural economies. A similar effort was, of course, also made in the United States in the nineteenth century, and many industrialized countries still attempt to shift the composition of their economies in the most profitable directions possible.

In the United States, the federal government has been relatively little involved in promoting structural change, with the major exception of regional programs such as the Tennessee Valley Authority and the Appalachian Regional Commission. Also, the federal government has been active in supporting and protecting defense industries, and those industries have certainly been crucial for the development of "high-tech" industries. If anything, the federal government has attempted to utilize trade policies, including quotas on imported products such as automobiles, as a means of slowing the structural change of the economy rather than accelerating it. Politically the federal government has difficulty in supporting one area of the country over another, and so it tends to use rather general instruments except when trying to protect industry from foreign competition that is perceived to be unfair.

State and local governments, on the other hand, have been extremely active in attempting to promote economic development and structural change, particularly through their tax systems.[35] States permit industries moving into their area to take tax credits for their investments and to write off a certain percentage of their profits against taxes for some years. Local governments have fewer tax options (property tax relief being the most important), but they can provide grants for industrial sites and other infrastructural developments to make themselves more attractive to industries. Building infrastructure, indeed, is an underappreciated mechanism for economic development; in the 1990s there was a very close relationship between investment in roads and other economic infrastructure and the growth of jobs in the states.[36]

Southern states have been especially active in promoting economic development through tax incentives; these policies, combined with favorable climate, more available energy, and low rates of unionization, have tended to reverse the traditional imbalance in economic growth between the North and the South.[37] The Frostbelt states have tended to grow more slowly than the Sunbelt states, although the general economic upsurge of the 1990s tended to bring the northern industrial states along, and many have been prospering. These states have been using their own incentives to induce industries to remain where they are instead of moving south and have actively sought new investment. Several northern states also have turned their economies around by relying on their educational and technological resources, instead of their industrial labor force,[38] and this strategy is likely to continue to be effective as the United States continues to lose manufacturing jobs overseas and increasingly must turn to its educational and technological capacity to compete (see Chapter 12).

In addition to the regional changes and the competition among areas of the country, a more general aspect of change in the economy has been increasing productivity in the workforce. Compared to those of other industrialized countries, the American workforce is highly productive, and investments in a variety of technologies have been increasing that productivity. The decline in employment in manufacturing jobs results in part from these productivity gains, as the application of technology and better working practices makes fewer and fewer workers necessary to produce the same number of automobiles, or whatever. Thus, while the share of employment in manufacturing has dropped by over 8 percent since 1990, the share of gross domestic product coming from manufacturing has remained almost constant.

The Instruments of Economic Policy

Governments have a number of weapons at their disposal to try to influence the performance of their economies. Analysts often speak of a dichotomy between monetary policy and fiscal policy,[39] and these are certainly two of the more important policy options, although other options are available, including regulations and control, financial supports for business and agriculture, public ownership, incentives, and moral suasion. Most governments use a combination of all of these tools, although the government of the United States tends to rely most heavily on the indirect instruments of fiscal and monetary policy.

There is also a debate about whether the traditional tools of national economic management will continue to be viable, given the increasing globalization of economic life. The argument is that capital is now so mobile, and trade so important, that any attempt to influence the economy (especially through monetary policy) is doomed to failure.[40] Further, there are a number of international agreements and arrangements—the General Agreement on Tariffs and Trade (GATT), the World Trade Organization (WTO), and the North American Free Trade Agreement (NAFTA), for instance—that restrict the capacity of American government to make autonomous decisions about economic policy.[41] The United States has played a major role in negotiating these agreements, and in continuing policymaking within them, so that the organizations and their policies are not totally beyond the control of the American government.

Trade policy remains controversial politically, because the groups harmed directly by increased trade do not recognize some of the more general benefits being created for the United States economy.[42] In particular, organized labor has resisted the appeal of freer trade, preferring to attempt to preserve the jobs union workers already have to accepting the promise of more and better jobs through trade. Government has attempted to compensate with job-retraining programs, but that effort also is seen as posing possible benefits in the future against real costs now.[43] And labor is far from the only opposition to free trade and globalization, as is indicated by the unusual alliances of labor activists, environmentalists, anarchists, and a host of other groups that greet every major international meeting on trade.[44] Even the George W. Bush administration, which has advocated free trade in principle, has found protection measures useful in handling some particular trade issues.[45]

Fiscal Policy

We have discussed the importance of the budgetary process as a mechanism for allocating resources among government agencies and between the public and private sectors of the economy. These decisions are also central to the Keynesian approach to economic management, which stresses the importance of the public budget in regulating effective demand. Simply stated, if government wants to stimulate the economy (i.e., to increase economic growth and to reduce unemployment), it should run a budget deficit. Such a deficit places in circulation more money than the government has removed from circulation, thereby generating greater demand for goods and services by citizens who have more money to spend. This additional money, as it circulates through the economy, multiplies in magnitude to an extent that depends on the propensity of citizens to spend their additional income rather than save it. Likewise, if a government wants to reduce inflation in an "overheated" economy, it should run a budget surplus, removing more money from circulation in taxes than it puts back in through public expenditures. This budget surplus leaves citizens with less money than they had before the government's action and so should lessen total demand.

The theory of fiscal policy is rather straightforward, but the practice presents several important difficulties. Perhaps the most important is that deficits and surpluses are not politically neutral. It is a reasonable hypothesis that citizens like to receive benefits from government but do not like to pay taxes to finance those benefits. Consequently, despite the American political rhetoric lauding the balanced budget,[46] there were forty-seven budget deficits in forty-eight years from 1950 through 1997. Deficits occurred even during the 1950s and 1960s, when the economy performed very well. Politicians have practiced "one-eyed Keynesianism"—reading the passages Keynes wrote about running deficits but apparently not reading the passages about running surpluses in good times.[47] The tendency toward running deficits was accentuated during the Reagan administration, when the administration's belief in "supply-side" economics produced large tax cuts without commensurate reductions in expenditure (see pp. 209–211). Although Keynes has been disavowed by many (or even most) economic policymakers, his ideas are still considered when the budget is made, and the influence of deficits (and at least in theory, surpluses) must be considered.[48]

Also, as noted, estimating the amount of revenue to be received, or the outlays of public programs, is not simple. Even the best budget planning cannot adjust precisely the level of a deficit or surplus (see table 8.4), although the automatic stabilizers built into the revenue and expenditure programs of government help regulate the deficit. For example, when the economy begins to turn downward, government revenues decline as workers become unemployed and cease paying income and Social Security taxes; these unemployed workers and their families also begin to place demands on a variety of social programs. The decline in revenue and the increase in expenditures then automatically push the budget toward a deficit without political leaders making any conscious choices about fiscal policy. Of course, if the recession is very deep or continues for a very long time, government may have to act with new programs that will further increase the deficits.

To assist in making decisions about the right-size budget deficit or surplus to aim for, the "full-employment budget" has been suggested, and to some extent used, as a decision-making aid.[49] The idea is that the budget should be in balance during periods of full employment, defined as 5 percent unemployed. Naturally, during times of higher unemployment there would be a deficit, given the fundamental Keynesian paradigm. Therefore, a budget is calculated that would be in balance at full employment, and then the added costs of unemployment in social expenditures and lost revenues are added to determine the full-employment deficit. That deficit is deemed justifiable because it results not from the profligacy of governments but from economic difficulties. Any deficit higher than that is seen as a political decision to spend money that will not be raised as taxes and as expenditures giving advantages to incumbent politicians facing reelection. A deficit also may be accepted for ideological reasons, as was true of the extremely large deficits of the Reagan-Bush administrations that resulted primarily from tax cuts. Likewise, when it became apparent that the U.S. budget would begin to run a surplus in the late 1990s, there were calls from the Republican right to reduce taxes immediately, rather than wait to see just what the effects of this change would be.[50]

The tax cut adopted in the first months of George W. Bush's administration was Keynesian economics dressed up to some degree as conservatism. Although the benefits of the tax cut did go disproportionately to the more affluent, some benefits were offered to most taxpayers, putting some money in the hands of the people most likely to spend it. The tax cut was not justified in terms of this Keynesian logic and effects, however, but in terms of a desire to reduce the eco-

TABLE 8.4   Federal Deficit and Debt, 1965–2001 (in millions of dollars)

	Deficit	Debt
1965	−1,411	322,318
1970	−2,342	380,921
1975	−53,242	541,925
1980	−73,835	908,503
1985	−212,344	1,816,974
1990	−220,740	3,206,374
1995	−163,899	4,821,018
1997	−125,591	5,453,677
1998	+69,200	5,467,300
1999	+124,600	5,606,100
2000	+236,400	5,629,000
2001	+280,700	5,625,000

Source: U.S. Office of Management and Budget, *Historical Tables,* annual.

nomic power of government and to let citizens make their own decisions. The 2003 tax cut, however, was justified more as an economic stimulant.

Making fiscal policy. Most fiscal policy decisions are made through the budgetary process outlined in Chapter 6. When the president and his advisers establish the limits under which expenditure decisions of individual agencies must be made, they do so with a particular budget deficit or surplus in mind. Given the rhetoric and conventional wisdom of American politics, it appears that most presidents initiate the process with the intention of producing a balanced budget, but few if any have actually succeeded; President Clinton, toward the end of his administration, was a notable exception. They are overwhelmed by the complexity of the calculations and, perhaps irresistably, by political pressures to spend but not tax. A president's intentions may also be overwhelmed by reliance on economic policies that are meant to produce rapid economic growth but cannot do that job once they are implemented.[51]

Fiscal policy is primarily a presidential concern, and it is a central issue for most presidents. Only at the level of the entire budget can global decisions about economic management be made and be somewhat shielded from special interests demanding special expenditures or tax preferences. Within the executive branch, however, the president receives both advice and pressure—largely in the direction of spending more. The president can attempt to rise above special interests, but his cabinet secretaries almost certainly cannot, given the close connections of agencies and departments to the clienteles that they serve; the cabinet secretaries may press appeals made to them by special interests on to the president and his budget director.

Furthermore, the president cannot make expenditure and taxation decisions alone. The involvement of Congress in these decisions has been increasingly important since the mid-1970s, when the creation of the Congressional Budget Office, combined with the increasing vigor of the Joint Economic Committee and the Joint Budget Committee, greatly enhanced its capacity to compete with the president over fiscal policy decisions.[52] The negotiations between the George H.W. Bush administration and congressional leaders when coping with a budget crisis in 1990 indicated the extent to which budgetary decisions, and decisions about fiscal policy, have become joint decisions.[53]

Similarly, the negotiations between the Clinton administration and Congress over the FY 1994 budget pointed to the enhanced importance of Congress as an economic policymaker.[54] Beginning with the budget originally proposed by the outgoing Bush administration, the Clinton administration attempted to adapt that budget to conform to the economic proposals made by candidate Clinton during the 1992 campaign. In particular, there was to be some increase in taxes and other revenues ($36 billion net) and some reduction in expenditures (over $50 billion net) in an attempt (to some degree successful) to reduce the size of the federal budget deficit. This initial round of negotiations was followed by a more significant one in 1997 that laid the groundwork for a more extensive shift in budget priorities and eventually for a balanced budget in 1998.[55]

Despite the competition of Congress, the budget is labeled a presidential budget, and the economic success or failure it produces (or at least with which it is coincident) generally is laid at the president's doorstep politically.[56] As a consequence, even if the budget is not the dominant influence on economic performance it is sometimes made out to be, a president will want to have his ideas implemented through the budget so as at least to be judged politically on the effects of his own policies, rather than those of Congress.

Leadership in economic policy has become as much a part of the president's role as being commander-in-chief of the armed forces. Any president who attempts to avoid responsibility for the economy will find difficulty in doing so and may be perceived as a weak domestic leader. President George H.W. Bush, for example, attempted to blame Congress for the recession of the early 1990s, but the public held him mostly responsible instead, and the media's focus on these economic problems was a major factor in his loss of the 1992 election. Similarly, the success of the economy in the late 1990s helped maintain President Clinton's popularity with the public when he was beset by a number of other serious political problems. President George W. Bush was able to overcome the economic downturn in the economy during the first year of his administration because of the tendency of the public to stand behind a president in times of national crisis, but otherwise he might have been in serious political difficulty. Presidents do receive some credit (or blame) for other types of policies, but it is still fiscal policy that most citizens regard as the source of economic fluctuations.

Supply-side economics. With the election of President Reagan in 1980 there came something of a revolution in fiscal policy in the United States, usually referred to as "supply-side economics."[57] Basically, this approach argued that, instead of inadequate demand in the American economy (the standard Keynesian critique), there was a dearth of supply, especially a dearth of investment. The fundamental idea of supply-side economics was to increase the supply of both labor and capital so that economic growth would take place. Further, this approach argued that government intervention, especially through high taxes, was the major barrier to full participation of labor and capital in the marketplace, and therefore any measures to reduce that role would in the (not very) long run produce rapid economic growth.

Some of the analysis supporting the supply-side policies had a great deal of face validity. In particular, the United States economy has had a dearth of savings and investment when compared with the economies of other industrialized countries (see table 8.5, p. 210). Savings are the capital from which business can borrow for new factories and equipment, but Americans choose to spend, and to borrow to spend more, rather than to save and invest.[58] This has been a real problem in the economy, although the recent record of tax cuts is that the public simply uses tax savings to spend more. This experience illustrates the point that many tools of economic policy depend on the behavior of the public to be effective, and this supply-side theory does not appear to have had much cooperation from the public. Capital accumulation in the American economy grew somewhat during the late 1990s, as the soaring level of the stock market attracted more and more small investors, but was still lower than in most other industrialized countries.[59]

The major instrument for implementing supply-side economics was the Economic Recovery Tax Act of 1981 (ERTA) which, over four years, reduced the average income tax of Americans by 23 percent. The tax reductions advantaged those in higher income brackets, presumably those most likely to invest any additional after-tax income. The fundamental assumption of ERTA was that if individuals had increased incentives to work and invest they would do so, and economic growth would result. Whereas Keynesian economics argued for providing people (usually the less affluent) with increased income through government expenditures, with the expectation that they would spend the money and create demand for goods and services, the supply-side solution, in contrast, argued for providing the more affluent with greater incentives to work and invest because they could retain more of what they earned.

The Economic Recovery Tax Act produced a massive increase in the federal

TABLE 8.5 Changes in Gross Capital Formation, 1980–2000

	1980	1988	1993	1996	1997	1998	1999	2000
United States	17.3	15.7	14.1	15.5	15.9	16.8	17.1	17.4
Australia	25.2	25.6	21.5	22.3	22.9	23.7	23.5	22.5
Canada	23.3	21.9	17.8	17.1	18.9	19.3	19.9	19.8
France	23.8	21.9	19.3	18.5	17.0	18.4	18.5	n.a.
Germany	22.6	19.6	23.0	21.7	21.4	21.1	20.5	n.a.
Japan	31.7	30.0	29.2	28.5	28.1	26.9	26.2	26.0
Sweden	20.1	20.2	14.2	15.7	14.9	15.8	16.6	17.1
United Kingdom	18.7	20.5	15.7	16.5	16.7	17.3	17.5	17.6

Source: International Monetary Fund, *International Financial Statistics,* monthly.

deficit (see table 8.4). Taxes were reduced significantly but, despite efforts by some members of the administration, federal expenditures were not reduced nearly as much. The fiscally conservative administration did not worry, however, because it believed that lower taxes would so stimulate economic growth that, over time, more revenue would come from lower tax rates; this sharp response of government revenues to tax reductions is referred to as the "Laffer curve," after economist Arthur Laffer.[60] Even after it became clear that the optimistic Laffer curve did not work, however, the Reagan administration did not raise taxes, and low taxation became a central feature of its (and the succeeding Bush administration's) economic policies and political appeals.

The deficit problem came to a head during the construction of the FY 1991 federal budget. The deficit projected for that year was a great deal more than that permissible under the Gramm-Rudman-Hollings rules (see Chapter 6), but neither President George H. W. Bush nor Congress wanted to take responsibility for raising taxes or reducing popular benefits. In response, congressional Democrats offered a very redistributive plan for increasing taxes that neither the president nor even some conservatives in their own ranks could accept. Bush was especially reluctant to increase taxes after having made a campaign pledge of "No New Taxes," but in the end he did have to propose some increased taxation. After several continuing resolutions to keep government operating without a formal budget and one failed budget bill, a compromise was finally reached in mid-October 1990. This compromise called for increasing some taxes (largely excise taxes on tobacco, alcohol, and gasoline) and reducing a few spending programs, but nothing that would have eliminated the deficit, or even reduced it significantly. Further, the deficit figure under discussion was actually a low estimate of the true federal deficit, for it excluded, for example, the costs of "bailing out" failed savings-and-loan institutions insured by the federal government and several other "off budget" expenditure programs.[61]

At the beginning of the twenty-first century, budget deficits appeared to be, at least in the short run, a thing of the past, and the end of large deficits was expected to have a number of potentially positive economic consequences. One was that less foreign capital would be required to fund the debt, and that the United States might lose its status as the world's largest debtor nation. Further, it was anticipated that lower federal borrowing would help to stabilize domestic interest rates. Finally, because government debt, like private debt, must be repaid (or, at a minimum, debt interest must be paid), the prospect of paying less debt interest (both because of a lower debt to GDP and lower interest rates) seemed likely to free some money for new programs. The largest continuing impact of the Reagan administration had been that debt interest had kept government from spending money on new social programs for years, but in 2000 it appeared that there might soon be financial latitude to make new initiatives.

That optimism waned significantly during 2001 and 2002. Terrorists attacks, corporate scandals, and a general slowdown in the economy combined with a tax cut and increased spending on defense and a few domestic programs to drive the budget into major deficits for fiscal 2003. All but the most optimistic analysts then projected that such deficits would continue for the foreseeable future, barring significant changes in the economy or in fiscal policies.

Monetary Policy

Whereas the basic fiscal policy paradigm stresses the importance of demand management through varying levels of revenues and expenditures, the monetary solution to economic management stresses the importance of the money supply in controlling economic fluctuations. Like additional public expenditures, increasing the amount of money in circulation is presumed to stimulate the economy. Extra money lowers interest rates, making it easier for citizens to borrow for investments or for purchases, and this in turn encourages economic activity. Likewise, reducing the availability of money makes it more difficult to borrow and to spend, thus slowing an inflationary economy.

In the United States, the Federal Reserve Board and its member Federal Reserve banks are primarily responsible for monetary policy. The Federal Reserve Board and the banks are intentionally independent from the executive authority of the president and, because their budget is only appended to the federal budget, it is also largely independent from congressional control through the budgetary process.[62] The Federal Reserve is independent, so its members exercise their judgment as bankers rather than submitting to control by political officials who want to manipulate the money supply for political gain. The Federal Reserve has exercised its independence and has refused several times to accede to presidential requests. For example, during the Johnson administration, Federal

Reserve Chairman William McC. Martin turned down the president's request to increase the money supply more rapidly to ease financial pressures created by the simultaneous expansion of domestic social programs and the Vietnam War. More recently, the Federal Reserve Board would not cooperate with the first Bush administration in its efforts to fund continuing deficits with minimal tax increases, nor with President Clinton in his efforts to keep the economic recovery moving as rapidly as possible during 1994.

The Federal Reserve has a variety of monetary tools at its disposal to influence the economy. Its three principal tools are open-market operations, the discount rate and federal funds rate, and reserve requirements. *Open-market operations* are the most commonly used mechanisms of monetary policy. These involve the Federal Reserve entering the money markets to buy or sell securities issued by the federal government. If it wishes to reduce the supply of money, the Federal Reserve attempts to sell securities, exchanging the bonds for cash that was in circulation. If it wants to expand the money supply, "the Fed" purchases securities on the market, exchanging money for the bonds. The success or failure of these operations depends, of course, on the willingness of citizens to buy and sell the securities at the time and at the interest rate the Federal Reserve thinks appropriate.

A more drastic option available to the Federal Reserve is to change the *discount rate* and the *federal funds rate*. These are the rates of interest at which member banks can borrow money from the Federal Reserve bank or from each other to cover shortages in the reserve requirement. Obviously, these rates affect interest rates in the economy as a whole, as member banks have to increase the interest rates they charge their customers to compensate if there is an increased cost of borrowing money from the Federal Reserve. And with the basic monetary paradigm, making money more difficult (or at least more costly) to borrow will slow down economic activity and, presumably, inflation. In some instances the Fed does not even have to change the discount rate; all its chairman has to do is to mention the possibility of a change, and the economy may react.[63]

The discount rate changes relatively infrequently and then only by a very small amount. For example, the rate had not changed for months prior to December 1990 when the Federal Reserve reduced the rate slightly to attempt to minimize an apparent recession. As that recession continued well into 1991, the Federal Reserve continued to make downward adjustments in the discount rate to attempt to stimulate investment and growth, and the rate reached its lowest level for over a decade. The discount rate had been very stable, and low, from early 1997 until 2001. Federal Reserve Chairman Alan Greenspan from time to time warned about the dangers of inflation and excessive demand, but in practice the rate was kept constant. As the economy began to slow during the first years of the George W. Bush administration, the discount rate was cut again and again, reaching one of the lowest levels on record in mid-2002.

Alan Greenspan (center right), chair of the Federal Reserve, chats with (from left to right) German Finance Minister Hans Eichel, International Monetary Fund Managing Director Horst Kohler, and U.S. Secretary of the Treasury John Snow during an IMF–World Bank meeting in Dubai on 20 September 2003. Although the world's richest and, arguably, its most politically powerful nation, the United States cannot isolate itself from international economic issues.

Finally, the Federal Reserve Board can change the *reserve requirement*. Member banks of the Federal Reserve system are required to keep reserves on deposit at the Federal Reserve banks to cover their outstanding loans. This is a percentage of the total amount they have out in loans, normally around 10 percent, that banks must retain on deposit. If the Federal Reserve raises the reserve requirement from 10 to 12.5 percent, then for each dollar a bank had out in loans before the change, it can lend only 75 cents. The bank will have to deposit more money, call in some loans, or reduce the pace at which it grants new loans. Any of these measures will reduce substantially the amount of money in circulation and should slow down economic activity. Conversely, reducing the reserve requirement makes more money available for loans and should increase economic activity. Changing the reserve requirement is a drastic action and is undertaken only if there is a perceived need to influence the economy dramatically and quickly.

The Federal Reserve has been a paragon of conservative economic policy. Its members traditionally have been bankers or businessmen who have tried to please a constituency of similar composition. The Federal Reserve's tight money policies have been criticized frequently for producing economic hardship and slow growth, as when it raised interest rates during the early days of economic recovery in 1993. On the other hand, Federal Reserve action has also been defended as appropriate, given threats of inflation fueled in part by fiscal policy. What is most important, however, is the possibility that a lack of coordination of fiscal and monetary policy will cause the two to cancel each other's effects and produce little or no effect, or the possibility that their coordination may produce an excessive amount of correction to the economy so that changes constantly overshoot the mark and economic fluctuations are exaggerated rather than minimized.

Regulations and Control

In general, regulation has been used not for the purpose of general economic management but for the sake of achieving other economic and social goals. Regulations have been associated with cleaning up the environment, making workplaces safer, or making consumer products safer. Obviously such regulations also have an effect on overall economic growth, because they make it more or less profitable to engage in certain activities. In addition, some regulatory activities, such as antitrust regulation, do have a pervasive impact on the economic structure of the society and perhaps on consumer prices for a range of goods.

Antitrust regulation has been one of the most important forms of government control of the economy.[64] Beginning with the Sherman Act in 1890, the federal government has sought to ensure that a few firms did not control an industry and then extract excessive profits.[65] The criminal nature of the sanctions in the Sherman Act, and the vagueness of its definitions of illegal actions, made enforcement difficult, however, and the Clayton Act was passed in 1914 at the same time that the Federal Trade Commission was created. This legislation gave clearer (although still far from unambiguous) definitions of actions that constituted "combinations in restraint" of trade and provided an enforcement mechanism that could act administratively rather than entirely through the courts.[66]

Antitrust regulation as a mechanism for fostering competition has been a significant tool in American economic policy, but it is possible that it has outlived its utility. A major economic policy concern since the 1990s has been for external *competitiveness*, rather than for internal *competition*. It may be that to be competitive with many foreign firms American firms will have to be larger and have a larger market share. Further, there may be a need for greater protection of patent rights and intellectual property rights, which, in turn, may create natural monopolies in certain areas. Consumers and nascent firms still need protection from the economic power of big business, but antitrust may not be the best tool in the current global economy.

Antitrust prosecution of Microsoft in 1998 brought some of the issues around antitrust policy into sharper focus.[67] An extremely successful company in international as well as domestic markets, Microsoft had been able to create a virtual monopoly in some areas of software. Should the firm be punished for being successful, and for making technological advances that put it in a dominant position? Would the software market be better served by more competition and more options for the consumer, even if there were to be some problems of compatibility? There were cogent arguments on both sides of this debate, and such issues may be more common in the future as technological changes and patents for them become more crucial for economic success. In the end, Microsoft escaped with little direct punishment for what were seen as anticompetitive actions, although the company was forced to alter future practices to enhance market entry by smaller firms.

The United States has had limited experience with wage and price controls like those that have been used in Europe, but the minimum wage has been a source of political contention in recent years. The minimum wage was first adopted during the New Deal as a means of ensuring that workers would have something like a living wage even in hard economic times. While the wage adopted at the time may have been a living wage, the need for Congress to act to increase that wage has meant that its real value has tended to fluctuate over time (see table 8.6). Businesses, especially small businesses, naturally do not want to have to pay higher wages, and they go to Congress to argue that a higher minimum wage would either put them out of business or force them to get rid of workers—neither of which is an option that congressmen like to entertain.[68]

Congress voted to increase the minimum wage *twice* in the 1990s, but even after these increases, the rate remains lower in real terms than it was in the 1950s. Nevertheless, conservatives continue to argue that it is a deterrent to hiring, especially hiring relatively inexperienced younger people. When the economy was booming in the 1990s, the minimum wage was less of an issue than it might have been in other times, and in many cities the demand for labor meant that most jobs—even the "hamburger flipping" jobs—paid above minimum wage. A slowdown in activity, however, has meant greater concern about the impact of this form of economic regulation, and a political movement for a "living wage" has also been gathering momentum.

The question of economic regulation through control of wages is especially relevant for the implementation of the "flexible labor market" that has been argued to be a major source of the Clinton administration's economic success.[69] The ability of workers to move quickly and easily to follow demand and the flexibility of wage rates to adjust to a "market clearing level" were crucial for high levels of employment and secondarily for high levels of growth. In the eyes of many Europeans, the relative insecurity of the American labor market and the

TABLE 8.6   The Value of the Minimum Wage

	Nominal value	Real value (in 2002 dollars)
1970	1.60	7.74
1974	1.60	5.91
1978	2.65	7.31
1980	3.10	6.86
1982	3.35	6.63
1986	3.35	5.93
1990	3.35	4.61
1994	4.25	5.41
1998	5.15	5.63
2000	5.15	5.39
2002	5.15	5.15

absence of an effective social safety net make working conditions in the United States very harsh, but the system has been more effective in generating jobs than the more regulated labor market structures found in Europe.

By the summer of 2002 many Americans were searching for a more regulated economy.[70] Revelations of malpractice at Enron, Worldcom, and Xerox, among other firms, indicated that businesses in the United States were, with the complicity of accounting firms, engaging in rather systematic deception both of their own investors and of the federal regulatory authorities. In particular, the Securities and Exchange Commission (established during the New Deal to regulate the integrity of the stock market) was proving to be ineffective in monitoring the activities of big businesses and the financial statements they were providing publicly.

Public Support for Business

In addition to regulating the conduct of business and providing support through tax incentives, governments provide a number of more direct subsidies to industry. In the United States the federal government has a share of the action in providing such subsidies, but a great deal of support also comes from state and even local governments. The majority of the direct expenditures benefiting business and industry are provided for research and development and for the subsidization of credit. Other forms of support for industry include promotion of inland water transportation by allowing use of locks and dams on rivers at well-below-market prices, services such as free weather reports and other economic information, and a variety of grants and loans for small business. Federal credit facilities are available for a host of business projects, including the facilitation of international trade through the Export-Import Bank and a variety of supports for agriculture and housing. Taken together, the federal government in 1997 sup-plied over $75 billion of direct and indirect support for business and industry.[71]

State and local governments tend to provide supports for business and in-dustry in a competitive environment. Just as they compete with one another with tax incentives in order to attract industries to their localities, so too can state governments use direct services and credits to attract industry[72]—in fact, there is some evidence that government services are more important than tax breaks in this effort. The services of state and local governments need not be ex-traordinary; they may need only do things that they usually do, such as supply-ing transportation, water, sewers, and similar services, and do them well. Of course, some expenditures of subnational governments are more extraordinary, possibly including the building of plants or more elaborate forms of infrastruc-ture for industries that agree to situate themselves in the locality.

All these supports for business must be examined in the context of a con-tinuing "industrial policy debate" in the United States. As the United States was falling behind Japan, West Germany, and even smaller countries like South Korea and Taiwan during the 1980s and thereafter in the production of basic commodities such as steel and finished products such as automobiles, the ques-tion "What is wrong with American industry?" became a central policy issue.[73] Numerous answers to that question have been offered, including inept manage-ment, avaricious unions, and meddlesome government. Another possibility is that government does not do enough to support American industry, and what it does is poorly organized—the implication being that a more comprehensive approach to the problems of American industry and its competitiveness in the international marketplace should be adopted. Such a program might include some or all of the following elements:

1. *Direct government grants for the modernization and expansion of industry.* Despite major improvements, some of the machinery of American heavy indus-try is outdated in comparison with that of our competitors. Government could help by supplying grants, loans, or both. There is some assistance through the tax system, but little or no direct aid.

2. *Trade policy.* American government has followed free-trade policies dur-ing most of the postwar period, using tariffs and other restrictions on imports infrequently; it could instead impose tariffs and other trade barriers to help American industry "get back on its feet." There are voluntary arrangements with Japan over the import of automobiles, but some advocate broader use of these powers. The United States continues to debate with the European Union over a number of trade issues, for example tariffs on steel imported from the European Union, although there are about as many European as American complaints about unfair competition and trade policies. Even the free-trade agreement with

neighboring Canada and Mexico is believed by some citizens, and some politicians, potentially to undermine the American economy.[74]

The increasing importance of international trade for the American economy makes trade policy all the more important. As noted earlier, the United States continues to run massive trade deficits. Indeed, the relative prosperity of the late 1990s tended to exacerbate the trade deficit, as Americans found they had more money to spend and chose to spend it on foreign-made products, trips to Europe, and the like.

3. *Deregulation.* Some sections of the business community argue that the numerous safety and environmental regulations of the federal government make it difficult for American industry to produce products at a price that is competitive on the world market. In particular, businessmen and unions alike are concerned with the number of jobs being lost to low-wage and low-regulation countries such as Indonesia, Mexico, and Brazil. They believe that deregulation would improve the competitiveness of business; even after ten years of Reagan and the first President Bush, American industry was more heavily regulated than in many competitor countries,[75] and despite the continuing efforts of the Republican Congress (and to some extent the Clinton administration) it remains heavily regulated. In addition, the United States tends to pursue regulatory policies such as antitrust laws with somewhat greater vigor than is true for most of the rest of the world, also potentially inhibiting competitiveness of American industry in world markets.

4. *Research and development.* American industry has a tradition of being among the most advanced technologically in the world. Unfortunately, this has become more of a tradition than a reality; except for a few industries, such as computers, American industry appears to be falling behind many countries. Government could make a major contribution to American industry by making more funds available for research.

5. *Regional policy.* The effects of declining industry have not been spread evenly over the United States but have been concentrated in the older industrial regions, especially in the Great Lakes area. Thus, as well as dealing with the direct problems of industry, there is a need to address some of the human problems created by a changing industrial base in many states and localities. In turn, these efforts may make those localities more attractive to industries considering relocation. More recently, the decline in defense industries has made Southern California one of the more economically depressed areas of the American economy.

Government has been involved in supporting industry for most of the history of the United States. Many of the great industrial ventures in this country, including the westward extension of the railroad, were undertaken with the direct or indirect support of government.[76] There may now be even greater need for government support for business and industry than in the past, given the declining industrial position of the United States. However, too much dependence on government to "bail out losers"—most recently the airline industry—may mean that American industry ceases to be responsible for its own revitalization and will simply wait for the public sector to rescue it. That "bail out" may come through direct subsidies or through protectionist trade policy.[77] Use of the trade policy avenue for adjusting the economy is, however, increasingly constrained by international agreements such as NAFTA and membership in the World Trade Organization.[78]

Public Ownership

Although it is not common in the United States, public ownership of certain kinds of industries may be important for economic management, especially influencing the location of certain industries. Even in the United States a number of public and quasi-public corporations are involved in the economy. In 1976 there were twenty wholly publicly owned and seven partly owned corporations in the federal government, and the general movement toward managerialism and privatization in government has led to an increased use of corporate forms of organization, even when the mode of organization appears inappropriate (the National Service Corporation, for example). Some of these industries have been privatized, but government remains more of an entrepreneur than most citizens realize.

At the state and local levels, numerous public enterprises are organized to carry out economic as well as some social policy functions. These enterprises range from publicly owned utilities, such as electricity, gas, and transportation, to functions usually associated with the private sector, such as insurance and banking. Although public enterprises ideologically are anathema in the United States, in practice this form of organization is actually increasingly popular as a means of providing service while at the same time attempting to be as efficient and business-like as possible.

These public corporations perform a variety of functions for government. One is to provide revenue—for example, local government utilities can buy electricity at commercial rates and then distribute it at rates that yield a profit. Also, public corporations can be utilized to regulate prices and certain essential services. Although many publicly owned transportation corporations run with a deficit, they maintain relatively low costs and provide greater service than could be given by a private firm, and local government considers those objectives important. At the federal level, corporate structures have been used for regional development in the Tennessee Valley Authority, a largely successful attempt to transform the economy of a backward region through public action and public ownership of electrical power production. Also, federal corporations have been active in promoting U.S. foreign trade, through the Export-Import Bank and the Overseas Private Investment Corporation (related to the goals of having a positive balance of payments), and in providing transportation to promote economic growth, through the St. Lawrence Seaway and Amtrak.

One interesting variation on public ownership is the use of loan guarantees and insurance to attempt to assure continuing employment and economic growth. One notable example of this policy option was the Loan Guarantee Board, which was charged with developing financing to keep the Chrysler Corporation in business and its workers in jobs. The federal government did not buy one share of Chrysler stock but used its economic powers to keep the company alive. Also, the federal government spent billions of dollars to make good on its insurance commitments to account owners of failing savings and loans and banks in the early 1990s. These activities helped to preserve employment, enabled one corporation to reverse its economic fortunes, and protected the savings of millions of citizens, while helping to preserve confidence in the financial institutions of the country. It might be argued that public involvement in moribund corporations is disguised social policy and may actually slow economic growth. At least for the short term, however, it represents an important economic policy instrument.

Incentives

Governments can also attempt to influence economic change by providing incentives for desired behaviors. Most such incentives are made available through the tax system and are directed primarily at encouraging investment and economic change. The tax reforms of the 1980s eliminated many of these incentives, but they still constitute a powerful economic weapon for government. We have already mentioned the role that state government tax incentives play in encouraging structural change in individual state economies, with some contribution to economic development in the country as a whole. The federal government also provides special incentives for selected industries and general incentives for businesses to invest, especially in research and development.

The major incentives for structural change in the U.S. economy have been the oil depletion allowance and similar allowances for other nonrenewable natural resources, which permit investors to write off against profits a portion of the investments they have made in searching for new supplies of a resource such as oil. The decontrol of "new oil" under President Carter's energy program was another means of encouraging exploration for domestic energy supplies. A variety of provisions of the federal tax code also serve to encourage investment in general by both corporations and individuals. The capital gains provisions of the tax laws permit profits made on investments held for over one year to be taxed at half the individual's normal tax rate, and in no case at higher than 25 percent.

Industries are also given extensive tax credits for new investments and allowed higher-than-average depreciation on investments during the first year. All these policies make it easier and more profitable for industries to invest and for economic growth to follow that investment, but none mandates that the industry make the investments. The administrative costs of incentive programs are comparatively small when subsidy programs are considered as the alternative, and those programs also are perceived as less intrusive into the market economy than the possible alternatives. But the dollar an industry saves from taxes is worth exactly the same as the dollar granted as a subsidy, and perhaps even more, since there are fewer strings and restrictions attached to the dollar saved from taxes.

Moral Suasion

When all else fails, or perhaps before anything else is tried, governments can attempt to influence citizens and industries by persuasion. Persuasion works best in times of national emergency, but economic circumstances may be sufficiently dire to create the perception of an emergency.[79] Presidents, using their power as spokesmen for the nation, are central to the use of persuasion to control economic behavior, and they can employ a variety of symbols to influence citizens. Attempting to speak for the nation as president and appealing to patriotism to get what he wanted, Lyndon Johnson exerted the power of the office when he "jawboned" industries to encourage them to restrain price increases. Ronald Reagan used his gifts as the "Great Communicator" to persuade citizens to accept his economic and tax policies. Even George H.W. Bush's purchase of a pair of socks in a shopping mall could be seen as an attempt, largely unsuccessful, to manipulate symbols to urge Americans to start buying again and lift the country out of a recession.

The effects of persuasion depend on the nature of the policy problem being addressed and on the character of the political leader attempting to employ the persuasion. Industrialists are unlikely to continue to provide jobs for workers in an unprofitable factory simply because they are asked to, but citizens may well try to "buy American" in order to improve the balance of payments. Political leaders who are trusted and respected will find it relatively easy to influence their fellow citizens, whereas those who are less popular may find more direct mechanisms for economic management more effective. Also, some economic problems—such as a budget deficit—may simply be too big to be attacked with words alone.

Summary

The management of the economy is a central concern of government. It is the area of policymaking on which governments are most frequently evaluated by their citizens. This is true not only because of the direct importance of the issues for citizens but also because of the frequent reporting of standard indicators such as the inflation rate and the level of unemployment. Even if an individual has a job and an income that keeps pace with the cost of living, he or she may believe the president is not doing a good job because of the aggregate numbers that regularly appear in the newspapers. The extent to which the performance of the economy is now laid at the feet of government, especially the president, is in marked contrast to the era before the depression, when the economy was not believed to be controllable by government. The president clearly plays a crucial role in economic management, because of his role as spokesman for government, because of the importance of the presidential budget in controlling the economy, and because of his influence on other areas of economic policy such as taxation.

It is important to understand, however, that the condition of the economy is not solely a presidential responsibility. Congress is involved with the president in determining the budget, which is the central instrument of presidential intervention in the economy. The actions of the Federal Reserve Board are almost totally beyond the control of the president. Furthermore, the federal structure of the United States is such that state and local governments' taxing and spending decisions have a significant impact not only on the overall stimulative or depressive effects of public expenditures but also on the attempts to move industries and labor geographically. Also, the success of national economic policies is increasingly dependent on decisions made by other nations, by international organizations such as the International Monetary Fund, and by global markets.

Finally, we citizens have a substantial impact on the state of the economy. Many presidential decisions on fiscal policy, as well as many Federal Reserve decisions about monetary policy, depend on citizens responding in the predicted fashion. Even major aggregates such as economic growth depend to a great extent on the perceptions and behaviors of citizens—citizen confidence is as good an economic indicator as many more objective indicators. If citizens and businesses believe that prosperity is coming, they will be willing to invest and thus may make their belief a self-fulfilling prophecy. Government can do everything in its power to try to influence the behavior of citizens, but ultimately most decisions are beyond its control. Nevertheless, the success of an economic policy is a major factor in determining whether citizens believe that government is doing a good job.

CHAPTER 9

Tax Policy

TAX POLICY IS a major component of economic policy, but it deserves some discussion in its own right. Here we are especially concerned with the choice of revenue instruments used to collect the money needed by government to pay for its programs. In addition to the basic decisions about raising adequate revenues to meet expenditure demands, taxes are used to address a number of other policy purposes. Raising the same amount of tax revenues by different means may have very different economic and political effects, and those effects should be understood when discussing tax policies.[1] For example, raising money by means of an income tax is more favorable to the poor than is raising that same amount of money through a sales tax. Also, raising money by different means may be more or less difficult administratively, so that governments may choose ease (and certainty) of collection rather than other values—equity or impacts on economic growth—when selecting their tax policies.

Table 9.1 (p. 224) shows the tax profile of the United States in comparison with those of other major Western countries, detailing the proportion of total tax revenue in each country derived from a number of possible revenue sources. The United States stands apart from its major trading partners in several ways. First, there is substantially less reliance on taxes on goods and services in the United States than in the other countries. Although most states and many localities collect sales and excise taxes, there is no national sales tax comparable to the value-added tax (VAT) used in almost all European countries.[2] Fiscal pressures, especially on the Social Security system (see Chapter 11), may one day make such a tax necessary, but it has been delayed longer in this country than elsewhere.

Second, the United States derives substantially more of its total tax revenue from property taxes than most other countries do. Property taxes are collected by state and local governments, and they are the principal revenue source for most local governments (see table 9.2, p. 225). This pattern appears to reflect an Anglo-Saxon tradition in revenue collection, for the United Kingdom, Canada,

TABLE 9.1 Kinds of Tax Revenues, 1998 (as percentage of total)

	Personal income tax	Corporate income tax	Employees' social security	Employers' social security	General consumption tax	Selective commodity taxes	Property tax	Customs	Other
Australia	43.3	15.2	0.0	0.0	8.5	12.5	9.5	2.1	8.9
Belgium	30.7	8.5	9.7	19.2	15.3	7.5	3.2	0.1	5.6
Canada	37.8	10.0	5.3	8.1	14.1	9.1	10.4	0.7	0.5
Denmark	51.6	5.6	2.4	0.7	19.6	12.1	3.6	0.1	5.0
France	17.4	6.0	8.7	25.2	17.5	8.4	7.3	0.1	10.7
Germany	25.0	4.4	17.9	19.9	17.9	8.4	2.4	0.1	1.2
Italy	25.0	7.0	6.3	20.5	14.2	10.2	5.8	0.1	10.9
Japan	18.8	13.3	15.0	19.6	8.9	7.7	10.5	0.7	5.5
Sweden	35.0	5.7	5.8	22.5	13.6	7.3	3.7	0.2	7.2
Switzerland	31.8	6.0	11.4	10.8	10.0	7.0	8.3	0.6	14.1
United Kingdom	27.5	10.4	7.3	9.4	18.1	12.8	10.7	0.1	4.2
United States	40.5	9.0	10.2	12.2	7.6	6.5	10.6	0.7	2.7

Source: Organization for Economic Cooperation and Development, *Revenue Statistics of OECD Member Countries, 1965–98* (Paris: OECD, 2000).

TABLE 9.2   Property Tax Revenue of Local Government, 1960–2000 (in millions of dollars)

	Current	Real	Percentage of total revenues
1960	15,798	17,851	47.8
1970	32,963	28,367	40.7
1980	65,607	26,594	28.2
1985	99,772	32,825	28.2
1990	149,765	38,116	26.9
1995	203,500	40,111	23.9
1998	229,200	39,875	23.2
1999	238,500	40,004	22.1
2000	248,500	41,653	21.7

Source: Statistical Abstract of the United States, annual.

and New Zealand all use the property tax more heavily than do most other industrialized countries.[3] In the late 1980s Britain dropped the local property tax in favor of a per capita "poll tax," but public opposition rather quickly forced a reversal of that policy innovation by the Thatcher government.[4] The local property tax is especially important as a source of funding for education (see Chapter 12), and tends to be the tax that local governments rely on more than any other for their fiscal independence.

Third, there is a relatively high reliance on corporate taxes in the United States. Given the characterization of American politics as dominated by special interests (especially business interests), high levels of corporate taxation may require further explanation.[5] Corporations rarely bear the full burden of corporate taxation; instead, the real tax burden falls on consumers of the firms' products (higher prices), on the companies' workers (lower wages), or on stockholders (lower dividends). Under many economic circumstances—such as the extremely high level of corporation taxation in Japan—firms can add taxes on to the price of their products as a cost of doing business. A more political explanation for this practice involves the tradition of populism in many states in the United States that place a relatively heavier burden of taxation on corporations than on individuals, and even the most conservative politicians on the national level must remember that corporations do not vote but individual taxpayers do.[6]

One thing that table 9.1 cannot demonstrate easily is the complexity of the tax system in the United States. Some of this complexity is a function of federalism and the numerous different tax systems existing at the state and local levels (see table 9.3, p. 226), but there are also a number of different taxes at the federal level. Further, as the tax system has evolved, even greater complexity has resulted from the numerous deductions, exemptions, and other special treatments ("tax expenditures" or "loopholes") that have been written into the tax laws (see table 9.4).[7]

TABLE 9.3   Taxes and Federalism, 2000 (in billions of dollars)

			Tax Type		
	Income	Sales	Excises	Social insurance	Property
Federal	1,211.8	0	66.9	652.9	0
State	203.4	164.4	29.2	238.9	11.7
Local	19.7	36.2	15.4	35.1	228.4

Source: Statistical Abstract of the United States, 2001.

The tax reforms of the 1980s closed some of the more egregious loopholes in the tax system, but a number still remain. While many of the remaining exclusions have good economic and social justifications (e.g., the deductibility of mortgage interest stimulates home ownership as well as the construction industry), some loopholes (capital gains or oil depletion allowances) appear to benefit primarily the wealthy and the well organized. Further, in almost every revenue bill since the major reform in 1986 some new special tax treatments have appeared, returning the tax system to the same "Christmas tree" it had been prior to reform.[8] One exception was legislation passed in 1996 that requires Congress to identify "limited tax benefits," that is, tax breaks that go only to a relatively few individuals or firms.[9] This requirement makes the creation of these special benefits more public, in contrast to the closed and expert nature of tax policy that has been crucial for its ability to confer benefits with a minimum of public awareness or discussion.

The magnitude of the impact of tax expenditures can be seen from the data in table 9.4, comparing the size of tax expenditures with federal spending for the

TABLE 9.4   Federal Spending vs. Tax Expenditures for Same Program Areas, 2002 (in billions of dollars)

	Federal spending	Tax expenditures
National defense	2,053.3	2.2
Social policy	769.4	175.6
Health	195.2	115.9
Education	71.7	6.8
Housing	32.1	134.3

Source: Budget of the United States Government, Fiscal 2003.
Note: The Office of Management of Budget discourages adding tax expenditure figures because of different assumptions underlying the different policy areas, and therefore these numbers are only suggestive.

TABLE 9.5   Distribution of Tax Expenditures by Income Level, 2001 (in percentages)

	<$10,000	$10,000– 30,000	$30,000– 50,000	$50,000– 100,000	>$100,000
Medical care	0.02	10.6	21.7	40.8	26.7
Mortgage interest	0.1	0.7	5.2	33.1	59.9
Real estate tax	0.01	0.8	4.9	29.6	64.6
Earned Income Tax Credit	18.4	68.2	6.1	7.3	0.0
Charitable contributions	0.01	1.3	5.2	24.4	68.9
Child care	1.1	15.6	18.4	34.5	30.4
Excludability of Social Security	0.1	19.1	39.7	37.4	2.7

Source: Joint Committee on Taxation, *Estimates of Federal Tax Expenditures for Fiscal Years 2002–2006* (Washington, D.C.: Government Printing Office, January 2002).

same objective. In at least one policy area (housing), the financial impact of tax expenditures is substantially greater than federal spending in the sphere, while direct expenditures are larger for most policies. However, even in two of the federal government's largest expenditure programs—Social Security and health care—tax expenditures amount to at least one-third of expenditures. Thus there is, as Christopher Howard has argued, a substantial "hidden welfare state" in the United States.[10]

As well as constituting a hidden welfare state, the prevailing structure of tax expenditures also tends to create a welfare state for the middle class. As shown in table 9.5, with the exception of the excludability of Social Security income and the Earned Income Tax Credit, the majority of the benefits of tax expenditures accrue to people earning over $50,000 per annum, and for some provisions of the tax code, the principal beneficiaries earn over $100,000. If the benefits that go to business are added to these personal benefits for the affluent, it can be argued that the tax system produces substantial negative redistribution. The apparent (and real) unfairness of many aspects of the tax system has helped to spawn tax reform in the past, but a number of apparent inequities remain and even more have been created.

Public Opinion and Taxation

Paying their taxes is not the favorite public policy activity of the American public, who would much prefer to consume the benefits produced by those taxes. At the same time, although they are not keen to pay taxes, Americans are not unrealistic, and most appear to realize that they do have to pay a good deal of their income in taxes. The major questions that arise in taxpayers' minds are whether the tax system is fair and whether they are getting "value for money" for what they pay to government. Further, Americans appear to want to have some control over how tax money is spent, and they prefer taxes that are linked to specific types of expenditures—usually called earmarked taxes—to taxes that go into the general fund.

Fairness

The public tends to have two concerns when thinking about the fairness of the tax system. One is the basic premise that everybody who benefits from government should pay at least something in taxes. Several surveys about taxes have found that the public appears to be willing to accept the basic principle of progressivity—that the more affluent should pay at a higher rate—so long as even the poor pay something. Indeed, there tends to be little public support for the principle of the flat tax, by which everyone pays the same tax rate, a concept that might be thought to be "fair" (see pp. 242–243). Americans do not appear to think that all taxpayers should pay the same rate so long as everyone is paying at least a little something to support government.

The public's other concern is whether all citizens are paying their "fair share" of taxes. Defining that fair share objectively is difficult, given the numerous alternative conceptions of fairness,[11] but taxpayers do not appear to have any difficulty in defining fairness subjectively, as table 9.6 shows. In the first place, it appears that although most Americans do think they pay too much in federal income tax, the numbers are not usually much over 50 percent. Further, the number of those who think they pay too much tends to vary with economic and political circumstances. Comparison of the low numbers at the beginning of the Kennedy administration and the very high numbers during the years of the Vietnam War and Watergate suggests that these reactions may be as much measures of discontent with government as measures of actual resistance to the taxes themselves.[12] Interestingly, after years of declining confidence in government, when asked just before income taxes were due in 1997, over half of a sample of taxpayers maintained that they thought their taxes were fair, and about half of taxpayers continue to think that the taxes they pay are generally fair.[13]

Citizens also have opinions about who else is, and should be, paying taxes. Table 9.7 (p. 230) points out that most people see the need for some progressivity in the income tax structure. On average they think that lower-income and middle-income people pay too much and the upper echelons of the income ladder pay too little. The large proportion who believe that middle-income people pay too much reflects in part the fact that most Americans think of themselves as middle-class and that they as individuals pay too much federal tax. Indeed, when these figures are broken down by income groups (not shown in this table), a strong element of self-interest comes through in the responses. This feeling

TABLE 9.6   Opinions on Income Tax, 1963–2001 (in percentages)

"Do you consider the amount of federal income tax you pay too high, about right, or too low?"

	Too high	About right	Too low	No opinion
1963	52	38	1	8
1973	65	28	1	6
1985	63	32	1	4
1990	63	31	2	4
1994	56	42	—	2
1996	64	33	1	2
1998	66	31	1	2
1999	65	29	2	4
2000	63	33	1	3
2001	65	31	1	3

Source: Gallup poll, various years.

about the unfair nature of taxation may be exacerbated by the tax cuts adopted during the first months of George W. Bush's administration, and again in 2003, which went differentially to higher-income taxpayers.[14]

Another aspect of who pays what in taxes, and the perceived fairness of the system, is the ability to avoid paying taxes legally through the use of loopholes. What does the public think of the loopholes built into the tax laws? Several surveys point to some similar findings (see table 9.8, p. 230). One is that the more commonly used deductions, such as the home mortgage deduction, are generally thought to be fair and desirable. Another is that exemptions and deductions going to particular classes of people with special needs—the elderly, the blind, for instance—are considered fair, while those that are used primarily by the affluent, such as business entertainment deductions, are not considered good public policy. Again, the populism of American political culture can be seen in this belief that programs benefiting the average citizen and the "deserving poor" in society are good policies.

Value for Money

The public also evaluate taxes according to what they believe that they receive in return—is the tax "price" for goods and services provided by government worth it or not? Americans tend to answer that question rather differently for different levels of government. In most surveys, local governments are perceived to deliver the most for the tax money, while the federal government delivers the least. This is perhaps to be expected, given that the federal government collects the most in tax revenue (almost 60 percent in 2000) and delivers the fewest direct services to the public. Citizens see local firemen and state workers repairing

TABLE 9.7   Perceptions of Paying Fair Share of Taxes (in percentages)

	Too high	About right	Too low	No opinion
Lower-income people				
1992	32	57	8	3
1994	43	42	12	3
1996	40	48	9	3
Middle-income people				
1992	36	57	5	2
1994	39	54	5	2
1996	34	58	5	3
Upper-income people				
1992	16	4	77	3
1994	20	10	68	2
1996	19	9	68	4

Source: Gallup poll, annual.

TABLE 9.8   Fairness of Tax Deductions and Exemptions (in percentages)

A. Perceived fairness of deductions

	Fair	Unfair	Percentage of respondents using this deduction
Charitable contributions	84	16	51
State and local taxes	76	24	32
Capital gains	51	49	12
Mortgage interest on second home	50	50	7
Fringe benefits at work	28	72	30
Business entertainment	22	78	7

B. Perceived legitimacy of deductions and exemptions

	Legitimate	Illegitimate
Elderly exemption	95	5
Blind exemption	95	5
Property tax on homeowners	93	7
Social Security income[a]	92	8
Home mortgage	92	8
Charitable contributions	71	29
Municipal bonds[b]	53	47
Capital gains	48	52

Source: "Tax Americana," *Public Opinion*, February/March 1986, 28.
a. When the question about the legitimacy of deductions was asked, Social Security was totally exempt from tax; it is now 50 percent exempt.
b. Interest on municipal bonds is not taxable by the federal government.

highways but relatively few federal employees at work. When a citizen does see a federal employee, it may be an Internal Revenue Service employee or a Customs agent going through his or her baggage. The federal government simply is not perceived as providing many direct services to the public.[15]

Citizens also tend to evaluate "sin taxes" positively. That is, they are likely to support taxation on alcohol, tobacco, gambling, and the like even if they would not support other types of taxation—voters in the state of Washington were willing to increase the price of cigarettes (most of which is taxation) to $5 a pack. The support for this type of taxation appears to come less from moral judgment than from a sense that people who spend money in those ways also have the money to pay in taxes; this feeling is heightened when the tax is earmarked for a popular policy such as education. Further, these taxes are easily avoidable, so people have only themselves to blame if they must pay them. Finally, governments tend to like these taxes because the demand for such products appears relatively inelastic—they are able to pile on high levels of tax and the public will still buy the products.[16] There is, however, some backlash against these excise taxes among conservatives, who argue that they are simply another government limitation on individual freedom to choose one's own way of life.[17]

Finally, both survey and behavioral evidence indicate that citizens want to have greater certainty about where their tax money is going. In surveys, citizens appear to support earmarked taxes, such as a gasoline tax to be spent on transportation needs, more than they do general taxation. Similarly, if asked simply whether they would vote to raise taxes, there tends to be a negative majority among survey respondents, but when the increase is linked to a particular expenditure—especially a popular one such as Social Security or public education—there tends to be a positive majority. It appears that if citizens are made aware of what their taxes will buy, they become more willing to bear the financial pain of paying.

The issue of willingness to pay taxes arose very clearly in early 2001 when newly inaugurated President George W. Bush worked hard to push through a tax cut. At the time, a substantial budget surplus had been accumulated, so there was a sense that sufficient money was available for spending programs, reducing the national debt, or reducing the level of taxation. When confronted with these possibilities, citizens said they would be willing to forego tax reductions in favor of preserving either Medicare or Social Security or both, but they favored a tax reduction over paying down the federal debt.[18] In another poll, over 60 percent of respondents said that health, education, and Social Security were more important than a tax cut.[19]

Responding in a survey that one would be willing to pay more taxes is relatively easy. A more pertinent question is whether one would actually behave that way. At the state and local levels, citizens are given the opportunity to vote for or against proposals for tax increases. For some time the approval of Proposition 13 in California made it appear that a "tax revolt" was under way and that citizens would not accept any new taxes.[20] It now appears, however, that voters have been making somewhat more sophisticated policy choices, being willing to support taxing measures that are associated with particular expenditure programs while tending to oppose more general increases in taxes. For example, in the 2000 election, voters approved almost two-thirds of tax referenda that had a clear expenditure linked to the tax. Citizens appear to demand a clear quid pro quo in taxation.

Choices in Tax Policy

Americans obviously have made a number of choices concerning taxation that are different from policy choices made in other industrialized countries, although tax reform in many countries has tended to make their tax policies increasingly similar.[21] Some of the growing similarity represents a response to globalizing economic forces, while some represents more a need on the part of governments to raise all the income they can.[22] The aggregate figures presented earlier (table 9.1, p. 224) represent taxation decisions made by many thousands of individual governments, although the federal government alone accounts for approximately three-quarters of all taxes. What criteria might these governments be employing when they make their decisions about taxes?

Collectibility

One criterion that must be considered is the ability of government to collect a tax, and even more important, the potential of that tax to yield large amounts of revenue for the investment made in collecting it. The administration of taxes is expensive, and it has political costs in addition to its economic costs. Therefore, a government should be sure that it can generate sufficient revenue from a tax to justify incurring those costs. One of the many critiques of the tax system of the United States (at the federal level, as well as the problems resulting from multiple levels of taxation) is that it is very difficult to administer, given its complexity. There are very large burdens on citizens, businesses, and government itself that might be alleviated by various alternative tax systems (see pp. 242–245).[23]

The two major tax "handles" for modern, industrialized governments are *income* and *expenditure*. By definition, almost all money in an economy is both income and expenditure, and governments can raise revenue by tapping either or both streams of economic transactions. Further, given that in modern economies most income is earned as salaries and wages in relatively large organizations, and most purchases are made through relatively large and identifiable organizations, governments can employ private bodies to do much of the tax collection for them.

Employers typically withhold a portion of their employees' incomes for income and Social Security taxes, and they are required to submit detailed accounting of sales and of profits for their own taxes. These collection procedures impose a cost on the private sector—one estimate is that it costs businesses over $7 billion to comply with tax laws—but they make the collection of revenue easier and less expensive for government.[24] Individual citizens also do a great deal of the work: the Internal Revenue Service has estimated that the average taxpayer requires 9.4 hours a year to keep records and to fill out and file the forms for the federal income tax; this amounts to over 1 billion hours of work a year for all taxpayers.[25]

Fiscal Neutrality

As well as being collectible, a "good" tax is one that does not produce any significant distortions in the economy.[26] That is, the tax system should not give preference to one kind of revenue or expenditure, unless there is a very good reason to do so. If the tax system were to advantage certain types of economic activities, it could direct resources away from their most productive economic use and probably reduce the rate of economic growth in the society. Prior to tax reform in 1986, the tax system in the United States contained a large number of special-interest provisions ("loopholes") that had been written into the law. These provisions provided citizens and corporations alike with incentives to use their money in ways that might be unproductive on economic grounds (investing in racehorses or in loss-making businesses) but that were quite lucrative given the character of the existing tax system.

Tax reform in 1986 made the tax system more fiscally neutral, but there are continuing efforts by special interests to gain special tax benefits for themselves. Every year since the passage of that major tax reform has seen some special preferences creep back into the tax laws.[27] Another attempt at major change in the mid-1990s actually resulted in more preferences being added to the tax system, and Congress and the president continue to battle over others, such as a tax deduction for tuition to private elementary and secondary schools (see Chapter 12). A tax break has been added for higher education but there is still a debate over other levels. Also, state and local tax systems provide a number of additional tax benefits that can distort economic activity, most importantly the numerous tax incentives used to attract new industry to one place or another. A tax reform adopted in 2001 added some general tax preferences for parents with children in higher education but not the targeted assistance sought earlier.

Buoyancy

Raising revenue is unpopular politically, so any tax that can produce additional revenue without any political activity is a valuable tax for government. A buoyant tax is one for which the yield keeps pace with, or perhaps exceeds, the pace of economic growth and/or inflation. In principle, the progressive income tax is a buoyant tax: as individuals earn more income, they pay not only higher taxes but higher rates of tax, so there is a fiscal dividend from the tax, with government automatically receiving a higher proportion of national income. Taxes that require reassessments or adjustments in rates in order to keep pace with inflation (e.g., the property tax) are not buoyant and hence may generate political difficulties if the real value of their yield is to be maintained—this effect was evident in the "tax revolt" against the property tax in a number of states.

The fiscal dividend that is associated with the progressive income tax during inflationary periods has led to legislation that indexes tax brackets. That is, as inflation increases the money income of citizens without increasing their real income, the income levels at which taxes are first charged and at which tax rates change are raised so that tax rates change at the same rate as real income. Everything else being equal, real tax income for government would therefore remain constant without legislative action to increase rates. This kind of change was a major thrust of tax reform during the first Reagan administration. In addition, the tax reform of 1986 reduced the progressivity of the tax system by lowering the number of tax brackets from fourteen to five, and then effectively to three (two rates plus a surcharge) in 1990. That basic system has remained in place since that time, albeit with some adjustments in the brackets, and some reductions of the rates in 2001.

Distributive Effects

Another thing that taxes can do for government is to alter the income distribution within society. This change is usually thought of as benefiting the less affluent at the expense of the more affluent. However, many taxes used by governments are actually regressive—that is, they take a larger proportion of income from the poor than from the rich. These regressive taxes (e.g., the Social Security tax and sales taxes) must be justified on other grounds, such as ease of collection or similarity to insurance premiums.

Analyses of the net impacts of taxes on income distribution are difficult to calculate, especially if attention is given to the effects of expenditures that the taxes finance. Nevertheless, there does seem to be a general finding in the United States that both the poor—especially the working poor—and the rich pay a higher rate of tax than the majority of citizens do, while the large majority of citizens pay approximately the same rate of tax.[28] This is true when federal, state, and local taxes are added together; the federal tax structure has been at least moderately progressive, although some changes made during the Reagan years, as well as those of the George W. Bush administration, have made it less so.

It is especially interesting that the working poor pay such a high rate of tax.

This is explained by their need to consume rather than save their income, which makes almost all their income subject to sales and excise taxes. Also, all of the income of poorer workers is covered by Social Security deductions, whereas the more affluent can earn substantial amounts of income above a threshold rate beyond which no additional Social Security tax is paid. Finally, the working poor are simply unable to take advantage of many of the loopholes in the tax system that the more affluent can use, and even if they could do so, the loopholes would be worth less at their lower tax rates.

Changes in the federal tax system over the past decade have tended to make the system somewhat less progressive. The top rates of income tax were reduced significantly (from 70 percent to 33 percent) during the Reagan and George H.W. Bush administrations, and the tax burden has been shifting slightly away from income taxation and toward excise and Social Security taxes, as well as toward user fees.[29] These changes have been offset in part by eliminating a number of the less defensible loopholes in the tax laws that primarily did benefit the rich. The decreased progressivity of the tax system was in large part effected very consciously. Part of President Reagan's "supply-side" strategy was to place more money in the hands of the affluent so they would invest. Further, the George H.W. Bush administration found that its pledge of "No New Taxes" meant, in practice, no new income taxes; excise taxes were more palatable, both to the administration and to most citizens.[30]

The Clinton administration reversed somewhat the trend toward a less redistributive tax system at the federal level. Early in his term of office President Clinton put through an economic reform package and a major budget bill that shifted some of the tax burden back to the more affluent, although critics argued that it was not the middle-class tax cut he had promised in the 1992 campaign.[31] This bill increased to 36 percent the tax rate on taxable incomes over $140,000 for couples ($115,000 for individuals), and although this change affected only a rather small percentage of the American public, it did raise approximately $27.5 billion in 1994. Another $7.5 billion was raised by increasing the top rate of corporation tax to 36 percent. The Clinton package was not entirely redistributive, however, for heavier taxes also were imposed on alcohol, tobacco, and energy—taxes that tend to fall disproportionately on the less affluent. Still, an estimated 70 percent of the new tax revenue came from households with yearly incomes over $100,000 (4.4 percent of all households).[32] As of 2000, approximately 47 percent of federal income tax revenues came from taxpayers with incomes over $100,000.

Visibility

Finally, public officials making decisions about taxes must be concerned about the political acceptability of taxes. This is often a crucial factor, for low taxes are related to the historical traditions of the country as well as to those of some states whose populist political cultures regard the property tax as a threat to the "little man" who owns a house. The political acceptability of taxes also may be a function of their visibility. Everything else being equal, the less visible a tax is, the more acceptable it will be.[33] Even though income tax is withheld from employees' checks at each pay period, the citizen is still required to file a statement each year on which he or she must see the total tax account for the year. Similarly, property-tax bills are typically sent to homeowners each year; in states and localities with high property taxes, these bills may seem huge. Both of these taxes are obvious to the taxpayer and therefore are likely to be resisted. The Social Security tax is less visible: although it is deducted from paychecks along with the income tax, there is no annual reckoning that might bring the total tax bill to the citizen's attention and, furthermore, half of the total Social Security bill is paid by the employer.

The lack of a total tax bill is a very important element in a country (such as the United States) with several levels of government, all of which levy taxes. These taxes are levied at different times and in different ways, so only the better-informed citizens are likely to know their total tax bills.[34] The United States is a low-tax country—in part because Americans want it that way—but the division among taxes and taxing units may make the total bill appear even lower than it is. The maintenance of the "fiscal illusion" created by multiple taxing units helps to make such taxes as do exist more palatable.[35] The political viability of the tax system is further enhanced because citizens tend to focus their ire on the federal level of government while permitting state and local taxes to creep upward.

The problem of tax visibility is one reason for considering a value-added tax (VAT) for the United States,[36] perhaps as a means of reducing the resurgent federal deficit. Unlike a sales tax, which is levied as the consumer pays for the commodity and is added on as a separate item, the VAT is levied at each stage of the production process and included in the price of the product when sold. As a result, the actual amount of the tax—and even the fact that a tax is being levied—may be largely hidden from the consumer; consequently, there may be less political mobilization opposing the tax. It is just that invisibility, however, that makes many fiscal conservatives extremely wary of the VAT, fearing that government could expand its activities without citizens understanding what the real increases in their tax bill had been.

The Politics of Tax Reform

Taxation is different from most other kinds of policy in that it is essentially something that no one really wants and everyone seeks to avoid whenever possible. Former Senator Russell Long of Louisiana, long a power on the Senate Finance Committee responsible for tax legislation, encapsulated the nature of tax politics in this little ditty: "Don't tax you, don't tax me, tax that fellow behind the tree." The nature of tax politics is to attempt to divert the burden of taxation on to others and to build in special privileges for oneself. Because virtually no one in contemporary economic systems can avoid taxes, the next best strategy is to ensure that everyone pays his or her fair share of the costs of government. This helps to explain why sales taxes are popular among all segments of society even though they are regressive.[37]

Compared with other forms of policymaking, tax policymaking has been relatively technical and legalistic.[38] The tax code is an extremely complex set of laws, and it is made even more complex by rulings issued by the Internal Revenue Service and tax courts concerning just what the tax code really means. In Congress, tax policymaking historically has been the preserve of a relatively few powerful and knowledgeable congressmen and senators (e.g., Senator Long and former Congressman Wilbur Mills).[39] Changes in Congress, such as opening committee deliberations to greater "sunshine," have tended to lessen the power of the tax committees and the venerable individuals who populate them, but finance committees still possess substantial political power.

The perceived (and real) complexity of tax policymaking allows many special interests to have desired provisions written into the tax code with little awareness on the part of the general public. These special interests are represented by members of Congress, whose constituencies may contain large concentrations of one kind of industry or another. Adding loopholes to a tax law often is an exercise in coalition-building through logrolling, as every member of Congress adds in his or her provisions in return for support of the legislation as a whole. This process has produced a federal tax system, especially an income tax system, that is perceived as highly unfair by many citizens: Harris surveys taken prior to tax reform in 1986 indicated that an average of 90 percent of respondents thought that the federal income tax was unfair.[40] Polls taken after the reforms were almost as negative about the tax structure, and the subsequent years have done little to enhance public confidence.

Any number of proposals for tax reform have been made in the United States, but the actual passage of a major tax reform in 1986 came as a surprise to most observers. What was perhaps even more surprising was that the reform passed was as sweeping and as comprehensive as it was.[41] It is relatively easy to criticize the reform and to point out its weaknesses, but given the history of tax policy in the United States, and indeed in most countries, the package actually put into effect was remarkable. The tax system was simplified for the average taxpayer, a large number of the more egregious loopholes were removed, and the impact of the tax system on the less affluent was made somewhat more equitable. A year, or even a few months, prior to passage, such a change in the tax laws would have been thought impossible.

What happened to produce this major reversal of tax policymaking as usual? There is no simple answer to that question, but apparently a confluence of forces, liberal and conservative, business and labor, producers and consumers, all wanted change. President Reagan wanted to reduce the progressivity of taxes, allowing the more affluent to keep more of what they earned. Some of his conservative allies wanted to eliminate special preferences for certain industries in order to produce a more level playing field for all industries as a means of stimulating economic growth.[42] Liberals also supported the elimination of these special preferences as a means of attempting to help middle- and low-income groups that could not take advantage of many of these loopholes. In addition, there were several policy entrepreneurs—Senator Bill Bradley, Congressman Dan Rostenkowski, Secretary of the Treasury Donald Regan, and others—who made heavy political investments to bring about this major policy change.[43] This was a rare "policy window" through which advocates of various tax reform proposals could jump to produce significant change in the tax structure.[44]

Naturally, the interests whose particular benefits were affected by this tax simplification were skeptical about the legislation. Among the first to question the efficacy of the legislation were mayors and governors, who argued that ending the deductibility of some state and local taxes would make it more difficult for subnational governments to increase taxes. These public officials were followed closely by business interests, who argued that the repeal of special investment credits, accelerated depreciation, and other benefits for investment would further slow the rate of capital formation in the United States and thereby slow economic growth. A standard place to begin any political analysis is to ask "whose ox is gored," and a large number of oxen would be gored by this tax reform legislation.[45]

Tax Reform in the 1990s and Beyond

Another significant tax reform came in the later 1990s, as President Clinton and the Republican Congress finally managed to agree on some transformation of the tax code. Unlike the 1986 reform, however, these changes tended to build in more special provisions and loopholes rather than to eliminate them. The final shape of the bill reflected a good deal of negotiation and logrolling between a conservative Congress and a more liberal president. In that way it represented a return to the old "Christmas tree" style of tax legislation, with something for everybody hung on it. Although this tax bill was presented as an effort to be fairer to American families, especially those in the middle class, in reality it tended to benefit as many or more special interests than it disadvantaged.

Perhaps the major change made in the 1997 legislation was in the treatment of capital gains—specifically, reducing significantly the rate at which this tax is charged. If a citizen invests in stocks, bonds, a piece of land, or whatever and later sells it at a profit, he or she has received a capital gain that is subject to taxes. The major exception is houses: if the money is reinvested into another house, no tax is incurred, and there is a one-time exclusion designed for aging people who want to move out of their family home into some other type of housing. Any other type of profit from investment (with very minor exceptions) is subject to taxation, although the tax rate on these profits has tended to be lower than that on ordinary income. For example, throughout much of the postwar period, capital gains were taxed at half the normal rate of income tax.

There has been a great deal of debate among politicians and economists about the desirability and effects of capital gains taxation. One argument is that this investment profit is income, and there is no justification for treating it differently from any other type of income. Indeed, given that only the more affluent in the society generally receive capital gains on anything other than houses, eliminating capital gains taxation would make the federal tax system less progressive than it is. Further, low or non-existent capital gains taxation would encourage speculation in all sorts of assets and might make the stock market and other financial markets more volatile than they already are.

There are also good arguments for lowering capital gains taxation or for eliminating it entirely. In the first place, as we have already noted (see Chapter 8), one problem for the American economy is a low rate of savings and investment. High capital gains taxes tend to discourage investment, or at least do not reward investors for making good choices; investments involve risk, and having to pay full tax rates if the risk is justified does not seem fair. Also, capital gains are generally counted in current dollar terms and do not take into account the effects of inflation, which may make an apparently large return on an investment actually trivial.[46] Finally, an aversion to paying capital gains taxes may encourage some investors to hold on to assets after they have ceased to be as productive as would alternative uses of the same money; this is another way in which the tax system may distort the use of resources in the economy and lower potential economic growth.

There was a great deal of agitation for reducing or even eliminating the capital gains tax during the Reagan administration, and especially during the George H.W. Bush administration. Little happened, however, until 1997, when the combination of a soaring stock market and fears about the viability of Social Security as a source of retirement income brought about a change in the structure of investment in the United States: many more people began to invest in the stock market, with over 40 percent of households placing some money in the market. Capital gains taxation thus became a more general issue, rather than just a concern for the wealthy.[47]

Despite public discontent with many aspects of the prevailing tax system, adopting a tax reform is a difficult undertaking politically. Making tax policy has traditionally been the preserve of the special interests, and it may be difficult to

Senior citizens and others gather on Capitol Hill to express opposition to a Repulican-drafted bill to offset proposed income tax cuts by reducing Medicare benefits.

prevent them from continuing their role in the process. In addition, many of the arguments advanced by those special interests may have social and economic validity. The repeal of credits for business investment contained in the 1997 reform may indeed have some long-term negative impact on economic growth in the United States. In short, tax reform was a desirable policy goal, but like almost any policy change, it was not without its critics and its negative consequences. Further, as American politics has become more ideological, tax policy tends to be an area in which the conflicts between conservative and progressive ideas about good public policy appear very stark.

Tax Reform in the Bush Administration

The most recent reforms of the federal tax system were enacted in 2001 and 2003, after President George W. Bush argued that tax rates needed to be reduced to encourage economic growth and to put money back in the hands of ordinary citizens.[48] This proposal reflected the ideological predispositions of the president and his supporters, and it was first made in the context of a large surplus projected for the federal budget. Tax rates were reduced for all taxpayers, and there was an immediate (or virtually so) refund based on making a retroactive reduction of the lowest tax rate charged, which was designed to provide an immediate boost for a slowing economy.

The tax "reform" of 2001 was, however, in many ways the reverse of the reforms that had preceded it, making the tax system more complex rather than simplifying it. A number of new loopholes were added, some of which benefited the more affluent citizens and corporations, and some of which—such as support for parents paying for the college education of their children—were more generally available.

Another aspect of tax reform introduced at the outset of the second Bush administration was the gradual reduction, and possible elimination, of the estate tax. The federal government for decades has collected a tax on estates over a certain size when their owners die. The Republican Party has been pushing for several years to have that tax eliminated, characterizing it as a "death tax" and arguing that this tax makes it more difficult for a small businessman to pass along the family business or farm to his or her children. Republicans also argue that the money in an estate has already been taxed once by income tax, so it is unfair to tax it again. Although the vast majority of estates in the United States—98 percent, in fact—fall below the threshold at which the tax is charged, these points have proven to be a powerful political argument.

The Democrats in Congress, on the other hand, have tended to favor retaining the estate tax, although they are generally willing, or even anxious, to raise the amount at which the tax is first imposed—$1 million in 2002.[49] Their basic justification for retaining the estate tax is that associated with all forms of progressive taxation—the ability to pay—combined with a desire to level the playing field between generations. Indeed, part of the argument for retaining the estate tax is the classic capitalist argument that everyone should have to earn his or her own way in the world, and the tax has been supported publicly by extremely wealthy individuals such as Bill Gates Sr.[50] In addition, Democrats have wondered where the money would come from to fill the revenue hole left if this tax were to be repealed—although it is less than 2 percent of total federal revenue, it still amounts to roughly $70 billion. The total repeal of the tax was defeated in 2002, but this issue seemed likely to become a recurring debate in the ideological conflicts between Democrats and Republicans.

Additional tax cuts were approved in 2003 under pressure from the Bush administration, which argued that they were both a means of stimulating a sluggish economy and a means of returning more money to the people who earned it. These cuts were, however, differentially beneficial to the more affluent and therefore seemed unlikely to have the stimulative effect intended. For example, a significant proportion of the total tax cut came in the form of reductions of taxes on dividends from stocks, an income source of little importance to the average worker.

Proposals for Further Fundamental Reform

The tax reforms of 1986 and the less comprehensive reforms of the mid-1990s made significant changes in the tax system, but they were all produced in the context of the progressive income tax, which is assumed as the basic source of revenue for the federal government. That assumption is, however, being questioned in a number of proposals for reform, which range from shifting the income tax to a flat rate on all income to shifting away from personal income to either integrated corporate taxation or consumption taxation. All of these reform proposals have some merit, but all also have political and economic costs. Perhaps the major cost of any sweeping reform of the tax system would be political: Americans may not like the existing tax system, but the move to a different system would be likely to make taxation more apparent and hence to emphasize the bite in the system.

The federal government may want to maintain its fundamental reliance on the income tax, but it can collect that revenue in rather different ways than it has been doing. As we pointed out earlier, the current structure of the income tax imposes different levels of tax on different income levels and also provides a number of deductions and exemptions—the loopholes already discussed. The tax system is therefore very complicated—the tax code is approximately 10,000 pages long—and requires a large amount of administration, both by government and by private citizens. The current system also may create inequities because some types of expenditures are considered worthy of deductions while others are not.

The flat tax. One logical alternative to the current system is to have a simple flat tax on all income regardless of its source, eliminating almost all deductions and loopholes for expenditures. The advocates of this reform, notably the publisher and Republican politician Steve Forbes, argue that this system would be fairer, treating all income and expenditure equally and treating all citizens equally. The simpler flat tax also could eliminate a good deal of the employment in the Internal Revenue Service and in the private-sector tax reporting industry, as well as reducing distress over the way in which people believe they are (mis)treated by the IRS.[51] On more technical grounds, the flat tax would be more fiscally neutral, so that decisions about how to invest could be made on economic, rather than tax, considerations.

As might be expected, the flat tax is not without its critics. First, it would almost certainly be a regressive move from the current tax structure, with the affluent having to pay less than they do now. The flat tax is usually discussed in the range of 17 percent of total income—a substantially lower rate than the more affluent now pay on average in income tax. Under such a plan, therefore, the very affluent seemingly would benefit at the expense of the remainder of the population. (Despite the political rhetoric about the ability of the affluent to avoid income tax through loopholes, on average they do pay high taxes.) The flat tax would also eliminate the possibility of using the tax system for other public policy purposes. There are certainly problems with some of the loopholes that have been created in the tax system, but the use of tax expenditures has also been a powerful tool for addressing other policy concerns, especially housing and support for charities.[52] Finally, a shift to a flat tax might require some shifting of state tax structures, given that several states calculate their own income taxes as a percentage of the federal tax.

National consumption tax.   A more extreme solution to the problems identified in the federal income tax system is to move from an income tax to a consumption tax. Americans are used to general consumption taxes (sales taxes) being levied by state and local governments, but the federal government has only used specific consumption taxes, such as those on alcohol, tobacco, and gasoline. This is in contrast to many other developed economies that raise a large proportion of their tax revenue through a national consumption tax, usually the VAT.

The logic of a consumption tax is, first, that it places the burden on spending rather than on earning money. If indeed one of problems of the American economy is that there is inadequate savings, it makes sense to tax spending rather than saving money. Another positive aspect of the consumption tax is that it would require everyone in the society to pay some part of the tax burden. We noted earlier that Americans want to be sure that all citizens "participate" in funding government, and a consumption tax would certainly require that. Further, the consumption tax would place the burden of recordkeeping on businesses rather than the general public, thus eliminating citizen frustrations with the tax system and with government more generally.

No tax is perfect, and there would certainly be some drawbacks to a consumption tax. First, in order to raise the amount of money now collected by the federal government, the tax rate would have to be roughly 30 percent on all purchases.[53] This is about four times higher than the highest rate of sales tax in the states, and would produce a huge, if one-time only, increase in prices.[54] Also, this alternative form of taxation would be regressive, because on average the poor tend to spend a much higher proportion of their income than do the more affluent. Like state and local sales taxes, a national consumption tax could be made less regressive by excluding items such as food, medicines, clothing, and the like, but then the tax rate on other goods and services would have to be all the higher. Finally, given that businesses rather than individuals would be liable for the consumption tax, government could not use the tax system for other purposes, such as providing the important Earned Income Tax Credit as a means of subsidizing the wages of the poor.

Some of the objections to a national consumption tax based on business transactions could be met by adopting a personal consumption tax, by which individual taxpayers would report all the money they had earned during the year and then subtract the amount they had saved. The difference would represent consumption, and it would be subject to tax.[55] This proposal might solve some problems but in turn would create others. This form of taxation would require personal filings and would therefore require as large and intrusive an IRS as there is at present. Indeed, it might be even more difficult for the average citizen to set a correct level of tax withholding throughout the year, so that more refunds and/or large payments could be due at filing. Further, determination of what "savings" are might be difficult with this form of taxation. Are consumer durable goods savings? A house almost certainly would be, but a car or a washing machine?

Conservatives voice several other complaints about a national consumption tax. One is that it could be more easily hidden from the public than other types of taxes, given that it probably would be a part of the price of the product rather than a separate item to be paid. At a rate of 30 percent, such a tax would be unlikely to go unnoticed by taxpayers, but at a lower rate, to supplement the income tax, it might. Further, some conservatives argue that taxing consumption would be a way of punishing the more affluent for their success rather than rewarding them for it, and therefore might be as much or more of an economic disincentive than the income tax.[56] This would be especially true if differential rates of consumption tax were charged for luxury items such as jewelry or expensive cars and boats.

Integrating corporate and personal taxation. A more technical recommendation for changing the existing tax code is to integrate corporate and personal taxation—usually called the Comprehensive Business Income Tax. The basic concept is that if most income-earners in the United States work for some sort of organization, then those organizations, rather than the individual citizens employed by those firms, would make the tax filings. Individual wages might be taxed, but this tax revenue could be collected at source, leaving primarily the self-employed having to make individual filings.

Such a change in the tax system is advocated for at least two reasons. The first is to make tax administration easier. If corporations, with their computerized recordkeeping, could be made responsible for most tax filings, the job of collecting income taxes would be much easier. If nothing else, that would mean "only"

24 million tax returns being filed, as compared to the current level of nearly 140 million returns.[57] Some individuals would still be responsible for filing tax forms for items such as capital gains, but the bulk of the work of recordkeeping and filing would be done by businesses with better capacities for keeping the records.

The other reason for pushing for an integration of personal and corporate taxation focuses instead on the economic consequences of the existing tax structure. Under the current system there is some double taxation of business profits—once when the corporation earns the profits and again when they are paid out to individuals as stock dividends. Double taxation is believed by many economists to tax corporate income excessively and therefore to deter investment (although it may also give firms an incentive to reinvest their profits rather than to distribute them). Integration of the two forms of taxation is argued, therefore, to facilitate investment and savings.

Conclusion

Taxation is one public policy that most citizens would prefer not to think about, but one that occupies a good deal of their time (and money). It is also the subject of a number of myths, not least of which is that the United States is a high-tax country.[58] Taxation may be anathema to most members of the public, but it is central for government because it is how government obtains the money it needs to survive and to provide public services. In addition to simply raising adequate revenue for survival, tax policy is also used to attain a number of policy goals, and the "tax expenditures" through which those goals are reached are among the most controversial features of tax policy. While in some ways an efficient means of reaching policy goals, they provide benefits to some segments of the society that may appear unfair to those who are not able to benefit from them.

Although many people are dissatisfied with the existing structure of taxation in the United States, reforming these programs remains extremely difficult. There has been one major tax reform in recent history, but that reform's success in making the tax system simpler and fairer appears to be further diluted with each passing year. The impacts of reforming capital gains taxation in 1997 are yet to be fully understood, and given the wider range of stock ownership, these reforms seem likely to have a wider range of impacts than would have been true even a few years ago. There are few powerful political forces on the side of tax reform but numerous forces attempting to utilize the tax system to feather their own economic and social nests. Even though most Americans are not keen on paying taxes, they would be more likely to tolerate, and comply with, a tax system that appeared fair and equitable.

CHAPTER 10

Health Care Policies

ONE GREAT MYTH about American political life and public policy is that we have a purely private health care system. In fact, in 1992 nearly 40 percent of all health care expenditures in the United States were made by federal government agencies of some sort, and many physicians who loudly proclaim the virtues of private medical care receive a substantial portion of their income from public medical programs such as Medicare, Medicaid, and the Children's Health Insurance Program (CHIPS) (see table 10.1). In 2001 that number rose to over 44 percent. Further, on average, 81,000 patients receive treatment in Veterans Administration hospitals every day, and millions of other patients are treated in hospitals operated by state and local governments. The public sector does make a much smaller proportion of total health expenditures in the United States than in most other industrialized democracies, but government involvement in the provision of health care is, nevertheless, significant.

The extent of American government involvement in health care can be seen in part in the health care programs listed in table 10.2 (p. 248). All three levels of government are to some degree involved in health care, and at the federal level a wide variety of public agencies are involved. Almost all cabinet-level departments of the federal government are to some degree involved with health care, as are a number of independent executive agencies. Their involvement ranges from directly providing medical care to some segments of the population (e.g., through the Department of Defense, the Department of the Interior, or the Department of Veterans Affairs), through funding medical care for the general public, through regulating some aspects of medical care or the environmental causes of disease, to subsidizing medical research.

Without involvement of the public sector, American health care would certainly be very different, and probably not as good as it is. Without government, health care certainly would not be as accessible to the poor, to children, and to the elderly, and the overall technical quality would probably not be as high as it

TABLE 10.1   Sources of Payment to Health Care Providers, 1992 (in percentages)

	Hospitals	Physicians	Other
Government			
Federal	39.9	27.4	20.1
State	15.3	6.7	11.1
Direct payments	5.0	19.1	47.6
Private insurance	35.1	46.8	17.7
Other private payers	4.7	0.1	3.5

Source: Sally T. Sonnefeld et al., "Projections of National Health Expenditures through the Year 2000," Health Care Financing Review 13 (Fall 1991).

currently is for those who nominally pay all their medical expenses privately. For one thing, the federal government is a major source of funds for medical research ($20.1 billion in 2000), without which many of the medical advances the average citizen is now familiar with would not have been made, or would at least have been delayed.

Although the role of government in health care is larger than most American citizens believe it to be, that role is still not as great as many people believe it should be. Rather than opt for greater involvement in medical care, the Reagan and George H.W. Bush administrations reduced the federal role by cutting back federal health funding and converting former categorical programs that subsidized health care at the state and local level into block-grant programs. The effectiveness of block-grant programs depends much more on the priorities of state governments for implementation, and there is some evidence that health care for the very poor has been significantly reduced in quantity and quality.[1] Medicaid has become an extremely expensive program for the states, and they have been searching for means to limit their financial exposure. By the late 1990s even many in the middle class were encountering difficulty in financing medical care for themselves and their families—in 2002, approximately 44 million Americans had no medical insurance, public or private.

The problems of cost and access to care have helped produce demands for more public involvement in health care, including some continuing interest in national health insurance.[2] A number of surveys indicate that well over half of the American public would support some form of national health insurance. For example, a survey in mid-1994 reported that 77 percent of respondents wanted some form of universal medical care, although they disagreed on the exact nature of the program.[3] More recent surveys indicate that health care continues to be an area that Americans believe requires substantial rethinking and a stronger public role.[4] This is one policy area in which the conservative policy ideas of past decades encounter substantial skepticism, for over half the population say that the federal

TABLE 10.2   Major Health Programs

Federal	State	Local

Department of Agriculture
    Meat inspections
	State hospitals
	State mental
	    hospitals
		City hospitals
		Sanitation and
		    public health

Department of Health and
    Human Services
    Food and Drug Administration
    Community Health Services
    Indian Health Services
    National Institutes of Health
    Substance abuse programs
    Health education
    HMO loan funds
    U.S. Public Health Service
    Medicare
    Medicaid
	Substance abuse
	Medicaid	

Department of the Interior Territorial health programs		
Department of Veterans' Affairs VA hospitals		

government should have a primary role in financing health care.[5] On the other hand, with typical ambivalence about the role of government, Americans appear to want universal access to medical care without large-scale government programs.

President Clinton placed health care reform at the top of his policy agenda when he came to office in 1993. He took a strong personal interest in this policy area and placed Hillary Rodham Clinton in charge of a task force to draft the reform. After a series of consultations around the country and long hearings before congressional committees, the administration drafted a bill that proposed a complex arrangement of purchasing organizations ("alliances") that would operate somewhat like existing health maintenance organizations (HMOs, discussed later). The most important aspect of the bill for the administration was that it guaranteed universal coverage to all citizens. The Clintons' health care plan generated several other proposals, ranging from a single-payer plan similar to that found in Canada (detailed later in this chapter) to very modest extensions of existing public- and private-sector programs relying on voluntary acceptance and tax subsidies.[6]

None of the plans for reform of health care was successful, and the net result of the 1993 effort was that Congress never actually voted on any of the attempts at comprehensive reform. We discuss this failure in some detail later in

TABLE 10.3   Percentage of Population Not Covered by Health Insurance, 1999

Low		High	
Rhode Island	6.9	New Mexico	25.8
Minnesota	8.0	Texas	23.3
Iowa	8.3	Louisiana	22.5
Missouri	8.6	Arizona	21.2
Pennsylvania	9.4	Nevada	20.7
	US Average: 15.5		

Source: U.S. Bureau of the Census, Current Population Reports P60-211.

the chapter, but it is indicative of some broader issues in health care policy. One is the public's ambivalence toward government involvement: Americans want health care reform in general, but they often oppose specific plans. A second point is the importance of health care not just for patients but also for the economy—one dollar in seven of GNP is in health care, and the lobbying surrounding health care reform therefore has as much to do with the economy as with patient care. Finally, beyond its pervasive economic effects, health care also touches every citizen who has been, or ever will be, ill. Thus, health care politics affects every member of society.

Although the major political concern is often with creating a *national* program of health insurance, the states have begun to put their own programs into place to cover the uninsured (see table 10.3). For example, Hawaii already has a public health care system that, along with private insurance, covers almost the entire population of the state, and Massachusetts has experimented with a similarly extensive plan.[7] Minnesota also has adopted a health care program, using HMOs, that approaches comprehensive coverage, while other states such as Pennsylvania have provided substantial health coverage for all children, if not for adults.[8] Individual states also have innovated in the manner in which they deliver Medicaid services to improve coverage and to lower costs (see pp. 266–267). Many states also have added substantial coverage for children, funded at least in part by the federal government as a part of the welfare reforms of 1996 and the adoption of the Children's Health Insurance Program in 1997.[9] The major question about the public role in health care appears to be the extent of the federal government's role, rather than whether or not the public sector should be involved.

One ironic outcome of the failure to adopt the Clinton health care reforms is that the American medical system now features many of the very elements that were perceived to be so undesirable in the Clinton plan—the controls over access to care, the giant bureaucracy, and the bewildering complexity—but without the greater equality that would have resulted from that plan.[10] That is, all the problematic components of the Clinton plan have survived in the managed care system that emerged during the 1990s, but that private system (despite the involvement of the public sector) still leaves over 40 million people without adequate health care coverage. We may have gotten the worst of both worlds.

Health care reform did not figure heavily in the presidential campaign of George W. Bush, whose general commitment to private-sector solutions to social problems makes advocacy of major changes in publicly provided health care unlikely under his administration. Substantial pressures are building, however, to improve health coverage—especially to alleviate some of the burden of costly prescription medications for the elderly.[11] Other health care issues, including a "patient's bill of rights"—which would require private health care providers to assume greater social responsibility for the ways in which their programs provide coverage—have taken a central place on the political agenda.[12] Finally, recognizing the need for more comprehensive coverage, President Bush has put forward some ideas for more indirect methods, such as tax incentives, for addressing this problem.[13]

Problems in Health Care

The United States is one of the richest countries in the world, and it spends a much larger proportion of its economic resources (as measured by gross domestic product) on health care than does any other industrialized nation (see table 10.4). The results of all those expenditures, however, are not so impressive. In infant mortality, a commonly used indicator of the quality of medical care, the United States ranks fourteenth in the world, behind most Western European countries and Japan.[14] Depending on one's perspective, these figures are made better or worse if the total is disaggregated by race. For the white population in the United States, the infant mortality rate is as low (6.0 per 1,000 live births in 1999) as that of all but a few Western European and Asian countries, but among minority populations, the infant mortality rate is closer to that of much poorer countries (see table 10.5). The infant mortality rates for African Americans (14.3 deaths) is closer to rates found in the countries of the former Soviet bloc and some South American countries. Further, the disparity between black and white infant mortality has actually increased since 1970.

Health care of absolutely the finest quality is available in the United States, but it may be available only to a limited (and perhaps declining) portion of the population. Vast disparities in access exist among racial, economic, and geographical groups in the United States; even with Medicare, Medicaid, and other public programs, the poor, the elderly, and those living in rural areas receive less medical care, and poorer care, than do white middle-class urban citizens. Individuals in those groups also report that their own health is poor, as compared to that of more advantaged Americans (see table 10.7, p. 253). Further, an increasing number of middle-class citizens are beginning to be squeezed out of the

TABLE 10.4   Health Expenditures as a Percentage of Gross Domestic Product, 1998

	Total	*Public sector*
United States	13.6	6.1
Germany	10.6	7.9
Switzerland	10.4	7.7
France	9.6	7.3
Canada	9.5	6.6
Sweden	8.4	7.0
Greece	8.3	4.7
Japan	7.6	6.0
United Kingdom	7.0	5.6
Hungary	6.8	5.2
Ireland	6.4	4.8

Source: Organization for Economic Cooperation and Development, *Health Data 2000* (Paris: OECD, 2000).

TABLE 10.5   Infant Mortality Rates, 2001 (per 1,000 live births)

Japan	3.9	Belarus	14.4
Netherlands	4.4	Sri Lanka	16.1
Belgium	4.7	Argentina	17.8
Germany	4.7	Malaysia	20.3
Spain	4.9	Syria	33.5
Canada	5.0	Bangladesh	69.9
United States (white)	6.0	Tanzania	79.4
Greece	6.4	Ethiopia	100.0
Cuba	7.4	Afghanistan	147.0
United States (black)	14.3	Angola	193.7

Source: U.S. Census Bureau, *Statistical Abstract of the United States, 2001* (Washington, D.C.: Government Printing Office, annual).

medical care market by rapidly increasing prices and by declining insurance benefits provided by employers. The problems that Americans confront in health care now are basically three: access, cost, and quality .

Access to Medical Care

If any medical care system is to function effectively, prospective patients must have access to that system. A number of factors can deter citizens from becoming patients, and one purpose of public involvement in the medical marketplace must be to equalize access for all citizens. Americans still differ on the extent to which they believe that equal access to medical care should be a right of citizenship, but most are willing to accept that all citizens require some form of pro-

TABLE 10.6   Distribution of Health Insurance Coverage, 1999 (in percentages)

| | Covered by insurance | | Not covered |
	Private	Public	
Total	71.0	13.5	15.5
Age			
Under 18	68.9	17.2	13.9
65 and over	61.5	37.2	1.3
Race			
White	73.9	11.9	14.2
Black	55.8	23.0	21.2
Income			
Under $25K	41.0	34.9	24.1
Over $75K	88.4	3.3	8.3
Below poverty	25.8	41.8	32.4

Source: Calculated from U.S. Census Bureau, *Statistical Abstract of the United States, 2001.*

tection against at least serious illnesses.[15] There is more marked difference in the role that citizens are willing to assign to government, especially the federal government, in achieving greater equality.

The most commonly cited barrier to access to health care is economics. As the majority of medical care in the United States is still paid for privately, those who lack the income or insurance to pay for it—again, there are approximately 44 million Americans who do not have health insurance (see table 10.6)—may not be able to afford medical care. Despite several public health care programs, medicine is still not as available to the poor as it is to the more affluent. As of 2000 almost 30 percent of all those with incomes below the official poverty line were not eligible to receive Medicaid benefits—they were poor, but not sufficiently poor to qualify under the means-testing criteria of Medicaid.[16] Only 20 percent of the poor have any privately financed health insurance, and only 10 percent of the poor have any non-hospital coverage.[17] Even the elderly poor, who have access to Medicare because of their age, must still pay for some components of their insurance, and at a rate that may well deter some from taking full advantage of the program.

The middle class now may find that the rising cost of medical care and the possibility of catastrophic illness make all but the very wealthy medically indigent. The federal government made a very brief foray into catastrophic coverage for Medicare recipients in the late 1980s, but financing and administrative and political difficulties led to the program's termination after only one year.[18] Further, the absence of medical insurance is not a problem only for the poor. In

TABLE 10.7   Personal Assessment of Health Status (in percentages)

	Excellent	Very good	Good	Fair or poor
Race				
White	42.8	34.8	21.7	10.1
Black	28.3	21.7	29.8	19.5
Family income				
Under $10,000	28.9	21.7	27.5	21.1
$10,000–14,999	34.0	24.7	27.0	13.7
$15,000–19,999	36.9	26.7	25.5	10.4
$20,000–34,999	43.7	27.1	21.9	6.9
$35,000 or more	52.8	26.1	15.9	4.6

Source: Department of Health and Human Services, *Health Status of the Disadvantaged: Chartbook, 1986* (Washington, D.C.: Public Health Service, 1986).

1994 almost 45 percent of all the uninsured had incomes over $25,000 per year, and one in five had incomes over $50,000. Over 80 percent of the uninsured live in families headed by people who work, usually for small firms in service industries, at least part of the year.[19] Over half the uninsured had someone in the family who worked full-time.[20] These numbers help to explain the continuing demand for reform of the American health care system.

The problem of inadequate health insurance coverage is not going away; if anything, it is getting worse. From 1990 to 1995 private health insurance coverage dropped from 75 percent to 70.5 percent of the population; the proportion with coverage in 1979 had been 80 percent.[21] This decline of coverage occurred across all economic classes, but it has hit hardest those earning between $10,000 and $40,000. In addition, workers covered by insurance arranged by their employers are currently being required to pay through their own contributions on average more than double the proportion of the total costs that their counterparts had to contribute several years ago.

In the contemporary American medical care system, having insurance, as well as not having it, can present troubles. Having insurance can minimize mobility in the economy. A worker with a job that provides health benefits may find it difficult to leave that job for one that may be better in other respects but does not offer health benefits. In some cases, even if the new job does provide insurance, that insurance will not cover preexisting conditions. If a prospective employee or family member has been diagnosed with any serious condition that cannot be covered by the new insurance, moving between jobs may be impossible. One reform that was enacted following the failure of the Clinton health care program was the Kennedy-Kassebaum bill, which mandated increased portability of medical insurance, so that fewer people would lose coverage if they changed jobs.[22]

Even if economic barriers to medical care were removed, there might still be significant noneconomic barriers. Interestingly, even under the almost entirely free medical care system of the United Kingdom, differences in health status by social or economic class have not narrowed significantly.[23] Each social class is on average healthier, but the disparities between the wealthy and the poor remain, indicating that there are other barriers to consuming health care and, perhaps more importantly, barriers to creating health, that are not removed simply by free access. Members of the poor and working classes may lose hourly wages if they go to the doctor, whereas salaried employees either do not lose pay or take personal-business leaves. Transportation is generally easier for the more affluent, whereas the poor rely on public transportation.

Perhaps the most important barrier to more equal access is becoming communication. More affluent and educated citizens know better how to get what they want from professional and bureaucratic organizations than do the poor, and they are more likely to be well treated by individuals and institutions than are the less-well-off. A doctor is more likely to pay serious attention to the description of symptoms coming from a middle-class patient than to that from a poor patient, and the middle-class patient is more likely to demand extra diagnostic and curative procedures. Also, there is some evidence that doctors do not pay adequate attention to the complaints of the elderly. Communication and bureaucratic skills are especially important in managed care, where numerous gatekeepers are used to try to limit expenditures; generally only the articulate and persistent are able to get what they want.[24] So even if all direct economic barriers were removed, there might still be serious barriers to gaining equality in medical care, especially as the poor are generally not as healthy to begin with as the more affluent and, as a consequence, may require greater medical care.

These socioeconomic differences in access to health care are manifested in differential health outcomes between racial groups in the United States. The clear difference in infant mortality by race has already been mentioned, but equally large differences also appear in any number of other indicators of health quality.[25] For example, maternal mortality among African Americans is over three times higher than for the remainder of the population, as is the incidence of tuberculosis. Deaths from diabetes-related causes in the African-American population are double the rate of those in the population as a whole. It is clear that the nonwhite population faces substantial problems of access to quality care. Further, there is ample evidence that medical personnel do not always provide the same quality of care to members of minority groups as they do to white Americans.[26]

In addition to economic conditions and racial considerations, geography plays a significant dual role in defining access to medical care. First, urban areas are generally better served with doctors and especially with hospitals than are rural areas. For example, in Standard Metropolitan Statistical Areas (SMSAs) in the United States, the average number of physicians per 100,000 population is 221, and the average number of hospital beds per 100,000 is 437. This contrasts with 93 physicians per 100,000 and 394 hospital beds per 100,000 in the non-SMSA regions of the country. Another example of the disparity in medical care resources is that eighteen rural counties in Texas alone have not a single physician, although there are more doctors in the United States than ever before. The geographical disparities in medical services would be even more pronounced if physicians' areas of specialization and hospitals' standards and equipment were also considered. This imbalance in care does not necessarily equate with health outcomes; the District of Columbia has one of the highest numbers of physicians in relation to population (758 per 100,000 population, as compared to a national average of 254) but also has perhaps the worst health outcomes in the country.[27]

Second, there are marked regional imbalances in access to medical care.[28] These can be related in part, but not entirely, to urban-rural differences. The places in the United States best served by physicians and hospitals are the Middle Atlantic states and the states of the Far West, while the worst served are the Upper Midwest and the Deep South. There are, for example, 422 doctors per 100,000 in Massachusetts and 379 per 100,000 in Maryland, but only 164 per 100,000 in Mississippi and 155 per 100,000 in Idaho. Although a variety of programs, public and private, have attempted to equalize personnel distributions, imbalances persist. This maldistribution does not, however, exist so clearly for hospital beds, as many small communities have been able to maintain hospitals, in part as a means of attempting to attract physicians and other health care workers.[29] Finally, there is some evidence that residents of poor and rural states do not receive the same quality of medical care even when services are available.[30]

Thus, in some parts of the United States, high-quality medical care may not be available, even for someone who can afford it, without a substantial investment in travel. For any serious emergency, distance places the affected individual at even greater risk. Several pilot programs to encourage young doctors to practice in rural, "underdoctored" areas have been tried, and more are being advocated, but pronounced inequalities persist. Many rural areas have tried on their own to attract physicians, sometimes offering to finance the medical education of a young person willing to practice in their town.[31] These issues of distribution must be addressed along with economic issues if there is to be greater equality in access to health care. The federal government has instituted a program for funding rural health clinics, but even those facilities appear to go to the largest settlements eligible for assistance.[32]

Finally, we should note that access alone may not be sufficient to ensure that medical care is successful. The relatively high rate of infant mortality (especially among the minority population) is often taken as an indicator of poor access to medical care, although there is some evidence that other factors may be as important in determining those health outcomes. For example, the highest rates of infant mortality (by state) tend to be less closely related to the availability of medical personnel and facilities in the state, or even to per capita income, than to the family situations into which children are born. Illegitimate births, for example, tend to have a much higher rate of infant mortality.[33] Likewise, smoking and alcohol abuse tend to be more prevalent among less affluent and less educated members of the society, exacerbating problems of access to medical care.

Cost

The second fundamental problem that has troubled health care consumers and policymakers is the rapidly rising cost of medical care; this is the health care "problem that won't go away."[34] Not only is it not going away, cost has in fact become the driving force in health policy, especially within the private sector. The majority of Americans with health insurance now participate in some sort of managed care plan, with cost-containment as its principal objective. Indeed, critics of such plans argue that cost concerns have become too dominant, and that they need to ensure quality as much as to minimize costs.

The total cost of medical care in the United States derives from two factors. The first is the number of medical procedures conducted. A growing number of procedures are performed in the United States, both because of the aging of the population and because of the increasing number and types of treatments made available by advances in medical science.[35] Controlling the number of procedures performed has become one of the key elements of managed care, which requires patients to get approval from case managers before an operation or other procedure will be covered by their insurance.[36]

The other contributing factor to the total cost of health care—the one that is most often discussed—is the general increase in prices for all medical procedures. Table 10.8 shows changes in prices for some components of medical care compared with the overall consumer price index (CPI) and with a composite medical care price index. It is clear from these data that medical costs as a whole have increased more rapidly than have total consumer costs and that, among the components of medical costs, hospital costs have increased most rapidly. These costs have increased 298 percent more over a forty-year period than have total consumer prices, while those for total medical care have increased "only" 46 percent more rapidly than has the CPI.

The rate of increase in medical costs slowed slightly during the 1990s but still outpaced general price increases. Further, many experts expect another surge in medical care costs in the immediate future. Most of the savings from implementing managed care have already been realized, so that the underlying dynamics of medical inflation may quickly reassert themselves.[37] Further, the aging of the American population means that there will be more elderly citizens re-

TABLE 10.8   Changes in Medical Care Costs Compared with Consumer Price Index
(1967=100)

	CPI	Total medicine	Hospitals	Physicians	Medical commodities
1960	66.7	79.1	57.3	77.0	104.5
1970	116.3	120.6	145.4	121.4	103.6
1980	246.8	256.9	418.9	269.3	168.1
1985	326.6	413.0	722.5	407.9	262.7
1990	421.8	592.9	1,096.1	533.1	388.4
1995	491.4	817.6	1,577.1	692.5	486.2
1996	512.5	847.8	1,638.6	717.0	500.3
1998	532.7	899.4	1,748.6	771.8	527.2
1999	544.4	930.9	1,821.9	788.2	548.8
2000	562.9	969.1	1,914.9	805.8	567.9

Source: Calculated from U.S. Bureau of the Census, *Statistical Abstract of the United States* (Washington, D.C.: Government Printing Office, annual).

quiring more health care and with that increased demand, more pressures on costs. Finally, because of the political pressure to ensure that patients in managed care have better access to a full range of treatment options, managed care may no longer be an effective barrier to medical inflation.

The importance of these cost data is that medical care is becoming more difficult for the average person to afford. Even if an individual's income keeps pace with the consumer price index, it will fall behind the increasing costs of medical care. The rapidly increasing prices mean that few people can afford to pay for a catastrophic illness requiring long-term hospitalization and extensive treatment; even the best medical insurance available will likely be exhausted by such an illness. Thus, it has become increasingly possible for even a person with a substantial income to be financially destroyed by a major illness. Another potential problem is that all the concern about the cost of medicine may serve to undermine the quality of medical care, something that may be especially evident in managed care.

Health care costs are a problem for government as well as for private citizens, as almost half the total medical care bill in the United States is paid by governments. But even its large share of the medical marketplace has not enabled government to exercise any significant control over health costs, perhaps because decisions about health care spending are made not by one government but by several governments. And within each government are several agencies interested in health care. Government's attempts to control medical costs have therefore been diffused, and they have encountered difficulty overcoming the technical and political power of health care providers. As we discuss later, however, government is attempting to move more effectively to assist citizens—both as tax-payers and as patients—in coping with the costs of health care.

To be able to control costs, we must understand why medical costs have been increasing so rapidly. A number of factors have been identified as causing at least part of the increase.[38] For hospitals, one factor has been a rapid rise in the cost of supplies and equipment, including large capital investments, such as magnetic resonance imaging (MRI) scanners, as well as more mundane items such as dressings and surgical gloves. In addition, labor costs for hospitals have been increasing rapidly, as many professional and nonprofessional employees unionize to bargain for higher wages. Also, there may be too many hospital beds for the number of available patients. Empty hospital beds involve capital costs and even some running costs that must be met, and these costs are spread among the patients who do occupy beds as increases in the room rates. The same consideration applies to overinvestment in technology; every hospital that buys an MRI scanner, for example, must pay for it whether or not it is used very often. For example, the United States has over 3,000 MRI systems (at several million dollars each), while Canada is able to get by with approximately 45.[39] Finally, the complex system of funding medical care in the United States costs a great deal of money. Some studies find that 25 percent of total hospital costs are in administration—about twice that in Canada, with its single-payer public insurance program.[40]

During the 1990s hospitals began reacting to increasing pressures from insurers (including government agencies) and also anticipating changes from national health reform. They attempted to reduce their operating costs by reducing the number of employees, managing patient loads more effectively, and consolidating expensive services such as CAT and MRI scanning units. Managed competition programs also were introduced to establish maximum payments for certain procedures and to encourage the insured to make the best use of their insurance dollars.[41] Hospital costs continue to increase, but the rate of increase has slowed. Further, since the best way to limit hospital costs is to keep patients out of hospitals, increasing numbers of surgical procedures are done on an out-patient basis, and stays in hospital are being shortened—at times to dangerous levels.

Physician costs also have been rising, although not as rapidly as hospital costs. In addition to the general pressures of inflation in the economy as a whole, doctor's fees have been affected by increases in equipment and supply costs, the increasing cost of medical malpractice insurance, and the need to practice "defensive medicine" to protect against malpractice suits by ordering every possible diagnostic procedure.[42] Some of the relatively high cost of physicians' services in the United States is due to the high level of specialization of American doctors.[43] Only 13 percent of the private physicians in office-based practice in the United States are in general practice, down from 18 percent in 1980 (see table 10.9), although when the number of internists (who often function as GPs) is considered, the shift away

TABLE 10.9   Distribution of Physicians by Type of Practice

	1980	1990	1995	2000
General medicine	17.6	17.0	14.0	13.1
Internal medicine	14.9	17.5	17.0	17.6
Obstetrics and gynecology	7.2	7.4	6.6	6.4
Surgery	16.0	15.2	12.4	12.9
Pediatrics	6.4	8.1	7.9	8.6
Other	38.9	34.8	44.1	41.2

Source: American Medical Association, *Physician Characteristic and Distribution* (Chicago: AMA, annual).

from general practice is not nearly so pronounced. In addition, a higher percentage of American doctors practice in hospitals than is the case in many other countries, and hospital care is much more expensive than out-patient care.

Physicians have cooperated increasingly with "preferred provider" programs in which large insurance carriers such as Blue Cross negotiate lower fees for their clients and monitor the charges imposed by physicians. These insurers also require second opinions for expensive procedures or for procedures that are often performed unnecessarily. Doctors sometimes resent interference in their clinical freedom, but these programs ensure them access to large pools of patients, all of whom by definition have insurance and who therefore present fewer problems in collecting fees than might other patients.[44]

The federal government has undertaken several programs to attempt to control physician costs for Medicare patients, generally using a "resource-based relative value scale" (RBRVS), which assigns reasonable costs to procedures based on the time involved as well as the doctor's direct costs and malpractice premiums.[45] Medicare then reimburses 80 percent of those "reasonable costs." As designed, this program assigns somewhat higher relative values to services provided by general practitioners than it does to those offered by specialists, a move designed to reduce medical costs. This program has had limited impact on Medicare costs,[46] however, and government is increasingly moving Medicare recipients into managed-care programs as a more effective mechanism for controlling health care costs.[47]

Finally, the method of payment for most medical care, especially hospital care, may influence costs. Well over 90 percent of all hospital costs and approximately 80 percent of all medical expenses are paid by third-party payers, which may be private (e.g., Blue Cross) or public (Medicaid or Medicare).[48] As a result, neither doctors nor patients have an incentive to restrict consumption of medical care; it has often been perceived as "free." Individuals may, in fact, want to use all the insurance benefits they can in order to recover the amount they have paid as premiums over the years. This is a phenomenon known as the "tragedy of the commons," in which the rational behavior of individuals creates irrationality for society as a whole.[49] To rectify some problems with third-party payment, the Reagan administration included in its 1985 budget a program to tax employer-financed health insurance above a certain value, thus increasing the cost of "first-dollar" coverage (i.e., coverage beginning from the first dollar spent for treatment). Managed-care programs also provide first-dollar coverage for some types of care, but they often impose co-payments to deter consumption or at least make the consumer conscious of the costs.

The states, which have the primary responsibility for administering Medicaid, the public medical program for the poor, have been encountering large cost increases. In addition to the usual programs for managed care and scrutiny of costs, at least one state, Oregon, adopted a more radical plan for cost containment. The state government decided that it wanted to be able to continue to provide care to all its citizens who could not afford private care, rather than lowering the amount of income at which individuals lost eligibility for the program. But the state also realized that it could not pay for everything for everybody.[50] It therefore decided that Medicaid in Oregon would pay only for a range of diseases—selected by cost, seriousness, and effectiveness of treatment—that fell above a line determined by the amount of money available. Medicaid would not pay for treatment of other conditions. So, for example, in 1991 Medicaid would pay for inflammation of the stomach (no. 587 on the list of disorders) but not for lower back pain (no. 588).[51] Also, the program would not pay for "heroic treatments" for extremely difficult cases, such as babies born weighing less than 500 grams.

The Oregon policy has had its critics, who argue that this program of rationing prevents the poor from getting equal treatment and that the selection of the cutoff point in care is arbitrary.[52] It was particularly attacked by groups representing the disabled and the chronically ill. Advocates, however, maintained that the program enabled the state to continue serving all the poor and to continue providing routine and cost-effective diagnostic procedures free of charge. At least in the short run, critics of the program won, and the program was eliminated because it was alleged to violate legal protections for the disabled.[53] This is but one of many difficult choices that rising medical costs may soon impose on American society and its government. Still, the specter of rationing continues to hang over medical care in the United States, whether it is done implicitly or explicitly.

Quality

Finally, both citizens and government must be concerned about the quality of medical care being provided. Citizens' obvious concern has been reflected in the increased number of malpractice suits and complaints against physicians and hospitals. Governments' concerns about quality extend from the general social responsibility for regulating the safety and effectiveness of medicines and medical devices on the market, to the quality of care provided to Medicare and Medicaid patients, to a perhaps more philosophical concern with the efficacy of modern medical care as a remedy for the health problems of American citizens.[54] Medical care is, however, a difficult product for which to judge quality. When a patient enters a physician's office—regardless of whether the resulting bill will be paid by Blue Cross–Blue Shield, by Medicaid, or out of pocket—he or she has the right to expect, at a minimum, competent medical care that meets current standards. Unfortunately, many patients do not receive such care, and they complain about receiving poor-quality care or medical treatment that they believe is delivered without any genuine humanity. The AMA's own statistics document a significant rate of error in diagnosis and treatment.

A more subtle problem is the way in which the quality of health care is eroded through both overtreatment and undertreatment of patients, both generally resulting from financial incentives. Overtreatment has appeared in a number of studies documenting excessive use of medical technology and drugs as a means of generating more income for physicians and hospitals. For the public sector, overtreatment means increased costs for Medicare and Medicaid patients, as well as the more human costs imposed on the patients. This problem of quality appears to be declining, however, as fewer and fewer patients have indemnity insurance, which pays providers on a fee-for-service basis.

The rise of managed care has raised even more questions about quality in the health care industry. Are patients being denied beneficial, or even necessary treatments, simply to minimize costs? Are patients being moved in and out of hospitals—so-called drive-through surgery—in order to maintain profit margins? Government has begun to make some regulatory interventions to address these issues, including regulating length of stay for some procedures. The current quality problem in health care is one of undertreatment, rather than the overtreatment of fee-for-service medicine, as managed care places pressures on providers not to provide services. Because they have an economic interest in not providing services, health maintenance organizations and other managed-care providers use screening devices to prevent patients from receiving certain types of care. One mechanism has been to prohibit doctors from informing patients about expensive treatments that might be beneficial for them. These "gag rules" have now been largely eliminated because of pressures from government and the medical providers.[55] Indeed, some states are beginning to make insurance companies and HMOs liable if they do not provide information and needed care.[56]

The medical profession itself is supposed to be the first line of defense in maintaining the quality of medical care. State medical associations and their review boards are expected to monitor the practice of medicine and handle complaints about incompetent or unethical practitioners. Other professional organizations are supposed to perform the same task for their members. While these organizations do have an interest in maintaining the integrity of patient care, they often find it difficult to discipline their fellow professionals and friends. More positively, the medical profession has taken a major stand in fighting some of the excesses of the managed-care industry and has sought to defend its members' clinical freedom in offering treatment.[57]

A more important philosophical question has been introduced into the discussion of the quality of care, in part by the comment of former Colorado governor Richard Lamm that "we all have the duty to die," meaning that the terminally ill perhaps should not be kept alive by heroic means when such intervention only "prolongs dying" rather than saves life.[58] Is it high-technology medicine that sustains a semblance of life that has lost most human qualities, or is it a high-technology ego trip for the physician? The physicians' first commandment, *primum non nocere* (first, do not harm), has traditionally been understood to require preserving life at all costs; modern technology has made that an expensive and possibly inhumane interpretation. Some patients' families have gone to court to have their loved ones removed from life-support systems, but the techniques available to sustain life appear to have outpaced the ethical, legal, and policy capacity to cope with the changes.[59]

The question of what care is appropriate for the very old and the terminally ill raises the question of rationing of health care. Although this issue is sometimes discussed primarily as a problem of cost, it also has a number of implications for a definition of quality care. Some countries have already begun to impose rather strict rationing of care—not performing organ transplants for patients over certain ages, for example.[60] This development in other systems has, in turn, produced fears that a more extensive public role in American medical care will also mean a greater possibility for such rationing. For consumers used to being able to purchase what they want (provided they have good insurance) in the medical marketplace, the imposition of rationing would seem prima facie a reduction of quality.

The proposal for a "patient's bill of rights" is a more recent public-sector initiative designed to improve the quality of health care services under managed care. Several versions of legislation designed to create such a mechanism were defeated in Congress in 2001, although compromise legislation was passed to provide patients greater opportunities for compensation from insurers and HMOs that deny care. The compromise that made passage of the bill possible included the provisions that state courts would be the locus for any suits involved and that there would be a ceiling on the amount of liability. Although useful for coping with some of the problems of managed care, this legislation depends on compensation after the fact rather than prevention as the means to address the issue of quality in health care.

Public Programs in Health Care

Government is deeply involved in health care services, despite the rhetoric about a free-enterprise medical care system in the United States. Existing public programs provide direct medical services to some segments of the population, offer medical care insurance for others, and support the health of the entire population through public health programs, regulation, and research. Many citizens question the efficacy of these programs, especially the regulatory programs, but they are evidence of the large and important role of government in medicine. We now discuss several major government programs in medical care, with some attention to the policy issues involved in each, and the possibilities of improving the quality of health care through public action.

Medicare

The government medical care program with which most citizens are familiar is Medicare, adopted as part of the Social Security Amendments of 1965. The program is essentially one of medical insurance for the elderly and the disabled who are eligible for Social Security or Railroad Retirement benefits. The program has two components. Part A, financed principally through payroll taxation, is a hospitalization plan. It covers the first 60 days of hospitalization but requires the patient to pay the first $812 (2002). The program also covers hospitalization during the 61st to 90th days but requires a co-payment of $203 per day, and then $406 per day for up to 60 more "lifetime reserve" days (total of 60 for each Medicare recipient over his or her lifetime). This portion of the plan also covers up to 100 days in a nursing-care facility after release from the hospital, with this coverage being subject to a $101.50 co-payment by the insured after the first 20 days (2002).[61]

Part B of Medicare is a supplementary insurance program covering doctors' fees and other outpatient services. These expenses are also subject to deductibles and to coinsurance, with the insured paying the first $100 each year, plus 20 percent of allowable costs. This portion of the Medicare program is financed by the insured, who pay a monthly premium of $54 (2002). Insured persons bear a rather high proportion of their medical expenses under Medicare, given that it is a publicly provided insurance program. The program is, however, certainly subsidized, and it is still a bargain for the average retired person, who might not be able to purchase in the private market anything like the coverage provided because the elderly have, on average, significantly higher medical expenses than the population as a whole.

Medicare is a better program than would be available to most of the elderly under private insurance programs—it requires no physical examination for coverage, covers preexisting health conditions, is uniformly available throughout the country, and provides some services that might not be available on private plans. The program does present some problems, however, perhaps the greatest of which is that it requires those insured to pay a significant amount out of their own pockets for coverage, even when they are hospitalized. Purchasing Part B of the plan requires an annual outlay of $648 (2002), which, although not much money for health insurance, may be a relatively large share of a pensioner's income. In addition, the costs of deductibles and coinsurance in both parts of Medicare may place a burden on less affluent beneficiaries of the program.

In addition to the costs to the recipient on expenses that are covered, Medicare does not cover all the medical expenses that most beneficiaries will incur. For example, it does not pay for prescription drugs, eye or dental examinations, eyeglasses or dentures, preventive examinations, or immunizations; nor does the program cover long-term care. In short, Medicare does not address many medical problems that plague the elderly population the program was intended to serve, and as a result it does not wholly meet the needs of the elderly poor, who are most in need of services. In fact, at least one study shows that the gap between the health status of rich and poor elderly people widened initially after the introduction of Medicare.[62] The more affluent can use the program as a supplement to their own assets or private health insurance programs, while the less affluent are still incapable of providing adequately for their medical needs, even with Medicare.

One attempt to solve the "medigap" problem has been the introduction of private health insurance programs to fill in the lacunae of Medicare coverage. Unfortunately, most existing policies of this type do not cover the most glaring deficiencies of Medicare—for example, the absence of coverage for extended nursing-home care. In addition, the policies do not cover preexisting health problems, and they frequently have long waiting periods for eligibility. In short, these policies often cost more money without providing the protection required. Congress passed legislation in 1980 imposing some standards on such insurance policies, but the law was directed more at outright fraud than at providing policies that truly cover the gaps in Medicare coverage. Additional legislation in 1990 tightened controls on insurers, but often there is still duplication and waste.[63]

On the government's side of the Medicare program, the costs of funding medical insurance for the elderly impose a burden on the working-age population and on government resources. The basic hospitalization coverage under Medicare is financed by a payroll tax collected as a part of the Social Security tax, taking 1.45 percent of each worker's salary. Since the policy was changed in 1991, the health insurance portion of the Social Security tax is extracted on all earned income, unlike the pension and disability portion, which is extracted only up to $65,400 per year (1997). With increasing opposition to Social Security taxes have come suggestions to shift the financing of Medicare to general tax revenues such as the income tax, leaving the entire payroll tax to fund Social Se-curity pensions.[64]

The increasing costs of medical care and the growing number of Americans eligible for Medicare mean that difficulties are likely to arise in financing the pro-gram for some years to come. Congress attempted to address these difficulties as a part of the balanced-budget bill in the summer of 1997.[65] A number of options are now available to Medicare recipients, including traditional "fee-for-service" medi-cine, managed care, preferred-provider plans, and medical savings accounts.[66] Any of the shifts from fee-for-service medicine will provide some cost savings, but some, such as the medical savings account, involve the recipient's taking a chance that he or she will remain relatively healthy during a particular time period, a risky gamble for most elderly people.[67] A major political battle was waged over adding prescription drug coverage in 2002, but the lack of a final decision pleased neither the elderly nor those concerned about cost containment. The Republican victory in the 2002 congressional elections seemed to promise a plan adopted, based on private insurance providers, but as of the end of 2003, there is still no plan.[68]

Finally, problems of quality and fair pricing for Medicare patients are also likely to persist. Medicare regulations allow the Health Care Financing Admin-istration (now the Centers for Medicare and Medicaid, or CMS) to pay "rea-sonable" costs to physicians and hospitals for services rendered to beneficiaries, and, of course, they also require that the providers give adequate and "standard" treatment. In some instances physicians have charged more than the amount designated as "reasonable," thereby imposing additional costs on the patient. In other instances physicians have employed generally unnecessary tests and proce-dures, knowing that the costs would be largely covered by Medicare.

The 1982 Tax Equity and Fiscal Responsibility Act created PROs (Peer Re-view Organizations), now called Quality Improvement Programs, to augment and then replace the earlier Physician Service Review Organizations (PSROs). These organizations are concerned with quality and attempt to work with providers to improve outcomes, but they are also increasingly involved in de-tecting and exposing outright fraud on the part of a few physicians who bill for patients whom they do not see or otherwise abuse the system.[69] Government ac-tions have been supplemented by efforts of private insurance firms, who also lose money through fraud.[70] But fraud is but one of many factors increasing the costs of medical care, and the need for effective cost control will remain an important issue for some time to come.

One move to control costs for public medical programs, called Diagnosis Related Groups (DRGs), is a form of prospective reimbursement. This program, adopted in 1983, has hospitals reimbursed for Medicare and Medicaid patients according to one of over 400 specific diagnostic groups (e.g., appendicitis).[71] The hospital is guaranteed a fixed amount for each patient according to the

DRG to which his or her complaint is assigned. A hospital that is able to treat a patient for less can retain the difference as "profit," but if the hospital stay costs more than is allowed under the DRG, the hospital must absorb the loss. This system is in large part responsible for the fact that hospital stays in the United States are the shortest in the world.

Despite some experience with DRGs, a number of questions remain about how they affect medical care. For example, the doctor determines the course of treatment more than the hospital does, and there has been increased conflict between hospital administrators and physicians about patient care. Also, this program may reduce the quality of care provided to Medicaid and Medicare patients or cause too-early dismissals of patients, shifting costs onto home medical care programs and community medicine; patients are discharged "quicker and sicker," and too often they are readmitted soon after discharge. Also, DRGs do not easily accommodate the multiple diseases and infirmities characteristic of so many Medicare patients. Nevertheless, the DRG program is an interesting attempt to impose greater cost consciousness on hospitals and physicians, and it has been copied by some private health insurers. This approach to cost control may be preferable to rationing approaches such as that imposed in Oregon for Medicaid patients (see p. 260).

Medicaid

While Medicare is directed toward the elderly and the disabled, Medicaid, the second major public health care program, is directed toward the poor. The Medicaid program was created at the same time as Medicare, to provide federal matching funds to state and local governments for medical care of welfare recipients and the "medically indigent," a category intended to include those who do not qualify for public assistance but whose income is not sufficient to cover necessary medical expenses. Unlike Medicare, which is a uniform national program, Medicaid is administered by the states, and as a consequence the benefits, eligibility requirements, and administration vary considerably. However, if a state does choose to have a Medicaid program (two states do not), it must provide medical care benefits for all welfare recipients and for those who receive Supplemental Security Income because of categorical problems—age, blindness, and disability.

Medicaid regulations require states to provide a range of services to program recipients: hospitalization, laboratory and other diagnostic services, X-rays, nursing-home care, screening for a range of diseases, and physicians' services. The states may also extend benefits to cover prescription drugs and other services. For each service, the states may set limitations on the amount of care covered and on the rate of reimbursement, and given the increasing costs, they have tended to provide little more than the minimum benefits required under federal law. Federal laws, however, are becoming increasingly stringent, thus imposing additional costs on the states that are difficult to fund.[72] Some states are reacting by using alternative service systems such as HMOs for their Medicaid clients—by 1999 over one-third of Medicaid recipients were in managed care.[73]

In addition to the variance in coverage and benefits across the country, Medicaid has other policy problems. The ones most commonly cited are fraud and abuse. It is sometimes estimated that up to 7 percent of total federal outlays for Medicaid are accounted for by abuse.[74] Almost all such abuse is perpetrated by service providers, rather than by beneficiaries—the patients—in part because of the complex eligibility requirements and procedures for reimbursement. Still, this pattern of fraud presents a negative image of the program to the public.[75] With a continuing strain on public resources, any program that has a reputation for fraud is likely to encounter funding difficulties—and this is true whether the fraud is committed by respected providers, such as physicians, or by their indigent clients.

The general strain on fiscal resources at all levels of government and increased medical costs also have produced more direct effects on the Medicaid program. States have been forced to cut back on optional services under the program and to reduce coverage of primary (physician) care in order to be able to finance hospital care for recipients. Also, some states have set limitations on the amount of physicians' reimbursement for each service. These reimbursements are significantly lower than the rates doctors would receive from private or even Medicare patients; the result is that an increasing number of physicians refuse to accept Medicaid patients. In part because of these trends, Medicaid has increasingly become a program of institutional medical care—which is, paradoxically, the most expensive method of delivering medical services. As with Medicare, however, institutional care through hospitals, hospital emergency rooms, and nursing homes is the one kind of medical care almost sure to be covered under the program. As a result, less than 2 percent of all Medicaid spending goes to home health services, while over 40 percent of all expenditures goes to extended-care facilities, many of which do not meet federal standards.

Like Medicare, the Medicaid program has done a great deal of good in making medical care available to people who might not otherwise receive it. Nevertheless, some significant Medicaid problems—notably costs and coverage—will remain political issues for years. Proposals for solving those problems range from the abolition of both programs to the establishment of national health insurance, with a number of proposals for internal readjustments of the programs or the use of private health insurance in between these more radical alternatives. There is a special drive to ensure that as many children as possible are included in the program.[76]

Health Maintenance Organizations: Managing Managed Care

A fundamental and frequently made criticism of American medical care is that it is, or at least has been, fee-for-service medicine. Medical practitioners were paid for each service performed and, as a consequence, had incentives to utilize their skills; surgeons made money by wielding their scalpels, and internists made money by ordering diagnostic procedures. Furthermore, critics have charged that American medical care has been primarily acute care. The system is oriented toward treating the ill rather than toward preventing illness. The most money is to be made through curing illness, not through promoting good health. This point is to some degree substantiated by the relatively low levels of immunizations among American children (see table 10.10). Despite all the expenditure on medical care in the United States, millions of children still are not fully immunized against normal childhood diseases.

The health maintenance organization (HMO) was developed as at least a partial response to those failings of the health care system.[77] First, the HMO provides prepaid medical care—members pay an annual fee in return for which they receive virtually all their medical care. They may have to pay ancillary costs (e.g., a small set fee for each prescription), but the vast majority of medical expenses are covered through the HMO. Under such a prepayment scheme, doctors working for the HMO have no incentive to prescribe additional treatments. If anything, given that the doctors commonly share in the profits of the organization or frequently own the HMO themselves, they have an incentive not to prescribe treatments, because any surgery or treatment that would cost the organization without providing additional income reduces profits. By the same reasoning, since a healthy member is all profit, while a sick member is all loss, doctors in an HMO have an incentive to keep the members healthy and to practice preventive medicine. By thus reversing the incentives usually presented to physicians, it is argued, HMOs can significantly improve the quality of health care and slow the rapid escalation of medical costs.

The formation of HMOs has been supported by the federal government. In 1973 President Nixon signed into law a bill directed at improving choice in the health care marketplace.[78] The legislation provided for planning and development grants for prospective HMOs, but at the same time it placed a number of restrictions on any HMO using federal funding. Most important, all HMOs had to offer an extensive array of services, including psychiatric care. An employer offering group insurance to employees had to make an equal contribution for any employee who wanted to join an HMO. The federal involvement in HMOs was reauthorized in 1978 for another three years, with additional support for the development of outpatient care facilities, which are important in minimizing expensive hospitalization. The HMO movement has also been as-

TABLE 10.10   Percentage of Children Immunized

	1995	*1999*
Diphtheria-pertussis-typhoid	95	96
Polio	88	90
Measles, mumps, rubella	90	92
Hepatitis B	68	88

Source: U.S. Centers for Disease Control, *Mortality and Morbidity Review,* July 2001.

sisted by federal efforts restricting the actions of physicians and private insurers who have sought to reduce the competition offered by HMOs, and continues to be supported by government.

HMOs and other forms of managed care now operate widely in the United States. There continues to be a good deal of skepticism about the quality of medical care provided by HMOs, however, and some citizens appear unwilling to adopt this significant departure from the traditional means of delivering health services. Although the concept does have critics—most of them members of the medical profession—it also has supporters. HMO plans have been supported by organized labor as one means of reducing medical inflation, and they are often favored by businesses as a means of reducing costs, a mechanism that is more palatable than direct government regulation. In one vote of confidence, the Reagan administration in 1984 allowed Medicare and Medicaid patients the option of joining HMOs for their medical care, believing that this option could reduce the government's costs for these programs with no loss of medical quality.[79] As pressures on medical costs have increased, and employers and individual consumers have sought lower-cost alternatives, an increasing proportion of the medical profession has moved into HMOs and similar organizations.[80]

HMOs were the first step in creating the concept of managed care, whose basic idea is that doctors cannot make all decisions about what sorts of care to provide nor patients (or their primary-care physicians) their own decisions about what specialists to consult. Physicians, hospitals, and other providers are connected in "networks" or "organizations," and referrals for specialized care are made within those networks. Further, health care managers make decisions about what sort of care is appropriate and can even prevent a patient's receiving the type of care that he or she, or the physician, wants. The patient may still go to an emergency room or other facility outside the network, but the service received there generally is not covered by insurance.

The managed care system has been successful in reducing the rate of increase in health care costs, but now pressures are building that are beginning to accelerate the price rise again—most important among them, that the system of insurance is becoming so general that many poorer and sicker people are being brought into managed care.[81] There are also some political pressures (in some cases successful) to require managed care plans to permit greater clinical freedom for physicians and to ensure that patients can make their own decisions about some aspects of care, especially visits to the emergency room.[82] President Clinton, for example, advocated a "patient's bill of rights"[83] to ensure that patients would have much greater control over their own medical care, despite the probability of higher costs; this innovation eventually was accepted in the early days of the administration of George W. Bush.

Even without the patient's bill of rights, the costs of HMOs were moving upward by the turn of the new century, along with the rest of medical care. A number of factors are responsible, including the aging of the population, the development of numerous expensive new treatments that can no longer be excluded by HMOs (or other managed care systems) as being "experimental," and the increased willingness of the medical profession to resist the controls that the plans attempt to impose.[84] These increasing costs are, in turn, adding to the incentives for businesses to drop health coverage for their employees or to increase the proportion of the cost to be contributed by the employees. In effect, the presumed remedy for the problem of health care costs has itself turned out to be expensive.

Health Care Regulation

Perhaps the most pervasive impact of government on the delivery of health care services in the United States has been through regulation, of which there are many kinds. The adoption of the Employment Retirement Income Security Act (ERISA) in 1974 put the federal government squarely in the center of regulation, often superseding state-level regulation.[85] Among the many targets of health care regulation, this chapter can only briefly discuss three types: costs, quality, and pharmaceuticals.[86]

Hospital Costs

Cost increases have been a major consideration in health care for some time, and hospital costs have been the most rapidly increasing component of medical costs. Further, as hospitals constitute a major component of the total health care bill (44 percent) and are readily identifiable institutions with better record-keeping than the average physician, it seems sensible to concentrate on them to control medical care costs. Approaches to controlling hospital costs have been varied. The Carter administration proposed direct regulation of hospital costs, which was sufficient to frighten the hospital industry to introduce its own voluntary effort (VE) program to slow increases in costs. Another major approach to controlling hospital costs has been prospective reimbursement; the federal version of this approach for Medicare patients is the Diagnostic Related Groupings mentioned earlier. In essence, DRGs constitute a market approach to cost containment, for they allow hospitals that are efficient to make a profit, while those that are not well run can sustain losses.

Although both the Carter program and DRGs attack the problem of hospital costs, neither attempted to address some other fundamental causes of price escalation. One problem was the fundamental principle of fee-for-service medicine, which gives hospitals and doctors an incentive to provide more services. Another was the related tendency of the medical profession to offer high-cost hospital treatment when lower-cost options would be as effective. This choice was made both for the convenience of the physician and because many health insurance policies will pay for hospital treatments but not for the same treatments performed on an outpatient basis. The regimen of DRGs and preferred-provider plans to limit costs in private insurance have helped to rein in this tendency somewhat, but American medical care remains more hospital-centered than that of many other countries. Finally, it is important to remember that hospitals do not have patients, doctors do, and hospitals must compete for doctors in order to fill their available beds. This competition takes place largely through the acquisition of high-cost technology (CAT scanners, magnetic resonance imaging systems, etc.), which must be amortized through the higher price of hospital care.

Health Care Quality

The regulation of quality is one of the most controversial areas of government intervention in the health care field. First, regulation operates directly against long-established canons of clinical freedom and the right of members of the medical profession to regulate their own conduct. Medical professionals, as well as most of the public, assume that the only person qualified to judge the professional conduct of a physician is another physician. The specter of bureaucrats intervening in medical care is not comforting to the average American.

In addition, private mechanisms for rectifying harm done by a physician in the conduct of his or her profession are well established. These include legal proceedings such as tort and malpractice lawsuits, which generate their own health care problems and have been cited as one factor causing rapid increases in medical care costs. Some effects of malpractice litigation are direct, as physicians pass their doubled or tripled malpractice insurance costs on to patients in higher fees. Although this direct impact of malpractice insurance fees on medical costs appears minimal, the indirect effects—the practice of "defensive medicine"—appear more substantial. A doctor fearing a malpractice suit may prescribe additional diagnostic procedures, extra days in the hospital, or extra treatments to lessen his or her chances of being found legally negligent, and the costs of these extra procedures also are passed on to consumers. Other effects of malpractice as a quality control are more systemic, as doctors in specialties such as obstetrics and neurosurgery, which are subject to frequent lawsuits, simply change to other specialties. This phenomenon can leave small towns and even small cities without certain types of medical care.

Despite some earlier opposition from the medical and legal profession, there is now a strong drive for increased quality regulation of medical care. As noted, much of this has come about because of apparent abuses by HMOs. Several surveys have found that significant majorities of the population want some protection from the economic power of managed care,[87] and so even some conservative Republican congressmen have advocated a stronger governmental role in the regulation of the managed care industry.[88]

As we mentioned when discussing Medicare, the major public instruments for regulating the quality of medical care are the Quality Improvement Programs. These organizations are designed in part to monitor costs of services provided to Medicare patients, but they necessarily become involved in the issue of appropriate and effective treatment as well, for treatments that are ineffective or dangerous can also be costly. Some quality organizations have gone so far as to establish standard profiles of treatment for common conditions and then to question physicians whose practice differs significantly from those patterns. Physicians who offer more extensive treatments may be imposing additional costs on the program, while those who are providing unusual or less extensive treatments may be threatening the health of the patient.

The growth of managed care is placing more pressure on government to regulate health care. Patients often believe that they are being denied adequate care by their HMOs or other forms of managed care, and their complaints have generated a number of regulatory interventions or proposals for regulations. For example, at least one state has enabled patients to sue HMOs for malpractice when care is inadequate, rather than placing all the onus on the individual physician.[89] Eighteen states have attacked one of the most infamous of the practices of managed care programs—the so called "gag rules" that prevent physicians from informing patients about more expensive, and perhaps more effective, treatments. The federal government also has become involved, as the patient's bill of rights has gone into effect as a means of ensuring that patients in managed care have some protections.

The attempts to regulate the managed care industry have been impeded to some extent by the early protection given to HMOs and similar organizations. When these forms of providing care were first being considered, they were regarded as a way of combating the dominance of fee-for-service medicine and were promoted both to limit costs and to place greater emphasis on preventive medicine.[90] These organizations were, in fact, made immune from lawsuits for their actions in restricting access to types of care. One of the subsequent proposals for boosting the quality of service in these organizations, however, is to use the legal system as the mechanism for quality control, as is done in most other aspects of the medical system, extending it to insurers as well as practitioners.[91]

Drug Regulation

The federal government is also deeply involved in the regulation of the pharmaceutical industry and in the control of substances in food and water that are potentially harmful to health. Its regulatory efforts in regard to food and drugs began in 1902, with extensive increases in its powers in 1938 and again in 1962, but the issues surrounding drug regulation have become substantially more heated since the early 1980s. The Food and Drug Administration (FDA), which is responsible for most drug regulation, has been under attack from all sides. Some argue that its regulations have been excessively stringent and have prevented useful drugs from coming to the market. The AIDS epidemic has brought this complaint to the fore and has actually produced some changes in the procedures for licensing new drugs.[92] Other critics of the FDA believe that its regulations have been too lax and excessively dominated by the pharmaceutical industry and that, as a result, potentially dangerous drugs have been certified for sale.[93] Also, the FDA and the drug industry have been criticized for not paying sufficient attention to the different reactions that women may have to many drugs that were initially tested only on men.[94]

The basic regulatory doctrine applied to pharmaceuticals is that a drug must be shown to be both safe and effective before it can be approved for sale. Several problems arise from this doctrine. First, almost any drug will have some side effects, so that proving its safety is difficult, and some criteria must be established for weighing the benefits of an individual drug against its side effects. The example commonly cited here is that because of the range of its known side effects, common aspirin might have considerable difficulty being certified for use under current standards. The safety and effectiveness of a drug must be demonstrated by clinical trials that are often time-consuming and expensive, and potentially important drugs are thereby delayed in coming to the public.

Critics of the drug industry point to other issues in drug regulation and in the pharmaceutical industry as a whole. For example, there are the problems of look-alike drugs and the use of brand names as opposed to generic drugs.[95] It is argued that a great deal of the attention in drug research is directed toward finding combinations of drugs that can be marketed under a brand name or in reproducing findings of already proven drugs so that they can be marketed with a different brand name. Because brand-name drugs are invariably more expensive than generic drugs, critics charge that the licensing of brand names actually aids the pharmaceutical industry by promoting the sale of higher-priced drugs. They also argue that drugs are sold and prescribed without adequate dissemination of information about their possible side effects. Some states have intervened to reduce the problem of inflated drug costs by allowing pharmacists to substitute a generic drug for a brand-name drug unless the physician specifically forbids such substitution. Many drugstores attempt to make their customers aware of this cost-saving option, so unless the physicians believes that a generic drug would not be effective (or opposes its use for some other, allegedly less noble reason), patients are able to choose a cheaper alternative.[96] In addition, American consumers have found ways to purchase cheaper drugs from Canada, either taking trips north of the border or using mail-order. Ironically, most of these cheaper drugs were manufactured in the United States.

A major attempt to modify drug regulation procedures was made in 1979 in a Senate bill proposed by Edward Kennedy, D-Mass. Among its most important proposals was shortening the review period required prior to marketing new drugs, especially so-called breakthrough drugs that offer great promise for serious illnesses and seem greatly superior to existing drugs. The proposed legislation also mandated that more information on drugs be disseminated to physicians and patients so that more informed decisions could be made about the drugs' use, and it attempted to limit certain drug-company promotional practices. With skilled political management, the bill passed the Senate easily, but it did not pass in the House of Representatives. This legislation represented, however, the future direction of drug regulation, as "fast tracking" of drugs has now become possible.

The Food and Drug Administration regulates food as well as drugs, especially the possibility of carcinogenic substances in food. The Delaney Amendment (passed in 1958) requires the FDA to remove from the market foods containing any substance that "induces" cancer in human beings or animals. An issue developed over this amendment during the late 1970s when studies in Canada showed that large amounts of the artificial sweetener saccharin tended to produce bladder cancer. Under the Delaney Amendment, the FDA was required to propose a ban on saccharin. Subsequent reports by the National Academy of Science then recommended that, instead of prohibiting all such substances, the government should establish categories of risk with attached regulations ranging from complete prohibition to warning labels to no action at all. It suggested also that such decisions take into consideration the possible benefits from the continued sale of the substance. Because many believed that saccharin was highly beneficial for some people and produced only a low risk, they suggested that it be allowed to remain on sale. These risk-benefit or cost-benefit considerations are a common aid to decision making in the public sector (see

Chapter 16), although they are perhaps of questionable validity when applied to risks of the occurrence of a disease such as cancer. Nevertheless, for whatever reasons, Congress reauthorized the continuing sale of saccharin.

Another issue related to the regulation of pharmaceuticals is the regulation of tobacco, and especially cigarette smoking. The surgeon general determined many years ago that smoking cigarettes is harmful, required warning labels on packages, and forbade advertising by electronic media. More recently, state and local governments have imposed bans on smoking in public places. The surgeon general and the FDA also have developed evidence on the thousands of deaths caused by smoking. In congressional hearings in 1994 the FDA presented evidence on the addictive nature of nicotine and began increasing its efforts to strengthen the regulations on the sale, advertising, and use of cigarettes. In particular, if it were to declare nicotine to be a drug, the FDA could regulate cigarettes as the delivery system for that drug, but the agency has never taken that step.

Cigarettes and their regulation also figure prominently in the discussion of financing health care. Several of the plans for national health insurance depend upon an increased tax on cigarettes for at least a part of the financing. Such a tax would function like a regulation if it were to encourage people to stop smoking, but that too would pay a benefit by reducing the estimated $65 billion spent on diseases caused by smoking. There are a number of efforts at the state level to improve enforcement of existing laws, especially laws against selling cigarettes to minors. The fundamental question of the capacity of government to control use of cigarettes continues to be pursued in the courts and in legislatures. The states have won major suits against the tobacco companies and some have used these funds to enhance the availability of medical care for their citizens, especially the less affluent.

Summary

Regulation is a common and pervasive form of public intervention into the health care industry in the United States. It is not without controversy, however, and almost all forms of regulation are under active review and reconsideration. Under Republican administrations, regulations are often replaced by competitive mechanisms using market forces to produce changes in the health service industry. The Clinton administration was by no means as negative about public intervention, but more regulations may be replaced. Even with the increasing public concern over health care in the early twenty-first century, some conservatives want to further reduce public attempts to control this industry while liberals seek to maintain and expand regulations. The passage of the patient's bill of rights was a major regulatory step, but liberals want increased controls over pricing and improved access to attempt to equalize access.

The Pursuit of National Health Insurance

The United States is the only Western industrialized nation without a significant program of national health insurance or direct health-service delivery by the public sector. As we have seen, this does not mean that the government has no role in medical care. In fact, approximately 14 percent of the American people now depend directly on the federal government for their health care, another group of the same size receive Medicaid funded jointly by the states and the federal government, and still others receive most or all of their care from emergency rooms in municipal hospitals. What the absence of national health insurance does mean is that citizens who do not fit into the particular categories eligible for public insurance—for example, the aged, veterans, the medically indigent—must rely on private health care, or the often substandard and usually time-consuming care available at emergency rooms in public hospitals.[97] Rising medical expenses, the ever-present possibility of catastrophic illnesses with equally catastrophic economic consequences, and the declining availability of health insurance as an employee benefit, however, have given rise to increasing pressures to extend the public role in medicine to the entire population.

The idea of a national health insurance program for the United States goes back at least to the Truman administration. (Indeed, Theodore Roosevelt, aware of health care programs then beginning in European nations, had proposed something like a national health program at the beginning of the twentieth century.) When President Harry Truman proposed a comprehensive national health insurance program in 1945 as a part of the Social Security program, it met with relentless opposition from the American Medical Association (AMA) and conservative business organizations, who called the plan "socialized medicine." The AMA spent millions of dollars on its successful campaign against national health insurance, and most Americans appeared to want to retain the private medical system. The adoption of Medicare in 1965 represented a first partial success for advocates of a national health insurance program, but pressures have continued to grow for a plan that would insure the entire population.

Interestingly, public opinion about health care has also changed. Although the AMA's arguments against socialized medicine were persuasive in the 1940s and 1950s, by 1973 a majority of Americans polled favored some system of public health insurance. By the mid-1990s as many as two-thirds of respondents in polls said they favored national health insurance of some sort.[98] The political importance of the issue was highlighted in a 1991 senatorial election in Pennsylvania in which a relatively unknown Democrat (Harris Wofford), campaigning heavily on the issue of national health care, soundly defeated a popular ex-governor and ex–U.S. attorney general (Richard Thornburgh). Democrats quickly identified the health insurance issue as a possible avenue to the White House in 1992, and Bill Clinton seized on it as a centerpiece of his campaign.

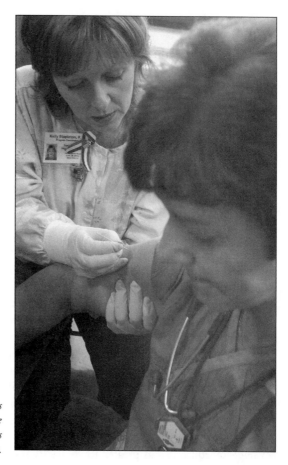

The threat of bioterrorism has increased awareness of the importance of immunizations and other public health measures.

One major difficulty in the drive for some sort of national health insurance in the 1990s was that several alternative plans were available. Some of the plans had the backing of powerful interests in the medical establishment (one was even proposed by the AMA), some had the backing of the Republicans in Congress and others of the Democrats in Congress, while still others were proposed by health care advocacy groups. The Clinton administration began the most recent active discussion of national health insurance, but its plan was but one among many. The political problem, therefore, was to get enough support to coalesce around any one plan to have it adopted and then implemented successfully.[99] As we have already pointed out, both the Clinton administration and the advocates of other plans failed in that effort.

We will now look at several broad alternative approaches to national health insurance[100] and then more specifically at several of the plans that have been under active consideration at one time or another.

"Play or Pay"

One approach to national health insurance is commonly called "play or pay." The idea is that all employers would have to provide at least minimal health insurance for their employees ("play") or contribute to a public insurance program that would cover their employees and everyone else not covered by private health insurance ("pay"). Most plans call for a payroll tax of 7 or 8 percent for companies not providing health benefits. These plans also depend to a great extent on the actions of the private sector, but they do include a public insurance program (usually an expanded Medicare program) to provide a safety net for the unemployed. A program like this is already in place in Hawaii; a more extensive program was tried in Massachusetts but encountered substantial financial difficulties when the economy in that state sustained a number of serious reverses.[101]

The play-or-pay system largely would preserve the existing insurance system, although probably with more extensive regulation, as well as the existing, fee-for-service medical-care system, again perhaps with greater regulation of costs. In addition, it would allow companies to provide better benefits to their employees than the minimums mandated under the law, although those benefits might be treated as taxable income for the recipients. The principal difficulty with this plan is the claim by many small employers that health insurance costs would force them out of business, much as many others were forced in the 1990s to drop medical coverage of their employees because of the costs.

The reform plan proposed by the AMA contains most elements of the play-or-pay system and would require all employers, over time, to provide medical care to their employees. Combined with this fundamental change in the status quo would be reform of existing public programs to ensure greater equality of coverage (Medicaid) and greater financial soundness (Medicare). Further, the plan would impose several cost-cutting ideas, such as limitation of malpractice claims. While this proposal is to some degree self-serving on the part of the medical care profession, it does demonstrate the pervasiveness of concern about access and cost issues in health care in the United States.

Canadian-Style Comprehensive Coverage

The most extreme proposals for public medical care would adopt something like the plan currently in operation in Canada—generally referred to as the "single-payer" system[102]—and would change the medical industry in the United States rather fundamentally, placing the public sector, not the private providers (doctors and hospitals), in the driver's seat in medicine. The simplest plan of this type would extend Medicare, with its deductibles and co-payments, to cover the entire population. Other plans involve issuing to all legal residents cards to be presented to providers, who would then receive reimbursement from the government. Fees would be set or maximum reimbursements established, and doctors and hospitals would be able to charge more if the patient were willing (and able) to pay.

Critics argue that this program would require large tax increases and would put existing health insurance providers out of business in favor of large public bureaucracies. Further, the critics claim that the experience of Canada is that health care innovation has been slower, and that there is some waiting for elective procedures. Advocates of the Canadian system, in contrast, argue that such charges are exaggerated and that these problems have had little real impact on the quality of care. Indeed, they assert that Americans are receiving too many needless tests and treatments because that is the only way for doctors to earn money in a fee-for-service environment. Further, these advocates of the single-payer system argue that those who are better served under the current system will have to pay some costs if a more equitable system of medical care is to be introduced.

The George H. W. Bush Administration

The administration of George H. W. Bush offered a plan for national health care reform toward the end of its time in office, in part as a means of preventing the Democrats from capturing this issue entirely. Several plans were actually broached by the White House and its allies, all quite minimal and depending largely on the private sector to provide most of the coverage and on the reduction of medical costs to make insurance plans affordable for individuals and small businesses.[103] The most basic proposal coming from that administration was a simple refundable tax credit to assist individuals who purchased private insurance.

A more complete plan that was favored by some in the administration was labeled "managed competition."[104] This plan would have had firms large enough to provide cost-effective medical insurance continue to provide insurance coverage for their employees as they have in the past. But these large companies would receive tax write-offs amounting to only 80 percent of the average current cost of providing similar medical care and would therefore be expected to pressure medical providers to give them preferential rates in exchange for the large volume of business they could offer. "Preferred provider plans" such as this are already used by insurers such as Blue Cross–Blue Shield, and this plan would have extended that idea to most private insurance.

The remainder of the population, whether employed or not, would receive health insurance from newly created agencies called "public sponsors." Individuals would be offered several prepaid plans (HMOs) and perhaps a conventional insurance plan, but the assumption was that the insurance plans would cost more and that the difference would have to be paid by the insured. This would mean that most people would choose to be covered through HMOs, which would therefore have a great deal of market power, like the insurers for large firms, and could bargain with providers for lower rates. This plan would have provided medical care to all citizens and might have stabilized or lowered medical care costs, assuming the market worked as expected.

The Clinton Administration Plan and Its Alternatives

The Clinton administration placed health care reform at the top of its domestic agenda when it took office in January 1993. Almost immediately Hillary Rodham Clinton began a series of meetings with "stakeholders" and with ordinary citizens to collect ideas for the reform. The plan that she and the administration proposed was a complex one, depending on "alliances" of health care providers. Very much as HMOs have done for years, these alliances would supply all the health care needs for their members for a set annual fee, although fee-for-service plans also would be available. According to the Clinton plan's provision, those fees would be fixed at an average of $1,800 for an individual and $4,200 for families, below existing private insurance rates for much of the population. Individuals would also be required to pay deductibles and co-payments for services on the fee-for-service plans. Businesses would be mandated to pay for their employees (up to 7.9 percent of their payrolls), with subsidies available for small business.

Universality was the central tenet of the Clinton proposals, and this was the issue over which the president said he would never compromise. The employer mandates that were central to universality also became a focus of criticism. For the unemployed or for people working for very small employers, insurance would be provided by the federal government, paid for by cigarette taxes and perhaps other taxes. Employers could provide insurance better than the national minimums, but those extra benefits could be treated as taxable income for the employee or made not deductible as a business expense for the employer. The Clinton program therefore would have tended to create much greater equality in access to medical care than is currently found in the United States. The program also provided for cost containment, initially through competitive incentives but later through regulated prices, if necessary to reduce medical inflation to the general rate of inflation.[105]

As might be expected, the Clinton plan produced substantial criticism from a number of directions. Many critics, even those who favored universality and mandates, regarded the plan as excessively complex and too heavily reliant on the alliances to both provide care and minimize costs. These critics often advocated instead a single-payer plan such as the Canadian system. Other critics disagreed with the concept of universality, believing that it was too costly and imposed excessive costs on employers to provide medical insurance. They sought alternatives more like that proposed by the previous administration, relying more on voluntary efforts and the private sector. They also saw the Clinton plan creating a huge and costly federal bureaucracy.

One principal alternative to the Clinton plan was devised and championed by Senator Robert Dole, R-Kans. This plan relied heavily on voluntary compliance and private insurance, and it did not seek universal coverage—the target was 91 or 92 percent of the population. The plan provided for subsidies for the less affluent for purchasing insurance, to be paid for by cost containment in Medicare and Medicaid. Further, by mandating portability of health insurance, this plan attempted to address the problem of workers being locked into jobs by fear of losing their insurance. There was also a "fail-safe" provision to prevent the program from adding to the federal deficit. Although it was supported by numerous Republican senators, Democratic control of Congress then prevented this plan from emerging from committee.

Several other plans also emerged in Congress, including one from the Senate Labor and Human Resources Committee, chaired by Edward Kennedy, D-Mass. This plan provided a number of alternative means for acquiring medical insurance, including private insurance, purchasing cooperatives at state level, and participation in the existing Federal Employees Health Benefit Plan. This plan had many elements of "play or pay," including the requirement that employers not providing insurance for their employees would have to pay a substantial payroll tax. The plan also would impose a fairly large tax on cigarettes to help fund the additional costs of the program.

The Senate Finance Committee chaired by Daniel Patrick Moynihan, D-N.Y., prepared another health insurance plan that was less universal than those advocated by President Clinton and by Senator Kennedy, with no employer mandates; participation in insurance purchasing alliances was voluntary. This plan proposed to increase rates of coverage of the population gradually over seven years, with a national commission making policy recommendations to Congress if 95 percent of the population were not covered by 2002. The plan was financed by increased cigarette taxes and by taxes on higher-priced private insurance plans.

The House Ways and Means Committee also authored a plan for national health insurance. This plan relied on the existing Medicare program (a new Part C) as the basis for providing health insurance to the uninsured and to Medicaid recipients, with most employees remaining on private insurance.[106] Thus, unlike the Clinton plan, it required no new federal bureaucracy but only the extension of an existing one. The bulk of insurance (80 percent) would still be private, provided by employers, with small employers eligible for subsidies of up to half the cost of insurance. Low-income insured workers would also be eligible for subsidized premiums. This proposal also would have had strong cost-control, with each state and the nation having a national limit for health care spending. The additional costs of the program would be financed by a gradual increase in the cigarette tax to 69 cents per pack and a tax on private insurance programs.

Finally, the House Education and Labor Committee developed its own plan, including many of the same features as the Clinton plan, although offering expanded benefits and avoiding the mandatory alliances. Instead, there would be purchasing cooperatives formed at the state level, with employers having more than 1,000 employees allowed to opt out and create their own insurance plans. The financing of this program was rather similar to that in the Clinton plan, with an additional tax on the large employers that opted out of the basic plans.

After the various committees had acted, the majority leadership in both houses of Congress attempted to blend their several proposals into two plans. In the House of Representatives, Richard Gephardt, D-Mo., presented a plan that had many of the features of the Clinton proposal, most notably the demand for universal coverage and employer mandates to cover 80 percent of the cost of the average individual policy. It differed in requiring a range of options for all citizens and in providing subsidies to people with much higher incomes (as well as a number of other technical details).

In the Senate, Majority Leader George Mitchell, D-Maine, developed a plan that attempted to reconcile the basic intentions of the Clinton plan with the arguments of its critics. In the first place, the Mitchell plan dropped the goal of immediate universality and replaced it with a goal of 95 percent coverage by the year 2000. If that goal were not reached by voluntary means, a system of mandates might be imposed by 2002. Most of the other features of the Mitchell plan were somewhat simplified versions of the Clinton plan.

Summary

In the end, none of these proposals for reforming health care could be passed by the 1994 Congress. As the debate wore on, more questions than answers emerged about health care.[107] Many citizens and many politicians raised a wide range of questions about the impacts of the various proposals for reform. The politicians also worried about the impact that voting for one or another proposal might have on their political careers, especially just before midterm elections, and this fear was exacerbated by the vast amounts of lobbying, especially by the insurance and health care industries.[108] Further, it was impossible for liberals and conservatives to put aside their ideological differences to find a compromise that all could accept. For all sides, the pursuit of a perfect plan was the enemy of selecting an acceptable plan.

All the reform proposals faced insurmountable obstacles to adoption and perhaps even greater barriers to effective implementation. All the plans were complex, grafting on top of an already complicated system one or another means of financing a health care program that could provide universal access. The plans all involved increases in the amount of money flowing through the public sector, although almost all were likely to reduce the total amount spent on medical care over what would have happened under the existing system. All the plans also involved imposing some costs on the private sector, although the degree of mandating varied substantially. These plans also all proposed to maintain choice for consumers, but many opponents of the Clinton plan and more comprehensive plans feared rationing and a decline in the quality of available care, especially for those with the resources to pay for it.[109]

The competition among these alternative plans for health care reform demonstrates a good deal about the politics of public policy in the United States. The conflict pitted a number of special interests and their resources against the interests of the uninsured and even the general public who might benefit from lower medical care costs. Further, it demonstrated very clearly the conflict that can arise between the president and Congress over both the substance of policy and their relative power in the process. It also illustrated the degree of fragmentation that exists within the individual institutions, as a number of congressional committees drafted their own reform plans.[110] Finally, this reform effort pointed to the importance of policy entrepreneurship. In this case several players—Hillary Rodham Clinton, Senator Dole, and Senator Moynihan—were all attempting to be successful entrepreneurs, whereas only one was likely to succeed, and in this case, despite their skills, none finally did so.

The failure of comprehensive health care reform did not end attempts at implementing some reforms. In particular, the federal government began to consider some regulatory reforms that could address some of the most egregious problems of the current health care system, and adopted proposals to require health insurers to cover preexisting conditions and to make insurance portable when workers change jobs.[111] Some thought is also being given to extending the federal employees health care plan to cover more Americans, after many Americans began to ask why they can't have health coverage as good as that of the people who voted down reform. Conservatives are discussing converting the system to one with more individual choice and more options, albeit under significant regulation.[112] Comprehensive reform of the health care system is extremely unlikely in the George W. Bush administration, despite its being forced to confront major demands for improving care such as prescription drug plans for senior citizens and coverage for the increasing number of citizens who continue to lack adequate health care insurance.

Although the federal government has failed so far to generate meaningful reforms, attempts at changing the health care system persist. One is a series of incremental reforms at the federal level.[113] Also, individual states have returned to making innovations in health care for their citizens, and are again serving as laboratories for a variety of reforms.[114] Already twenty states are experimenting with the idea of alliances for small business and individuals to purchase insurance at rates lower than they could obtain individually. Other states (Washington and Oregon) attempted to mandate that employers provide and pay half the cost of health insurance for full-time workers, but they are currently blocked by federal regulations from doing so. All states are in some way now involved in providing health care to all children, but the means through which this idea is implemented vary substantially. While all these efforts are encouraging, they risk creating a patchwork of laws and regulations that may make it more difficult for companies to do business and that may give some states competitive advantages over others.

Conclusion

Changing and reforming policies is always difficult, and health care is perhaps a particularly difficult policy field in which to produce change. There are a number of powerful interests—doctors, hospitals, pharmaceutical companies, and the like—with a direct interest in the area. Further, as issues of universal coverage arise, business interests become concerned about the costs that may be imposed upon them. Citizens also worry that by attempting to provide better medical care for the entire population, government may undermine the high quality of care that is currently available to the most fortunate segments of the society.

Although restoring or encouraging competition is appealing to many Americans as a solution to the problems we have identified in the health care industry, there may be difficulties in implementing this concept. The health care industry differs from other industries in important ways that reduce the utility of competition as a remedy for its problems. In particular, the dominance of professionals in determining the amount and type of care consumed by patients makes the usual competitive mechanisms less applicable. Those characteristics of the industry may, in turn, require a stronger role for the public sector if effective control over costs, quality, and access is to be attained.

First, very little information on the price or quality of medical care is available to the consumer. Prices for health care services are rarely advertised; frequently the consumer does not even consider them when making decisions about care. In fact, in a somewhat perverse way, consumers often choose a higher-priced rather than a lower-priced service in the belief (often correct) that the more expensive service will be superior. And, beyond hearsay, little information is available to patients about the quality of services provided by individual physicians or hospitals. The public sector has begun to intervene to make more information about health care quality available, and the increasing competition among health insurers and health care providers has provided another source of information, albeit biased, but it is still difficult for the average consumer to make choices.

In addition, the provision of health care is, in many ways, a monopoly or cartel. Entry into the marketplace by potential suppliers is limited by licensing requirements and further controlled by the professions themselves, that is, by limiting the number of places available in medical schools. Thus, unlike some industries, the health care field makes it difficult for competition to develop among suppliers. One possible means of promoting competition would be to break down the medical profession's monopoly by giving nurse practitioners and other paraprofessionals greater opportunity to practice, but the medical profession resists such changes. Hospitals do compete increasingly for patients, however, and with that competition has come some greater attention to the quality of care.

Bringing about any significant reforms in the delivery of health services in the United States will be difficult because of the power of the professions, large medical organizations such as hospitals, and, increasingly, managed-care organizations. The strongest pressures are to preserve the status quo, although physicians are becoming increasingly concerned by the control that insurers are exerting over their services in the name of cost containment. It may well be that only introduction of a large-scale reform such as national health insurance will be sufficient to break the existing system of finance and delivery and to provide better and more equitable medical care for most Americans.

CHAPTER 11

Income Maintenance: Social Security and Welfare

THE UNITED STATES has frequently been described as a welfare state "laggard" because its levels of expenditures on social policies are low compared with those of other industrialized nations and because it has not adopted certain public programs, such as child benefits and sickness insurance, that are common in other countries.[1] Although this is true, the gap between the United States and other Western democracies has narrowed as American expenditures for social programs continue to increase, while program services and expenditures in almost all other countries have been reduced or stabilized since the 1980s. The increased level of expenditures in the United States reflects some new programs, but mostly rising expenditures for established programs, particularly Social Security. U.S. social programs, broadly defined, in 2000 cost almost $700 billion and provided services to millions of clients. These social programs now account for approximately *one-third* of all federal expenditures; social expenditures are approximately *40 percent* of total public expenditures.

The debate over social programs in the United States has shifted rather dramatically since the early 1990s. Throughout most of the existence of what has been called the American welfare state, aid to individuals who could in principle work but who did not has been a controversial issue. In 1996 the existing "welfare" program—Aid to Families with Dependent Children (AFDC)—was replaced with a program that is referred to colloquially as "workfare." The new program eliminated many of the complaints that conservatives—and many ordinary citizens—had expressed about aid for the poor, and this issue was effectively defused. The Reagan and George H.W. Bush administrations had cut the growth of the programs of social aid substantially prior to this fundamental transformation of the system.

While the controversy over "welfare" has thus been minimized, the Social Security program has become instead the center of major political conflict. This program has been a great success since its inception in the 1930s and has been widely supported by the public. However, threats to the solvency of the system and fears about the continuation of benefits made Social Security a central issue in the 2000 presidential campaign. As the Republican candidate, George W. Bush pressed for a large private-sector role in providing for retirement incomes for citizens, then Vice President Al Gore, the Democratic candidate, argued for more incremental changes that would preserve the integrity of the program without fundamentally altering its public character. The subsequent deadlocked election seemed to reflect the less than full confidence of the voters in Bush's partial privatization proposals, and his electoral college victory then set the stage for a continuing discussion of this program and the nature of social support in the United States.

What are these social programs that cost so much and touch the lives of so many citizens? Leaving aside programs such as public housing, education, and health care, all of which have obvious social importance, we are left with an array of programs that themselves provide a broad range of services and benefits. The largest programs in terms of costs and number of beneficiaries are *social insurance* programs such as Social Security (old-age and disability pensions), unemployment insurance, and workmen's compensation (see table 11.1). Means-tested benefits such as "workfare," food stamps, and Supplemental Security Income—which are available only to individuals willing to demonstrate that their earnings fall below the level of need designated by each program—also are significant in terms of expenditures. These *social assistance* programs involve significant state and local expenditures as well as federal expenditures; the federal government actually spends relatively little on means-tested social programs. Finally, there are *personal social services* directed toward improving the quality of life for individuals through services such as counseling, adoption, foster care, and rehabilitation.

These three major kinds of social programs address different needs and usually benefit different clients. Likewise, each has its own particular programmatic and political problems, which we address in this chapter. Despite their apparent vulnerability to political pressures in a society that has emphasized the virtues of self-reliance, some characteristics of social programs, especially such social insurance programs as Social Security, make it difficult to reduce them and also produce some demands for increases. Too many people (and/or their aging parents) depend on social insurance programs for their livelihood for politicians to be anxious to cut spending for these programs—despite rhetoric in the 2000 electoral campaign about the need for fundamental change. The pressures to preserve and enhance those programs will be especially insistent as the population continues to age and the full range of effects of potential reforms becomes

TABLE 11.1   Costs of Income Maintenance Programs, 1970–1999 (in millions of dollars)

	1970	1980	1990	1995	1999	Percentage increase
Social Security	29,686	117,118	244,100	327,667	379,905	1,279
Unemployment	3,819	18,327	17,644	21,864	20,016	523
Public aid	16,800	43,544	63,481	100,444	104,137	619
Food stamps	577	9,100	14,741	22,447	15,492	2,684
Public housing	702	7,200	16,300	23,451	29,511	4,214
Other	19,660	73,200	48,800	45,300	47,982	243
Total	71,300	298,200	496,100	541,173	597,043	837
Percentage of public expenditures	20.1	28.2	37.4	38.0	38.2	

Source: *Statistical Abstract of the United States* (Washington, D.C.: Government Printing Office, annual).

evident. Social programs are therefore likely to remain a major political battleground in the United States.

Social Insurance

The largest single federal expenditure program of any type is Social Security. Although generally thought of as providing pensions for retired workers, the program also offers other protections to those who contribute to it. It provides cash benefits, for example, for the survivors of workers who die before retirement, including benefits for a deceased worker's children until they reach the age of eighteen, if they are not employed. The program also offers disability protection for workers who become incapable of earning a living, so that they and any dependents can receive benefits. Finally, Medicare is linked with Social Security for financing purposes. In addition to Social Security, there are two other significant social insurance programs in the United States. One program, unemployment insurance, is managed by the states with a federal subsidy, while the other, workers' compensation, is managed by the states with employers bearing the major financial burden for the program. This latter program is the American equivalent of industrial accidents insurance common in other industrialized countries.

Table 11.2 (p. 289) provides information about the recipients of social insurance benefits. By far the largest number of recipients are retired workers, although significant numbers of citizens receive benefits under other social insurance programs. Likewise, the largest share of social insurance goes to retired persons, although the highest average benefit paid in 2000 was for the unemployed, followed closely by disabled workers. Many social changes are responsible for the growing number of social insurance recipients. The most important

TABLE 11.2   Social Insurance Recipients, 2000

Program	Number
Social Security	
Retired workers and families	34,100,000
Disabled workers and families	7,243,000
Survivors	7,205,000
Unemployment insurance	2,188,000
Workers' compensation	2,416,000

Source: Social Security Administration, Social Security Bulletin, *Annual Statistical Supplement,* 2002.

is that the average age of Americans is increasing, making more people in the U.S. eligible for retirement benefits. Also, the passage of the Americans with Disabilities Act in 1991 made other groups more conscious of their rights to disability benefits. Social insurance programs are all entitlement programs, meaning that citizens who have paid in to them cannot be denied benefits once they meet the criteria for eligibility.

We must understand several important characteristics of social insurance programs, especially Social Security, if we are to comprehend the programs and the political debates that sometimes surround them. First, social insurance programs do relatively little, given the volume of expenditure, to redistribute income across economic classes.[2] Instead, these programs tend to redistribute income across time and across generations. Unlike a private annuity, in which an individual pays in money that accumulates in a personal account, Social Security is not an actuarially sound insurance program; it is a direct transfer program that taxes working people and their employers and pays out that money to the beneficiaries. The major purpose of Social Security is to distribute income across time—workers and their employers pay their taxes into the fund while employed, thereby reducing their income at that time, but receive benefits when they retire or if they become disabled.

Second, although they are not actuarially sound, these programs are conceived as insurance rather than government "giveaway" programs. Citizens believe they are purchasing an insurance policy through payroll taxes collected during their working lives. Defining the programs as social insurance has been crucial in legitimating them, as many citizens would not have been willing to accept a public pension to which they had not contributed; they would regard it as charity. Further, most congressmen in 1935 (when the programs were enacted) would not have been willing to vote for the programs if they had not been defined as insurance. This insurance element is also important because of the implicit contract between the citizen and the government. More than any other public program, Social Security is an entitlement program—citizens believe they have a legal and moral claim to receive benefits in large part because they have contributed throughout their working lives.

The insurance nature of Social Security programs also helps explain their financing, which is accomplished through payroll contributions, paid equally by employers and employees.[3] Social Security taxes are paid not on all earnings, but on only the first $84,900 (in 2002) of earnings each year; the health insurance component is now paid on all earnings. As shown in table 11.3, rates of tax and the threshold at which individuals stop paying social insurance taxes have increased over time in order to pay for the rising costs of the program. Thus, instead of being a general tax, Social Security "contributions" are limited in much the same way as are premiums for a private insurance policy, although not all workers will pay the same amount for social insurance if they earn below the threshold. Because it was envisioned as an insurance program and not a vehicle for redistributive social policy, the Social Security tax has been a flat-rate, rather than progressive, tax—all income earners pay the same rate on their income up to the annual limit.

Social Security is funded through an earmarked tax: all the money collected by this payroll tax is devoted to Social Security benefits, and only Social Security taxes are available for financing the benefits.[4] The restrictiveness of the financial system makes the tax, and the program in general, more palatable to many citizens, but it also severely constrains its financial base. In recent years the

TABLE 11.3 Increasing Rates of Social Security Taxation, 1960–2002

	Tax Rate		On earnings	Maximum
	OASDI[a]	HI[b]	up to:	tax[c]
1960	3.00	n.a.	$4,800	$144
1965	3.625	0.35	4,800	174
1970	4.20	0.60	7,800	374
1975	4.95	0.90	14,100	825
1980	5.08	1.05	25,900	1,588
1985	5.70	1.35	39,600	2,792
1990	6.20	1.45	51,300	3,924
1993	6.20	1.45	57,600	4,406
1994	6.20	1.45	60,600	4,636
1995	6.20	1.45	61,200	n.a.
1998	6.20	1.45	68,100	n.a.
2000	6.20	1.45	76,200	n.a.
2001	6.20	1.45	80,400	n.a.
2002	6.20	1.45	84,900	n.a.

Source: Social Security Administration.
a. Old Age, Survivors, and Disability Insurance.
b. Health insurance (Medicare).
c. Until 1995 health insurance was capped at the same level as OASDI; after 1995 HI is charged on all earnings, so there is no maximum tax.

specter of the Social Security system "going bankrupt" has been a part of the political debate. Both candidates in the 2000 presidential campaign presented plans to prevent that occurrence, but the aging of the population places continued pressure on this program. Despite some optimistic forecasts about economic growth and its associated higher tax revenues, the spending demands for Social Security is expected to begin to outstrip revenues by around 2020.

The second aspect of financing that is crucial for understanding the contemporary debate is the Social Security Trust Fund. During the past several decades—while the large "baby boom" generation born in the years immediately after World War II has been employed and has enjoyed reasonably high rates of economic growth—the Social Security System has been receiving more income from taxes than it has been spending on benefits. As this generation begins to retire in large numbers around 2010, however, more money will flow out than flows in, and the money that has been accumulating in the trust fund will begin to run out. Conservatives argue that this is all the more true given that these funds have been invested in relatively low-yield (but extremely safe) government securities rather than in the stock market. Their preference for a larger private-sector element in Social Security has produced sweeping proposals to permit citizens to invest at least a part of their Social Security taxes in the market.

Social Security now includes almost all working people—in 2000 well over 90 percent of employed Americans were covered by the program. This figure includes a large number of self-employed individuals, who pay a self-employment tax (equal to the employees' and employers' contributions) instead of having their contributions matched by an employer. The principal groups now excluded from the program are federal government employees hired before 1984, employees of many state and local governments, and some farm workers. These exclusions are made for administrative convenience or because of constitutional inhibitions on the federal government's ability to tax state or local governments, but many employers who could avoid the system opt into it to provide protections for their employees.

Finally, the benefits of the program are only partially related to earnings.[5] Those who pay more into the program during their working lives receive greater benefits when they retire, but those at the bottom of the income ladder receive a larger rate of return on their contributions and a higher level of replacement of their earnings upon retirement than do those with higher earnings (see table 11.4). Social Security is not intended to be a welfare program, but it is slightly redistributive in that it attempts thus to ensure that those at the bottom of the earnings ladder have something approximating an adequate retirement income. Still, it is difficult to argue that anyone living entirely on Social Security, even at the full benefit level, receives enough money to live comfortably. The average worker and his or her family receives about 76 percent of preretirement income

TABLE 11.4 Replacement Ratios of Earnings in Social Security, by Income Groups
(in percentages)

	Monthly Earnings					
	$100	$500	$1000	$1387	$1800	$2033
Worker alone (aged 65+)	167	74	60	51	44	41
Worker with spouse (aged 65+)	250	112	80	77	66	62

under Social Security; at the upper threshold level of Social Security taxes, the family would receive 43-percent replacement.[6]

The redistributive element of Social Security has been increased by raising taxes on benefits paid to more affluent recipients. For most of the program's history, the pensions paid to retired Americans have not been taxable, regardless of income. Beginning in 1984, however, 50 percent of Social Security benefits became taxable for recipients with taxable incomes and tax-free interest income over $25,000 (for an individual) or $32,000 (for a couple).[7] One part of a more radical reform (see p. 303) would make all benefits taxable. These past changes and proposals for extending the taxation of benefits do make the system more redistributive, but in the process they risk making it more like a welfare program.

Problems in Social Security

Although Social Security is widely accepted and generally very popular with the public, several problems in the program should be considered. These problems arise when the program is considered for renewal or modification, and they were central to the work of the 1996 and 2001 commissions that reviewed the program. These policy problems have political ramifications that affect the program's treatment in Congress and by the president. They also reflect the difficulties encountered in making adjustments to a successful program that is threatened with very severe impacts of social and demographic change.[8] Social Security has been maintained with incremental adjustments for over sixty years, but at the beginning of the twenty-first century there may be a need for more fundamental reform.

The retirement test. One problem that is being eliminated gradually is the retirement test—the penalty imposed on recipients of Social Security who wish to supplement their benefits by working. As the program is currently managed, if a recipient earns a certain amount of money (excluding income from private retirement funds or investments), a penalty is imposed on the benefits paid to him or her. In 2002 Social Security recipients up to the age of sixty-four could earn $11,280 a year without penalty but would lose $1 in benefits for every $2 earned over that amount. In the year an individual reaches sixty-five, a worker earning over $30,000 a year loses $1 for every $3 earned; over sixty-five, earnings are unlimited with no penalty on benefits.[9] For the person younger than sixty-five, there is, in effect, a 50-percent tax on earnings over the income allowed, a tax rate higher than that imposed on any individual paying the federal income tax.

There are several good reasons for removing, or at least relaxing, the retirement test. First, if the program is conceived as social insurance rather than as a means-tested benefit, recipients should receive benefits as a matter of right, much as the recipients of private annuities do. The retirement test thus gives the lie to the idea of Social Security as an insurance program. As it becomes unrewarding for retirees to work, or to gradually move out of the labor force, they will stop working and cease paying Social Security taxes, whereas if they continued to work they could pay some of their own benefits through taxes. The higher tax cost for the program borne by the working-age population becomes especially troubling as the population ages and there are fewer active workers to pay for the benefits of retirees.

There are also humane reasons for eliminating or modifying the retirement test. As the life expectancy of American citizens has increased, many individuals are capable of continuing to work after the usual retirement age. In a society that frequently defines an individual's worth on the basis of his or her work, the inability to work without paying a penalty for it may impose severe psychological as well as economic burdens on the retiree. More flexible or unlimited earnings would allow Social Security recipients to participate in the labor market, although perhaps not to the extent they did previously, and would permit phasing out employment rather than a sudden and often traumatic retirement.

On the other side of the argument, allowing retirees to continue working could have a significant effect on the job prospects of other potential employees, especially those just entering the labor market: every retiree who continued to work would mean one less job for a young person. Youth unemployment (especially for minority groups) is a significant problem, and the needs of the elderly must be balanced against the needs of younger people. Additionally, allowing retirees to continue working while still receiving benefits would amount to a direct transfer of income from the young to the old, based simply on age rather than on participation in the labor market. The strong economy in the late 1990s created a continuing need for the skills and abilities of workers who might otherwise have retired under the Social Security system, but as the economy slowed, it became apparent that opening opportunities for younger workers might be more beneficial.

Fixed retirement age. Related to the problem of a retirement test is the question of a fixed retirement age. Under existing laws, the standard retirement age was sixty-five for a number of years, then increased gradually to sixty-seven. For women the retirement age had been set earlier, but workers of both sexes now have the same retirement age. Under the Social Security system, individuals receive only a slight additional benefit for working after this age, although they must continue to pay Social Security taxes on their earnings. In addition, if individuals choose to retire before reaching the official retirement age, their benefits are reduced even if they have been paying into the system for years. These rules provide an incentive for workers to retire at the official age, and under current law all individuals are expected to retire at that age regardless of health or financial situation.

Good justifications can be found both for raising and for lowering the retirement age. One main argument for raising the age is cost containment in a system that is facing severe financial problems; others are based on humane considerations. If the retirement age were raised, total program costs would be reduced, for people would not depend on the program as long. When Social Security was adopted in 1935, only about half the male population could expect to live to age sixty-five, and those who reached sixty-five could expect to live about twelve years longer. By 1990, however, over 72 percent of the male population would live to sixty-five and they would then live, on average, fifteen years on Social Security. By 2010, 78 percent are expected to live to sixty-five and to be on the program for over sixteen years thereafter.[10] Thus, there are more retirees and each retiree costs more today, so total program costs are increasing. In addition, the health status, the nature of work, and the educational levels of workers have all been improving. As the baby boom generation prepares to retire around 2010, there will be an additional 77 million recipients; delaying their retirement could help maintain the solvency of Social Security—one preliminary recommendation of the 1998 National Commission on Retirement Policy was to raise the retirement age to seventy.[11] Also, some workers' lack of private pension plans may mean that they cannot maintain their lifestyles if they are forced to retire.

On the other side of the argument are some good reasons to lower the retirement age. Many people who have retirement incomes in addition to Social Security may want to retire while they are still in good health and capable of enjoying more years of leisure.[12] At the systemic level, the lowering of the retirement age might create additional job openings for unemployed youths. In addition, the availability of a flexible retirement age could make it easier to modernize the nation's workforce, as workers with obsolete skills might move to Social Security more readily, as a consequence reducing some of the human costs of modernization and economic change.

Some policies for determining benefits and appropriate retirement ages may have to be retained, but there are good reasons for making this policy more flexible and for balancing different needs. Such flexibility could benefit individuals as well as the economy and society as a whole. However, care would need to be taken that this flexibility took into account the needs and wishes of workers, as well as administrative convenience and the financial problems of government. Balancing these demands in the context of the financial problems of the system is a severe political and policymaking challenge. Further care must be taken to mesh any changes in public retirment programs with private-sector retirement and health programs.

The treatment of women and families.   The treatment of women under the Social Security system is another continuing issue. When the system was designed, the vast majority of women were housewives who did not work outside the home and who remained married to the same men for their entire lives. Those characteristics would hardly describe the average woman in the United States today, and therefore some aspects of the treatment of women under Social Security now appear outdated and even blatantly discriminatory. For example, if a woman is married to a covered employee for fewer than ten years, a divorce cancels her access to the former husband's benefits, and for Social Security purposes it is as if they had never been married. And, as we have noted, the benefits an individual receives are roughly based on contributions, so that even if a woman who has not been working returns to work or begins to work after such a divorce, she will find it difficult to accumulate sufficient credits for a significant retirement benefit. Given that, on average, marriages that end in divorce last seven years, this means that a significant number of women (and increasingly some men) lose the Social Security benefits of having been married.

Also, if both husband and wife work, as is now true for many if not most married couples in the United States, the pair receive little additional pension if they remain married. This is true even though they may pay twice as much in Social Security contributions as a couple with only one worker. Benefits are based on each partner's individual work record, and there is no spousal benefit unless one worker would receive more from a spousal benefit than her or his own work. Therefore, on average, the replacement rate for a one-worker couple with average earnings is 61 percent; for two-earner couples the replacement rate is 44 percent. At higher rates of income, this "marriage penalty" is even more severe.[13]

An even broader question is whether a woman, or a man, who chooses not to work outside the home should not in fact receive some Social Security protection based on her or his contributions to the household and to society through this work in the home. The idea of a "homemaker's credit" in Social Security has been advanced so that these individuals would have their own protection within Social Security. This kind of protection may be especially important for disability insurance, for if the homemaker should become disabled, especially with children still in the home, this would impose additional personal or financial burdens on the family, as other family members would have to do the work he or she had once performed in the home, or pay to have it done. With the current financial pressures on Social Security, however, there is little likelihood of homemakers' benefits being expanded; and, if anything, the treatment of women under Social Security may become even less generous.

The disability test. In addition to providing benefits in retirement or if a breadwinner in a family dies, Social Security also protects families whose breadwinner is unable to work because of sickness or injury. The "substantial gainful employment" test in the program is an important problem for people seeking to qualify for those benefits. The test, as administered, is rather harsh, requiring that a person be totally disabled before he or she can receive benefits.[14] The individual must be disqualified from any "substantial gainful employment" that is available within the area of the potential beneficiary and for which he or she has the requisite skills.[15] These standards are much more stringent than those applied in private disability programs, which require only the inability to engage in one's customary occupation, or in other public programs such as the Black Lung program or veterans' programs.[16] At present, well under 50 percent of all applicants for disability receive benefits. In addition, the Social Security Amendments of 1980 mandated frequent reexaminations of the eligibility of program claimants, with the result that significant numbers of people have been removed from the program.[17] Also, there has been a movement to tighten eligibility for people with substance abuse problems, but efforts to reduce eligibility even further are often difficult to implement.[18]

The stringency of the disability test requires workers who have any disability to leave the workforce almost entirely if they are to receive disability benefits. A situation may well arise, however, in which an individual is too unhealthy to earn an adequate income and yet not unhealthy enough to receive benefits under the existing disability program. For both social and financial reasons it would be beneficial to have a more graduated disability test to assist those who have a partial disability but who wish to continue to be as productive as they can. A person could be assigned a percentage disability and compensated accordingly. Such a test is already used in the Veterans Administration, and it could be implemented for civilian disability benefits.

Workers' compensation is another accident and disability program in the United States, although it is managed by the states rather than by the federal government (except for the program covering federal employees). The disability tests employed in this program vary markedly from state to state, but generally they are less stringent than the Social Security test.[19] Further, there are provisions for permanent partial disability payments that enable a person to continue working in some occupation other than his or her original occupation. Workers' compensation programs now cover almost 90 percent of the American workforce but provide different levels of benefit by state.[20] Also, although the options available for granting limited disability are in many ways beneficial, they are also the source of a great deal of litigation.

Social Security and the Economy

Social Security also affects the American economy. The most commonly cited effect is the reduction of individual savings and the consequent reduction in the amount of capital available for investment, compared with the situation if there were no public insurance program. Because individuals know that their retirement will be at least partly financed by Social Security, they do not save as much during their working lives as they might otherwise. Further, because Social Security as it is currently managed does not accumulate as large an amount of reserves to pay future benefits as it might if it were a private annuity program, there is less capital accumulation in the U.S. economy than there might otherwise be.[21] Estimates of the magnitude of savings lost as a result of the Social Security program vary widely, but most experts agree that there has been some reduction in savings as a result of Social Security. Most also think that the disincentive effects are less than many conservative critics of the program have argued.[22]

The second major effect of Social Security on the economy is the lessening of labor market participation by older workers. As noted, the retirement test and the standard retirement age tend to provide disincentives for those over sixty-five to continue working. As with the economic effect of reduced savings, estimating the magnitude of this effect on total growth and productivity is difficult, but several empirical studies have documented that there is some effect. Also, as the number of young workers entering the labor market decreases, the skills of older workers become increasingly valuable to the economy.

Financing Social Security

We now come to the most frequently discussed question concerning Social Security, especially following the 2000 presidential campaign: how can the program be financed in a way that will maintain the benefits expected by the people who have paid into the system? Periodically since the 1960s there have been reports that Social Security was going bankrupt, raising the specter that many elderly people would be left with no income for their old age. In 1984 President Reagan said that he did not believe that citizens currently making contributions to the system would ever receive much back in benefits.[23] Many citizens came to believe that negative prognosis, and by the mid–1980s less than half of all Americans expressed confidence in Social Security; in one survey only 36 percent of working Americans said they expected to receive any significant help with their retirement from Social Security.[24] The lack of confidence has been rather stable since that time, with just over a third of the population expecting reasonable Social Security benefits.[25]

The concern about the crisis in Social Security may appear foolish, given that the system is still running a surplus and has accumulated a significant trust fund (see table 11.5). However, within the next several decades the impending retirement of a huge age cohort—the "baby boomers" born between 1945 and 1952—threatens to send the system into deficit and to exhaust the reserve fund that continues to increase in the early twenty-first century. The exact date at which the funds would run out varies according to the assumptions used, but under most assumptions the funds would be exhausted by around 2020—although if the economic slowdown that began in 2001 were to continue much longer, that date would be even sooner.

Given the entitlement nature of the program, such dire outcomes are extremely unlikely. Indeed, at other times the Social Security system has run large surpluses that politicians have used to balance an otherwise unbalanced federal budget.[26] The debates during the 2000 presidential campaign stressed the need to separate Social Security from other parts of the budget by putting the fund in a "lock box." Indeed, without the surplus accumulated by this program, the huge budget surplus that politicians were discussing at that time would have been rather modest. But the Social Security system as a program financed entirely by payroll taxes may be in long-term difficulty.[27] Current projections suggest that younger workers may be called on to finance the program with ever higher payroll taxes, but they may be reluctant to do so if they fear that they will not later receive the benefits themselves.

There are several reasons for the financial difficulties of the Social Security program. The most obvious problem is the increasing number of aging Americans, a trend that began in the 1960s and is projected to continue if the birth rate remains low. In 1960 only 9 percent of the American population was over sixty-five; by 1990 that figure had increased to almost 13 percent, and it is expected to increase to almost 20 percent by 2025. In other words, in 1984 each Social Security beneficiary was supported by the taxes of approximately 3.3 active workers. In 2001 there were actually 3.4 workers for each beneficiary, but that ratio then began to fall rapidly. By 2030, it is estimated that each beneficiary will be supported by only 2.1 workers, and by 2050, by less than 2.0 active workers.[28] This declining ratio obviously implies either an increasing burden on active workers or a modification of the existing financial structure of the program.

Another factor increasing the difficulties in financing Social Security has been indexing benefits to match increases in prices and wages. Under existing

TABLE 11.5   Changes in Social Security Trust Fund 1980–2000 (in billions of dollars)

	_1980_	_1985_	_1990_	_1995_	_1998_	_1999_	_2000_
Income	105.3	182.1	288.8	332.9	424.9	457.1	490.5
Benefits paid	105.1	167.2	223.0	291.6	326.8	334.4	352.7
Assets	22.8	35.8	214.2	458.5	681.6	798.8	931.0

Source: U.S. Social Security Administration, _Annual Report of the Board of Trustees_ (Washington, D.C.: SSA, annual).

arrangements, the initial benefit levels paid retirees are adjusted annually to reflect changes in the average wages paid in the economy. In addition, in every twelve-month period during which prices increase more than 3 percent, benefits are adjusted so that retirees have approximately constant purchasing power from their pensions. Indexing benefits (a cost-of-living adjustment, or COLA as it is called) is an obvious target for those seeking to control social program costs. As Social Security faced one more crisis in 1983, legislation was passed that imposed a one-time delay of six months in the COLA. Another suggestion, by a group of economists at the usually moderate-to-liberal Brookings Institution, would be to eliminate the COLA in a year in which inflation was less than 5 percent; if inflation were greater than 5 percent, the correction would be the rate of inflation less 5 percent. Another suggestion would have the COLA pegged several percentage points lower than the inflation rate.[29] All these suggestions encounter opposition from the expanding and active lobbying organizations for the elderly.

The rationale for attacking indexing benefits as a means of reducing some financial problems in Social Security is twofold: it is a relatively simple change to make, and it has the potential to save significant amounts of money. For example, it is estimated that the six-month COLA delay in the 1983 legislation saved $40 billion from fiscal 1983 through fiscal 1988. However, such measures may well produce serious hardships for some elderly recipients of Social Security—one study has estimated that a COLA three percentage points below inflation would put over a million elderly below the official poverty line within several years. Many people wonder why the burden of making the federal budget and the Social Security system solvent should have to be placed on the backs of the elderly;[30] even President Reagan, who was openly skeptical about the future of Social Security, agreed in July 1984 that even if inflation fell below the 3 percent figure, the COLA adjustment would still be made. Congress rapidly agreed with the president (there was an election looming), and there is every reason to expect indexing of Social Security to continue.

Considering the financial pressures on Social Security, it is reasonable to question whether the system can afford to continue financing itself entirely through payroll taxes. And there are questions about the payroll tax itself, perhaps the most important being that the tax is basically regressive, exacting a higher percentage of tax from low-paid workers than from the more affluent. This regressive characteristic is the result of the threshold above which individuals earning additional income do not pay additional tax. In 2002 individuals paid a payroll tax of 7.65 percent on the first $84,900 of covered employment (see table 11.3, p. 290); beyond that amount, they paid no more taxes for the old age, survivors, or disability programs.[31] Thus, everyone who earned the threshold amount or less paid the same 7.65 percent of their income, while some earning $100,000 paid less than 6.5 percent of their income as Social Security taxes, and some with incomes of just over $200,000 paid only 3 percent.

In addition, the Social Security tax is applied only to salaries and wages, not to earnings from dividends or interest. These disparities are justified, however, because the system is conceptualized as providing insurance and not as providing benefits directly proportional to earnings; once you have paid your annual "premium" on the insurance policy, there is no need to pay more. The payroll tax for Social Security is regressive in another way as well. Most economists argue that workers actually bear the burden of the employers' contributions (the same 7.65 percent of salaries and wages up to the threshold) because employers count their contributions as a part of the cost of employing a worker and then reduce wages, or the number of employees, accordingly.[32]

The payroll tax has the further disadvantage of being relatively visible to employees.[33] They see the money deducted for Social Security from each paycheck, and they have some idea of how much money they pay into the system. This visibility means that the level of payroll taxation may be limited by real or potential taxpayer resistance. Using this visible tax in conjunction with the personal income tax, however, makes the total tax "bite" on wages less obvious than if there were a single tax on income to be used for social benefits as well as general government purposes.

The earmarked payroll tax does have one advantage that some people believe is worth retaining: because the receipts from this tax are relatively limited, politicians are prevented from using the Social Security system for political gains. That is, because general tax revenue (from the income tax primarily) is not used to finance the system, it is difficult for a president or Congress to increase rates of benefits just before an election to attempt to win votes from the elderly—although the COLA adjustment of benefits may have some of that potential because changes in benefits tend to go into effect shortly before election time in November. A final benefit of the earmarked tax is that it makes the system appear to most citizens to be a contributory insurance program instead of a welfare program.

Reforming Social Security

Various proposals have been made to alleviate some of the financial problems of

Social Security (see tables 11.6 and 11.7, p. 302). Among the simple, incremental changes would be to remove the financing of Medicare from the payroll tax and finance that program through general revenues. This would leave Social Security with more money while retaining the existing rates of payroll taxation; in 2001, 1.45 percent of the 7.65 percent payroll deduction was used to finance Medicare. Another mechanism, already mentioned, would be to change the COLA adjustment and timing, although in a period of high inflation such a change might work a considerable hardship on the elderly. Raising the retirement age, or at least making it more flexible, is another possible solution to the rising costs of Social Security, as would be a reduction of some of the welfare-like benefits attached to the program (e.g., the spouses' benefits). One such minor benefit—the burial allowance—has in some cases already been eliminated.

Another way of tinkering with the program would be to make it truly comprehensive, including all workers; new federal government employees are now in the system but state and local government employees can still opt out. Adding these workers to the membership in the program would provide a larger financial base of white-collar workers who earn better-than-average incomes and could help to shore up the system for some time. There might also be psychological benefits to pointing out that all citizens share in the same Social Security system. A large majority of Americans support the idea of making the system totally inclusive, but there are legal barriers that may prevent that happening.[34] Further, given the financial difficulties facing the system, this change might only add claimants while adding little revenue.

A rather more significant change would be to change the entire basis of Social Security financing from payroll contributions to general revenue, either through the income tax or through a value-added tax (VAT) like that used in Europe.[35] The VAT is a tax levied on businesses at each stage of production, based on the value that each business adds to the raw materials used to create the product it sells. The VAT has the advantages of being virtually invisible, its cost reflected only in the price of a product, and of being somewhat less regressive than the payroll tax, especially if commodities such as food and prescription drugs are untaxed. The invisibility of the VAT would be an advantage for those managing Social Security, although many citizens might not regard it as such; using VAT funds would allow Social Security income to expand with less restraint than the present system of finances.

Social Security finance is likely to remain an important policy issue. The average age of the population continues to increase, and program costs will keep growing, probably more rapidly than will the yield from the payroll tax. Unfortunately for the program's managers, the form of finance is now deeply entrenched, and it may be difficult to modify it without changing the insurance concept of the system and perhaps thereby reducing general support for the pro-

TABLE 11.6   Opinions on Coping with Problems in Social Security, 1999 (in percentages)

"In order to deal with shortfalls in Social Security funds, would you prefer raising the Social Security tax rate, reducing benefits for all recipients, or a combination of the two?"

Raising tax rate	20
Reducing benefits	5
Combination	56
Not sure	19

"If the federal government were to reduce Social Security benefits, which one of the following methods would you prefer?"

Cut in COLA	30
Increasing taxes	18
Raising retirement age	35
None/other	11
Not sure	6

Source: NBC News poll, 4–7 March 1999.

TABLE 11.7   Trade-offs of Taxes and Reducing Benefits

Avoid any tax increases	34
Avoid any benefit cuts	53
Neither/Don't know	13

Source: Princeton Survey Research Associates, June 2000.

gram. Also, it has been suggested that all Social Security benefits should be counted as taxable income. The 1983 amendments to the Social Security Act permitted the taxation of benefits received by retirees with incomes at the higher end of the scale: $25,000 for individuals, $32,000 for a couple. But the passage of any provision to tax benefits draws attention to the perceived crisis in Social Security financing and threatens in effect to make Social Security a means-tested program.

Radical Reforms

All the reforms of Social Security discussed so far amount to tinkering. Some reformers are proposing an almost complete overhaul of the system.[36] At the extreme, libertarian and conservative critics of Social Security would like to move toward complete privatization of the system. Beginning with younger workers, the funds that now go to Social Security would be invested privately, much as existing plans such as 401(k) now do.[37] These reformers argue that current participants in the program are much worse off than they would have been if they had been investing in the stock market, or even in safer money-market funds. The reform proposals made by candidate George W. Bush during his run for the presidency in 2000 were to move the system toward full privatization for younger workers, while attempting to protect the retirement income of older workers. Later, as president, he appointed a panel to study reforming the system, and it produced, not surprisingly, rather similar recommendations.

The idea of fully privatizing Social Security presents a number of problems. One is the transition to the new, private arrangements. As already noted, the ability of the program to pay benefits to current beneficiaries is in part dependent upon the continuing influx of funds from current workers—if those workers were no longer paying into the system, the feared bankruptcy would become even more likely. The reformers have developed plans for the transition, involving phasing out benefits and taxes over an extended period of time, but even then there is a significant threat to the solvency of the system.

The privatization of Social Security also would place a great burden on the individual participant in the process. He or she would need to be willing to take the risk of investing in the stock market and would have to understand that the certainty of Social Security was being sacrificed for the possibility of higher gains, or high losses, in the market (see table 11.8). Many such proposals for reforming public retirement looked extremely promising when the stock market was experiencing unprecedented growth in the late 1990s, but the economic uncertainties and falling stock markets of 2001 and 2002 caused many citizens to reconsider the virtues of continuing with the old system, and some of the excitement about moving toward full privatization waned, even among conservatives.

In addition to these plans for complete privatization of Social Security, there have been more moderate proposals for involving the private sector more directly. One of the more prominent proposals is to begin to move the population away from social insurance as we have known it toward something resembling a private annuity program. Senator Daniel Patrick Moynihan once proposed a "2 percent solution" to the long-term problems of Social Security: reducing Social Security taxes by 2 percent and permitting participants to invest that money in private retirement accounts.[38] Other congressmen and some economists have favored diverting even more money into private accounts. Benefits for recipients with private accounts would be scaled back, saving public money and ensuring long-term solvency of the program for the people who depend on it.

Like full privatization, the concept of partial privatization of the system was spurred in part by the boom in the stock market during the late 1990s. The assumption of partial privatization is that the greater use of the private sector would give the average retiree more money for retirement, while relieving the public sector of a major potential financial burden. Even with moving some people into such a new system, however, there would remain questions about the solvency of

TABLE 11.8 Preferences for Reform of Social Security

	Favor	Oppose	Don't know
Allow workers to invest Social Security payroll taxes in stock market	51	36	13
Of those favoring: Still favor if it reduces seniors' benefits	33	57	10

Source: Princeton Survey Research Associates, June 2000.

the system as well as calls for reform by raising the retirement age and making all income taxable. Likewise, the same transitional problems that would affect a fully privatized system would be relevant for less drastic changes in Social Security. In the short term, there would be uncertainty about the reliability of the new system, and indeed there should be some concern whether a privatized system would be able to provide the level of pensions expected by the reformers, or even the rate of return available under the existing social insurance scheme.

Summary

Social Security is a large, complex, and expensive program. As a result, several important policy issues concerning its effects on citizens and on the economy continue to be debated. It seems clear, however, that the program will persist, albeit in modified form, for some way must be found to finance a program of public retirement that will provide an adequate, or at least minimal, income for pensioners without bankrupting the working-age population. Likewise, some response must be made to increasing demands that government remove some of the rigidities and discrimination from the system, making it more humane and responsive to changing social and economic conditions. The Social Security system, in all probability, will continue to be a major success story in public policy but one that will remain prominent on the policymaking agenda.

Means-Tested Programs

The second major category of social programs is the means-tested program. To qualify for benefits under such a program, an individual must satisfy a means test—or, more accurately, an absence-of-means test. Applicants cannot earn more than a specified amount or have any major assets if they are to qualify for most means-tested programs. Rather obviously, then, these programs benefit groups of people, defined by economic criteria, that are generally neither the most influential in society nor the easiest to mobilize politically. Also, the means testing itself tends to stigmatize, and to some extent degrade, individuals who must apply for the benefits. These programs are not entitlements in the strict sense of the term, although political and judicial actions have tended to make them more matters of right than in the past.[39]

Means-tested programs have been the focus of a good deal of ideological debate, even in a country that tends to have more pragmatic than ideological politics.[40] Some citizens who regard means-tested benefits as "handouts" or "giveaways" often describe recipients of such benefits as "lazy welfare cheaters" and sing songs about "welfare Cadillacs." President Reagan once referred to recipients of the Aid to Families with Dependent Children (AFDC) program as "welfare queens."[41] More intellectual critics of the programs have blamed them for social disintegration, family breakups, and rising rates of urban crime. Racial issues are also involved in attitudes toward means-tested benefits, for although the majority of welfare recipients are white, a disproportionate share of blacks and Hispanics receive them. Means-tested benefits, including the AFDC program and its successor, the Personal Responsibility and Work Opportunity Reconciliation Act (PRWORA), as well as food stamps, Supplemental Security Income, and a variety of other programs, provide the only livelihood for many citizens, and they are criticized by some as both inadequate and demeaning.[42] What is clear is that these programs raise several important social, political, and economic issues.

AFDC and PRWORA: From Welfare to Workfare

The largest means-tested program, and the one that generated the most political controversy, was AFDC, or "welfare." This program benefited more than 14 million Americans, including approximately 8 million children, in 1994. The program cost the federal government over $14 billion, or less than 1 percent of its overall expenditures and was responsible for less than 5 percent of the federal deficit that year. AFDC took a larger share of state government expenditures, especially as the welfare rolls increased substantially during the early 1990s.[43] AFDC was expensive—if perhaps not so expensive as some believed—and because the program provided benefits on the basis of need rather than contributions, it was controversial in a market-oriented society. In addition, AFDC was growing in numbers and expense, and that produced heavy pressure for reform. Although this program was replaced during the Clinton administration, it is important to understand the nature of the reforms and the ways in which American social policy has been changing in recent years.

It is especially interesting that the controversy over AFDC arose during the 1960s and 1970s, rather than in the 1930s when it was adopted. The program originated as a part of the package that produced Social Security, but at that time the major controversy was over Social Security rather than AFDC; it was assumed that

AFDC would be used by a relatively small number of widows with children, rather than by women who were unmarried, divorced, or separated.[44] But while Social Security has since become a widely accepted part of American life, AFDC was long perceived as a problem by the taxpayers who funded the program, as well as by its recipients. Changing family patterns also played a part in the low status of AFDC recipients; as many more women went to work in the economy, women generally began to be regarded as perfectly capable of earning their own way.

Before we discuss the 1996 major reform of the program, it is important to understand why the reform was so important. In general, AFDC recipients were women with children, with virtually no income, and with no one living in the household capable of supporting the children. Actually, some males also qualified for AFDC; an increasing number qualify for assistance under the Family Support Act. By 1988 fewer than 15 percent of the recipients were widows, wives of disabled men, or unemployed—those for whom the program was intended. Most AFDC recipients were in fatherless families, in approximately half of which the parents were never married, the other half being separated and divorced mothers.

AFDC, although a national program, was administered by states and localities. Despite several attempts at reform and "nationalization" of the program, it remained decentralized. The federal government provided a small subsidy to the states for the program; the remainder of the benefits came from state and local funds. The benefits varied widely across states. In January 1992 the highest monthly benefit for a family of three was $924 in Alaska. If we leave aside Alaska and its extremely high cost of living, the highest payment was $680 in Connecticut, while the lowest AFDC payment for a family of three was $120 in Mississippi; the average across the nation was $395 per month. None of these benefit levels was particularly munificent, and the substantial disparities were only partly due to differences in the cost of living in the various localities.

The states also used AFDC payments to regulate the behavior of recipients.[45] The image of the "welfare mother" having illegitimate children in order to qualify for benefits was one that gave supporters of the program difficulties when attempting to improve benefits. Several states reacted against this common image by refusing to increase payments for mothers who had additional children while on AFDC, with one state actually reducing benefits if there were an additional child.[46] Likewise, at least one state eliminated general assistance payments to individuals not eligible for AFDC, and others reduced the size and duration of payments. Other states gave lower AFDC benefits to recipients who had just moved in from out of state. There were a number of other regulations on the behavior of AFDC recipients: several states reduced benefits for AFDC recipients whose children did not attend school regularly; other states cut off AFDC payments to teenage mothers who did not live with a parent or legal guardian; and some states even required all welfare recipients to be fingerprinted to help reduce fraud.[47]

The AFDC program was not without major problems, but those problems were often exaggerated in the popular mind. First, as shown earlier, AFDC was not a big spending program—it actually cost the federal government relatively little. Further, once on welfare most people did not remain on the program for life; in 1994 more than one-third of AFDC recipients had been on the program one year or less, and over 78 percent had been on it for five years or less; the median time on the program was twenty-two months. Also, almost as many whites as African Americans were on AFDC. Finally, as might have been expected from the transitional nature of the program, divorce and separation rather than childbearing without benefit of marriage were the major reasons for accepting AFDC. Nevertheless, a number of problems commonly associated with AFDC persisted.

Means testing.   Programs that require recipients to prove that they are indigent stigmatize the recipients, especially in a society that places a high value on success and income as symbols of personal worth. Most recipients of welfare benefits are relatively powerless and the stigma attached to being on AFDC lessened their feelings of self-worth. That stigmatization, in turn, may have helped to perpetuate the problems that caused their indigence in the first place. Unfortunately, the program as designed tended to perpetuate indigence rather than to allow people to work their way out of poverty.

Punishment for working.   The one aspect of AFDC that appeared to make the least sense was that individuals who attempted to work their way out of poverty were penalized for doing so. An individual could work no more than 100 hours per month, no matter what the rate of pay, and after a certain amount was earned each year (the sum varied by state), the recipient was required to return $2 in benefits for every $3 earned—in effect a higher rate of tax than any current income tax.[48] Obviously, such a high rate of "tax" on earnings provided little incentive for individuals to work. In addition, because other benefits, such as food stamps and Medicaid, might be tied to receiving AFDC, going out to take a job meant the loss of a great deal more than the AFDC check.[49]

Family structure.   AFDC also had negative effects on family structure. As noted, under most circumstances a woman with children could not receive benefits if an able-bodied male resided in the home. This meant that traditional families, whose virtues were stressed by politicians such as Bill Clinton and Dan Quayle, usually were not eligible for AFDC. This requirement also made it more difficult for a woman on AFDC to work, since she must either care for the children herself or find suitable day-care facilities. It also had deleterious effects on children, who grew up in fatherless households. These latter problems in the program were becoming less unusual, however, as single-parent families became more common in the United States.[50]

Costs and benefits. Depending on whom you ask, the benefits of AFDC were either too high or too low. Critics concerned about the costs of the program argued that "generous" benefits encouraged people to stay on welfare rather than find a job. On the other side of the argument, most recipients of AFDC benefits would point out that even the highest monthly state benefit ($924) was hardly sufficient for a life of leisure and that the average benefit across the country was only $395. Recipients and their supporters thus argued that the benefits were too low to provide a decent living for the recipients and their children, and that the children inherited poverty along with the substandard housing, low-quality education, family disruption, and poor diet commonly associated with AFDC households.

The Family Support Act

The problems inherent in the AFDC program did not go unnoticed by lawmakers, and one reaction was passing the Family Support Act of 1988.[51] This act, which was associated especially with Senator Daniel Patrick Moynihan, D-N.Y., attempted to break the "cycle of poverty" that had led to several generations of family members following one another as recipients of AFDC. Although it represented mere tinkering when compared to later reforms, it did address some of the most egregious problems in the program. Among the provisions of the act were the following:

1. *Greater help for families with two parents.* The act required the states to amend their AFDC programs to provide at least six months' benefits per year (AFDC-UP) to families with both parents unemployed.

2. *Improved child support enforcement.* This was intended to reduce the number of children requiring assistance from AFDC, as well as to have some impact on strengthening parental responsibility toward children.

3. *Job training.* States were mandated to provide enhanced job training and child-care services so that AFDC recipients would be able to get and keep reasonable jobs in the economy.[52]

4. *Enhanced medicare benefits.* People who left welfare for work would not automatically lose medical insurance, a major impediment to those wishing to leave AFDC, given that a declining number of jobs for which most people leaving welfare were qualified would offer health benefits.[53]

The Family Support Act certainly was not a cure-all for the problems of the AFDC program, and it did not eliminate poverty in the United States. Further, the requirements for implementation by the states produced substantial variations in the generosity of the benefits and the speed of their adoption.[54] Still, this program's adoption was a recognition of the types of changes that were needed to cope with the problems inherent in the basic system of providing financial support for the indigent.

The 1996 Reforms

As noted earlier, there was a major reform of the welfare system in 1996. Usually referred to as "workfare," the new program put in place was the result of an agreement between the Clinton administration and the Republican Congress on reforming the system to place much greater emphasis on work and to severely limit the time that any individual could receive social assistance. This program built on reforms that were already underway in several states, notably Wisconsin, and it fundamentally altered the nature of welfare in the United States.[55] There are six basic provisions of workfare, or, more formally, the Personal Responsibility and Work Opportunity Reconciliation Act of 1996 (PRWORA).[56]

1. *Ending AFDC.* This act terminated AFDC as developed during the 1930s and substituted a temporary, work-oriented program. The bill also brought together the funding for a number of other means-tested benefits such as Supplemental Security Income, food stamps, and child-support enforcement into a single block grant to the states.

2. *Restriction of eligibility.* The reform restricted the time period for which an individual is eligible for benefits. A standard critique of the pre-reform AFDC system was that people never left the program once they were on it. This was actually not the case,[57] but it was certainly the perception and an important stimulus to the politics of reform. The reforms adopted in PRWORA limited benefits to two years at any one time, and to five years over a lifetime. Further, food stamps benefits were limited to three months in any three years.

3. *Demands for work.* The reform's basic rationale was that prohibiting recipients' ability to remain on the program indefinitely would force them to find some other way of gaining sufficient income to survive. The PRWORA reforms tend to hasten recipients along the path to self-sufficiency by requiring that they either get a job or prepare themselves for a job in order to receive benefits. This requirement means that state and local governments must develop new job opportunities, but the assumption is that people will work. The Clinton administration's proposed tax breaks for businesses that provide job opportunities for former welfare recipients and the long-term unemployed were delayed,[58] but by 2002 these incentives were in place and appeared to be having some effect.

4. *Treatment of immigrants.* Another provision of the PRWORA was a limitation on welfare benefits available to immigrants, even legal immigrants, who

were made ineligible for food stamps. Despite the conviction that the basic provisions should save money, especially for states like California with large numbers of immigrants,[59] there was some rethinking of this provision in the course of implementation, and in 2002 President Bush revoked it, a move that was thought to be motivated by both humane and political concerns.[60]

5. *Vigorous enforcement of child support.* One means of saving government money was to have fathers (or, in a few cases, mothers) of children provide for those children. The Family Support Act of 1988 stressed enforcement, but the 1996 reform placed even greater pressure on the states to find "dead-beat dads" and extract child-support money from those who could provide it.

6. *Implementation by the states.* Like AFDC, the new welfare program was to be implemented by the states, but unlike AFDC, PRWORA was designed to give the states a good deal of latitude in how they interpreted and implemented the policy.[61] Indeed, some states have chosen to work with private firms as implementation agents[62] or to decentralize implementation even further to local governments.[63] The legislation also funds the program through a limited block grant rather than an open-ended subsidy, so that, in addition to being given greater latitude, the states are relieved of the requirement to match federal funding as in the previous regimen. Program benefits, or Temporary Assistance to Needy Families—TANF—benefits, are variable across states just as they were under AFDC (see table 11.9), but the states were to begin losing part of the block grant in 2002 if they did not meet work participation targets for their program recipients.

The provisions of PRWORA appear extremely punitive, and in some ways they are. However, the final legislation is not as severe as some proposals that were offered, especially in the Republican Congress, where one zealous reformer proposed to deny benefits to teenage mothers and to encourage them to put their children up for adoption. Interestingly, the very politicians who generally talk most about individual autonomy were central in placing so many controls on personal behavior in this bill.[64] There remains some question whether this program is really the best thing for welfare recipients, and especially the children. There is some evidence that children do better—in school, socially, and, ultimately, economically—when they have at least one parent at home regularly to care for and nurture them.[65] This point has been stressed by conservatives such as former Vice President Dan Quayle, but it has also been recognized by more liberal child advocacy groups. The emphasis on work is appealing to most Americans for ideological and financial reasons, but in the long run it may actually exacerbate the cycle of dependency that the reforms are intended to break. While AFDC had negative consequences for family life, workfare may have even more negative consequences for children. President George W. Bush and his administration have pushed this argument further, trying to use welfare money to promote marriage and to reduce divorce rates among recipients of public assistance.[66]

TABLE 11.9   Variations in Average Benefits from Temporary Assistance to
Needy Families, September 1999

High		Low	
Alaska	$632.44	Mississippi	$109.50
Hawaii	518.23	Texas	138.91
California	494.70	Alabama	140.88
Massachusetts	494.61	South Carolina	150.22
Vermont	471.26	Louisiana	151.66

Source: U.S. Agency for Children and Families.

Note: U.S. average = $357.27.

TABLE 11.10   Proportion of TANF Recipients Involved in Work (Fall 2001)

High		Low	
Washington	93	Georgia	6
Wisconsin	91	Mississippi	18
Montana	89	Connecticut	23
Kentucky	86	Vermont	22
California	81	New Hampshire	25
National Average = 56			

Source: U.S. General Accounting Office, *TANF Time Limits and Work Requirements* (Washington, D.C.: USGAO, 2002), GAO-02-770.

It is far too early to say what the final impacts of this legislation will be.[67] It is not yet clear whether people with relatively few job skills can support themselves and their families adequately—there have been a number of evaluations of the program, largely on a state-by-state basis, with somewhat mixed results. Also, as administrators gain more experience with the program there are pressures for change, including proposals for supporting more educational opportunities as a means of improving long-term economic prospects for the recipients.[68] What is certain is that this reform has changed the nature of American social policy in a rather fundamental way—and that further policy interventions will be required to provide child care, as well as programs for chemical dependency, job placement, and a number of other needs that arise out of this one change.[69] The success of the new program, and of the overall substitution of work for welfare, depends very much on the ability of the economy to provide the needed jobs.[70] Otherwise, the program may simply push the poor into short-term public-sector jobs rather than meaningful work in the private sector. Getting people off welfare may prove much easier than keeping them off.[71]

Implementing Workfare

After the adoption of PRWORA, this major change in social policy had to be put into effect by the states. As noted, the program was designed to provide state governments with substantial latitude in deciding how to make the program work, and the states have availed themselves of that opportunity. As a result, there are marked differences in the severity with which the regulations are enforced and hence the proportion of recipients who are being denied benefits or being allowed to engage in training rather than actually take a job.

One important intended consequence of the 1996 reforms of AFDC was to reduce the number of people receiving benefits. This goal was largely achieved, although at different rates in different states: although on average over 50 percent of public assistance recipients were removed from the rolls by late 2001,[72] Rhode Island, for example, had only 21 percent fewer welfare recipients, while Idaho had eliminated 94 percent and Wyoming 90 percent. There were some apparent political considerations involved in these changes, as states controlled primarily by Republicans since the adoption of the reforms had eliminated on average 56 percent of their recipients, while those under Democratic control had reduced their welfare rolls by 46 percent. This pattern indicates that there is some generalized support for the reforms, but it also shows some party differences.

The implementation of PRWORA was fortunately timed. The late 1990s were a period of extremely high employment and rapid economic growth, which meant that a person who wanted to find a job had a better chance of doing so than at almost any other time in recent history. Further, the salaries that could be earned by workers with even minimal qualifications had increased substantially. Despite the propitious timing, however, numerous studies have found that the creation of jobs that pay enough to support a family adequately and yet are suitable for people without considerable education and skills has lagged behind the need created by the workfare reforms. Dependence on a job that paid only minimum wage, for example, would put a family below the federal poverty line, and other benefits such as Medicaid might not be available. As the American economy went into recession in late 2001, the capacity of this, and other means-tested programs, to meet demands from increased unemployment and underemployment was seriously threatened.[73]

In addition to finding adequate employment opportunities, recipients and former recipients face some other problems as a result of this act. One of these is the need to provide for child care and other supports for workers, such as adequate public transportation. Child care is expensive, but it is crucial for women with small children who are now expected to enter the labor force.

Finally, the time limits adopted as a part of the program produced no major impact in the early years after its adoption, but as more and more recipients began to exhaust their eligibility, the consequences of this provision became clearer.[74] The early evidence showed that people were moving off welfare and getting jobs but that those jobs often were not very good and were threatened by the slowdown of the economy. Further, maintaining employment is to some extent a function of other government programs such as child-care support and public health insurance.

Alternatives for Further Reform of Income Support

With this one major reform implemented, various options for additional reforms—some of which are common in Western Europe—have been seriously proposed in the United States. The general characteristic of these alternative programs is the provision of benefits for less affluent citizens without the stigma, or the administrative complexity, of existing means-tested programs. Most such alternatives would, however, require a significant change in contemporary attitudes about the poor and about social policy in the United States. American popular opinion would have to shift toward providing universal benefits for all citizens and creating more of a welfare state in order for these options to be politically acceptable.

Family allowances. One alternative that is employed in virtually all other democratic, industrialized societies is the family allowance,[75] by which families are given a monthly benefit check from the government, usually based on the number of children. For the more affluent, this simply becomes additional taxable income, while for the poor it may be a major source of support. But the most important aspect of the program is that it includes everyone, or at least all households with children. The stigma of receiving government benefits is therefore removed, and the program is substantially easier to administer than PRWORA. If adopted in the United States, the program would need to provide a level of benefit for each child sufficient to match the current level of benefits, and this would mean that a great deal of money would have to pass through the public sector as taxes and expenditures, but the effects would perhaps justify accepting that difficulty, given the negative consequences of means-tested programs.

The negative income tax. A second alternative to the existing income support program is the negative income tax,[76] under which a minimal level of income would be determined, based on family size. Each family would then file its tax statement, with those earning below the established minimum receiving a rebate or subsidy, while those above that level would pay taxes much as usual. Such a program would provide a guaranteed annual income for all citizens and would be administratively simpler than PRWORA. The recipients themselves would provide a good deal of the information necessary to calculate benefits, instead of having to rely on state and local welfare offices. In addition, this program would establish equal benefits across the United States, with perhaps some adjustments for different costs of living in different parts of the country. The negative income tax, as it is usually conceptualized, would also make it easier to work one's way out of poverty because it imposes only a one-third or one-half reduction of benefits for any money earned.

The negative income tax, or something like it, was seriously proposed for the United States in a family assistance plan offered by President Richard Nixon.[77] If this program had been enacted, it would certainly have been the most sweeping reform of the welfare system ever made in this country, guaranteeing an annual income for all citizens. The program was defeated in Congress, however, by a coalition of liberals who thought its benefits too meager and conservatives who were ideologically opposed to the concept of a guaranteed minimum income. In addition, social workers and other professionals believed that their jobs were threatened by a program that placed the major burden of proving eligibility on the individual citizen.

Although the program has not been adopted in its entirety, there have been some movements toward a negative income tax in the United States. Most importantly, the Earned Income Tax Credit operates through the tax system to benefit low-income taxpayers with at least one child in the family. The ideas behind this program (introduced in 1975) were to offset the effects of the Social Security tax on low-income individuals and to encourage people to work rather than to take AFDC. This program now provides benefits (reduced taxes, or in some cases direct cash transfers) to over 56 million Americans, and therefore ranks as by far the most widely used means-tested benefit in the country. Administered through the tax system, it also is inexpensive to manage and less intrusive than many other social programs.

Faith-based initiatives in social policy.   During the 2000 campaign for the presidency, George W. Bush emphasized the possibilities of involving faith-based organizations more directly in addressing social problems in the United States. This approach was linked to his interest in reducing both the intrusiveness of government and government expenditures, as well as to his commitment to establishing a more prominent place for religion in American life. The assumption was that these private-sector organizations could help people in need without the bureaucratic "red tape" and with more flexibility than public organizations.

Early in his administration President Bush appointed a director for an Office of Faith-Based Programs and began to move toward the greater involvement of various religious organizations in the delivery of social programs. Despite the general American involvement in volunteerism and the relative strength of religious organizations in comparison to other industrial democracies, however, this program did not get off to the expected strong start. There was even some resistance from within the religious community itself, given the fear of excessive involvement of government with these groups' freedom to serve their clienteles as they would prefer.

Child support.   Although the popular image of the welfare recipient is that of a woman who has a child out-of-wedlock, in reality almost half of those served by the program find themselves in need of assistance because of divorce or separation. They are women left with children to support and they often lack significant job skills and work experience. Even in cases in which a legal divorce or separation decree has awarded child support, many men have not paid this support regularly, if at all. Several studies have found that a large percentage of the children whose families receive welfare have fathers who are not paying child support.

The federal government has now begun (with the assistance of the states) to enforce child support, especially in cases in which the mother otherwise would be receiving government benefits such as PRWORA or food stamps. The Family Support Act of 1988 required the states to establish enforcement plans, and in 1994 employers were required to deduct support payments from the wages of fathers who were not in compliance with legal mandates to support their children. These compliance plans now involve rather complex systems to identify fathers and then to extract the required support from them. These efforts have been somewhat successful, making recoveries of over $16 billion from almost 7 million absent parents in 1998.[78]

This approach to the problem of poor children is not without its difficulties, however.[79] First, the delinquent fathers (or mothers) must be identified and located. And then, a federal study has found, these irresponsible parents tend to be relatively poor themselves, with 29 percent living below the poverty line, and therefore have little income to extract for support of the children.[80] In spite of those barriers, the states have adopted increasingly vigorous programs of enforcement and now are able to collect 80 percent of in-state support.[81] Some states go so far as to confiscate the property as well as to garnish the wages of fathers who violate support orders.[82] Other states have begun to impose other penalties, such as loss of driver's licenses, on fathers who fail to provide support.[83]

Full employment.   Perhaps the simplest means of eliminating many of the problems of means-tested programs is to guarantee jobs rather than social benefits to those who need them. The federal government has been involved in a number of programs for job training and subsidized employment, the most prominent being the Comprehensive Employment and Training Act (CETA) in the 1970s and early 1980s,[84] and then J.O.B.S in the later 1980s. The purpose of these programs was to enable people to acquire job skills by working with local private contractors and then to subsidize the employment of those trainees for several years until they could be expected to have improved their productivity sufficiently to be able to earn a decent wage in the labor market. Although

CETA continued in operation until 1981, it was severely criticized on several grounds—for using inefficient and corrupt prime contractors, for example, and for training people to do nonexistent jobs.

The combination of an economy in recession and continuing pressures to solve the problems of poverty and welfare led the George H.W. Bush administration to place renewed emphasis on jobs and job-training. The president announced "Job Training 2000" as part of his economic program during the reelection campaign in 1992. Initially the details were far from clear, but the idea that jobs were superior on almost all counts to welfare was clearly stated. The difficulty the president faced at that time was the shortage of good jobs in the American economy even for workers with well-developed skills and ample job experience—qualifications that most welfare recipients lack.

The Clinton administration continued to place significant emphasis on developing jobs as the best means for addressing social problems. Robert Reich, President Clinton's first secretary of labor, as both an academic and a practitng analyst of changing employment patterns in the world, pressed the need for the U.S. economic system to adjust to the globalized economy.[85] The welfare reforms implemented by the Clinton administration (discussed earlier) emphasized work as a solution to the problem of welfare, but they did not rely entirely on the private sector to develop those jobs. Stressing education and training, and targeting many programs for young people, these programs built on a number of job programs that the federal government already had in place, but whose multiple, and often competing, goals had limited their effects.[86]

Job-training programs have not had a positive image in the United States, but they are gaining added importance under "workfare" programs. Although they are argued to be beneficial in the long run, in the short run these programs do not appear to be addressing the immediate needs of many poor citizens. Also, as they have been developing under PRWORA, the resources available for job training have been put to very differential use by different groups. Many white recipients have been using the money for college, while many nonwhite recipients have opted for trade schools or more vocational programs. In both instances, existing education and training programs rather than specially designed federal programs are utilized, and although the differences in the programs chosen may make little difference in the short run in an era of full employment, they may well produce major differences in earnings in the long run.

The War on Poverty

Another attempt at a comprehensive solution to the problems of poverty and means-tested benefits was the Johnson administration's War on Poverty. During the administration of John F. Kennedy, poverty had been "rediscovered" in the

United States, becoming a popular political issue, especially among liberals. Following Kennedy's assassination, President Lyndon Johnson used his formidable political talents and the memory of his slain predecessor to implement legislation that was designed to break the cycle of poverty. The War on Poverty differed from other social programs of the time in that it was directed less toward the short-term amelioration of deprivation than toward changing longstanding patterns and conditions of the very poor.[87]

War on Poverty programs did more than just hand out money—although they certainly did a good deal of that—by attempting to attack the cultural and social conditions associated with poverty. They also sought to involve the poor in the design and implementation of the programs more directly than had the more paternalistic efforts common at the time. The umbrella organization for the programs of the War on Poverty was the Office of Economic Opportunity, created as a separate agency outside the (then) Department of Health, Education, and Welfare (HEW). It was feared that the bureaucratic nature of HEW, and its commitment to social insurance programs as the mechanism for solving social problems, would hinder the activism envisioned for the War on Poverty, and consequently an independent organization was established.

One aim of the War on Poverty was to educate the children of the poor so that they could compete successfully in school and in the economy, and one of its most popular programs was Head Start, which attempted to prepare poor children to compete with other children when they entered school. The program sought to provide the skills that middle-class children generally have when they enter kindergarten but that children from economically deprived households frequently lack. Despite the popularity of Head Start, however, its demonstrable effects have been rather modest. Children who participated in the program were better prepared to enter kindergarten than children who had not been in the program, but their "head start" rapidly vanished. Without continuing extra assistance, after several years the Head Start children were not significantly different from children who had not participated.[88] Of course, depending on one's point of view, this could be an argument either that the program had failed or that it needed more follow-up once the children reached elementary school. Additionally, a college work-study program was initiated to try to make it more possible for students from low-income families to attend college, a program that has been expanded and continues after the demise of the War on Poverty.

For adults, the War on Poverty initiated a variety of programs intended to provide employment or to prepare people from poor households for productive employment. These programs commonly involved cooperation between the federal government and either state and local governments or private businesses. In addition to the employment-related projects, many smaller programs provided

Rediscovery of the depressing economic plight of families with children in the 1960s gave rise to a comprehensive series of programs intended to break the cycle of poverty.

counseling, loans for small businesses, family planning, and a whole range of other social services. In general, the War on Poverty provided something for almost everyone who needed and wanted work or help.

By the early 1980s, however, most of the programs of the War on Poverty had been dismantled, reduced, or modified. This retreat reflected changes in political ideologies as well as a diminishing availability of tax money as economic growth became less certain.[89] The major programs that have survived are Head Start and College Work-Study. Were the programs of the War on Poverty, and perhaps the whole war itself, a massive failure or at best a noble experiment in social change? Did they fail, or were they never really tried? These programs represented a major departure from the traditional means of attempting to solve, or at least ameliorate, poverty in the United States, and their impact may actually be more enduring than short-term evaluations indicate. Certainly the need to address the problems of poverty in the midst of affluence remains as pressing at the beginning of the new century as it was in 1965 when the War on Poverty was initiated. Whether the means to change is to come through better jobs in the private sector or through public programs, at least 30 million Americans—a large proportion of them children—live below the official poverty line, still waiting to enter the economic mainstream of American life.

That having been said, the continuing economic progress of the economy has been reducing slowly the level of poverty.[90] The data in table 11.11 (p. 320) show that during the economic boom period of the 1990s the poverty rate in the United States dropped significantly. At the same time, however, inequality actually increased, as the very affluent captured an even larger share of the economic pie. Also, poverty rates among the elderly continue to fall as most retirees now have at least a Social Security pension.[91] The socioeconomic profile of the United States is therefore a "half-full–half-empty" picture, with continuing inequality yet declining rates of deep poverty. The slowed economy and policy changes pushed poverty levels back up by 2002.

Other Means-Tested Programs

Although cash assistance programs have been the most common topic of discussion when the issue of means-tested benefits arises, there are also a number of other benefits available to less-privileged citizens. For example, food stamps are generally available to people on welfare as well as to other people who are working but whose income falls below prescribed limits. This program requires that participants purchase the stamps at a discount and then use them to buy food and certain other necessities. Unlike most other social programs, food stamps cannot be used legally other than for these strictly defined necessities, so that some of the common complaints against "welfare"—misuse of the funds for alcohol, gambling, and the like—can be controlled. Further, this program helps to increase demand for American agricultural products, so it gains support from those interests as well as from the interests that support social assistance. A similar program called WIC (Women, Infants, and Children) provides specified nutritional benefits to women and children. As noted, these programs, too, have been impacted by the general moves to reform welfare and now are much less available than in the past.

Supplemental Security Income (SSI) is another important means-tested program, which as of 2000 provided benefits to over 6.5 million people. The largest number of these recipients qualify by falling into the categories of aged, blind, or disabled. These were the categories in earlier state programs of assistance programs, but in 1974 these programs were federalized, thus removing them from the weaker financial provisions then available at the state level. These benefits have been indexed since that time, so that the assistance now offered to these groups is probably substantially superior to what it would have been if the program had remained at the state level.

TABLE 11.11   Changes in Poverty Rates, 1960–2002 (in percentages)

	1960	1970	1980	1985	1990	1995	1998	2000	2002
Total	22.2	12.6	13.0	14.0	13.5	13.8	12.7	11.3	12.1
African Americans	55.1	33.5	32.5	31.3	31.9	29.3	26.1	22.1	24.1
Children	26.9	15.1	18.3	20.7	20.6	20.8	18.9	16.2	16.7
Female-headed households	n.a.	38.1	36.7	37.6	37.2	36.5	33.1	27.9	28.4
Over 65 years of age	35.2	24.6	15.7	12.6	12.2	10.5	10.5	10.2	10.4

Source: U.S. Bureau of the Census, *Current Population Reports,* Series P-60, annual.

The Persistence of Poverty in the United States

We began our discussion of agenda setting with a discussion of the impact of Michael Harrington's book, *The Other America*, on the development of a poverty program in the United States.[92] Despite the attention such analysts brought to the problem and programs such as the War on Poverty, in the early twenty-first century poverty is nearly as great a problem as it was in the mid-1960s when President Johnson declared war on it. Poverty began declining during the 1960s and 1970s, but it began to increase again in the early 1990s. Moreover, the poverty rate is not uniform across the population but is concentrated among female-headed households, blacks and Native Americans, and children. Seventeen percent of all children under the age of eighteen now live below the official poverty line; one-third of all black children and over 30 percent of Hispanic children lived in poverty in 1999. Both of these rates of poverty reached their height in the early 1990s, and although they have since decreased slightly, they remain higher than during the 1970s. In contrast, the poverty rate for the elderly has improved substantially; that poverty rate is now less than half what it was in 1970, despite a growing elderly population. The economic growth of the 1990s had a major impact in reducing poverty, as the large number of jobs created enabled many people previously excluded from the labor market to get and keep a job.

In general, the social policies of the Reagan and George H.W. Bush administrations seem to have forced more people to live in poverty than would have been true if earlier social policies had been continued. A number of other factors, such as slower economic growth and changing demographics may have had some impact on the increasing poverty rate,[93] but public policy has been an important element. The Clinton administration returned to some of the social activism of previous Democratic administrations, although in a somewhat more restrained manner, placing its emphasis for the most part on developing more jobs and preparing people for those jobs rather than on direct grants to improve the situation of the poor. In contrast, poverty has hardly been discussed as an issue by the George W. Bush administration.

More than just jobs may be needed, however, if poverty is to be eliminated. As we pointed out earlier, a minimum-wage job will not pull a family of three or four above the poverty line, and in most areas will not do so even for an individual.[94] The minimum wage has been raised on occasion, but it still is lower than in 1995 when inflation is considered (see table 8.6, p. 216), and an increasing proportion of jobs in the United States are at the minimum-wage level. Given that many if not most of the families involved have a single wage-earner (usually female), there is little possibility of combining incomes to bring these families above the poverty line. There may be a need to link social benefits—food stamps, energy assistance, Medicaid—with work more closely than in the past. Such linkage has played a part in welfare reform efforts, but it may need to be extended to families already working as well as those receiving welfare.[95]

Poverty is a symbolic issue, but it is also a matter of careful counting.[96] How do we know who is living in poverty and who is not? The official definition of poverty for 2002 was a family of four living on an income of $18,558 or less; income includes government cash benefits, and adjustments are made for family size, urban versus rural areas, and so on. This definition does not include as income all noncash public benefits, such as food stamps, Medicare or Medicaid, and housing subsidies. In addition, no allowance is made for levels of taxation that could reduce income below poverty levels.

Because of the availability of numerous public benefits and the relationship of poverty status to eligibility for other public programs, conservative economists during the Reagan-Bush years argued for a change in the definition of poverty.[97] Such a change would have shown that many fewer people were in poverty and would thereby have benefited administrations that consistently argued that their policies had not harmed the poor. In addition, such a change in definition might have had the effect of a "reverse Harrington"—if the problem could be defined out of existence, it could be eliminated from the public agenda. The Clinton administration and Congress, however, reasserted concern about the definition of poverty and its current level, although they chose to address the problem indirectly—through employment programs and welfare reform—rather than directly.

The Homeless

In addition to the large number of people living in poverty in the United States, there are an increasing number of homeless, who often are not included in the official poverty figures because they are not caught in the statistical nets used to calculate those figures. Instead, the homeless live on the margins of society, often without government benefits of any sort, sleeping in shelters or on the streets and eating in soup kitchens.[98] Were it not for their visibility in many urban areas, the homeless might not really be counted as a part of the society at all.

The reasons for homelessness are numerous. Government policies have reduced the number of subsidized low-income housing units and so have forced many people—including families—onto the streets.[99] Further, changes in mental health laws requiring minimal possible restraint led during the 1970s to the release of many patients from institutions to poorly prepared community mental health programs, and some of those patients have since found their way to the streets.[100] Increases in chemical dependency have also contributed to homelessness in the United States, as has the declining number of jobs at which a person with low levels of education can earn a wage sufficient to support a family, or even him or herself. The latter problem was ameliorated by the economic boom of the 1990s, but it was by no means eliminated, and in fact it made something of a comeback as economic growth slowed in the first years of the twenty-first century.

For whatever reason, homelessness is now a significant social policy problem that is not being addressed effectively. The federal government has little or no policy for coping with the issue of homelessness—indeed, the only federal program of any consequence is the McKinney Act, which authorizes several types of emergency assistance, including housing, food, health care, and drug and alcohol treatment. For this purpose the federal government appropriated over $5 billion from 1987 to 1998, with most of this amount being spent through state and local governments.[101] Although this appears to be a significant amount of money, it is a rather meager amount compared with the magnitude of the need, and the program does not address the fundamental causes of the social problem.[102] More homeless persons now are being assisted by private organizations than by governments at any level. This emphasis on the private sector corresponded well with the emphasis on volunteerism during the Reagan and (both) Bush administrations, as well as in the post-1994 Republican Congress, but it has done little to solve the underlying problems. Further, city governments have begun to crack down on the homeless as a part of policing programs proclaiming "zero tolerance" that have sought to eliminate all forms of perceived antisocial behavior.

Approaches to homelessness were not altered significantly after the return to a Democratic administration in 1992. This was in part because of the absence of any clear policy solution to a multidimensional problem. Because people are homeless for a variety of reasons, addressing the problem would require an equally broad and probably expensive strategy. Further, many of those reasons, such as addiction and mental illness, might prove difficult for public policies to "solve" through conventional policy instruments. The Clinton administration had a number of other domestic policy priorities—such as health and welfare reform—and so relied on state and local governments, and especially the private, charitable sector to address the problem of homelessness. The George W. Bush administration followed in that path, depending even more heavily on "faith-based" organizations to do much of the work in alleviating poverty and homelessness.

Private Social Programs

Finally, we should point out that although most Americans tend to think about social programs as benefits provided directly by government, a huge number of social benefits are actually conferred by the private sector, usually with the indirect support of government. Pensions are a good example. We discussed earlier the very large and important program for public pensions provided through the Social Security Administration, but a huge number of citizens have private pensions. Over 92 million workers had pension rights through their employers or unions in the late 1990s, and millions of others have purchased private annuities or have contributed to individual retirement accounts—almost 31 million participate in 401(k) plans as means of tax-sheltering investments for retirement. Even many ordinary workers have pension rights through their employers, through their unions, or through their own savings and investments, and the tax system has assisted millions of people in creating Individual Retirement Accounts (IRAs) that are designed generally to supplement other forms of retirement income.

The federal government supports these private social benefits in at least two ways. First, an employee can deduct from his or her taxable income most contributions made to these programs, while the contributions made by the employer are not taxable until the employee begins to receive the pension. In addition, the federal government now supervises and guarantees pensions through the Pension Benefit Guaranty Corporation, much as it does bank deposits through the Federal Deposit Insurance Corporation. Pension schemes also are regulated through the Employee Retirement Income Security Act (ERISA). Given that most recipients of private programs are members of the middle class, these supports amount to a major (disguised) social benefit for that segment of the population. Much the same preferential economic distribution holds true for federal support for private medical insurance, disability insurance, and owner-occupied housing through the tax system.

The collapse of the Enron corporation in 2002 brought to light the weakness of the regulations on private pension schemes, and it produced a call for more stringent regulation.[103] Under the legislation of the time, a corporation was allowed to put all the funds invested by its employees in its own stock, therefore making those employees totally dependent upon the success of that one company, although most financial advisers would urge any investor to diversify and spread risk. Further, companies could restrict the timing of withdrawals of these funds and thereby force employees to lose their savings if the firm were to collapse, as was the case at Enron. Congress passed a law demanding greater corporate integrity during the summer of 2002, but the protections applied more to investors than to employees hoping for a company pension at the end of their working lives; what had long been a major benefit of working for a large corporation had become major worry instead.

Summary

The disjuncture between the poor and the nonpoor is not evident in Social Security, but it is apparent in almost all other elements of social policy in the United States—and in most other countries as well.[104] Especially in the United States, this dual pattern makes the politics of social policy very difficult for reformers as the political struggle quickly translates into a conflict of "us versus them" or between the "haves" and the "have nots." This struggle is exacerbated when the economy is not growing, so that any benefits granted the poor are perceived as directly reducing the standard of living of the middle classes. Even during periods of affluence there are always alternative uses for money that might be spent on social programs.

The social services are composed of a large number of rather diverse programs that are held together by an overriding concern with individual needs and conditions, some economic and some personal. The programs that have been tried and remain in operation represent attempts by government to improve the conditions of its citizens, although these programs by no means represent entirely satisfactory solutions to the problems. Several of the programs have been as unpopular with their clients as with the taxpayers who fund them. This chapter has described some approaches to modifying existing programs, as well as some more sweeping changes in program structure that might benefit both government finances and program clients. These social problems will not go away; if anything, the late 1990s and the first years of the twenty-first century have brought increasing demands for services, especially for the elderly and the homeless. What must be found is a means of providing adequate benefits through a humane mechanism that will not bankrupt the taxpayers. This is no easy task, but it is one that policymakers must address.

The emerging globalized market and its effects on wages, earnings, and employment will place even greater pressures on social policy in the United States. One of the enduring problems likely to be exacerbated by this tide of internationalization is the number of people who work full-time but who still earn wages that keep them in poverty. Further, if average real wages continue to fall as they did for much of the 1980s, the amount of money available to fund retirement benefits will also decrease and financial pressures on Social Security will increase.

The Reagan administration (1981–1989) reduced the rate at which social expenditures were expanding at the federal level. The amount spent on social programs in 1988 was at least as great as when that administration took office, although the amount spent was approximately 10 to 12 percent less than would have been spent under pre-1981 laws.[105] The gradual erosion of spending for social benefits continued during the George H.W. Bush administration, leaving social spending less as a percentage of total federal spending in 1992 than it was before 1985. The welfare state was not really dismantled during that period, but its rate of expansion was slowed.

President Clinton placed welfare reform on the agenda during his presidential campaign and pressed Congress for those reforms after his election.[106] He and the Republican Congress agreed on a major reform in 1996, with the new program beginning to be implemented in 1997. That reform has been described in a number of settings as "welfare to work," its basic premises being that the eligibility for social assistance be limited in time and that individuals must prepare to support themselves in the economy. This reformed welfare program almost certainly will be more expensive than the previous program, but it is hoped that these costs will be short-term and that over time the new program will move people off public assistance and into productive jobs.[107] Interestingly, the social policies of the United States and Europe are coming together on this issue, as a number of European countries are beginning to implement welfare reforms similar to those of the United States.[108]

CHAPTER 12

Educational Policy

EDUCATION POLICY TRADITIONALLY HAS HAD a central position among American public policies. Although the United States as a nation was and has been slow to adopt other social programs—pensions, unemployment insurance, national health insurance, and the like—it has always been among the world leaders in public education. Some 17 percent of all public spending and more than one-third of all public employment in the United States are devoted to education. Most public involvement in education has been at the state and local levels; the federal government has become directly involved in elementary and secondary education only relatively recently. Still, by the early twenty-first century the federal government has become a major actor in educational policy at all levels, exerting its influence through direct expenditures as well as through a variety of indirect instruments.

The Clinton administration sought to make the federal government an even more important player and placed a great deal of emphasis on expanded funding and regulation of all areas of education. Nevertheless, the adequacy of American education continues to be questioned, as American students perform at or near the bottom of some international standardized tests, and poor education has become identified as a major problem in American economic competitiveness.[1] President Clinton argued for the federal government to play a more significant role in addressing these deficiencies, and the American public appeared to agree. In a survey in 1998, when asked what to do with any budget surplus that might become available, almost a quarter mentioned education as the first priority—it was the most frequently mentioned use.[2]

Republicans in Congress, on the other hand, have continued to argue that education is a local, family issue and that the federal government should not expand its activities in this area. Recalling that the Reagan and George H.W. Bush administrations' plans to terminate the federal Department of Education hurt the electoral fortunes of their party, Republicans have not recently called for the federal government to get out of education entirely, but they do fight expansion of its role. The Republican-controlled Congress of the late 1990s chose not to challenge the existence of the Department of Education so directly, although it did oppose efforts to impose more federal controls over teacher competence and to provide more support for educational facilities. Also, given the electoral appeal of education, Republican leaders in Congress have advanced some programs of their own, mostly involving vouchers or tax credits supporting private schools.

Education was a central theme of the presidential campaign of George W. Bush, as it had been for his father. Although he tended to favor a smaller role for government in general—and especially for the federal government—the second President Bush did advocate a stronger role for the federal government in education. This involvement was to be primarily regulatory, monitoring the quality of education offered by local schools and providing resources, in the form of vouchers, to enable students to leave schools that are continually failing. This enhanced role for government in education appealed to the president's conservative supporters, who saw it as a means of providing additional funding for private schools.

Background

The public role in education began very early in the United States, with the state of New York adopting free public education in 1834. Education later became compulsory in all states until a student reached a certain age. (This provision was temporarily revoked in some southern states as a means of avoiding racial integration.) Even in the early years of the Republic, the federal government had some role in education. The Northwest Ordinance of 1787, in planning the organization of the Northwest Territories of the United States, divided the land into townships and the townships into sections. One of the sixteen sections in every township was to be set aside for supporting free common education. In 1862 Congress passed the Morrill Act, granting land and a continuing appropriation of federal funds to establish and maintain in each state a college dedicated to teaching "agriculture and mechanical arts." From this act grew the system of land-grant colleges that has produced such major educational institutions as Cornell, Texas A&M, and the Universities of Wisconsin, Illinois, and Minnesota. In addition to their broader educational activities, the research and extension activities of these institutions have been important for the expansion of American agricultural productivity.

By the end of the twentieth century the federal government had a large-scale involvement in education.[3] In 2000 the federal government spent approximately $91 billion on education. This may appear to be a huge amount of money, but it actually represents a smaller percentage (4.7 percent) of total federal spending than was devoted to education in 1980 (5.8 percent). In addition to the amount of money being spent, a wide variety of federal organizations provide assistance for education. In 1997 all cabinet departments except one (Commerce) had some involvement in education, as did a variety of other federal agencies, such as the National Science Foundation, the National Aeronautics and Space Agency, the Agency for International Development, and the National Endowments for the Arts and Humanities.

There are several important characteristics of American education and educational policy. First, the emphasis on education is indicative of the general attitude Americans have taken toward social mobility and social change, the belief that education is important because it gives people "chances, not checks."[4] The prevailing American ethos is that government should attempt to create equal opportunity through education rather than equal outcomes through social expenditure programs. Individuals who have the ability are presumed to be able to better their circumstances through education and to succeed no matter what their social or economic backgrounds may have been. It is perhaps important to note that despite the evils of segregation, blacks in the South prior to *Brown v. Board of Education* (1954) were given access to public schools and public educational opportunities through the level of the doctoral degree. One cannot realistically argue that the opportunities were equal, but education was more easily available to African Americans than might be expected, given their social status in those states. The norm of educational opportunity appeared to cover even social groups that were systematically discriminated against.

Related to the role of education in social mobility is the importance of American public schools for social integration and assimilation. The United States has absorbed a huge number of immigrants, 8 million of whom arrived in the first decade of the twentieth century alone. The institution that was most important in bringing those new arrivals into the mainstream of American life was the public school system. This was certainly true for adults who learned English and civics in "Americanism" classes in the evenings. Also important in this regard is that the public schools in the United States traditionally taught all the children living in the community. Only a very few wealthy families sent their children to private schools; everyone else in the community went to the same school, often all the way through their elementary and secondary years.[5] The tradition of comprehensive schools that provided a variety of educational opportunities, from college preparatory through vocational, was important in reinforcing the ideology of a classless society and in at least promoting social homogeneity, if not achieving it.

The 1980s and the 1990s were also a period of large-scale immigration to the United States, and the public schools continued to play a role in assimilating the children of those millions of new Americans. But the social and economic realities of the late twentieth century appear to have broken down some of the homogenizing impact of the public schools, and education became increasingly ethnically and economically segregated.[6] To some degree the lack of homogenization has been by choice, as "multiculturalism" became a rallying cry for those who want a more diverse society and a more diverse educational system to support that society.[7] Deciding how to manage increasing social diversity while still meeting the educational needs of all segments of the society is a major question now facing American education. Bilingual education is another part of the battle, especially in such states as California and Florida, which have large immigrant populations.

Despite the centrality of public education at the elementary and secondary levels, there has never been a state monopoly on education. Existing alongside the public schools are religious schools—almost 11 percent of the elementary students in the United States in the late 1990s attended parochial schools—and other private schools. This diversity is especially evident in postsecondary education, with over 22 percent of all college students attending private institutions.[8] Almost anyone can open a school, provided it meets the standards set by government or other accrediting bodies. If anything, the diversity of options for students has been increasing. The sense that the public schools are not doing an adequate job has spawned a variety of new educational providers, ranging from very strict schools concentrating on the "Three Rs" to unstructured attempts to promote greater creativity and free exploration of ideas.

Finally, the emphasis in American education has always been on local and parental control. Of all the major activities of government, education is the one clearly retaining the greatest degree of local control and local funding. In fact, the largest single category of public employment in the United States is made up of the public school teachers who are employed by local governments. And the control that government exercises over education is generally also local. There are almost 14,000 local school boards in the United States, as well as over 22,000 counties and cities that frequently play a substantial role in providing public education. Despite all those opportunities for local political action, there are pressures for even greater local control and parental involvement—from white suburbanites, from inner-city minority parents, and from ideologues, all of whom believe that the public schools should be doing things differently.

Although the local school has traditionally been a positive symbol of local government and the community, there are now a number of doubts about education and increasing pressures for change. These problems are to some degree reflected in the evaluations Americans give their schools. When asked to grade schools, respondents to national polls have tended to give their own community schools a grade of C, while they give schools nationally a very low C—barely passing (see table 12.1). In another poll less than half of respondents said they were satisfied with the quality of education in the United States.[9] It should be noted, however, that parents with children in public schools offer substantially higher evaluations of public schools than do people with no children in school

TABLE 12.1 Public Grades for Public Education, 1975–2001

	School in own community	Schools nationally		School in own community	Schools nationally
1975	2.38	—	1988	2.40	2.10
1977	2.33	—	1989	2.35	2.02
1978	2.21	—	1990	2.44	2.11
1979	2.21	—	1991	2.47	2.08
1980	2.26	—	1992	2.41	2.01
1981	2.20	1.94	1993	2.37	2.05
1982	2.24	2.01	1994	2.31	2.00
1983	2.12	1.91	1995	2.28	1.97
1984	2.36	2.09	1996	2.31	1.98
1985	2.39	2.14	1998	2.31	1.93
1986	2.36	2.13	2000	2.47	1.98
1987	2.44	2.18	2001	2.47	2.01

Source: Phi Delta Kappan, annual.

Note: 4.0 = A; 3.0 = B; 2.0 = C; 1.0 = D; <1.0 = F.

or with children in private schools. The assessment of education is another aspect of public life affected adversely by publicity and negative media coverage.

The negative image of public schools is reinforced by numerous findings that American students do not do as well on standardized tests as do students in Western Europe, Taiwan, Korea, or Japan. Even here, however, the evidence is not as bleak as it sometimes appears. Students in some states, especially those in the upper Midwest, do as well or better than students overseas.[10] Further, American students have been improving in their performance on these tests, and they tend to do better on other types of testing. The perceived problems and the reforms proposed to deal with them are discussed later in this chapter.

The Federal Government's Role in Education

The involvement of the federal government in education has been a matter of controversy, especially during the Reagan administration, which set out to further reduce the federal role. President Reagan's first secretary of education, Terrel Bell, came into office pledging to dismantle the recently created Department of Education, but the need for educational improvement and increased educational funding became more apparent as the administration progressed, and eventually the department was saved and even authorized to launch new initiatives for improving American education. President Reagan's second secretary of education, William Bennett, reversed the administration's initial direction, replacing it with a federal effort to improve what he considered to be the deplorable state of American education. His campaign was based on his personal view of good education—a highly structured curriculum stressing basic skills and the canon of Western civilization.[11] Waged more with rhetoric than with resources, it did highlight the importance of a national educational policy in a highly competitive, postindustrial world. By most objective indicators, however, the quality of education did not improve under Bennett.

The George H. W. Bush Administration

George H.W. Bush campaigned in 1988 on a pledge to be the "education president," but the first several years of his administration provided little clarification of that vague promise. He promoted several programs for magnet schools and rewards for schools that improved student achievement, but although education policy remained important nationally, the immense federal budget deficit and the generally conservative nature of his administration did not permit substantial federal funding for education during the first half of its tenure, despite state and local officials' pleas for assistance. Administration spokesmen advocated better education at every possibility but did relatively little to provide local school districts with additional resources to meet those educational goals.

In 1991, however, President Bush unveiled a plan to meet his campaign pledges on education. An ambitious blueprint, entitled "America 2000: An Education Strategy," was announced by the president and his new secretary of education, Lamar Alexander. This plan featured the following four major elements:

1. *National testing.* Unlike competency testing, the national tests proposed were to be diagnostic and open to the public in order to enable communities to judge how well their local schools were doing and to exert political pressure for better education. The scores on the tests (in principle voluntary) could also be used by prospective employers, thereby pressing both students and schools to do better.

2. *New schools.* The federal government would fund 535 new schools (one for the district of each representative and senator) that would serve as models of what could be done with public education. Federal funding was to be supplemented by funds from business so that the new schools could "break the mold" of existing educational programs.

3. *Improving teachers.* "America 2000" offered several recommendations for improving the quality of the teachers in America's schools, including merit pay and alternative means of certifying competency for teaching (especially in mathematics and science), rather than depending on state certification.

4. *Choice.* Consistent with the market-oriented philosophy of many Republicans, President Bush proposed creation of a market model in education, giving parents more opportunity to choose and placing schools under more pressure to perform.

Despite the ambitious goals of this plan, in practice almost nothing actually happened in education at the federal level during the four years of the first Bush administration.

The Clinton Administration

Unlike healthcare and welfare reform, education was not a central element of Bill Clinton's campaign for the presidency, but his administration hardly ignored the necessity to address the educational needs of the society. During the first Clinton administration, education policy had three principal concerns: the role of education in economic competitiveness and in sustaining the place of the United States in the world economy, the importance of education in coping with the social and economic disparities existing within the United States, and the need to support early childhood education by increasing the funding for such programs as Head Start.[12]

Several major pieces of legislation were indicative of the Clinton administration's approach.[13] One of the first was "Goals 2000," a linear descendant of the previous administration's education efforts. This was a broad-scale reform act promoting state and local efforts for improving American education to make it equal to that in other industrialized democracies. There was a great deal of emphasis on testing and improving the qualifications of teachers. The administration also advocated reauthorization of the 1965 Elementary and Secondary Education Act (ESEA), the major source ($10 billion) of federal support for education.

Another important educational initiative of the Clinton administration was the School-to-Work Opportunities Act,[14] an attempt to coordinate the activities of the Department of Education and the Department of Labor to help those students who do not get a college degree (almost three-quarters of the total) to prepare themselves for good jobs in a rapidly changing economy. Not only an educational program, this act was also an effort to cope with the global competitiveness problem. The program was to be implemented by state and local governments, and it would require cooperation between two bureaucracies that had not always agreed on how best to meet education and training needs.[15]

The Clinton administration also emphasized the need to reduce class sizes and to improve the general standards of teaching in schools.[16] While few people disagreed that these measures would improve the quality of education, there remained questions about whether the states or the federal government should play the major role in improving education. The Republican Congress, for example, had an anti-Washington education agenda that emphasized instead the role of states, local governments, and families. In response, the Clinton administration insisted that only by working at the national level could real educational progress be made for the country as a whole. Relying on state and local governments, it argued, might only perpetuate the inequalities that exist among those governments.

As noted, this emphasis on the federal role in education has persisted into the administration of the second President Bush. Educational quality remains central to this policy preferenc. It is a goal that could be pursued at the state or local level but often has not been because it often involves higher costs and therefore higher local taxes, and because state and local governments may not wish to have their own weaknesses and failures noted. The Bush plan of "naming and shaming" failing schools through the No Child Left Behind Act has been derailed to some extent by the intrusion of other priorities, by underfunding by Congress, and by the lack of interest by many state and local governments, but there is an underlying commitment to improving educational quality.

Local Financing and the Federal Role

We should discuss one aspect of local control in education because it conditions the need for federal involvement. This is the traditional funding of public education through the local property tax, which has presented two significant problems in recent years. One is that property tax revenues generally have not kept pace with inflation. The administration of the property tax involves assessing property values and applying a rate of tax to the assessed value. In an inflationary period, assessments may not reflect the real value of the property, and certainly not the costs of goods and services, unless revaluation is done frequently. Thus, many local school boards find that their funding is no longer adequate for their needs. The second problem is that, even if there were no inflation, the tax base available to some school districts would be markedly different from that available to others. To provide the same quality of education, parents living in poorer districts have to tax themselves at higher rates than those in more affluent areas. This is an extremely regressive way to finance a basic public service, as the poor have to pay a higher rate of tax to obtain the same level of education as the better off.

The usual result of this pattern of funding is that the education provided to poorer children is not as good as that provided to wealthier students.[17] Thus, it is argued that the local property tax is an inequitable means of financing education and that some alternative, such as federal or state general revenues, should be used to equalize access to education. Both federal and state contributions to educational funding have been declining slightly over the past decade (see table 12.2), leaving localities to bear an increasing responsibility for funding education. As we discuss later, the court system has already begun to bring about some changes in school finance in the direction of greater equality and greater state funding, but the inadequacy of local taxation remains an important reason for federal involvement in education.

TABLE 12.2 Sources of Educational Funding (in percentages)

	1970	1980	1990	1995	2000
		All Education			
Federal government	10.7	11.4	8.2	8.8	8.7
State government	31.5	38.8	37.2	34.4	34.8
Local government	32.1	26.1	27.1	26.0	25.6
All other	25.7	23.6	27.4	30.8	31 .8
		Elementary and Secondary Education			
Federal government		9.1	5.6	6.7	6.4
State government		43.3	43.6	41.4	41.9
Local government		40.3	40.7	41.8	42.1
All other		7.3	10.1	10 .1	9.6

Source: National Center for Educational Statistics, *Digest of Educational Statistics* (Washington, D.C.: U.S. Department of Education, annual).

Higher Education

It has traditionally been more acceptable for the federal government to be involved with higher education—perhaps because the students are almost adults and are assumed to have formed their basic value systems before the central government could influence them or perhaps because of the higher per student expense. At any rate, the federal government began to assist institutions of higher education somewhat earlier than it did elementary schools. During the Lincoln administration the federal government initiated the land-grant college system, which continues to receive substantial federal support, especially for its agricultural extension activities. The federal government also runs or supports the service academies, Gallaudet University (for the deaf), and Howard University. In addition to directly funding almost eighty colleges and universities, the federal government provides substantial indirect support for almost every college and university.

The major form of indirect federal subsidy for colleges and universities involves the funding of individual students. These programs obviously benefit students directly, but they also help to support many colleges that might have to close if they lost the many students who could not attend without federal assistance. The largest of the federal programs that have aided college students has been the GI Bill, enabling veterans of World War II, Korea, and, to a lesser extent, Vietnam and the Gulf War to attend college with the government paying virtually all the costs. For nonveterans, one of the largest programs of student aid was also justified as a defense program. The National Defense Education Act, passed in 1958 just after the Soviet Union launched *Sputnik I,* was intended to help the United States catch up in science, although students in the social sciences and foreign languages benefited as well.

Federal assistance began to reach beyond defense-related concerns during the 1960s and 1970s. The College Work-Study program was adopted as part of the War on Poverty but was moved from the Office of Economic Opportunity to the Office of Education, where it began to benefit a wider range of students. Likewise, the Education Amendments of 1972 instituted something approaching a minimum income for college students—the Basic Educational Opportunity Grant (often referred to as a Pell grant), the centerpiece of the program, gave a student $1,800 (a figure later increased slightly to account for inflation) minus what the student's family could be expected to contribute. While this was not much help if the student wanted to attend Harvard or Yale, it provided the means to attend at least some institution of higher education. Pell grants are subject to considerably stricter eligibility requirements and lower levels of funding for each student than other sources of aid such as loans.

The federal government also assists students by guaranteeing student loans (Stafford loans) and even providing some student loans for very low-income students (Perkins loans). The guaranteed loans are particularly important because they permit government to leverage a great deal of private money for students in higher education with minimal direct federal outlays. The federal government guarantees to a private lending institution that the money the institution lends a student will be repaid even if the student reneges—as many have done. In turn, the money is offered to the student at a lower interest rate than would otherwise be available, and repayment does not have to begin until after the student leaves higher education. The failure of many students to repay their loans and the fraudulent use of the loans by some trade schools (whose students are also eligible for loans) have brought this program into question, but it remains a major source of funding for students in higher education—some 6.2 million students received some benefit from the guaranteed loan program in 2000, with an average loan of $4,025.

All the above-mentioned programs primarily benefit students entering college just out of high school, but there is one federal program designed to benefit more mature students. Provisions of the income tax code that provide deductions for students who go to school to maintain or improve their job skills support a variety of trade and technical schools as well as academic institutions. For colleges and universities, the tax program stimulates attendance, especially among a segment of the population that might not otherwise attend college, although the university never sees the money. A 1997 tax act permits parents to develop educational savings accounts for future expenses and provides some limited tax deductions for tuition payments made by lower- and middle-income parents. The benefits are rather small in comparison to rising tuition costs, but they do offer some relief.

Finally, the federal government supports higher education in other indirect ways—for example, by providing aid for facilities through the Higher Education Facilities Act of 1963 and for dormitories through the Department of Housing and Urban Development. Federal research money (almost $19 billion in 2000) helps institutions of higher education meet both direct and indirect costs, and there are specialized federal grant programs for such fields as public service and urban studies. In short, the federal government has become central to the maintenance of American higher education in the twenty-first century.

But the large amounts it invests in higher education give the federal government a substantial amount of control over the policies of the universities, as has been manifested primarily through efforts to promote the hiring of women and members of minority groups as faculty members. In *Grove City College v. Bell* (1984),[18] however, the Supreme Court diminished to some degree the influence of the federal government in ensuring greater equality in higher education programs. Before that decision, a college found to be discriminating might lose all its federal money, but in its 1984 ruling the Court found that only the funds directly supporting the activity in which the discrimination occurred could be withdrawn. So, for example, if discrimination were found in the programs covered by Title IX (athletics and student activities), the government could not withdraw money from student support or from federal research grants. During the George H.W. Bush administration, discrimination was not pursued vigorously either by the Department of Education or the Department of Justice. One member of the administration argued against scholarships being given on the basis of race to needy students even in private institutions, although he was forced to recant, and the administration later offered a moderate plan to eliminate most race-specific scholarships.[19]

This policy thrust was to some extent modified by the Clinton administration, which favored a more vigorous program of affirmative action and attempts to improve the status of minority populations. Those intentions, however, were in some ways thwarted in 1999 when the Supreme Court overturned admission and scholarships awarded on the basis of race.[20] In June 2003, the Supreme Court issued decisions in two cases involving the University of Michigan. The Court held that race could be taken into consideration in university admissions and established rough guidelines on how it should and should not be used.

Funding for Higher Education

Since 1980 federal funding for students in higher education has not fared well. The Reagan administration cut back on federal support, reducing the base level of the Pell grant by $80 and tightening the income restrictions; this resulted in approximately 100,000 fewer Pell grant recipients in 1983 than in 1981. There was also a drop of some 460,000 in the number of new guaranteed student loans, as well as reductions in federal funding of social science and humanities research through cuts in the budgets of the National Science Foundation and the National Endowment for the Humanities. Clearly the policy of the Reagan administration was that higher education is primarily a state and local government function, if government is to be involved at all, and that the federal government should be only minimally involved.

The general commitment of the George H.W. Bush administration to education was manifested in a somewhat more supportive attitude, but although that administration continued to proclaim that education was a central priority, federal funding for programs such as the National Science Foundation was only slightly increased above that in the Reagan administration.[21] The Clinton administration struggled to reverse that trend somewhat, but it had to face severe budget restraints while attempting also to fund a variety of other policy priorities such as welfare and health care reform. The Clinton education budget sought to increase the level of direct federal support for higher education and to provide more money for current and prospective students. One of the more creative of these efforts was the "Americorps" program, which provides scholarship money for students who spend several years in service positions. They receive small salaries while in those positions, but a good deal of the reward for participation comes when they go on to pursue educational opportunities. This program, and much of the rest of the existing support for education, has been changed little by the George W. Bush administration.

Elementary and Secondary Education

The role of the federal government in secondary and elementary education has been less significant historically and remains less significant today than its involvement in higher education. However, there is definitely a federal role in precollegiate education. Other than the planning provisions of the Northwest Ordinance, the first involvement of the federal government in elementary and secondary education resulted from the passage of the Smith-Hughes Act (1917), which made funds available for vocational education. In the 1930s surplus commodities and money were provided to school districts for hot lunch programs, and those programs were expanded during the War on Poverty to include breakfasts for children from poor families. The Lanham Act of 1940 made federal funds available to schools in "federally impacted areas," which was understood to mean areas with large numbers of government employees and especially areas in which tax-exempt government properties reduced the tax base used to fund education. In 1958 the National Defense Education Act authorized funds to improve science, mathematics, and foreign language teaching in the elementary and secondary schools as well as at the college level.

The federal government's major involvement in elementary and secondary education currently is through the Elementary and Secondary Education Act of 1965, which was the culmination of the efforts of numerous education and labor groups to secure more federal funding for education.[22] This legislation was passed, along with a number of other social and educational programs, during the Johnson administration, and like so much of that legislation, it could not have been passed without the substantial legislative skills of Lyndon Johnson and the memory of John Kennedy. But before it could become law, legislators had to remove the barriers that had blocked previous attempts.

One of these barriers was the general belief that education should be controlled locally. The federal aid that had been given to schools previously had been peripheral to the principal teaching functions of the schools—the exception being the National Defense Education Act—in the belief that such aid could not influence what was taught in the classroom. The Elementary and Secondary Education Act (ESEA) involved direct, general subsidies for education, and it was initially feared that this federal presence would influence what was taught. However, as the federal government was already becoming increasingly involved in many aspects of education and social life through other mechanisms, such as the courts, this fear of federal control diminished.

Another issue that arose in relation to federal subsidies for education was the potential availability of funds for parochial schools, which raised constitutional questions about the separation of church and state. Most Protestant groups opposed aid to parochial schools as a violation of that principle, while Catholic groups opposed any federal aid to education that did not provide assistance to parochial schools. ESEA funds eventually went to parochial as well as public schools, although the money could not be spent for teaching religious subjects. The legislation specified that the federal money was to go to the students, not to the schools directly, which helped defuse some criticism based on separation of church and state.

Federal aid to education had also encountered opposition prior to the 1965 act because of the possibility that the money might be used to support segregated school systems in the South. The Civil Rights Act of 1964, however, prohibited using federal funds in any program that discriminated on the basis of race, and this provision meant that the issue was largely settled by the time the 1965 legislation was considered. On the other side, southern school systems had been afraid that federal subsidies would be used to enforce desegregation, using a carrot instead of a stick approach. However, these school systems were already under pressure from the courts to desegregate, and so accepting ESEA money was a minor additional step toward their eventual desegregation.

The 1965 ESEA legislation was part of the War on Poverty, but as implemented it provided assistance to almost all school districts in the United States—only 5 percent of all school districts in the country received no ESEA money.[23] The legislation provided funds for hiring teachers' aides, stocking libraries, purchasing audiovisual materials, and developing compensatory programs. The basic intention of the program was to enable students from poor families to perform better in school and to learn to compete more effectively in the labor market. Federal funds from ESEA were allocated to the states according to a formula, as is true of a number of federal programs. The formula adopted for ESEA in 1965 granted to each state federal funds equal to one-half of its annual per pupil educational expenditure multiplied by the number of low-income children. These funds were to be used for remedial programs (Title I) and to purchase materials, but the principal policymaking and programming came from the federal government rather than from the local school boards. The 1965 formula thus aided the high-income states more than low-income states, as it was based on the amount of money already being spent, but it quickly came under attack and was amended in 1967 to provide greater assistance to the poorer states. Under the new formula, each state received half of its own per pupil expenditures or half of the national mean per pupil expenditure, whichever was higher. Also, the definition of low-income students was eased so that school districts could claim more students and receive more federal funding. The 1967 amendments equalized funding between richer and poorer states and produced rapid increases in ESEA expenditures.

During the Nixon administration, the categorical nature of the funds allocated through ESEA came under severe attack, as a part of the "new federalism."[24] Efforts to convert ESEA funding into another of the block grants that characterized that administration's approach to federal assistance did not succeed, however, and the federal government retained nominal control over the ways in which the money was to be spent. What did change was the formula for computing aid. In 1974 a new formula was adopted that put both rich and poor states at a disadvantage, as measured by their per pupil expenditures. That formula narrowed the range of allowable per pupil grant funds from 80 to 120 percent of the national mean—the very wealthy states could claim only 120 percent of the national average per low-income pupil when computing aid, while the very poor states could claim only 80 percent of the national average (not the national average). And instead of receiving 50 percent of its per pupil figure, each state could receive only 40 percent. These changes reduced the amount a state would probably receive from ESEA funding, although amendments to the legislation did specify that no state would receive less than 85 percent of what it had received under the previous formula.

As with so many public programs, implementation was crucial to the success of the ESEA programs. And in many ways ESEA represents a classic example of a program being modified through implementation. The U.S. Office of Education, which was charged with implementing ESEA, was quite passive in ensuring the attainment of the stated goal of the program: equalization of educational opportunity for economically deprived children. The tendency of those who implemented the program at the state and local levels was to pork-barrel the funds, spreading them around among all school districts regardless of the concentration of low-income students. As a result, wealthier suburban school districts used ESEA funds to purchase expensive "frills," while many inner-city and rural school districts still lacked basic materials and programs that might compensate for the poorer backgrounds of their pupils.[25]

The initial failure in implementation of ESEA resulted in part from the close ties between the U.S. Office of Education and local school districts and in part from the misinterpretation of the intention of Congress, which had established the program not as general assistance to education, but strictly as a compensatory program. After some changes in the Office of Education and greater attention to the use of the funds, the implementation of ESEA was improved, although a number of questions remained about the ways in which the funds were being used. The Title I money—that portion of the program that is most directly compensatory (now part of the Compensatory Education Program)—is now targeted more clearly toward the poorer districts, but money available under other provisions of the act is still widely distributed and used by wealthier schools and school districts to supplement their programs.

In addition to its impact on education through its spending programs, the federal government also has a substantial impact through numerous regulations and mandates. Among the most important of the legal mandates is the Education for All Handicapped Children Act of 1975, which mandated that all handicapped or "exceptional" students be educated in a manner suitable to their special needs. This legislation was intended primarily to assist children with learning disabilities and physical handicaps in receiving education through the public schools. The meaning of the act, however, has been extended to include educationally gifted children, so that school districts are now required to provide a variety of special programs for a variety of different students. Bilingual education has also been mandated in some circumstances for minority students. All of these programs add to the costs of providing public education but impose most of the costs on state and local governments.

Has all this federal aid and regulation really improved the quality of American education? There is some evidence that the ESEA Title I reading programs have been successful in raising the reading levels of low-income students.[26] Further, to the extent that additional funding can aid education in any number of ways, some of which are difficult to quantify, these programs have certainly produced benefits. It is ironic, however, that in spite of all the federal money directed at it (almost $21 billion in 2000), the issue of the quality of American education remains as prominent in the early twenty-first century as at any time since the launching of *Sputnik I* in 1957. As was true then, much of the concern centers on education in science, mathematics, and engineering. The difference is that in recent years the perceived need has been to improve competitiveness

First Lady Laura Bush, shown here in a Delaware classroom, has long been a staunch advocate of literacy and education.

against the Japanese and West Europeans rather than to protect the country against a perceived Soviet military threat. In that competition, there is a strong sense that American education is failing and that the American workforce is decreasingly capable of competing. Some of the blame for these failures is placed on families that do not nurture students sufficiently and some on the students themselves, but a great deal of the blame is directed at the public schools.

Issues of Educational Policy

Even with the victory of advocates of federal funding for elementary and secondary education, a number of problems remain in public education, and some new ones are arising. In general, the public schools and their teachers have lost some of the respect with which they were traditionally regarded, and educational policy has been the subject of more heated discussion than was true during most of our history. In fact, it is not uncommon for politicians or analysts nowadays to charge that the public schools have failed and to call for significant change. President George W. Bush's program for improving the schools, like that of his father, is but one statement of this sentiment. Some would counter this argument by pointing out that it is perhaps not so much that the schools have failed as that too much has been demanded of them—that the schools cannot be expected to solve all of the society's problems. These defenders would argue that the resources and tasks given the schools have not been equal, and that too much has been expected for too little money. Several specific issues illustrate both sides of this argument, but what may be most important is that the U.S. educational system, which was long regarded as one of the great success stories of American public policy, is no longer considered quite so successful.

Quality of Education

One common complaint against schools that has persisted since the 1950s is that "Johnny can't read"—that is, that the schools are failing in their fundamental task of teaching basic skills. In addition to reading, this criticism has extended to progressive teaching techniques such as the "new math." Substantial evidence that would appear to support this point includes the decline in SAT scores since the early 1960s (see table 12.3, p. 343). It should be noted, however, that an increasing proportion of high school students began taking the SATs in the early 1980s, so the reduction in scores since that time may reflect to some degree the averaging in of scores from a number of students not intending to go to college but being required to take the test solely to judge the quality of their education. Beginning in the early 1980s the test scores registered a series of small changes up and down, but by the late 1990s an upward turn in scores gave rise to some sense that perhaps investments in education, and some school reforms, were beginning to have a real impact on the quality of education.

The charge about the schools' failure to teach basic skills can be contrasted to the complaints of other critics who regard the existing educational system as excessively rigid and stultifying. Some believe that public schools destroy the innate creativity of children; they would prefer more "open" education with fewer rigid requirements and greater emphasis on creativity and expression. Others feel that the existing public schools are excessively narrow in teaching a single class or racial perception of the world, instead of providing a broader perspective on the human experience; they demand a broader curriculum, or perhaps different schools for minority children. Quality in education, therefore, is not a self-evident attribute but may have definite class and racial components, and it may include creativity as well as the ability to solve math problems.[27]

Even if schools were serving the needs of the majority, they still might not be doing a good job for disadvantaged students, whose special needs are not met through many conventional classrooms. Title I of the Elementary and Secondary Education Act sought to meet those needs, but its widespread distribution and the uncertainty about methodologies has limited its success.[28] When ESEA was reauthorized in 1994, a number of suggestions were made for making

TABLE 12.3   Scholastic Aptitude Test Scores, 1967–2000

	Verbal	Mathematical
1967	543	516
1970	537	512
1975	512	498
1980	502	492
1985	509	500
1990	500	501
1995	504	506
1998	505	512
2000	505	514

Source: College Entrance Examination Board, *National College Bound Seniors* (Princeton, N.J.: CEEB, annual).

it more effective. Unfortunately, the tendency of Congress to convert any legislation possible into pork-barrel programs meant that it would remain difficult to keep this act from distributing funds as widely as it had in the past.

Vouchers and "Choice"

While the various complaints about education sometimes appear worlds apart, they have in common the desire to modify the type of education offered through the public schools. One possible response to these complaints would be to decentralize the school system, which would be in the tradition of local control over education but would merely alter the definition of what the appropriate local area is. In New York City in the 1980s, the conflict between parents in Ocean Hill-Brownsville and the city's public schools represented one of the most explosive events of this movement. Later, Chicago and then Milwaukee decentralized much of their school systems to the individual school level, giving parents a great deal of direct managerial authority over teachers and curriculum. These experiments in local control have been judged by many to be successes, but for most pressing problems in public education, decentralization may not be the answer in all situations.[29] If a local school does not have the right leadership (professional and parental), it could prove disastrous to decentralize.[30]

Related to the idea of decentralization is the possibility of choice among schools within a school system. In almost any school system some schools have the reputation, and perhaps the reality, of being better than others. These schools are often in middle-class neighborhoods, with parents who place pressure on the school board, principals, and teachers for high-quality education. Some school systems also utilize "magnet" (specialized or selective) schools to promote educational quality and to achieve racial integration. One proposed solution to the general problems of quality in education is to allow any student in a public school system to attend any school in the system, thus creating something approaching the market system implied in voucher plans but keeping all the funds in the public school system.

A more common policy option proposed to address the problem of quality education is the use of educational vouchers—giving each student's parents a "check" equal to some specified amount of money that would be applicable only for education.[31] The parents could spend that voucher either in the public schools, where it would pay the entire cost of the child's education, or at some other school where it might not cover the entire cost and the parents would have to make up the difference. Under the voucher plan, parents would have significantly greater control over the kind of education their children would receive, choosing among open schools, fundamental schools stressing basic skills and discipline, religiously oriented schools, and any other schools that meet state standards. One voucher or choice program implemented in Milwaukee was specifically targeted for low-income students and did not require additional parental funds.[32]

The idea of educational vouchers has been around for several decades, but it received a large boost from the work of John Chubb and Terry Moe.[33] These scholars argued that the fundamental problem with public education was organizational—schools and school systems were too bureaucratic to provide good education. They argued that the only way to remedy that problem was to create competition and offer choice to parents and students. Although Chubb and Moe argued that vouchers would not be necessary, they came to be considered a part of their proposed reforms. The George H.W. Bush administration's advocacy of choice in education placed voucher plans at the center of the debate over improving American education.

More recently, the Republicans in Congress began placing great emphasis on vouchers as a means of improving education, in particular for students in the District of Columbia. In 1998 they proposed giving a limited number (2,000 out of 78,000) of students vouchers to attend private or suburban schools. The logic was that the financially strapped schools in the nation's capital were among the worst-performing in the United States and the city's children should be given the opportunity to escape them. President Clinton responded by arguing that this proposal would only divert needed money from the public schools, and he promised to veto the legislation.[34] The George W. Bush administration came to office emphasizing the need for vouchers but was willing to bargain that away in order to gain passage of other educational reforms, especially those that would punish "failing schools."

Although the voucher plan is appealing as a means of offering choice in education and thereby improving education, a number of questions have been raised about its potential effects on the educational system.[35] Perhaps the most fundamental question is whether it would increase stratification in education;

one of the fundamental virtues and goals of American education, after all, has been its attempt to promote social homogeneity and integration. If a voucher plan did not cover the full price of a child's education, many low-income parents would not be able to make up the difference between the value of the voucher and the tuition of private schools, especially the better private schools. The plan might simply end up subsidizing middle-class parents without improving the quality of education for the poor, who need that improvement the most—plans like that in Milwaukee are an obvious exception. In fact, such a plan might well undo the racial integration that resulted from years of effort and policymaking. All these questions are reinforced by the Coleman Report and numerous other studies of education, which point out that the child's home background is crucial to educational success.[36] A voucher plan would tend to benefit children who would probably succeed anyway, and it might divert funds from schools and children who need the most help.

Also, although educational vouchers could be used only for schools that meet established state standards, questions remain about the propriety of spending public money for education over which the state has no control and about the possibility that the voucher system might actually lower the quality of education. It is not entirely clear where the capital—both human and physical—required to implement this reform of the education system would come from. As a consequence, a full-scale voucher plan might result in the formation of a number of small and inadequate schools, none of them providing the quality of education that could be offered by large, comprehensive public schools. It may be that education is a service that is not amenable to market logic and competition. That having been said, nearly half the American public now say that they believe vouchers are an acceptable policy instrument in education, although three-quarters also want to ensure high levels of accountability for the use of funds.[37]

Finally, the idea of the voucher plan is justified by the market ideology. Some analysts think that the introduction of competition into the education marketplace will improve the quality of education by increasing the choices available to consumers and by placing competitive pressures for improvement on existing public schools. For this education marketplace to function effectively, however, the consumer must have access to information about the "product" being produced. This might be difficult if a number of new schools were started in response to a voucher plan. After all, even in established systems of public and private education, it is difficult to assess quality, especially because much of the difference in the educational success of students is accounted for by family backgrounds, and much of the effect of education may not be evident until far in the future.

"Charter schools" are a means of providing choice more on a collective rather than an individual basis. These schools are organized by parents or by providers as a means of opting out of the local schools, albeit with public financial support.[38] Many states have passed legislation providing funding for charter schools, provided they meet accreditation standards. Although these schools offer some of the same basic benefits as vouchers, they provide a collective rather than an individual choice, and they may be a way of expanding the educational opportunities available in a society, rather than simply subsidizing the existing array of educational institutions. Still, charter schools may also drain away some resources from the mainstream of public education. For that reason, educational unions and local school boards have tended to provide little political support for this innovation in education.[39]

Finally, schemes to provide "tuition tax credits" for parents sending their children to private schools are similar to vouchers. This option was actively supported by the Reagan administration as a means of providing education that would be better and more in line with the "cultural and moral values" of the parents, and the proposals surfaced again several times during the George H.W. Bush administration, and again in the 1997–1998 Republican Congress. The political and educational arguments for tuition tax credits are similar to those for vouchers: they promote greater pluralism and allow parents greater choice. In addition, as many minority students have performed better in private (especially Roman Catholic) schools, this program could be of substantial benefit to them.

Those opposed to tuition tax credits, such as the National Education Association, the Parent-Teacher Association, and the American Federation of Teachers, argue that they would only undermine public education by creating a two-class educational system. Parents of minority students would still have to have the means of paying anything over the amount of the tax credit, so the beneficiaries again would be middle-class students, who may not need the benefit. Finally, programs such as this, which would tend to benefit parochial and other religiously based schools, raise the continuing question of the separation of church and state.

Thus, while few educators or policy analysts would claim that the American educational system is currently what most citizens want it to be, it is not entirely clear that a voucher plan, or other plans promoting choice, would improve it all that much. The benefits of a voucher plan might be as much psychological as real—it would appear to offer parents more choices and to allow them greater control over their children's education. However, the effects on the general quality of education might be difficult to measure. This would be especially true if one effect of the program were to siphon significant amounts of money away from public education for the benefit of private schools. For most students, the effect of "choice" would be less money for their public schools, and most likely therefore, a poorer-quality education.

Competency Testing

Another potential response to concerns about educational quality is competency testing.[40] This plan would address the claim that students are being promoted who have not mastered the material required at each grade level, that they are being promoted simply to get them through the school system, with the result that students who cannot read and write are graduating from high school. Competency testing would require a student to pass a test on basic educational skills—reading, writing, and computation—before being awarded a high school diploma, thus ensuring that at least minimal standards of quality are enforced. Advocates of competency testing also argue that it would provide more incentives for students to learn and for teachers to teach.

Although many leaders of minority communities have argued that the public schools do not adequately prepare minority students, they have not been supporters of competency testing. The program has been attacked as racist, because a disproportionate share of the students who fail the tests in states where such programs are in operation (most notably in Florida) are nonwhite. These competency tests, continuing to be challenged in the courts, are claimed to be biased against nonwhites because they employ standard English and are based on values and concepts that are derived from white middle-class culture. Such tests are, at best, a minimal demonstration of educational quality, but the poor scores are, nevertheless, indicative of the poor quality of education being offered some students.

The federal government has long been an advocate of various forms of competency testing for the public schools. It has supported the National Assessment of Educational Progress, a test given in the fourth, eighth, and eleventh grades, for twenty years.[41] In addition, the George H.W. Bush administration's 1991 proposals for improving education were based heavily on the efficacy of standardized testing and something close to a national curriculum. The proposed tests would not have prevented a student from graduating from high school, but they could have been used to compare student performance so that, in essence, poor performers might as well not have graduated in the eyes of prospective employers. These tests were also intended to provide parents and taxpayers with a measure of the effectiveness of their schools that could be used to generate political pressures on poorly performing school systems. The Clinton administration also stressed national testing as a means of promoting educational quality, while congressional Republicans tended to oppose it, favoring more decentralized forms of accountability.[42]

Even without national testing, or the use of standardized testing as a means of determining whether a student can graduate, educational testing has become an issue in education. On the one hand, parents and state legislatures want some way to hold teachers and educational officials accountable for their activities, and they see standardized testing as a means of determining if their schools are doing a good job and, if not, trying to find out why. On the other hand, critics argue that students are already spending too much time on such tests, to the detriment of other types of learning. For example, eighth graders in thirty-nine states take some statewide tests, as do eleventh graders in thirty-five states.[43] Further, some critics charge that teachers now teach students to do well on these tests, rather than giving them the skills they will require in future life.

The Clinton administration entered the battle over testing, proposing the use of national tests. Again, the logic was to use the tests as diagnostics to determine if local schools were doing the job, and if not, to mobilize local pressure to improve the schools. More conservative politicians interested in maintaining local control, as well as some leaders of advocacy groups concerned about the validity of testing among minority and economically deprived students, came out in opposition to the general testing plans. As these issues continue to be fought over in Washington, they make it clear that education has become an important topic of national politics, not just a local issue.

President George W. Bush campaigned on using national testing and identifying "failing schools" from which parents would be able to obtain some relief. The "No Child Left Behind" legislation is designed to give parents the opportunity to move their children out of schools that continue to fail to meet standards. The states have been slow to respond to the challenges put to them by the administration, in part because of the power of teachers unions as well as the fears of disruption in the school systems, but this issue is unlikely to go away. The triumph of the Republicans in the 2002 congressional elections has returned vouchers to a more central place in the educational debate.

Testing Teacher Competence

In addition to testing the quality of the product of the schools—the students—a number of reformers have argued that the producers—the teachers—should also be tested. The tradition had been that once a teacher graduated from a school of education, he or she would be given a certificate, usually renewable after additional coursework, and he or she would soon receive tenure and could then teach for life. Numerous parents and education experts who thought that the traditional system was insufficient to guarantee that teachers could indeed educate students effectively proposed that all teachers should be tested. This policy was widely supported by the public (85 percent in one poll), and some form of competency testing for teachers has been adopted in forty-four states.

Initial scores on the teachers' tests appeared to justify the arguments from the critics of the existing educational system. In several southern states, only about half the teachers who took a test in the early 1990s passed it the first time. As the testing became more general across the United States, the failure rate dropped significantly, and testing has become a standard part of the certification process for new teachers. Even though it is now widely used, there are still a number of complaints about the policy. First, just as for pupil competency testing, it is argued that the tests are discriminatory; indeed, a much higher proportion of nonwhites than whites fail the test. Also, teachers' unions argue that the test—especially if given to established classroom teachers—does not adequately measure all the things a teacher must do to be effective. Finally, testing is seen as just one more hurdle that can keep teachers out of the classroom where they are needed.

Competency testing itself certainly cannot guarantee a supply of good teachers in the United States. There are other problems, including low teachers' salaries, a problem that the Reagan administration identified as a major focus of its efforts to improve education. Another problem is the declining interest in teaching among young women, who were once the major source of talent in elementary and secondary education but now have numerous other, more lucrative, careers open to them. Yet another problem is presented by the working conditions encountered in many schools, especially problems of discipline and personal safety.[44] Finally, teachers no longer appear to command the respect that they traditionally enjoyed in American society, and many of the psychic rewards of teaching have disappeared for much of the teaching profession. Unless the public schools can attract enough qualified and dedicated teachers, all the other reforms in educational policy may be to little avail.[45]

School Facilities

Americans are fond of saying they will do anything for their children, but if an impartial observer were to walk into many of America's schools, he or she would doubt the sincerity of those statements. Many American schools are dilapidated, and they appear to be unlikely places in which to find excellence in education. The General Accounting Office conducted a survey that concluded that one school building in three in the country was inadequate, and almost six in ten had at least one inadequate feature, such as a leaking roof.[46] There were, however, marked differences across the country in the condition of school buildings (see table 12.4), for half of the schools in the District of Columbia were labeled inadequate, but less than 19 percent of schools in Iowa were found to be so. In the District of Columbia, 91.1 percent of schools had at least one inadequate feature, as compared to only 37 percent of schools in Georgia. In addition to the differences by state, there are intrastate differences, with inner cities having generally worse school facilities.

In 1998 the Clinton administration began to push a national campaign to improve the quality of the facilities available to schoolchildren.[47] The federal government already had begun to be involved with school building issues through a number of mandates, especially access for the disabled. President

TABLE 12.4   Schools with Deficiencies, 1999 (in percentages)

		Type of School District		
	Total	Central city	Suburban	Rural	Poor[a]
Temporary buildings	39	45	44	29	43
At least one inadequate feature	50	56	44	52	63
Needing some additional spending to bring to overall good condition	76	74	81	70	84

Source: National Center for Educational Statistics, *Digest of Educational Statistics, 2001* (Washington, D.C.: U.S. Department of Education, 2002).

a. Over 70 percent of pupils in school lunch programs.

Clinton argued that there was a pressing need for improving facilities, in some cases to guarantee basic safety and in many others to ensure that students had a positive learning environment. The schools would also need a range of electronic equipment and access if they were to be adequate to the task of educating for the emerging economy and society. This campaign produced a number of positive public relations events for the administration and in the end produced some real improvements in facilities.

The Separation of Church and State

The First Amendment both forbids the establishment of a religion and ensures the free exercise of religion in the United States. In public education, these two clauses have caused a number of controversies about education and government's role in education. The two clauses may, in fact, be interpreted as being in conflict. For example, if schools require a prayer, this is deemed an establishment of religion (*Engle v. Vitale*, 370 U.S. 421 [1962]). Conversely, prohibiting prayer is seen by some as a limitation on the free exercise of religion.

Issues of church and state arise over two areas in education. The first is the school prayer issue. Since 1962, when the Supreme Court outlawed official school prayer, religious groups have attempted to have prayer returned to the schools, either through a constitutional amendment specifically permitting prayer or through compromise measures such as silent meditation and voluntary attendance at prayers. The issue of prayer in school resurfaced in 1984, when a Reagan administration proposal directed at improving the quality of American education contained a provision allowing local school boards to permit a moment of silent meditation at the beginning of the school day; this was presumed to promote discipline as well as moral education. When individual states have attempted to impose such plans, they have been struck down by the Supreme Court (*Wallace v. Jaffree*, 472 U.S. 38 [1985]); the federal mandate was not adopted. In 1990, the Court did, however, permit religious groups formed by students to use school facilities for their meetings after school hours, and this may be a wedge for greater use of the public schools for religious exercises.

If the Supreme Court followed the election returns, the justices would have sided with President Reagan, both Presidents Bush, and their fundamentalist supporters on the issue of school prayer. Large majorities of the population have favored permitting prayer in schools, but as with many other issues, opposing groups have successfully countered, raising issues of civil liberties. Thus, attempts at passing a school-prayer amendment have been unsuccessful. The standard legislative tactic has been to block consideration by procedural mechanisms rather than by a vote that would make it clear to constituents how legislators feel about school prayer.

The second area of controversy concerning the separation of church and state is public support for religious schools. In deciding this issue, the Supreme Court has been forced to make a number of difficult decisions, but over the years it has tended to allow increasing public support for religious education. For example, in 1930 the Court upheld the right of states to provide textbooks to children in parochial schools on the same basis that books were provided to students in public schools.[48] In 1947 the Court upheld bus transportation for parochial school students at public expense. Both rulings were upheld on the grounds that these expenditures benefited the students, not the church.[49]

In contrast, in 1971 the Court struck down a Pennsylvania law that directed the state to pay part of parochial school teachers' salaries, arguing that this was of direct benefit to the church and created excessive entanglement between church and state.[50] Also, the Court has permitted states to provide teachers for exceptional students in parochial schools, but not on the premises of these schools. In a somewhat contradictory move, the Court in 1976 upheld general grants of public money to church-affiliated colleges.[51] In 1994, the Court ruled that the state of New York had violated the separation principle by creating a school district that served only the disabled children of a Hasidic Jewish sect that did not want its children to attend public schools.[52]

The reasoning behind these decisions is tortuous, but three principles do stand out. The first is that aid to students and their families is more acceptable than aid to religious institutions. Second, institutions of higher education are permitted more entanglement between church and state than are elementary and secondary schools. Finally, the public sector should not have to spend additional money on education because of the special religious demands of a group, but neither should it impose additional financial burdens on the religious groups.

Unionization and Management

The image of the American "schoolmarm" is ingrained in the popular mind. Leaving aside any sexist stereotypes about all elementary and secondary school teachers being female, the point here is that the image of the schoolteacher has been the positive one of a person dedicated to education and to students. The teacher and the school were considered integral parts of the American community.

The image of the teacher is now changing, however, in part because of increasing unionization and a growing number of teachers' strikes.[53] No longer the representatives of culture and learning in small towns, teachers are now more likely to be employed by large school districts and to be members of organizations that bargain collectively for improved wages and benefits. One of the two major teachers' organizations is the American Federation of Teachers, affiliated with the AFL-CIO. This organization, which is clearly a union, has been quite willing to employ the strike weapon in its dealings with school districts. The second major teachers' organization, the National Education Association, is a professional organization, but its local chapters operate as collective bargaining units. The NEA has been more reluctant to use the strike to gain its ends, although certainly a number of its local chapters have struck. As of 1999 approximately 77 percent of the teachers in the United States were members of these organizations or of local teachers' unions. In almost any year there are several hundred strikes by public schoolteachers. The sight of teachers picketing and of children out of school until October and even November has changed the once-positive image of the teacher. As local government budgets continue to be squeezed, there will be demands for more students in each classroom and less money for raises, and the teachers' strike may become an even more common phenomenon.

In addition to forcing parents to make arrangements for their childrens' care during strikes, labor unrest in education has other, more important consequences. As discussed earlier, many Americans believe that the quality of American education is not as high as it should be. The sight of educators on strike tends to erode the public image of education even further. Of course, those who favor the more militant actions by teachers quite rightly point out that good teachers will not work for the salaries they are sometimes offered, and that fewer good students will be attracted into careers in teaching. There are, however, important problems of symbolism and public image when teachers take to the picket line.

The impact of educational unions extends beyond the possibility of strikes. The high level of unionization in education also poses significant problems for administrators in their day-to-day management of their schools. For example, as we have already noted, school principals and superintendents are under increasing pressure to demonstrate the adequate or superior performance of their schools. They must do that with less control over personnel than they would have in private industry or even in other areas of the public sector.

Equalization of Resources

As mentioned earlier, most public education is financed by local property taxes, and this basis of finance can produce substantial inequities in education. Local school districts with poor resource bases must either tax their poorer constituents more heavily or, more commonly, provide inferior education to the district's children.[54] Also, given that poorer school districts frequently have concentrations of minority group families, this form of educational financing affects racial and cultural integration and the perceived fairness of government. The resulting inequalities in educational opportunity may, in turn, perpetuate racial differences in economic and social opportunities.

Reliance on the local property tax to finance public schools has been challenged successfully in the courts, although they have not provided any definite answers to the questions involved. In *Serrano v. Priest* (1971), the California Supreme Court ruled that the great disparity between richer and poorer school districts in the Los Angeles area violated provisions of both the state and federal constitutions. In particular, this disparity constituted a denial of equal protection for the residents of the poorer district. The court did not, however, make any direct recommendations on how this disparity could be ameliorated to meet constitutional standards. One common assumption was that the state might have to either take over educational financing entirely or alter the formula for distributing state equalization payments.

In a similar case, *San Antonio School District v. Rodriguez* (1973), the Supreme Court ruled that the differences between two Texas school districts were not so great as to constitute a violation of the equal protection clause; the Court did not say how much of a difference would constitute such a violation. This decision left open the constitutionality of the continuation of these disparities between school districts, but the problems local districts face in attempting to provide for decent education from a low taxable property base remain quite tangible.[55]

One answer to these enduring questions came in the 1990s, when various state courts decided that the existing system of school financing violated their state constitutional requirements for "an efficient system for the general diffusion of knowledge." The Texas Supreme Court ordered the state of Texas to find some means of redressing the differences among its 1,044 school districts.[56] Those school districts exhibited massive disparities: the richest 5 percent of school districts spent $11,801 per pupil, while the poorest 5 percent spent $3,190 per pupil.[57] The state legislature first opted for regional tax sharing, but the voters rejected this amendment to the state constitution.[58] The final plan called for wealthier school districts to transfer some of their taxable property to poorer districts so that those poorer districts could provide a better education for their pupils.[59]

The question was settled in Texas through the courts, as it has been in the courts in seventeen other states, but this is a general problem for all fifty states.[60]

Some states have begun to address questions of equality of funding for education without direct court intervention. The most important example is Michigan, which acted following several embarrassing events, such as the closing of a school district in northern Michigan several months before the scheduled end of the term because of lack of funds. State leaders decided to substitute a 2-percent sales tax and a tripling of the cigarette tax for the property tax as the source for educational financing, after voters chose this option over an increase in the state income tax.[61] These consumption taxes were statewide, and the revenue was to be divided according to the relative needs of the school districts. As this example shows, the states have a variety of mechanisms for equalizing the access to funding, and ESEA money can also be used for that purpose.[62] One state—Kentucky, which historically had one of the most unequal and least effective school systems in the country—even attacked the problem directly by centralizing the funding of schools, with a great deal of apparent success.[63]

Disparities in funding and quality persist across the country, however, and many children continue to receive substandard education because of inadequate resources in the state, county, or neighborhood. As a part of its Goals 2000: Educate America Act, the Clinton administration proposed some equalization funding for poorer districts.[64] This plan was supported by many educational groups but was naturally opposed both by more affluent districts and by a Republican Congress that favored preservation or enhancement of local control. While generally more concerned with content than with funding, congressional emphasis on local power in education does tend to preserve inequalities.

The school district in which a student lives may affect the quality of his or her education, but the state in which that school district operates may also make a difference. There are pronounced variations in the level of funding for public education by state (see table 12.5). There are also substantial variations in the average salaries offered to teachers in different states; in 1998 the highest average salary (New Jersey) was 88 percent higher than that in South Dakota. The relatively poor states of the South and upper Midwest fare the worst in terms of support for public education, while the industrial states of the Northeast tend to do the best.

These data illustrate that there is yet no national education policy or standard, and a child's life chances may depend upon geography. The differences in actual educational outcomes, however, may not be as disparate as the money being spent. Some states with very low levels of per pupil expenditures, such as Iowa, South Dakota, and Utah actually have very good results on standardized tests such as the SAT.[65] In fact, there is actually a slight negative statistical relationship between the amount of money spent per pupil and scores on the SAT.[66] Some of this success may be attributed to relatively homogenous populations in these states, while some of it may be a function of the smaller schools in rural America and the closer personal attention the pupils receive in those settings.

TABLE 12.5 Inequalities in Educational Funding

A. Average Teacher Salaries (1999)

National average = $39,278

Five highest		Five lowest	
NEW JERSEY	$50,284	SOUTH DAKOTA	$27,875
ALASKA	49,140	NORTH DAKOTA	28,213
NEW YORK	48,712	MISSISSIPPI	28,229
CONNECTICUT	48,009	NEW MEXICO	30,042
PENNSYLVANIA	47,542	MONTANA	30,617

B. Per Pupil Expenditures (1998)

National average = $6,189

Five highest		Five lowest	
NEW JERSEY	$9,643	UTAH	$3,969
CONNECTICUT	8,904	MISSISSIPPI	4,288
NEW YORK	8,852	ARIZONA	4,595
ALASKA	8,271	SOUTH DAKOTA	4,699
RHODE ISLAND	7,928	ARKANSAS	4,708

Source: U.S. Department of Education, *Digest of Educational Statistics* (Washington, D.C.: Government Printing Office, 2002).

Further, students in small rural schools do not have to cope with as much crime and social disruption as is found in urban areas where more money is spent.

Desegregation and Busing

Finally, the issues of desegregation and busing have created longstanding controversy. The important question here is whether the school system can be expected to solve all of society's problems or whether it should concentrate more narrowly on education. The argument is that little is being done elsewhere in society to change the underlying causes of segregation, especially segregated housing, and that the only institution that has been subjected to such stringent requirements for desegregation is the public school system. Frequently, busing affects popular support for public education, and the decline of public education after desegregation becomes a self-fulfilling prophecy as white parents either remove their children from the integrated schools and send them to private schools or move their families out of the affected areas. The latter move is more probably more destructive, since it erodes the financial base of the schools.

The administration of George H.W. Bush began to remove some federal pressure for desegregation in 1992 as it joined with a Georgia school district to seek release from court-directed desegregation. The courts in general have become less active in forcing desegregation, and the early months of the Clinton administration saw no particular activism by the Department of Justice or the Department of Education on behalf of new efforts at desegregation. The George W. Bush administration has sought to address inequalities of education more through attempts to eliminate failing schools (many of them serving poor and minority students) rather than through pressure for desegregation.

On the other side of the argument is the central importance of education in the formation of the values and attitudes. Desegregation appears to benefit minority children by improving not only the quality of their education but also their children's self-image. It may also be important in reducing the social isolation of white children from minority children. Social integration has traditionally been one purpose of American public education, and it may be important to continue to pursue that goal through desegregation. After years of fighting for an end to segregation, however, some minority groups now have somewhat paradoxically come to favor a resegregation of students. They argue that the curriculum of most public schools does not reflect the interests or needs of their community and that students can learn better without racial tensions and when taught by teachers of their own race. Such resegregation may be occurring de facto, especially in northern cities, as residential patterns become increasingly segregated.[67]

The new and old issues surrounding desegregation can be, and have been, debated at length, but the issue of busing has been so emotionally charged that rational discourse is frequently impossible. The connection between educational quality and racial equality is an important one for the society that must be pursued within both policy domains.[68] Some argue that education is too central to the formation of the social fabric of the United States to be allowed to become isolated from other social concerns. However, education also may be too important in a highly technological society to be compromised in any way in an attempt to solve other social problems, and it may be that too many social responsibilities are being placed on schools and their teachers. How this debate is resolved may say a great deal about the future of American society and the American economy.

If busing has been the most divisive issue in desegregating elementary and secondary schools, affirmative action admission and scholarships have been its analogue at the level of higher education. Under pressure from the federal Department of Education and the Department of Justice as well as from their own state legislatures, a number of state university systems were providing preferences for minority students. In 1997 California and Texas courts found that the states were unlawfully discriminating on the basis of race in providing these preferences, and enjoined the state universities from doing so in the future. In 2003 the Supreme court ruled that race could be used as one of several factors in determining admissions.[69] This may be just one more event in the ongoing

TABLE 12.6 Increases in Cost of Higher Education, 1976–2000 (average tuition)

	Current	Real
1976	$924	$1,584
1980	1,163	1,479
1985	1,985	1,734
1990	2,839	1,926
1995	4,044	2,236
1998	4,755	2,462
2000	5,244	2,538

Source: U.S. Department of Education, Digest of Educational Statistics (Washington, D.C.: annual).

struggle to reconcile different interpretations of the word *equality* as it applies to education and other public policies.

Desegregation efforts have usually been the primary issues of contention, but in fact race permeates many other aspects of American education. For example, discipline in schools appears to be meted out differently by race,[70] and nonwhite students may be encouraged to pursue nonacademic programs at a higher rate than white students. Now added to race are issues of language and immigrant status that divide school populations and often place the focus of education less on learning and more on pursuit of social justice.

Higher Education Costs

We have already pointed out that the federal government provides a good deal of support for students attending institutions of higher education, as well as a variety of supports for those institutions themselves. There is a great deal of money available for student support, but the country still encounters problems in making higher education available for every student who might want to pursue it. This longstanding problem has been somewhat exacerbated by continuing increases in the cost of attending college or university. As shown in table 12.6, the costs of college have been increasing more rapidly than have overall costs in the economy.

These rising costs of higher education are a function of a variety of factors. One is that, as labor-intensive organizations, universities have less ability than other industries do to reduce their costs by investing in capital. Indeed, emphasis on quality has an influence in higher education as well as at lower levels of the educational system, including demands for smaller classes and more personal attention, all of which increase staffing demands and costs. Further, part of the emphasis on quality in higher education also involves investment in more technology in laboratories, computer centers, and the like—all of which is necessary (and expensive) but may not really improve the productivity of the institution.

Summary

Education has been and remains a central concern of American public policy. While traditionally the concern of state and local government, it is increasingly influenced by federal policy, in part because of education's close connection to other goals such as economic growth. But while education has been an important and highly respected public function, it is currently under attack. The quality of education, the competence of school personnel, and the place of education in social change are all topics of vital concern to many Americans. Several policy instruments have been proposed to rectify the perceived difficulties in these areas, the most commonly discussed being the voucher plan, but few statements on educational policy have gained wide public acceptance.

The debate over education policy is in part a result of the absence of a widely accepted theory of causation in education. Unlike science policy, educational policy is a subject about which reasonable people often disagree radically. Voucher plans are intended in part to allow people to make individual choices concerning education without having to pay too great an economic price. The role of government as the funding agent for these programs, however, requires greater attention to the real benefits of certain forms of education and a decision about just how far the use of vouchers can be allowed to extend. This is a task for rational policy analysts who recognize that such analysis must be subjected to serious political and social scrutiny. This is especially true because education is an issue about which almost everyone has an opinion; and because the students involved are the children of those opinionated people, there will be controversy.

CHAPTER 13

Energy and the Environment

AT THE BEGINNING of the twenty-first century the United States continues to face two significant problems that affect the relationship between its economy and the physical world. One is a virtually insatiable demand for energy that is much higher per capita than that of other industrialized economies. The other policy problem is the need to manage the effluents of an industrialized society, and to preserve as much of the natural environment as possible. These two policy areas will be discussed together here, in part because they are interconnected in several crucial ways.

First, the high consumption of energy, especially the use of fossil fuels, produces huge quantities of pollution, and the periodic shortages and high prices of petroleum and natural gas place pressure on industries to burn cheaper coal, which creates even higher levels of pollution. Even the transportation of fossil fuels, especially oil, presents several well-known and politically visible threats to the environment—the *Exxon Valdez* spill in Alaska being one of the more infamous examples. Failure to address the energy problem by exploring nontraditional sources of energy or by engaging in extensive conservation efforts will almost certainly exacerbate the environmental problem.

Also, some regulations issued by the Environmental Protection Agency to reduce pollution (e.g., emission controls on automobiles) have tended to require using more energy than would otherwise be used. Both energy and environmental issues also have a large technical and scientific element, and governments have at times required the development of new technologies to meet their environmental demands.[1] Ultimately, however, changes in human behavior—including such simple approaches as energy conservation and recycling used paper, plastic, and metal—may be more important than technological change in producing improvements in the environment.

Both energy and environmental policy are also closely linked with continuing concerns about the American economy. Uncertainties about energy supplies, including those arising from frequent political instability in the Persian Gulf, and rising energy prices make investment decisions more difficult for businesses and contribute to inflation. In an industrial economy the price of almost every product is influenced by the cost of energy, so increases in energy prices have a pervasive impact on the economy. Likewise, critics charge that strict environmental controls make economic development projects more expensive or in some cases impossible. On the other hand, if the economy picks up, all the more pollution will be produced.

Finally, both energy and environmental policies are linked increasingly to global considerations. Pollution is no longer a national question about clean water and clean air. It has taken on a pronounced international dimension, including widespread concerns about global warming, ozone depletion, transborder pollution, and decreasing biological diversity.[2] On the other hand, as the economy is increasingly affected by international competition, it is argued that weaker environmental standards in other countries gives them an advantage over American firms. The United States is not a signatory of the Kyoto agreement on global warming,[3] and, especially under the George W. Bush administration, is widely perceived as a laggard in environmental policy.

Energy, too, is an international concern, not only because the United States imports so much of its energy needs, but also because the immense demand of the United States and other industrialized countries tends to increase the price and to lower availability for the developing countries. Because energy is one of the most widely traded international commodities, excessive demand in one part of the world economy tends to distort much of the market. This chapter examines energy and environmental problems, the responses of governments to these problems, and some possible alternative policies.

Energy: Problems and Policies

Energy is a crucial component of the American way of life. We are accustomed to using, and squandering, energy to a degree unimaginable even in other affluent industrialized societies. The typically large American automobile, and more recently the massive "sports utility vehicles," have been symbols of that attitude toward energy usage, as is the single person driving an automobile to work each day. Car size tended to decrease when energy was expensive in the 1980s and early 1990s, but by the late 1990s Americans had reverted to even larger and heavier vans and SUVs. The United States consumes over 4 percent of all the energy used in the world—90 percent more energy per capita than Sweden but slightly less per capita than Canada (both of which have standards of living similar to that of the United States).[4] While high energy usage is related to industrialization and higher standards of living, the United States appears to use much more than is required to maintain the comfortable standard of living to which most of its citizens have become accustomed.

This high level of energy usage was not perceived to be a problem until the OPEC (Organization of Petroleum Exporting Countries) embargo on oil shipments to the United States in 1973 demonstrated the extent of our dependence on imported oil.[5] Thereafter, the rapidly escalating price of oil that resulted from OPEC price-fixing, restricted production, and then a second embargo emphasized the dependence of the United States on foreign oil to supplement relatively large quantities of domestic oil, natural gas, and coal. The experiences of the 1970s made it clear that American energy policies need to be reexamined and probably altered in some ways. That policy lesson does not appear to have been learned, as cheaper oil in the 1980s and 1990s restored more relaxed attitudes toward energy use that persisted despite further alarms during the Iran-Iraq war and later the Gulf war. In addition, the policies of the Reagan and (especially) both Bush administrations have stressed exploration and exploitation rather than conservation as the best way to eliminate energy difficulties. The possibilities of another major conflict in the Gulf helped to drive energy prices higher in late 2002 and again in 2003, and energy is a long-term policy that government will have to grapple with more seriously at some time in the near future.

Energy Sources

In spite of the importance of foreign petroleum and the American love affair with the automobile, petroleum is not our only energy source, and other available sources of energy could be more highly developed. Oil is, however, the major energy source for the United States, accounting for 38 percent of all energy consumed, a percentage that has fluctuated little in the past several decades (see table 13.1, p. 362). Approximately 48 percent of the oil consumed in the United States is imported, so a little simple arithmetic reveals that roughly 19 percent of the total U.S. energy supply is imported oil.[6] Again, the total amount of oil we import has been increasing as domestic supplies have become more difficult (and expensive) to extract and as demand has continued to grow. This has produced political pressures to open exploration in environmentally fragile areas such as the Alaska Wildlife Refuge, some areas of the Rockies, and off the Florida coast. The George W. Bush administration began lobbying soon after taking office to open the Alaska refuge, but the proposal met strong legal and political opposition and was eventually defeated in a Democratic-led Senate.[7] Very quickly, however, the administration began to look for exploration options in other parts of the United States.[8]

This reliance on imported oil produces a number of problems. First, it makes energy supplies for the United States extremely uncertain and places the

TABLE 13.1 Sources of Energy, 1970–1999 (in percentages)

	Petroleum	Natural gas	Coal	Nuclear	Renewable sources
1970	43.4	34.7	16.5	0.3	5.2
1980	43.6	25.9	18.7	5.4	7.1
1990	42.3	23.4	22.9	6.1	6.3
1995	36.7	24.2	22.1	7.2	7.7
1999	38.4	23.6	22.0	7.9	7.1

Source: U.S. Energy Information Agency, *Annual Energy Review* (Washington, D.C.: Department of Energy, annual).

American economy in the position of a hostage to foreign powers. Continuing instability in the Middle East makes this dependence on foreign oil all the more problematic.[9] Second, the money paid for foreign oil goes outside the United States and is difficult to match with exports. The U.S. negative balance of payments increased in the 1990s, which has serious consequences for the domestic economy (see chapter 8). Over 11 percent of U.S. imports are energy, without which the balance of payments deficit would be approximately half of what it actually is.[10] Also, oil is a finite resource, and proven world reserves of oil are sufficient only for a limited number of years at current rates of consumption. This means that eventually the American economy will have to convert to some other form of energy; continued reliance on foreign oil will only delay the hard economic, social, and technological choices that will have to be made when this particular energy resource is depleted. Finally, although other energy sources pose environmental risks as well, on average almost a million gallons of oil is spilled into U.S. waters each year. Most oil spills are not nearly as destructive as the *Exxon Valdez* in Alaska, but all have some environmental consequences.

Natural Gas

The United States has been more blessed with reserves of natural gas than with petroleum. Currently, almost all natural gas used in this country comes from domestic sources. Natural gas is also a limited resource, however, for only somewhere between thirty-five and sixty years' worth of proven reserves are available at current and predicted rates of consumption.[11] Therefore, natural gas does not constitute a long-term alternative for the United States. In addition, natural gas is so valuable for industrial uses—in the fabrication of plastics and synthetic fibers, for example—that it may be inefficient to use it to heat buildings and cook meals.

Alternatives to domestically produced natural gas include importing gas in liquid form from Algeria or the former Soviet Union. These sources would extend the availability of natural gas supplies but would present the same political and economic problems as imported oil. In addition, the technology involved in transporting liquid natural gas has not yet been fully developed, so massive explosions could occur if great care is not exercised. Given the environmental dangers already encountered with oil spills, the difficulty of developing a new technology for transporting natural gas simply to preserve that relatively short-lived energy supply may not be politically acceptable.

Coal

America's most abundant energy resource is coal. The United States has enough coal to last approximately 200 years, and it exports substantial quantities of coal to Japan and to some parts of Europe. In addition to supplying relatively cheap energy, coal can be used as a raw material for industrial purposes, as can natural gas. If coal usage were developed more fully, the demand for natural gas and petroleum might be reduced. Coal has several disadvantages as an energy resource, however. First, there is the environmental problem: coal does not burn as cleanly as oil or natural gas, and a good deal of American coal is rather high in sulfur. When this coal is burned, it forms sulfur dioxide (SO_2), which then combines with water to form sulfuric acid (H_2SO_4)—a major source of the "acid rain" that threatens forests and wildlife in the northern United States and Canada. Also, the soot that comes from coal-fired plants allegedly claims 12,000 lives per year, which has prompted the George W. Bush administration's plans for gradually cleaning up coal-fired plants, beginning in 2008.[12]

The extraction of coal presents further environmental difficulties, since much of the available coal is most efficiently extracted by strip-mining, a method that deeply scars the landscape and may render the land unusable for years. Improved methods for reclaiming strip-mined land have been developed, but the recovery still takes time and money, and the original natural landscape is lost forever.[13] On the other hand, mining coal by building tunnels presents huge health and safety problems for the miners.[14]

In addition to the environmental problems, no technology yet exists for using coal to power automobiles or trucks. The "synfuels" project that was one component of President Carter's energy plan was intended to find a way to extract a liquid fuel from coal ("gassification"), but at present no such technology exists at a reasonable price.[15] Thus, coal can be used to generate electricity and heat, but not for transportation, which accounts for 26 percent of energy use in the United States. The development of other technologies (e.g., improved storage batteries and better electric cars) may help to expand its utility, but at present coal remains of limited use for transportation.

Finally, there are massive logistical problems in using coal as a major energy source. Coal is more difficult to transport than petroleum or natural gas, which may be readily moved through pipelines. Furthermore, a good deal of the available coal is located at substantial distances from the points of principal energy demand, and American railroads at present do not have sufficient rolling stock or suitable roadbeds to manage major increases in coal shipments. Water transportation might be a better option, but even that possibility would require investment in boats or barges to make greater use of coal a more practical choice than it is at present.

Nuclear Power

As of 1998 the United States had 110 nuclear power plants that produced approximately 8 percent of the total energy used in this country, and almost 22 percent of all electricity. By 2002 those numbers had dropped to 103 plants and 21 percent of electricity. In several states, two-thirds of electrical power still comes from nuclear power. At one time it was believed that nuclear power would meet future energy needs as, particularly with fast-breeder reactors, the supply of energy appeared almost endless. But after the near-disaster at the Three Mile Island nuclear plant in 1979, and the very real 1986 disaster at Chernobyl in the former Soviet Union, the possibility of a nuclear future appears less likely. This is true in part because, without the breeder reactor and its potential dangers, producers must deal with a limited supply of fissionable uranium. More important, safety and environmental problems, and the very real dilemmas of disposing of nuclear waste, have called the feasibility of nuclear power into question for the public as well as for many experts.[16]

The Three Mile Island and Chernobyl incidents pointed to the possibility that nuclear power plants might present health and safety hazards for citizens living near them and possibly even for people living hundreds of miles away. Had the "China syndrome" occurred—melting of the reactor core—the likely extent of damage to the health of citizens is difficult to estimate. If a nuclear power plant has no incidents of this sort, the additional radioactivity in its vicinity is indeed negligible, but there remains the possibility—although advocates of the technology argue that it is remote—of a serious accident. The accident at Chernobyl caused at least 330 deaths during the first four years after it occurred, and there are estimates of up to a half million additional deaths as a result of this one nuclear accident.[17] The American nuclear industry emphasizes the contrast between the inadequate design of the Soviet reactor and the ever safer designs available in the United States, but many Americans remember only the atomic horrors produced in the Ukraine.

Even if there were no danger of accidents, the environmental and health problems associated with nuclear waste disposal would present difficulties. Some nuclear wastes lose their radioactivity very slowly—the half-life, or time required for half the nuclear activity to be exhausted, of plutonium-239 (one by-product of nuclear reactors) is 24,000 years. This means that the nuclear industry (and ultimately government) must find a means of disposing of these wastes so as to prevent contamination of the environment. There are proposals for burying these wastes, but almost no one wants the facilities near their home—the NIMBY phenomenon is very strong in this field.[18] Government must also find a means to prevent terrorists from gaining control of the radioactive material, because it would constitute a powerful instrument for blackmail. The disposal of nuclear wastes therefore presents both environmental problems and serious dangers in guarding large areas against possible terrorist attacks and thefts. In 2002 the Bush administration settled on Yucca Mountain, Nevada, as the repository for nuclear wastes after years of debate, but the court challenges to that decision will persist.[19]

Finally, the construction of nuclear power plants has been so slow and so expensive that many electrical utilities have become frustrated and abandoned the projects. The requirements for extensive inspection and reinspection of the plants as they are built, because of the dangers of accidents and contamination, have slowed the construction of the plants significantly, as have the lawsuits filed by opponents of nuclear power. Operating costs of nuclear power plants will certainly be less than those of fossil-fuel plants, but the initial capital investment and the relatively short operating life of a nuclear plant (often 30 years or less) have caused many private utilities to cancel plans to build these facilities; no new plans have been initiated in almost two decades. These problems put much of the burden for energy production back on to fossil fuels, with their associated pollution and finite global supply.

The regulatory difficulties of coping with nuclear power in the United States are indicated by the long controversy over the Seabrook nuclear plant in New Hampshire.[20] The Public Service Company of New Hampshire originally announced plans to build twin reactors at Seabrook in 1972. A series of legal disputes and demonstrations, as well as rising costs, caused the cancellation of one of the reactors in 1984, even after $800 million had been spent on it. Construction of Unit 1 was completed in July 1986, but the Chernobyl accident had occurred a few months earlier and it led the surrounding states and their utility companies to withdraw their cooperation in further work on the plant. Having invested $2.1 billion in Seabrook without generating a single kilowatt, Public Service Company of New Hampshire filed for bankruptcy protection in 1988. After intervention by the Reagan administration, the Nuclear Regulatory Commission (NRC) permitted testing of the plant beginning in June 1989, and on 1 March 1990, the NRC granted an operating license to the new owner, Northeast Utilities.[21] While this scenario represents the extreme case, it is little wonder that all nuclear power plants ordered since 1974 have now been cancelled.

Other Energy Sources in Use

Several other energy sources are currently being used in the United States, although none accounts for a significant percentage of total energy capacity. These include hydroelectric power, wood, and some solar and geothermal power. To date, with the exception of hydroelectric power, these potential sources have not offered much hope for rapid development, although a great deal is promised for solar power, and geothermal power (power produced with the heat from natural sources in the earth) is apparently successful in Iceland and parts of Europe. Wood, perhaps our oldest power source, is a renewable energy source. However, constraints on the amount of wood available, its cost, and the pollution problems it presents limit its usefulness, in spite of a growing number of Franklin stoves and wood-burning furnaces in the northern United States.

Unconventional Energy Sources

As the problems with America's energy future have become more apparent to citizens, politicians, and scientists, a number of alternatives to fossil fuels and nuclear power have been explored. The search has been for energy sources that are renewable, clean, safe, and compatible with the American lifestyle. Of the four criteria, the last has become least important as some understanding of the uniqueness of that lifestyle has begun to penetrate our collective consciousness. At present, there appear to be five major possible alternative energy sources, two of which—extraction of oil from the shale found in Colorado and Wyoming and nuclear fusion (rather than fission)—are variations on existing power sources. The oil-shale technology, if developed, would have an immense environmental impact, much like that of strip-mined coal. Further, extracting the shale oil would require huge amounts of water in an area already short of water and would produce a number of undesirable effluents in areas that are both beautiful and environmentally fragile. And all of these environmental problems would produce a relatively small amount of oil, when compared with current levels of consumption and other modes of production.

The technology of fusion power is still in the beginning stages despite significant research and development expenditures. The idea of this power source is to approximate, in a laboratory or power station, the processes that produce the energy of the sun. This will require temperatures of tens of millions of degrees and the technology to create and then contain a superheated "plasma" of charged particles.[22] In other words, fusion will require massive technological developments, but it may someday produce cheap and virtually limitless supplies of energy, with much less radioactivity than is caused by nuclear fission. European researchers have been able actually to produce some limited amounts of power using a fusion technique, and American researchers also have produced a brief sustained fusion.[23]

Limited amounts of solar power are also in use in the United States, heating some houses and businesses and heating water for home use. But the use of solar power to produce electricity for mass distribution ("big solar") will require technological breakthroughs as well as answers to some environmental questions. Although theoretically there is a limitless source of solar power, many areas of the United States may not receive a sufficient amount of sunlight when they need it most. For example, northern cities need energy most during the winter, for heating, but they receive little sunlight then; one possible use for solar energy, however, may be to provide supplementary power needed during peak-loading periods from air-conditioning in the summer.

The photovoltaic cell—the means of converting sunlight into electrical energy—is at present underdeveloped and inefficient. Thus, to make sufficient quantities of electricity with "big solar" projects will require devotion of large land areas to solar panels, which some environmentalists may regard as just another form of pollution. Solar power is, however, also being harnessed for use in automobiles. There are engineering contests for solar-powered vehicles, although none of the winners so far—most of them extremely small and slow (as were the first gasoline-powered automobiles)—appears likely to be available in automobile showrooms any time in the foreseeable future.

There has also been a great deal of discussion about using wind power to generate electricity. The windmill, which once dominated rural landscapes, is to many people also the symbol of the energy future. Like solar power, wind power has already been put to use in small and decentralized ways, but the unreliability of the source and the prospect of thousands of windmills dotting the American plains and coasts have reduced the attractiveness of this alternative.[24] Possibly, with better means of storing electricity, wind power will become a more practical means of meeting at least some of America's future energy requirements, but in the short term it does not appear to be a particularly attractive alternative.

Finally, there is the possibility of using the agricultural productivity of the United States as a means of addressing energy needs. Gasohol, a combination of gasoline and methyl (wood) alcohol produced from plants, is already sold in some areas of the United States as a fuel for automobiles. The same plant material used for gasohol could be converted into methane gas and used like natural gas to heat homes. There are also a number of options for using the substantial forest reserves of the United States and the by-products of timber production as alternative energy resources.

The production of energy from biomass has several advantages. One is that it is renewable. Use of rapidly growing plants—or agricultural by-products such as cornstalks—would have less impact on the environment than some other en-

Power generating windmills line a California highway, offering one of several kinds of pollution-free energy sources available to that state's electricity consumers.

ergy sources. The methane gas that is one usable product of the biomass process, however, has been demonstrated to be at least as much a culprit in the "greenhouse effect" as carbon dioxide. In addition, massive parcels of land would have to be cultivated to produce the necessary quantities of organic material. This means of energy production has the decided advantage for Americans of producing a product that—unlike solar, wind, or fusion power—can be burned in automobiles. More efficient electric automobiles and storage batteries may be developed someday, but gasohol or even pure methanol already can be burned in a modified internal combustion engine, and the technology for burning methane gas in automobiles is also being developed. Thus, biomass production may serve the American lifestyle better than other alternative forms of energy production. At present, cost is a major barrier to the production of significant quantities of methanol, for the price of alcohol has been higher than the price of gasoline. As petroleum prices rise and fluctuate while methanol production increases, however, methanol may yet become a more competitive energy source.

Policy Options

Broadly speaking, there are two ways of addressing the energy problems of the United States (and the world). One strategy is conservation, or discouraging energy consumption by citizens and industry, and the other is producing more energy. The conflict between these two approaches can be seen easily in the history of American energy policy following the crises over oil supplies in the 1970s. This history also reflects some fundamental ideological differences in approaches to energy policy, with liberals tending to favor conservation and conservatives more likely to support increased production.

Conservation was the Carter administration's principal approach to the energy problem. For example, there were specifications for the temperature range in public buildings, as well as tax incentives for insulation and other energy-saving modifications for homes. But more than anything else, the issue of conservation was highlighted by controversies over deregulation of oil and natural gas prices, especially for so-called new oil and gas. The idea was that any gas and oil discovered after the passage of the legislation would be priced at a rate determined by the market, rather than at the controlled price of domestic oil and gas, which was then below world prices. This would allow the price of oil and gas to rise, thereby encouraging conservation, but it would also create huge "windfall" profits for oil and gas companies. To attempt to spread the impacts of decontrol more equitably across the society, the Carter energy package therefore included a windfall profits tax on oil companies.

Another important aspect of the Carter approach to energy problems was the Synthetic Fuels Corporation, intended to develop substitutes for petroleum from coal and other resources. As noted earlier, this research has yet to produce any economically feasible results, although there have been some significant advances. Finally, a stockpile of petroleum—the Strategic Petroleum Reserve—was created to delay the effects of any future oil embargoes on the United States. The mere mention by President Bush that this reserve could be used, for example, served to stabilize petroleum prices during the Gulf war.

The Reagan administration's approach to energy was more market- and production-oriented. During his 1980 campaign, candidate Reagan stressed the need for the market to deal with energy problems and condemned the Department of Energy as a "wasteful bureaucracy."[25] Reagan's first administration assumed that price deregulation would encourage the market to produce more energy and that price increases would make it profitable to exploit some remaining energy sources (e.g., oil in old wells). Also, the administration—with the special attention of Interior Secretary James Watt—sought, largely unsuccessfully, to exploit energy resources on public lands, such as the Alaska lands "locked up" under the Carter administration. There was some leasing of federal lands for coal mining—some 16,000 acres in the Powder River Basin of Montana and Wyoming, for example—but the favorable prices offered to private coal companies when the coal market was glutted were condemned as poor resource management and as a national "fire sale." This sale was especially vulnerable to criticism because of the environmental sensitivity of the area leased. The declining price of petroleum on the international market, however, has made the planned exploitation of shale oils in equally sensitive areas of the West less attractive, and that development has ended.

The lowered price of oil had other effects on national energy policy in the 1980s. First, it facilitated the development of the Strategic Petroleum Reserve, which by January 1984 had reached 360 million barrels (almost a month's supply). Further, as shale oils became less attractive, so did synthetic fuels, and the Synthetic Fuels Corporation had a difficult time maintaining any interest in the private sector.[26] In 1984 President Reagan persuaded Congress to rescind funding for the Synthetic Fuels Corporation.[27] Stable energy prices also made the continued deregulation of oil and natural gas feasible, with this policy continuing in the 1990s to include competition among home suppliers.

In summary, energy policy was not a major concern during the Reagan administration. Energy prices were relatively stable, and the international market had plentiful oil. Also, energy consumption in the United States was declining; existing supplies and sources were more than adequate, and the market-oriented strategies of the administration were largely successful. Not surprisingly, the administration of George Bush favored a similar approach to energy policy. In general, President Bush pursued a policy of finding and exploiting new fossil fuel resources, but in the National Energy Strategy announced in early 1991, however, he offered a more diversified approach to energy policy. He advocated increasing domestic oil production to 3.8 million barrels a day but also called for a research and development program on alternative energy sources such as biomass and solar power.[28] On the other hand, many critics—even some in business—argued that the president did not place adequate emphasis on energy conservation.

The Clinton administration made few if any major initiatives in energy policy. Coming to office at a time of relatively plentiful energy and bringing a host of other agenda items with him, President Clinton invested little political capital in energy issues. His secretary of energy—Hazel R. O'Leary—was a very visible figure, but not because of any bold initiatives in new policy. Instead, she received very high marks from the public and from Washington insiders for her opening of numerous files on U.S. atomic testing during the height of the Cold War. These files pointed to a number of severe abuses by government, and she began a program to compensate the victims of some of the most egregious of those abuses.[29]

The George W. Bush administration came to office in 2001 with a clear preference for producing more energy rather than limiting use—as was to be expected, given the backgrounds of both the president and the vice president in the energy industry and the large contributions to the Bush campaign by numerous energy companies.[30] Unlike either the Clinton administration or his father's administration, the second President Bush has attempted to formulate a more or less comprehensive energy plan. The process of formulation, however, became a major political problem because the consultations organized by Vice President Cheney to seek advice on the plan were in essence held in secret. Public interest groups sued successfully to find out at least who was involved in those consultations; when eventually published, the list consisted only of producer groups.[31] Not surprisingly, given the interests of that advisory faction and the predispositions of the administration itself, the plan's major directives were for increasing production and expanding exploration for and exploitation of domestic resources. The principal instruments involved were to be subsidies (direct and through the tax system) for energy producers, with some little incentive for conservation.[32] The emphasis on increased production was heightened by the terrorist attacks of September 2001, and the perceived need to make the United States less dependent on foreign energy sources.

During the 1970s it was popular to talk about the energy "crisis" in the United States, as prices soared and supplies dwindled, but by 2001 polls showed that although the public still regarded energy as a problem, it had little sense of crisis.[33] Fears of energy shortages now appeared exaggerated, and Americans continued to favor provision of low-cost and plentiful energy even for potentially wasteful uses. Even when U.S. gasoline prices reached an average of $1.60 per gallon in the summer of 2001—very high by our standards—they were still less than half of those found in most countries in Europe.

Yet there was reason to believe that this halcyon period might be only a brief respite from an ongoing energy problem. Supplies of fossil fuels in the world are finite. The easing of immediate pressures in energy procurement therefore provides a false sense of security and prevents the search for viable long-term energy sources. This is especially true in view of the fact that many citizens are suspicious of technological solutions (e.g., nuclear power) to energy problems. Further, continuing U.S. dependence on foreign oil may make its economy and society hostage to forces over which we have no control. Yet another energy "crisis" may be required before citizens and government are willing to return to the active consideration of alternative energy futures for the United States.

The States and Energy Policy

The preceding discussion has been about the role of the federal government in energy policy, but as in most policy areas in the United States, local and state governments have some role. In particular, a good deal of the regulation of energy distribution is done at the state level. The traditional model for this regulation has been to create virtual monopolies in electricity and gas and then regulate rates to provide the privately owned utilities a set return on capital investment (profit) while attempting to offer energy to consumers as inexpensively as possible.[34] In some cities, the local government purchases energy in bulk and distributes it at cost to citizens, resulting in even lower consumer costs.

The spread of neoliberal ideas has led to the deregulation of energy supplies in many states. On the assumption that competition in the market could produce even better outcomes for consumers and also remove the "heavy hand" of government regulation, about half the states had undertaken some form of deregulation as of 2001. In some cases this practice has been very successful—energy costs in Pennsylvania dropped by over one-third.[35] On the other hand, deregulation was at least partially responsible for a major energy crisis that hit the state of California in 2000 and 2001.[36] It seems unlikely that energy will ever be as tightly controlled as it once was, but there does appear to be a need to monitor the markets if not exert some control over energy distribution.

Hard and Soft Energy Options

One of the most provocative presentations of the policy options facing the United States with respect to energy is Amory Lovins's discussion of "hard" versus "soft" energy paths.[37] Although there have been numerous criticisms of the apocalyptic conclusions reached by Lovins, his analysis of the policy alternatives is important. The hard route is to continue to increase energy consumption as fast or faster than national economic growth and to rely on fossil fuels, especially coal, or on nuclear power to supply that energy. This option is both production-oriented and centralized in its use of large-scale energy production and distribution, primarily through existing electrical utilities. The soft route, on the other hand, would allow energy use to grow less rapidly than national economic growth and would promote conservation. The soft route would also stress decentralized production of energy, with each family or small community having its own power source, usually of a renewable variety.

Lovins's analysis is significant for several reasons. First, economic growth is often linked with energy consumption. In fact, the usual assumption has been that these two are inextricably linked, although they need not be in Lovins's decentralized vision of the future. Second, as an environmental activist, Lovins focuses on the connection between environmental issues and energy issues, as we have been doing here. Finally, he stresses the links between political decision making, political structures, and energy sources. He fears the centralization that might occur in politics as a result of large-scale use of nuclear power, with the attendant need to protect waste storage sites and even the power plants themselves.

The ongoing energy "crisis" implies a need for Americans to change our lifestyle so as to conserve energy, to live more frugally, and with different forms of energy, or to locate additional sources of petroleum, natural gas, and uranium—or to pursue some part of all these options. There are few clear answers to the problems posed for the country by its expanding energy needs and the eventual exhaustion of our traditional resources. Americans tend to believe that technological solutions can be found to all problems that face them, but the application of technology has yet to make a significant dent in the continuing problems of energy policy.

Also, it is important to discuss the political and social effects of the American energy problem and not just its technological aspects. As mentioned, the choices made about energy supplies may well be so fundamental that they affect the manner in which governments function; in more extreme versions, they may affect even the level of government that citizens regard as most important. In a future characterized by highly decentralized energy, a centralized federal government may be less important than the community government. The community, rather than the large urban area, may become the appropriate unit of social organization. Like so many other policy areas, energy policy may be too important to be left to the experts—there must be active citizen understanding and involvement to shape humane as well as technologically feasible politics.

Environmental Policies

Just as Harriet Beecher Stowe's *Uncle Tom's Cabin* is supposed to have helped initiate the Civil War, and as Michael Harrington's *The Other America* is believed to have helped initiate the War on Poverty, so it is sometimes said that Rachel Carson's *The Silent Spring* helped to launch the environmental movement in the United States. Her description of the horrors of a spring without the usual sounds of life associated with that time of the year made citizens and policy-makers understand the possible effects of the pollutants—especially insecticides—being poured into the air and water of the United States.

The environment remains no small problem. Even after several decades of increased environmental awareness, tons of pollutants are still dumped into the air and water or stored in rusting barrels with the potential to poison the land for years. It is difficult to determine the amount of disease and the number of deaths that result from such pollution or to estimate the amount of property damage it causes, but the damage produced in each of these categories is clearly substantial. That economic damage, however, may be minimal compared to the human and aesthetic damage that is produced by uncontrolled pollution. Against the images of natural beauty in the country can be set scenes of wastelands made by unthinking human activities.

The United States obviously has a pollution problem. Further, we have found that this problem is not confined to our own air and water but is, instead, global. Scientific research published during the 1980s identified a gradual warming trend in the earth's atmosphere—the "greenhouse effect"—that could alter climates and even produce massive coastal flooding if the polar ice caps were to melt. This warming appears to be largely the product of putting carbon dioxide into the atmosphere by burning fossil fuels.[38] Many people have raised doubts about the validity of these theories, but recent experience of uncommon weather-related occurrences, such as severe floods and droughts and (often pleasantly) mild winters, has caused increasing numbers of Americans to believe that something is upsetting the natural order and that it may well be global warming.

Other scientists have pointed to the destruction of ozone in the earth's atmosphere, which will permit more ultraviolet radiation to reach the surface and thus increase the risk of skin cancers. Much of this atmospheric change is a result of the release of chlorinated fluorocarbons (CFCs) into the atmosphere from aerosol cans, refrigeration units, and numerous industrial applications. Still other scientists have warned of the destruction of the tropical rain forests that supply not only much of the world's oxygen but also a large number of as yet undiscovered useful plants.[39] Even outside the tropics, a gradual erosion of biodiversity has been observed in the United States and in the rest of the world. Also, the United States both exports acid rain to Canada and imports some water and air pollution from Mexico and Canada. It no longer appears sufficient to address environmental problems within the context of a single country; concerted international action and policies are needed.

Within the context of the United States, environmental problems have been addressed through a variety of statutes now enforced largely by the Environmental Protection Agency (EPA).[40] Few people now question the desirability of a clean environment, but some would like to see that value balanced more carefully with other important values, such as economic growth, jobs, and controlling inflation. The slowdowns of the American economy during the late 1980s and early 1990s, and again in 2001, have led many citizens to question whether the nation could afford stringent controls on pollution, especially when many U.S. jobs are perceived to be going to countries that place less stringent environmental controls on manufacturers. It is also argued that environmental controls could contribute to inflation by making some commodities, such as automobiles, more expensive than they would otherwise be. Great progress has been made in environmental policy, but the challenges have changed to some extent, and the connections between energy policy and economic policy are now even clearer.

The Politics of Pollution

It would be difficult to find a group that actively favors environmental degradation. Instead, the politics of pollution is generally phrased in terms of what are acceptable trade-offs between environmental values and other values. There is sufficient public concern about the environment that it would be almost impossible to make wholesale retreats from existing environmental programs. For example, in 1990, 71 percent of the respondents to a national poll said they would support environmental protection laws regardless of the costs, while only 21 percent disagreed with that proposition. This unequivocal support for environmental protection is up from less than 50 percent in the early 1980s, and by 1997 over two-thirds of Americans considered themselves environmentalists.[41] At the same time, individuals who want to preserve their own jobs and firms that want to preserve their industries are willing to sacrifice at least part of the environment for those ends.

There are numerous examples of the conflict between environmental and economic interests. For example, loggers and environmentalists in the Pacific Northwest fought over the preservation of the habitat of the spotted owl and then continued to dispute over more general concerns about those forests. Environmentalists wanted to save old-growth forests to protect that endangered species, while loggers saw primarily the loss of their livelihoods if the owl were to be saved.[42] Both sides had powerful reasons to support their positions, and the resolution will affect the long-term trade-off between the values of the environment and the economy.[43] The conflict in 2002 over the preservation of caribou herds that might be threatened by drilling in the Arctic areas of Alaska will certainly not be the last battle of this type.[44]

Some trade-offs have to be made. When the U.S. economy slowed during the 1980s, some of the blame for the slowdown was placed on the more stringent environmental controls in the United States than in other countries. The continuing globalization of the economy then led to the use of this argument for protecting American jobs by loosening environmental laws, as well as by imposing protective devices such as tariffs. Similarly, a portion of the inflation problem of that era was blamed on regulations of all kinds, including environmental regulations; the cost of the average American automobile increased by several hundred dollars because of environmental controls.[45] These same environmental controls made the automobile somewhat less energy efficient, so in this case energy conservation and environmental concerns constituted another trade-off. A similar energy versus environment trade-off can be seen in coal mining; the cheapest means of mining coal, strip-mining, is extremely destructive of the environment. Further, potential petroleum reserves have been found in environmentally sensitive areas in Alaska and along the Florida coast. Even if all Americans are to some degree in favor of a clean environment, it is difficult to find much agreement on how such trade-offs among values should be made in individual cases.

The stakeholders in the environmental arena are obvious. Industry is a major actor, for many environmental regulations restrict the activities of businesses. Local governments are also the objects of environmental controls, for much water pollution is produced by poorly treated sewage coming from local government sources; federal and state governments have imposed expensive mandates on local governments requiring them to clean up their water supplies. More recently, mandates have been imposed for controlling runoff from storm drains, or, in the language of environmental policy, "non-point sources," as in the runoff from farms that has become an increasing problem. Again, most of the interests affected by pollution legislation have not opposed the legislation so much on ideological grounds as on technical grounds, arguing that many of the regulations are technologically infeasible, or are so expensive that enforcing them would make the cost of doing business prohibitive.[46] Local governments in particular have argued that they simply do not have the money to comply with all the rules being imposed on them.

On the other side of the debate are the environmental interest groups, such as the Sierra Club, the National Wildlife Federation, and the Friends of the Earth. A few of these organizations—most notably the Sierra Club—have been in existence for years, but the majority are the products of the environmental mobilization of the late 1960s and 1970s. By the early part of the twenty-first century there were approximately 9.5 million members of national environmental groups, with more members of local organizations.[47] Yet there are disagreements among members of these groups as to the tactics that they want to follow and their willingness to make trade-offs with other values, such as economic growth. Some environmental groups have been highly confrontational, employing tactics such as placing large spikes in trees to make them dangerous to cut with power saws and harassing hunters and the wearers of fur coats. Environmentalists no longer all fit the image of the mild-mannered bird watcher; some are militant advocates of their political and moral positions.

Finally, government itself is an active participant in environmental politics. The major actor in government is the Environmental Protection Agency (EPA), organized in 1970 to take the lead in environmental regulation for the federal government. Given its mission and the time at which it was formed, many employees of the EPA were, and are, committed environmentalists. This commitment put them in conflict with political appointees of the Reagan administration who did not share those values. Before her ouster, for example, agency director Anne Burford Gorsuch had numerous conflicts with employees of the EPA who did not accept her values and thought she was too much in league with industry. Given the commitment to environmental politics by Vice President Al Gore[48] among others in the Clinton administration, there was a somewhat stronger commitment to environmental protection in the 1990s, although by no means as strong as environmentalists would have liked.[49] In 2000, the former governor of New Jersey (the most polluted state in the United States by many counts), Christine Todd Whitman, was appointed administrator of the EPA by President George W. Bush, and she proved more active in pressing the usual agenda of her agency than many critics had predicted. She resigned in 2003, alledgedly under pressure from those in the administration opposed to an active environmental policy.

The EPA is not, however, the only federal agency with environmental concerns; one enumeration found almost thirty federal organizations with some environmental regulatory responsibilities. Some, such as the Department of the Interior, which manages federal lands, have a substantial impact on federal policies but may have their own ideologies that are not purely environmental. The Forest Service in the Department of Agriculture, for example, tends to consider forests as crops rather than as natural assets, and therefore it seeks to make a profit by harvesting them. This preference accords well with the George W. Bush administration's emphasis on the use of federal lands managed by Interior and the Forest Service for economic, rather than environmental, purposes.[50] The Department of Defense also has massive environmental responsibilities, including cleaning up large-scale pollution on military bases.[51] This widespread administrative involvement in the environment has meant some lack of coordination, but consequent attempts to coordinate and to produce greater uniformity in regulation have enjoyed little success because of the diverse interests in this policy community.[52]

Also, although most attention in environmental policy is focused on the federal government, the states have become major players in the field, as was to some extent intended by the major laws in the field that depend in part upon the states for implementation.[53] Although the states thus play major roles in protecting the environment, they often have counterincentives to be relatively permissive in their enforcement, in order to attract industry.[54] During the Clinton administration there was often a high level of conflict between state and local governments and the EPA, even though both the president and his leading EPA administrators had experience as state officials.[55] For example, the states became increasingly aggressive in using the courts to oppose the interventions of the EPA.[56]

Making environmental policy is in part a technical exercise. There are a huge number of complex technical questions about the nature of environmental problems and about the feasibility of solutions offered for problems. Making environmental policy is also an ideological exercise on the part of many of the actors involved, and now especially for the environmental groups. The technical dimensions can be used to mask the economic interests and the ideologies involved in this debate, but fundamentally, making environmental policy means finding trade-offs among environmental values, technical feasibility, and economic growth that can satisfy the multiple constituencies involved in this policy area.

Given the complex trade-offs involved in this policy area, there has been increased interest in risk-based decision making. The logic of this approach is that rather than focusing on absolute prohibitions against all hazards, government policymakers should focus on the most dangerous pollutants and seek to reduce those hazards to levels that are deemed to be "safe."[57] Further, this approach calls for balancing of the costs and benefits in the production of potentially dangerous substances. Of course, this approach offends committed defenders of the environment who would prefer to retain the traditional "command and control" regulatory regimens.[58] The Environmental Protection Agency has been attempting to tailor its regulatory interventions more closely to the characteristics of particular industries. Also, beginning in the George H.W. Bush administration and continuing into the Clinton and George W. Bush administrations, the EPA has sought to be more cooperative in its approach to regulation.[59]

Finally, as in so many other areas of federal policy, the courts are also important decision makers. This role has been manifested on some substantive issues, such as the implementation of the Endangered Species Act, but it has been particularly important in defining the procedural rules under which the EPA must function. In particular, the Supreme Court has been tending to minimize some of the procedural requirements in environmental laws, including environmental impact statements, and to permit somewhat more rapid decisions on implementing other types of environmental policy actions. The courts also have been important in defining the standing to sue of environmental groups—the Rehnquist court tending to diminish the capacity of those groups to bring suits in federal court.[60]

The Legislation

Except for some older regulatory initiatives (e.g., the Refuse Act of 1899), the principal pieces of environmental legislation were passed during the 1960s and 1970s. Most of this legislation had built into it specific guidelines for the expiration of its authorization after a certain number of years. The reauthorization of these acts, each with some variations on the original legislation, were the cause of major political and ideological battles in the mid-1990s.[61] Those discussions revealed that even among those very committed to environmental protection there is some interest in developing alternatives to direct regulation as the means of reducing pollution.[62] The need to build policy regimens that produce greater compliance, less impact on economic performance, and lower administrative costs is recognized by many people in the field. We now discuss each area of legislation and the enforcement of environmental policy, as well as the alternatives proposed to the existing system of regulation.

Water pollution. Federal interest in water pollution goes back to the Refuse Act of 1899, which was intended to prevent the dumping of refuse in navigable waters and was enforced by the Army Corps of Engineers. This legislation provided the principal federal means of attacking water pollution until more stringent legislation was passed in the 1970s. Another piece of relatively early federal legislation was the Water Pollution Control Act of 1956, which allowed interested parties around a polluted body of water to call a conference concerning that pollution. The recommendations of the conference would be passed on to enforcement officials in the states involved, and if the states did not act within six months, the federal government (through the Department of the Interior) could intervene and seek an injunction to stop the polluting. Although there were possibilities of more stringent enforcement through the court system, only one injunction was issued during the fifteen years the 1956 law was in effect. However, by making federal matching funds available for the construction of sewage treatment facilities, the act did encourage cities and towns to clean up their water.

As this early legislation on water pollution proved ineffective, the federal government took a major step forward in 1965 with the Water Quality Act, which relied on the states, as had the 1956 act, but made the first steps toward establishing criteria for water quality. Each state submitted to the Department of Health, Education, and Welfare (after 1970 to the Environmental Protection Agency) standards for water quality. These standards were to be in measurable quantities (e.g., the number of bacteria per unit of water). After HEW or the EPA approved these quality standards, they were to be translated into specific effluent standards (e.g., an industry would release only so many tons of pollutants each month). It was then anticipated that the states would enforce these standards; if they did not, the secretary of HEW was given the authority to enforce the standards approved by the state within that state's boundaries.

The state basis of the Water Quality Act proved to be its undoing. Because states were competing with one another to attract industries, those that adopted more stringent water-quality standards might be at a disadvantage. Thus, water-quality standards tended to converge on the lowest common denominator. Even then, the states rarely if ever enforced their standards. The federal government, in turn, did little to encourage more vigorous enforcement by the states, and nothing to enforce the standards themselves. It became clear that the states had little incentive to enforce pollution standards to clean up their own water and that therefore more effective national standards would be required.

Those national standards were developed through the 1972 Clean Water Act (CWA). Technically amendments to the Water Pollution Control Act, this legislation established national goals, setting 1983 as the deadline for all streams to be safe for fish and for human swimming, and 1985 as the date when all harmful discharges into navigable streams must stop. Those goals had to be abandoned after a flood of lawsuits and an enumeration of the costs persuaded government that they was too optimistic. Still, the legislation required that all private concerns were to adopt the "best practicable technology" by 1977 and the "best available technology" by 1983. Standards for public sewage treatment were less demanding, with all wastes to receive some treatment by 1977 and with the "best practicable technology" standard applied by 1983 as the policy guidelines.[63] As the regulatory regime for water quality has developed, risk assessment has become a more important tool for analysis.

This legislation established a nationwide discharge permit system, enabling the Environmental Protection Agency to specify the amount of effluents that could be released and to monitor compliance with the technology requirements. As noted, this legislation established nationwide standards, although a good deal of the implementation actually was done at the state level. The states could not use low water-quality standards as a means of competing for industry, but their implementation of the standards continued to differ substantially in severity.

President Reagan vetoed the reauthorization of the CWA in 1986, arguing that compliance was too expensive for industry and local governments, but Congress overrode the veto, with the perhaps unexpected support of many industrial organizations. Industry appeared to accept the existing set of standards as a reasonable compromise between what it might want and what more militant environmentalists might want.[64] As a part of the general pattern of devolution of authority in the federal system, the Reagan administration also placed greater reliance on the states.[65] Amendments and rewriting during the Clinton administration then strengthened some aspects of the legislation but also weakened some important regulations, including those on control of chlorine and the various compounds formed from chlorine in water.[66]

Also, in 1986 amendments were made to the Safe Drinking Water Act that added eighty-six contaminants to the list of substances prohibited from public drinking water. This act was originally passed in 1974 and, like a good deal of all environmental legislation, had faced implementation difficulties because of its reliance on state and local governments, as well as suits by citizens as means of bringing problems to the attention of the EPA. The growing emphasis on non-point sources of pollution also depends heavily on state and even local governments for its success. Despite the numerous enforcement problems, and the problems of vagueness in the legislation itself, there has been progress in cleaning up the water in the United States (see table 13.2), as levels of all contaminants continue to drop.

Air Pollution. Air pollution did not become a matter of federal concern as early as did water pollution, perhaps because of the lack of a clear constitutional peg on which to hang any attempt at enforcement. (Federal control over navigable streams provided such a legal peg for water pollution legislation.) In addition, the effects of air pollution failed to produce much public attention—despite the deaths of twenty people during severe air pollution in Donora, Pennsylvania, in 1948, and even though an obvious smog problem plagued the Los Angeles area as early as the 1950s.

TABLE 13.2 Improvements in Water Quality (percentage of tested watersheds exceeding permissible standards)

	1975	*1980*	*1985*	*1989*	*1995*
Coliform bacteria	36	31	38	20	35
Dissolved oxygen	5	5	3	3	1
Phosphorus	5	4	3	3	4
Lead	n.a.	5	<1	<1	<1

Source: Bureau of the Census, *Statistical Abstract of the United States*, annual.

The first federal legislation against air pollution was the Clean Air Act of 1963. This legislation was similar to the 1956 Water Pollution Act in that it relied on conferences, voluntary compliance, and possible HEW enforcement. Only once during the seven years in which the act was in effect did HEW attempt to force a firm to cease polluting. Also, in 1965 the act was amended to authorize the secretary of HEW to set standards for automobile emissions, using measurable standards like those of the Water Pollution Control Act Amendments of 1972.

The Clean Air Act was significantly amended in 1970, directing the EPA to establish ambient ("surrounding") air-quality standards. There were to be two sets of standards, primary and secondary. Primary standards, those necessary to protect public health, were to be attained by 1975, while secondary standards, those necessary to protect vegetation, paint, buildings, and so forth, were to be attained within "a reasonable time." Also, the EPA was given the authority to establish emissions standards for certain new manufacturing plants, such as cement and sulfuric acid factories and electrical generating stations fired by fossil fuels ("point sources"), which had greater-than-average potential for significant air pollution. The 1977 amendments to the Clean Air Act required developing state plans for controlling new point sources of pollution and establishing higher standards of protection for certain types of areas (e.g., parks) within a state.

The Clean Air Act amendments also addressed emissions from automobiles, which continue to constitute the principal air pollution problem in most American cities. The 1970 standards superseded the weak standards obtained in the 1965 Motor Vehicle Air Pollution Control Act, mandating a 90-percent reduction in the level of hydrocarbons and carbon monoxide emissions by 1975, with similar reductions in oxides of nitrogen to be achieved by 1976. Although the standards set by the amendments were tough, a variety of factors slowed their implementation. Primarily, the technology for achieving these reductions was difficult and expensive to develop, and some of it, such as the catalytic converter, had side effects that are perhaps as dangerous as the emissions they were designed to eliminate. In addition, many pollution controls reduced gasoline

TABLE 13.3   Improvements in Air Quality (million metric tons emitted)

	1970	1980	1985	1990	1995	1997	1998
Particulates	13,042	7,119	4,831	5,057	4,579	4,743	4,450
Sulfur dioxide	31,161	25,905	23,685	23,660	19,181	19,622	19,647
Nitrogen oxides	20,928	24,384	23,198	24,049	24,921	24,824	24,454
Carbon monoxide	129,444	117,434	117,013	98,523	93,353	94,410	89,454
Volatile organic compounds	30,982	26,079	26,336	20,936	20,817	18,876	17,917
Lead	220,879	74,153	22,890	4,975	3,929	3,952	3,973

Source: U.S. Environmental Protection Agency, *National Air Quality and Emissions Trends Reports* (Washington, D.C.: EPA, annual).

mileage, and increasing energy shortages brought the conflict between environmental concerns and energy problems to the attention of citizens and policymakers alike. The concern about pollution and energy use began to place a great deal of unwelcome pressure on automobile manufacturers to create more fuel efficient and cleaner-running automobiles, and after some delays, those standards were largely met. The success of this first round of "technology forcing" standards, however, produced demands for even greater reductions in automobile emissions, which then ran up against countervailing resistance from industry that stalled further changes in air pollution legislation from 1977 to 1990. (Interestingly, the George W. Bush administration in 2002 began advocating technology-forcing legislation to require that an increasing proportion of automobiles be powered by electricity rather than gasoline, despite the higher costs than more conventional alternatives.[67]) Despite the stagnant legislative scene, the quality of air in the United States continued to improve, in large part a function of the old legislation (see table 13.3).

The legislative impasse over air pollution legislation was broken in 1990 with a major set of amendments to the Clean Air Act, which dealt with some of the traditional concerns over air quality within the United States but also began to address larger, global issues such as the greenhouse effect and acid rain. The amendments included the following provisions:

1. Protection of the ozone layer by banning use of CFCs in aerosol sprays and regulation of their use as refrigerants.
2. Plans to reduce acid rain by halving emissions of sulfur dioxide and nitrogen oxides and by considerably strengthening environmental requirements on fossil-fuel power plants.
3. Further emission requirements on automobiles and requirements for oil companies to create cleaner-burning fuels.[68]

4. Increased restriction on "toxic air pollutants," with the EPA given the power to control emissions of over 200 substances from a variety of sources, ranging from coke and steel mills to dry cleaners, and to demand installation of new technologies to limit or eliminate emissions.

The 1990 amendments to the Clean Air Act depended largely on traditional "command and control" regulation. These regulations were not well received in the George H.W. Bush administration, which, despite being led by the "environmental president," sought to maximize use of market mechanisms to solve social and economic problems. The Environmental Protection Agency, on the other hand, received something of a new lease on life from this legislation and the 1990 Pollution Control Act, which invested it with the power to exert greater pressures to clean up America's air.

In line with the general movement of environmental controls away from strict hierarchical regulatory regimens, there is an increasing emphasis on negotiation and accommodation in air pollution policy. For example, in late 1994 the Environmental Protection Agency negotiated an agreement with ten northeastern states to reduce air pollution from factories (especially electrical power plants).[69] In 2003, however, some of those restrictions were eased by the administration of George W. Bush. This followed a similar agreement (among twelve states) to reduce significantly the amount of air pollution coming from automobiles. The outcomes of these negotiations were not all that either industry or environmentalists would have wanted, but the bargaining involved in making these pacts produced agreements that all affected interests, including the states that would implement the agreements, could live with. Citizens complain because some of the provisions of these agreements, such as the use of reformulated gasoline during summer months, impose additional costs on them, but there has been a substantial social benefit from reduced pollution. Interestingly, during the early days of his administration, President George W. Bush chose to maintain some of the strict air quality standards adopted during the Clinton administration, despite the opposition of many industrial groups.

General environmental legislation. In addition to the legislation addressing specific kinds of pollution described earlier, the National Environmental Policy Act (NEPA) of 1970 established guidelines for environmental controls for projects involving the federal government. The principal component of this legislation was the Environmental Impact Statement, which was required for any federally funded project that might affect environmental quality. Before a project can be approved, the Environmental Impact Statement must be filed, detailing the environmental impact of the project, its potential negative consequences, and possible alternatives. These statements must be prepared well in advance of the proposed starting date of the project in order to allow citizen participation and review, and then they are filed with the Council on Environmental Quality in the Executive Office of the President.

The NEPA rules also allow citizens to challenge a project on environmental grounds, and over 400 court cases were filed during the first five years after the act went into effect. The legislation requires that environmental considerations be taken into account when a project is planned, but it does not indicate the weight that is to be attached to these considerations as compared with other costs and benefits of the project. This ambiguity in the legislation has been the source of many court cases and many difficult decisions for the judges involved. In the case of the Alaska pipeline, special legislation was required to allow the project to continue in the face of determined opposition and court challenges by conservation groups. That case also illustrated the increasing conflict between energy needs and environmental protection, and similar conflicts are emerging over proposals to open the Alaska National Wildlife Refuge to oil exploration.

One of the continuing goals of industry is weakening, or terminating, the Environmental Impact Statement. The court challenges already mentioned have had some effects on this instrument, but there are also political pressures. Under the second Bush administration there have been proposals to weaken or eliminate requirements for environmental assessments for programs, especially in defense and energy.

Toxic Waste

Toxic wastes are one by-product of a society that has become dependent on synthetic products for its way of life. The usual estimate of the volume of hazardous waste in the United States, cited by the EPA, is that around 250 million tons is created each year—one ton per citizen in the United States.[70] Only about 10 percent of this waste is disposed of safely.[71] In addition to the hazard itself, the problem with hazardous wastes is that they tend to be persistent chemicals that have to be kept away from people and their water and food supplies for years or even centuries. Such storage is expensive, and before there was a full understanding of the dangers, or proper regulation, industries disposed of these wastes in a very haphazard manner, thus endangering many citizens.

The issue of hazardous wastes first came to widespread attention in 1977 when the Love Canal dump near Buffalo, New York, spilled wastes into a nearby residential neighborhood. Eventually several hundred residents had to be moved out of their homes and most never returned. Hazardous wastes again made headlines in 1982 when it was found that the town of Times Beach, Missouri, had been contaminated with the extremely toxic chemical dioxin and so had to be evacuated. Although these have been the most obvious manifestations of the toxic waste problem, there are approximately 30,000 toxic waste dumps across the United States, and several thousand of them pose serious threats to the health of citizens. It is estimated that up to $50 billion would be required to clean up existing waste dumps and dispose of all the chemicals stored in them in an environmentally safe manner.

The federal government adopted two major pieces of legislation to address the problem of toxic wastes. The first was the Resource Conservation and Recovery Act (RCRA) of 1976, which was reauthorized in 1980, and allowed to continue in effect since then. This act required the EPA to determine what chemicals were hazardous and the appropriate means of disposing of them and to establish a system of permits to ensure that hazardous chemicals were indeed disposed of properly. Because of the technical complexity of the task, and the low priority attached to the exercise during the Carter administration, the necessary regulations were not promulgated until 1980.[72] The regulations were attacked by industry as being too stringent and by environmentalists as being too lenient, but by the time President Carter was ready to leave office, toxic waste issues were beginning to be assigned a high priority in the EPA.

When the Reagan administration came into office in 1981, it began almost immediately to attack the "regulatory excess" believed to be characteristic of the RCRA. Specifically, using the authority of the Paperwork Reduction Act and an executive order promoting deregulation, the Office of Management and Budget sought to dismantle some of the reporting and permit regulations of the RCRA, and it cut funding for the RCRA by almost 25 percent.[73] The attempts by the Reagan administration, under the leadership of its EPA director, Anne Burford Gorsuch, met strong opposition from environmental groups and some congressmen, however, and the EPA did not achieve the degree of deregulation desired. When scandals within the EPA forced Gorsuch from office, the new EPA administrator, William Ruckelshaus, began to restore some teeth to a law that had become almost unenforced. Under the first Bush administration, the "Quayle Commission," established to review and eliminate regulations, again tended toward weakening the provisions of the RCRA.

The second major program for dealing with toxic wastes is the Superfund, which applies funds from a tax on oil and chemical companies for cleaning up hazardous waste sites. The program, as first proposed by the Carter administration, contained regulations requiring industry to clean up its own sites, as well as providing funds to clean up particularly hazardous sites. Finally adopted just before the Reagan administration came into office, the act imposed substantially weaker penalties for industries violating the act than had been proposed, but it did provide a means of addressing some of the worst hazardous waste sites in the United States.

The Reagan administration quickly moved away from the regulatory strategy and rapid timetable of the Carter administration and toward "negotiated settlements" between the industries and the Office of Waste Programs Enforcement in the EPA. There was a great deal of emphasis during this time on having industries clean up their own sites and on avoiding conflict with industries. But as members of Congress grew increasingly impatient with what they regarded as a slowing of the planned cleanup schedule and a change in the intended mechanisms for achieving cleanups, they investigated the Superfund for alleged mismanagement and removed its head from office. They also passed the Superfund amendments of 1986 (SARA), requiring the manufacturers of toxic chemicals to monitor the types and releases of those chemicals.[74]

The EPA under Ruckelshaus soon began to pursue cleaning up dumps more actively. Even with that increased activity, only about a third of the 1,600 hazardous sites on the "National Priority List" had been cleaned up by 1998.[75] This slowness was in part a function of the costs—in the late 1980s it cost on average over $21 million to clean up one site, and by the early 1990s that figure had increased to over $30 million.[76] Against that level of need, Congress has been appropriating in the vicinity of $9 billion over five years. Indeed, an increasing number of sites requiring cleanup continue to be discovered, and with them an increasing demand on the limited resources available. If anything the implementers of Superfund seem to believe that they are falling behind as the level of toxic pollution in the United States becomes more apparent and more sites are added to the list. Despite the magnitude of the problem, the George W. Bush administration has made some efforts to defund the Superfund.[77]

Both the RCRA and the Superfund are potentially important for addressing the problem of a massive amount of toxic waste threatening the environment. The implementation of these programs was slowed by difficulties in writing the necessary regulations and by partisan and ideological opposition during the Reagan and George H.W. Bush administrations. Also, somewhat paradoxically, the "strict liability" provisions of the legislation, which make the producers of toxic wastes responsible for them over their entire lifetime, have deterred enforcement. It is often cheaper for producers to take the risk of criminal prosecution and to dispose of wastes illegally than to identify the wastes to the EPA and then bear the costs of their safe disposal.[78] The delays and the enforcement difficulties have only made the toxic waste problem more serious, and despite more vigorous attempts at cleanup during the Clinton administration, the number of dangerous sites has fallen little.

There is a need for a large-scale effort to identify existing waste sites, clean them, and devise regulatory mechanisms for the safe disposal of such wastes in the future. The government has a number of policy tools at its disposal for addressing these tasks, including prosecution, accommodation, and negotiation, as well as direct federal action to remove the toxic materials.[79] All of these approaches have some advantages and disadvantages for coping with problems arising from private-sector wastes. The problem is, however, being confounded by the large volume of toxic wastes generated by the federal government itself, especially the Department of Defense.[80] Emissions of toxic wastes have been slowed but they will remain a serious environmental problem for the United States for decades to come.

Endangered Species Act

One of the more controversial pieces of environmental legislation is the Endangered Species Act, originally passed in 1973. This act, which depends more on the Department of the Interior than the EPA for enforcement, enables the Fish and Wildlife Service (FWS) to designate species as endangered or threatened (as over three hundred have been since the act was passed) and then permits them to protect the crucial habitats of the species. There have been a number of famous (and infamous) instances in which a seemingly insignificant species (such as the snail darter) blocks a major public or private project, although as noted, the most famous case was that of the spotted owl in the Pacific Northwest and its impact on the logging industry.

The Endangered Species Act has produced some significant results, including bringing back the bald eagle population from its formerly depleted state, but it remains controversial in spite of those accomplishments. The legal and philosophical concept of "takings" has been applied particularly against enforcement of this act, although other environmental legislation has some aspects of takings. The idea is that such acts deprive landowners of the use of their property without just compensation.[81] There is little doubt that there has been procedural due process, given that the takings result from an act of Congress, but there is some question as to whether the substance of these acts is indeed legitimate. The courts have begun to examine environmental legislation from this perspective, and to find in favor of landowners.[82]

The issue of endangered species is one of many instances in which government must balance a range of interests and a range of principles. In a society founded on ideals of free enterprise, property rights are important, but they must be weighed against other desirable policy goals such as preservation of the environment. Likewise, economic development goals are being weighed against these environmental goals. Different politicians and citizens groups make highly varying judgments about the relative merits of these goals, and the political process must find ways to accommodate this range of perspectives on good policy.

Implementation of Environmental Controls

The principal organization charged with the implementation of environmental control legislation is the Environmental Protection Agency, organized in 1970 and conceived as an executive agency, responsible to the president but independent of any cabinet department. The agency was charged with implementing a variety of air, water, and toxic waste programs, but in so doing it encountered a number of difficulties, some of which were political, involving the relationship between the EPA and other federal agencies and the states. The EPA was given a rather broad set of responsibilities and a wide field of action that inevitably brought it into conflict with other federal and state agencies. When the EPA sought to flex its environmental muscles, it almost inevitably ran into conflicts with agencies that wanted to build dams, roadways, or waterways, or with the heads of private industries who believed that the standards imposed on them by the EPA were too stringent and impeded their ability to compete in the marketplace, especially the world market. The EPA was given an unenviable task to perform, but because it was made up mostly of people committed to the environmental movement, it set out to accomplish that task with some zeal. The difficulties it encountered were intensified because many of the projects it sought to stop were pet projects of some congressman or senator, and the agency's reputation on Capitol Hill was not the best.

The EPA was also given a difficult administrative task. Congress was relatively specific about the dates by which certain levels of pollution reduction were to be achieved, giving the agency little latitude and little opportunity to bargain with polluting industries. Also, in attempting to specify so precisely the conditions for alleviating pollution, Congress often wrote into legislation several contradictory paragraphs, which in turn created more implementation difficulties for the EPA. Finally, the strategy adopted for a good deal of the program—technology-forcing regulations—created substantial difficulties for implementers and for industries seeking to comply with the legislation.[83] When standards were adopted to reduce air pollution by 1975 to 10 percent of what it was in 1970, the technology to produce that improvement in air quality simply did not exist. It was believed that passage of the legislation would spur development of the technology, but the actual result was a delay in implementation rather than any technological breakthroughs. Certainly a number of improvements have been made, especially in the internal combustion engine, as a result of this legislation, but the major innovations anticipated have not materialized.

One major implementation problem associated with environmental policies has been standard setting. We noted that such phrases as "primary and secondary standards of air quality" and "best available technology" were not clearly defined in legislation. Even if they had been defined, it would still have been necessary to convert those standards into permissible levels of emissions from individual sources of pollution (e.g., for each factory and municipal waste treatment facility). Overall goals for pollution reduction are relatively easy to establish, but great difficulty is encountered in translating those goals into workable and enforceable criteria. And the criteria developed must be applicable to polluters, not just to pollution, if any significant improvements in environmental quality are to be achieved. At times the difficulty of setting those standards has forced the EPA to adopt a "best practice" doctrine: if a plant is doing things in the same way as every other plant, then it must be doing things right. Also, the standard setters have been under pressure to accept more risk and to be less strict about environmental controls so as to promote economic growth and competitiveness.[84]

The enforcement of established criteria has presented several interesting questions. First, should a mechanism exist for making trade-offs between environmental protection and economic growth? For example, the Sierra Club succeeded in obtaining a court ruling that the air pollution legislation did not allow any degradation of existing air quality, an interpretation that had been resisted by the EPA. This ruling meant that people living in an area with very clean air— probably an area with little or no industry—might be forbidden to bring in any industry. A related question is how to allocate any proposed reductions in effluents among industries or other polluters. For example, should there be across-the-board percentage reductions, requiring each polluter to reduce pollution by 20 percent or whatever, or should attention be paid both to the level of emissions and the technological feasibility of reducing pollution at each source? For some industries even minor reductions in effluents might be very difficult to attain, while others might be able virtually to eliminate their effluents with only a limited investment. How should these considerations be taken into account?

Second, although environmental protection legislation is replete with legal weapons to force compliance from polluters, including the authority to close down an offending industry, in reality the enforcement of the legislation has been much less draconian. Politically, the EPA cannot afford to close an industry that provides a major source of employment, either nationally or in a single community. Thus, frequently the agency's hands are tied, and the level of compliance desired or mandated has not been achieved. This element of political vulnerability may be functional in some ways, given the evidence that cooperation is more effective than adversarial relationships in generating compliance.[85]

Finally, although the Environmental Protection Agency has been given a number of legal and administrative mechanisms for improving air and water quality, its efforts are frequently hampered by the complex systems for standard setting and implementation. State governments, for example, are essential in devising plans for reducing pollution, and local communities have to become involved in building new waste-treatment facilities. And the EPA itself is not responsible for distributing matching federal funds for those treatment facilities, so instead of being distributed on the basis of the severity of the pollution problem, the funds are allocated on a first-come, first-served basis. Consequently, instead of developing definitive standards and practices, the enforcement of environmental legislation is frequently only a by-product of compromise, negotiation, and bargaining.[86] This characteristic does not, of course, distinguish environmental policy from most other policy, but it does run counter to some of the rhetoric about the EPA "running roughshod" over the interests of industries and local communities.

Alternatives to Regulation

As we have been demonstrating, the principal means of addressing environmental problems has been through direct regulation—the mandating of certain actions or the attainment of certain standards—enforced through legal penalties or possible closings. It has been argued that a more efficient means of producing improvements in the environment would be to impose effluent charges or taxes.[87] In other words, instead of telling an industry that it could emit only a certain number of tons of effluents each year, government would allow it to emit as much as it desired. The polluter would, however, have to pay a tax based on the amount of pollution discharged, and therefore the greater the quantity, the higher would be the total cost. And some means of graduating the charges could be devised so that the greater the volume of effluents, the higher the rate of payment.

The presumed advantage of effluent charges is that they would allow more efficient industries to pollute, while less efficient industries would either have to close down or improve their environmental standards. The more efficient industries could afford to pay the effluent tax and still make a profit, while less efficient industries could not. This market-oriented solution to the pollution problem would be compatible with economic growth and efficiency.[88] It is argued that it would be a definite improvement over direct regulation as a means of forcing the trade-off between those competing values, and it would give most industries a real incentive to improve their environmental performance as well as their economic efficiency. Some of these ideas for market reform were implemented during the Clinton administration as components of the "Reinventing EPA" program and, adopting the "Common Sense Initiative," were very successful, while others demonstrated the difficulties of making markets perform as wished by politicians.[89]

Another component of the market-oriented approach to environmental regulation is to issue tradeable permits to pollute. The 1990 amendments to the Clean Air Act permit utility firms to trade rights to pollute, particularly in sulfur dioxide and later in chlorinated fluorocarbons. The initial allocation of these allowances was related roughly to the amount of pollution the firms emitted in 1987. These amendments required the firms to begin to reduce their total emissions by 1995, with each firm being given the choice either to invest in pollution control devices or to buy pollution rights from other utilities that are reducing their emissions.[90] Again, the assumption is that this mechanism will produce an efficient allocation of resources as well as reduced pollution.[91]

Effluent taxation and tradeable permits have been criticized, however, especially by environmentalists, some of whom regard them as mechanisms for buying the right to pollute, and even to kill. To those critics, the value of a clean environment is greater than the value of economic growth in almost any circumstance, and they cannot accept the idea of balancing the two. Another problem is that enforcing a pollution tax might be even more difficult than enforcing existing regulatory standards. Effluents would have to be monitored almost continuously to determine the total amount of discharge, whereas under the present regulatory system less frequent monitoring often is sufficient, as is less exact measurement.

The air and water of the United States are much cleaner in the early twenty-first century than they were before the passage of the environmental legislation. Fish have returned to streams that were once biologically dead, and cities such as Pittsburgh, which was once constantly shrouded in smoke and grit, now can be seen from a distance. Despite these successes, the EPA and its legislation have come under a great deal of criticism. The agency has been attacked from both sides—for being insensitive to the needs of industry and for being too soft on polluters. And questions about the role of the EPA are likely to become even more important as scarce resources and slow economic growth raise the average citizen's concern about national priorities. The Reagan administration began early during its term of office to question the efficacy of many standards and to soften environmental regulations, especially on automobile-caused pollution. This relaxation of standards was intended to assist the depressed automobile industry by allowing American automobiles to compete with imported automobiles, at least on price.

Decisions in one policy area often impinge on many other areas. Environmental policy cannot be discussed apart from energy policy, or from policies concerning economic growth. The institutions of government, however, frequently do not provide mechanisms for rectifying these conflicts of values. Each policy area is treated separately, according to its own constellation of interests and professional standards, and each seeks to maximize the returns from political activities for the participants in the policymaking. As both national resources and government resources dwindle, however, decisions by such "subgovernments" may be a luxury we can no longer afford. There is a need for enhanced policy coordination between these areas as well as many others, but Washington tends to work better *within* policy areas than across them, and conflict rather than cooperation is the common outcome.

The early years of the twenty-first century may be the decade during which some important questions about the relationship between Americans and their physical environment are decided. We as a nation must decide how much value to attach to a clean and relatively unspoiled environment, as compared with the amount of value we attach to the mastery of that environment through energy exploration and economic growth. Although renewable energy resources and some shifting of attitudes about the desirability of economic growth may soften these hard choices, the choices must still be made. These choices will arise with respect to specific questions, such as whether to open more Alaskan lands to energy exploration or how to manage the oil shale of the western states. They may also arise over issues such as the disposal of increasing quantities of toxic industrial wastes and the need to develop cleaner means of producing the goods to which we have become accustomed. In the process, Americans will be asked what they are willing to give up for a cleaner environment. Are styrofoam cups worth the emission of CFCs into the environment and the swelling of solid waste dumps? Are we willing to spend an hour or so every week recycling materials to prevent pollution and conserve energy? The sum of these individual choices, along with the regulatory choices made by government, will say a good deal about the quality of life in the United States for years to come.

CHAPTER 14

Protective Policies: Defense and Law Enforcement

THE U.S. CONSTITUTION lists "to provide for the common defense" as a primary purpose of the government of the United States. Going back to Lexington and Concord and the Minutemen, military defense has been a visible and sometimes extremely expensive function in a country favoring small government and few government employees.[1] Not all threats to peace and order are foreign, and from the beginning, law enforcement has also been a major public function. In the United States policing has been largely a state and local function, but, like education, it has seen an increasing involvement of the federal government. Some of that involvement has been purely financial, but increasingly the federal government is directly concerned with enforcing the law. Following the terrorist attacks of 11 September 2001, it began to take an even more active role in directing and coordinating law enforcement.

This chapter examines these two government functions, both of which are in general salient to the public but have varied in their relevance. Until September 11th, defense had been declining in relevance to the average citizen, while law enforcement had been a growing concern for some years. In many surveys during the 1990s, crime and personal safety were considered the most pressing problems of government (see table 14.1, p. 394). The events of late 2001, however, have placed both of these policies at the very center of public concern. These two policy areas have obvious similarities, including the use of force in the name of the public, but there are also some more subtle similarities, such as their potential threats to civil liberties. There are some obvious and important differences between them as well.

TABLE 14.1 Most Important Issues for Americans (in percentages, up to three mentions recorded)

	Nov. 1991	Aug. 1992	Jan. 1993	Sept. 1993	Jan. 1994	Jan. 1997	Jun. 2000
Unemployment	23	27	22	20	18	21	20
Economy (general)	32	37	35	26	14		
Drugs	10	6	6	6	9	17	16
Health care	6	12	18	28	20	7	12
Crime	6	7	9	16	37	23	20

Source: Gallup Poll Monthly, September 1992, 11; January 1994, 43; January 1997, 20.

Defense Policy

Providing for the common defense is now a much more complex and expensive task than it was when an effective military force could be raised by calling for each man in the community to take down the rifle from over the fireplace. Military spending accounted for 16.5 percent of federal spending in 2000, down from 35 percent in 1980. In 2000 military spending was 3.3 percent of gross national product (see table 14.2)—$3.00 out of every $100 in the economy went for military defense, down from 6.5 percent of GNP in 1985. In some parts of the United States such as Norfolk, Virginia, and Southern California, defense (whether the military itself or civilian defense contractors) is a dominant component of the local economy.

Defense policy became even more controversial after the end of the Cold War and the short Gulf War. The demands placed on the defense establishment now involve even greater complexity and even greater uncertainty than when the adversary was clear and the types of weapons needed, at least for deterrence, were largely agreed upon.[2] Further, although many Americans expected a "peace dividend" at the end of the Cold War, most government leaders were not as anxious to dismantle the military establishment. Still, military leaders had accepted the necessity of reducing defense expenditures in a less supportive political and financial climate, but the 2003 budget of the George W. Bush administration proposed a significant increase in defense spending, for both new technology and for manpower. That increase reversed some years of decline, and further increases were implicitly promised in recognition that the world had again become a dangerous place.

Even before the increases of the Bush budget estimates, however, there were some pressures for an increase in defense spending within a very few years, as a number of weapons systems under contract would begin to be delivered and existing systems modernized, posing the obvious question of whether those weapons were still necessary.[3] Also, the shift from nuclear deterrence to conven-

TABLE 14.2   Military Expenditures as Percentage of Gross Domestic Product, 2000

North Korea	27.5
Saudi Arabia	14.5
Israel	9.7
Russia	5.8
Pakistan	5.7
Syria	5.6
Greece	4.6
Taiwan	4.6
United States	3.3
France	3.0
United Kingdom	2.7
Sweden	2.5
Germany	1.6
Canada	1.3
Japan	1.0

Source: U.S. Department of State, *World Military Expenditures and Arms Transfers*, annual.

tional warfare and an increased emphasis on peacekeeping seemed likely to make defense more expensive. A missile can sit in a silo for some time with minimal maintenance costs, but soldiers and sailors have to be paid every month and fed every day. They may cost even more when the economy is good and recruits are difficult to attract. Deciding on defense policy has never been easy, but it is likely to become even more difficult because most of the former certainties about strategy have been changed in a very short period of time and there is little certainty about the future.

The Environment of Defense Policy

A number of factors condition the manner in which defense policy is made and the likely outcomes of the process. Unlike many other policy areas, defense policy is influenced by forces that are, to a great extent, beyond the control of the government officials making the decisions. In part because of the uncertainty involved in making defense policy, there may be greater perceptual differences among individuals involved in the process than is true for other policy areas.[4] For example, the degree of threat that any decision maker perceives in the international environment will affect his or her willingness to allocate resources to defense. These perceptual differences have been exacerbated since the clear threat of the Soviet Union has been largely ended, leaving the United States to contend with the possibility of smaller-scale, but still dangerous, conflicts around the world. Further, terrorism and unconventional threats to American security now loom much larger, and they require a different type of military posture.[5]

The prospect of smaller-scale conflicts also raises the question of whether the U.S. role should be that of global policeman or of merely one more nation in the international community, albeit the only remaining superpower.[6] Further, if the United States is to act as an international policeman, should it do so alone or in concert with international organizations such as the United Nations, NATO, and the Organization of American States?[7] The actions in Iraq gave a very unilateralist answer to this question. An even more basic question is whether the national interests of the United States are really served by using its military forces for such peacekeeping and relief functions around the world, no matter how desirable those tasks may be on humanitarian grounds?[8]

Adversaries and potential adversaries. For most of the past half-century, the fundamental factor shaping defense policy was the relationship between the United States and the Soviet Union. Almost as soon as the two superpowers ceased being allies after World War II, they became adversaries on a global scale. Early stages of that adversarial relationship included the Berlin blockade and the Korean War, followed by the U-2 incident, the Cuban missile crisis, Vietnam, and Afghanistan, not to mention hundreds of more minor incidents.[9] None of these incidents involved direct conflict between troops of the two superpowers, although confrontations between the troops of one superpower and those of allies or surrogates of the other occurred several times. The degree of hostility expressed between the United States and the Soviet Union varied, however; there were periods of détente ameliorating the tensions of the Cold War and some important negotiated agreements (e.g., the nuclear test ban treaty and the SALT agreements) that lessened tensions, at least for a while.

In addition to conventional conflicts, the nuclear arms race drove each country to develop massive stockpiles of nuclear weapons, capable of destroying the world several times over. Nuclear weapons have not been used since World War II, and there were several successful attempts to reduce their numbers (or at least reduce their rate of growth) even during the peak Cold War years. As more historical materials from the Cold War period become available to scholars and analysts, it is even clearer that the nuclear threat did serve as a major deterrent to conflictual behavior, but also that the number of near-disastrous accidents had made the world a very dangerous place indeed.[10]

The remaining stockpiles of these weapons represent a crucial factor that defense policymakers must always take into account, especially since the former Soviet Union has disintegrated into a number of smaller states. Several of these new states retain large quantities of weapons and have national ambitions that may lead them to rattle the nuclear saber, if not actually use the weapons.[11] In 2002 Russian President Vladimir Putin and President George W. Bush reached agreement on a major reduction in the nuclear stockpiles of the two countries, further limiting the possibilities of a nuclear confrontation.[12] Nevertheless, both countries retain hundreds of warheads, quite enough to destroy each other and much of the rest of humanity as well.

Thus, the world was very dangerous during the Cold War and the nuclear stockpiling by the two superpowers, but it may be even more dangerous since "peace" has broken out. Instead of being one Soviet Union with nuclear weapons, a number of the new republics now possess those weapons. The Gulf War also highlighted the presence of nuclear, chemical, and biological weapons in a number of other countries, and the apparent willingness of those countries to use force to attain their own political and economic goals. Some potential adversaries, such as North Korea,[13] still appear to be fighting the Cold War and persist in the rhetoric of fighting against global capitalism. Other adversaries such as Iraq were pursuing more nationalistic or economic goals. Further, there is some evidence that the new nuclear powers are not nearly as cautious as the former Soviet Union in how they develop and deploy weapons.[14] India and Pakistan have both developed and exploded nuclear weapons, and although their primary target is not the United States, the existence of more nuclear powers adds another variable to an already difficult set of strategic calculations. Finally, there is the fear, if little tangible evidence, that terrorist groups also possess weapons of mass destruction.

Although many potential adversaries are small and relatively weak militarily, they are widely dispersed around the globe, and the American defense establishment must decide how quickly, and in how many simultaneous situations, it must be prepared to respond.[15] Further, those planners must decide how much force both we and the potential adversaries can, and should, bring to bear in these potential conflicts. There is a danger that the United States military has been so attuned to large-scale international conflicts that it will not be capable of coping effectively with seemingly mundane low-level conflicts that appear more probable in the post–Cold War era. The "bottom-up review" of defense policy undertaken in 1994 was an attempt to develop a new strategic doctrine, premised on the possibility of several smaller conflicts, such as the Gulf War.[16] The question then became how many of these "major regional conflicts" should the American military be able to cope with simultaneously? The basic answer was two, with one being contained while the other was being won.

The possibilities of war with Iraq have increased the stakes in the debate over the force structure of the United States. There has been an ongoing debate within the military policy community over first whether this is indeed the right force structure to plan for, and second whether the existing forces of the United States are adequate for these demands. The experiences of the Gulf War and Iraq indicated that the U.S. was capable of mounting a major effort at an extreme distance from its own borders, but could it have managed another such conflict, even to contain it, until more forces were available?[17] There has been some re-ordering of force structures to attempt to make divisions capable of responding more quickly to threat, but concern remains about whether the forces still think about more intense conflicts than those with which the immediate future may challenge them. Beginning in late 2001, the military was involved in a relatively small conflict in Afghanistan, indicating that it had learned some of the lessons of conducting small-scale conflicts. In addition, the new "Bush doctrine," which argued for preemptive action against potential adversaries (especially terrorists), has placed even greater burdens on the military.

Allies.   The United States also has friends in the world, although its allies do not always agree with it on defense and foreign policy issues. The United States has important defense agreements with Japan, South Korea, Israel, and Australia, but its most important alliance has been the North Atlantic Treaty Organization (NATO), which has linked nations in Europe and North America for their mutual defense since the late 1940s. NATO has been responsible for the defense of Western Europe and the North Atlantic, and the United States has committed by far the largest share of men and matériel to the alliance.[18] The collapse of the Soviet threat in the late 1980s, however, made many people—defense analysts and ordinary citizens alike—question the continuation of NATO, at least in its traditional format. Further, economic problems at home and the continuing economic and political integration of Western Europe mean that there is less need for a large American military presence in Europe, and almost all of the divisions stationed in Germany since the end of World War II have come home. Similarly, the United States was willing to give up major military bases in the Philippines, in the belief that they would be much less valuable in a world without direct East-West confrontations.

Although these alliances are apparently now less valuable, the experience of the Gulf War showed that Western nations, and even some former adversaries from the Warsaw Pact, could band together to confront a perceived common threat. The United Nations stamp of approval on their actions in the Persian Gulf made the alliance more viable, but there had been a sense that the United States does have friends around the world that can be counted on in many military situations. In the Iraq war there were a few old friends who joined in the conflict. The alliances may be ad hoc arrangements rather than continuing treaty commitments, but they can still generate collective action to maintain international security. Further, economic and social issues (including human rights) may become more important in defining security arrangements in the near future, so the United States needs to adjust its own thinking about how to make and maintain international alliances.[19]

The importance of U.S. involvement in NATO was evident in the attempts to maintain the peace in the former Yugoslavia in the 1990s. A variety of European members of NATO had made attempts to control the violence in Croatia and Bosnia but had little success until American troops became involved.[20] The deployment of these troops as a NATO activity helped to legitimate the operations of the peacekeeping forces, but the presence of American troops remained crucial. The initial commitment of troops for one year had to be extended for an indefinite period in order to maintain the uneasy peace. The George W. Bush administration was extremely skeptical of this involvement when it first came to office but after learning more of the situation there, it has maintained some U.S. role in the Balkans. Again, these activities indicate the extent to which the traditional role of the U.S. military has been altered.

The American attack on Afghanistan in late 2001 also involved the creation of a small alliance against the Taliban government accused of harboring al Qaeda terrorists. Most important was creating a working agreement with Pakistan, which served as the staging ground for much of the campaign. A few other long-standing allies such as Britain became involved, but the operation was primarily American. The split within NATO became more pronounced in the Iraq conflict. This military initiative demonstrated not only the capacity of the American government to project power across the globe but also the fact that alliances in the future may be purpose-made rather than stable and enduring.

Technology

The technology of modern warfare has advanced far beyond that available even during the Vietnam conflict or the Gulf War of 1991.[21] Nuclear armaments are a major part of the technological change, but systems for delivering weapons have improved even more rapidly. In the 1950s it took hours for a plane to fly from the former Soviet Union to the United States; a missile can now make a comparable journey in fifteen minutes, and a missile launched from a submarine offshore could arrive in a few minutes. There even are plans for war in space, with "killer satellites" and orbiting weapons as part of an antimissile system ("Star Wars").[22] The technology of conventional warfare now includes the advanced laser-guided weapons, infrared night-vision scopes, stealth airplanes, computers, and antimissile defenses featured prominently during the Gulf War. The wars in Afghanistan and in Iraq demonstrated even more technological capacity to increase the effectiveness and safety of the armed forces.[23] There is also discussion of a whole new generation of weapons, including the potential for laser weapons, that would have been found only in science fiction a few years ago.

Advancing weapons technology has several implications for defense policy. One is that defense is a constant activity; there is no longer time to raise an army and then go to war. A standing army historically has been something of an anathema to many Americans, but in the late 1990s the U.S. military numbered approximately 2 million uniformed personnel plus almost 1 million civilian employees in the Department of Defense. Another feature of the increased technology of modern warfare is cost, which is in part a function of having to maintain a large military establishment but goes beyond that. One new B-1 or B-2 bomber costs almost $1 billion; one army tank now costs approximately $10 million, and one proposed new carrier for the navy could cost several billion dollars.[24] Therefore, any discussion of improving the technical quality of American military forces must be conducted in the context of very high costs.[25]

Public Opinion

Finally, American defense policy is made in a relatively open political arena where it is definitely influenced by public opinion. As is often the case, however, public opinion about defense is ambiguous. There are few committed advocates of unilateral disarmament in the United States, especially after September 11th, and virtually all American politicians advocate a strong defense. Nevertheless, a number of questions remain about program costs, about whether many of the high-technology weapons purchased actually contribute significantly to national security, and about how the military power of the United States should be used (e.g., in the Caribbean, Central America, or other parts of the Third World). These questions involve political calculations as well as technical military issues, and they will continue to be fought out in Congress and the media as well as in the Pentagon.

Nuclear weapons constitute an even greater public opinion problem. A significant portion of the American populace, although favoring a strong defense, were opposed to the nuclear arms race between the United States and the Soviet Union. The public has generally applauded the negotiated freezes on nuclear weapons and the reduction in the numbers of such weapons stockpiled by both sides. There is virtual unanimity on one point: the United States should never be the first country to use nuclear weapons in a conflict.[26] This is true whether the conflict be one among superpowers or more limited conflicts such as the Gulf War. The spread of nuclear weapons to other countries such as India and Pakistan makes the issues of the safety and control of nuclear weapons all the more relevant.

With the negotiated reduction in nuclear readiness between the United States and the former Soviet Union, the issue of nuclear weapons did not, however, vanish. The one remaining superpower, and the successor states to the former one, still possess substantial stocks of nuclear weapons, as well as the means to deliver those weapons. Further, despite the existence of the nuclear nonproliferation treaty, and the efforts of the United Nations to enforce that treaty, nuclear weapons appear to be spreading around the globe, potentially to terrorist groups as well as legitimate governments such as North Korea.[27] The threat of nuclear weapons is something that the United States (not to mention the rest of the world) must live with for the foreseeable future. Simple agreement among Americans that the weapons are an immense danger will not eliminate the fact of their existence.

U.S. Force Configurations

Table 14.3 (p. 402) lists the strategic weapon holdings of the United States, Russia, and China. With the end of the Cold War, much of this vast arsenal appears to be dinosaurs left from an earlier age. Early pledges from Boris Yeltsin, leader of the Russian federation, and from President George H.W. Bush to dismantle much of the strategic forces meant that these weapons were to follow the path of intermediate range weapons in Europe and be destroyed.[28] More than a decade later, each country retains a nuclear arsenal, but neither is of the magnitude that characterized them at the height of the Cold War. In particular, most of the missiles are being fitted with a single warhead, rather than the multiple warheads formerly found on many missiles. In downsizing, the United States has held on to its submarine-launched weapons most dearly, being more willing to trade away other parts of its "triad."[29] As promising as these developments are, the uncertainty about whose "finger is on the button," and indeed how many buttons there are, in the former Soviet Union leaves the world still a dangerous place and makes maintaining some nuclear deterrent an important feature of American defense policy.

The balance in nonstrategic forces in the world is less easy to define. Table 14.4 (p. 402) details the balance of conventional forces between the United States and several other potential adversaries. The countries formed out of the former Soviet Union have a very large military force, but the fragmentation among and within them may make those forces less dangerous than they might otherwise be. Still, the actual force levels of the United States are smaller than those of some other countries. In any conflict with those countries, the superior technical capabilities of some of the American weapons, as well as superiority in the number of attack aircraft, would be needed to level the field.

Table 14.5 (p. 402) shows the balance of naval forces between the United States and the former Soviet Union, as well as several other countries. The United States has fewer surface ships and far fewer general-purpose submarines, but numerical inferiority may in fact underestimate the strength of the U.S. Navy, given the capabilities contained in one attack-carrier battle group. In ad-

TABLE 14.3   Nuclear Warheads Possessed by United States and Major Potential Adversaries

Deliverable by	United States	Russia	China
Bombers	2,900	1,374	150
ICBMs	2,000	2,000	110
Submarine launched missles	3,520	2,600	24

Source: International Institute of Strategic Studies, *The Military Balance 1997–98* (London: Oxford, 1998).

TABLE 14.4   Conventional Land Forces of United States and Major Potential Adversaries

	United States	Russia	China	North Korea
Personnel	670,000	500,000	200,000+	950,000
Main battle tanks	8,200	16,800	8,500	2,500
Artillery	8,200	18,400+	14,500+	10,200

Source: International Institute of Strategic Studies, *The Military Balance, 1997–98* (London: Oxford, 1998).

TABLE 14.5   Naval Forces of United States and Major Potential Adversaries

	United States	Russia	China	North Korea
Submarines	95	133	63	25
Carriers	12	1	0	0
Other major surface vessels	132	165	54[a]	3

Source: International Institute of Strategic Studies, *The Military Balance, 1997–98* (London: Oxford, 1998).

a. Excludes numerous patrol craft.

dition, the superior detection equipment and satellite tracking devices on American vessels make the submarines of other countries relatively less effective. Thus, despite reduction in naval construction, and the far-flung missions that its navy must serve, on balance the edge seems to go to the naval forces of the United States.

If nothing else, toting up personnel and weapons systems demonstrates the huge destructive potential that can be unleashed in a few moments by a number of countries in the world. Such great power carries with it great responsibility and the need for effective strategic doctrines to prevent the use of nuclear weapons—or, if possible, any weapons. The doctrines of a bipolar world, such as "mutually assured destruction," are no longer valid, and because of that there is perhaps less security than even during the height of the Cold War. The increased emphasis on terrorism and "rogue states" in defense policy has led to the promulgation of the "Bush doctrine," which argues for preemptive strikes against any threats to the United States.[30]

Problems of Defense Policy

Maintaining the defenses of the United States presents several significant policy problems, none of which can be solved readily. One is how to manage nuclear strategy in a multipolar world. Other problems are more narrowly focused, such as the interaction of specific defense issues (e.g., the acquisition of weapons and manpower) with either fundamental features of the economic system or fundamental American values. These problems have only grown more complex as the uncertainty about the military future of the United States makes the choices more difficult and more risky.

Military Procurement

The first major defense problem is that of acquiring new weapons systems.[31] In a modern, high-technology military force, new weapons are not bought "off-the-shelf" but represent years or even decades of research and development. This in turn presents several problems for the military managers who seek to acquire the weapons. One problem is attempting to predict years in advance just what sort of weapons will be required to ensure American national security. For example, during the Reagan years a great deal of money was funneled into the Strategic Defense Initiative (SDI, or "Star Wars").[32] Given changes in the strategic environment, that program now appears to be of limited utility, as there is relatively less chance of strategic missiles being launched at the United States, and much greater chance of terrorism or small, limited wars. Despite that, the George W. Bush administration has been pushing ahead with a missile defense program, renouncing the Anti-Ballistic Missile Treaty with Russia at the same time.

Another problem for procurement officials is deciding what form of competition to demand among potential suppliers of the weapons. One option is to have possible competitors develop full-scale operating systems and then to test those prototypes against each other. The other option is to settle on one or a limited number of vendors very early in the development process and then work with the contractor to develop the weapon. Although the former option corresponds to the standard procedures for bidding out contracts in order to get the most "bang for the buck" from the Department of Defense's money, it may ultimately produce more expensive and less effective weapons. If a manufacturer must develop fully operational weapons in order to compete for a program, it may choose simply not to compete; hence many potentially useful ideas (especially from smaller firms) might be lost. Second, if this full-scale competition were carried out, any firm competing for government contracts might have to amortize its failures across winning contracts in order to make a profit, and consequently the costs of weapons systems as a group would increase. Another option would be to sell the weapons to other countries, a strategy that came back to haunt several countries, including the United States, during the Gulf War and thus may not be the best strategy for reducing the level of military tension in the world.

On the other hand, awarding contracts for major weapons systems on the basis of only prototypes and engineering projections may produce numerous disappointments and cost overruns. Despite screening by skilled military and civilian personnel in the Department of Defense, ideas that look good on the drawing board may not work when they are brought to full-scale production and deployment. There are numerous examples in recent weapons systems: the Sergeant York (DIVAD) antiaircraft cannon, the Bradley fighting vehicle, the C-17 aircraft, and several missile systems have not performed as expected.[33] Even if a manufacturer is capable of making the system work as promised, there may be large cost overruns; the delivered price of the C-5A military transport plane was several times the projected price.

Given that most weapons procurement contracts are "cost plus," therefore virtually guaranteeing the manufacturer a profit, those contractors have a strong incentive to bid low on projects and allow costs to escalate. The Department of Defense has instituted controls to try to prevent the most flagrant violations of this contracting system, but it is difficult to control genuine cases of cost underestimation when a project is well into production. If a workable product can be attained, it will almost certainly be better to go ahead with the project despite cost overruns than to begin again.

Another problem arising from the procurement process is that a manufacturer awarded a contract for a particular weapons system becomes the "sole source" for that system and for the parts that go along with it. This allows firms to charge exorbitant prices for spare parts and tools—simple wrenches worth a dollar or less have been billed to the Department of Defense for several thousand dollars. Some revelations about these apparent excesses have been more media events than real cost problems, and curbs have been instituted to stop some of the greatest abuses, but the underlying problem in weapons procurement remains.

The division among the armed services may also produce problems in procuring weapons, or at least may make weapons cost more than they should. Again, there are two options: to attempt to force the services to use the same weapons whenever possible, or to allow each of the services to acquire the systems most suited to its particular needs. For example, since both the air force and the navy fly airplanes that perform similar missions, why can they not use the same planes? In addition to coordination problems caused by the long-standing rivalries between the services, however, there could be a danger that weapons resulting from an integrated procurement process would be neither fish nor fowl. For example, the weight added to a plane to make it strong enough for carrier landings for the navy might make it less suitable as an air-superiority interceptor for the air force.

On the other hand, procurement of a number of different weapons may produce higher costs, for the research and development costs of each can be amortized across fewer units of production. In addition, the budgetary process of the United States presents problems for weapons procurement. Unlike most other countries, the United States has an annual defense budget, creating the possibility (and some real examples) that an ongoing weapons system may not be funded. This possibility, of course, presents problems for both contractors and for the military. To date, proposals for a multiyear procurement process have been adopted only in part, for Congress wishes to maintain its control over the public purse.[34]

Continuing fiscal constraints on the federal government after the end of the Cold War have introduced other budget problems into the procurement process. Some procurement plans continue to develop prototypes of new weapons systems and to test these prototypes, but not to produce the systems in any quantity.[35] The idea is that the armed forces can remain technologically modern, yet do so at limited expense; if there were an outbreak of hostilities, then the weapons systems could go into production. On the one hand, this approach to procurement appears to violate some of the assumptions about contemporary military preparedness mentioned earlier, in which speed of response is an essential element. On the other hand, this may be the only way to maintain the technological edge first demonstrated during the Gulf War while also reducing the amount of money spent on the military.

The process of equipping a modern army is a difficult one, and it is made more so by the budgeting process and the budget problems of the United States. It is made even more difficult by the close ties between the Department of Defense and its defense contractors—the military-industrial complex, or the fifth branch of the armed forces—that may make an independent evaluation of some proposed weapons systems more difficult. These problems are harder to solve because Congress wants to preserve its budgetary power, while the defense establishment needs the cooperation and capabilities of contractors. Given the importance of hardware and technology for the modern military, however, significant attention must continue to be given to solving these problems.

Updating the Strategic Deterrent

Much of the strategic deterrent force of the United States is aging; in some cases, it already may be obsolete. The B-52 bomber, which entered service in the 1950s, is, despite updates and modifications, a very old weapon. The Minuteman missile is by no means obsolete, but it was vulnerable to a Soviet first strike. These problems with existing weapons led to the development of three new weapons systems—the B-1 and B-2 bombers and the MX missile—all of which have been at the center of controversy.

The B-1 bomber was designed as a supersonic penetrating intercontinental bomber that could fly to a target and return, depending on speed and electronic countermeasures for its survival. After several prototypes were built and tested, the Carter administration canceled the project in 1977, arguing that bombers might not be as efficient as Cruise missiles, and that the development of "stealth" technology, which would make an airplane less visible to radar, would make the B-1 obsolete quickly. This decision caused a great deal of negative reaction in the military—especially in the air force—and was reversed by the Reagan administration, which called for a force of one hundred B-1 bombers. Eventually, however, continuing problems with the prototypes of the B-1, and the rapid development of stealth technology incorporated into the B-2, led to the end of the B-1. Then, B-2 production was stopped after production of only twenty planes, a victim of the end of the Cold War and tight Pentagon budgets.

Updating the U.S. missile fleet has presented an even more difficult problem. The MX was designed to reduce the vulnerability of the current Minuteman missiles, as well as to upgrade the accuracy and number of warheads in the U.S. nuclear arsenal. While the existing Minuteman III missiles had three MIRVed warheads, the MX could carry ten. The Reagan administration decided to produce one hundred MX missiles and appointed a bipartisan Commission on Strategic Alternatives (the Scowcroft Commission) to make suggestions for basing the MX. This commission recommended the development of a new, small, and highly mobile missile—which soon came to be known as the "Midgetman"—that could be fired from a mobile launcher and therefore moved almost anywhere, much as Cruise missiles can be. The Midgetman would have only a single, rather small warhead, but given its relatively low cost and its relative invulnerability, it could present a serious deterrent, especially given the destructive capacity of even a small warhead. Nevertheless, this missile was not purchased, despite plans for up to six hundred, and only fifty MXs were purchased. Instead, defense planners opted for a rapid development and deployment of less expensive Cruise missiles.

While all these advances in weapons technology were once of tremendous importance for the defense of the United States, their importance is not now clear. Are they really necessary or useful to meet the threats that may be posed by smaller nuclear powers, or will these weapons and a host of other strategic weapons become merely rather quaint relics of the past? Already the long journeys of Trident submarines have an element of the Flying Dutchman about them,[36] and in late 1991 the B-52s that had been on constant alert since the 1950s stood down. Again, there is an apparent need for a thorough and careful examination of just what military purchases of the future should be.

The All-Volunteer Military

During the Vietnam War, the use of conscription to provide manpower for the armed forces became increasingly unpopular in the United States. Therefore, in 1975, the draft was phased out and replaced by an all-volunteer force. While this was politically desirable at the time, and almost certainly is still so today, that policy decision presents several problems for the armed forces.[37] These problems had been reduced but by no means eliminated by the "build-down" of forces prior to involvement in Afghanistan and the Gulf.[38]

The most obvious problem is that the military must now compete directly with civilian employers for the same pool of young people, instead of being able to train young people in the military for a short time and then perhaps induce some of them to remain in the service. Given the risks associated with serving in the military, it is not surprising that there have been difficulties at times in filling enlistment quotas. There are special difficulties in attracting educated and skilled personnel, for these are the people whose services are most in demand in the civilian labor market. Thus, for much of its history, the all-volunteer force has been plagued by stories of low-quality recruits. In the Gulf War, Afghanistan, and in the possible second war in the Gulf much of the burden has fallen on reservists called up from civilian occupations, often with substantial disruptions for them and for their employers.

The recruitment problems diminished during the recession of the early 1980s and again in the 1990s, when any job seemed attractive, and there were long queues of potential enlistees waiting to enter the armed forces. When the economy was booming in the late 1990s, military enlistment was not nearly as attractive an opportunity. The military also has reduced its demand for young men somewhat by placing women in jobs formerly filled by males (although still not in all combat positions) and by using civilians in jobs once filled by uniformed personnel. Problems persist, however, in attracting enough highly skilled personnel—there seems to be an increasing disparity between the skills required to function effectively in a military increasingly dominated by technical weapons systems and the recruits generally available, although performance of the all-volunteer forces and the reserves in the Gulf War allayed these fears somewhat.

Associated with the problem of attracting personnel is that of compensating them. An obvious means of attracting and retaining people in any job is to pay them adequately, and this is especially true for the military, given the dangers and hardships associated with serving in the armed forces. Unfortunately, however, military pay is generally not competitive with private-sector pay, even when the value of allowances and benefits is included in the comparison. Military pay is much better than it was before the introduction of the all-volunteer military, but it is not yet capable of attracting as many of the best personnel in the labor market as the armed forces require. Also, with the end of the Cold War, the patriotic appeal of defending the United States became less effective in recruitment. Nevertheless, military pay has become more expensive in the aggregate and now accounts for a larger percentage of the defense budget than it did before the all-volunteer force.

In addition to the general problem of low pay for military personnel is the special difficulty of retaining those that the armed forces have trained. For example, an individual who trains as a pilot in the air force is frequently able to command at least twice his military pay working for a private airline. Even skilled enlisted personnel, such as machinists and radar operators, have found that the private sector offers them much greater economic rewards than does continuing in the military. As military pay failed to keep pace with wages in the private sector, many military personnel have found themselves in a difficult economic position.[39] The retirement option available to military personnel (full retirement benefits after thirty years) may make staying in the service more desirable, but the loss of crucial skilled personnel continues, and there are some pressures to make military retirement less generous.

Finally, there are philosophical and constitutional questions about the development of an all-volunteer military. Given historical patterns and some continuing discrimination in the labor market, an all-volunteer force may be composed increasingly of members of minority groups, and this effect may be seen as imposing an excessive national defense burden on these groups. More generally, the traditional ideal of the U.S. military has been that of the "citizen-soldier"; historically we have rejected the idea of a professional standing army. The all-volunteer force policy, however, makes a professional armed services more likely and implies that large numbers of young Americans will no longer be serving for a time in the armed forces.

This pattern of recruitment, in turn, may make the military more of a group apart from the rest of society and perhaps may make it less amenable to civilian control. Thus, paradoxically, although we may need a professional military to be able to handle the highly sophisticated weapons in the contemporary arsenal and even the skills needed for covert actions,[40] we may find that we thereby lose some control over those weapons and their potential for massive destruction. In addition, the end of the Cold War, and the resultant sense that the military is not really that necessary any longer, may (again, paradoxically) make the military a more discrete element of the society. The issue of the distinction between civilian and military is even more important as terrorism brings war into the homeland, and the military may be called upon to serve in what might normally be civilian functions. There is little evidence to support a claim that a "warrior caste" has developed in the United States, but the current personnel system of the armed forces may make that development more likely than it would be with the conscription system.

Other Personnel Issues

The military of the United States cannot be isolated from the social issues that influence life in the country as a whole. In particular, the issues of how to integrate women into the armed forces and how to deal with homosexuality have become important concerns for the military. Women have been involved unofficially in the military for the entire history of the United States,[41] but they have been a part of the military officially only since 1942. Most of this involvement has involved support roles, including clerical duties, nursing, and a variety of other activities far removed from actual fighting; for example, women were traditionally not allowed to serve on ships in the navy.

During the late 1980s and early 1990s, however, the military began to allow women into more positions. Having already begun to allow women on some ships, the navy extended that to include all ships except submarines. The air force began to train women for combat positions, and some actually participated in combat missions during the Gulf War, Afghanistan, and Iraq. The army now permits women to serve in all positions except frontline combat positions. If the United States should engage in armed conflicts in the future, it is clear that women will be involved more directly than in the past and that there will almost certainly be more women casualties than ever before. Despite these changes, many women believe that they are still being denied full equality within the military.[42]

A number of highly publicized sexual harassment and "fraternization" cases have focused attention on the issue of the interaction of the two sexes in the military. Some critics claim that harassment of women is endemic in the military,[43] while others argue that the issue has been blown of proportion.[44] Whatever the reality, this is a public relations problem for the military. One of the solutions has been to return to training in single-sex units, something the marines alone had retained in the 1990s. Training and constant monitoring are also offered as remedies, but there appear to be no quick and easy answers.[45] Fraternization between men and women, especially between officers and enlisted personnel, is hardly new, but again there are issues about how to maintain discipline and how to enforce military codes of conduct. To some critics, especially women's groups, these rules are being implemented unfairly, citing the case of a female air force pilot forced out of the service for a relationship with an enlisted man, while a male general was not punished nearly as severely.[46]

The issue of the rights of homosexuals to serve in the armed forces has been even more controversial than the integration of women into combat. During his first presidential campaign President Clinton promised to give homosexuals full rights to serve, but once in office he faced strong pressures from within the military to modify that stance. The suggested compromise position was referred to as "Don't ask, don't tell," meaning that recruiters should not inquire about sexual preference and recruits should not volunteer that information. Sexual orientation would not in itself be a cause for dismissal from the armed forces, but such action would result from involvement in homosexual acts or causing disruptive incidents.[47]

This compromise position satisfied neither side in the dispute.[48] Members of the homosexual community believed that the president had reneged on his promise, that the compromise position still did not accord homosexuals the same rights to military service as those of the heterosexual community. On the other hand, opponents in the military services and in Congress believed that this compromise would undermine military discipline and would reduce the effectiveness of the armed forces. Not surprisingly therefore, the courts have become involved in the controversy and issued a number of rulings, most of which have tended to reinforce the right of homosexuals to serve in the military. For example, a ruling in 1994 reinstated a homosexual officer who had been dismissed earlier for publicly stating that he was gay.[49] Other cases, however, have been settled in favor of the military and its need to maintain discipline.[50] This continues to be a controversial and potentially harmful area of conflict in personnel policy.

Conventional Forces and Strategies

Despite all the concern about nuclear weapons and nuclear disarmament, the most likely use of force by the United States would involve conventional forces. Such forces were used twice under the Reagan administration—once in Lebanon and once in Grenada—and three times during the George H.W. Bush administration—in Panama, in the Gulf War, and finally in Somalia. The Clinton administration chose to use military force to deal with problems in Haiti, in the Balkans, and then in Afghanistan and the Sudan in response to terrorism. In addition, the navy has been used frequently to "show the flag" in the Caribbean, the Mediterranean, and the Persian Gulf. While these activities were taking place, American troops remained on duty in Western Europe, South Korea, Okinawa, Guantanamo Bay in Cuba, and several other places around the globe. The ability of the

United States to respond to threats to its national interests around the world with conventional forces remains an important element in defense planning.

One of the important elements in this ability of the United States to project its presence around the world is the Rapid Deployment Force. These are troops that are ready to be deployed by air on very short notice. Materials have been positioned in places around the world to supply these troops until seaborne supplies can be delivered to them. Under a program called POMCUS, the Carter and Reagan administrations positioned supplies for up to six divisions in Western Europe and the Persian Gulf region; in the event of a confrontation, troops could be flown in without the need to airlift heavy equipment and munitions. These programs are designed to make the U.S. armed forces more flexible and mobile.

Technology plays a major role in that flexibility and mobility. For example, the deployment of the M-1 tank during the Gulf War indicates that it is an extremely reliable, fast, and effective weapon despite its technological sophistication. The problem then becomes acquiring enough of these weapons to meet the needs of the armed forces. But what are those needs? What should the armed forces be preparing for? Current doctrine holds that the armed forces should be preparing for one-and-a-half wars; that is, the armed forces should be preparing for one major and one minor conflict to occur at any one time.[51] Even that level of conflict might strain the available resources, especially if the conflicts involved the logistical problems of the Gulf War and did not include a convenient friendly power such as Saudi Arabia, as the Iraq war has shown.

Planning to meet contingencies with conventional forces is important not only for the ability to utilize U.S. forces to implement national policy but also because strong conventional forces make the use of weapons of mass destruction, meaning primarily theater nuclear weapons, less likely. Plans exist for using such weapons in the event of apparent defeat by conventional forces, but once those weapons are used, it will be difficult to contain their escalation. The problem of nuclear escalation has largely been eliminated in Europe, but it would definitely be possible in dealing with smaller powers and might also escalate to include chemical and biological weapons. Thus, the availability of nuclear weapons makes conventional forces that much more important.

Having an effective conventional deterrent also depends upon the readiness of those forces to fight when needed. There is some fear among military leaders, as well as military analysts, that reductions in spending will reduce the military's capacity to meet the demands that may be placed upon it. Some fear has been expressed that American defense forces have become "hollow"—that they do not have sufficient readiness to meet another crisis on the order of the Gulf War.[52] The ability to respond effectively and quickly in Afghanistan and Iraq put those fears to rest.[53] The demands now are to create forces that are even lighter and more mobile. As times change dramatically, Russia has now become at least an associate member of NATO, and other NATO members have appeared willing to shoulder some additional burdens, at least for peace-keeping in Europe.[54]

Defense and/or Jobs

As the Cold War ended and many if not most Americans were ready for a significant cut in the defense budget, we found that cutting back was not as simple as it seemed. The economic prosperity of the United States rests in part on its military-industrial complex, so that reducing defense expenditures means reducing employment, both for the men and women in the armed services and for employees in defense industries. By early 1998 there were somewhat less than 2 million personnel in the armed forces, another 900,000 civilian employees in the Department of Defense, and an additional 1 million people employed in defense industries.[55] There were some job losses in the 1990s in defense industries but concerns about terror and potential conflicts in the Gulf ratcheted defense employment back up by 2002.

Economically, the end of the Cold War arrived at a difficult time for the United States. Unemployment was already high without soldiers returning to the domestic labor force or workers in aircraft factories or tank factories being laid off. Even when the economy is better, defense cuts have a major impact on the politics of the defense budget. Most congressmen are in favor of reducing the budget in principle but are much less interested in the idea when it directly impacts their own districts. In an interesting Freudian slip, Senator Dianne Feinstein (D-Calif.) once argued that the B-2 bomber did not deliver a "big enough payroll." Thus, to a great extent, defense spending has been reconceptualized as a means of providing jobs, and as a (thinly) disguised industrial policy.[56] Also, the United States is a successful exporter of arms when it wants to be, so promoting defense industries may be one way to address our balance of payments problem.

In addition to general economic problems, downsizing the military may have other costs as well. For the military it may mean the loss of a great deal of talent, especially in the officer corps and in career nonenlisted personnel, that could be important for any future military activities. For the individuals who joined the all-volunteer military in the hope of a career, it may mean a huge adjustment of life plans and career prospects. Even for military personnel who remain in the service force, reductions can mean very slow promotions[57] and probably some career frustration.

One strategy the armed forces can use to ensure continued employment for its personnel and continued funding from Congress is to find new tasks on which to employ its capabilities. The most obvious opportunity for the use of the military is in the "war" on drugs. Obviously the rhetoric on the issue is already suited to use of the military, as some missions in that war may also be. There are, however, questions concerning the desirability of military involvement in this policy area. For example, do we want to use American military might to attack the drug problem in other countries, especially those in Latin America, which have many unpleasant memories of previous U.S. military expeditions? Finally, is the military really capable of doing the police work necessary to be effective in drug control? As right as such involvement may seem for supporting the military budget, it may be wrong for a variety of other reasons.

As noted, another occasional use of the military has been in peacekeeping. This is in some ways thinly disguised military action, with the hope that weapons do not actually have to be used. In other ways peacekeeping is police work, involving detection of violations of cease-fires or of agreed borders, or perhaps arresting alleged war criminals. This is difficult work, given that it is often dangerous and generally places the troops between two adversaries, neither of which may particularly want them to be there. Still, it is a crucial role in a dangerous world, still divided by numerous ethnic and national divisions, if no longer by the Cold War.

Making defense policy is exceedingly difficult. It involves planning for an uncertain future and dealing with adversaries whose strength and strategies are not readily predictable, as well as allies whose commitment to a common purpose and a common set of policies may be uncertain. Defense policy also involves making prospective decisions about weapons that may take years or even decades to develop and that may not perform as intended. Finally, defense involves huge costs that may be politically unpopular even when the public strongly supports a strong U.S. military posture. Defense policymaking is a series of gigantic gambles about the future, gambles that most of those involved hope never actually have to be taken.

Defense policy was the subject of intense and sustained political debate during the Reagan administration. Although Ronald Reagan came into office promising to modernize and strengthen America's armed forces and won reelection stressing the same themes, his ambitious program of military procurement and expansion came into conflict with an increasing federal deficit. After Reagan left office, some programs were delayed, while others were scaled back and a few eliminated. President George H.W. Bush's use of the military in the 1991 Gulf War renewed its confidence and its sense of mission, but even that success was not enough to save the military budget in an era of declining resources and declining threat. The Clinton administration came to office seeking to cut defense further but soon found both conventional military and more novel humanitarian tasks for the armed forces to perform. The position of military defense gained a renewed importance after 11 September 2001 and the promulgation of the Bush doctrine of a more pro-active American role in defending its interests.

Law Enforcement

Defense involves the use of force, or the threat of the use of force, outside the borders of the United States. Law enforcement involves the legitimate use of coercion within the borders of the country. Most of the policies we have talked about—taxation is a notable exception—confer benefits on citizens. Law enforcement tends to be directed at penalizing certain citizens, while at the same time providing significant benefits to other citizens. Policing traditionally has been a concern of state and local governments in the United States, but as with most other policy areas the federal government has begun to play a larger and larger role. This is true in terms of financial support for the subnational governments, as well as in the direct provision of police protection to the public.

Crime has been a very salient policy issue in the United States in the past several decades.[58] Politicians have competed with one another over who could be the toughest on crime; one presidential candidate, Michael Dukakis, suffered badly when he was perceived as being too soft on crime while governor of Massachusetts. Public concern about crime remained high even after crime rates declined significantly during the 1990s (see table 14.6). These declines—due to very good economic conditions, more effective policing (including "zero tolerance" in cities such as New York),[59] and demographic change[60]—reduced crime in the United States to levels not much greater than in Western Europe. The major exception to that generalization was murder, especially murder involving firearms. An uninformed observer, however, would not have known of that reduction either from political advertisements or from public opinion polls.

After almost a decade of decline, however, violent crime began to increase again in 2001, reflecting the confluence of several factors. One was the release from prison of large numbers of criminals who had been incarcerated in the early days of crackdowns in the early 1990s, few of whom had been rehabilitated by their time in prison. In addition, as the economy was cooling off, more people were turning to crime to make a living. Also, the FBI was in some disarray and federal law enforcement did not appear as credible as it once had.[61] This increase in crime seemed likely to make the public even more conscious of the impact of crime on their lives.

Federal Law Enforcement

The role of the federal government in police protection is not entirely new. Indeed, the first organization formed at the federal level—the U.S. Coast Guard—

Following the loss of hundreds of emergency personnel in the September 11 World Trade Center attacks, renewed attention and respect has been given to those who serve and protect. This wall in New York City's Battery Park honors those law enforcement officers fallen in the line of duty.

was established primarily to catch smugglers. Countless western movies and television programs have portrayed the role of the U.S. marshal as the principal peace officer in the territories of the American West before they gained statehood. In less dramatic settings federal marshals have been responsible for the implementation of the orders of federal courts. The military has also served this function in our history, especially when there is a threat of major violence or civil disorder. One notable example was President Eisenhower's use of federal troops to prevent violence when Central High School in Little Rock, Arkansas, was integrated in 1957.

Terrorism has strengthened the federal role in law enforcement, with the Patriot Act of 2002 providing the federal government new powers of search into previously privileged personal records and activities. Likewise, the federal government has become more central in coordination of state and local law enforcement efforts.

Perhaps the most familiar law enforcement organization in the federal government is the Federal Bureau of Investigation (FBI). A component of the Department of Justice, this organization is responsible for enforcing a number of federal laws, especially those against kidnapping and bank robbery. During the

TABLE 14.6 Crime Rates (crimes per 100,000 population) 1980–1999

	Violent crimes			Property crimes		
	Total	Murder	Assault	Total	Burglary	Car theft
1980	596.6	10.2	298.5	5,353.3	1,684.1	502.2
1985	556.6	7.9	302.9	4,650.5	1,287.3	462.0
1990	731.8	9.4	424.1	5,088.5	1,235.9	657.8
1992	757.5	9.3	441.8	4,902.7	1,168.2	631.5
1995	684.6	8.2	418.3	4,591.3	987.1	560.4
1997	611.3	6.8	382.3	4,318.7	919.4	506.0
1998	567.5	6.3	361.3	4,051.8	863.0	459.8
1999	524.7	5.7	336.1	3,742.1	770.0	420.7

Source: Federal Bureau of Investigation, *Crime in the United States* (Washington, D.C.: FBI, annual).

Cold War the FBI also had major responsibility for finding and apprehending foreign agents. That function continues, although now directed against the agents of different countries, and the agency's role has expanded in efforts to protect against terrorism, as in the flying of dozens of its agents to Africa to investigate the American embassy bombings in 1998. This organization gained a reputation for efficiency and incorruptibility during the many years in which J. Edgar Hoover was the director,[62] and although the Bureau's reputation has declined somewhat, it remains a very effective law enforcement organization.

In addition to the FBI, the Coast Guard, and federal marshals, a number of other law enforcement bodies exist within the federal government. The Secret Service, based in the Department of Homeland Security, is responsible both for protecting the safety of the president and the vice president and for catching counterfeiters of U.S. currency. Within the Justice Department, the Bureau of Alcohol, Tobacco, Firearms, and Explosives (ATF) is responsible for enforcing a variety of federal taxes and other laws having to do with the three commodities in its title.[63] The Drug Enforcement Administration (DEA) enforces federal laws concerning the sale and possession of illegal drugs. Postal inspectors are responsible for enforcing laws concerning the use of the mail for fraudulent or other illegal purposes. The Customs Bureau is responsible for enforcing laws about imports into the United States, including some aspects of drug laws and the protection of endangered species. Finally, the Bureau of Citizenship and Immigration Services and the Border Patrol are responsible for enforcing immigration laws. This is a rather long list of organizations for a government presumably having a minimal role in law enforcement.[64]

The federal government's role in law enforcement is predicated on several powers given to it in the Constitution. One of these is the power to tax; the activities of the ATF and Customs stem largely from that very basic power. Many of the FBI's concerns derive from the powers of the federal government to deal with issues that transcend state borders. For example, kidnapping became a federal concern after the kidnapping of the Lindbergh baby and the interstate flight of the criminal in the 1920s. The federal government also exercises its authority over interstate commerce to regulate the sale and distribution of certain drugs, with the DEA obviously deriving most of its powers from that source. Finally, the federal government's duty to protect its own officials and the value of its currency gives the Secret Service its constitutional justification.

Federal Support to State and Local Governments

In addition to providing police protection directly, the federal government supplies some support for state and local governments that bear the major burden of policing. The type and amount of this support has tended to vary across time, but there is some ongoing support for this important activity coming from Washington. Fighting crime is not usually a controversial issue, so politicians usually can feel safe in spending for this function even when there are pressures to reduce the size of the federal budget.

John DiIulio has argued that there have been two federal "wars on crime," with a third being initiated in the 1990s.[65] Echoing the founders of the programs, he claimed that the first was the War on Poverty, whose programs were an attack on the root causes of crime as well as of poverty. This war was also fought with a number of more direct weapons, such as the Omnibus Crime Control and Safe Streets Act of 1968, which provided substantial federal funding for local governments through the Law Enforcement Assistance Administration (LEAA)—more, in fact, than the entire Department of Justice budget in 1968.

The second federal "war on crime" opened a more direct attack on crime and criminals. This initiative, occurring during the Reagan administration, was spearheaded by the Comprehensive Crime Control Act of 1984 and the Anti-Drug Abuse Act of 1988. The LEAA was phased out, and with it much of the federal support for local law enforcement (other than for antidrug programs). This war focused instead on providing stiffer sentences for perpetuators of federal crimes and especially on the linkage between illegal drugs and other crimes.

As is discussed later in this chapter, the third "war" on crime contained some elements of the strategy of each of the two previous ones. Like DiIulio's first war, it provided a good deal of money for local law enforcement—presumably 100,000 more police officers were to be on the streets because of the 1994 Crime Control Bill. That bill also contained a strong element of crime prevention and social policy.[66] Like the second war, this latest effort focuses attention on federal crimes and federal law enforcement, specifying new death penalties for sixty federal crimes. Given public fears of crime in the mid-1990s, there was little question that the federal government should be taking an active role in fighting crime; the policy question was what form that assault should take.

Issues in Law Enforcement Policy

As in most policy areas, there are a number of enduring issues that help illustrate the complexity of law enforcement policy. It is sometimes easy to think that, because the government has long been in the business of enforcing laws and policing, the issues and approaches to solving them would be well established. This is not the case, however, in part because this policy area involves the intersection of a variety of issues—whose complexity is becoming more apparent all the time—as well as interactions with a number of other policy areas.

The Causes of Crime

The most fundamental issue is identifying the root causes of crime. On one side is the belief that crime results from the failure of society to enforce its values on people who do not share those values. The advocates of this position argue that the best and perhaps the only way to address problems of crime is to ensure that convicted criminals receive swift, sure, and even harsh punishment.[67] Further, supporters of this view complain that current programs of parole and pardon put criminals back onto the streets too quickly. For example, there has been a move in several states and at the federal level toward a "three strikes and you're out" approach to sentencing, whereby an individual convicted of three felonies must be imprisoned for life without the possibility of parole.[68]

The contrary position is that crime results from social and economic problems, including problems in family structure. From this perspective, the best and most efficient means of dealing with crime is to address those socioeconomic issues.[69] It is argued that instead of punishing the criminal after he or she has already decided to commit a criminal act, an emphasis on the social roots of crime instead would help to prevent crime. In addition to general programs for improving socioeconomic conditions, advocates have stressed the need for efforts to help parents learn how to raise their children without the violence that appears to breed additional violence.[70] Even some police forces have begun to think of their role as dealing with "problems" rather than clearing up crime "incidents."[71] Part of the Clinton administration's crime control program, for example, was to emphasize "community-oriented policing," which attempts to develop a more positive social fabric as well as enforcing the law.

The selection of one model of causation or another for crime in turn initiates a series of choices about how to spend public funds. If the punishment route

TABLE 14.7   Attitudes toward Punishment and Rehabilitation, 1971–1993 (in percentages)

"Is the primary task of prisons to punish criminals or rehabilitate them?"

	1971	*1976*	*1980*	*1989*	*1993*
Punish	15	21	32	38	61
Rehabilitate	76	65	53	48	25

Source: George Pettinico, "Crime and Punishment: America Changes Its Mind," *Public Perspective,* September 1994, 30–31.

is selected, government must spend a great deal of money for police protection and for prisons—it costs approximately $60,000 per year to keep a prisoner in state prison[72] (nearly double the cost of sending a student to a private university for a year).[73] In contrast, focusing on the social roots of crime requires a good deal of expenditure on education, social services, family support, and other similar programs, as well as on rehabilitative services for prisoners already in jail.

Neither policy choice is without its costs and benefits, and the choice itself involves fundamental value decisions. Some of these values will be expressed by professional policy analysts and policymakers. Like education, however, crime and punishment are issues about which the average American is likely to have an opinion, as can be seen in the responses to polls about the basic purpose of prisons (see table 14.7). The American public has tended to agree that criminals can be rehabilitated and deserve a second chance, but a spate of violent crime in the 1990s reversed that opinion dramatically, and now most Americans seem to be seeking retribution rather than rehabilitation in the prison system. Likewise, states are passing legislation removing educational and recreational facilities from prisons, simply as a means of punishing prisoners as harshly as possible.[74]

Gun Control

Many citizens now identify violent crime as the most important problem in their lives. Probably the major instrument of that violence is the firearm. There are an estimated 60 million handguns in the United States, and millions of other firearms, including semiautomatic assault weapons, are in the hands of private citizens. The Second Amendment to the Constitution gives citizens the "right to bear arms," although that right is phrased in the context of the need for a militia.[75] The advocates of gun control point to the number of murders by handguns each year (approximately 7,500 in 1999—well over half the total number of murders[76]) to argue for their control, especially the cheap "Saturday Night Specials" that are bought and used in the heat of the moment. Opponents of gun control counter that criminals will always find a way to get guns and that law-abiding citizens need some means of protecting themselves, their families, and their property.

State and local governments have begun to regulate the ownership and sale of firearms. Nearly all large local governments require that handguns be registered. Some also require a waiting period between application for purchase of a handgun and the delivery of the weapon, in order to give the police time to check on the reliability of the purchaser. Further, the federal government has regulated automatic weapons and other especially dangerous weapons since the days of Prohibition and the fight against gangsters. More recently, it began to regulate sales of weapons through the mail, and in 1993 Congress passed the "Brady bill," which imposed a federal requirement for a five-day waiting period between application for a handgun and its delivery.[77] The states have their own laws on gun sales, making firearms more available in some states than in others, although guns are often purchased in one state and then used in another.

It is clear that there is no absolute right for a citizen to own any type of gun he or she wants, or to get it anytime he or she wants; the question is what sort of restrictions are permissible under the Constitution—and politically possible. The National Rifle Association (NRA) has developed into an active, well-financed, and usually successful lobbying organization that is dedicated to opposing gun control. The passage of the Brady bill was seen by some as a signal of the declining influence of the NRA,[78] however, and that power appeared to wane even further when its lobbyists were ultimately unsuccessful in removing the ban on assault weapons from the 1994 Clinton crime bill (see pp. 424–426). As attorney general of the United States, John Ashcroft has been more favorable to the gun lobby than previous holders of that office and the pressure on limiting all types of firearms sales has been reduced.

Despite lobbying by the National Rifle Association, gun control tends to be popular among the American populace. For example, in a poll taken in late 1993, some 87 percent of Americans (and 79 percent of gun owners) favored the Brady bill, while 77 percent of respondents (66 percent of gun owners) favored a ban on cheap handguns and 72 percent a ban on all handguns. The only question for which there was not majority support was an absolute ban on guns, although 39 percent of respondents did favor a measure of that sort.[79] There has been little change in public opinion since that time, despite NRA efforts to improve its image by sponsoring more programs for children and choosing actor Charlton Heston as its head and spokesman in a number of political advertisements.

The Death Penalty

Related to the question of punishment of criminals is whether government should impose the ultimate sanction, the death penalty. In general, Americans answer yes to that question, which leads to the subsidiary question, under what circumstances it should be imposed. Thirty-seven states now have prisoners under a sentence of death; some, such as Florida and Texas, apply the death penalty vigorously, while in other states the penalty is rarely imposed. The federal government also enforces the death penalty for certain federal crimes, the number of which was increased dramatically in the 1994 crime bill. The increase in the use of the death penalty appears to suit most Americans: 72 percent of respondents favored the death penalty in a 1993 survey.[80] The 1997 execution in Texas of a woman who appeared to have reformed significantly since committing her crime produced some doubts about the practice, but the public continues to support the ultimate penalty for many major crimes.

The arguments centered on this issue are practical, constitutional, and moral.[81] The practical questions revolve around the question of whether the death penalty is really an effective deterrent to violent crime. Advocates believe that it is, although some of the states with the highest murder rates are also among those that impose the penalty most readily. Proponents also contend that it is a certain deterrent in preventing the criminal in question from committing any more crimes. Opponents of the death penalty argue that it is not really a deterrent, and that most of the acts for which it is now imposed are more the product of the passion of the moment than calculated choices by the perpetrators. The opponents also point out that the legal work now required to implement the penalty is very often monumental and often costs a government more than might be spent in keeping the convicted criminal in jail for life. Also, the number of errors in convictions uncovered in 2001 and 2002, using DNA evidence in particular, have led some states such as Illinois to suspend the death penalty and to review all cases.

The constitutional questions revolve around the issue of whether the Eighth Amendment to the Constitution, which outlaws "cruel and unusual punishment," does in practice prohibit the death penalty. Supporters of the penalty argue that when this amendment was written, the death penalty was used widely, so that it could not be considered *unusual*—this term, they claim, referred instead to practices such as torture. The opponents of the death penalty, on the other hand, argue that it is indeed *cruel*, under contemporary interpretations of that word. For several decades the Supreme Court tended to side with the opponents and in effect outlawed the execution of prisoners.[82] The Court, however, reversed its stand in 1976 and began to permit the use of the penalty in certain defined situations. In 2002 the Court ruled, in *Adkins v. Virginia*, that executing retarded criminals constituted "cruel and unusual" punishment, and battles to determine the limits of action in this area continued.[83]

A second constitutional question concerning the death penalty is whether the act as currently administered violates the "equal protection" clause of the

Fourteenth Amendment. Opponents of capital punishment argue that African Americans and other minorities are much more likely to be put to death than are whites, even when they have committed roughly comparable crimes.[84] They also point to a pronounced economic bias in the imposition of the penalty, for poor defendants often have difficulty in securing adequate legal counsel to prevent their being sentenced to death.[85] Supporters of the death penalty argue, however, that more violent crimes are committed per capita by members of minority groups and that the differential rate of executions merely reflects an unfortunate social reality.

Finally, there is a moral question about the use of the power of the state to put people to death. Critics of the death penalty argue that this practice makes government and society little better than the criminals that they are punishing and that the finality of the sentence runs the risk of executing innocent people who then have no meaningful recourse. As with decision theory, the probability (even if small) that the decision to execute is incorrect will produce social costs that may be greater than any benefits created. The supporters of the death penalty recognize the severity of the punishment, and few if any take the imposition of the death penalty lightly, but they argue that individuals who commit extremely brutal crimes and crimes involving certain types of victims (children, for example) have forfeited their right to live in a civilized society.

The debate over the death penalty continues. Supporters hailed the inclusion of a large number of new death penalties in the Clinton crime bill and the Supreme Court's decision to reduce the capacity of convicts on death row to receive stays of their sentences.[86] Opponents of capital punishment were buoyed when Justice Harry Blackmun, near retirement, wrote a dissenting opinion saying that he would no longer take part in any decisions to execute prisoners, despite the fact that he had voted a number of times previously to permit states to impose the death penalty.[87] This statement by a respected justice did cause some reassessment, but there have been no shifts in the legality or use of this punishment.

The Rights of the Accused

In addition to protections against cruel and unusual punishment, the Bill of Rights grants a number of protections to the accused. For example, the accused are protected against self-incrimination (Fifth Amendment) and against unlawful search and seizure of their persons and property (Fourth Amendment). They are assured a trial by a jury of their peers, and they are guaranteed that the writ of habeas corpus is available to them so that they will know why they are being arrested and so that they cannot be held for long periods of time without some formal charge being filed against them (Article I, section 9). Finally, accused citizens have a right to legal counsel when they go to court (and now as soon as they are arrested).

This is an impressive list of protections. In fact, some critics believe that the list is too long and that the police are being "handcuffed" in their attempts to arrest and convict criminals. This feeling has become all the more pronounced over the past several decades as the courts have tended to interpret the rights of the accused more broadly and to require the police to be more careful in how they treat the accused. For example, when arrested, a suspect must now be advised of his or her legal rights, including the right to counsel.[88] Also, the courts have tended to interpret the protections against unreasonable search more strictly, so that the police must have sound reasons to obtain a search warrant, and even stronger justification if they search without first receiving a warrant. (Still, in the media event that was the O.J. Simpson trial, the judge admitted some crucial evidence gathered before a search warrant had been issued because it was discovered incidental to other proper police activities.)[89] All these protections for the accused have produced a number of cries that too many criminals are able to escape conviction on mere "technicalities."

The defenders of the current restrictions on police behavior contend that civil liberties are more than "technicalities," they are fundamental to the nature of the American political system and the judicial process. They argue that if police and prosecutors cannot make sustainable cases against defendants within these restrictions, they are not doing their jobs properly. Further, they point out that the police now have a number of powerful scientific tools, such as DNA testing, that should enable them to gain convictions without having to resort to more suspect means of investigation. These defenders, in fact, would be willing to trade off a few convictions in order to ensure that the fundamental civil liberties of all Americans were protected. Concerns about terrorism have placed civil liberties under greater strain in the United States, with some prisoners being detained without even being identified and domestic surveillance being increased.

Associated with the perceived difficulties in prosecuting accused criminals is the issue of pardon and parole. Newspapers often feature accounts of paroled convicts committing major crimes, sometimes within days of having been released from prison. On the other hand, the possibility of parole is often a motivating factor for cooperation by prisoners in what could otherwise be extremely dangerous settings.[90] In addition, prisons in most states are filled to capacity— the United States has the highest rate of per capita incarceration of any industrial democracy. Without the option for early release, even more prisons would have to be built, imposing further demands on state and local resources. As with most policy problems, there is no quick and easy answer.

Youth Crime

A final issue in law enforcement became more evident in the late 1990s—the problem of violent crimes committed by children. A number of cases involving children taking guns to school and attacking their classmates and teachers in 1997 and 1998 produced real feelings of shock and made the public highly aware of this issue, although the evidence is that there has always been a much higher rate of crime than is usually realized.[91] The continuing spate of violent crimes by children and teenagers, including one of the Washington snipers in 2002, has kept this issue at the center of the debate on criminal justice.

In light of the earlier discussion of gun control, it is important to note that all of these notorious incidents of juvenile violence involved guns. This in turn led to calls for requirements for locking all guns so that they cannot be accessed by children or others who may want to use them unwisely. Not surprisingly, this proposal has been opposed by the National Rifle Association and other pro-gun groups. Another question raised by these killings was how to treat crimes committed by the young. Should they be prosecuted in the same manner as any other crime, or should they, as is true in almost all instances, be subject to separate legal standards? Two boys who killed four people in Arkansas, for example, can only be kept in jail (or other institutions) until they reach the age of twenty-one.

The Clinton Crime Bill

Given the degree of public concern about crime, and particularly violent crime, the Clinton administration developed and advocated a major federal crime bill in 1994. The nature of this bill and the politics that surrounded it illustrate a number of points we have been making about the policy process in the United States. The first point has to do with the social and political construction of the issue of crime.[92] While the majority of the efforts and money mandated in the Clinton bill were dedicated to direct law enforcement, the legislation also contained some recognition of the socioeconomic roots of crime. Approximately one-third of the expenditures called for in the original draft were to go for social and educational programs designed to prevent crime—especially among the young. These proposed expenditures, however, permitted opponents of the bill to describe it as a social welfare program rather than a "tough" anticrime bill,[93] and they were able eventually to force some reductions in social spending.

A second point is that the crime bill was designed to provide state, and especially local, governments with large amounts of new money for hiring additional police and for a number of other purposes. Critics of the bill characterized these provisions as "pork-barrel legislation" rather than an attempt to address the fundamental problems of crime.[94] The bill did require a distribution of benefits, with a large proportion of spending—perhaps larger than might be justified by their relative rates of violent crime—going to rural and suburban communities rather than to the large central cities. That windfall for their constituents did not stop conservative critics from rural areas from arguing that the bill really was no more than a subsidy for the cities.

A third point about the Clinton bill is that it tended to anger a range of groups in the society. As finally written, the bill offended many members of minority groups, as well as the congressmen who represented them. One of the original drafts of the bill had contained a strong racial justice provision that would have addressed perceived disparities in sentencing, especially in the use of the death penalty, between white and nonwhite criminals.[95] The negotiations over the final version of the law deleted these provisions, causing several potential supporters to abandon the bill, although the leadership of the Congressional Black Caucus maintained its support. On the other side of the ideological spectrum, the National Rifle Association lobbied extremely hard against the bill because it contained provisions banning the sale of certain types of weapons, mostly semiautomatic assault rifles. As noted earlier, this once omnipotent interest group had recently lost a major battle over the Brady bill and felt that it could not lose another.

A final point is that the Clinton crime bill illustrates the tendency of problems to float upward in a federal system, despite the construction of the Constitution reserving powers to the states. The crime bill gave the federal government a role in investigating a number of crimes, especially domestic violence, that previously had been the almost exclusive preserve of state and local governments. In part, it was good politics for federal legislators to be seen as concerned about the rising crime rate, so they agreed to intervene. Further, the perception that the federal government has more resources than the other levels of government to "solve" these problems has tended to push the problems upward.

Given all the objections, the bill could not be passed as first proposed, and that failure illustrates another very important point about the process of legitimating public policies. The bill's critics appeared to fix their attention on the one or two features they could not support, rather than on those they might have approved. Adopting legislation almost invariably involves making compromises, and the failure to do so may be a major barrier to effective governmental action. This is perhaps especially true in the United States, given the inherent tendency of the system toward gridlock.[96] In the end, an acceptable compromise was forged so that the bill could finally be passed by Congress and signed by the president.

The legislation that was passed still contained a mixture of punishment and prevention.[97] Of the $30.2 billion allocated over six years, the bulk of the money went to hiring local police officers ($8.8 billion), building prisons ($7.9 billion), the incarceration of criminal aliens ($1.8 billion), and other programs directed at catching and punishing criminals ($4.8 billion). After cuts, there was still $6.9 billion for prevention programs such as fighting violence against women ($1.6 billion), noncriminal "drug courts" ($1 billion), and recreation opportunities for inner-city children ($562 million).[98] The bill also had a number of regulatory features, the most important being outlawing the sale of nineteen kinds of assault rifles and gun clips holding more than ten bullets, extending the federal death penalty, and allowing adult treatment of thirteen-year-olds charged with major crimes.

Whether as a result of the Clinton crime bill or not, substantial reductions in crime (especially violent crimes) soon made it appear that crime was becoming less of a problem for American society than it had been. This meant politically that candidates would find it more difficult to play the crime card, which had been especially useful for conservative politicians, and that some money might be saved from policing and from jailing convicted criminals. Open questions remained about whether this reduction in crime could survive either welfare reform, with its potential for creating more poverty, or, indeed, any economic downturn of consequence. In the short term, however, there did appear to be some good news in this policy area.

Conclusion

We have been discussing the ways in which governments in the United States attempt to protect their citizens from "enemies, domestic and foreign." This is one of the defining duties of any government,[99] and it is one in which governments have been engaged since their inception. The issues involved in this policy area have, however, become more complex in recent years. First, in defense, there is no longer a clearly identifiable enemy against which to plot strategy. Instead, the task is one of preparing for a wide range of different threats to national security, including some for which the military is not particularly well adapted. Further, there are demands for the use of military for a range of purposes that go well beyond conventional national defense and require it to fulfill virtually a social mission on the international scene. Finally, domestic social and political concerns have invaded the world of the armed forces, requiring some rethinking of the values and mores of that world.

Crime is an equally complex policy and political problem. It is perhaps even more complex than defense, given that the United States attempts to combat crime while maintaining an open and free society. Police measures that might be effective in curtailing the growth of crime are simply not possible if the tradition of the open society is to be maintained. Even without the complications of civil liberties, there would be other difficulties for a government attempting to solve a serious crime problem, not least of which is understanding the root causes of this social pathology and therefore the best means of addressing the problem.

CHAPTER 15

Culture Wars in American Politics: Regulating Social Life

THE AMERICAN REPUBLIC was founded with a conception of separation of church and state enshrined in the first amendment to the Constitution. Despite the attempt to create a secular republic, issues having strong moral or religious dimensions—slavery, civil rights, peace in Vietnam—have become defining political issues. During the past several decades, politics has again injected intense moral and religious conflicts into the heart of policy process.[1] Issues such as abortion, school prayer, stem-cell research, human cloning, and equal treatment of same-sex partnerships are all prominent on the political agenda. And even when American government is not actively engaged in making decisions on these matters, they nevertheless figure as litmus tests for candidates for office at all levels of government. The conflicts over these issues have been described as "culture wars," given that they tend to divide citizens sharply on the basis of religious, social, and culturally based conceptions of right and wrong.

Before proceeding to discuss some of these conflicts in more detail, we should recognize some general characteristics of these issues that have (often profound) political consequences. Although these moral concerns raise a range of constitutional questions, they do have some characteristics in common. Unfortunately, most of those shared characteristics are what make these issues difficult for the political process to handle effectively, in ways that will satisfy the participants in the process. All political problems divide people, but the fissures created by these moral issues are deeper and more difficult to contain within the civil and constrained discourse of the conventional political process. The term *culture wars* is indeed apt, given the intensity with which those involved are likely to approach the conflict between fundamentally different notions of what is acceptable or appropriate in society.

The most obvious point about these issues is that they tend to be nonbargainable for the participants. Most issues that arise in government are resolved through a process of bargaining and compromise, with each side gaining something and each side having to accept some losses. These moral issues, however, are nonbargainable for two reasons. The first is simply that they are conceived of as fundamental questions of right and wrong: abortion is either an appropriate means of limiting fertility or it is a sin, and there is little ground for compromise. Further, the claims for right and wrong in the case of abortion and many other such issues are based on different moral foundations. For "right to lifers," abortion is primarily a religious issue, while "pro-choice" advocates approach the issue as the woman's human right to choose about how her own body is to be used. These groups have a great deal to scream about but little to talk about.

The difficulty of finding a middle ground on this type of issue was well illustrated by President George W. Bush's decision to permit limited federal funding for research on embryonic stem cells.[2] This was an attempt to compromise by allowing federal support for research on existing "lines" of stem cells, while prohibiting funding for creating or doing research on any new lines.[3] The president's decision angered religious conservatives, who regard any stem-cell research as using human beings for research purposes and as potentially encouraging abortions as the means of obtaining those cells. On the other side, many scientists believed that this decision did not provide enough freedom for them to pursue the research needed to find potential cures for Alzheimer's, Parkinson's, and other major diseases. These scientists also implied that the decision demonstrated, at least to their minds, a greater commitment to religious than to scientific values, and at least a few top medical researchers then went to Europe, where they felt the climate for research on stem cells was less restrictive. Thus the president's attempt to create a Solomonic compromise was not acceptable to the strong advocates on either side of the issue, while perhaps the only factor preventing an even greater political uproar was the difficulty that the average citizen encountered in attempting to understand the scientific and moral issues involved in this area of medical research.[4] Bush then sought to defuse some of the conflict over stem-cell research and related issues by appointing an expert bioethics panel, but that may only have delayed resolution of the fundamental conflicts involved.[5]

The second reason for the inutility of bargaining over such moral issues is that most such issues are not amenable to solution through the application of money. No amount of funding provided for sex education, or adoption, or any other alternative to abortion will make the continuation of those procedures acceptable in the eyes of the opponents. No amount of money spent on support for benefits for same-sex partners—no matter how desirable that may otherwise be—will make up for an absence of legal recognition for same-sex marriages in the eyes of proponents.[6] In short, although money is the standard lubricant in the political process, it is not likely to be effective in ameliorating conflicts based on fundamental moral and ethical disagreements over these highly charged issues. Indeed, even the suggestion of a monetary response may be considered insulting or demeaning by activists in these policy areas.

The futility of monetary solutions to these policy problems underscores their nonutilitarian nature. Most policy disputes are framed primarily on pragmatic, utilitarian principles—will the program in question work, and will society be better off (usually measured in economic terms) if it does work?[7] The moral issues we are discussing here, however, are more often framed in terms of absolute values. It is not likely to matter to the parties involved whether the society would be better off economically, if fundamental moral precepts were to be violated in order to achieve that utilitarian benefit. In this corner of the policy world, the ends most definitely do not justify the means.

Another common characteristic of these policies is that their politics is often carried on as intensively outside formal institutions as within them, which opens wider the potential for extremists to become activated by the intensity of the arguments in the policy area. This characteristic has been most evident in the continuing abortion controversy, but it has also figured in debates over homosexual rights and was clearly manifested during the early civil rights struggles. Despite the abundant legislation—and even more attempted legislation—on abortion, the majority of the debate appears to have taken place in the streets. Indeed, the extremists have gone so far as to use guns and bombs in attempts to enforce what they believe to be the correct moral choice and to punish their enemies. For a country in which politics has been largely nonideological and in general rather tame, this militant style of political behavior is both unexpected and more difficult to accept than it might be in other countries.

Further, the politics generated by these moral issues often involves constitutional disputes that must be decided in the courts, rather than through legislation. This characteristic has been evident for abortion (*Roe v. Wade*) and for school prayer (*Engel v. Vitale*), on which the principal contemporary debates have been sparked by court cases rather than by acts of Congress or state legislatures. Ever since the Supreme Court ruled that school prayer violated the separation of church and state, proponents of the practice have been attempting to find a formulation—silent prayer, a moment of silence, voluntary prayer—that could permit religious activity while still passing constitutional muster. Even if one or more of these watered-down options is eventually found acceptable by the courts (see below), such compromise is unlikely to please committed advocates of prayer, who will still want to make conventional religious observance a part of the school day. Similarly, there have been any number of legislative attempts to restrict access to abortion services, but the courts have been the final arbiters of what is constitutional and what is not.

The three public policy areas to be discussed in this chapter vividly illustrate the set of common characteristics we have identified for moral issues in politics. Among the most contentious issues in American politics, these policy areas have been fought over by activists who are willing to go to jail, and even to kill those with whom they disagree, because of their strong commitment to the principles involved. The issues vary in the intensity with which they have been contested in the streets, in the courts, and in legislative bodies, but all provoke reactions that surpass those typically expressed in response to matters of policy. Further, governments and the courts have made decisions about these issues that have served as merely temporary truces in the continuing battles over values, as the losers in any one decision are unwilling to accept it as final and so continue to soldier on in the culture war.

Abortion and Reproductive Rights

If any issue best illustrates the points made earlier about moral and cultural politics, it is abortion. In 1972 a woman, who was referred to as Jane Roe in legal documents in order to preserve her privacy and anonymity, sought to have an abortion that did not meet the current legal criteria for the procedure in Texas. At that time in Texas the only possible condition acceptable in law was to preserve the life of the mother, but other states permitted terminations under these conditions: (a) that it endangered the life or health (including mental health) of the woman; (b) that it was likely to result in a severely deformed infant; or (c) that it was the consequence of rape or incest. When the *Roe* case finally reached the Supreme Court, the Court ruled in 1973 that, based on the right of privacy, a woman had a constitutionally protected right to terminate a pregnancy within the first trimester, regardless of the reason or possible consequences of the pregnancy.[8]

Abortion had been illegal in most of the United States for some years, although it was not criminalized until the mid-nineteenth century—therapeutic abortions, albeit often extremely unsafe, were common in the early days of the United States, as they were in Europe at that time.[9] During the American equivalent of the Victorian period in Britain, individual states began to enact legislation limiting abortion and making anyone performing this procedure, and sometimes the woman herself, subject to severe criminal penalties. As a consequence of those laws, although an unknown number of abortions apparently were performed, almost all were done by untrained individuals in settings less than ideal for the health of the woman involved. The result was often death or severe illness, although the illegality of the procedure meant that any accurate enumeration of abortions was unavailable.

In part because abortion had been illegal not just in most of the United States but almost universally until the decision in 1973, the religious basis of the laws adopted by the states was not manifest. Indeed, religious groups do not appear to have been directly involved in the criminalization of abortion in the nineteenth century. However, following the familiar political dictum that major policy decisions motivate the losers, the Supreme Court decisions in *Roe v. Wade* and *Doe v. Bolton* activated the Roman Catholic Church and other elements of the religious right, injecting them into American politics to a degree that had rarely been seen previously.[10]   Likewise, prior to the time at which the two women in question brought their cases through the court system, there had been relatively little political mobilization around the abortion issue, even among feminists and other elements of the women's movement. Once the Court had acted, however, activist groups on both sides of the issue, but particularly on the anti-abortion side, sprang to battle on all political fronts.

It is important to note that the decisions rendered by the Court in *Roe* and *Doe* had little or no basis in the establishment clause of the First Amendment, as might have been expected. Instead, the decisions were based directly on the (implied) right of privacy of the woman not to have government intervene in her personal, reproductive life. This argument, which is essentially individualistic in its import, might have been thought to please conservatives, but the result was actually the opposite. Abortion politics brought together a wide range of activists on the political right to defend what they considered traditional moral and religious values. The coalition of religious groups cut across conventional political and denominational lines, bringing together Roman Catholics, Orthodox Jews, fundamentalist Protestants, and Mormons, among others. Abortion was not only (in the view of most of these groups) murder, it was also a threat to "family values" as they defined them.

As well as being a rallying cry for the religious (and less religious) right, abortion rights have been, and continue to be, a touchstone issue for women's political organizations and their supporters, as well as for civil libertarians. In *Roe* the Supreme Court created what was in essence a new right for women, and many (if not most—see table 15.1, p. 432) are loath to relinquish that right. Further, as more time passes, fewer and fewer women who are active politically can remember a time when they did not have the "right" to a legal, safe abortion should they desire one. The argument of most pro-choice groups is that although abortion is far from the preferred option for controlling fertility, it is one that they want and demand to have available if required.

The Rhetoric of Abortion Politics

The nature of the rhetoric surrounding this issue, as should be evident from the discussion above, serves to illustrate some of the points made earlier about issues of this type. Each side in the controversy tends to employ arguments and ter-

TABLE 15.1   Public Attitudes to Abortion, 1996–2002 (in percentages)

	Always legal	*"Abortion should be . . ."* Legal under some circumstances	Never legal	No opinion
February 2002	26	54	18	2
March 2001	26	51	18	5
January 2000	26	56	15	3
January 1998	23	59	17	1
July 1996	25	58	15	2

Source: CNN/*USA Today* polls.

minology that are dear to the hearts of their supporters but that tend to demonize and alienate the opposition. At times, the extremist rhetoric and graphic symbols used may alienate even some moderates, but ideological purity tends to be more important than coalition building in this policy area. As one analyst of the contemporary political scene has called it, this debate over abortion rights has no neutral ground.[11]

Even the naming of the opposing sides in the debate is calculated to create political advantage and to emphasize the values that the advocates are attempting to promote. On one side, the opponents of abortion use the term *pro-life* to describe their movement. It is difficult to be against life, although this term begs the question of when life begins, but these activists claim that they are favoring life while their opponents are sending thousands of innocent "children" to their deaths. This rhetorical frame has created a powerful argument for the opponents of abortion, but the attempt to illustrate it by the use of graphic pictures of fetuses has lessened the appeal to the less committed.

On the other side of the debate, the defenders of the woman's right to a legal abortion define their position as being *pro-choice.* Although this term does not carry the emotional appeal of supporting life, in a democratic society the notion that individuals should have the ability to make their own choices is a powerful political argument. Again, activists on this side of the debate do not advocate abortion as a positive or desirable action but as an option that should be available if a woman deems it necessary. Further, the principle at the center of this side's arguments is that the choice should be made by the woman herself, rather than by a doctor or by a public authority of any sort.

Political and Policy Reactions to Roe and Doe

Almost as soon as the Supreme Court announced its decisions legalizing abortion, governments, as well as the foes of abortion, began to find ways to circumvent what appeared to be a sweeping acceptance of abortion rights. Religious and political foes of these rulings engaged in a variety of direct political and social actions, including blockading clinics and even hospitals providing abortion services. In reaction to that direct action by anti-abortion forces, leaders of the pro-choice movement then developed programs to escort women wanting to go to those facilities through the gauntlets of protestors, and in some cases they also were able to get police protection for the clients of the clinics.

Not only was there direct political mobilization around the abortion issue, but interest groups also began to mobilize in order to support, and especially to oppose, freely available abortion services. The early supporters of abortion rights were women's organizations such as the National Organization for Women (NOW), but after the increased politicization of the issue, more narrowly focused organizations such as the National Abortion and Reproductive Rights Action League, or NARAL (now NARAL Pro-Choice America), were formed to protect the rights that had been secured through the court decisions. On the other side of the political conflict, interest groups and religious organizations have been mobilized to attempt to reverse *Roe*, and they have focused on an annual event at the National Mall and at the Supreme Court building that has brought out thousands of abortion opponents.

Abortion politics demonstrate the capacity of intense political mobilization to shape policies. When asked in public opinion polls, the majority of Americans (and a large majority of women) favor preserving a woman's right to seek an abortion in some or all cases. In 2000 only 19 percent of Americans would ban abortions entirely, and another 20 percent would permit them only in cases of threat to the mother's life. Thus, the majority of Americans would permit abortions in a relatively wide range of cases, yet the majority of legislatures have passed laws that would severely restrict access. Also, in 2003 Congress passed a federal ban on "partial-birth" abortions. The Christian Coalition, the Roman Catholic Church, and their allies have been able to influence legislatures to make policies that do not correspond closely to public opinion on the issue.

Abortion law has been made primarily at the state level in the United States. The major court decisions brought the federal government more into the policy area—by striking down state laws that were deemed unconstitutional—but they did not by any means end the dominant state role. Since the time of *Roe* and *Doe,* state legislatures have generated a large number of policy responses, most being attempts to prevent abortions through means other than direct prohibition, such as restricting availability of the procedure without directly confronting the rulings of the Court. A common strategy has been to require women below a certain age to obtain the consent of one or both parents or guardians before having an abortion.[12] The courts, however, have tended to disallow such blanket requirements again in the interest of privacy and have required the states to provide alternative mechanisms for approval, usually through the judicial system (*Bellotti v. Baird*, 1976; *Hodgson v. Minnesota*, 1990). Likewise, a number of states have adopted provisions requiring the woman's male partner to consent to an abortion, but these restrictions have also been disallowed by the courts.

Another regulatory strategy has been to impose waiting periods and detailed reporting requirements on hospitals and doctors. The logic of this approach seems to be that the trouble of having to come to a hospital or center twice may persuade a woman to abandon the attempt, or that it may offer abortion opponents the chance to identify women seeking the procedure so as to attempt to dissuade them. The courts, however, have tended to throw out restrictions imposed upon abortions and abortion providers without clear medical reasons to justify them and to negate specific medical requirements imposed by legislation.

The control of public spending has been a major means by which governments have attempted to discourage abortion. In general, this policy instrument has been more successful than have the regulatory instruments described above.[13] At the federal level, the Hyde Amendment to the appropriations bill for Labor and Health, Education and Welfare in 1976 (named after Illinois Republican Rep. Henry Hyde) prohibits the use of federal funds for abortions. At the state level, public hospitals have been prohibited in many states from performing abortions except in the most extreme cases.

On the other side of the controversy, there have been some legislative and administrative attempts to defend women's access to abortion services. For example, the courts have upheld the use of antiracketeering legislation to punish conspiracies directed at using violence against abortion providers. Also, Congress has passed legislation—the Freedom of Access to Clinic Entrances Act (FACE)—that attempts to protect women from harassment when they go to an abortion clinic and also provides some protection to the abortion providers. This legislation was designed to limit the use of physical intimidation by abortion opponents, and it has been deemed constitutional by the Court, in part because it protects individuals and organizations engaged in interstate commerce.[14]

Finally, both pro-choice and pro-life groups have been active in scrutinizing judicial appointees and in placing pressure on the president and governors to appoint judges who will conform to the groups' preferred policies on the issue. The pro-life groups, who want abortion to be the litmus test for appointees to public office, were very active in the early days of the administration of George W. Bush, hoping to ensure that another "stealth" pro-choice justice not be appointed to the Supreme Court, as had occurred during the administration of his father.[15] The pro-choice groups also have been active in scrutinizing candidates, but they have not been so vociferous in promoting this single criterion for judging prospective judicial appointees.

Gay Rights: Politics Comes Out of the Closet

Abortion policy has been conceptualized by pro-choice groups as an issue that affects all women, even if only a very small number of women may actually have the need or the desire to utilize this procedure for controlling fertility. The issue of the rights of gay and lesbian citizens likewise affects, directly or indirectly, all members of those groups, who nevertheless constitute a relatively small segment of the American population. Political mobilization around the issue of rights and protections for homosexuals grew most rapidly during the 1980s and 1990s, although the event usually cited as the movement's beginning point was the Stonewall riots in New York in 1969, directed against police harassment of a gay bar by that name. By 1993 the movement could muster 300,000 supporters for a march in Washington.[16]

Perhaps even more so than abortion, homosexuality historically and traditionally has been suppressed by law and custom in most societies. Western societies had, and continue to have in some cases, laws that punish homosexual activities rather severely. The social stigma has been at least as powerful, with gay people bearing the brunt of jokes, exclusion, and violence. Thus, most members of the homosexual community opted to stay "in the closet" and to deny publicly their sexual preference. For much of history, keeping that sexual preference secret was a wise strategy, given that openly admitting it might well involve loss of employment, social ostracism, and even personal violence.

The politics surrounding gay and lesbian issues is about identity as well as rights. One important motivation for this political mobilization is to claim the right of individuals with sexual preferences different from those of the majority of the population to be treated as the equals of the majority. Slogans such as "Gay Pride" have been used to rally supporters and to create a greater sense of belonging within the homosexual community. The idea of such political rhetoric is that not only is it acceptable to be gay, but it also has become a source of pride and activism for many members of the community. In response, the opposition has attempted to deny the appropriateness of that pride, and even that identity, and to drive the gay movement and its members back into the closet.

The coalition that has opposed gay rights is rather similar to that which has opposed abortion rights for women. In this case, however, the Roman Catholic Church is not so prominent as it has been in the abortion battle, leaving conservative, fundamentalist Protestants to lead the fight instead. While the Catholic church has hardly been supportive of gay and lesbian rights, its condemnation of homosexuality has not been so overt despite denying homosexuals the opportunity to be priests.[17] The political opposition to gay rights has argued that these groups are seeking special rights and special protections for which there is no constitutional basis. At the extreme, these opponents also insist that gay rights groups' demands for recognition and acceptance are undermining the moral standards of the country[18] and are opposed to "family values"—a phrase that has to some extent become a code name for conservative, fundamentalist conceptions of morality.

Members of gay and lesbian groups, on the other hand, regard their political activity as simply demanding the right to equal treatment. For example, when claiming employee benefits for same-sex partners, gays and lesbians argue that all they want is to have their relationships be treated like any other stable partnerships, qualifying them for the same legal and financial benefits that are routinely extended to heterosexual married couples. The opposition forces, again often basing their arguments on traditional religious values, characterize these claims as something more.[19] They argue, for example, that employee benefit packages are intended for married couples only, and that in many cases unmarried heterosexual couples are not eligible, even if they are in stable relationships.

The conflict over the status and rights of the gay population has not been extended as broadly throughout the political community as has that over abortion rights. Some interest groups have been formed, and some lobbying and other attempts to influence policy have been initiated. Rather than a collection of interest groups, however, mobilization of the gay community initially assumed the form of a social movement, whose approach was less one of direct contact with government and bargaining over specific policies than of attempting to raise the issues of concern to the group through broader public appeal and to create solidarity among the members of the movement.

Again, the battle is often joined not so much in the legislative arena as in the courts. In particular, legal cases have been filed to prevent landlords from discriminating in housing and employers from dismissing workers simply on the basis of their sexual orientation. While not as visible as *Roe v. Wade*, these cases are as important to the members of the gay community—as well as to their opponents.

Gay Rights and Public Policy

Gay rights is in itself an important public policy issue with strong elements of civil rights and equality involved in it. However, the political mobilization of the gay community has also raised a number of more immediate policy issues, some of which have had impact only on the homosexual community, while others have had wider relevance, including strong links to some areas such as AIDS research and treatment. As we noted earlier, the style of political activism invoked on gay rights issues has been less that of the interest group and more that of the movement. Still, as that movement has become better institutionalized, so too have the forms of interaction between it and government.

One of the most important political milestones in that interaction occurred with respect to military service during the Clinton administration. During his first presidential campaign, Clinton had advocated greater rights for the gay community and had received overwhelming support from those voters. One issue that his gay supporters wanted addressed was possible elimination of the prohibition against homosexuals serving in the military. Once elected, however, President Clinton encountered substantial resistance from the military to any change in the existing policy. Military leaders defended their traditional stance of excluding homosexuals by arguing that permitting homosexuals to serve alongside heterosexual soldiers would be detrimental to morale.

The solution that the Clinton administration developed was labeled "don't ask, don't tell," meaning that there would be no efforts on the part of the military to seek out gays within its ranks so long as those individuals did nothing that was indeed detrimental to the morale or good conduct of their unit. Again, compromises are rarely entirely satisfying when dealing with issues of this sort, and this was no exception. The gay community thought that President Clinton had reneged on his commitments once elected and faced with opposition. On the other hand, many leaders in the military believed that this policy did indeed undermine discipline and morale and that a president with no military experience had intervened in an unacceptable manner.

In addition to the issues of identity, the gay community's political involvement focused on how to combat HIV/AIDS. When the nature and epidemiology of this disease became known during the 1980s, it sparked widespread recognition within the gay community that, rather than being a question of lifestyle, politics in the gay community had become a question of life. This produced high levels of mobilization and political organization in cities such as San Francisco, with the gay community becoming heavily involved in public health and safe-sex campaigns. At the national level, this mobilization also produced campaigns to increase funding for research for a cure for HIV/AIDS, and it spurred a massive increase in this research, which has led to drug regimens that can at least hold the disease in check if not cure it.

One interesting consequence of this campaign for new treatments for HIV/AIDS is that it involved putting pressure on the Food and Drug Administration for "fast-tracking" drugs that might be beneficial for treating the disease. That is, rather than accepting the usual lengthy approval process required before most drugs are allowed to go on the market, interest groups, such as Human Rights Campaign, Lambda Legal, and National Gay and Lesbian Task Force (NGLTF) exerted pressure to speed up approval for drugs that might help. Pointing out that individuals with this disease were in imminent danger of death, the AIDS activists argued that trying something was better than just letting the victims die. This successful campaign then opened the door for more rapid approval of drugs for other extremely deadly diseases. There have been some cases of drugs reaching the market that do have extreme side-effects or relatively little efficacy for treating the disease, but most people with such diseases appear willing to opt for a chance while they are living rather than a certainty after they are dead.

Another unusual aspect of the political conflict over the rights of homosexuals is that referendums attempting to guarantee rights to equal treatment in employment and housing have been contested in a number of localities. These elections were in some cases promoted by the advocates of equal rights for gay and lesbian citizens, while in other cases they were prompted by the opponents, generally in response to actions by state or local governments that extended such rights to the homosexual communities. The arguments advanced in these elections are rather predictable: the advocates of guaranteeing rights contend that gays and lesbians should not be discriminated against because of their sexual preference and that they are entitled to the same protections as other minority groups in the society; some opponents base their objections on religious grounds, asserting that government has no place in protecting a lifestyle that they believe to be in contradiction of biblical teachings, while others more simply maintain that there is no constitutional basis for this kind of protection and therefore it is not appropriate.[20]

Referendums on gay rights have achieved highly variable outcomes, winning in some unlikely places and failing in others where success seemed more likely. As is often the case in the referendum process, the precise wording of the proposition on the ballot plays a role in determining the outcome. So, for example, referendums expressed in terms of granting rights appear to be less successful than those phrased in terms of preventing negative discrimination against gay and lesbian people. In general, however, the concept of defending the rights of all segments of society appears to have substantial appeal to the public.

There have been some significant pieces of legislation passed by Congress and state legislatures. Some of this legislation has been designed to create greater rights for members of the gay and lesbian communities, although such efforts have been relatively infrequent, given that much of the voting population is still rather conservative on issues of sexual preference and the opposition tends to be well-organized and vocal. Nevertheless, some legislation has been passed at the state level that supports the policy goals of gay activists. For example, Vermont has passed legislation permitting same-sex civil unions, and a number of states have prohibited discrimination on the basis of sexual preference on the same principle as that used to ban discrimination based on race or gender. That legislation, however, has not been unchallenged, and it has in a number of instances led to further legal and political conflicts over the extension of alleged "special treatment" to these groups.

In contrast to the pro–gay rights legislation, some measures have been introduced to defend the position of the straight community and to limit the use of

Bruce Deming, left, and Jeff Byrne—with their daughter Anna Byrne-Deming—were denied a marriage license by senior legal process clerk Maggie Zevallos, right, who told the couple that under California law, only an unmarried male and an unmarried female may wed. While considerable strides have been made in the area of gay rights, many feel that there is still a long road to walk.

public funds for support of any programs that advance the goals of the gay and lesbian community. For example, the Marriage Protection Act of 1996 stated that for purposes of any federal programs, marriage was to be defined as between two people of the opposite sex and, further, that no state would be required to recognize same-sex marriages permitted in another state. Couples coming from those few states that have sanctioned same-sex marriages thus may find themselves in a legal limbo if they move, or even travel, to another state.[21]

The Separation of Church and State: School Prayer and Other Issues

The First Amendment to the U.S. Constitution forbids the establishment of a national religion and also ensures the free exercise of religion. That is, the framers, on the one hand, attempted to prevent government from endorsing or supporting any particular religion, while, on the other hand, forbidding it to interfere with individuals practicing their own version of religion, whatever that religion might be. While the framers may have thought those two provisions were compatible, many contemporary citizens do not—they contend that rulings designed to prohibit establishment of religion instead prevent them from free exercise of their religious beliefs. This conflict between the two dimensions of religious liberty arises in part because the courts have decided against permitting any religious observance at publicly funded events. Citizens committed to the free exercise of religion regard any restrictions on public observance—even when other people are involved who may be of different religions or who profess no religion at all—as an infringement of their rights. This attitude is all the more likely when there is a dominant religious community that sees no reason why it should not have religious observances at public events.

Public education has been one of the principal battlegrounds in this continuing conflict. The two clauses of the First Amendment regarding religion have caused a number of controversies. For much of American history it was considered quite common, and indeed expected, for the school day to begin with a prayer, which was almost invariably Christian in tone and often was prescribed by the school board or some other public body. The clear and direct role of government in prescribing these prayers led the Supreme Court to deem them an establishment of religion.[22] That decision began an ongoing series of political and legal fights over the limits of government-mandated prayer and other religious observance in the public schools, in which the judiciary has struggled to find some way to balance the establishment and free exercise clauses. These controversies themselves are, somewhat ironically, often resolved by a Supreme Court that opens its own sessions with a prayer.

Issues of separation of church and state in education arise within two principal areas. The first is school prayer, specifically, the attempts of local school boards to permit some form of prayer at school. Since 1962, when the Supreme Court outlawed official school prayer, various religious groups have attempted to reintroduce it, either through a constitutional amendment permitting prayer in schools or through mechanisms such as silent meditation and voluntary attendance at prayer sessions. The issue resurfaced in 1984 when a Reagan administration proposal directed at improving the quality of American education included a provision allowing local school boards to permit a moment of silent meditation at the beginning of the school day; this practice was presumed to promote discipline as well as moral education. Individual states' attempts to impose such plans have been struck down by the Supreme Court,[25] but in 1990, the Court did permit religious groups formed by students to use school facilities after school hours, and this seemed likely to be an entering wedge for greater use of the public schools for religious exercises. Indeed, in 2000 the Court allowed even more general use of school buildings for religious functions, further narrowing the separation of public-sector facilities and religious observance.

A range of other issues about religious observance in public education have arisen since the early 1980s, reflecting in part the rising political involvement of the Christian Coalition and other fundamentalist Protestant organizations. For example, in a number of jurisdictions, questions have been raised about religious expression at events held outside normal school hours—at football games and graduations in particular—but in most instances the Court has maintained that these events are still a part of the public education system and that therefore the inclusion of religious ritual is a violation of the establishment clause. The Court's general direction has been to maintain the principle of separation between the system of public education and the church, even where there appears to be strong public support for breaching the wall.

If the Supreme Court were to follow the election returns, the justices would have sided with President Reagan, both Presidents Bush, and their fundamentalist supporters on the issue of school prayer. Large majorities of the American population have expressed opinions in favor of permitting prayer in schools. As in many other issues, however, political elites tend to be more sensitive to the issues of minority rights involved in school prayer, and so attempts at passing a school-prayer amendment in Congress have been unsuccessful. The usual tactic of opponents has been to block consideration of the issue through procedural mechanisms in the legislature rather than by calling for formal votes that would make it clear to constituents how their congressmen dealt with school prayer.

The second area of controversy concerning the separation of church and state is public support for religious schools. In deciding this issue, the Supreme Court has been forced to make a number of difficult decisions. Over the years, however, the Court has been tending to allow greater public support for religious education. For example, in 1930 it upheld the right of states to provide textbooks for children in parochial schools on the same basis that books are provided to students in public schools,[24] and in 1947 the Court ruled in favor of providing bus transportation for parochial school students at public expense.[25] Both policies were upheld on the grounds that these expenditures benefited the students involved, not the church.

In contrast, in 1971 the Supreme Court struck down a Pennsylvania law that had the state pay part of parochial school teachers' salaries, arguing that this was of direct benefit to the church (essentially subsidizing church employees) and created excessive entanglement between church and state.[26] The Court has also permitted states to provide teachers for exceptional students in parochial schools, but not on the premises of these schools. In a somewhat contradictory fashion, the Court in 1976 upheld general grants of public money to church-affiliated colleges.[27] They later restricted the ability of those institutions to use the funds for religious purposes.[28] Then, in 1994 the Court ruled that the State of New York had violated the separation principle by creating a school district that served only the disabled children of a Hasidic Jewish sect that did not want its children to attend public schools.[29]

The issue of government support of religious education continues to be pressed on both sides, in part because of the importance of vouchers and charter schools in the contemporary debate over education—as we noted when discussing education policy (see Chapter 12). Parochial schools and other religiously based schools would likely be the principal beneficiaries of any greater use of vouchers. As in the case of abortion, public support for religious schools brings together a rather unlikely coalition, the Roman Catholic Church and fundamentalist Protestant sects that have been forming their own schools in order to incorporate school prayer and religious instruction into their educational program. The opposition has been based in a coalition of secular proponents of public education, along with mainstream Protestant churches and some liberal Jewish leaders. In 2002 the Supreme Court ruled in a landmark case that the use of vouchers supporting religious schools did not violate separation of church and state.[30]

All these court decisions on funding religiously based education feature reasoning that may appear tortuous, but three guidelines do stand out. The first is that aid to students and their families is more acceptable than is aid to institutions that are connected to churches. If parents and children have made their own choice to seek a religious education, they should be able to do so. These citizens are, in principle, as much entitled to public support for education as are their fellow citizens who choose public schools for their children—as one aspect of the concept of "free exercise of religion." Second, institutions of higher education are permitted more entanglement between church and state than are elementary and secondary schools. The assumption is that more mature students are less vulnerable to the influence of any overt religious teachings. Third, the public sector should not have to spend additional money on education because of the special religious demands of a group, but neither should it impose additional financial burdens on the religious groups.

Finally, the conflict between church and state has also been manifested in conflicts over control of the curriculum being taught in the public schools—particularly over the teaching of evolution. Religious conservatives prefer that evolution be replaced or at least supplemented by creationism, or "creation science," which accepts the biblical version of the divine creation of all species on earth at once, as written in Genesis. At a minimum, these conservatives want evolution taught as a speculative theory rather than as settled scientific fact. They argue, for example, that gaps in the fossil record make it impossible to demonstrate that evolution did in fact occur as argued by its proponents.[31]

Whereas most of the battle over church and state has been fought within the court system, the battle over curriculum has been more overtly political, being joined in states and local communities with elected school boards. The religious right has been extremely successful in organizing politically to take control of these boards, which have been able in turn to shift the curriculum to reflect their own views about evolution, as well as to take on other curricular issues such as sex education. The most extreme case of this type of mobilization occurred in Kansas, where the elected state board of education was captured for a short time by the creationists. A subsequent election returned control of the board to a more moderate group, but the power of well-organized activist groups in education politics had been demonstrated rather clearly. Political polling indicates that these groups generally do not hold majorities in the communities in which they are successful, but the religious right's ability to get out the vote of citizens who feel intensely about these issues enables it to win elections.

The issue of the public school curriculum also arises with respect to the growth in home schooling and the spread of charter schools (see Chapter 12). Parents who do not want their children exposed to ideas opposed to their own creationist perspectives either remove their children from schools and educate them at home or band together to create charter schools, which are supported at least in part by public funds but allow greater control to be exercised by the parents. Even then, they may not be able to escape completely the curriculum of public education, given that state departments of education establish regulations on what must be offered at home or in the charter schools. Education is central in shaping culture, and in the culture wars that are becoming increasingly important in American political life, it occupies a pivotal position.

Summary

Moral and cultural issues have become central to contemporary policy debates in the United States. The Puritan tradition has been strong and influential in American social and political life, and it has tended to shape much of national policy. However, the spate of moral issues arising in politics in recent decades has created intense political divisions within the United States; the issues are important, but they are extremely difficult for the political system to process effectively. While most of the other policy issues we have discussed to this point can be addressed through bargaining and compromise, moral issues generally are not open to compromise, for participants in the process usually are unwilling to trade off their values in these debates.

The problem for government is that these issues are unlikely to go away, and indeed they may intensify. The scientific progress in the area of reproductive technology and the increasing social, cultural, and religious diversity of American society all but guarantee that there will continue to be conflicts of this type. Further, the political parties have become somewhat aligned along cultural lines as well as along a left-right continuum, ensuring that these issues will continue to be carried directly into political debates. Also, moral and political issues tend to create rather unusual political and even religious coalitions that make political calculations all the more difficult for policymakers and so may contribute to additional conflict and instability within the policymaking system.

PART FOUR
Policy Analysis

CHAPTER 16

Cost-Benefit Analysis

MUCH OF THIS BOOK has been concerned with the process through which policies are adopted and with the characteristics of policies adopted in the United States. This chapter extends that discussion to examination of the principal method of policy analysis used when making policy choices, cost-benefit analysis. Because governments operate with limited resources and limited ability to predict the future, they must employ some techniques to help them decide how to utilize those scarce resources. Cost-benefit analysis is the most commonly employed technique, other than the informal promptings of intuition and experience. The fundamental principle of cost-benefit analysis is that any project undertaken should produce a benefit for society greater than its cost.[1] Second, when several projects promise to yield positive net benefits and when all cannot be undertaken because of limited resources, the project that creates the greatest net benefit to the society should be selected. This technique is perhaps most applicable to capital projects, such as building highways or dams, but it can also be applied to other types of public programs. In fact, cost-benefit analysis was adopted as a means of assessing all proposed regulations during the Reagan administration, in an attempt to curb the growth of government involvement in the economy.

Obviously there is a decided utilitarian bias underlying cost-benefit analysis.[2] The costs and benefits of a project are all compared along the single measuring rod of money, and those that create the greatest net benefit are deemed superior. This implies that the dominant value in society is economic wealth and, further, that more is always better. Total wealth is presumed to be of paramount importance, even if rather perverse distributional consequences arise from the program. I discuss the philosophical and practical issues that arise with cost-benefit analysis later in the chapter; its implications may be sufficiently troubling, especially in a democratic political system, for some critics to argue for alternative means of evaluating policies. But cost-benefit analysis does have the advantage of reducing all the costs and benefits of public programs to that single economic dimension, whereas other forms of analysis may produce confusion because of the lack of such a common standard of comparison. On that single dimension, cost-benefit analysis can give an answer as to whether a project is desirable or not, while other methods tend to produce more ambiguous results.

Principles of Cost-Benefit Analysis

In the world of cost-benefit analysis, more is always better. Although it does have serious intellectual foundations, the method is in many ways no more than a systematic framework within which to collect data concerning the merits and demerits of a public program. And it is not a new idea: the Army Corps of Engineers used the technique as early as 1900 to evaluate the merits of proposed improvements to rivers and harbors. The basic procedure is to enumerate the positive features of a program and attach a monetary value to them, and at the same time to enumerate the negative features and attach a monetary value to those features. The net balance of costs and benefits will then determine if a program is economically feasible, although many other questions about its desirability may remain.

One principal concept underlying cost-benefit analysis comes from the tradition in welfare economics that has sought to develop an acceptable social welfare function, or a socially desirable means for making collective policy decisions.[3] That is, how can societies take the numerous and often conflicting views of their citizens and generate the policy choices that are the most acceptable to the society? One of the first welfare criteria of this sort was the Pareto principle, which argued that a policy move was optimal if no move away from it could be made to benefit someone without hurting someone else.[4] Stated another way, a Pareto optimal policy move would be one that benefits at least one person without hurting anyone. Clearly, in the real world of political decision making, policies of this kind are rare indeed, and politics is frequently about who gets what at the expense of whom. Therefore, using the Pareto principle would be extremely conservative, supporting very few public interventions.

A substitute welfare criterion was advanced by Nicholas Kaldor and John Hicks, who argued that a policy change is socially justified if the winners gain a sufficient amount to compensate the losers and still have something left for themselves.[5] This does not imply that those winners necessarily *will* compensate the losers or that government can even identify the losers, but it presumes that the society as a whole is better off because of the overall increase in benefits. This welfare criterion obviously is a justification of the reliance of cost-benefit analysis on the production of the greatest possible net benefit; it can be hoped that at least part of the benefits created will somehow find their way to the individuals who may have been harmed by the policy choice, but at least those benefits have been created. Intellectually, this approach has another problem: it requires aggregating utilities across a range of individuals, and that requires doing the nearly impossible—making interpersonal comparisons of utility.[6]

A second fundamental idea underlying cost-benefit analysis is that of the consumer's surplus.[7] Stated simply, this is the amount of money a consumer would be willing to pay for a given product, minus the amount he or she must actually pay. Consumers tend to value the first unit of a product or service they receive more highly than the second, and the second more highly than the third: the first quart of milk where there has been none is more valuable than the second. But the units of a product are not priced marginally; they are sold at an average price, which means that the utility of increased production will give consumers a surplus value from the production. Thus, any investment that reduces the cost of the product or service produces a benefit in savings that increases the consumer surplus. The investment by government in a new superhighway that reduces the cost to consumers of driving the same number of miles—in time, in gasoline, and in potential loss of life and property—creates a consumer surplus. And as the time, gasoline, and lives saved by the new highway may be used for other increased production, the actual savings represent a minimum definition of the improvement to society resulting from the construction of the new highway.

Also important in understanding cost-benefit analysis is the concept of opportunity costs: any resource used in one project cannot be used in another. For example, the concrete, steel, and labor used to build the superhighway cannot be used to build a new dam. Consequently, all projects must be evaluated against other possible projects to determine the most appropriate way to use resources—especially financial resources. Projects are also compared, implicitly if not explicitly, with taking no action and allowing the money to remain in the hands of individual citizens. Again, the basic idea of getting the most "bang for the buck" is important in understanding cost-benefit analysis.

When identifying and assessing costs and benefits, the analyst must also be concerned with the range of effects of the proposed program and the point at which he or she disregards effects as being too remote for consideration.[8] For example, building a municipal waste incinerator in Detroit, Michigan, will have pronounced effects in Windsor, Ontario, Canada, that must be considered—even though that city is outside the United States. The prevailing air currents may mean that some ash and acid from the incinerator also reach Norway and Sweden, but those effects may be so minimal and so remote that they can safely be disregarded. Engaging in this form of analysis requires making judgments about what effects are sufficiently proximate and important to be included in the calculations.

Finally, in evaluating costs and benefits, we must be concerned about time. The costs and benefits of most projects do not occur at a single time, but accrue over a number of years. If our superhighway is built, it will be serviceable for fifty years and will be financed over twenty years through government bonds. Policymakers must be certain that the long-term costs and benefits as well as the short-term consequences are positive. This, of course, requires some estimation of the nature of the future. We may estimate that our new superhighway will be useful for fifty years, but oil shortages may so reduce driving during that period that the real benefits will be much less than anticipated. Or, conversely, the value of gasoline may increase so much that the savings produced are more valuable than assumed at present. These kinds of assumptions about the future must be built into the model of valuation if it is to aid a decision maker.

In part because of the uncertainty over future costs and benefits, and in part because of the general principle that people prefer a dollar today to a dollar next year, the costs and benefits of projects must be converted to present values before useful cost and benefit calculations can be made. That is, the benefits that accrue to the society in the future have their value discounted and are consequently worth less than benefits produced in the first year of the project. Likewise, costs that occur in future years are valued less than costs that occur in the first few years. Thus, cost-benefit analysis would appear to favor projects that offer quick payoffs rather than greater long-term benefits, but perhaps higher maintenance and operation costs as well. While there may be a good logical justification for these biases in the method, they do certainly influence the kinds of programs that will be selected, and that fact will have definite social implications, not least of all for future generations. Other forms of analytic aids for government decision makers, such as "decision trees", include probabilities of outcomes as a means of coping with the uncertainties of the future, but cost-benefit analysis tends to rely instead on discounting future costs and benefits.

Doing Cost-Benefit Analysis

To better understand the application of cost-benefit analysis, we now work through the steps required to justify the construction of a new dam on the Nowhere River. This project is being proposed by the Army Corps of Engineers, and we have to determine whether or not the project should be undertaken. We must first decide if the project is feasible and acceptable on its own, and then if it is preferable to other projects that could be funded with the same resources. Again, this decision is being made first on economic grounds, although we may have to bring other forms of analysis (politics) and other criteria (the environment may be trumps) into the decision process at a later time.

While the TVA's multiple hydroelectric projects provide cheap power, stimulate industrialization, and create new recreational opportunities in remote areas, the costs of maintenance, upkeep, and restoration of these immense structures can be considerable.

Determining Costs and Benefits

One of the most important factors to consider when performing a cost-benefit analysis, especially of a public project, is that all costs and benefits should be enumerated. Thus, unlike projects that might be undertaken in the private sector, public projects require an explicit statement of the social, or external, costs and benefits. In the public sector, projects whose strictly economic potential outweighs their costs may be rejected because of the possibility of pollution or the loss of external benefits such as natural beauty. In fact, one of the principal logical justifications for the existence of the public sector is that it should take into account these external factors and attempt to correct them in ways not possible in the private sector.[9] Even with that social justification, however, the values of the costs and benefits are usually computed in economic terms just as if they were to accrue in the private market. This reliance on market logic for non-market decisions is one of the fundamental ironies in cost-benefit analysis.[10]

Thus, for our dam project, we can think of two lists of attributes (see table 16.1). On one side are the costs of the project, the main one being the economic

TABLE 16.1   Costs and Benefits of Dam Project

Costs	Benefits
Construction costs	Hydroelectric power
Flooded land	Flood control
Relocation of families	Irrigation
Loss of recreation	New recreational opportunities

cost of constructing the dam, which should reflect the market valuation of the opportunity costs of using the same resources for other purposes. Also, the dam will impose an economic cost by flooding the houses and farmland of present inhabitants of the area, and there are social, or human, costs involved as well, for these farms have been in the same families for generations, and the farmers have resisted the project from the beginning. Finally, there are additional social costs in that the proposed dam will impound a river that currently has some recreational value for canoeists and is essentially an unspoiled natural area.

On the other side of the ledger are the benefits of the program. First, the dam will provide hydroelectric power for the region. In so doing it will provide a source of electric power that does not consume scarce fossil fuels and does not create the air pollution that would result from producing the same amount of electricity with fossil fuels. Also, the dam would help control the raging Nowhere River, which every spring overflows its banks and floods a number of towns, cities, and farms downstream. In addition, the impounded water behind the dam will provide irrigation water for the remaining farmers, enabling them to grow crops more reliably than if they had to rely on rainfall alone. Finally, although canoeists will lose some recreational benefits as a result of the building of the dam, citizens who enjoy power boating and water skiing will benefit from the large lake formed behind the dam. Thus, although this proposed dam does impose a number of costs on the society, it also provides a number of benefits in return. To proceed with this analysis, we must now begin to attach some quantitative values to these costs and benefits in order to be able to make a decision as to the feasibility and desirability of the project.

Assigning Value

Assigning a real monetary value to all the costs and benefits of this mythical project would be difficult. The market directly provides a value for some aspects: we know, or can estimate accurately, the costs of building the dam and the market value of the hydroelectric power it will produce. Although such costs are generally measurable through the market, the market may not fully reflect the costs and benefits. For example, if our dam is to be built in a remote area with little more than subsistence agriculture, bringing in a large number of highly skilled and highly paid workers may distort prices and increase the costs of building the dam. Similarly, not only is the hydroelectric power salable, but it may produce substantial secondary benefits (or perhaps costs) by stimulating industrialization in this remote rural area. The experience of the Tennessee Valley Authority and its impact on the Tennessee Valley as a result of the development of cheap electric power illustrates this point rather nicely.[11] We cannot fully predict these secondary benefits, nor can we rely on them to make the project feasible, but they do frequently occur.

Some other costs and benefits of the project, although not directly measurable through the market, can be estimated in other ways. For example, we have to estimate the dam's recreational value to the people who will use the lake for waterskiing and its cost to those who will no longer be able to use the river for canoeing. We can do this by estimating the people's willingness to pay for their recreation[12]—just how much time and money are they willing to invest to enjoy these recreational activities? Evidence for this calculation can be gained from surveys of recreation participants, or from their actual behavior in renting equipment and travel to recreation sites. These calculations will offer some measure of the economic value of the lake, and of the free-flowing stream, to the population.

The creation of the dam and the lake behind it help illustrate another point about valuing costs and benefits. The lake will produce lakefront property, which tends to have higher market value than does other nearby property, so something of the aesthetic value of the impoundment can be calculated. This method of valuation is analogous to estimating the value of clean air by comparing prices of similar housing in polluted and less polluted areas of a city.[13]

This method of valuation returns to the concept of the consumer's surplus. The first unit of a particular commodity is valued more highly than any subsequent units, so that as production is increased, each unit is marginally less valuable to the consumer. In our dam example, if there already have been a number of impoundments in the area—as there have been in the Tennessee Valley—a new lake will have less value to recreation consumers, and they will be less willing to pay than if this were the first lake in an area with a large number of free-flowing streams. Likewise, one more hydroelectric power station in an area that already has cheap electrical power is less valuable than it would be in an economically backward area, and consequently citizens will be less willing to pay for that new power plant.

Finally, on some aspects of the project the market provides little or no guidance about valuation. For the farmers who are displaced by the project, we can calculate the economic value of their land, their houses, and their moving costs, but we cannot readily assign an economic value to those houses that are the ancestral homes of families and are therefore more valuable psychologically than ordinary houses.[14] Similarly, there is some value in not disturbing a natural setting, simply because it is natural, and this is a difficult thing to which to assign an economic value. As a result, absolute prohibitions are sometimes built into legislation to prevent certain actions, so planners cannot depend entirely on net-benefit ratios. The Environmental Protection Agency's guideline for preserving the habitats of endangered species, which resulted in the now notorious case of the snail darter in the Little Tennessee River and the more recent case of the delta smelt in California, is an example of the application of regulations to prevent some actions regardless of the relative economic costs and benefits.[15]

The willingness-to-pay approach to valuation questions the people directly involved with the project about their own valuation of costs and benefits. For some of those costs and benefits, the population at large may be equally important as judges of the value. Federal regulators are now under congressional mandates to find ways to assess the value that the public assigns to the costs of environmental problems such as oil spills. These "contingent value" measurements by passive users are now being undertaken by survey methods. The first of these was conducted by the National Oceanic and Atmospheric Administration and gained broad support from environmental groups.[16] This method of valuation has, however, met general opposition by business concerns and has been contested in the court system.[17]

It is fortunate that the dam we are building does not require any direct decisions about loss of life or injury to human beings. With projects that do—for example, building the superhighway as a means of saving lives—we come to perhaps the most difficult problem of valuation: estimating the value of a human life.[18] Although it is convenient to say that life is priceless, in practice decisions are made that deprive some people of their lives even when that loss of life is preventable, and when this is the case, some subjective, if not objective, evaluation is being made of the worth of lives. One standard method of making such a judgment involves discounted future earnings: the life of the individual is worth whatever the individual could have earned in the course of his or her working life, discounted to present value. Therefore, by this method, a highly paid corporate executive's life is valued more highly than a housewife's or a college professor's. This mechanism for evaluating lives clearly conforms to the basic market valuation, but it can clearly be contested on humane grounds—its use in distributing compensation payments to the families of those who died in the terrorist attacks of September 11th has generated a great deal of political controversy.[19]

Another method of assessing the value of lives as a basis for cost-benefit analysis utilizes the size of awards to plaintiffs in legal cases involving negligence or malpractice that resulted in loss of life. In other words, what do panels of citizens or judges consider a human life to be worth? This method constitutes yet another version of the market criterion, albeit one in which considerations of

TABLE 16.2   Hypothetical Costs and Benefits of Dam Project for Twenty Years

										Year										
	1	2	3	4	5	6	7	8	9	10	11	12	13	14	15	16	17	18	19	20
Costs	5	8	7	2	1	1	1	1	1	1	1	1	1	1	1	1	1	1	1	1
Benefits	0	0	0	3	4	5	5	5	5	5	5	5	5	5	5	4	4	4	3	2

human suffering and "loss of companionship" have a greater—some would say too great because of the emotionalism involved—impact on the economic valuation than does earning power. This valuation also is affected, particularly in the minds of insurance companies responsible for most of the payments, by emotional appeals by attorneys.

Another means of assessing the value of a human life is somewhat similar to the "willingness to pay" criterion. In theory, individuals would be willing to pay almost anything to preserve their own lives and the lives of their loved ones. However, individuals engage in risky behavior and risky occupations all the time, and when they do so, they make a subjective statement about the value of their lives.[20] Because we know how much more likely it is for a coal miner to be killed at work—either in the mines or as a result of black lung disease—than it is for a construction worker, we can estimate from any differences in wages how much these individuals would appear to value their lives. This method does, of course, imply a certain level of knowledge that individuals may not have, and it assumes that the collective bargaining process, through which wages of coal miners and construction workers are determined, accurately reflects both individual preferences and the market values of lives. This method does, however, offer another feasible means of estimating the value of life, one that uses assessments by individual citizens rather than by the market or the courts.

Discounting

We now return to the problem of time. The costs and benefits of a project do not all magically appear as soon as the project is completed, but typically are stretched over a number of years. Table 16.2 shows the stream of benefits coming from the dam on the Nowhere River over a twenty-year period. This is the projected feasible lifetime of the project because the Nowhere River carries a great deal of silt, which is expected to fill the lake behind the dam by the end of that period. How do we assess these benefits and come up with a single number to compare with costs in order to determine the economic feasibility of the project?

To calculate such a figure, we must compute the present value of the future benefits. We have already decided on the time span of the project; the only task that remains is to determine the discount rate that should be applied to a public investment. And, as with the valuation of costs and benefits, disagreements may arise about what that rate should be.[21] One method is to use the opportunity costs of the use of these funds. Presumably any money used in a project in the public sector will be extracted from the private sector by some means such as taxation or borrowing, and consequently the rate of return these resources could earn if they were invested in private-sector projects is the appropriate rate of discount for public-sector projects. This is not always a practical solution, however, as rates of return differ for different kinds of investments, and investors apparently choose to put some money into each kind of investment. Is building a dam more like speculative mining investments, building a steel mill, or investing in an insured savings account? Which of the many possible rates of return should be selected?

Several other issues arise with respect to the selection of a discount rate. First, in discussing projects for which most benefits are to accrue in the future, there is an element of uncertainty. In our example we have assumed that the probable life span of the dam will be twenty years, but in reality the lake may fill up with silt in fifteen years. Consequently, it may be more prudent to select a discount rate higher than that found in the market because we cannot be sure of the real occurrence or real value of the benefits. And because these benefits are expected to be further away in time, they are less certain; therefore, even higher rates of discount should be applied. Also, considering the effects of inflation and the uncertainties about the development of new energy sources, we may need to be more conservative about discount rates.

Second, some analysts argue that there should be a "social rate of discount" lower than that established by the market.[22] Such an arbitrarily set discount rate would be justified on the basis of the need for greater public investment in order to provide a capital infrastructure for future generations. Further, as the size of the public sector is to some degree determined by the rate of discount, that rate should be set not by the market but by more conscious political choices concerning the appropriate level of public activity. The economic counterargument is that, in the long term, the society will be better off if resources are allocated on the basis of their opportunity costs. If a public project is deemed infeasible because of the selection of a market-determined discount rate, then the resources that would have been used in that project would, it is argued, produce greater social benefit in a project that is feasible under that rate of discount; this would be true regardless of whether the project is in the public or the private sector. If no such project is available, then the money would be better saved until such a project does materialize.

Finally, a question arises about intergenerational equity. What do we owe to posterity, or, to put it the other way around, what has posterity ever done for us?

TABLE 16.3   Costs and Benefits of Alternate Projects (in millions of dollars)

Projects	Costs	Benefits	Net benefit
A	70	130	60
B	75	120	45
C	200	270	70
D	150	250	100

If the discount rate is set lower than that determined by the market, we will tend to undertake more projects that have an extended time value and that will benefit future generations. But we will also deprive the present generation of opportunities for consumption by using those resources as investment capital. This is as much a philosophical as a practical issue, but it is important for our understanding of alternative consequences arising from alternative choices of a rate of discount for public projects.

Using several discount rates, we now work through the example of levels of benefit from the dam. Let us assume that the prime interest rate in the United States is approximately 8 percent. If we use this market-determined interest rate, the $100 in benefits produced after one year would be worth

$$V = \$100/1.08 = \$92.59.$$

And $100 in benefits produced after two years would be worth

$$V = \$100/(1.08)2 = \$85.73.$$

And $100 in benefits produced in the twentieth year of the project would be worth only $21.45 in present value. Thus, if we use this market rate of discount in evaluating a public project, the net benefit of that project at present value is positive. This project has a rather high cost during its early years, with the benefits occurring gradually over the twenty years. At a higher discount rate, however, such a project is not feasible. If we use a discount rate of 18 percent, which would have seemed very reasonable in the late 1970s (but absurd in the 1990s), the net benefit of the dam at present value would be negative and the project would be economically infeasible.

Discounting is a means of reducing all costs and benefits of a project to present value, based on the assumption that benefits created in the future are worth less than those created immediately. Philosophically or ideologically one might desire a low discount rate in order to encourage public investment but object to the entire process of discounting. Should we not simply look to see if the stream of benefits created is greater than the total costs, no matter how and when they occur? This would, of course, be equivalent to a discount rate of zero. This point may be valid philosophically, but until the argument is accepted by economists,

TABLE 16.4   Choosing a Package of Projects by Net Benefit Ratio (in millions of dollars)

Project	Costs	Cumulative costs	Benefits	Net benefits	Net benefit ratio
A	2	2	12	10	5.0
B	4	6	20	16	4.0
C	10	16	40	30	3.0
D	10	26	35	25	2.5
E	8	34	28	20	2.5
F	16	50	51	35	2.2
G	2	52	6	4	2.0
H	15	67	42	27	1.8
I	10	77	26	16	1.6
J	18	95	45	27	1.5

financiers, and government decision makers, public investment decisions will be made on the basis of present value and on the basis of interest rates that approximate the real value of the rate of return in the private sector.

Choosing among Projects

We have determined that our dam on the Nowhere River is feasible, given that a benevolent deity has provided us a discount rate of 8 percent for this project. But it is not yet time to break ground for the dam. We must first compare our project with the alternative projects for funding. Thus, the opportunity cost question arises not only with respect to the single project being considered and the option of allowing the money to remain in private hands but also with regard to choices made among other possible projects in the public sector.

We have argued that the fundamental rule is to select the project that will produce the greatest total benefit to society. If we apply the Kaldor-Hicks criterion, we see that this project is justified simply because it will create more benefits to spread around in the society and presumably will compensate those who have lost something because the project was built. Thus, in the simplest case, if we were to choose to undertake only a single project this year—perhaps because of limited manpower for supervision—we would choose Project D from table 16.3 simply because it creates the highest level of net benefit. By investing less money in Projects A and B we could have produced slightly more net benefit for society, but we are administratively constrained from making that decision and must choose only the one most productive investment.

More commonly, however, a particular resource—usually money—is limited, and with that limitation in mind, we have to choose one or more projects that will result in maximum benefits. Let us say that the ten projects listed in table 16.4 are all economically feasible and that we have been given a budget of $50 million for capital projects. Which projects should we select for funding? In such a situation, we should rank the projects according to the ratio of net benefits to initial costs (the costs that will be reflected in our capital budget), and then we should begin with the best projects, in terms of the ratio of benefits to initial costs, until the budget is exhausted. In this way, we will get the greatest benefit for the expenditure of our limited funds. And projects that we might have selected if we were choosing only a single project would not be selected under these conditions of resource constraint.

This problem of selecting among projects demonstrates the first of several problems that arise from the application of the basic rule of cost-benefit analysis. Given the budgetary process and the allocation of funds among agencies, we may produce a case of "multi-organizational sub-optimization." This is a fancy way of saying that if our agency has been given $50 million, we will spend it, even if other agencies have projects that will produce greater benefits for society but do not have adequate funds in their budgets. Thus, if I had the money, I would continue to fund the projects listed in table 16.4 even though several of them have relatively low net-benefit ratios and even though there might be better projects that other government bureaus wanted to fund. Of course, I will have been asked what benefits my proposed projects would produce when the capital budget was being considered, but because of political considerations arising in the process my budget is excessive in light of the benefits that could be produced from alternative uses of the money. This is not, of course, a flaw in the method; it is a flaw in the application of the method in complex and competitive government settings.

A not unrelated problem is that cost-benefit analysis places relatively little importance on efficiency or cost effectiveness. It looks primarily at total benefits produced rather than at the ratio of benefits to costs. It could be argued that this method tends to favor the axe over the scalpel as a cutting tool; in other words, it tends to favor large projects over small projects. This may be an inefficient use of resources, and it may lock government into costly projects, whereas smaller projects might provide greater flexibility and greater future opportunities for innovation. Capital projects are inherently lumpy, so that only projects of a certain size are feasible, but the concentration on total net benefits in cost-benefit analysis may exaggerate the problems of size and inflexibility.

We have now worked our way from the initial step of deciding what costs and benefits our project provides to deciding if it is the best project to undertake, given limited budgetary resources and the competing uses of the money. At each stage of the process we have had to adopt a number of assumptions and approximations to reach a decision. Thus, although cost-benefit analysis does provide a "hard" answer as to whether or not we should undertake a project, that answer should not remain unquestioned. We now discuss some criticisms of cost-benefit analysis and some possible ways of building greater political and economic sophistication into the application of the methodology.

Extensions

We have so far been discussing a very basic approach to the method of cost-benefit analysis. There are, however, a number of extensions and modifications that are important for thinking about the utility of the method. First, other techniques such as cost-effectiveness analysis have many things in common with cost-benefit analysis but offer their own particular perspectives. For example, cost-effectiveness analysis does not require the assessment of the value of various outcomes to the extent required in cost-benefit analysis, but rather assumes that an outcome is desirable.[23] Unlike cost-benefit analysis, this technique cannot tell the analyst whether an outcome is beneficial, only what it will cost to achieve a specified quantity of the outcome. Therefore, cost-effectiveness analysis tends to be used frequently in health policy and medicine, where curing a disease is a prima facie good; the question is how much will it cost.[24] Even then, however, some physicians do not like the concept of attaching a price to a cure and thinking about efficiency in medical care.[25]

Criticism and Modification

Such things as the difficulty of assigning monetary values to nonmonetary outcomes, the choice of time ranges and discount rates, and the reliance on total net benefit as the criterion all introduce uncertainties about the usefulness of the outcome. We now discuss more basic problems that arise concerning the method itself and its relationship to the political process. Perhaps the most important is that some naive politicians and analysts might let the method make decisions for them, instead of using the information derived from the analysis as one among many elements in their decision-making process. If the method is thus used naively and uncritically, its application can result in decisions that many people would deem socially undesirable. For example, all costs and benefits are counted as equal in the model, and even if they could be calculated accurately, some individuals would argue that the cost of death might be more important than other costs. Thus, we might wish to first reduce deaths to the lowest possible level and then perhaps apply a cost-benefit analysis to other aspects of the project. We might use this "lexicographic preference" as a means of initially sorting projects, when a single dominant value such as life or the preservation of an endangered species is involved. That is, we would take only projects that "pass" the one crucial test and then subject those to cost-benefit analysis.

Perhaps the most socially questionable aspect of cost-benefit analysis is that it gives little attention to the distributive questions involved in all policies.[26] All benefits and costs are counted equally in the method, regardless of who receives or bears them. A project that increased the wealth of a wealthy man by several million dollars and was financed by regressive taxation of $100,000 would be preferred in cost-benefit calculations to a project that produced a benefit of $900,000 for unemployed workers and was financed by progressive taxation of $200,000. This is an extreme example, but it does point to the distributional blindness of the method. Of course, advocates of the method justify it by saying that the society as a whole will be better off with the greatest increase in benefits, and presumably winners can later compensate losers. In reality, however, winners rarely if ever do so, and usually losers cannot be directly identified anyway. Redistributional goals may be included directly in the analysis, by attaching some weight greater than one to positive changes in the salaries of low-income or unemployed persons, or they may be imposed on the analysis after the fact. However, because government exists in part to attempt to redress some of the inequities produced in the marketplace, some attention must be given to redistributional goals when evaluating public projects.

Furthermore, the utilitarian and "econocratic" foundations of cost-benefit analysis may not be entirely suitable for a functioning political democracy.[27] Money alone is the measure of all things, and decisions made according to this method can be expected to be based on economic rather than the political values. In Chapter 17 I discuss some possible ethical alternatives that may be more suitable in a democracy. The difficulty is that these other criteria lack the apparent precision of cost-benefit analysis and also its ability to provide a clear-cut answer to questions about the desirability of a policy intervention.

Finally, cost-benefit analysis has been referred to as "nonsense on stilts."[28] This rather rude description implies that there are so many assumptions involved in the calculations, and so many imponderables about the future effects of projects, that cost-benefit analysis is the functional equivalent of witchcraft in the public sector. Although this criticism has been phrased in exaggerated language, to some degree it is well taken. It is difficult if not impossible to know the value of eliminating an externality, just as it is difficult to know just how much life, health, and snail darters are worth economically. Cost-benefit analysis can be used to avoid difficult political decisions and to yield responsibility to experts who can supply the "correct" answer. Of course, this fundamental abdication of political responsibility is indeed an "insidious poison in the body politick." Only when the results of analysis are integrated with other forms of analysis, including ethical analysis, and then combined with sound political judgment, can the "correct decision" ever be made.

CHAPTER 17
Ethical Analysis of Public Policy

ALL THE MATHEMATICAL and economic capabilities in the world and all the sub-stantive knowledge of policy areas are of little consequence if we have no moral or ethical foundation on which to base our evaluation of policies.[1] Most of the important questions concerning policy analysis have as much to do with the "should" questions as with the "can" questions. That is, most important policy decisions involve an assessment of what should be done by government as much as they involve the feasibility question of what government can do. The range of technical possibilities for action is frequently broader for policymakers than is the range of ethically justifiable possibilities for acting "in the public interest." But, unfortunately, many values that should affect policy decisions in the pub-lic sector conflict with one another. Analysts frequently confront choices among competing positive values, rather than clear-cut decisions about options that are either completely right or completely wrong.

In making almost all decisions about allocating resources among the pro-grams of government, policymakers must choose among worthy ends; they do not have the luxury of picking the only acceptable policy. Which is more im-portant, the jobs of 500 loggers or an endangered species of owl? Also, policy-makers must choose among alternative means to reach their desired goals, and those means themselves may have substantial ethical implications. Finally, in at-tempting to make decisions on ethical grounds, decision makers are confronted with an overwhelming utilitarian bias in the discussion and implementation of public policy.[2] As noted earlier in our consideration of cost-benefit analysis, the prevailing conception is that government should do what creates the greatest economic value for the society rather than worry too much about the "softer" values we discuss in this chapter.

The basic concept behind utilitarianism—producing the greatest net bene-fit to society—is in the main admirable, but it can be used to justify actions that violate procedural norms as well as usual conceptions of fair distribution of the benefits of society. Further, this approach tends to reduce all considerations to economic ones, although there are a variety of other values that may be equally important for determining the proper course of government action. This chapter presents several important ethical premises that constitute alternatives to utilitarianism and that can be used to guide policy decisions. It also discusses some of the difficulties of implementing those alternative ethical and moral values in real public-sector decisions.

Fundamental Value Premises

Any number of premises have been used to justify policy decisions, ranging from such concepts as "Americanism," "Aryan purity," "the principles of Marxism-Leninism," and that old standby, "the public interest," to such philosophical or religious principles.[3] The main difficulty in ethical analysis of policy decisions is finding principles that can be consistently applied to a number of situations and that produce acceptable decisions in those situations.[4] Words such as *justice, equity*, and *good* are tossed about in a rather cavalier fashion in debates over public policies. The analyst must attempt to systematize his or her values and learn to apply them consistently to issues. The policy analyst therefore must be a moral actor as well as a technician, or else remain what Arnold Meltsner refers to as a "baby analyst" throughout his or her career.[5] As we pointed out when discussing application of cost-benefit analysis (see Chapter 16), values are involved throughout the policy process, embedded in policy options and in commonly used analytic methods. In order to understand what one wants, one must explicate and examine those values.

In this chapter I discuss five important nonutilitarian value premises for making policy decisions: preservation of life and individual autonomy, and concepts of truthfulness, lying, and desert. These values would probably be widely accepted by the public as important standards for assessing policies, and they have a wide range of applicability across policy issues. As I point out, however, these values cannot be applied unambiguously, and the conflicts they encounter are embedded in each issue as well as ranging across the several issues. In many cases there are even conflicts among the values themselves, so that the analyst will have to decide how to weight the different values.

The Preservation of Life

The preservation of human life is one of the most fundamental values that we could expect to see manifested in the policy process. The sanctity of life is, after all, a fundamental value of Judeo-Christian ethics and is embodied in all professional codes of ethics.[6] Despite the universal acceptance of this value as an ethical criterion, a number of conflicts arise over its application in real-world decision-making situations. These are "tragic choices" because the resources available often do not permit everyone to be aided, and those not aided are condemned to die earlier than they might otherwise.[7] The ethical question then becomes which lives to preserve.

One obvious conflict over the use of resources to save lives exists between identifiable lives and statistical lives. Here we are faced with the tendency of individuals to allocate resources differently when known lives of specific individuals are at stake than they would in cases where some unspecified persons would be saved at some time in the future. If we know that particular individuals will die in the near future, we tend to provide them the resources they need to save themselves, even though the same resources could save many more unidentified lives in the future if allocated differently.

In medical care this problem is manifested in the conflict between acute and preventive medicine. Preventive medicine is almost certainly the most cost-effective means of saving lives from the dangers of cancer, circulatory diseases, or accidents, but it is difficult to identify the direct beneficiaries. However, the victims of the disease are clearly identifiable, they have identifiable families, and consequently it is more difficult to refuse care to them than to the unknown statistical beneficiaries of preventive medicine. This pattern of decision making was described in Chapter 3 as the "mountain-climber syndrome," by which we feel compelled to spend thousands of dollars to save a stranded mountain climber, even though many more lives could be saved if the same amount of money were spent on highway accident prevention. It is virtually impossible to say no to stranded mountain climbers and their families although, if the appropriate ethical criterion is to save as many lives as possible, that is perhaps what we should do.

But even if all the lives at stake in a decision are identifiable, allocative decisions must be made in some instances. Table 17.1 (p. 465), although it concentrates on a relatively small number of individuals who are potential recipients of a liver transplant, illustrates the broader problem of being forced to choose among lives. Each individual described in the table is worthy of receiving the lifesaving treatment simply because he or she is a human being, but because organs for transplants are scarce and the demand for them far exceeds the supply, decisions must be made that will allow some people to live and force others to die. What criteria can be applied in making such a choice? One might be the conventional utilitarian criterion: the individuals who will contribute the most to the community (especially economically) should be allowed to live. Another criterion might be longevity: the youngest persons should be allowed to receive the treatment, thus saving the greatest number of person-years of life. Another criterion might be autonomy: the individuals who have the greatest probability of returning to active and useful lives after treatment should receive the treat-

TABLE 17.1 Who Shall Live and Who Shall Die? (liver transplant candidates)

Patient	Sex and age	Occupation	Home life	Medical stability	Civic activities and other considerations
A	M 55	Cardiac surgeon on the verge of a major new technique	Married; two adult children	Bad long-term prognosis, maybe 2 years	Philanthropist with very high net worth; rumors of unfaithfulness
B	F 38	Owner of successful designer shop	Widow; three children, ages 4, 8, and 13	Good	From out of state; excellent violinist in community orchestra
C	M 46	Medical technician	Married; six children, ages 8 to 14	Good	Union boss
D	M 29	Assembly-line worker	Single	Good	Retarded—mental age, 10 years; ward of the state
E	F 36	Well-known historian, college professor; Ph.D.	Divorced; custodian of one son, age 5; ex-husband alive	Fair prognosis, but odd case that would allow perfection of new surgical technique	Excessive eater, drinker, and smoker; very popular professor; other medical conditions
F	M 60	Ex-state senator, now retired	Widower	Good	Criminal record (extortion)
G	M 45	Vice-president of local bank	Happily married; three sons, ages 15 to 25	Good	Deacon of local church; member of Rotary Club

Source: Washington Post, 22 March 1981.

ment.[8] Another criterion might be whether or not the disease requiring the treatment is self-inflicted. For example, should chronic alcoholics be given the same preference for receiving a new liver as other patients? At least one state in the United States has ruled that Medicaid should not pay for such treatments for active alcoholics and drug abusers.[9]

A variety of other criteria could be used to justify the choice of one transplant candidate over another, but a choice must still be made among real lives. In addition, some even broader allocative questions arise from this example: How many transplant centers should be developed in American hospitals? Should there be sufficient capacity to help all the patients who might need this treatment, regardless of the cost and the underutilization of the facilities most of the time? Or should only enough centers be developed to meet average demands? Should individuals who can afford to pay be allowed to jump ahead of others in line to receive new organs if their payments can fund future surgeries for the less fortunate?

These questions have arisen in a very real way in the debate over the allocation of the limited supply of donor organs among transplant centers around the country. One model of allocation would keep the organ in the catchment area where it was procured and permit the local transplant center to use it, while another would have a more centralized system of allocation, providing the organ to the patient who is most in need, that is, the nearest to death.[10] Given that the sicker patients tend to cluster at a few major transplant centers, this alternative might put smaller centers out of business. This conflict in turn raises several ethical questions: Why should an individual's chance of survival depend on where he or she lives rather than on medical criteria? Should there not be some attempt to keep more centers open and promote the technology for longer-term benefits?

Even though the preservation of life may be an important or even dominant value for public policymaking, in many situations the definition of life itself is subject to debate, legally as well as morally. The use of therapeutic abortion as a means of birth control presents one problem of this sort: determining when human life begins.[11] This issue has been fought in the court system and in the streets of many American cities and towns, but no resolution has been found that both sides can accept. Even here the question is not always clear-cut, for many abortion opponents would accept abortions in the case of rape or incest, while many abortion supporters would reject the procedure as a means of determining gender. Issues concerning artificial means of prolonging life even when a person would be considered dead by many clinical criteria illustrate the problem of defining life at the other end of the life cycle.[12]

The possibility of assisted suicide for the terminally ill has raised conflicts between the values of preserving life and of preserving autonomy (a concept that is discussed later in this chapter).[13] If an adult wants to end his or her life—

Actor Christopher Reeve (far right), paralyzed in a 1995 riding accident, has been a vocal advocate of stem cell research. Shown here with James Thomson (left), professor of Anatomy, University of Wisconsin-Madison and John Gearhart, Armstrong Professor of Medicine, Institute for Cell Engineering, Johns Hopkins, Reeve has lobbied Congress for legislation and funding of this area. Critics, however, raise ethical concerns about the morality of using tissue from unborn fetuses for such research.

because of a terminal and painful disease, for example—should government have the obligation, or even the right, to prevent that adult from doing so? Should the individual have access to assisted suicide if he or she is simply depressed or despondent? Thus, while all policymakers and all citizens may agree on the importance of preserving human life, serious disagreements arise over just what constitutes a human life and who can dispense with it.

Finally, in some situations the government sanctions and actively encourages the taking of human lives. The most obvious example is war; others are capital punishment and, in some instances, the management of police officers' response to threats to their own lives and safety. The question that arises here is what criteria governments can use to justify the taking of some lives while we deplore and prohibit the taking of others?[14] Obvious criteria that we might apply are self-preservation and the protection of society against elements that could undermine it or take other lives. But there is some degree of inconsistency in the arguments here, and government must justify placing higher values on some lives than on others. Again, the fundamental point is that although there may be broad agreement in society on the importance of preserving human lives as a goal of all public policies, this criterion is not obviously and unambiguously enforceable in all policy situations. We must have a detailed analysis of all such situations and some understanding of the particular application of the criterion in each of those varied situations.

The Preservation of Individual Autonomy

Another important value for public policy, especially in a democracy, is maximization of the autonomy of each citizen to make decisions about his or her own life. This principle underlies a considerable body of conservative political thought, which assumes that the interests of the individual are, everything else being equal, more important than those of the society as a whole.[15] It also assumes that individuals may at times select alternatives that many other people, and society as a whole acting through government, might deem unacceptable. Thus, child labor, sweatshops, and extremely long working hours with low wages were all justified at one time because they preserved the right of the individual to "choose" his or her own working conditions.[16]

In adherence to an extreme definition of individual autonomy, which includes the right to choose conditions or products that are inherently harmful, the public sector would be excluded from almost all forms of social and economic activity. Even using this extreme version of autonomy, however, the state has been able to intervene to protect individuals against fraud and breach of contract, and it has to some degree protected children and other less competent individuals more than it does adults, who presumably are able to make their own decisions. In contrast, advocates of an enhanced role for the public sector have argued that the welfare state, by increasing the options available to citizens, especially less advantaged citizens, actually enhances individual freedom and autonomy.[17]

Several interesting questions arise in the public sector in regard to individual autonomy. One involves the legitimacy of state intervention: what groups in society should the state attempt to protect, either against themselves or against those who would defraud them or otherwise infringe on their rights? Children have traditionally been protected—even against their own parents—because they have been assumed to be incapable of exercising full, autonomous choice,[18] and the state has been empowered to operate in loco parentis to attempt to preserve the rights of children. Likewise, the state has protected mentally incompetent adults who cannot make rational, autonomous choices. Less justifiably by most criteria, the state has operated to limit the choices of welfare recipients, unwed mothers, and individuals who, although they may have full mental capabilities, are stigmatized in some fashion by society and punished for making questionable choices in the past. As Desmond King points out, liberal societies such as the United States have at times adopted extremely illiberal policies, policies that limit exercise of free choice of the individual, when they believe there is some compelling state interest involved.[19] Again, the question is what criteria should be used to decide which groups the state should treat as its children?

The state may also intervene to protect the life of an individual who has made an autonomous decision to end his or her life. Legislation that makes suicide a crime and attempts to prevent individuals from purposely ending their lives reflects a judgment that the value of preserving life supersedes the value of preserving individual autonomy. In this hierarchy of values, the decision to end one's own life by definition indicates that the individual needs the protection of the state. The same principle is apparently applied to individuals who have made it clear that they do not wish to be kept "alive" by artificial means when all hope of recovery to a fully conscious and autonomous life is lost. Such instances raise several conflicting values and return us to the question of what actually constitutes a human life? Does it matter that an individual may have declared while in good health that he or she does not want to be kept alive by artificial means?[20] The potentially conflicting principles of preserving life and preserving autonomy become even more confused here because an individual who once made an autonomous choice about how he or she would like to be treated may at the crucial time be no longer able to decide anything autonomously and may, in fact, never be able to do so again.

In less extreme instances, the state may also restrain the autonomy of an individual for the sake of protecting him or her from the adverse consequences of a personal choice. Consumer protection is an obvious example—government may disregard the traditional principle of caveat emptor and simply prohibit the sale of potentially harmful products in order to protect the citizen. On the one hand, the conservative who is interested in preserving individual choice would argue that such protections are harmful inasmuch as the paternalistic actions of government prevent citizens from being truly free actors. On the other hand, the complexity of the marketplace, the number of products offered for sale, and the absence of full information may prevent individuals from making meaningful judgments.[21] As a consequence, government is justified in intervening, especially because many of the products banned would affect persons incapable of making their own informed choices—for example, children. A less extreme example is government's requirement of labeling and full disclosure of information so that citizens are able to make more rational and informed autonomous decisions about the products they purchase.

At times government also forces citizens to consume certain goods and services because they are presumably for the citizens' own good. Two examples of these "merit goods" that have been of concern recently are requirements that people riding in automobiles should have to wear seat belts and that people riding motorcycles should have to wear helmets.[22] These measures have been supported by a number of safety organizations and by many citizens, but other citizens argue that they should be "free to be foolish," to make their own choices, and to assume certain risks.[23] As appealing as that argument sounds within a free society, there are also potential costs from risky decisions that extend beyond the individual who is willing to take the chance. Their families are potentially harmed, both emotionally and economically, by such risky behavior. The society as a whole may have a stake in the individual decision because public money may well have to pay for a long and expensive hospitalization from a preventable injury. Thus, as with all of the ethical principles that can be applied to public decisions, there tend to be few absolutes and a great deal of balancing of ideas and ethical criteria when government must act to make policy.

Professional licensing and laws that control the licensing of drugs also have been criticized as unduly restricting the free choice of individuals. It is argued that individuals should have the right to select the form of treatment they would like, even if the medical establishment deems it quackery. So, for example, activists for AIDS victims have criticized the U.S. Food and Drug Administration for delaying approval of some drugs that may have potential for ameliorating the symptoms of AIDS and slowing the progress of the disease.[24] The criticisms have been particularly pointed because these drugs already are licensed and available in other industrialized countries. Similar arguments were made earlier about the failure of the FDA to approve laetrile as a drug for the treatment of cancer. In both cases, the individual is being denied the right to choose courses of treatment for a deadly disease.

Of course, the counterargument from the Food and Drug Administration is that these restrictions are justified because they increase the probability that the individual will receive treatments that are known to have some beneficial effects. If there were no licensing the individual might rely on a treatment without any real therapeutic value until it was too late to use other treatments. The question from the perspective of ethics is who should be able to make the choice about the best treatment—the individual affected or a government organization?

Lying

Most systems of ethics and morality prohibit lying.[25] People generally regard lying as wrong simply "because it is wrong," but it can also be considered wrong because it allows one individual to deprive another of his or her autonomy. When one person lies to another, the liar deprives the other person of the ability to make rational and informed decisions. In some instances, telling "little white lies" may prevent awkward social situations, but perhaps more stringent criteria should be applied to justify lies told by government, especially in a democracy.

Lying to the public by public officials has been justified primarily as being in the public's own good. Political leaders who accept this paternalistic argument assume that public officials have more information and are unwilling to divulge it either for security reasons or because they believe that the information will only "confuse" citizens. They may therefore lie to the public in order to get average citizens to behave in ways that they—the public officials—prefer. They also seem to believe that the citizens would behave in that same way if they had all the information available to the political leader, but even if citizens would not behave as public officials want them to, officials think that they *should* behave in that manner, and the lie is therefore justified as a means of protecting the public from its own irresponsibility or ignorance.

Such lying obviously limits the autonomy of the average citizen when making policy choices or evaluating the performance of those in office. Even white lies are questionable—the importance of autonomy in democratic political systems may demand much closer attention to honesty, even though the short-term consequences of telling the truth may not benefit incumbents. In times of war officials may need to lie, or at a minimum withhold information, for security reasons or to maintain morale, but even that largely justifiable behavior will tend to undermine the legitimacy of a democratic system. In part, citizens may find it difficult to know when the lying has stopped—a problem that became very evident during the Cold War.[26]

Other white lies told to the public involve withholding information that might cause panic or other responses that are potentially very dangerous. For example, a public official may learn that a nuclear power plant has had a minor and apparently controllable accident that is not believed to endanger anyone. The official may withhold this information from the public in the belief that doing so will prevent a panic; a mass flight from the scene could cause more harm than the accident. But, as with other ethical situations, the decision to lie about one thing and not about others makes it difficult for the official (and government as a whole) to behave consistently. Perhaps the only standard that can be applied with any consistency in this case is the utilitarian criterion: the harm prevented by the lie must outweigh the ill effects caused by the lie. Determining this utilitarian ratio is relatively easy when we are balancing the possible few deaths and limited property damage from a minor nuclear accident against probable widespread and violent panic. Continued lying, however, will eventually generate a public loss of trust in government and its officials, and the cost of such skepticism is difficult to calculate.[27]

A special category of lying is the withholding of information by public officials to protect their own careers. This is a problem for the "whistle blowers" who would expose deceit, as well as for the liars, and it happens in the private as well as in the public sector.[28] Attempting to act ethically and responsibly has placed many individuals in difficult situations. For example, the man who blew the whistle on government cost overruns on the Lockheed C-5A airplane lost his job; so did the EPA official who exposed the agency's shortcomings under Rita Lavelle, as well as many other conscientious officials in less dramatic circumstances.[29] The problem caused when someone blows the whistle is especially difficult to analyze when the individual at fault does not lie directly but simply does nothing to expose errors made in government.

The whistle blower must go to some lengths in order to make the information about official lying known to the public and must accept substantial career risks. Because of these difficulties, policymakers may want to devise means to encourage whistle blowers and to protect them against reprisals. The federal government and many state and local governments in the United States have devised programs to protect whistle blowers, but there are still substantial risks for the individual who chooses to act in what he or she considers the responsible manner. In conjunction with, or in the absence of, programs encouraging officials to divulge information, other legislation such as the Freedom of Information Act can at least make it more difficult for government to suppress information.[30]

Thus, in addition to the general moral prohibition, lying carries a particular onus in the public sector because it can destroy an individual citizen's ability to make appropriate and informed choices about government. Although a lie may be told for good reasons (at least in the mind of the liar), it must be questioned unless it has extremely positive benefits and is not told just for the convenience of the individual official. The long-term consequences for government of even "justifiable" lying may be negative. Citizens who learn that government lies to them for good reasons may soon wonder if it will not lie to them for less noble reasons, and they may find it difficult to believe the official interpretation of anything. In the United States, for example, the Vietnam War, Watergate, and "Irangate" have created a sense of distrust toward government among an entire generation of citizens that manifests itself in somewhat general disaffection with government.[31]

If strictures against lying are to some degree dependent on a desire to preserve the political community and the sense of trust within it, somewhat different rules may apply in international politics. Although there is a concept of an international community of nations, the moral bonds within that community tend to be weaker than the bonds that exist within a single nation. Further, a national political leader's paramount responsibilities are to his or her own citizens. Therefore, lying in international politics may be more acceptable; political leaders regularly face the problem of "dirty hands," which seems to be part of the job of being a political leader in an imperfect world.[32] That is, leaders may be forced to engage in activities that they know to be wrong in most circumstances, such as lying, in order to serve the (largely utilitarian) goals of protecting and preserving the interests of their own country.

Fairness

Fairness is a value to which citizens expect government to assign maximum importance. One standard justification for the existence of government, even for conservatives, is that it protects and enforces the civil and political rights of all individuals, with as much equality as possible. Further, it is argued (at least by liberals) that government has the legal and economic capacity to redress inequities in the distribution of goods and services that result from the operations of the marketplace.[33] Government, then, is charged with ensuring that citizens are treated fairly in the political system and perhaps in the economy and society.

But just what is "fair treatment of citizens"? As employed by different schools of social and political thought, the word *fair* has had different meanings. To a conservative, for example, fairness means allowing individuals maximum opportunities to exercise their own abilities and to keep what they earn in the marketplace through those abilities. Some conservatives consider it fair that people who cannot provide for themselves should suffer, along with their families, although they disagree about how much suffering is acceptable.[34] Similarly, many conservatives do not consider it fair for government to take property from some citizens in order to benefit others; in this view, property has rights, just as people do.[35]

The familiar Marxist doctrine of "from each according to his abilities to each according to his needs" suggests a very different standard of fairness, implying that all members of the society, provided they are willing to contribute their own abilities (however limited), are entitled to have their material needs satisfied.[36] According to this standard, those with lower earning capacities need not suffer, although the doctrine does not guarantee absolute equality. There is, however, no uncontested definition of "needs," so this standard could be an open-ended entitlement for citizens were it to be accepted.

The standard of fairness applied in most contemporary welfare states is something of a mixture of the conservative and Marxist standards, although it generally lacks the intellectual underpinnings of either extreme.[37] The mixed-economy welfare state that operates in industrialized societies usually allows productive citizens to retain most of their earnings and at the same time requires them to help build a floor of benefits so that the less fortunate can maintain at least a minimal standard of living. Unlike the situation in the Marxist state, this redistribution of goods and services to the less fortunate from the more success-ful is conducted in the context of free and open politics.

As well as being concerned with fairness across classes and among individu-als, governments increasingly must be concerned about fairness across genera-tions. The current generation is custodian of the natural resources of the society and must make decisions about the use of those resources. Is it *fair* for the cur-rent generation to consume such a large share of the proven reserves of resources such as oil, copper, chromium, and the like? Further, is it *fair* for this generation to incur a massive public (and private) debt that will impose burdens on, and re-strain the opportunities of, future generations? What principles can be used to justify choices that have intergenerational consequences?[38] How can those prin-ciples be included in the analytic techniques used to make policy decisions?[39]

Can these operating principles of the contemporary welfare state—prin-ciples that arise largely from political accidents and a pragmatic evolution process—be systematized and developed on a more intellectual plane? One promising approach to such a systematic justification of the welfare state can be found in philosopher John Rawls's concept of social justice. In his essay "Justice as Fairness,"[40] Rawls develops two principles of justice for a society. The first is that "each person participating in a practice, or affected by it, has an equal right to the most extensive liberty compatible with like liberty of all." This is a re-statement of the basic right of individuals to be involved in governmental deci-sions that affect them, a principle not incompatible with the cry "No taxation without representation!" This first principle of justice would place the burden of proof on anyone who would seek to limit participation in political life; it can therefore be seen as a safeguard for procedural democracy in contemporary so-cieties. Thus, Rawls places a pronounced emphasis on the decision-making pro-cedures employed when evaluating the fairness of those decisions and the fairness of the institutions of society. This may present great difficulties for the citizen and the analyst, however, if the decisions reached by participatory means conflict with more substantive conceptions of fairness.

The second principle of fairness advanced by Rawls is more substantive and also more problematic. Referred to as the "difference principle," it states that "social and economic inequalities are to be arranged so that they are both: (a) to the greatest benefit of the least advantaged; and (b) attached to offices and po-sitions open to all under conditions of fair equality of opportunity."[41] This prin-ciple places the burden of proof on those who attempt to justify a system of inequalities, which can be seen as just only if all other possible arrangements would produce lowered expectations for the least-well-off group in society. To help a society that is striving for equality, citizens are asked to think of their own place in society as shrouded behind a "veil of ignorance," so that it cannot be known to them in advance.[42] Would they be willing to gamble on being in the lowest segment of the society when they decide on a set of inequalities for the society? If they would not, then they have good reason to understand the society's need to equalize the distribution of goods and services. Of course, it is impossible to apply the logic of the veil of ignorance within existing societies, but it is a useful concept for understanding the rational acceptance of redistributive government policies, and in justifying such policies politically.

Several interesting questions arise with respect to Rawls's difference principle. One is the place of natural endowments and individual differences in producing and justifying inequalities. Should individuals who have special natural abilities be allowed to benefit from them? This borders on the basic ethical principle of desert, or the degree to which any individual deserves what he or she receives in the world (this concept is discussed in the next section). The question then is reminiscent of a Kurt Vonnegut story in *Player Piano*, in which individuals' particular talents are balanced by the "great handicapper."[43] Individuals who can run particularly fast, for instance, are required to wear heavy weights to slow them down, and those who have creative gifts are required to wear earphones through which come loud and discordant noises to distract them from thinking and using that creativity. Does Rawls regard such a homogeneous and ultimately dull society as desirable or fair? One would think not, but he does point out that natural endowments are desirable primarily because they can be used to assist those in the lowest segment of society. Thus, noblesse oblige is expected of those who possess natural talents.

Does the same expectation hold true for those whose endowments are economic rather than physical or intellectual? It would appear that in Rawls's view equality is a natural principle that can be justified by decision making that occurs behind the veil of ignorance, as well as by the cooperative instincts that Rawls believes are inherent in humans. Again, in his view, economic endowments should exist only to the extent they can be used for the betterment of the lowest segments in society.

In contrast, critics point to what they consider the natural rights of individuals to retain their holdings,[44] and to the potential incentives for work and investment that are inherent in a system of economic inequality. Inequalities are argued to be functional for a society because they supply a spur to ambition and an incentive to produce more—both artistically and economically—which in turn can be considered to benefit the entire society.[45] Thus, to critics of Rawls's philosophy, the tendency toward equality may be inappropriate on ethical grounds because it would deny individuals benefits that they have received through either genetics or education, and it may be wrong on utilitarian grounds because it reduces the total production of the society along several dimensions.

Finally, the Rawlsian framework is discussed primarily within the context of a single society, or a single institution in which cooperative principles would at least be considered, if not always followed. Could these principles be applied to a broader context; in particular, should they be applied to a global community? In other words, should the riches accumulated in industrialized countries be used to benefit the citizens of the most impoverished countries of the world?[46] Such a policy would, of course, be politically difficult to implement, even if it could be shown to be morally desirable. Nevertheless, the ethical underpinnings of foreign aid must be considered, especially as the world moves into an era of increased scarcity as well as increased interdependence.

Although we have been discussing issues of fairness primarily in economic terms, increasingly these issues are conceptualized in terms of race, ethnicity, and gender. The same logic of analysis may well be applicable, however, for fairness could be maximized by assuming the same veil of ignorance for making decisions about these social differences as it is when used for decisions about economic differences. These social categories, however, also raise issues of compensation for past injustices, along with a perceived need to create structures and programs that will encourage future achievement of the previously disadvantaged groups.

Such remedy for past unfairness, in turn, creates resentments on the part of those who feel that their natural endowments of skills and abilities are being devalued. This kind of resentment arises in response to scholarships granted on the basis of race or gender, hiring quotas, and a variety of other "affirmative action" policies intended to change existing social and economic patterns.[47] Further, although economic inequalities may be justified as providing incentives for individuals to do more for themselves and to change their own conditions, it is generally not feasible for individuals to change gender or race. No question of equality and fairness is easy to resolve, but these issues of race and gender have proved to be among the most difficult for the political system to cope with.

While opinions may differ as to the applicability of Rawls's ideas in the real world of policymaking, and even to the desirability of such application, his work does raise interesting and important ethical questions for those attempting to design public policies. Many industrialized democracies have been making redistributive economic policy decisions for years, often justifying them on pragmatic or political grounds rather than on ethical principles.[48] The work of Rawls provides intellectual underpinnings for these policies, even though no government has gone as far in redistributing income and wealth as Rawls's difference principle would demand. These governments are now facing more decisions about race and gender inequalities, and there too some guidance beyond simple political expediency may be required.

The Concept of Desert

Discussion of the values of the welfare state raises the question of *desert*. What does a citizen deserve as a member of the society, and what does the individual deserve as a human being with particular needs and virtues? As discussed earlier, the American people enjoy some rights by virtue of the Constitution and the Bill of Rights. The existence of these rights is largely incontestable, although there certainly are multiple interpretations of their meaning. The more interesting cases, however, involve benefits coming from government that have come to be considered rights but are much less clearly grounded in the basic law of the land.

The concept of "entitlement" is the most important instance of desert being constructed by policy and then being accepted by the population.[49] Social insurance programs are the clearest example of entitlements, for the citizen has paid for the program over his or her working lifetime and has received a commitment from government to provide the benefits when the citizen needs them—because of retirement, unemployment, or disability. These programs were designed to be regarded not as charity or a government "handout" but rather as a right. Further, entitlement programs were designed to make it difficult for subsequent generations of politicians to dismantle them.[50]

When we move away from social insurance and other contributory programs, however, the concept of desert becomes more difficult to sustain within the public sector in the United States. It is clear that young people do have a right to a free public education, but only through high school—why does this right not extend through college, or even through graduate school?[51] Likewise, the debate over health care reform in 1994 raised the question of whether citizens have a right to health care, and if so to what level of health care? If there is a right to basic health care, is there also a right to the most advanced and expensive treatments available? If the rights are restricted to basic services, where does the entitlement stop and why? Certain public goods, such as clean air and water, also are often conceptualized as the entitlements of citizens. Why?

Can there be a "negative desert"? Do some citizens deserve certain punishments and sanctions? It is sometimes argued that the perpetrators of certain crimes "deserve" the death penalty.[52] It is also argued that those responsible for economic or environmental crimes "deserve" certain severe (but not death) penalties. On what basis can it be said that people deserve a specified form of punishment, particularly one as severe and final as the death penalty? At a less extreme level, do people who have other perceived failings, such as having to accept public assistance, deserve to be punished or controlled in other ways? In Chapter 11 we noted the increasing number of restrictions and regulations being imposed on welfare recipients; do those people "deserve" that treatment, and if so why?

A final point about desert is that it is often defined in terms of particular communities, with those outside the community being excluded. In a search to find alternatives to big government and utilitarian values, one strand of communitarian thinking in the United States has argued for greater devolution of decision making to communities. Empowering such communities to make decisions for themselves, however, could easily lead to an "us versus them" conception of governing, with (paradoxically) a great deal of mutuality within the community and substantial exclusion of outsiders. For example, would equalization of school funding be an appropriate policy under communitarian governance? The concept of community has a powerful appeal to many Americans, but its restrictive concept of desert raises a number of questions about membership in the community.

Ethics and Public Policy: Alternatives to Utilitarianism

The ethical system most often applied to public policy analysis is *utilitarianism*, by which actions are justified as producing the greatest net benefit for the society as a whole. As noted in Chapter 16, this principle undergirds the dominant analytic approaches in the field, such as cost-benefit analysis. In this chapter we have discussed several ethical questions that arise in making and implementing public policies, as well as some possible answers to these questions. Most of the discussion of these questions presented here reflects a nonutilitarian perspective. Ultimately, however, just as no one can provide definitive answers to these ethical questions in public policy, public officials may face policy questions that have no readily acceptable answers, economically, politically, or ethically. Values and ethical principles are frequently in conflict, and sometimes the policymaker must violate one firmly held ethical position in order to protect another.

Despite these practical difficulties, it is important for citizens and policymakers to think about policy in ethical terms. Perhaps too much policymaking has been conducted without attention to anything but the political and economic consequences. Of course, such utilitarian values are important as criteria on which to base evaluation of a program, but they may not be the only relevant criteria. Both the policymaker and the citizen must be concerned also with matters of justice and trust in government. Indeed, it may be that justice and social trust ultimately make the best policies—and even the best politics.

Notes

Chapter 1

1. U.S. Bureau of the Census, *1997 Census of Governments* (Washington, D.C.: Government Printing Office, 1998). The number of governments increased by an average of more than 300 per year during the early 1990s.
2. See Lester Salaman, "Introduction" in Salaman, ed. *Handbook of Policy Instruments* (New York: Oxford University Press, 2001).
3. Richard Nelson, *The Moon and the Ghetto* (New York: Norton, 1977).
4. Richard Rose, "The Programme Approach to the Growth of Government," *British Journal of Political Science* 15 (1985): 1–28.
5. Alison Mitchell, "Clinton Promotes Education Testing, Gingrich Opposes," *New York Times*, 8 September 1997.
6. Brian W. Hogwood and B. Guy Peters, *The Pathology of Public Policy* (Oxford: Oxford University Press, 1985); and Craig W. Thomas, "Public Management as Interagency Cooperation," *Journal of Public Administration Research and Theory* 7 (1997): 221–46.
7. Helen Ingram and Anne Schneider, "Improving Implementation through Framing Smarter Statutes," *Journal of Public Policy* 10 (1990): 67–88; Stephen H. Linder and B. Guy Peters, "The Study of Policy Instruments," *Policy Currents* 2 (May 1992): 1, 4–7; and B. Guy Peters and Frans K. M. Van Nispen, *Tools and Public Policy* (Cheltenham, England: Edward Elgar, 1998).
8. Private actors do, of course, have recourse to law as a means of influencing policy and forcing government action. This is especially true in the United States where the courts are so important for determining policy. For example, in addition to the enforcement activities of the Federal Trade Commission and the Antitrust Division of the Department of Justice, private individuals also bring suit to enforce antitrust laws.
9. *Bragdon v. Abbott*, 97 SC 156 (1997).
10. B. Guy Peters and Martin O. Heisler, "Thinking about Public Sector Growth," in *Why Governments Grow: Measuring Public Sector Size*, ed. C. L. Taylor (Beverly Hills, Calif.: Sage, 1983). *See also* Giandomenico Majone, *Regulating Europe* (London: Routledge, 1996).
11. The costing of these regulatory interventions was made popular by Murray Wiedenbaum. See his "The High Costs of Government Regulation," *Challenge*, November

1979, 32–39. These costings were not without their political motivations, e.g., to demonstrate the high costs of government, and they usually failed to include the off-setting value of the benefits of regulation.

12. William T. Gormley, *Privatization and Its Alternatives* (Madison: University of Wisconsin Press, 1991).

13. Penelope Lemov, "Jailhouse, INC," *Governing* 6 (May 1993): 44–48.

14. Donald F. Kettl, *Government by Proxy: (Mis)Managing Federal Programs?* (Washington, D.C.: CQ Press, 1988); and Patricia W. Ingraham, "Quality in the Public Services," in *Governance in a Changing Environment*, ed. B. Guy Peters and Donald J. Savoie (Montreal: McGill/Queens University Press, 1995).

15. Charles H. Levine and Paul L. Posner, "The Centralizing Effects of Fiscal Austerity on the Intergovernmental System," *Political Science Quarterly* 96 (1981): 67–85.

16. James D. Chesney, "Intergovernmental Politics in the Allocation of Block Grant Funds for Substance Abuse in Michigan," *Publius* 24 (1994): 39–46; and Doug Peterson, "Block Grant 'Turn-Backs' Revived in Bush Budget," *Nation's Cities Weekly* 15 (3 February 1992): 6.

17. Neal R. Pierce, "Bush 'Turnback' Plan Sounds Nice but It's 'Irrelevant'", *Nation's Cities Weekly* 14 (18 February 1991): 12.

18. Stanley S. Surrey and Paul R. McDaniel, *Tax Expenditures* (Cambridge, Mass.: Harvard University Press, 1985).

19. Aaron Wildavsky, "Keeping Kosher: The Epistemology of Tax Expenditures," *Journal of Public Policy* 5 (1985): 413–31.

20. Charles L. Schultze, *The Public Use of Private Interest* (Washington, D.C.: Brookings Institution, 1977).

21. See, for example, F. Anderson, *Environmental Improvement through Economic Incentives* (Baltimore: Johns Hopkins University Press, 1977); and Richard C. Hula, *Market-based Public Policy* (New York: St. Martin's, 1990).

22. Barry P. Bosworth, Andrew S. Carron, and Elisabeth Rhyne, *The Economics of Federal Credit Programs* (Washington, D.C.: Brookings Institution, 1987).

23. Thomas Anton, *Moving Money* (Cambridge, Mass.: Oelgeschlager, Hain and Gunn, 1980).

24. Johan Fritzell, "Income Inequality Trends in the 1980s: A Five-Country Comparison," *Acta Sociologica* 36 (1993): 47–62; and Sheldon Danzinger and Peter Gottschalk, *Uneven Tides: Rising Inequality in America* (New York: Russell Sage, 1993).

25. On taxation, see B. Guy Peters, *The Politics of Taxation: A Comparative Perspective* (Oxford: Blackwells, 1991). On conscription, see Margaret Levi, *Consent, Dissent, Patriotism* (Cambridge, England: Cambridge University Press, 1997).

26. Anthony King, "Ideas, Institutions and Policies of Government: A Comparative Analysis," *British Journal of Political Science* 5 (1975): 418.

27. See Linda M. Bennett and Stephen Earl Bennett, *Living with Leviathan: Americans Coming to Terms with Big Government* (Lawrence: University of Kansas Press, 1990).

28. Lloyd A. Free and Hadley Cantril, *The Political Beliefs of Americans* (New York: Simon and Schuster, 1968).

29. David O. Sears and Jack Citrin, *Tax Revolt: Something for Nothing in California*, rev. ed. (Berkeley: University of California Press, 1991).

30. See "Opinion Pulse," *The American Enterprise*, March/April 1997, 92.

31. Peter Bachrach and Aryeh Botwinick, *Power and Empowerment: A Radical Theory of Participatory Democracy* (Philadelphia: Temple University Press, 1992).

32. Michael T. Hayes, *Incrementalism* (New York: Longman, 1992).

33. See, for example, Charles O. Jones, *The Reagan Legacy* (Chatham, N.J.: Chatham House, 1989).

34. Robin Toner, "House Democrats Support Abortion in Health Plans," *New York Times*, 14 July 1994.

35. See William Schneider, "What Else Do They Want?" *National Journal*, (16 May 1998): 1150.

36. See Robert Reich, *The Work of Nations* (New York: Norton, 1991); and Ann O. Kreuger, *The Political Economy of American Trade Policy* (Chicago: University of Chicago Press, 1995).

37. Andrew Hacker, *Two Nations: Black and White, Separate, Hostile Unequal* (New York: Scribners, 1992).

Chapter 2

1. Charles H. Levine, "Human Resource Erosion and the Uncertain Future of the U.S. Civil Service: From Policy Gridlock to Structural Fragmentation," *Governance* 1 (1988): 115–43.

2. Peter H. Stone, "Tobacco's Road," *National Journal* (1 January 1994): 19–23. Increasing concern over the health effects of tobacco is making any support less palatable.

3. See Terry Sanford, *Storm over the States* (New York: McGraw-Hill, 1967), 80.

4. Deil S. Wright, *Understanding Intergovernmental Relations*, 3d ed. (Belmont, Calif.: Brooks/Cole, 1988), 83–86.

5. Ibid.

6. For a somewhat different view, see Jae-Won Yoo and Deil S. Wright, "Public Policy and Intergovernmental Relations: Measuring Perceived Changes in National Influences," *Policy Studies Journal* 21 (1993): 687–99.

7. John Kincaid, "From Cooperative to Coercive Federalism," *The Annals* 509 (1990): 139–52.

8. Angela Antonelli, "Promises Unfilled: Unfunded Mandates Reform Act of 1995," *Regulation* 19, no. 2 (1996): 44–52.

9. *New York Times*, 13 October 1991.

10. U.S. Bureau of the Census, *Census of Governments, 1997* (Washington, D.C.: Government Printing Office, 1998).

11. Jerry Mitchell, *Public Authorities and Public Policy: The Business of Government* (New York: Greenwood, 1992); Kathryn A. Foster, *The Political Economy of Special Purpose Government* (Washington, D.C.: Georgetown University Press, 1998).

12. During the mid-1980s the states averaged over 11 percent surpluses in their total budgets. See the Tax Foundation, *Facts and Figures on Government Finance, 1991* (Baltimore: Johns Hopkins University Press, 1991), table E2.

13. On the concept of "veto points," see Ellen Immergut, *Health Politics: Interests and Institutions in Western Europe* (Cambridge, England: Cambridge University Press, 1992).

14. Mark Peterson, *Legislating Together* (Cambridge, Mass.: Harvard University Press, 1992).

15. See, for example, James Q. Wilson, *Bureaucracy* (New York: Basic Books, 1989).

16. See Cornelius Kerwin, *Rulemaking*, 2d ed. (Washington, D.C.: CQ Press, 2000).

17. George Krause, *A Two-Way Street: The Institutional Dynamics of the Modern Administrative State* (Pittsburgh: University of Pittsburgh Press, 2000).

18. Morris P. Fiorina, "An Era of Divided Government," *Political Science Quarterly* 107 (1992): 387–410; and James L. Sundquist, *Constitutional Reform and Effective Government*, rev. ed. (Washington, D.C.: Brookings Institution, 1992).

19. For example, other Democrats were active in developing and promoting alternatives to the Clinton health care reform proposals (see chapter 10). See also Viveca Novak, "It Still Takes Two," *National Journal* (25 September 1993): 2301–3.

20. David Mayhew, *Divided We Govern* (New Haven: Yale University Press, 1991); Charles O. Jones, *The Presidency in a Separated System* (Washington, D.C.: Brookings Institution, 1994); Nelson Polsby, *Policy Innovation in America* (New Haven: Yale University Press, 1984); and John E. Schwartz, *America's Hidden Success*, rev. ed. (New York: Norton, 1988). For a critique, see Alberto Alesina and Howard Rosenthal, *Partisan Politics, Divided Government and the Economy* (Cambridge, England: Cambridge University Press, 1996).

21. Michael T. Hayes, *Incrementalism* (New York: Longman, 1992).

22. Charles E. Lindblom, *The Intelligence of Democracy: Decision Making through Mutual Adjustment* (New York: Free Press, 1965).

23. For example, a poll in late 2003 found that 79 percent of the American populace supported health care for all Americans even if it meant higher taxes; see *Washington Post* poll, 13 October 2003.

24. Brian W. Hogwood and B. Guy Peters, *Policy Dynamics* (Brighton, England: Wheatsheaf, 1982); and Robert E. Goodin, *Political Theory and Public Policy* (Chicago: University of Chicago Press, 1986).

25. The classic statement is J. Leiper Freeman, *The Political Process: Executive Bureau-Legislative Committee Relations* (New York: Random House, 1965).

26. The classic statement of this point is Theodore J. Lowi, *The End of Liberalism*, 2d ed. (New York: Norton, 1979).

27. Peter L. Hall and C. Lawrence Evans, "The Power of Subcommittees," *Journal of Politics* 52 (1990): 335–55.

28. See D. Roderick Kiewiet and Mathew D. McCubbins, *The Logic of Delegation* (Chicago: University of Chicago Press, 1991).

29. Gregory J. Wawro, *Legislative Entrepreneurship in the U.S. House of Representatives* (Ann Arbor: University of Michigan Press, 2000).

30. D. McCool, "Subgovernments as Determinants of Political Viability," *Political Science Quarterly* 105 (1990): 269–93.

31. André Blais and Stéphane Dion, *The Budget-Maximizing Bureaucrat* (Pittsburgh: University of Pittsburgh Press, 1992).

32. Peter B. Natchez and Irvin C. Bupp, "Policy and Priority in the Budgetary Process," *American Political Science Review* 67 (1973): 951–63.

33. See Robert H. Salisbury, J. P. Heinz, R. L. Nelson, and Edward O. Laumann, "Triangles, Networks and Hollow Cores: The Complex Geometry of Washington In-

terest Representation," in *The Politics of Interests*, ed. Mark P. Petracca (Boulder, Colo.: Westview, 1992).

34. Rufus E. Miles, "A Cabinet Department of Education: An Unwise Campaign Promise or a Sound Idea?" *Public Administration Review* 39 (1979): 103–10.

35. For example, the Cooperative Extension Service in the Department of Agriculture eliminated hundreds of county offices.

36. See Jack L. Walker, *Mobilizing Interest Groups in America* (Ann Arbor: University of Michigan Press, 1991).

37. Charles O. Jones, *The United States Congress* (Homewood, Ill.: Dorsey, 1982).

38. Try it!

39. Some scholars make a great deal over the differences between these concepts, with a community being a more unified and tightly knit set of groups than a network. See Martin J. Smith, *Pressure, Power and Policy* (Pittsburgh: University of Pittsburgh Press, 1994).

40. See Rose and Peters, *Can Government Go Bankrupt?*

41. William T. Gormley, *Privatization and Its Alternatives* (Madison: University of Wisconsin Press, 1991).

42. See Linda L. M. Bennett and Stephen Earl Bennett, *Living With Leviathan: Americans Come to Terms With Big Government* (Lawrence: University of Kansas Press, 1990).

43. Jonas Prager, "Contracting Out Government Services: Lessons from the Private Sector," *Public Administration Review* 54 (1994): 176–84; and Steven Rathgeb Smith and Michael Lipsky, *Nonprofits for Hire: The Welfare State in the Age of Contracting* (Cambridge, Mass.: Harvard University Press, 1993).

44. B. Guy Peters, "Public and Private Provision of Services," in *The Private Provision of Public Services,* ed. Dennis Thompson (Beverly Hills, Calif.: Sage, 1986).

45. This form of organization has not been typical in the United States. See Robert H. Salisbury, "Why No Corporatism in America?" in *Trends toward Corporatist Intermediation*, ed. Phillipe C. Schmitter and Gerhard Lehmbruch (Beverly Hills, Calif.: Sage, 1979); and Susan B. Hansen, "Industrial Policy and Corporatism in the American States," *Governance* 2 (1989): 172–97.

46. Donna Batten and Peter D. Dresser, eds., *Encyclopedia of Government Advisory Bodies,* 1992–93 (Detroit: Gale Research, 1993).

47. For a more complete treatment of public employment, see Hans-Ulrich Derlien and B. Guy Peters, *Who Works for Government and What Do They Do?* (Bamberg: University of Bamberg, Administrative Sciences, 1998).

48. See Jonathan R. T. Hughes, *The Governmental Habit Redux: Economic Controls from Colonial Times to the Present* (Princeton: Princeton University Press, 1993).

49. The figures for later years would be somewhat lower, but with a significant number of jobs still being created by defense purchases.

50. Tax Foundation, *Facts and Figures on Government Finance, 1996* (Baltimore: Johns Hopkins University Press, 1997).

51. Howard Banks, "The Costs of the Fed's Ketchup and Other Rules," *Forbes* 151 (15 February 1993): 39.

52. See Thomas D. Hopkins, "OMB's Regulatory Accounting Report Falls Short of the Mark," *Policy Study* 142 (St. Louis: Washington University Center for the Study of American Business, November 1997).

Chapter 3

1. See Michael Harrington, *The Other America: Poverty in America* (New York: Macmillan, 1963). The huge number of more recent books explicitly on the topic of poverty include Loretta Schwartz-Nobel, *Growing up Empty: The Hunger Epidemic in America* (New York: HarperCollins, 2002); Robert Asen, *Visions of Poverty: Welfare Policy and Political Imagination* (East Lansing: Michigan State University Press, 2002); Judith A. Chafel, *Child Poverty and Public Policy* (Washington, D.C.: Urban Institute Press, 1993); Jonathan L. Freedman, *From Cradle to Grave: The Human Face of Poverty in America* (New York: Atheneum, 1993); and Christopher Jencks, *Rethinking Social Policy* (Cambridge, Mass.: Harvard University Press, 1992).

2. But see Barbara J. Nelson, *Making an Issue of Child Abuse* (Chicago: University of Chicago Press, 1984).

3. James Agee, *Let Us Now Praise Famous Men* (Boston: Houghton Mifflin, 1941). This is a book of photographs and text about the plight of rural America during the Depression, funded by the Farm Security Administration. The book clearly had some impact, but that impact was more limited than a comprehensive attack on poverty.

4. Anthony Downs, "Up and Down with Ecology: 'The Issue Attention Cycle,' " *Public Interest* 28 (1972): 28–50; and B. Guy Peters and Brian W. Hogwood, "In Search of the Issue-Attention Cycle," *Journal of Politics* 47 (1985): 238–53.

5. Peter Hennessey, Susan Morrison, and Richard Townsend, "Routines Punctuated by Orgies: The Central Policy Review Staff," *Strathclyde Papers on Government and Politics*, No. 30 (1985). This reference has nothing to do with the sexual harassment issue discussed above.

6. Frank Baumgartner and Bryan D. Jones, *Agendas and Instability in American Politics* (Chicago: University of Chicago Press, 1993). The same description could be applied to individual policy areas as is being applied to the system as a whole.

7. See also Bryan D. Jones, *Reconceiving Decision-Making in Democratic Politics* (Chicago: University of Chicago Press, 1994).

8. Michael D. Cohen, James G. March, and Johan P. Olsen, "The Garbage Can Model of Organizational Choice," *Administrative Science Quarterly* 17 (1972): 1–25; and John Kingdon, *Agendas, Alternatives, and Public Policy*, 2d ed. (Boston: Little, Brown, 1993).

9. Joel Best, *Images of Issues* (New York: Aldine DeGruyter, 1989).

10. Roger W. Cobb and Charles D. Elder, *Participation in American Politics* (Baltimore: Johns Hopkins University Press, 1983), 85.

11. This is what Peter Bachrach and Morton S. Baratz referred to as the "second face of power." See their "Decisions and Nondecisions: An Analytic Framework," *American Political Science Review* 57 (1964): 632–42; and Steven Lukes, *Power: A Radical View* (London: Macmillan, 1974).

12. Cobb and Elder, *Participation*, 86.

13. Ibid., 96.

14. U.S. Department of Defense, *Quadrennial Defense Review Report* (Washington, D.C.: Department of Defense, 30 September 2001).

15. This has often been the case for social policy programs, given that in the United States these programs generally have low status, and so politicians may be able to score political points by reducing expenditures and benefits dispensed by them.

16. Jack L. Walker, "Setting the Agenda in the U.S. Senate: A Theory of Problem Selection," *British Journal of Political Science* 7 (1977): 423–45.
17. See David Dery, "Rethinking Agenda Setting," unpublished paper, Department of Political Science, Hebrew University of Jerusalem, June 2002.
18. See A. Grant Jordan, "The Pluralism of Pluralism: An Anti-Theory," *Political Studies* 38 (1990): 286–301.
19. For another, similar setting, see B. Guy Peters, "Agenda-Setting in the European Community," *Journal of European Public Policy* 1 (1994): 9–26.
20. C. Wright Mills, *The Power Elite* (New York: Oxford University Press, 1961); and Charles E. Lindblom, *Democracy and the Market System* (New York; Oxford University Press, 1988).
21. Carter A. Wilson, "Policy Regimes and Policy Change," *Journal of Public Policy* 20 (2000): 247–74.
22. E. E. Schattschneider, *The Semi-Sovereign People* (New York: Holt, Rinehart and Winston, 1969).
23. Lance deHaven Smith, *Philosophical Critiques of Policy Analysis: Lindblom, Habermas and the Great Society* (Gainesville: University of Florida Press, 1988). Habermas proposes the development of a more participatory "dialogical democracy" as a means of effectively including all interests. See also Jon Elster, ed., *Deliberative Democracy* (New York: Cambridge University Press, 1998).
24. Bachrach and Baratz, "Decisions and Nondecisions," 632–42.
25. Bachrach and Baratz, "The Two Faces of Power."
26. Martin J. Smith, *Pressure, Power and Policy* (Pittsburgh: University of Pittsburgh Press, 1993).
27. K. Beckett, "Media Depictions of Drug Abuse: The Impact of Official Sources," *Research in Political Sociology* 7 (1995): 161–82.
28. J. Leiper Freeman, *The Political Process: Executive Bureau-Legislative Committee Relations* (New York: Random House, 1965).
29. Advisory Commission in Intergovernmental Relations, *The Federal Role in the Federal System* (Washington, D.C.: ACIR, 1980).
30. Nelson Polsby, *Policy Innovation in America* (New Haven: Yale University Press, 1984); and John E. Schwartz, *America's Hidden Successes*, rev. ed. (New York: Norton, 1988). More recently Paul C. Light, *Government's Greatest Achievements* (Washington, D.C.: Brookings Institution, 2002).
31. Charles O. Jones, *Separate but Equal Branches: Congress and the Presidency* (Chatham, N.J.: Chatham House, 1994).
32. See Robert S. Gilmour and Alexis A. Halley, eds., *Who Makes Public Policy? The Struggle for Control between Congress and the Executive* (Chatham, N.J.: Chatham House, 1994).
33. See, for example, Baumgartner and Jones, *Agendas and Instability.*
34. Best, *Images of Issues*; and Anne Schneider and Helen Ingram, "Social Construction of Target Populations: Implications for Policy and Politics," *American Political Science Review* 87 (1993): 34–47.
35. John W. Kingdon, *Agendas, Alternatives and Public Policy* (Boston: Little, Brown, 1984); Nancy C. Roberts, "Public Entrepreneurship and Innovation," *Policy Studies Review* 11 (1992): 55–73.

36. See James Q. Wilson, *The Politics of Regulation* (New York: Basic Books, 1980).

37. Robert H. Salisbury, "The Paradox of Interest Groups in Washington—More Groups, Less Clout," in *The New American Political System*, ed. Anthony King (Washington, D.C.: American Enterprise Institute, 1990).

38. Theodore R. Marmor, *The Politics of Medicare* (Chicago: Aldine, 1973).

39. Julie Kosterlitz, "All Together Now," *National Journal* (13 November 1993): 2704–8.

40. Brian W. Hogwood and B. Guy Peters, *Policy Dynamics* (Brighton, England: Wheatsheaf, 1983).

41. See Christopher Howard, *The Hidden Welfare State: Tax Expenditures and Social Policy in the United States* (Princeton: Princeton University Press, 1997).

42. Aaron Wildavsky, "Policy as Its Own Cause," *Speaking Truth to Power* (Boston: Little, Brown, 1979), 62–85.

43. Advocates for the victims of the disease argue that there were significant delays in responding to the issue, in part because of "homophobia." See Gregory M. Herek and Beverly Greene, *AIDS, Identity and Community* (Beverly Hills, Calif.: Sage, 1995). On the other hand, the National Institutes of Health now spends $33,513 in research for every AIDS death in the country, as opposed to $1,162 for each heart disease death. "Panel Criticizes NIH Spending," *USA Today*, 9 July 1998.

44. One education bill advanced by the Clinton administration in fact contained an explicit reference to the need for improving competitiveness through education.

45. Jonathan Weisman, "Linking Tax to Death May Have Brought Its Doom," *USA Today*, 21 May 2001.

46. But see Peter Self, *Government by the Market?: The Politics of Public Choice* (Boulder, Colo.: Westview, 1991).

47. James M. Buchanan, *The Demands and Supply of Public Goods* (Chicago: Rand-McNally, 1958): 3–7.

48. A classic statement of the issue is R. H. Coase, "The Problem of Social Cost," *Journal of Law and Economics* (1960): 1–44.

49. Charles Wolf Jr., *Markets or Governments?* (Cambridge, Mass.: MIT Press, 1987).

50. The issue remains central to the political agenda, with politicians being evaluated very much on the performance of the economy. See chapter 8.

51. Cohen, March, and Olsen, "Garbage Can Model."

52. Abraham Kaplan, *The Conduct of Inquiry* (San Francisco: Chandler, 1964).

53. On instruments, see Christopher Hood, *The Tools of Government* (Chatham, N.J.: Chatham House, 1986); Lester M. Salamon with Michael S. Lund, *Beyond Privatization* (Washington, D.C.: Urban Institute Press, 1989); and Stephen H. Linder and B. Guy Peters, "Instruments of Government: Perceptions and Contexts," *Journal of Public Policy* 9 (1989): 35–58.

54. Richard F. Elmore, "Instruments and Strategy in the Study of Public Policy," *Policy Studies Review* 7 (1987): 174–86.

55. For example, organizational resistance to privatizing Social Security within government, as well as political pressure from outside, may save the program when it is under threat. See chapter 11.

56. They are argued to be so by, among others, William Niskanen, *Bureaucracy and Representative Government* (Chicago: Aldine/Atherton, 1971). But see André Blais and Stéphane Dion, *The Budget-Maximizing Bureaucrat* (Pittsburgh: University of Pittsburgh Press, 1991).

57. Kenneth J. Meier, *Politics and the Bureaucracy*, 3d ed. (Pacific Grove, Calif.: Brooks/Cole, 1993).

58. Mark A. Eisner, "Bureaucratic Professionalism and the Limits of Political Control Thesis: The Case of the Federal Trade Commission," *Governance* 6 (1992): 127–53.

59. John DiIulio, ed., *Deregulating Government* (Washington, D.C.: Brookings Institution, 1994); and B. Guy Peters, *The Future of Governing* (Lawrence: University of Kansas Press, 1996).

60. See Charles L. Heatherly, ed., *Mandate for Change: Policy Management in a Conservative Administration* (Washington, D.C.: Heritage Foundation, 1981).

61. The conservative end of the policymaking dimension is also populated by the Cato Institute, which tends to offer advice from an almost philosophical libertarian position. On George H. W. Bush, see Colin Campbell and Bert A. Rockman, eds., *The Bush Presidency: A Midterm Assessment* (Chatham, N.J.: Chatham House, 1991).

62. See, for example, *The Work of Nations: Preparing Ourselves for 21st Century Capitalism* (New York: Knopf, 1991); and *Education and the Next Economy* (Washington, D.C.: National Education Association, 1988).

63. Again, try it!

64. Michael Malbin, *Our Unelected Representatives* (New York: Basic Books, 1980). For a conservative critique, see Eric Felten, "Little Princes," *Policy Review* 63 (1993): 51–57.

65. See W. Kip Viscusi, "The Value of Risks to Life and Health," *Journal of Economic Literature* 31 (1993); 1912–46; Richard Zeckhauser and W. Kip Viscusi, "Risk within Reason," *Science* 248 (4 May 1990); 559–64; and R. Hahn, *Risks, Costs and Lives Saved* (Oxford: Oxford University Press, 1996).

66. Robert Eisner, *The Misunderstood Economy* (Cambridge, Mass.: Harvard Business School, 1994).

67. There have been a number of books and articles about "crises" in Social Security, but the pattern of decision making tends to be more incremental. See Theodore R. Marmor, *Social Security: Beyond the Rhetoric of Crisis* (Princeton: Princeton University Press, 1988); and Martha Derthick, *Agency under Stress: The Social Security Administration in American Government* (Washington, D.C.: Brookings Institution, 1990).

68. See Richard Topf, "Science, Public Policy, and the Authoritativeness of the Governmental Process," in *The Politics of Expert Advice*, ed. Anthony Barker and B. Guy Peters (Pittsburgh: University of Pittsburgh Press, 1993).

69. R. Kent Weaver, "Setting and Firing Policy Triggers," *Journal of Public Policy* 9 (1989): 307–36.

70. Paulette Kurzer, "The Politics of Central Banks: Austerity and Unemployment in Europe," *Journal of Public Policy* 8 (1988): 21–48.

71. Indeed, reducing values such as clean air, natural beauty, and social equality to dollars and cents (as is necessary to make cost-benefit analysis work) represents an extreme form of utilitarianism.

72. See Henry J. Aaron, Thomas E. Mann, and Timothy Taylor, *Values and Public Policy* (Washington, D.C.: Brookings Institution, 1994).

73. Moshe F. Rubenstein, *Patterns of Problem Solving* (Englewood Cliffs, N.J.: Prentice-Hall, 1975).

74. The political risks for the mayor may be different than the actual risks to the city and its people. The mayor does not want to be seen as panicking in the face of a cri-

sis, but the unnecessary loss of life may be the most damaging possibility of all for a political leader.

75. Stephen H. Linder and B. Guy Peters, "From Social Theory to Policy Design," *Journal of Public Policy* 4 (1984): 237–59; and Davis Bobrow and John S. Dryzek, *Policy Analysis by Design* (Pittsburgh: University of Pittsburgh Press, 1987).

76. Anne L. Schneider and Helen M. Ingram, for example, argue that policy design runs directly opposite to the pluralistic politics that dominates policymaking in the United States. See their *Policy Design for Democracy* (Lawrence: University of Kansas Press, 1997).

Chapter 4

1. Peter G. Brown, *Restoring the Public Trust* (Boston: Beacon Press, 1994); and Rodney Barker, *Political Legitimacy and the State* (Oxford: Clarendon Press, 1990).

2. The government of the United Kingdom suspended civil liberties in Northern Ireland in response to the sectarian violence there. For at least a portion of the population, this action reduced its legitimacy. For other citizens, the extreme crisis of sectarian violence and terrorism justified the action.

3. Donald L. Westerfield, *War Powers: The President, the Congress, and the Question of War* (Westport, Conn.: Praeger, 1996).

4. See, for example, Alan Brinkley, "What's Wrong with American Political Leadership?" *Wilson Quarterly* 18, no. 2 (1994): 46–54.

5. The very high figure in 1991 appears to be at least in part a function of the Gulf War (see also the figure for the military in that year)—presidents often get a popularity boost from wars. George W. Bush has enjoyed the same high levels after 11 September 2001.

6. Robert Z. Lawrence, "Is it Really the Economy, Stupid?" in *Why People Don't Trust Government*, ed. Joseph S. Nye, Philip D. Zelikow, and David C. King (Cambridge, Mass.: Harvard University Press, 1997).

7. On indexation, see chapter 11.

8. This is to some degree what Aaron Wildavsky meant when he argued that policy analysts must engage in *Speaking Truth to Power* (Boston: Little, Brown, 1979).

9. Arnold J. Meltsner, "Political Feasibility and Policy Analysis," *Public Administration Review* 32 (1972): 859–67; and Giandomenico Majone, "The Feasibility of Social Policies," *Policy Sciences* 6 (1975): 49–69.

10. Joel D. Aberbach, *Keeping a Watchful Eye: The Politics of Congressional Oversight* (Washington, D.C.: Brookings Institution, 1991).

11. *Immigration and Naturalization Service v. Chadha* 462 U.S. 919 (1983). See also William West and Joseph Cooper, "The Congressional Veto and Administrative Rulemaking," *Political Science Quarterly* 98 (1983): 285–304.

12. Louis Fisher, "The Legislative Veto: Invalidated, It Survives," *Law and Contemporary Problems* 56 (1993): 273–92; and Jessica Korn, *The Power of Separation: American Constitutionalism and the Myth of the Legislative Veto* (Princeton, N.J.: Princeton University Press, 1997).

13. Walter J. Oleszek, *Congressional Procedures and the Policy Process* (Washington, D.C.:

CQ Press, 1988); and Sarah A. Binder and Steven S. Smith, *Filibustering: Politics or Principle* (Washington, D.C.: Brookings Institution, 1997).

14. There are, therefore, a number of "veto points," a concept not dissimilar to "clearance points" in implementation theory. See Ellen Immergut, *Health Care Politics* (Cambridge, England: Cambridge University Press, 1992).

15. There have been majorities in favor of reforming medical care for some time, but there is as yet no major change. Likewise, there was substantial political pressure for a tobacco settlement in 1998 but the proposal died under an onslaught of interest-group pressures and concerns about economic impacts. See Barry Meier, "Talks Stall in Efforts to Reach Accord," *New York Times*, 5 August 1998; and Donley Studlar, Tobacco Control (Peterborough, Ont.: Broadview Press, 2002).

16. Charles E. Lindblom and Edward J. Woodhouse, *The Policy-making Process*, 3d ed. (Englewood Cliffs, N.J.: Prentice-Hall, 1993).

17. In many ways these programs were more successful in reaching these goals than in reaching the social and housing goals toward which they were nominally directed. See Clarence Stone and Heywood T. Sanders, eds., *The Politics of Urban Development* (Lawrence: University of Kansas Press, 1987).

18. James Buchanan and Gordon Tullock, *The Calculus of Consent* (Ann Arbor: University of Michigan Press, 1962), 120–44.

19. See John A. Hamman, "Universalism, Program Development and the Distribution of Federal Assistance," *Legislative Studies Quarterly* 18 (1993): 553–68.

20. Morris P. Fiorina, *Congress: The Keystone of the Washington Establishment* (New Haven: Yale University Press, 1981).

21. Douglas R. Arnold, *Congress and the Bureaucracy* (New Haven: Yale University Press, 1979).

22. Many programs will do that; the question is whether there is also a broader public interest involved.

23. James Kitfield, "The Battle of the Depots," *National Journal*, 4 April 1998.

24. William R. Riker and Peter Ordeshook, *Positive Political Theory* (Englewood Cliffs, N.J.: Prentice-Hall, 1973), 97–114.

25. Kenneth Arrow, *Social Choice and Individual Values*, 2d ed. (New York: John Wiley, 1963).

26. Joel D. Aberbach, *Keeping a Watchful Eye* (Washington, D.C.: Brookings Institution, 1991).

27. These terms come from Mathew McCubbins and Thomas Schwartz, "Congressional Oversight Overlooked: Police Patrols versus Fire Alarms," *American Journal of Political Science* 28 (1984): 165–79.

28. "GOP, to Its Own Delight, Enacts House Rule Changes," *Congressional Quarterly Weekly Report* 53, no. 1 (7 January 1995): 13–15.

29. Cornelius M. Kerwin, *Rulemaking: How Government Agencies Write Law and Make Policy* (Washington, D.C.: CQ Press, 1994).

30. Marc Allen Eisner, *Regulatory Politics in Transition* (Baltimore: Johns Hopkins University Press, 2000).

31. Kerwin, *Rulemaking*, 18–19.

32. Margaret T. Kriz, "Kibitzer with Clout," *National Journal*, (30 May 1987): 1404–8.

33. Thomas O. McGarity, *Reinventing Rationality: The Role of Regulatory Analysis in the Federal Bureaucracy* (Cambridge, England: Cambridge University Press, 1991).

34. Viveca Novak, "The New Regulators," *National Journal,* (17 July 1993): 1801–4.

35. Martin Shapiro, "APA: Past, Present and Future," *Virginia Law Review* 72 (1986): 447–92.

36. Jerry L. Mashaw, "Prodelegation: Why Administrators Should Make Political Decisions," *Journal of Law, Economics and Organization* 5 (1985): 141–64.

37. Even then, there was a concentration of participation, with only a few interest groups taking advantage of this opportunity. See Barry Boyer, "Funding Public Participation in Agency Proceedings: The Federal Trade Commission Experience," *Georgetown Law Journal* 70 (1981): 51–172.

38. See Glen O. Robinson, *American Bureaucracy: Public Choice and Public Law* (Ann Arbor: University of Michigan Press, 1991), 139–47.

39. Stephen Williams, "Hybrid Rulemaking under the Administrative Procedures Act: A Legal and Empirical Analysis," *University of Chicago Law Review* 42 (1975): 401–56.

40. *International Harvester Co. v. Ruckelshaus* 478 F. 2nd. 615 (1973).

41. William Gormley Jr., *Taming the Bureaucracy* (Princeton, N.J.: Princeton University Press, 1989), 94–97.

42. Philip Harter, "Negotiated Rulemaking: A Cure for the Malaise," *Georgetown Law Review* 71 (1982): 1–28; and Thomas McGarrity, "Some Thoughts on Deossifying the Rulemaking Process," *Duke Law Journal* 41 (1992): 1385–1462.

43. David Pritzker and Deborah Dalton, *Negotiated Rulemaking Sourcebook* (Washington, D.C.: Administrative Conference of the United States, 1990).

44. Philippe C. Schmitter, "Still the Century of Corporatism?" *Review of Politics* 36 (1974): 85–131.

45. See Robert Kvavik, *Interest Groups in Norwegian Politics* (Oslo: Universitetsforlaget, 1980).

46. Mike Mills, "President to Stage Timber Summit," *Congressional Quarterly Weekly Report* 51 (13 March 1993): 593.

47. See Colin S. Diver, "A Theory of Regulatory Enforcement," *Public Policy* 29 (1980): 295–96.

48. Theodore J. Lowi, *The End of Liberalism,* 2d ed. (New York: Norton, 1979).

49. Richard A. Harris and Sidney M. Milkis, *The Politics of Regulatory Change* (New York: Oxford University Press, 1989).

50. David Schoenbrod, *Power without Responsibility* (New Haven: Yale University Press, 1993).

51. Martha Derthick and Paul J. Quirk, *The Politics of Deregulation* (Washington, D.C.: Brookings Institution, 1985).

52. Robert A. Kagan, "Adversarial Legalism and American Government," *Journal of Policy Analysis and Management* 10 (1991): 369–406; and Robert J. Samuelson, "Whitewater: The Law as Bludgeon," *International Herald Tribune,* 8 March 1994.

53. Federal Judge Frank Johnson in Alabama literally took over the prisons and mental hospitals of that state. See *Wyatt v. Stickney* 344 F. Supp. 373 (M.D. Ala 1972) and *Pugh v. Locke* 406 F. Supp. 318 (M.D. Ala 1976).

54. Thomas J. Cronin, *Direct Democracy* (Cambridge, Mass.: Harvard University Press,

1989). See also Ian Budge, *The New Challenge of Direct Democracy* (Cambridge, Mass.: Polity Press, 1996).

55. James Bohman, *Public Deliberation: Pluralism, Complexity and Democracy* (Cambridge, Mass.: MIT Press, 1990); Benjamin R. Barber, *Strong Democracy: Participatory Politics in a New Age* (Berkeley: University of California Press, 1984). For a less philosophical discussion, see Phil Duncan, "American Democracy in Search of Debate," *Congressional Quarterly Weekly Report* 51 (16 October 1993): 2850.

Chapter 5

1. Michael Lipsky, *Street Level Bureaucracy* (New York: Russell Sage, 1980).

2. Gary Bryner, *Bureaucratic Discretion* (New York: Pergamon, 1987); Cass Sunstein, *After the Rights Revolution: Reconceiving the Regulatory State* (Cambridge, Mass.: Harvard University Press, 1990).

3. See U.S. Senate, Committee on Governmental Affairs, *The Federal Executive Establishment: Evolution and Trends* (Washington, D.C.: Government Printing Office, 1980): 23–63.

4. Harold Seidman and Robert S. Gilmour, *Politics, Position and Power*, 4th ed. (New York: Oxford University Press, 1986).

5. The degree of central control in Defense can be exaggerated. See C. Kenneth Allard, *Command, Control, and the Common Defense* (New Haven: Yale University Press, 1990).

6. At various times in its history, the Coast Guard has been lodged in those other two departments.

7. John Hart, *The Presidential Branch*, 2d ed. (Chatham, N.J.: Chatham House, 1994).

8. B. Guy Peters, R. A.W. Rhodes, and Vincent Wright, eds., *Administering the Summit* (London: Macmillan, 1998).

9. Frederick C. Mosher, *The GAO* (Boulder, Colo.: Westview, 1979); and Ray C. Rist, *Program Evaluation and Management of Government* (New Brunswick, N.J.: Transaction, 1990).

10. Daily reports from the General Accounting Office can be found at www.gao.gov.

11. Marc Alan Eisner, *Regulatory Politics in Transition* (Baltimore: Johns Hopkins University Press, 1993).

12. The classic statement is Samuel P. Huntington, "The Marasmus of the ICC," *Yale Law Review* (April 1952): 467–509. For a very different perspective, see Jonathan R. Mezey, "Organizational Design and Political Control of Administrative Agencies," *Journal of Law, Economics and Organization* 8 (1992): 93–110.

13. In addition, the growth of the consumer movement has placed additional pressures on regulatory agencies to escape capture. See Michael D. Reagan, *Regulation: The Politics of Policy* (Boston: Little, Brown, 1987).

14. Annemarie Hauck Walsh, *Managing the Public's Business* (Cambridge, Mass.: MIT Press, 1980), 41–44.

15. See Peter Passell, "The Sticky Side of Privatization: Sale of U.S. Nuclear Fuel Plants Raises Host of Conflicts," *New York Times*, 30 August 1997.

16. Michael Dorf, "Artifactions: The Battle over the National Endowment for the Arts," *Brookings Review* (winter 1993): 32–35.

17. On 25 June 1998, the Court argued that there is no right to a grant, so artists could not argue that this denied them any fundamental rights. *National Endowment for the Arts v. Finley*, SC 97–371.

18. Herman Schwartz, "Governmentally Appointed Directors in a Private Corporation—The Communications Satellite Act of 1962," *Harvard Law Review*, December 1965, 350–64.

19. Seidman and Gilmour, *Politics, Position and Power*, 274.

20. Marc Alan Eisner, *Antitrust and the Triumph of Economics* (Chapel Hill: University of North Carolina Press, 1992).

21. Martin Landau, "The Rationality of Redundancy," *Public Administration Review* 29 (1969): 346–58; Jonathan R. Bendor, *Parallel Politics* (Berkeley: University of California Press, 1985).

22. James L. Sundquist, "Needed: A Political Theory for a New Era of Coalition Government in the United States," *Political Science Quarterly* 108 (1988): 613–35.

23. U.S. Senate, Committee on Governmental Affairs, *Federal Executive Establishment* (Washington, D.C.: Government Printing Office, 1980), 27–30.

24. "In God We Trust," *Harvard Political Review* 28 (2001): 15–27.

25. Woodrow Wilson, "The Study of Administration," *Political Science Quarterly* 1 (1887): 197–222.

26. This is perhaps especially true of American government given the number of "veto points" that exist within the system. See Ellen Immergut, *Health Care Politics: Ideas and Institutions in Western Europe* (Cambridge, England: Cambridge University Press, 1992).

27. See Else Oyen, S. M. Miller, and S. A. Samad, *Poverty: A Global Review* (Oslo: Scandinavian University Press, 1996).

28. Daniel Patrick Moynihan, *The Politics of Guaranteed Income* (New York: Vintage, 1973), 240.

29. The importance of laser technologies is demonstrated in William Broad, *Teller's War: The Top-Secret Story behind the Star Wars Initiative* (New York: Simon and Schuster, 1992).

30. That difference is discussed well in Richard R. Nelson, *The Moon and the Ghetto* (New York: Norton, 1977).

31. Robert B. Stevens, ed., *Income Security: Statutory History of the United States* (New York: McGraw-Hill, 1970): 639–59.

32. That decision eventually was rescinded after a public outcry. However, in 1998, another decision by the Department of Agriculture made salsa a vegetable for school lunches, provided it was made from fresh vegetables (there's that word again).

33. Tax legislation is sufficiently complex that it is possible to hide benefits for particular groups even in legislation claiming to be general tax relief. See Paul Krugman, *Fuzzy Math: The Essential Guide to the Bush Tax Plan* (New York: Norton, 2001).

34. Theodore J. Lowi, *The End of Liberalism*, 2d ed. (New York: Norton, 1979), 42–63.

35. Christopher Hood, *The Limits of Administration* (New York: John Wiley, 1976).

36. Ronald Randall, "Presidential Power versus Bureaucratic Intransigence: The Influence of the Nixon Administration on Welfare Policy," *American Political Science Review* 73 (1979): 795–810.

37. Paul R. Portney, "Natural Resources and the Environment," in *The Reagan Record*, ed. John Palmer and Isabel Sawhill (Washington, D.C.: Urban Institute Press, 1984).

38. Burt Solomon, "Twixt Cup and Lip," *National Journal*, (24 October 1992): 2410–15; and Paul C. Light, *Thickening Government: Federal Hierarchy and the Diffusion of Accountability* (Washington, D.C.: Brookings Institution, 1995).

39. A classic description of the dangers of this occurring is found in Herbert Kaufman, *The Forest Ranger* (Baltimore: Johns Hopkins University Press, 1960).

40. Janet Schrader, "Lost on the Road to Reform: Some of My Clients Can't Do the Jobs Out There," *Washington Post*, 11 May 1997.

41. Jan Horah and Heather Scott, *NIMBYs and LULUs: Not-in-my Back-Yard and Locally-Unwanted-Land-Use* (Chicago: Council of Planning Librarians, 1993).

42. See Jack DeSario and Stuart Langton, *Citizen Participation in Public Decision Making* (New York: Greenwood, 1987).

43. See Henry Tam, *Communitarianism: A New Agenda for Politics and Citizenship* (London: Macmillan, 1998).

44. Donald F. Kettl, *Reinventing Government? Appraising the National Performance Review* (Washington, D.C.: Brookings Institution, 1995).

45. See Ortwin Renn, Thomas Webler, Horst Rakel, Peter Dienel, and Branden Johnson, "Public Participation in Decision Making: A Three-Step Procedure," *Policy Sciences* 26 (1993): 189–214.

46. Peter M. Blau, *The Dynamics of Bureaucracy* (Chicago: University of Chicago Press, 1955), 184–93.

47. Eugene Bardach and Robert A. Kagan, *Going by the Book: The Problem of Regulatory Unreasonableness* (Philadelphia: Temple University Press, 1982).

48. This is now often phrased in terms of a "principal" controlling its agents. See Dan Wood and Richard Waterman, *Bureaucratic Dynamics: The Role of Bureaucracy in a Democracy* (Boulder, Colo.: Westview, 1994).

49. Martha A. Derthick, *Agency under Stress: The Social Security Administration in American Government* (Washington, D.C.: Brookings Institution, 1990).

50. Elaine Sciolino, "Nuclear Anxiety: The Blunder," *New York Times*, 16 May 1998.

51. Arthur Stinchcombe, *Information and Organizations* (Berkeley: University of California Press, 1990).

52. James G. March and Herbert A. Simon, *Organizations* (New York: John Wiley, 1958).

53. On the other hand, too much similarity in backgrounds and training enhances the possibilities of "group-think" and an absence of error-correction within the organization. See Paul 't Hart, Eric K. Stern, and Bengt Sundelius, *Beyond Groupthink: Political Group Dynamics and Foreign Policy-Making* (Ann Arbor: University of Michigan Press, 1997).

54. The Gore Commission (National Performance Review) reforms have had the effect of reducing drastically the number of levels in organizations with the presumed effect of empowering employees at lower levels of organizations, and improving internal communications.

55. James McGregor Burns, *Roosevelt: The Lion and the Fox* (New York: Harcourt, Brace, 1956).

56. Harold Wilensky, *Organizational Intelligence* (New York: Basic Books, 1967), 130–45.

57. Hood, *Limits of Administration*, 85–87.

58. Ibid., 192–97.

59. For a good compilation, see Peter Hall, *Great Planning Disasters* (London: Weidenfield and Nicolson, 1980). We should remember, however, that these failings are as common in large private organizations as in the public sector, but there they tend to be less publicized. See Charles T. Goodsell, *The Case for Bureaucracy: A Public Administration Polemic*, 4th ed. (Chatham, N.J.: Chatham House, 2003).

60. Paul R. Schulman, *Large-Scale Policy Analysis* (New York: Elsevier, 1980).

61. Richard A. Rettig, *Cancer Crusade* (Princeton, N.J.: Princeton University Press, 1977).

62. This assumes that this disease is similar to cancer in requiring a more decentralized research format.

63. Benny Hjern and David O. Porter, "Implementation Structures: A New Unit of Organisational Analysis," *Organisational Studies* 2 (1981): 211–28.

64. Eugene Bardach, "Turf Barriers to Interagency Collaboration," in *The State of Public Management*, ed. D. F. Kettl and H. B. Milward (Baltimore: Johns Hopkins University Press, 1996).

65. See Kevin P. Kearns, *Private Sector Strategies for Public Sector Success* (San Francisco: Jossey-Bass, 2000)

66. Jeffrey L. Pressman and Aaron Wildavsky, *Implementation* (Berkeley: University of California Press, 1979).

67. Ibid., 145–68.

68. Judith Bowen, "The Pressman-Wildavsky Paradox," *Journal of Public Policy* 2 (1982): 1–22; and Ernst Alexander, "Improbable Implementation: The Pressman-Wildavsky Paradox Revisited," *Journal of Public Policy* 9 (1989): 451–65.

69. See David Osborne and Ted Gaebler, *Reinventing Government* (Reading, Mass.: Addison-Wesley, 1992); and B. Guy Peters, "Can't Row, Shouldn't Steer: What's a Government to Do?" *Public Policy and Administration* 12, no. 2 (1997): 51–61.

70. Peter J. May, "Mandate Design and Implementation: Enhancing Implementation Efforts and Shaping Regulatory Policy," *Journal of Policy Analysis and Management* 12 (1993): 634–63.

71. Rochelle L. Stanfield, "Between the Cracks," *National Journal*, 11 October 1997.

72. William T. Gormley, "Regulating Mr. Rogers's Neighborhood: The Dilemmas of Day Care Regulation," *Brookings Review* 8 (1990): 21–28.

73. Barry Meier, "Fight in Congress Looms on Fishing," *New York Times*, 19 September 1994.

74. R. Lewis Bowman, Eleanor C. Main, and B. Guy Peters, "Coordination in the Atlanta Model Cities Program," mimeo, Department of Political Science, Emory University, 1971.

75. Jon Pierre, "The Marketization of the State: Citizens, Consumers and the Emergence of Public Markets," in *Governance in a Changing Environment*, ed. Donald Savoie and B. Guy Peters (Montreal: McGill/Queens University Press, 1995).

76. Richard F. Elmore, "Backward Mapping and Implementation Research and Policy Decisions," in *Studying Implementation*, ed. Walter Williams (Chatham, N.J.: Chatham House, 1984).

77. M. Kiviniemi, "Public Policies and their Targets: A Typology of the Concept of Implementation," *International Social Science Quarterly* 108 (1986): 251–65.

78. Elmore, "Backward Mapping"; Paul A. Sabatier, "Top-Down and Bottom-Up Models of Policy Implementation: A Critical Analysis and Suggested Synthesis," *Journal of Public Policy* 6 (1986): 21–48; and Stephen H. Linder and B. Guy Peters, "Implementation as a Guide to Policy Formulation: A Question of 'When' Rather Than 'Whether,' " *International Review of Administrative Sciences* 55 (1989): 631–52.

79. Linder and Peters, "Implementation as a Guide."

80. Giandomenico Majone, "The Feasibility of Social Policies," *Policy Sciences* 6 (1975): 49–69.

81. Malcolm L. Goggin, Ann O'M. Bowman, James P. Lester, and Laurence J. O'Toole, *Implementation Theory and Practice: Toward a Third Generation* (New York: Harper/Collins, 1990).

Chapter 6

1. Jan-Erik Lane, *The Public Sector: Concepts, Models, and Approaches* (London: Sage, 1994).

2. Rather than a question of the efficient division of resources between the public and private sectors, this is an intergenerational equity question.

3. Charles Stewart III, *Budget Reform Politics* (New York: Cambridge University Press, 1989).

4. Louis Fisher, *Presidential Spending Power* (Princeton: Princeton University Press, 1975).

5. "After Years of Wrangling, Accord Is Reached on Plan to Balance Budget by 2002," *New York Times,* 3 May 1997.

6. Frederick C. Mosher, *The GAO: The Quest for Accountability in American Government* (Boulder, Colo.: Westview, 1979), 65–96.

7. U.S. General Accounting Office, *Biennial Budgeting for the Federal Government* (Washington, D.C.: USGAO, 7 October 1993), GAO/T-AIMED–94–4; and Louis Fisher, "Biennial Budgeting in the Federal Government," *Public Budgeting and Finance* 17, no. 3 (1997): 87–97.

8. "Federal Capital Budgeting," *Intergovernmental Perspective* 20 (1994): 8–16; Beverly S. Bunch, "Current Practices and Issues in Capital Budgeting and Reporting," *Public Budgeting and Finance* 16, no. 2 (1996): 7–25.

9. See *Washington Post,* "The Long Path to the Federal Budget," 4 February 2002.

10. Charles L. Schultze, "Paying the Bills," in *Setting Domestic Priorities,* ed. Henry J. Aaron and Charles L. Schultze (Washington, D.C.: Brookings Institution, 1992).

11. Paul E. Peterson and Mark Rom, "Macroeconomic Policymaking: Who Is in Control," in *Can the Government Govern?* ed. John E. Chubb and Paul E. Peterson (Washington, D.C.: Brookings Institution, 1989).

12. This official was Murray Weidenbaum—see David Stockman, *The Triumph of Politics* (New York: Harper and Row, 1986), 104.

13. David E. Rosenbaum, "Answer: Trim Entitlements. Question: How Do You Do It?" *New York Times,* 8 June 1993.

14. See Roy T. Meyers, *Strategic Budgeting* (Ann Arbor: University of Michigan Press, 1994), 52–60.

15. Aaron Wildavsky, *The New Politics of the Budgetary Process* (Glenview, Ill.: Scott, Foresman, 1986), 100–118.

16. Ibid., 81–82.

17. U.S. Office of Management and Budget, *Preparation and Submission of "Current Services" Budget Estimates*, Bulletin 76–4 (Washington, D.C.: OMB, 13 August 1975), 2–4.

18. Maurice Wright describes volume budgeting in "From Planning to Control: PESC in the 1970s," *Public Spending Decisions*, ed. Maurice Wright (London: Allen and Unwin, 1980), 88–119.

19. See Thomas W. Wander, F. Ted Hebert, and Gary W. Copeland, *Congressional Budgeting* (Baltimore: Johns Hopkins University Press, 1984); and Robin Toner, "Putting Prices on Congress's Ideas," *New York Times*, 21 August 1994.

20. John W. Ellwood and James A. Thurber, "The Politics of the Congressional Budget Process," in *Congress Reconsidered*, ed. Lawrence C. Dodd and Bruce Oppenheimer, 2d ed. (Washington, D.C.: CQ Press, 1981). There has been some tendency to disperse this power, with appropriations committees now handling only about two-thirds of the total budget. See John F. Cogan, "Congress Has Dispersed the Power of the Purse," *Public Affairs Report* 35 (September 1994): 7–8.

21. Paul Starobin, "Bringing It Home," *National Journal*, 27 March 1993.

22. D. Roderick Kiewiet and Mathew D. McCubbins, *The Logic of Delegation* (Chicago: University of Chicago Press, 1991).

23. John R. Gilmour, *Reconcilable Differences: Congress, the Budget Process and the Deficit* (Berkeley: University of California Press, 1990), 115–23.

24. See Irene Rubin, *The Politics of Public Budgeting*, 4th ed. (Chatham, N.J.: Chatham House, 2002), 75–76; and James Thurber, "Congressional Budget Reform: Impact on Congressional Appropriations Committees," *Public Budgeting and Finance* 17, no. 3 (1997): 62–73.

25. Carl Hulse, "Whistle-Stops and War Whoops Bury Budget Woes," *New York Times*, 1 October 2002.

26. Fischer, *Presidential Spending Power.*

27. Mosher, *The GAO*, 169–200; and Ray C. Rist, "Management Accountability: The Signals Sent by Auditing and Evaluation," *Journal of Public Policy* 9 (1989): 355–69.

28. Technically, the general fund is borrowing the money from the Social Security Trust Fund, although the presentation of deficit figures does not make that distinction clear. See General Accounting Office, *Retirement Income: Implications of Demographic Trends for Social Security and Pension Reform* (Washington, D.C.: USGAO, July 1997), GAO/HEHS–97–81.

29. Glenn Kessler, "Use of Retirement Funds to Widen Debt Limit Fight," *Washington Post*, 3 April 2002.

30. See Robert D. Reischauer, "The Unfulfillable Promise: Cutting Nondefense Discretionary Spending," in *Setting National Priorities: Budget Choices for the Next Century*, ed. Reischauer (Washington, D.C.: Brookings Institution, 1997).

31. Rob Norton, "Every Budget Tells a Story, and This Is No Exception," *Washington Post*, 10 March 2002.

32. Jeff Shear, "The Untouchables," *National Journal*, 16 July 1994.

33. A variety of federal loan programs account for over $200 billion in outstanding direct

loans and over $700 billion in guaranteed loans. The Tax Foundation, *Facts and Figures on Government Finance, 1993* (Washington, D.C: The Tax Foundation, 1994).

34. Ben Wildavsky, "After the Deficit," *National Journal*, (29 November 1997): 2408–10.

35. General Accounting Office, *Budgeting for Federal Insurance Programs* (Washington, D.C.: GAO, September 1997), GAO/AIMD–97–16.

36. Office of Management and Budget, *Budget of the United States, FY 1997, Analytical Perspectives* (Washington, D.C.: Government Printing Office, 1997).

37. Peter Passell, "Despite All the Talk About Tax Cuts, People Can Expect to Pay More, *New York Times*, 17 November 1991.

38. For Canada, see Richard B. Simeon, *Federal Provincial Diplomacy* (Toronto: University of Toronto Press, 1974); for Germany, see Russell J. Dalton, *Politics in Germany*, 2d ed. (New York: HarperCollins, 1993), 372–77.

39. These surpluses tended to be, on average, 11 percent of total state revenues, although some 15 percent of total state revenues came from grants from the federal government.

40. William D. Berry, "The Confusing Case of Budgetary Incrementalism: Too Many Meanings for a Single Concept," *Journal of Politics* 52 (1990): 167–96.

41. M. A. H. Dempster and Aaron Wildavsky, "On Change: Or, There is No Magic Size for an Increment," *Political Studies* 28 (1980): 371–89.

42. See David Braybrooke and Charles E. Lindblom, *A Strategy for Decision* (New York: Free Press, 1963).

43. Otto A. Davis, M. A. H. Dempster, and Aaron Wildavsky, "A Theory of the Budgetary Process," *American Political Science Review* 60 (1969): 529–47. These findings are now quite old, but there is little evidence that the process or the outcomes have changed significantly.

44. Aaron Wildavsky, *Budgeting: A Comparative Theory of the Budgetary Process*, rev. ed. (New Brunswick, N.J.: Transaction, 1986): 7–27.

45. Michael T. Hayes, *Incrementalism and Public Policy* (New York; Longman, 1992), 131–44; see also Meyers, *Strategic Budgeting*.

46. Peter B. Natchez and Irvin C. Bupp, "Policy and Priority in the Budgetary Process," *American Political Science Review* 64 (1973): 951–63.

47. Dempster and Wildavsky, "On Change."

48. John R. Gist, " 'Increment' and 'Base' in the Congressional Appropriation Process," *American Journal of Political Science* 21 (1977): 341–52.

49. Robert E. Goodin, *Political Theory and Public Policy* (Chicago: University of Chicago Press, 1983): 22–38.

50. Brian W. Hogwood and B. Guy Peters, *The Pathology of Public Policy* (New York: Oxford University Press, 1985), 124–26.

51. David Novick, *Program Budgeting: Program Analysis and the Federal Budget* (Cambridge, Mass.: Harvard University Press, 1967).

52. Robert H. Haveman and Burton A. Weisbrod, "Defining Benefits from Public Programs: Some Guidance from Policy Analysts," in *Public Expenditure and Policy Analysis*, ed. Haveman and Julius Margolis, 3d ed. (Boston: Houghton-Mifflin, 1983); and Philip G. Joyce, "Using Performance Measures for Federal Budgeting: Proposals and Prospects," *Public Budgeting and Finance* 13 (1993): 3–17.

53. Aaron Wildavsky, "Political Implications of Budgetary Reform," *Public Administration Review* 21 (1961): 183–90.

54. Lenneal J. Henderson, "GPRA: Mission, Metrics, and Marketing," *Public Manager* 24, no. 1 (1995): 7–10; and Beryl A. Radin, "The Government Performance and Results Act (GPRA): Hydra-headed Monster or Flexible Management Tool?" *Public Administration Review* 58 (1998): 307–16.

55. Richard W. Stevenson, "Bush Budget Links Dollars and Deeds in Judging Agencies," *New York Times*, 1 February 2002.

56. USGAO, *Managing for Results: Agency Progress in Linking Performance Plans with Budgets and Financial Statement* (Washington, D.C.: General Accounting Office, January), GAO–02–236.

57. These solutions are examples of "formula budgeting," which substitutes formulas for political judgment and political will. See Eric A. Hanushek, "Formula Budgeting: The Economics and Politics of Fiscal Policy under Rules," *Journal of Public Analysis and Management* 6 (1986): 3–19.

58. James D. Savage, *Balanced Budgets and American Politics* (Ithaca, N.Y.: Cornell University Press, 1988).

59. *Bowsher v. Synar* 478 U.S. 714 (1986); see also Lance T. LeLoup, Barbara Luck Graham, and Stacey Barwick, "Deficit Politics and Constitutional Government: The Impact of Gramm-Rudman-Hollings," *Public Budgeting and Finance* 7 (1987): 83–103.

60. Congressional Budget Office, *The Economic and Budget Outlook, 1992–96* (Washington, D.C.: Government Printing Office, 1991).

61. Philip G. Joyce, "Congressional Budget Reform: The Unanticipated Implications of Federal Policy Making," *Public Administration Review* 56 (1996): 317–24.

62. Allen Schick, *The Federal Budget: Politics, Policy and Process* (Washington, D.C.: Brookings Institution, 1995), 40–41.

63. Karl O'Lessker, "The Clinton Budget for FY 1994: Taking Aim at the Deficit," *Public Budgeting and Finance* 13 (1993): 7–19.

64. Alvin Rabushka, "Fiscal Responsibility: Will Anything Less than a Constitutional Amendment Do?" in *The Federal Budget*, ed. Michael J. Boskin and Aaron Wildavsky (San Francisco: Institute for Contemporary Studies, 1982), 333–50. See also Henry J. Aaron, "The Balanced Budget Blunder," *Brookings Review* (spring 1994): 41; and James V. Saturno and Richard G. Forgette, "The Balanced Budget Amendment: How Would It Be Enforced," *Public Budgeting and Finance* 18, no. 1 (1998): 33–53.

65. Rudolph G. Penner and Alan J. Abramson, *Broken Purse Strings: Congressional Budgeting 1974–1988* (Washington, D.C.: Urban Institute Press, 1989), 95–100. For more recent figures, see Bill Montague, "New Budget Forecasts 'Solid'," *USA Today*, 13 December 1995.

66. Updated by author from Rudolph G. Penner, "Forecasting Budget Totals: Why We Can't Get It Right," in Boskin and Wildavsky, *Federal Budget*, 89–110. See also Donald F. Kettl, *Deficit Politics* (New York: Macmillan, 1992), 109–17.

67. U.S. House of Representatives, *Committee on the Budget, The Line-Item Veto: An Appraisal* (Washington, D.C.: Government Printing Office, 1984).

68. See Norman Ornstein, "Why GOP Will Rue Line-item Veto," *USA Today*, 18 November 1997.

69. Viveca Novak, "Defective Remedy," *National Journal*, 27 March 1993.

70. These included one provision that would have provided $84 million to one sugar

beet processor in Texas, and another that benefited certain potato growers in Idaho. See Robert Pear, "Justice Department Belatedly Finds New Defense of Line-item Veto," *New York Times*, 26 March 1998.

71. Daniel Tarschys, "Rational Decremental Budgeting: Elements of an Expenditure Policy for the 1980s," *Policy Sciences* 14 (1982): 49–58.

72. Allen Schick, "Micro-Budgetary Reform," *Public Administration Review* 48 (1988): 523–33.

73. President's Private Sector Survey on Cost Containment (Grace Commission), *Report to the President* (Washington, D.C.: PPSSCC, 1984).

74. Charles T. Goodsell, "The Grace Commission: Seeking Efficiency for the Whole People?" *Public Administration Review* 44 (1984): 196–204; and B. Guy Peters and Donald J. Savoie, "Civil Service Reform: Misdiagnosing the Patient," *Public Administration Review* 54 (1994): 418–25.

75. Sar A. Levitan and Alexandra B. Noden, *Working for the Sovereign* (Baltimore: Johns Hopkins University Press, 1983), 85.

76. The National Performance Review, *Making Government Work Better and Cost Less* (The Gore Report) (Washington, D.C.: Government Printing Office, 1993).

77. Aaron Wildavsky, "A Budget for All Seasons: Why the Traditional Budget Lasts," *Public Administration Review* 38 (1978): 501–9. See also Dirk-Jan Kraan, *Budgetary Decisions: A Public Choice Approach* (Cambridge, England: Cambridge University Press, 1996).

Chapter 7

1. For a good summary of the issues involved in evaluating public sector programs, see Evert Vedung, *Public Policy and Program Evaluation* (New Brunswick, N.J.: Transaction Publishers, 1997).

2. Geert Bouckaert and A. Halachmi, *Organizational Performance and Measurement in the Public Sector* (Westport, Conn.: Quorum Books, 1997).

3. Elaine Morley, Scott P. Bryant, and Harry P. Hatry, *Comparative Performance Measurement* (Washington, D.C.: Urban Institute, 2001).

4. J. N. Noy, "If You Don't Care Where You Get To, Then It Doesn't Matter Which Way You Go," in *The Evolution of Social Policy*, ed. C.C. Abt (Beverly Hills, Calif.: Sage, 1976): 97–120.

5. David L. Sills, *The Volunteers* (Glencoe, Ill.: Free Press, 1956): 253–68.

6. To get some idea of the current orientation of the organization, take a look at the Bureau of Indian Affairs Web site: www.doi.gov/bureau-indian-affairs.html.

7. Daniel A. Mazmanian and Jeanne Nienaber, *Can Organizations Change?* (Washington, D.C.: Brookings Institution, 1979).

8. There is a growing literature on the means of minimizing and controlling changes in the mission of regulatory agencies. See Mathew D. McCubbins, Roger G. Noll, and Barry R. Weingast, "Structure and Process, Politics and Policy: Administrative Arrangements and the Political Control of Agencies," *Virginia Law Review* 75 (1989): 431–82; and Jonathan R. Mezey, "Organizational Design and the Political Control of Regulatory Agencies," *Journal of Law, Economics and Organization* 8 (1992): 93–110.

9. Robert K. Merton, "Bureaucratic Structure and Personality," *Social Forces* (1940): 560–68.

10. Anthony Downs, *Inside Bureaucracy* (Boston: Little, Brown, 1967), 92–111.

11. See Paul Light, *Tides of Reform* (New Haven: Yale University Press, 1998).

12. Morley, Bryant, and Hatry, *Comparative Performance Measurement*.

13. See Christopher Hood, B. Guy Peters, and Helmutt Wollmann, "Sixteen Ways to Consumerise the Public Sector," *Public Money and Management* 16, no. 4 (1996): 43–50.

14. William Alonzo and Paul Starr, *The Politics of Numbers* (New York: Russell Sage Foundation, 1987).

15. Geert Bouckaert, Derry Ormond, and B. Guy Peters, *A Potential Governance Agenda for Finland* (Helsinki: Ministry of Finance, 2000).

16. Richard N. Haass, *The Reluctant Sheriff: The United States after the Cold War* (Washington, D.C.: Brookings Institution, 1997).

17. I. C. R. Byatt, "Theoretical Issues in Expenditure Decisions," in *Public Expenditure: Allocation among Competing Ends*, ed. Michael V. Posner (Cambridge, England: Cambridge University Press, 1977), 22–27.

18. That is especially true for the federal government, which delivers few identifiable services to the public, and it explains in part why the federal government is often evaluated as the least effective of the three levels of government in the United States.

19. Lester M. Salamon, "The Time Dimension in Policy Evaluation: The Case of New Deal Land Reform," *Public Policy* (spring 1979): 129–83.

20. See Robert E. Goodin, *Political Theory and Public Policy* (Chicago: University of Chicago Press, 1983), 26–29.

21. Debra Viadero, "'Fade-Out' in Head Start Gains Linked to Later Schooling," *Education Week* 13 (20 April 1994): 9.

22. For a discussion of this point, see Henry J. Aaron, *Politics and the Professors* (Washington, D.C.: Brookings Institution, 1978), 84–85. More recent research indicates that there may be some more durable effects; see Edward Zigler and Susan Muenchow, *Head Start: The Inside Story of America's Most Successful Educational Experiment* (New York: Basic Books, 1992).

23. Gerald Schneider, *Time, Planning and Policymaking* (Bern: Peter Lang, 1991).

24. On social experiments, see William Dunn, *The Experimenting Society* (New Brunswick, N.J.: Transaction Books, 1998); and Norma R. A. Romm, *Accountability in Social Research: Issues and Debates* (New York: Kluwer, 2001).

25. Donald T. Campbell and Julian C. Stanley, *Experimental and Quasi-Experimental Design for Research* (Chicago: Rand-McNally, 1966); and Richard E. Neustadt and Ernest R. May, *Thinking in Time: The Uses of History for Decision-Makers* (New York: Free Press, 1986).

26. See, for example, Edward D. Berkowitz, *America's Welfare State: From Roosevelt to Reagan* (Baltimore: Johns Hopkins University Press, 1991). The welfare reform passed in 1996 (see chapter 11) represents yet another milestone on this long road.

27. Campbell and Stanley, *Experimental and Quasi-Experimental Design for Research*, 44–53.

28. For a discussion of the role of experimentation in assessing social policy, see R. A. Berk et al., "Social Policy Experimentation: A Position Paper," *Education Research* 94 (1985): 387–429.

29. Peter Passell, "Like a New Drug, Social Programs Are Put to the Test," *New York Times*, 9 March 1993. Also, the reforms of Medicare after the Balanced Budget Act involve an experiment of 300,000 using Medical Savings Plans.

30. Helen Ingram and Ann Schneider, "The Choice of Target Populations," *Administration and Society* 23 (1991): 149–67; and Anne Schneider and Helen Ingram, "Social Construction of Target Populations: Implications for Politics and Policy," *American Political Science Review* 87 (1993): 334–47.

31. Karen Davis, "Equal Treatment and Unequal Benefits," *Milbank Memorial Fund Quarterly* (1975): 449–88.

32. See Rochelle L. Stanfield, "Jump Start," *National Journal*, (12 February 1994): 364–67.

33. Peter Townsend, ed., *Inequalities in Health* (The Black Report) (London: Penguin, 1988).

34. Brian W. Hogwood and B. Guy Peters, *The Pathology of Public Policy* (Oxford: Oxford University Press, 1985).

35. Welfare had already tended to be short-term for many of the recipients, so the fact that many people could move on should have been no surprise.

36. Barbara J. Holt, "Targeting in Federal Grant Programs: The Case of the Older Americans Act," *Public Administration Review* 54 (1994): 444–49.

37. Peter H. Rossi and Howard E. Freeman, *Evaluation: A Systematic Approach*, 4th. ed. (Newbury Park, Calif.: Sage, 1989), 135–37.

38. Sam D. Sieber, *Fatal Remedies* (New York: Plenum, 1980).

39. Arnold Meltsner, *Policy Analysts in the Bureaucracy* (Berkeley: University of California Press, 1976).

40. Eleanor Chelimsky, "The Politics of Program Evaluation," *Society* 25 (November 1987): 24–32.

41. See B. Guy Peters, *The Future of Governing: Two Decades of Administrative Reform* (Lawrence: University of Kansas Press, 1996).

42. U.S. General Accounting Office, *Managing for Results: Critical Issues for Improving Federal Agencies' Strategic Plans* (Washington, D.C.: USGAO, 16 September 1997), GAO/GGD–97–180. A full range of information on GPRA can be obtained from the GAO's Web site: www.gao.gov/sp/.

43. See B. Guy Peters, "The Rise and Fall and Rise of Evaluation in American Government," unpublished manuscript, Nuffield College, Oxford.

44. Donald F. Kettl and John J. DiIulio, eds., *Inside the Reinvention Machine: Appraising Governmental Reform* (Washington, D.C.: Brookings Institution, 1995).

45. Rochelle L. Stanfield, "Education Wars," *National Journal*, (7 March 1998): 506–9.

46. Michael Nelson, "What's Wrong with Policy Analysis," *Washington Monthly* (September 1979): 53–60. See also Dan Durning, "Participatory Policy Analysis in a Social Service Agency: A Case Study," *Journal of Policy Analysis and Management* 12 (1993): 297–322.

47. Brian W. Hogwood and B. Guy Peters, *Policy Dynamics* (Brighton, England: Wheatsheaf, 1983).

48. Ibid.

49. Peter DeLeon, "A Theory of Policy Termination," in *The Policy Cycle*, ed. Judith V.

May and Aaron Wildavsky (Beverly Hills, Calif.: Sage, 1978): 279–300; and Janet E. Franz, "Reviving and Revising a Termination Model," *Policy Sciences* 25 (1992): 175–89.

50. Kirk Victor, "Uncle Sam's Little Engine," *National Journal*, 23 November 1991.

51. Laurence E. Lynn Jr. and David deF. Whitman, *The President as Policymaker: Jimmy Carter and Welfare Reform* (Philadelphia: Temple University Press, 1981).

52. Anthony Downs, *Inside Bureaucracy* (Boston: Little, Brown, 1967).

53. Rufus E. Miles, "Considerations for a President Bent on Reorganization," *Public Administration Review* 37 (1977): 157.

54. Gary Mucciaroni, "Public Choice and the Politics of Comprehensive Tax Reform," *Governance* 3 (1990): 1–32; and Timothy J. Conlan, Margaret T. Wrightson, and David R. Beam, *Taxing Choices: The Politics of Tax Reform* (Washington, D.C.: CQ Press, 1990).

55. Jean-Claude Thoenig and Eduard Friedberg, "The Power of the Field Staff," in *The Management of Change in Government*, ed. Arne F. Leemans (The Hague: Martinus Nijhoff, 1976).

56. E. H. Klijn and G. R. Teisman, "Effective Policymaking in a Multi-Actor Environment," in *Autopoeisis and Configuration Theory*, ed. L. Schap et al. (Dordrecht: Kluwer, 1991).

57. On the network concept, see Edward O. Laumann and David Knoke, *The Organizational State: Social Change in National Policy Domains* (Madison: University of Wisconsin Press, 1987); and R. A. W. Rhodes, *Understanding Governance: Policy Networks, Governance, Reflexivity and Accountability* (Buckingham, England: Open University Press, 1997).

58. See Jan Kooiman, "Socio-Political Governance," in *Debating Governance*, ed. Jon Pierre (Oxford: Oxford University Press, 1998).

59. R. Kent Weaver, "Setting and Firing Policy Triggers," *Journal of Public Policy* 9 (1989): 307–36.

60. William T. Gormley Jr., *Taming the Bureaucracy: Muscles, Prayers and Other Strategies* (Princeton, N.J.: Princeton University Press, 1989), 205–7.

61. John L. Palmer and Isabel V. Sawhill, *The Reagan Record: An Assessment of America's Changing Domestic Priorities* (Cambridge, Mass.: Ballinger, 1984).

62. Colin Campbell and Bert A. Rockman, eds., *The Clinton Presidency: First Appraisals* (Chatham, N.J.: Chatham House, 1996).

Chapter 8

1. See Michael Stewart, *Keynes and After* (Harmondsworth, England: Penguin, 1972); and Peter A Hall, *The Political Power of Economic Ideas: Keynesianism across Nations* (Princeton: Princeton University Press, 1989).

2. Robert Skidelsky, *Politicians and the Slump* (London: Macmillan, 1967).

3. Walter Heller, *New Dimensions of Political Economy* (Cambridge, Mass.: Harvard University Press, 1966).

4. Paul Ormerod, *The Death of Economics* (London: Faber and Faber, 1994).

5. On the other hand, politicians who tell the truth about the economic future, and especially about higher taxes, are regarded with even greater skepticism.

6. Herbert Stein, *Presidential Economics: The Making of Economic Policy from Roosevelt to Clinton*, 3d rev. ed. (Washington, D.C.: American Enterprise Institute, 1994).

7. Jonathan Rauch, "The Visible Hand," *National Journal*, (9 July 1994): 1612–17.

8. G. Feketekuty, ed., *Trade Strategies for a New Era: Ensuring U.S. Leadership in a Global Economy* (New York: Council on Foreign Relations, 1998).

9. "Pathbreaking CBO Study Shows Dramatic Increases in Income Disparities in 1980s and 1990s" (Washington, D.C.: Center for Budget and Policy Priorities, 31 May 2001); and Congressional Budget Office, *Historical Effective Tax Rates 1979–1997* (Washington, D.C.: CBO, May 2001).

10. John Maggs and David Baumann, "The Stimulus Skirmish," *National Journal*, 15 October 2001.

11. "Decade of Deficits," *The Economist*, 22 June 2002.

12. This trade-off is referred to as the "Phillips Curve." See "A Cruise around the Phillips Curve," *The Economist*, (19 February 1994): 82–83; and A. J. Hallett-Hughes and M. L. Petit, "Stagflation and Phillips Curve Instability in a Model of Macroeconomic Policy," *Manchester School of Economic and Social Studies* 59 (1991): 123–45.

13. In fairness, they often have been promised more of everything by politicians, and often without any associated costs. See Isabel V. Sawhill, "Reaganomics in Retrospect," in *Perspectives on the Reagan Years*, ed. John L. Palmer (Washington, D.C.: Urban Institute Press, 1986).

14. We will point out, however, that although the average has been getting higher, the degree of inequality of distribution of the benefits of growth has also been increasing.

15. For a discussion of this "treble affluence," see Richard Rose and B. Guy Peters, *Can Government Go Bankrupt?* (New York: Basic Books, 1978).

16. Lester Thurow, *The Zero-Sum Society* (New York: Basic Books, 1979).

17. Service industries include a wide range of activities such as insurance, medical care, computer services, and banking in addition to dry cleaners, restaurants, etc.

18. William B. Johnston and Arnold H. Packer, *Workforce 2000: Work and Workers in the 21st Century* (New York: Hudson Institute, 1987); and U.S. Bureau of Labor Statistics, *Monthly Labor Review*, November 1996.

19. U.S. Bureau of Labor Statistics, *Employment and Earnings*, March 2002.

20. Although employment in manufacturing has been declining, value added has been relatively stable. Industries are finding ways to produce with less labor, or are shifting toward high value-added products such as computers and other information technologies.

21. Fred Hirsch and John H. Goldthorpe, *The Political Economy of Inflation* (Cambridge, Mass.: Harvard University Press, 1978).

22. R. Kent Weaver, *The Politics of Indexation* (Washington, D.C.: Brookings Institution, 1987).

23. This is the so-called Baumol's disease, named after the economist William J. Baumol; see his "The Macroeconomics of Unbalanced Growth: The Anatomy of Urban Crisis," in *Is Economics Relevant?* ed. Robert L. Heilbroner and A. M. Ford (Pacific Palisades, Calif.: Goodyear, 1971).

24. See B. Guy Peters, "Public Employment in American Government," paper

presented at annual Workshops of European Consortium for Political Research, Bern, Switzerland, March 1996.

25. John T. Woolley, *Monetary Politics: The Federal Reserve and the Politics of Monetary Politics* (Cambridge, England: Cambridge University Press, 1987).

26. Gösta Esping-Anderson, *The Three Worlds of Welfare Capitalism* (Princeton: Princeton University Press, 1990).

27. In 1999 imports equaled just over 22 percent of Gross National Product in the United States. They averaged 49.2 percent of GNP in Western Europe and 33.2 percent of GNP in all OECD countries.

28. These factors were further exacerbated by a strong U.S. dollar that made selling goods overseas more difficult. The dollar is seen as a "safe haven" in times of crisis and the price of the dollar was driven up on international money markets.

29. William S. Harat and Thomas D. Willett, eds., *Monetary Policy for a Volatile Global Economy* (Washington, D.C.: AEI Press, 1991).

30. Martin Tolchin and Susan Tolchin, *Buying into America: How Foreign Money Is Changing the Face of Our Nation* (New York: Times Books, 1988).

31. See Susan Strange, *The Retreat of the State: The Diffusion of Power in the World Economy* (Cambridge, England: Cambridge University Press, 1996).

32. Michael M. Weinstein, "Twisting Controls on Currency and Capital," *New York Times*, 10 September 1998.

33. M. Hallerberg and S. Basinger, "Internationalization and Changes in Tax Policy in OECD Countries: The Importance of Domestic Veto Players," *Comparative Political Studies* 31 (1998): 321–52.

34. David Vogel, *Trading Up: Consumer and Environmental Regulation in a Global Economy* (Cambridge, Mass.: Harvard University Press, 1995).

35. Susan B. Hansen, *The Politics of State Economic Development*, unpublished paper, Department of Political Science, University of Pittsburgh.

36. Fred R. Bleakley, "Infrastructure Dollars Pay Big Dividends," *Wall Street Journal*, 12 August 1997.

37. Robert J. Reinshuttle, *Economic Development: A Survey of State Activities* (Lexington, Ky.: Council of State Governments, 1984).

38. Fox Butterfield, "New England's Siren Call of the 1980s Becomes Echo of Depression," *New York Times*, 15 December 1991.

39. Paul E. Peterson and Mark Rom, "Macroeconomic Policymaking: Who Is in Control?" in *Can the Government Govern?* ed. John E. Chubb and Paul E. Peterson (Washington, D.C.: Brookings Institution, 1989).

40. See Strange, *Retreat of the State*; and K. Ohmae, *The End of the Nation State* (New York: Free Press, 1995). For a contrary view, see Linda Weiss, *The Myth of the Powerless State* (Cambridge, England: Cambridge University Press, 1998).

41. Alexander Kouzmin and Andrew Hayne, *Essays in Economic Globalization, Transnational Policies, and Vulnerability* (Washington, D.C.: IOS Press, 1999).

42. For one view, see Robert B. Reich, "Trade Accords That Spread the Wealth," *New York Times*, 2 September 1997.

43. John Maggs, "Back from the Dead," *National Journal*, (2 February 2002): 304–7.

44. See Robert E. Litan, "Trade Policy: What Next?" *Brookings Review*, (fall 2000): 41–44.

45. Paul Magnusson, "Bush Trade Policy: Crazy Quilt Like a Fox," *Business Week*, 15 April 2002.

46. James D. Savage, *Balanced Budgets and American Democracy* (Ithaca, N.Y.: Cornell University Press, 1988).

47. Rose and Peters, *Can Government Go Bankrupt?* 135–41; and James M. Buchanan and Richard Wagner, *Democracy in Deficit: The Political Legacy of Lord Keynes* (New York: Academic Press, 1978), 38–48.

48. When listening to the debates about the impacts of budgets in most parliaments or central agencies, it is clear that the ideas of Keynesianism are far from dead.

49. Henry Aaron et al., *Setting National Priorities: The 1980 Budget* (Washington, D.C.: Brookings Institution, 1979). For a critique, see William H. Buiter, "A Guide to Public Sector Deficits," *Economic Policy* 1 (1985): 3–15.

50. Richard W. Stevenson, "House Republicans to Seek Big Tax Cuts," *New York Times*, 10 September 1998.

51. President Reagan's belief in supply-side economics is an obvious case in point.

52. G. Calvin Mackenzie and Saranna Thornton, *Bucking the Deficit: Economic Policymaking in America* (Boulder, Colo.: Westview, 1996).

53. See chapter 6; and Lawrence J. Haas, "Deficit Doldrums," *National Journal*, 7 December 1991.

54. "Budget Resolution Embraces Clinton Plan," 1993 *CQ Almanac* (Washington, D.C.: CQ Press, 1994): 102–21.

55. "Pact Aims to Erase Deficit by 2002," 1997 *CQ Almanac* (Washington, D.C.: CQ Press, 1998), 2-18–2-23.

56. Douglas A. Hibbs, *The American Political Economy: Macroeconomics and Electoral Choice* (Cambridge, Mass.: Harvard University Press, 1987).

57. Paul Craig Roberts, *The Supply-Side Revolution: An Insider's Account of Policymaking in Washington* (Cambridge, Mass.: Harvard University Press, 1984), esp. 27–33.

58. B. Douglas Bernheim, *The Vanishing Nest Egg: Reflections on Saving in America* (New York: Twentieth Century Fund, 1991).

59. American industry tends to be financed more by equity capital than do most European and Japanese companies, which depend more on close relationships with banks. Therefore, investment in the stock market does supply business the capital it needs.

60. Bruce Bartlett and Timothy P. Roth, eds., *The Supply-Side Solution* (Chatham, N.J.: Chatham House, 1983). George H. W. Bush once referred to this assumption as "voodoo economics."

61. James T. Bennett and Thomas J. DiLorenzo, *Underground Government: The Off-Budget Public Sector* (Washington, D.C.: Cato Institute, 1983); and Bruce R. Bartlett, *The Federal Debt: On-Budget, Off-Budget and Contingent Liabilities*, Study Prepared for Use of Joint Economic Committee (Washington, D.C.: Government Printing Office, 1983).

62. Donald F. Kettl, *Leadership at the Fed* (New Haven: Yale University Press, 1986). For a more muckraking account, see William Greider, *Secrets of the Temple: How the Federal Reserve Runs the Country* (New York: Simon and Schuster, 1987).

63. In September 1998, when Greenspan mentioned that rates might be lowered to continue the expansion of the economy, markets reacted almost instantly.

64. See B. Guy Peters, "Institutionalization and Deinstutionalization: Regulatory Insti-

tutions in American Government," in *Comparative Regulatory Institutions*, ed. G. Bruce Doern and Stephen Wilks (Toronto: University of Toronto Press, 1998).

65. Marc Alan Eisner, *Antitrust and the Triumph of Economics* (Chapel Hill: University of North Carolina Press, 1991).

66. The Department of Justice had been the only enforcement agency. It retained its powers after the passage of the Clayton Act, and both it and the Federal Trade Commission enforce antitrust legislation.

67. Joel Brinkley, "Strategies Set in Microsoft Antitrust Case," *New York Times*, 14 September 1998.

68. Some of this argument appears specious given that all firms will face the same wage increases.

69. See Stein, *Presidential Economics*.

70. William Pfaff, "Deregulation Is a False God," *Los Angeles Times*, 27 June 2002.

71. Author's calculation based on the federal budget documents.

72. J. C. Gray and D. A. Spina, "State and Local Government Industrial Location Incentives: A Well-stocked Candy Store," *Journal of Corporation Law* 5 (1980): 517–687.

73. William S. Dietrich, *In the Shadow of the Rising Sun: The Political Roots of American Economic Decline* (University Park: Pennsylvania State University Press, 1991).

74. The most famous was Ross Perot, who characterized the predicted large loss of jobs to Mexico under NAFTA as a "large sucking sound." See also G. Bruce Doern and Brian W. Tomlin, *Faith and Fear: The Free Trade Story* (Toronto: Stoddard, 1991).

75. Jonathan Rauch, "The Deregulatory President," *National Journal*, (30 November 1991): 2902–6.

76. Jonathan T. R. Hughes, *The Governmental Habit Redux: Economic Controls from Colonial Times to the Present*, 2d ed. (Princeton: Princeton University Press, 1991).

77. That support may come through direct subsidies or through protection from foreign competition. See David B. Yoffie, "American Trade Policy: An Obsolete Bargain," in *Can the Government Govern?* ed. John E. Chubb and Paul E. Peterson (Washington, D.C.: Brookings Institution, 1989).

78. North American Free Trade Agreement and the World Trade Organization.

79. See Marie-Louise Bermelmans-Videc, Ray C. Rist, and Evert Vedung, eds., *Carrots, Sticks and Sermons: Policy Instruments and their Evaluation* (New Brunswick, N.J.: Transaction Books, 1998).

Chapter 9

1. Henry J. Aaron and William G. Gale, *Economic Effects of Fundamental Tax Reform* (Washington, D.C.: Brookings Institution, 1996).

2. Charles E. McClure, *The Value Added Tax: Key to Deficit Reduction?* (Washington, D.C.: American Enterprise Institute, 1987). Part of the drive to ensure competition in the European Union is to have relatively common tax systems, including the value-added tax, in all member nations.

3. B. Guy Peters, *Taxation: A Comparative Perspective* (Oxford: Blackwells, 1991).

4. David Butler, Anthony Adonis, and Tony Travers, *Failure in British Government: The Politics of the Poll Tax* (Oxford: Oxford University Press, 1994).

5. See Cathie Jo Martin, "Business Influence and State Power: The Case of U.S. Corporate Tax Policy," *Politics and Society* 17 (1989): 189–223.

   For a somewhat polemical account of recent developments, see Christopher Lasch, *The Revolt of the Elites and the Betrayal of Democracy* (New York: Norton, 1995). William F. Holmes, *American Populism* (New York: D.C. Heath, 1994) provides a more scholarly treatment of populism.

6. David Brunori, *State Tax Policy: A Political Perspective* (Washington, D.C.: Urban Institute).

7. Stanley S. Surrey and Paul R. McDaniel, *Tax Expenditures* (Cambridge, England: Cambridge University Press, 1985).

8. Richard W. Stevenson, "The Secret Language of Social Engineering," *New York Times*, 6 July 1997.

9. Robert Pear, "Now, Special Tax Breaks Get Hidden in Plain Sight," *New York Times*, 1 August 1997.

10. Christopher Howard, *The Hidden Welfare State: Tax Expenditures and Social Policy in the United States* (Princeton: Princeton University Press, 1997).

11. The two standard ideas are "ability to pay," justifying a progressive system of taxation, and "benefits received," which can justify more of a flat-rate system of taxation.

12. See O. Listhaug and Arthur H. Miller, "Public Support for Tax Evasion: Self-interest or Symbolic Politics?" *European Journal of Political Research* 13 (1985): 265–82. See also John T. Scholz and Mark Lubell, "Adaptive Political Attitudes: Duty, Trust and Fear as Monitors of Tax Policy," *American Journal of Political Science* 42 (1998): 903–20.

13. Gallup poll, 24–26 March 1997; March 25–27, 2001.

14. Robert Greenstein, *How Would Families at Different Income Levels Benefit from the Bush Tax Cut?* (Washington, D.C.: Center for Budget and Policy Priorities, April 2001).

15. It does, of course. Leaving aside how one counts the protective services delivered by the military, there is the Veterans Administration and its hospitals, the Postal Service, the National Park Service, agricultural extension agents, and a host of others.

16. This is, however, bad news for health advocates who are attempting to use the cigarette tax as a means of deterring smoking. It may be more of a deterrent for the main target group—teen smokers—who have less disposable income.

17. See William F. Shugart, ed., *Taxing Choices: The Predatory Politics of Fiscal Discrimination* (New Brunswick, N.J.: Transaction, 1997).

18. CBS News poll, April 2001.

19. ABC News poll, March 2001.

20. David O. Sears and Jack Citrin, *Tax Revolt: Something for Nothing in California*, enl. ed. (Cambridge, Mass.: Harvard University Press, 1985).

21. Allan M. Maslove, *The Economic and Social Environment of Tax Reform* (Toronto: University of Toronto Press, 1995).

22. There is some evidence, however, that globalization may not be as pervasive an influence on taxation as is usually assumed.

23. Joel Slemrod, "What is the Simplest Tax System of Them All?" in Aaron and Gale, *Economic Effects of Fundamental Tax Reform*.

24. F. Vaillancourt, "The Compliance Costs of Taxes on Businesses and Individuals: A Review of the Evidence," *Public Finance* 42 (1989): 395–414.

25. Even at the minimum wage of $5.15 per hour, this will amount to over $5 billion in free work by citizens.

26. Richard A. Musgrave, *Fiscal Systems* (New Haven: Yale University Press, 1969).

27. For somewhat different views, see Robert S. McIntyre, "Thrown for a Loop," *New Republic* 208 (15 March 1993): 17, 19ff; and Laura Sanders, "The Campeau Coup and the May Maneuver," *Forbes* 142 (31 October 1988): 98–99.

28. Joseph A. Pechman, *Who Paid the Taxes, 1966–85?* (Washington, D.C.: Brookings Institution, 1986).

29. Paul E. Peterson and Mark Rom, "Lower Taxes, More Spending and Budget Deficits," in *The Reagan Legacy*, ed. Charles O. Jones (Chatham, N.J.: Chatham House, 1988).

30. See B. Guy Peters, *The Politics of Taxation* (Oxford: Basil Blackwell, 1992), 166–73.

31. See the extended analysis of the Clinton proposals in the *New York Times*, 18 February 1993.

32. Gwen Ifill, "President Assures Middle Class over Income Taxes," *New York Times*, 17 February 1993.

33. Harold Wilensky, *The "New Corporatism," Centralization, and the Welfare State* (Beverly Hills, Calif.: Sage, 1976).

34. The author, for example, pays four separate income taxes, three property taxes, sales and excise taxes, etc. Some of these taxes are small, but they do add up.

35. W. W. Pommerehne and F. Schneider, "Fiscal Illusion, Political Institutions and Local Public Spending," *Kyklos* 31 (1978): 381–408.

36. McClure, *Value-Added Tax.*

37. Peters, *Politics of Taxation*, 165–67.

38. Sven Steinmo, *Taxation and Democracy* (New Haven: Yale University Press, 1992).

39. J. M. Verdier, "The President, Congress and Tax Reform: Patterns over Three Decades," *The Annals* (1988): 114–23.

40. Even after reform, the federal income tax is considered the least fair tax by a plurality of respondents in surveys. See Advisory Commission on Intergovernmental Relations, *Changing Public Attitudes on Government and Taxes* (Washington, D.C.: ACIR, annual).

41. Timothy J. Conlan, Margaret T. Wrightson, and David R. Beam, *Taxing Choices: The Politics of Tax Reform* (Washington, D.C.: CQ Press, 1989); and J. H. Birnbaum and A. S. Murray, *Showdown at Gucci Gulch* (New York: Random House, 1987).

42. Gary Mucciaroni, "Public Choice and the Politics of Comprehensive Tax Reform," *Governance* 3 (1990): 1–32.

43. Conlan, Wrightson, and Beam, *Taxing Choices.*

44. John W. Kingdon, *Agendas, Alternatives, and Public Policies* (Boston: Little, Brown, 1984).

45. See Cedric Sandford, *Successful Tax Reform* (Bath, England: Fiscal Publications, 1993).

46. For example, if I had invested in a piece of land in 1970 for $100, and then sold it in 1998 for $500, there would be an apparent profit of $400. If, however, inflation were taken into account, the "real" profit would be less than $200 (in 1998 dollars). On what basis should I be taxed?

47. In 1995, 82% of all returns reporting capital gains cited incomes less than $100,000, although 76% of all capital gains income does go to people earning over $100,000.

48. Henry J. Aaron and William A. Gale, "Truth in Taxes," *Brookings Review* (spring 2000): 12–15.

49. William Gale and Joel B. Slemrod, *Rethinking the Estate and Gift Tax* (Ann Arbor: University of Michigan Business School, January, 2001).

50. Carl Hulse, "Battle on Estate Tax: How Two Well-Organized Lobbies Sprang into Action," *New York Times*, 14 June 2001.

51. This resentment came to a head in 1997 and 1998 with a series of congressional hearings about the Internal Revenue Service and its treatment of citizens. See Daniel J. Murphy, "IRS: An Agency Out of Control?" *Investor's Business Daily*, 1 October 1997; and "It's April at the IRS," *USA Today*, 2 April 1998.

52. But see Aaron Wildavsky, "Keeping Kosher: The Epistemology of Tax Expenditures," *Journal of Public Policy* 5 (1985): 413–31.

53. See Robert S. McIntyre, "The 23 Percent Solution," *New York Times*, 23 January 1998.

54. Psychologically that may create demands for increases in wages, even though people should have a great deal more take-home pay with the elimination of the income tax.

55. See David F. Bradford, *Untangling the Income Tax* (Cambridge, Mass.: Harvard University Press, 1986); and U.S. General Accounting Office, *Tax Administration: Potential Impact of Alternate Taxes on Taxpayers and Administrators* (Washington, D.C.: GAO, January 1998), GAO/GGD–98–37, Appendix VIII.

56. See Thomas J. DiLorenzo and James T. Bennett, "National Nannies Seek Taxes on All We Consume," *USA Today*, 23 December 1997.

57. That is, 24 million business returns plus 115 million personal returns.

58. Ben Wildavsky, "A Taxing Question," *National Journal*, 28 February 1998.

Chapter 10

1. The evidence is that most states have not replaced the health care money they lost in the transition to block grants. See George E. Peterson et al., *Block Grants* (Washington, D.C.: Urban Institute, 1984).

2. Marilyn Werber Serafini, "Oh Yeah, the Uninsured," *National Journal*, (15 November 1997): 2300–2303.

3. Judi Hasson and Jessica Lee, "Poll: 43% Back Clinton Health Plan," *USA Today*, 30 June 1994.

4. For example, in a 1996 poll, half of the respondents said that providing affordable medical care for all was one of the top national priorities, and 22 percent said it was the highest priority. See Robert D. Reischauer, Stuart Butler, and Judith R. Lave, eds., *Medicare* (Washington, D.C.: National Academy of Social Insurance, 1998), 300.

5. "Federal, State, Local, or Private Action," *American Enterprise*, November/December 1997, 94; and Gina Kolata, "An Economist's View of Health Care Reform," *New York Times*, 2 May 2000.

6. Adam Clymer, "House Bill Asks 8.4% Payroll Tax for Canadian-Style Health Plan," *New York Times*, 28 January 1994.

7. Deane Neubauer, "Hawaii: The Health State," in *Health Policy Reform in the United States: Innovations from the States*, ed. Howard Leichter (Armonk, N.Y.: M. E. Sharpe, 1992); Camille Asccuaga, "Universal Health Care in Massachusetts: Lessons for the Future," in Leichter, *Health Policy Reform in the United States*; General Accounting Office, *Health Care in Hawaii: Implications for National Reform* (Washington, D.C.: GAO, February 1994), GAO/HEHS-94-68); and Anna Konderatas, Alan Weil, and Naomi Goldstein, "Assessing the New Federalism," *Health Affairs* 17 (1998): 17–24.

8. Robin Turner, "Health Care in Minnesota: Model for U.S. or Novelty?" *New York Times*, 9 October 1993. Children and the elderly again can be seen to hold a privileged position, with programs for them permissible even if more general programs are not.

9. With the loss of welfare also came a loss of Medicaid coverage, but another federal law funded care for children in states that adopted a suitable program. See Peter T. Kilborn, "States to Provide Health Insurance to More Children," *New York Times*, 21 September 1997; and Thomas M. Selden, Jessica S. Bathin, and Joel W. Cohen, "Trends: Medicaid's Problem Children: Eligible But Not Enrolled," *Health Affairs* 17, no. 3 (1998): 192–200.

10. See B. Guy Peters, "Is it the Institutions? Explaining the Failure of Health Care in the United States," *Public Policy and Administration* 11, no. 1 (1996): 8–15.

11. Dennis Cauchon, "Campaign Rx Could Be Wrong Prescription," *USA Today*, 1 November 2000.

12. Rebecca Adams, "Could Patients' Rights Law Bring Clarity to an Industry of Uncertainty?" *CQ Weekly* 59 (4 August 2001): 1902–3.

13. Marilyn Werber Serafini, "Piling Up the Health Care Bills," *National Journal*, 8 September 2001.

14. World Health Organization, *World Health Statistics Annual* (Geneva: WHO, annual).

15. "The Public Decides on Health Care Reform," *Public Perspective* 5 (September/October 1994): 23–28. A very large proportion support care for the elderly, with Medicare now being highly institutionalized.

16. These are primarily the working poor, who are often employed in jobs without health care benefits and who are not eligible for Medicaid as they would be if they were on welfare.

17. Henry J. Aaron, *Serious and Unstable Condition: Financing America's Health Care* (Washington, D.C.: Brookings Institution, 1991): 47–57.

18. Ibid., 45–47.

19. Robert Pear, "Tough Decision on Health Care If Employers Won't Pay the Bill," *New York Times*, 9 July 1994.

20. *New York Times*, 11 July 1994.

21. General Accounting Office, *Private Health Insurance: Continued Erosion of Coverage Linked to Cost Pressures* (Washington, D.C.: GAO, July 1997), GAO/HEHS-97-122.

22. Despite its good intentions, the indications are that Kennedy-Kassebaum is not as effective as it might be because the rates at which the portable insurance can be charged are not adequately controlled. See Robert Pear, "High Rates Hobble Law to Guarantee Health Insurance," *New York Times*, 17 March 1998.

23. Peter Townsend, ed., *Inequalities in Health: The Black Report* (London: Penguin, 1988).

24. Lisette Alvarez, "A Conservative Battles Corporate Health Care," *New York Times,* 12 February 1998.

25. Peter T. Kilborn, "Black Americans Trailing Whites in Health, Studies Say," *New York Times,* 26 January 1998.

26. Sheryl Gay Stolberg, "Race Gap Seen in Health Care of Equally Insured Patients," *New York Times,* 21 March 2002.

27. The infant mortality rate is more than double the national average. In 1995 it was more than 50 percent higher than the next highest unit—Mississippi.

28. Steven Greenhouse, "The States' Stakes in Clinton's Health Plan," *New York Times,* 10 October 1993.

29. Rural areas tend to have a number of hospital beds but very low occupancy rates, thereby driving up costs.

30. Dan Verango, "The Operation You Get Often Depends on Where You Live," *USA Today,* 19 September 2000. See www.dartmouth.edu/~atlas.

31. Peter T. Kilborn, "Roving Doctors Paying House Calls to Towns," *New York Times,* 16 April 2000.

32. *Rural Health Clinics: Rising Program Expenditures Not Focused on Improving Care in Isolated Areas,* Testimony of Bernice Steinhardt (Washington, D.C.: General Accounting Office, 13 February 1997), GAO/T-HEHS-97-65.

33. Nicholas Eberstadt, "Why Are So Many American Babies Dying?" *American Enterprise* 2 (September 1991): 37–45. This finding, of course, gives comfort to conservatives who stress individual responsibility and minimize the need for government intervention in the medical marketplace.

34. See Henry J. Aaron, *The Problem That Won't Go Away: Reforming U.S. Health Care Financing* (Washington, D.C.: Brookings Institution, 1995).

35. For example, CAT scans and MRIs are now common diagnostic techniques but were used scarcely—if at all—until relatively recently. Each is billed at over $1,000 per use.

36. These constraints are now being challenged in the courts. Mark Carriden, "High Court Hears Suit on HMO Referrals," *Dallas Morning News,* 15 January 2002.

37. Milt Frendenheim, "Many H.M.O.'s Easing the Rules on Specialists' Care," *New York Times,* 2 February 1997.

38. Henry J. Aaron, *Serious and Unstable Condition: Financing America's Health Care* (Washington, D.C.: Brookings Institution, 1991): 8–37.

39. The U.S. population is approximately eleven times as large as that of Canada, while we have approximately one hundred times as many MRI units.

40. Spencer Rich, "Hospital Administration Costs Put at 25%," *Washington Post,* 6 August 1993.

41. John K. Inglehart, "Health Policy Report: Managed Competition," *New England Journal of Medicine* 328 (22 April 1993): 1208–12; and Joshua M. Wiener and Laura Hixon Illston, "Health Care Reform: Six Questions for President Clinton," *Brookings Review* 11 (Spring 1993): 22–25.

42. Aaron, *Serious and Unstable Condition,* 45–47.

43. Julie Kosterlitz, "Wanted: GPs," *National Journal,* 5 September 1992.

44. Susan Hosek et al., *The Study of Preferred Provider Organizations* (Santa Monica, Calif.: RAND Corporation, 1990). Doctors are beginning to fight back against managed care. See Reed Abelson, "A Medical Resistance Movement," *New York Times*, 25 March 1998.

45. Paul B. Ginsburg et al., "Update: Medicare Physician Payment Reform," *Health Affairs* 9 (Spring 1990): 178–88.

46. Sandra Christenses and Scott Harrison, *Physician Payment Reform under Medicare* (Washington, D.C.: Congressional Budget Office, 1990).

47. See Stan Jones, "The Medicare Beneficiary as Consumer," in *Medicare: Preparing for the Challenges of the 21st Century*, ed. Robert D. Reischauer, Stuart Butler, and Judith Lave (Washington, D.C.: Brookings Institution, 1997).

48. 1995 figures. Health Care Financing Administration, *Health Care Financing Review*, annual.

49. Garrett Hardin and John Baden, *Managing the Commons* (San Francisco: W. H. Freeman, 1977).

50. This approach has not been popular with a number of groups, including the Children's Defense Fund. See Timothy Egan, "Oregon Health Plan Stalled by Politics," *New York Times*, 17 March 1993.

51. Susan Ferriss, "Plan in Oregon Would Expand Health Coverage to Poor Citizens," *Pittsburgh Post Gazette*, 20 December 1991.

52. Susan Feigenbaum, "Denying Access to Life-Saving Technologies: Budgetary Implications of a Moral Dilemma," *Regulation* 16, no. 4 (1994): 74–79.

53. Thomas J. Marzen and Louis W. Sullivan, "ADA Analyses of the Oregon Health Care Plan," *Issues in Law & Medicine* 9 (1994): 397–424.

54. On the latter point, see Ivan Illich, *Medical Nemesis* (New York: Pantheon, 1976).

55. Abelson, "Medical Resistance Movement"; and "The Tricky Business of Keeping Doctors Quiet," *New York Times*, 22 September 1996.

56. As of spring 1997, eight states had comprehensive laws providing managed care rights to citizens, two others had regulations and were writing legislation, and nineteen others had legislation under active consideration.

57. These efforts to regain control often have been less than successful. See Nancy Wolff and Mark Schlesinger, "Clinicians as Advocates: An Exploratory Study of Responses to Managed Care by Mental Health Professionals," *Journal of Behavioral Health Services & Research* 29: 274–88.

58. The same questions arise concerning developments in medical technology, such as artificial hearts. See "One Miracle, Many Doubts," *Time*, 10 December 1984, 10ff.

59. Henry R. Glick, *The Right to Die* (New York: Columbia University Press, 1994).

60. Rudolf Klein and Patricia Day, *Managing Scarcity: Priority Setting and Rationing in the National Health Service* (Buckingham, England: Open University Press, 1996).

61. In addition to the ninety days covered per stay, each participant has sixty "reserve days" during his or her life that can be used after any ninety-day period of hospitalization, although these have a copayment of $382.

62. Karen Davis, "Equal Treatment and Unequal Benefits," *Milbank Memorial Fund Quarterly* (Fall 1975): 449–88; and Robert Ball, "What Medicare Had in Mind," *Health Affairs* 14 (1995): 62–72.

63. "Tougher Standards for Medigap Insurance," *Aging* 362 (1991): 44–45.

64. Advisory Council on Social Security, *Report on Medicare Projections by the Health Technical Panel* (Washington, D.C.: Government Printing Office, 1991).

65. Marilyn Werber Serafini, "Brave New World," *National Journal*, (16 August 1997).

66. See section on Medicare financing in *Health Affairs*, 17, no. 1 (1998).

67. In a medical savings account, Medicare buys the patient a catastrophic care policy and covers part of the deductible payments for care under the policy. If there are any savings over the year, for example, the recipient is healthy and actually spends less than under the standard program, then he or she gets to keep the difference.

68. Robert Pear, "Republicans Plan to Push through Prescription Drug Coverage for the Elderly," *New York Times,* 10 November 2002.

69. In 1997 the Office of the Inspector General of the Department of Health and Human Services uncovered $23 billion a year in fraud and waste in Medicare.

70. Julie Kosterlitz, "Health Rip-Offs," *National Journal*, 20 June 1992.

71. Louise B. Russell and Carrie Lynn Manning, "The Effect of Prospective Payment on Medicare Expenditures," *New England Journal of Medicine*, 16 February 1989, 439–44.

72. Jeffrey A. Buck and Mark S. Kamlet, "Problems with Expanding Medicaid for the Uninsured," *Journal of Health Politics, Policy and Law* 18 (1993): 1–25. In 1999 Medicaid spending accounted for approximately one dollar in five of state expenditure.

73. Health Care Financing Administration, *Health Care Financing Review*, annual.

74. Paul Jesilow and Gilbert Geis, "Fraud by Physicians Against Medicaid," *Journal of the American Medical Association* 266 (18 December 1991): 3318–22.

75. Leslie G. Aronovitz, *Medicaid: A Program Highly Vulnerable to Fraud* (Washington, D.C.: General Accounting Office, 25 February 1994), GAO/T-HEHS–94–106.

76. See endnote 9.

77. Karen Davis et al., *Health Care Cost Containment* (Baltimore: Johns Hopkins University Press, 1990), 222ff.

78. Patricia Baumann, "The Formulation and Evolution of Health Maintenance Organization Policy, 1970–73," *Social Science and Medicine* (1976): 129–42.

79. This conforms to the general tendency of the Reagan and both Bush administrations to use market and quasi-market devices as means of reducing the costs of government.

80. Elisabeth Rosenthal, "Doctors Who Once Spurned H.M.O.s Now Often Find Systems' Doors Shut," *New York Times*, 25 June 1994.

81. See Lester C. Thurow, "As HMOs Lose Control, Patient Costs Head Skyward," *USA Today*, 16 December 1997.

82. Milt Freudenheim, "Big H.M.O. to Give Decisions on Care Back to Doctors," *New York Times*, 9 November 1999.

83. Robert Pear, "Clinton Picks Panel to Draft Bill of Rights in Health Care," *New York Times*, 27 March 1997.

84. Julie Appleby, "HMOs: What Happens When the Band Aids Run Out?" *USA Today*, 8 December 2000.

85. Stephen Linder and Pauline Vaillancourt Rousseau, "Health Care Policy," in *Developments in American Politics* 4, ed. Gillian Peele et al. (Basingstoke, England: Palgrave, 2002).

86. One of the older forms of health care regulation, the control of facilities through certificates-of-need, has ceased to be of great relevance, given the emphasis on cost containment in managed care.

87. Peter H. Stone, "Ready for Round Two," *National Journal*, 3 January 1998; and "Health Care Reform," *Public Perspective*, February/March 1998, 39.

88. In particular, Congressman Charles Norwood, R-Ga., has been leading a campaign for more extensive regulation of HMOs. This has him making common cause with Senator Edward Kennedy, D-Mass., one of the more liberal members of the Senate.

89. Sam Howe Verhovek, "Texas Is Lowering H.M.O. Legal Shield," *New York Times*, 5 June 1997.

90. There is some evidence that managed care systems do invest more in preventive care. Steven Findlay, "Survey Shows HMO Care Varies Widely," *USA Today*, 2 October 1997.

91. Tort actions may not be as effective as ex ante controls, but they do at least force the industry to consider the long-run costs of any decisions it may make.

92. Peter S. Arno and Karyn L. Feiden, *Against the Odds: The Story of AIDS Drug Development, Politics and Profits* (New York: HarperCollins, 1992).

93. Susan Okie, "Medical Journals Try to Curb Drug Companies' Influence on Research," *Washington Post*, 5 August 2001; and Dennis Cauchon, "FDA Advisers Tied to Industry," *USA Today*, 25 September 2000.

94. General Accounting Office, "Drug Safety: Most Drugs Withdrawn in Recent Years Have Greater Health Risks for Women," GAO–01–286R, 10 January 2001.

95. "Look-alike" drugs are virtually identical chemically with another drug, but have some slight modification to avoid patent restrictions.

96. See Sheryl Gay Stolberg and Jeff Gerth, "How Companies Stall Generics and Keep Themselves Healthy," *New York Times*, 23 July 2000.

97. The "substandard" here is a function largely of inadequate preventive care, and lack of consistent follow-up, rather than the quality of the individual treatments.

98. Gallup poll, January 1996.

99. For a discussion of these problems, see chapter 4.

100. Julie Kosterlitz, "A Sick System," *National Journal*, 15 February 1992.

101. Howard Leichter, *Health Policy Reform in America: Innovations from the States*, 2d ed. (Armonk, N.Y.: M. E. Sharpe, 1997).

102. Although it is referred to as "Canadian" in the American debates over health care, this type of plan is actually found in most developed democracies.

103. Some aspects of the plan have been implemented in various states, under the same name. See, for example, A. C. Enthoven and S. J. Singer, "Managed Competition and the California Health Economy," *Health Affairs* 15 (1996): 39–57.

104. See above.

105. Robert Pear, "Bill Passed by Panel Would Open Medicare to Millions of Uninsured People," *New York Times*, 1 July 1994.

106. See Peters, "Is It the Institutions?"

107. Katherine Q. Seelye, "Lobbyists Are the Loudest in the Health Care Debate," *New York Times*, 16 August 1994.

108. The degree of choice actually existing in the current medical care system appeared to have been exaggerated by the opponents of reform. See Robin Toner, "Ills of Health System Outlive Debate on Care," *New York Times*, 2 October 1994.

109. Richard E. Cohen, "Into the Swamp," *National Journal*, 19 March 1994.

110. Adam Clymer, "With Health Overhaul Dead, A Search for Minor Repairs," *New York Times*, 28 August 1994.

111. Robert Pear, "Health Care Debate to Shift to Federal Employees' Plan," *New York Times*, 7 September 1994.

112. Marilyn Werber Serafini, "A New Prescription," *National Journal*, 14 March 1998, 572–75.

113. Clymer, "With Health Overhaul Dead, A Search for Minor Repairs."

114. Robert Pear, "States Again Try Health Changes as Congress Fails," *New York Times*, 16 September 1994.

Chapter 11

1. See Harold Wilensky, *The Welfare State and Equality* (Berkeley: University of California Press, 1975), 32–36. For a different view, see Theodore R. Marmor, Jerry L. Mashaw, and Philip L. Harvey, *America's Misunderstood Welfare State* (New York: Basic Books, 1990).

2. Donald O. Parsons and Douglas R. Munro, "Intergenerational Transfers in Social Security," in *The Crisis in Social Security*, ed. Michael J. Boskin (San Francisco: Institute for Contemporary Studies, 1977): 65–86.

3. Self-employed persons pay a rate equal to the combined sum of contributions of employers and employees.

4. This separation of pensions and other social insurance benefits from general taxation is unusual in the rest of the world. See Margaret S. Gordon, *Social Security Policies in Industrial Countries: A Comparative Analysis* (Cambridge, England: Cambridge University Press, 1990).

5. Michael D. Hurd and John B. Shoven, "The Distributional Impact of Social Security," in *Pensions, Labor and Individual Choice*, ed. David Wise (Chicago: University of Chicago Press, 1985).

6. As income goes up, replacement rates go down; at $100,000 per year, the rate would be 28 percent.

7. The actual determination of taxability is somewhat more complicated. See David Pattison and David E. Harrington, "Proposals to Modify the Taxation of Social Security Benefits: Options and Distributional Effects," *Social Security Bulletin* 56 (Summer 1993): 3–13.

8. This program has been, like so many, "path dependent," and its initial formulation has largely determined its development. See Ellen Immergut, *Health Policy* (Cambridge, England: Cambridge University Press, 1991).

9. Joseph Bondar, "Beneficiaries Affected by the Annual Earnings Test, 1989," *Social Security Bulletin* 56 (Spring 1993): 20–34.

10. Social Security Agency, Office of the Actuary, *Life Tables for the United States Social Security Area, 1900–2080* (Baltimore: SSA, 1992).

11. "Commission: Raise Retirement Age to 70," *USA Today*, 19 May 1998.

12. There has been a tendency for people to retire earlier, especially among the more affluent, who have retirement income in addition to Social Security.

13. C. Eugene Steuerle and Jon M. Bakija, *Retooling Social Security for the 21st Century* (Washington, D.C.: Urban Institute Press, 1994), 97.

14. Deborah Stone, *The Disabled State* (Philadelphia: Temple University Press, 1985).

15. General Accounting Office, *SSA Disability Programs: Fully Updating Disability Criteria Has Implications for Program Design* (Washington, D.C.: GAO, 11 July 2002), GAO–02–919T.

16. General Accounting Office, *SSA and VA Disability Programs: Re-Examination of Disability Criteria Needed to Help Ensure Program Integrity* (Washington, D.C.: GAO, 9 August 2002), GAO–02–597.

17. Bernadine Weatherford, "The Disability Insurance Program: An Administrative Attack on the Welfare State," in *The Attack on the Welfare State*, ed. Anthony Champagne and Edward J. Harpham (Prospect Heights, Ill: Waveland Press, 1984).

18. General Accounting Office, *Social Security Disability: SSA Needs to Improve Continuing Disability Review Program* (Washington, D.C.: GAO, July 1993), GAO/HRD–93–109.

19. "Workers' Compensation," *Social Security Bulletin* 56 (Winter 1993): 28–31.

20. The maximum payment in Connecticut is $737 per week, while that in Georgia is $225 per week.

21. As noted, Social Security does accumulate funds in its trust fund but not at a rate needed to finance future benefits—much of which continue to be paid from current revenues from Social Security taxation.

22. For a detailed analysis, see Henry J. Aaron, Barry P. Bosworth, and Gary Burtless, *Can America Afford to Grow Old? Paying for Social Security* (Washington, D.C.: Brookings Institution, 1989), 55–75.

23. Practical politics, however, prevented President Reagan from doing anything to reduce Social Security benefits. See Paul E. Peterson and Mark Rom, "Lower Taxes, More Spending, and Budget Deficits," in *The Reagan Legacy*, ed. Charles O. Jones (New York: Chatham House, 1988), 224–25.

24. Princeton Survey Research survey reported in *USA Today*, 27 July 1998.

25. Princeton Survey Research survey, June 2000.

26. Jonathan Rauch, "False Security," *National Journal*, 14 February 1987, 362–65.

27. Aaron, Bosworth, and Burtless, *Can America Afford to Grow Old?* (Washington, D.C.: Brookings Institution, 1993).

28. Board of Trustees of the Federal Old-Age, Survivors, and Disability Insurance Trust Funds, *Annual Report, 2001* (Washington, D.C.: Government Printing Office, 2001). These figures are based on intermediate assumptions about the future of the system. Under less optimistic assumptions, there would be only 1.7 workers per recipient in 2050.

29. Linda E. Demkovich, "Budget Cutters Think the Unthinkable—Social Security Cuts Would Stem Red Ink," *National Journal*, 23 June 1984.

30. Ibid.

31. As noted, the health insurance component of the payroll tax (1.45 percent) is applied to all income.

32. George F. Break, "The Economic Effects of Social Security Financing," in *Social Security Financing*, ed. Felicity Skidmore (Cambridge, Mass.: MIT Press, 1981), 45–80.

33. See B. Guy Peters, *The Politics of Taxation* (Oxford: Basil Blackwell, 1992).

34. See "Americans Want Everyone in Social Security," *USA Today*, 29 July 1998.

35. Charles E. McClure, "VAT Versus the Payroll Tax," in *Social Security Financing*, ed. Felicity Skidmore (Cambridge, Mass.: MIT Press, 1981).

36. For a review of the proposals, see Henry J. Aaron and Robert D. Reischauer, "Should We Reform Social Security?" *Brookings Review* (Winter 1999): 6–11.

37. These retirement plans take their name from the section of the U.S. Internal Revenue Code that governs their creation and use.

38. Ben Wildavsky, "The Two Per Cent Solution," *National Journal*, 11 April 1998: 794–97.

39. R. Shep Melnick, *Between the Lines* (Washington, D.C.: Brookings Institution, 1994).

40. Most of these critics are on the political right, for example, Charles Murray, *Losing Ground* (New York: Basic Books, 1984) and his "Stop Favoring Welfare Mothers," *New York Times*, 16 January 1992; and Lawrence M. Mead, *The New Politics of Poverty* (New York: Basic Books, 1992). There are, however, also critics on the left, for example, David T. Ellwood, *Poor Support: Poverty and the American Family* (New York: Basic Books, 1988); and Frances Fox Piven and Richard Cloward, *Regulating the Poor*, 2d ed. (New York: Vintage Books, 1993).

41. M. Gilens, *Why Americans Hate Welfare: Race, Media and the Politics of Anti-Poverty Policy* (Chicago: University of Chicago Press, 2000).

42. See James L. Morrison, *The Healing of America: Welfare Reform in a Cyber Economy* (Brookfield, Vt.: Ashgate, 1997).

43. Penelope Lemov, "Putting Welfare on the Clock," *Governing*, November 1993, 29–30.

44. Edwin W. Witte, *The Development of the Social Security Act* (Madison: University of Wisconsin Press, 1962), 5–39.

45. Julie Kosterlitz, "Behavior Modification," *National Journal*, 1 February 1992, 271–75. The earlier attempts to control behavior pale in comparison to those of the 1996 reforms.

46. Ibid.

47. Kevin Sack, "Fingerprinting Allowed in Welfare Fraud Fight," *New York Times*, 9 July 1994.

48. Some evidence appearing just as workfare was being implemented placed some doubt on the efficacy of permitting greater earnings. See Jason DeParle, "More Questions about Incentives to Get Those on Welfare to Work," *New York Times*, 28 August 1997.

49. As noted, despite those disincentives to leave, the majority of people on AFDC did not stay long. The other problems with the program, and the relatively meager benefits, attracted few long-term beneficiaries.

50. Julie Kosterlitz, "Reworking Welfare," *National Journal*, 26 September 1992.

51. Michael Wiseman, "Research and Policy: A Symposium on the Family Support Act of 1988," *Journal of Policy Analysis and Management* 10 (1991): 588–89.

52. Kay E. Sherwood and David A. Long, "JOBS Implementation in an Uncertain Environment," *Public Welfare* 49 (1991): 17–27.

53. This problem would, of course, have been rectified if the Clinton plan, or any other plan, for universal health insurance had been adopted. Any comprehensive reform of that sort currently is off the agenda.

54. Sherwood and Long, "JOBS Implementation in an Uncertain Environment."

55. Amy L. Sherman, "The Lessons of W-2," *The Public Interest* 140 (Summer 2000): 36–46.

56. The title of the bill is a masterpiece of symbol manipulation in the process of agenda-setting and legitimation.

57. For a discussion of this and other myths, see Steven M.Teles, *Whose Welfare? AFDC and Elite Politics* (Lawrence: University Press of Kansas, 1996).

58. Robert Pear, "Clinton Will Seek Tax Break to Ease Path Off Welfare," *New York Times*, 28 January 1997.

59. Robert Pear, "Governors Limit Revisions Sought in Welfare Law," *New York Times*, 3 February 1997.

60. The political motivation was to please Hispanic voters, given the number of immigrants from Mexico and other Latin countries who had been denied benefits.

61. See Jonathan Rabinowitz, "Connecticut Welfare Law Cuts Hundreds Off the Rolls," *New York Times*, 3 November 1997; and Richard Wolf, "Some States Still at Welfare Impasse," *USA Today*, 2 July 1997.

62. Nina Bernstein, "Giant Companies Enter Race to Run State Welfare Programs," *New York Times*, 15 September 1996.

63. Judith Havemann, "Welfare Reform Still on a Roll as States Bounce It Down to Counties," *Washington Post*, 29 August 1997.

64. Dilys Hills, "Social Policy," in *Developments in American Politics III*, ed. Gillian Peele et al. (New York: Chatham House, 1998).

65. Rochelle L. Stanfield, "Valuing the Family," *National Journal*, 4 July 1992: 1562–66.

66. Marilyn Werber Serafini, "Get Hitched, Stay Hitched," *National Journal*, 9 March 2002, 694–97.

67. Rochelle L. Stanfield, "Cautious Optimism," *National Journal*, 2 May 1998, 990–93.

68. Laura Meckler, "Bush Outlining Welfare Plans," Associated Press, 26 February 2002.

69. See General Accounting Office, *Welfare Reform: States Are Restructuring Programs to Reduce Welfare Dependency* (Washington, D.C.: USGAO, 18 June 1998), GAO/HEHS–98–109. Oregon, for example, has found that half the welfare caseload will require treatment for chemical dependency before they are likely to be employable.

70. D. Card and R. M. Blank, *Findings Jobs: Work and Welfare Reform* (New York: Russell Sage, 2000).

71. Stanfield, "Cautious Optimism."

72. Administration for Children and Families, Department of Health and Human Services, *U.S. Welfare Caseloads Information* (Washington, D.C.: ACF, monthly).

73. Marilyn Werber Serafini, "As More Jobs Vanish, the Worries Mount," *National Journal*, 29 September 2001.

74. Ibid.

75. Sheila Kammerman and Alfred Kahn, "Universalism and Testing in Family Policy; New Perspectives on an Old Debate," *Social Work* 32 (1987): 277–80.

76. Hermione Parker, *Instead of the Dole: An Enquiry into the Integration of Tax and Benefit Systems* (London: Routledge, 1989).

77. M. Kenneth Bowler, *The Nixon Guaranteed Income Proposal: Substance and Process in Policy Change* (Cambridge, Mass.: Ballinger, 1974).

78. Office of Child Support Enforcement, *Annual Report to Congress*.

79. Irwin Garfinkel, Sara S. McLanahan, and Philip K. Robins, *Child Support and Child Well-Being* (Washington, D.C.: Urban Institute Press, 1994).

80. General Accounting Office, *Child Support Assurance: Effects of Applying State Guidelines to Determine Fathers' Payments* (Washington, D.C.: GAO, January, 1993), GAO/HRD–93–26.

81. Nadine Cohodas, "Child Support: No More Pretty Please," *Governing*, October 1993, 20–21.

82. Mimi Hall, "Child Support: States Pay If Parents Don't," *USA Today*, 28 March 1994.

83. At least one state has already done so; see "In Maine, No Child Support, No Driving," *New York Times*, 28 June 1994.

84. For a general discussion of employment policy, see Margaret Weir, *Politics and Jobs* (Princeton: Princeton University Press, 1992).

85. Robert B. Reich, *The Work of Nations: Preparing for 21st Century Capitalism* (New York: Knopf, 1991).

86. General Accounting Office, *Multiple Employment Training Programs: Conflicting Requirements Hamper Delivery of Services* (Washington, D.C.: GAO, January 1994), GAO/HEHS–94–78.

87. Sar A. Levitan, *The Great Society's Poor Law: A New Approach to Poverty* (Baltimore: Johns Hopkins University Press, 1969).

88. Some later research, however, finds some latent effects of Head Start, much like the "sleeper effects" described in chap. 7. See William Celis 3d, "Study Suggests Head Start Helps Beyond School," *New York Times*, 20 April 1993. See also Carlotta C. Joyner, "Head Start: Research Insufficient to Assess Program Impact," Testimony to Subcommittee on Early Childhood, Youth and Families, Senate Labor and Human Resources, 26 March 1998.

89. Richard Rose and B. Guy Peters, *Can Government Go Bankrupt?* (New York: Basic Books, 1978).

90. "'90s Boom Has Broad Impact," *Washington Post*, 5 June 2002.

91. Gary Burtless, "Growing Inequality," *Brookings Review* (Winter 1999): 31–37.

92. For a more recent view, see Michael Harrington, *The New American Poverty* (New York: Holt, Rinehart, and Winston, 1984).

93. Paul Starobin, "Unequal Shares," *National Journal*, 11 September 1993, 2176–79.

94. Sar Levitan, Frank Gallo, and Isaac Shapiro, *Working But Poor: America's Contradiction*, rev. ed. (Baltimore: Johns Hopkins University Press, 1993).

95. Ibid., 99–125.

96. Patricia Ruggles, *Drawing the Line: Alternative Poverty Measures and Their Implications for Public Policy* (Washington, D.C.: Urban Institute Press, 1990).

97. John L. Palmer, Timothy Smeeding, and Barbara Boyle Torrey, eds., *The Vulnerable* (Washington, D.C.: Urban Institute Press, 1988).

98. The current fashionable phrase for these problems, made popular by the Labour government in Britain, is "social exclusion."

99. Maybeth Shinn and Colleen Gillespie, "The Roles of Housing and Poverty in the Origins of Homelessness," *American Behavioral Scientist* 37 (1994): 505–21.

100. Ann Braden Johnson, *Out of Bedlam: The Truth about Deinstitutionalization* (New York: Basic Books, 1990); and Julian Leff, *Care in the Community: Myth or Reality* (New York: John Wiley, 1997).

101. General Accounting Office, *Homelessness: McKinney Act Programs Provide Assistance but Are Not Designed to be the Solution* (Washington, D.C.: GAO, May 1994), GAO/RCED–94–37.

102. Ibid.

103. General Accounting Office, *Private Pensions: Key Issues to Consider Following the Enron Collapse,* Testimony by David M. Walker (Washington, D.C.: GAO, 27 February 2002), GAO–02–480T.

104. Martin Rein and Lee Rainwater, *Public-Private Interplay in Social Service Provision* (Armonk, NY: M. E. Sharpe, 1988).

105. For one analysis, see Fred Englander and John Kane, "Reagan's Welfare Reforms: Were the Program Savings Realized?" *Policy Studies Review* 11 (1992): 3–23.

106. Jeff Shear, "Pulling in Harness," *National Journal,* 4 June 1994, 1286–90. Several of the designers of the original program quit in protest over the program eventually adopted in 1996.

107. Robert E. Crew and Joe Eyerman, "Finding Employment and Staying Employed after Leaving Welfare," *Journal of Poverty* 5 (2001): 67–91.

108. See Helen Fawcett, "Workfare: The Politics of Policy Transfer," paper presented at Conference of Structure and Organization of Government Research Committee, Lady Margaret Hall, University of Oxford, July 1998.

Chapter 12

1. Catherine S. Mangold, "Students Make Strides but Fall Short of Goals," *New York Times,* 18 August 1994.

2. "Poll Readings," *National Journal,* 14 February 1998, 368.

3. National Center for Education Statistics, *Digest of Education Statistics* (Washington, D.C.: Government Printing Office, 1992).

4. Richard Hofferbert, "Race, Space and the American Policy Paradox" (paper presented at the Conference of the Southern Political Science Association, 1980).

5. In areas in which parochial schools were important, these schools also tended to draw from a wide range of social classes if not religions.

6. Karen De Witt, "Nation's Schools Learn a Fourth R: Resegregation," *New York Times,* 19 January 1992.

7. For diverse views on this topic, see Gerald Graff, *Beyond the Culture Wars: How Teaching the Conflicts Can Revitalize American Education* (New York: Norton, 1992); and Russell Jacoby, *Dogmatic Wisdom: How the Culture Wars Divert Education and Distract America* (New York: Doubleday, 1994).

8. U.S. Bureau of the Census, *Statistical Abstract of the United States,* 1997 (Washington, D.C.: Government Printing Office, 1998).

9. "Poll Readings," *National Journal,* 19 January 1998. Twelve percent of respondents said they were very satisfied, and 32 percent were somewhat satisfied.

10. Students in Iowa and North Dakota on average scored as well as those in Korea and better than those in any European country on math and science tests. Tamara Henry, "Math, Science Gains May Spark More School Reform," *USA Today,* 26 March 1996.

11. See William Bennett, *Our Country and Our Children: Improving America's Schools and Affirming Our Common Culture* (New York: Touchstone, 1988). There have been

a number of books advocating such a traditional curriculum for American schools, including Allan Bloom, *The Closing of the American Mind* (New York: Touchstone, 1987).

12. Jeffrey L. Katz, "Head Start Reauthorization," *Congressional Quarterly Weekly Report* 52 (18 June 1994): 1653–55.

13. Rochelle L. Stanfield, "Standard Bearer," *National Journal*, 2 July 1994, 1566–70.

14. *Evaluating the Net Impact of School-to-Work: Proceedings of a Roundtable* (Washington, D.C.: U.S. Department of Labor).

15. Rochelle L. Stanfield, "Team Players," *National Journal*, 13 November 1993, 2723–27.

16. Anemona Hartcollis, "Educators Say Clinton's Plan on Class Size Faces Problems," *New York Times*, 29 January 1998.

17. Jonathan Kozol, *Savage Inequalities: Children in America's Schools* (New York: Crown Publishers, 1991).

18. *Grove City College v. Bell*, 465 U.S. 555 (1984).

19. Scott Jashik, "Secretary Seeks Ban on Grants Reserved for Specific Groups," *Chronicle of Higher Education* 38 (11 December 1991): A1, A26.

20. See *Texas et al. v. Lesage* (1999). The Michigan cases are *Gratz v. Bollinger* (2003) and *Grutter v. Bollinger* (2003).

21. Rochelle L. Stanfield, "We Have a Tradition of Not Learning," *National Journal*, (7 September 1991): 2156–57.

22. Norman C. Thomas, *Educational Policy in National Politics* (New York: David McKay, 1975).

23. The figure is now roughly 8 percent.

24. Michael D. Reagan, *The New Federalism* (New York: Oxford University Press, 1972).

25. Jerome T. Murphy, "Title I of ESEA: The Politics of Implementing Federal Educational Reform," *Harvard Education Review*, 1971, 35–63.

26. *Title I of ESEA: Is It Helping Poor Children?* (Washington, D.C.: NAACP Legal Defense Fund, 1969).

27. Some recent polls show that minority parents, like majority parents, want good basic education instead of a distinctive curriculum. See "Minority Parents Seek Quality over Diversity," *USA Today*, 29 July 1998.

28. Rochelle L. Stanfield, "Making the Grade?" *National Journal*, (17 April 1993).

29. Robert Guskind, "Rethinking Reform," *National Journal*, (25 May 1991): 1235–39.

30. It seems that in Milwaukee there has been a good deal of effective and committed leadership in the schools. Emily Van Dunk and Annliese Dickman, "School Choice Accountability," *Urban Affairs Review* 37 (2002): 844–56.

31. Myron Lieberman, *Privatization and Educational Choice* (New York: St. Martin's, 1989).

32. John Witte, "The Milwaukee Parental Choice Program Third Year Report," *LaFollette Policy Report* 6 (1994): 6–7.

33. John E. Chubb and Terry M. Moe, *Politics, Markets, and America's Schools* (Washington, D.C.: Brookings Institution, 1990).

34. Rochelle L. Stanfield, "Education Wars," *National Journal*, (7 March 1998).

35. Jeffrey R. Henig, *Rethinking School Choice: Limits of the Market Metaphor* (Princeton: Princeton University Press, 1994).

36. James S. Coleman, *Equality of Educational Opportunity* (Washington, D.C.: Government Printing Office, 1966). Since that time Coleman has modified his view to be substantially less supportive of busing.

37. Gallup poll, "Public Attitudes to Education," annual.
38. For a positive view, see James N. Goenner, "Charter Schools: The Revitalization of Public Education," *Phi Delta Kappan*, September 1996.
39. "States Ignore Traps Tripping Up Charter Schools," *USA Today*, 2 April 2002.
40. D. M. Lewis, "Certifying Functional Literacy: Competency and the Implications for Due Process and Equal Educational Opportunity," *Journal of Law and Education*, 1979, 145–83; and Chubb and Moe, *Politics, Markets, and America's Schools*, 197–98.
41. John L. Palmer and Isabel V. Sawhill, eds., *The Reagan Record* (Washington, D.C.: Urban Institute Press, 1984), 364–65.
42. Alison Mitchell, "Clinton Promotes Education Testing; Gingrich Opposes," *New York Times*, 8 September 1997.
43. Association of Chief School Officers, reported in Tom Squiteri, "Are Kids Tested to Death?" *USA Today*, 7 October 1997.
44. Jessica Portner, "Educators Keeping Eye on Measures Designed to Combat Youth Violence," *Education Week* 13 (9 February 1994): 21.
45. For some discussion of the lengths to which school systems may go to recruit teachers, see Jacques Steinberg, "As Demand for Teachers Exceeds Supply, Schools Sweeten Their Offers," *New York Times*, 7 September 1998.
46. U.S. General Accounting Office, *School Facilities: America's Schools Report Differing Conditions* (Washington, D.C.: GAO, June, 1996), GAO/HEHS-96-103.
47. Richard W. Stevenson, "Clinton Proposes Spending $25 Billion on Education," *New York Times*, 27 January 1998.
48. *Cochran v. Board of Education*, 281 U.S. 370 (1930).
49. *Everson v. Board of Education*, 330 U.S. 1 (1947).
50. *Lemon v. Kurzman*, 403 U.S. 602 (1971).
51. *Roemer v. Maryland*, 426 U.S. 736 (1976).
52. *Board of Education of the Kiryas Joel School District v. Grument*, 114 U.S. 2481 (1994).
53. See, for example, Lonnie Harp, "Michigan Bill Penalizes Teachers for Job Actions," *Education Weekly* 13 (27 April 1994): 9.
54. Stephen M. Barro, "Countering Inequity in School Finance," vol. 3, *Federal Policy Options for Improving the Education of Low-Income Students* (Santa Monica, Calif.: Rand Corporation, 1994).
55. Another equity funding case was contested in Alabama—*Alabama Coalition for Equity, Inc. v. Guy Hunt*.
56. *Edgewood v. Kirby*, 804, S.W.2D 491 (Tex. 1991).
57. Sam Howe Verhovek, "Texas to Hold Referendum on School-Aid Shift to Poor," *New York Times*, 16 February 1993.
58. Lonnie Harp, "Texas Voters Reject Finance Plan: Consolidation Called Last Resort, *Education Week* 12 (12 May 1993): 1, 16.
59. Lonnie Harp, "Texas Finance Ruling Angers Both Rich, Poor Districts," *Education Week* 13 (12 January 1994): 18.
60. Tamar Lewin, "Patchwork of School Financing Schemes Offers Few Answers and Much Conflict," *New York Times*, 8 April 1998.
61. William Schneider, "Voters Get an Offer They Can't Refuse," *National Journal* 26 (26 March 1994): 754.
62. Rochelle L. Stanfield, "Equity and Excellence," *National Journal*, (23 November 1991): 3860–64.

63. Reagan Walker, "Blueprint for State's New School System Advances in Kentucky," *Education Week* 9 (7 March 1990): 1, 21.

64. Rochelle L. Stanfield, "Learning Curve," *National Journal*, (3 July 1993): 1688–91.

65. Dirk Johnson, "Study Says Small Schools Are Key to Learning," *New York Times*, 21 September 1994.

66. The Spearman rank-order correlation is –0.26. This finding is to some degree confounded by the different percentages of students taking the SAT in different states. Many of the high-scoring states had a small percentage of students taking the SAT.

67. De Witt, "Nation's Schools Learn a Fourth R."

68. Rochelle L. Stanfield, "Reform by the Book," *National Journal*, (4 December 1994): 2885–87.

69. "Minority Admissions Dip at U. of California," *New York Times*, 1 April 1998.

70. For example, in 1998 blacks constituted 17 percent of the school population but had 31 percent of all expulsions (U.S. Department of Education).

Chapter 13

1. See, for example, Glennda Chui, "Scientific American Gives California High Marks for Technology," *San Jose Mercury News*, 12 November 2002.

2. Constance Mungall and Digby J. McLaren, eds., *Planet under Stress: The Challenge of Global Change* (New York: Oxford University Press, 1990).

3. Timothy Wirth, "Hot Air over Kyoto: The United States and the Politics of Global Warming," *Harvard International Review* 23 (2002): 72–77.

4. Statistical Office of the United Nations, *Yearbook of World Energy Statistics 1990* (New York: United Nations, 1998).

5. Robin C. Landon and Michael W. Klass, *OPEC: Policy Implications for the United States* (New York: Praeger, 1980).

6. U.S. Department of Energy, *Annual Energy Review 1997* (Washington, D.C.: DOE, 1998).

7. Eric Pianin, "A Stinging Repudiation Engineered by 3 Democrats," *Washington Post*, 19 April 2002.

8. Dan Morgan and Ellen Nakashima, "Search for Oil Targets Rockies," *Washington Post*, 19 April 2002.

9. Peter H. Stone, "Mixing Oil and Instability," *National Journal*, 10 November 2001.

10. International Monetary Fund, *Balance of Payments Statistics* (Washington, D.C.: International Monetary Fund, monthly).

11. There may well be more natural gas available, but relatively low prices have deterred exploration. See Mark Fischetti, "There's Gas in Them There Hills," *Technology Review* 96 (1993): 16–18.

12. Traci Watson, "EPA: Power Plant Plan Could Save 12,000 Lives per Year," *USA Today*, 3 July 2002.

13. James M. McElfish and Ann E. Beier, *Environmental Regulation of Coal Mining* (Washington, D.C.: Environmental Law Institute, 1990).

14. Some forty or more coal miners still die in accidents each year, while many others die slowly from lung diseases such as "black lung" and silicosis.

15. Processes of this type have existed for some time; Germany used a process like this in World War II. The process is not, however, economically feasible at anything like current energy prices.

16. Felicity Barringer, "Four Years Later, Soviets Reveal Wider Scope to Chernobyl Horror," *New York Times*, 28 April 1990; and David Marples, *The Social Impact of the Chernobyl Disaster* (New York: St. Martin's, 1988).

17. John L. Campbell, *Collapse of an Industry: Nuclear Power and the Contradictions of U.S. Policy* (Ithaca, N.Y.: Cornell University Press, 1988).

18. Richard Balzhiser, "Future Consequences of Nuclear Non-Policy," in *Energy: Production, Consumption, Consequences*, ed. John L. Helm (Washington, D.C.: National Academy Press, 1990).

19. U.S. General Accounting Office, *Nuclear Waste: Uncertainties about the Yucca Mountain Repository Project* (Washington, D.C.: GAO, 21 March 2000), GAO–02–539T.

20. Henry F. Bedford, *Seabrook Station: Citizen Politics and Nuclear Power* (Amherst: University of Massachusetts Press, 1990).

21. Matthew L. Wald, "License Is Granted to Nuclear Plant in New Hampshire," *New York Times*, 2 March 1990.

22. Rodman D. Griffin, "Nuclear Fusion," *CQ Researcher* 3 (22 January 1993): 51–64.

23. Michael Kenward, "Fusion Becomes a Hot Bet for the Future," *New Scientist* 132 (16 November 1991): 10–11.

24. Todd Wilkinson, "Gone With the Wind," *Backpacker* 20 (September 1992): 11.

25. *New York Times*, 2 March 1980.

26. Michael M. Crow and Gregory Hager, "Political versus Political Risk Deduction and the Failure of U.S. Synthetic Fuel Development Efforts," *Policy Studies Review* 5 (1985): 145–52.

27. Regina S. Axelrod, "Energy Policy: Changing the Rules of the Game," in *Environmental Policy in the 1980s: Reagan's New Agenda*, ed. Norman J. Vig and Michael E. Kraft (Washington, D.C.: CQ Press, 1984).

28. "Briefing on Energy Policy," *Weekly Compilation of Presidential Documents* 27 (25 February 1991): 188–90.

29. Eugene Feingold, "Finding Trust in Government," *Nation's Health* 24 (May 1994): 2; and "DOE's Growing Fallout," *Environmental Action* 26 (Spring 1994): 6.

30. *Reliable, Affordable and Environmentally Sound Energy for America's Future: Report of the National Energy Development Group* (Washington, D.C.: Executive Office of the President, May, 2001).

31. Natural Resources Defense Council, "Energy Department Documents Verify Industry Influence over Bush Policies," 21 May 2002.

32. See "Wasteful Handouts Skew Energy Benefit's Plan," *USA Today*, 30 May 2001.

33. An NBC-*Wall Street Journal* poll in April 2001 showed that 25 percent of the respondents thought there was a crisis, but 60 percent did see a distinct problem.

34. Claudia Golden and Gary D. Libecap, *The Regulated Economy* (Chicago: University of Chicago Press, 1994).

35. Center for the Advancement of Energy Markets website: www.caem.org, 1 February 2001.

36. T. Munroe and L. Baroody, "California's Flawed Deregulation: Implications for the State and Nation," *Journal of Energy and Development* 26 (2001): 159–79.

37. Amory B. Lovins, *Soft Energy Paths: Toward a Durable Peace* (New York: Harper and Row, 1979); and L. Hunter Lovins, Amory B. Lovins, and Seth Zuckerman, *Energy Unbound* (San Francisco: Sierra Books, 1986).

38. See National Academy of Sciences, *Our Earth, Our Future, Our Changing Global Environment* (Washington, D.C.: National Academy Press, 1990); and S. George Philander, *Is the Temperature Rising? The Uncertain Science of Global Warming* (Princeton: Princeton University Press, 1998).

39. The journal entitled *Diversity* is a good source of information about the resources existing in these settings.

40. One can, however, identify some twenty-seven other organizations with environmental responsibilities; see Walter A. Rosenbaum, *Environmental Politics and Policy* (Washington, D.C.: CQ Press, 1998).

41. Riley E. Dunlap, "Trends in Public Opinion toward Environmental Issues, 1965–1990," *Society and Natural Resources* 4 (1991): 285–312; and Jerry Spangler, "Survey Shows Environmental Values Deeply Rooted," *Desert News*, 9 October 1997.

42. Margaret E. Kriz, "Jobs vs. Owls," *National Journal*, 30 November 1993, 2913–16.

43. Another manifestation of the issue was the congressional use of a rider on an EPA appropriations act in 1996 to permit more lumbering of old-growth forests. For the consequences of these conflicts, see E. Niemi and E. Whitelaw, "Bird of Doom, or Was It?" *Amicus Journal* 22 (1997): 19–25.

44. On the caribou issue, see Paul Feine, "Beware Porcupine Caribou," *Energy Economist* 2 (1995): 2–19.

45. Murray Weidenbaum, "Return of the 'R' Word: The Regulatory Assault on the Economy," *Policy Review* 59 (1992): 40–43.

46. For example, the Safe Drinking Water Act requires monitoring for eighty-three substances although a number have never been found in any public water supply. See Margaret E. Kriz, "Cleaner Than Clean?" *National Journal*, (23 April 1994): 946–49.

47. Christopher J. Bosso, "After the Movement: Environmental Activism in the 1990s," in *Environmental Policy in the 1990s*, ed. Norman J. Vig and Michael E. Kraft, 3d ed. (Washington, D.C.: CQ Press, 1997). Updated from websites, personal conversations.

48. Vice President Gore's book on environmental politics became a part of the presidential campaign in 1992. See Al Gore, *Earth in the Balance: Ecology and the Human Spirit* (Boston: Houghton Mifflin, 1992).

49. Margaret Kriz, "That Was the Week That Was," *National Journal*, (2 February 1994): 393.

50. Margaret Kriz, "Working the Land: Bush Aggressively Opens Doors to New Drilling and Logging in Federal Lands," *National Journal*, (23 February 2002).

51. U.S. General Accounting Office, *Federal Facilities: Issues Involved in Cleaning Up Hazardous Wastes* (Washington, D.C.: GAO, 28 July 1992), GAO/T-RCED–92–82.

52. This has been described as "bureaucratic pluralism," with some even within the EPA itself. See Walter A. Rosenbaum, "Into the 1990s at EPA," in Vig and Kraft, *Environmental Policy in the 1990s*.

53. Evan Ringquist, *Environmental Protection at the State Level* (Armonk, N.Y.: M. E. Sharpe, 1994).

54. On the possibilities of a "race to the bottom," see Mary Graham, "Environmental Protection and the States," *Brookings Review* (Winter 1998): 22–25.

55. Margaret Kriz, "Feuding with the Feds," *National Journal*, (9 August 1997): 1598–1601.
56. West Virginia, for example, opposed attempts to impose nitrous oxide standards in 1997.
57. Richard N. L. Andrews, "Risk-Based Decisionmaking," in Vig and Kraft, *Environmental Policy in the 1990s*.
58. Donald T. Hornstein, "Reclaiming Environmental Law: A Normative Critique of Comparative Risk Analysis," *Columbia Law Review* 29 (1992): 562–633.
59. Margaret Kriz, "The Greening of Environmental Regulation," *National Journal*, (18 June 1994): 1464–67.
60. *Lujan v. Defenders of Wildlife*, 112 S. Ct. 2130 (1992). The courts tend to limit suits to those who have experienced a direct loss because of an action.
61. See Michael E. Kraft, "Environmental Policy in Congress: Revolution, Reform or Gridlock?" in Vig and Kraft, *Environmental Policy in the 1990s*.
62. James R. Kahn, *An Economic Approach to the Environment and Natural Resources* (New York: Dryden Press, 1995).
63. For a review of developments, see Debra S. Knopman and Richard A. Smith, "Twenty Years of the Clean Water Act," *Environment* 35 (1993): 17–20, 34–41.
64. "Oil Officials Fear Stricter Water Act Provisions from New Congress," *Oilgram News* 74, no. 218 (1986): 2.
65. James P. Lester, "New Federalism and Environmental Policy," *Publius* 16 (1986): 149–65.
66. Margaret E. Kriz, "Clashing Over Chlorine," *National Journal*, (19 March 1994): 659–61.
67. Paul Raeburn, "Hybrid Care: Less Fuel but More Costs," *Business Week*, 15 April 2002, 107.
68. Margaret Kriz, "Clean Machines," *National Journal*, (16 November 1991): 2789–94.
69. James C. McKinley Jr., "10 States Agree on a Program for Air Quality," *New York Times*, 2 October 1994.
70. Mark Crawford, "Hazardous Waste: Where to Put It?" *Science* 235 (9 January 1987): 156.
71. Peter A. A. Berle, "Toxic Tornado," *Audubon* 87 (1985): 4.
72. See Charles E. Davis, *The Politics of Hazardous Waste* (Englewood Cliffs, N.J.: Prentice Hall, 1993).
73. Steven Cohen, "Federal Hazardous Waste Programs," in Vig and Kraft, *Environmental Policy in the 1980s*.
74. Thomas Church and Robert Nakamura, *Cleaning Up the Mess: Implementation Strategies in Superfund* (Washington, D.C.: Brookings Institution, 1993).
75. Environmental Protection Agency, Office of Emergency and Remedial Response, *Superfund Facts* (annual).
76. Environmental Protection Agency, *A Preliminary Analysis of the Public Costs of Environmental Protection, 1981–2000* (Washington, D.C.: EPA, May 1990); and Milton E. Russell, William Colglazier, and Bruce E. Tonn, "U.S. Hazardous Waste Legacy," *Environment* 34 (1992): 12–15, 34–39.
77. Katharine Q. Seelye, "Bush Slashing Aid of E. P. A. Cleanup at 33 Toxic Sites," *New York Times*, 1 July 2002.

78. Zachary A. Smith, *The Environmental Policy Paradox* (Englewood Cliffs, N.J.: Prentice Hall, 1991), 179–86.
79. Church and Nakamura, *Cleaning Up the Mess.*
80. *Superfund: Backlog of Unevaluated Federal Facilities Slows Cleanup Efforts* (Washington, D.C.: General Accounting Office, July 1993): GAO/RCED–93–119.
81. Richard A. Epstein, *Takings: Property Rights and the Power of Eminent Domain* (Cambridge, Mass.: Harvard University Press, 1985).
82. Nancie G. Marzulla and Roger J. Marzulla, *Property Rights: Understanding Takings and Environmental Regulation* (Rockville, Md.: Government Institutes, 1997).
83. Charles O. Jones, "Speculative Augmentation in Federal Air Pollution Policymaking," *Journal of Politics* 42 (1975): 438–64.
84. Graeme Browning, "Taking Some Risks," *National Journal*, (1 June 1991): 1279–82.
85. L. J. Lindquist, *The Hare and the Tortoise* (Ann Arbor: University of Michigan Press, 1986).
86. Some analysts have argued that there may be *insufficient* negotiation in the enforcement of environmental legislation, and that better compliance could be achieved through bargaining rather than conventional regulatory enforcement. See Eugene Bardach and Robert Kagan, *Going by the Book* (Philadelphia: Temple University Press, 1983); and David Vogel, *Trading Up: Consumer and Environmental Regulation in a Global Economy* (Cambridge, Mass.: Harvard University Press, 1995).
87. A. Myrick Freeman, "Economics, Incentives and Environmental Regulation," in Vig and Kraft, *Environmental Policy in the 1990s*; and Robert N. Stavins, "Lessons from the American Experience with Market-based Environmental Policies," in *Market-based Governance*, ed. John D. Donahue and Joseph S. Nye (Washington, D.C.: Brookings Institution, 2002).
88. Barnaby J. Feder, "Sold: $21 Million of Air Pollution," *New York Times*, 30 March 1993. For a somewhat skeptical view, see U.S. General Accounting Office, *Environmental Protection: Implications for Using Pollution Taxes to Supplement Regulation* (Washington, D.C.: GAO, February 1993), GAO/RCED–93–13.
89. See Walter A. Rosenbaum, *Environmental Politics and Policy*, 5th ed. (Washington, D.C.: CQ Press, 2001), 109–10; and Robert N. Stavins, "Lessons from the American Experiment with Market-Based Environmental Policies," in *Market-based Governance*, ed. John D. Donahue and Joseph S. Nye (Washington, D.C.: Brookings Institution, 2002).
90. Margaret Kriz, "Emission Control," *National Journal*, (3 July 1993): 1696–1701.
91. See Renee Rico, "The U.S. Allowance Trading System for Sulphur Dioxide: An Update on Market Experience," *Environmental and Resource Economics* 5 (1995): 115–29.

Chapter 14

1. For some sense of the ups and downs of defense employment (civilian and uniformed), see B. Guy Peters, "Public Employment in the United States," in Richard Rose et al., *Public Employment in Western Democracies* (Cambridge: Cambridge University Press, 1985); and "The United States" in H.-U. Derlien and B. Guy Peters, eds., *Who Works for Government and What Do They Do?* (forthcoming, 2003).

2. See "Building Arms for the Wrong War," *New York Times*, 10 May 2002.

3. John D. Steinbruner and William W. Kaufmann, "International Security Reconsidered," in *Setting National Priorities: Budget Choices for the Next Century*, ed. Robert D. Reischauer (Washington, D.C.: Brookings Institution, 1997).

4. See, for example, Robert K. Jervis, *Perception and Misperception in International Politics* (Princeton: Princeton University Press, 1976).

5. For example, there have been a number of assertions about marked differences in policy preferences among members of the Bush administration following September 11.

6. Joseph S. Nye, *Bound to Lead: The Changing Nature of American Power* (New York: Basic Books, 1992).

7. Gregory L. Schulte, "Bringing Peace to Bosnia and Change to the Alliance," *NATO Review* 45 (March 1997): 22–25.

8. *Does UN Peacekeeping Serve U.S. Interests?* Hearing before U.S. House of Representatives, Committee on International Relations, 9 April 1997.

9. See, for example, James A. Nathan and James K. Oliver, *United States Foreign Policy and World Order*, 2d ed. (Boston: Little, Brown, 1981).

10. Paul Boyer, *Fallout: A Historian Reflects on America's Half-century Encounter with Nuclear Weapons* (Columbus: Ohio State University Press, 1998).

11. Dunbar Lockwood, "Purchasing Power," *Bulletin of the Atomic Scientists* 50 (March 1994): 10–12; and "Former Soviet Republics Clear Way for Nunn-Lugar Monies," *Arms Control Today* 24 (1994): 28–29.

12. At the same time, this amounted to the end of the Anti-Ballistic Missile Treaty, one of the early attempts to negotiate arms control in the Cold War. See D. E. Sanger and M. Wines, "With a Shrug, a Monument to Cold War Fades Away," *New York Times*, 14 June 2002.

13. Even recent evidence points to continuing nuclear weapons development in North Korea, despite agreements with both South Korea and the United States. See David E. Sanger, "North Korea Site an A-Bomb Plant, U.S. Agencies Say," *New York Times*, 17 August 1998. In 2002 President George W. Bush characterized North Korea, Iraq, and Iran as the "Axis of Evil." In October 2002 North Korea admitted that it was pursuing a nuclear weapons program after having agreed earlier not to do so. David E. Sanger and Tim Weiner, "US and 2 of Its Allies Warn North Korea on Atom Arms," *New York Times*, 27 October 2002.

14. Bradley Graham, "Missile Threat to U.S. Greater than Thought," *International Herald Tribune*, 17 July 1998.

15. Patrick E. Tyler, "As Fear of a Big War Fades, Military Plans for Little Ones," *New York Times*, 3 February 1992.

16. David C. Morrison, "Bottoming Out?" *National Journal*, (17 September 1994): 2126–30. See also Donald J. Savoie and B. Guy Peters, "Comparing Programme Review," in *Programme Review in Canada*, ed. E. Lundquist and D. J. Savoie (Ottawa: Canadian Centre for Management Development, 1999).

17. The worst-case scenario appeared to be an outbreak of war on the Korean Peninsula.

18. Julian Critchley, *The North Atlantic Alliance and the Soviet Union in the 1980s* (London: Macmillan, 1982).

19. Robert L. Bernstein and Richard Dicker, "Human Rights First," *Foreign Policy* 94 (1994): 43–47; and William Korey, *The Promises We Keep: Human Rights, the Helsinki Process and American Foreign Policy* (New York: St. Martin's, 1993).

20. See Christoph Bluth, Emil Kirchner, and James Sperling, *The Future of European Security* (Aldershot, Hants: Dartmouth, 1995).

21. For example, the much heralded accuracy of "smart bombs" during the Gulf War apparently would be crude in comparison to that of contemporary weapons.

22. For an analysis of the famous Reagan Strategic Defense Initiative program, see Congressional Budget Office, *Analysis of the Costs of the Administration's Strategic Defense Initiative, 1985–89* (Washington, D.C.: CBO, May 1984). This basic idea was revived in the 1990s.

23. James Dao and Andrew C. Revkin, "Machines Are Filling In for Troops," *New York Times*, 16 April 2000.

24. Lawrence J. Korb, "The 1991 Defense Budget," in *Setting National Priorities: Policy for the Nineties* (Washington, D.C.: Brookings Institution, 1990). See also David C. Morrison, "How Many Carriers Are Enough?" *National Journal*, (4 September 1993): 2162.

25. Gordon Adams, *The Politics of Defense Contracting: The Iron Triangle* (New Brunswick, N.J.: Transaction, 1981); and "Mission Implausible," *U.S. News & World Report*, (14 October 1991): 24–31.

26. Of course, the United States is the only country that has ever used these weapons in war.

27. There were a number of reports of plutonium from Russia being available for sale, potentially to terrorists. The economic crisis in the Soviet Union, especially failures to pay the armed forces adequately, provides more incentives to sell parts of the tons of weapons grade material still available.

28. William Newman, "Causes of Change in National Security Processes: Carter, Reagan, Bush Decision Making on Arms Control," *Presidential Studies Quarterly* 31 (2001): 69–103.

29. Owen Cote, "The Trident and the Triad," *International Security Quarterly* 16 (1991): 117–36.

30. Frank Rich, "The Bush Doctrine, R. I. P.," *New York Times*, 13 April 2002.

31. Pat Towell, "Pentagon Banking on Plans to Reinvent Procurement," *Congressional Quarterly Weekly Report* 52 (16 April 1994); and Lauren Holland, "Explaining Weapons Procurement: Matching Operational Performance and National Security Needs," *Armed Forces and Society* 19 (1993): 353–76.

32. The program and its sequels have cost approximately $5 billion per year since the mid-1980s.

33. The General Accounting Office has done a number of evaluations of these and other poorly performing weapons systems, e.g., *More Effective Review of Proposed Inventory Buys Could Reduce Unneeded Procurement* (Washington, D.C.: GAO, June 1994), GAO/NSIAD–94–130. See also Scott Shuger, "The Stealth Bomber Story You Haven't Heard," *Washington Monthly* 23 (January 1991): 1–2, 14–22.

34. Korb, "1991 Defense Budget," 136–38.

35. Eric Schmitt, "Military Proposes to End Production of Most New Arms," *New York Times*, 24 January 1992.

36. Eric Schmitt, "Run Silent, Run Deep, Beat Foes (Where?)," *New York Times*, 30 January 1992.

37. Martin Binkin, *America's Volunteer Military* (Washington, D.C.: Brookings Institution, 1984).

38. David McCormick, *The Downsized Warrior: America's Army in Transition* (New York: New York University Press, 1998).

39. *New York Times*, 12 June 1994.

40. By this I mean the skills needed by hostage rescue and counterterrorist groups in the military.

41. For example, Molly Pitcher played a partly real, partly mythical part in the Battle of Monmouth during the Revolutionary War.

42. See Andrea Stone, "They're 'Not an Experiment Anymore,'" *USA Today*, 11 January 2002.

43. Linda Bird Francke, *Ground Zero: The Gender Wars in the Military* (New York: Simon & Schuster, 1997).

44. See James Kitfield, "Front and Center," *National Journal*, (25 October 1997).

45. Ibid.

46. The Department of Defense argued that the fundamental reason for dismissal of the female pilot was her lying about the existence of a relationship and then continuing once ordered to terminate it.

47. Michael R. Gordon, "Pentagon Spells Out Rules for Ousting Homosexuals; Rights Group Vows a Fight," *New York Times*, 23 December 1993.

48. Tamar Lewin, "At Bases, Debate Rages over Impact of New Gay Policy," *New York Times*, 24 December 1993.

49. Jane Gross, "Navy Cannot Discharge Gay Officer, Court Rules," *New York Times*, 1 September 1994.

50. Eric Schmitt, "How is This Strategy Working? Don't Ask," *New York Times*, 19 December 1999.

51. Tim Weiner, "Proposal Cuts Back on Some Weapons to Spend More on Personnel," *New York Times*, 8 February 1994. Another version of this is to fight one war while maintaining a holding action in another.

52. William W. Kaufman, "'Hollow' Forces," *Brookings Review* 12 (1994): 24–29.

53. Thom Shanker and Eric Schott, "Military Would be Stressed by a New War, Study Finds," *New York Times*, 24 May 2002.

54. David Sanger, "NATO Formally Embraces Russia as a Junior Partner," *New York Times*, 25 May 2002.

55. Other estimates show substantially greater employment generated by defense purchases. These are rather conservative estimates from the Department of Labor.

56. James Kitfeld, "The New Partnership," *National Journal*, 6 August 1994.

57. David C. Morrison, "Painful Separation," *National Journal*, (3 March 1990): 768–73.

58. John DiIulio, "Federal Crime Policy," *Brookings Review*, (winter 1999): 17–21.

59. V. Beiser, "Why the Big Apple Feels Safer," *Macleans* 108 (11 September 1995): 39ff.

60. Generally young adults are the most prone to commit crimes; this group has been declining rapidly as a percentage of the American population.

61. See Dan Eggen, "Major Crimes in US Increase: 2001 Rise Follows 9 Years of Decline," *Washington Post*, 23 June 2002.
62. Hoover himself had a somewhat more complex career. See Anthony Summers, *Official and Confidential* (New York: Putnam, 1993).
63. This organization became very visible during the siege of the Branch Davidian compound in Waco, Texas, in 1993.
64. Actually it does not exhaust the list of federal enforcement activities, e.g., law enforcement by park rangers (Department of the Interior) in national parks.
65. John DiIulio, "Crime," in *Setting Domestic Priorities: What Can Government Do?* ed. Henry J. Aaron and Charles L Schultze (Washington, D.C.: Brookings Institution, 1992).
66. Included here was the (in)famous "midnight basketball"—keeping recreation centers in poorer areas open long hours to give young people something more constructive to do than commit crimes.
67. For a discussion of this controversy in the context of the Clinton crime bill, see W. John Moore, "Shooting in the Dark," *National Journal*, 1(2 February 1994): 358–63.
68. See "Crime in California: Three Strikes, You're Out," *Economist* 330 (15 January 1994): 29–32; and Michael G. Turner, "Three Strikes and You're Out Legislation: A National Assessment," *Federal Probation* 59 (1995): 16–35.
69. Committee on Ways and Means, U.S. House of Representatives, "Children and Families at Risk" (Washington, D.C.: Government Printing Office, January 1994).
70. This appears to be especially true for child and spousal abuse. See David J. Kolko, "Characteristics of Child Victims of Physical Abuse," *Journal of Interpersonal Violence* 7 (1992): 244–76; and Cathy Spatz Widom, "Avoidance of Criminality in Abused and Neglected Children," *Psychiatry* 54 (1991): 162–74.
71. Herman Goldstein, *Problem-Oriented Policing* (New York: McGraw-Hill, 1990).
72. U.S. Bureau of Justice Statistics, *State Prison Expenditures,* annual.
73. Some students appear to think that the two experiences are equally pleasant.
74. Most correctional officials oppose these changes, arguing that all this will do is make the prison population more restive and difficult to control.
75. The amendment is worded as follows: "A well regulated Militia, being necessary to the security of a free State, the right of the people to keep and bear Arms, shall not be infringed."
76. Federal Bureau of Investigation, *Crime in the United States* (Washington, D.C.: Government Printing Office, annual).
77. The act was named after James Brady, President Reagan's press secretary, who was wounded severely in the attempted assassination of Reagan in 1981. After that experience, his wife, Sarah Brady, became a vigorous advocate of gun control.
78. Peter H. Stone, "Under the Gun," *National Journal* 25 (5 June 1993): 1334–38; and Holly Idelson and Paul Nyhan, "Gun Rights and Restrictions: The Territory Reconfigured," *Congressional Quarterly Weekly Report* 51 (24 April 1993): 1021–27.
79. "Gun Owners Don't Fit Stereotypes," *USA Today*/CNN/Gallup poll, reported in *USA Today*, 30 December 1993.
80. George Pettinico, "Crime and Punishment: America Changes Its Mind," *Public Perspective* 5 (September/October 1994), 29.

81. Welsh S. White, *The Death Penalty in the Nineties: An Examination of the Modern System of Capital Punishment* (Ann Arbor: University of Michigan Press, 1991).

82. *Furman v. Georgia*, 408 U.S. 238 (1972).

83. Linda Greenhouse, "Justices Bar Death Penalty for Retarded Defendants," *New York Times*, 21 June 2002.

84. Gregory D. Russell, *The Death Penalty and Racial Bias: Overturning Supreme Court Assumptions* (Westport, Conn.: Greenwood, 1994).

85. This may not be strictly a constitutional argument, since the Constitution and its amendments do not mention economics as a forbidden category for differentiating among individuals.

86. Stephen Reinhardt, "The Supreme Court, the Death Penalty and the Harris Case," *Yale Law Journal* 102 (1992): 205–22.

87. Marcia Coyle, "Blackmun's Turnabout on the Death Penalty," *National Law Journal* 16 (7 March 1994): 39.

88. This is called "Mirandizing" an arrestee, after Ernesto Miranda, whose conviction was overturned because he was not told of his right to remain silent (*Miranda v. Arizona*, 384 U.S. 436 [1966]).

89. Kenneth B. Noble, "Ruling Helps Prosecution of Simpson," *New York Times*, 20 September 1994.

90. Prisons are already dangerous enough. See Mark S. Fleisher, *Warehousing Violence* (Newbury Park, Calif.: Sage, 1989); and George M. Anderson, "Prison Violence: Victims behind Bars," *America* 159 (26 November 1988): 430–33.

91. W. A. Corbitt, "Violent Crimes among Juveniles," *FBI Law Enforcement Bulletin 69* (June 2000): 18–21.

92. See a discussion of this idea in chapter 3.

93. Moore, "Shooting in the Dark."

94. Senator Alphonse D'Amato (R-N.Y.) went on the Senate floor singing a parody of "Old MacDonald Had a Farm" to complain about the "pork" in the legislation.

95. "Crime Control Issues," *Congressional Digest* 73 (June 1994): 169–70.

96. Morris P. Fiorina, "An Era of Divided Government," *Political Science Quarterly* 107 (1992): 387–410. But see Charles O. Jones, *The President in a Separated System* (Washington, D.C.: Brookings Institution, 1994).

97. Neil A. Lewis, "President Foresees Safer U.S.," *New York Times*, 27 August 1994.

98. Contained in this total is the "midnight basketball" that was so prominent in the negative comments about the bill. See Don Terry, "Basketball at Midnight: 'Hope' on a Summer Eve," *New York Times*, 19 August 1994.

99. See Richard Rose, "On the Priorities of Government," *European Journal of Political Research* 4 (1973): 247–89.

Chapter 15

1. See John Kenneth White, *The Values Divide: American Politics and Culture in Transition* (New York: Chatham House, 2002).

2. See Gilbert Meilaender, "The Point of a Ban, or How to Think about Stem Cell Research," *Hastings Center Report* 31 (2001): 9–16; and "Stem Cell Research: Confronting Scientific and Moral Issues," *Congressional Digest* 80 (2001): 225–56.

3. By "line," scientists mean a collection of cells derived from a common background. The common genetic background of the cells makes research less subject to possible spurious findings.

4. "The Politics of Genes: America's Next Ethical War," *The Economist* 359 (14 April 2001): 21–24.

5. Neil Munro, "Changing the Cloning Debate," *National Journal*, 26 January 2002.

6. School prayer may approach being bargainable in this way. If enough vouchers are made available, parents who want their children in schools where prayer is permitted may be able to find those opportunities, while the public schools remain more secular. Some advocates, however, believe that the absence of school prayer undermines the fundamental values of the country, while opponents argue that public support for religious schools is fundamentally wrong.

7. On policy framing, see D. A. Schon and M. Rein, *Frame Selection: On Solving Intractable Policy Disputes* (New York: Basic Books, 1994).

8. The right of privacy is itself implied rather than stated in the Constitution. See Madeleine Mercedes Plascenia, *Privacy and the Constitution* (New York: Garland, 1999).

9. Lawrence Tribe, *Abortion: The Clash of Absolutes* (New York: Norton, 1992), 29.

10. In *Doe v. Bolton* (1973) the Court ruled that not only could abortions not be criminalized, but the states could not make then unreasonably difficult to obtain.

11. Karen O'Connor, *No Neutral Ground: Abortion Politics in an Age of Absolutes* (Boulder, Colo.: Westview, 1996).

12. The logic is that this is a major decision that is irreversible. Further, many other medical procedures for males or females may require parental approval. The intended effect, of course, is to prevent the female minor from having the procedure, either because the parent will not approve it or because there is fear of even discussing the possibility.

13. On instruments, see chapter 5.

14. The interstate commerce clause (Article 1, section 8, clause 3) has been used in a variety of settings to provide Congress with the power to regulate in areas that might not appear to be so directly economic, for example, civil rights.

15. Justice David Souter was assumed to be pro-life when appointed by President George H. W. Bush in 1990, but, instead, he has tended to side with the pro-choice majority on the Court.

16. Barry D. Adam, *The Rise of the Gay and Lesbian Movement* (New York: Twayne, 1995).

17. The position, along with that of most mainstream Protestant churches, has been to "hate the sin but love the sinner."

18. One of the more extreme examples occurred after the 2001 terrorist attacks in New York and Washington D.C. Religious right leaders Jerry Falwell and Pat Robertson argued that the terrorists were facilitated by the undermining of the moral fiber of the country by gay rights advocates, as well as other "secularists." See Gustav Niebuhr, "Falwell Apologizes for Saying an Angry God Allowed Attacks," *New York Times*, 18 September 2001.

19. Mike Allen, "Bush Allows Death Benefits to Gays," *Washington Post*, 26 June 2002.

20. This was in many cases simply a more polite and legalistic version of the first argument.

21. This appears to come in conflict with the "full faith and credit" provisions of the Constitution.

22. *Engle v. Vitale*, 370 U.S. 421 (1962).

23. See *Wallace v. Jaffree*, 472 U.S. 38 (1985).

24. *Cochran v. Board of Education*, 281 U.S. 370 (1930).

25. *Everson v. Board of Education*, 330 U.S. 1 (1947).

26. *Lemon v. Kurzman*, 403 U.S. 602 (1971).

27. *Roemer v. Maryland*, 426 U.S. 736 (1976).

28. See *Mitchell v. Helms* (2000).

29. *Board of Education of the Kiryas Joel School District v. Grument* (1994).

30. Charles Lane, "Court Upholds Ohio School Vouchers," *Washington Post*, 28 June 2002.

31. In fairness, a number of scientists are concerned about those gaps. For a defense, see Stephen Jay Gould, *The Structure of Evolutionary Theory* (Cambridge, Mass.: Harvard University Press, 2002).

Chapter 16

1. Edward C. Gramlich, *Benefit-Cost Analysis for Government Programs* (Englewood Cliffs, N.J.: Prentice Hall, 1981).

2. Steven Kelman, "Cost-Benefit Analysis: An Ethical Critique," *Regulation*, 1981, 33–40.

3. Kenneth Arrow, *Social Choice and Individual Values* (New York: Wiley, 1963); and Allan Feldman, *Welfare Economics and Social Choice Theory* (Boston: Martinus Nijhoff, 1986).

4. P. Hennipman, "Pareto Optimality: Value Judgment or Analytical Tool?" in J. S. Cramer, A. Heertje, and P. Venekamp, *Relevance and Precision* (New York: North-Holland, 1976).

5. Nicholas Kaldor, "Welfare Propositions of Economics and Interpersonal Comparisons of Utility," *Economic Journal* 49 (1939): 549–52; and John R. Hicks, "The Valuation of the Social Income," *Economica* 7 (1940): 105–24.

6. Richard Posner, *The Economics of Justice* (Cambridge, Mass.: Harvard University Press, 1983).

7. E. J. Mishan, *Cost-Benefit Analysis*, exp. ed. (New York: Praeger, 1967), 24–54.

8. David Whittington and Duncan MacRae Jr., "The Issue of Standing in Cost-Benefit Analysis," *Journal of Policy Analysis and Management* 5 (1986): 665–82.

9. E. J. Mishan, "The Post-War Literature on Externalities: An Interpretative Essay," *Journal of Economic Literature* 16 (1978): 1–28; and Neva R. Goodwin, *As If the Future Mattered: Translating Social and Economic Theory into Human Behavior* (Ann Arbor: University of Michigan Press, 1996).

10. John Martin Gilroy, "The Ethical Poverty of Cost-Benefit Methods: Autonomy, Efficiency and Public Policy Choice," *Policy Sciences* 25 (1992): 83–102.

11. "The TVA—Hardy Survivor," *The Economist* 312 (1 July 1989): 22–23.

12. Edith Stokey and Richard Zeckhauser, *A Primer for Policy Analysis* (New York: Norton, 1978), 149–52.

13. This is referred to as a "hedonic price model," in which the contributions of intangibles to price are assessed. See Paul Portney, "Housing Prices, Health Effects and

Valuing Reductions in the Risk of Death," *Journal of Environmental Economics and Management* 8 (1981): 72–78.

14. Robin Gregory, Donald McGregor, and Sarah Lichtenstein, "Assessing the Quality of Expressed Preference Measures of Value," *Journal of Economic Behavior and Organization* 17 (1992): 277–92.

15. *The Road Back: Endangered Species Recovery* (Washington, D.C.: U.S. Department of the Interior, 1998). See chapter 13.

16. Peter Passell, "Polls May Help Government Decide the Worth of Nature," *New York Times*, 6 September 1993. See also J. A. Hausman, *Contingent Valuation: A Critical Assessment* (Amsterdam: North-Holland, 1993).

17. Robert E. Niewijk, "Misleading Quantification: The Contingent Valuation of Environmental Quality," *Regulation* 17, no. 1 (1994): 60–71.

18. Steven E. Rhoads, ed., *Valuing Life: Public Policy Dilemmas* (Boulder, Colo.: Westview, 1980); and W. Kip Viscusi, "Alternative Approaches to Valuing the Health Impact of Accidents: Liability Law and Prospective Evaluations," *Law and Contemporary Problems* 46 (1983): 49–68.

19. "What's a Life Worth? 9/11 Fund Stirs Anger," *USA Today*, 8 January 2002; and David W. Chen, "Hundreds of 9/11 Families File for Right to Sue Port Authority," *New York Times*, 10 July 2002.

20. Jack Hirschleifer and David L. Shapiro, "The Treatment of Risk and Uncertainty," in *Public Expenditure and Policy Analysis*, 3d ed., ed. Robert H. Haveman and Julius Margolis (Boston: HoughtonMifflin, 1983), 145–66.

21. For a general discussion of the problems of discounting, see Robert E. Goodin, "Discounting Discounting," *Journal of Public Policy* 2 (1982): 53–71.

22. William J. Baumol, "On the Social Rate of Discount," *American Economic Review* 10 (1968): 788–802.

23. Marthe R. Gold et al., *Cost-Effectiveness in Health and Medicine* (New York: Oxford University Press, 1996).

24. Ray Robinson, "Cost-Effectiveness Analysis," *British Medical Journal* 307 (25 September 1993): 793–95.

25. David M. Eddy, "Cost-Effectiveness Analysis: Will It be Accepted?" *Journal of the American Medical Association* 268 (1992): 132–36.

26. Alphonse G. Holtman, "Beyond Efficiency: Economists and Distributional Analysis," in *Policy Analysis and Economics: Developments, Tensions, Prospects*, ed. David L. Weimer (Boston: Kluwer, 1991); and Elio Londero, *Benefits and Beneficiaries: An Introduction to Estimating Distributional Effects in Cost-Benefit Analysis*, 2d ed. (Washington, D.C.: Inter-American Development Bank, 1996).

27. Peter Self, *Econocrats and the Policy Process: The Politics and Philosophy of Cost-Benefit Analysis* (London: Macmillan, 1975).

28. Peter Self, "Nonsense on Stilts: Cost-Benefit Analysis and the Roskill Commission," *Political Quarterly* 10 (1970): 30–63; and Kelman, "Cost-Benefit Analysis."

Chapter 17

1. See Alan F. Zundel, "The Futility of Empirical Policy Analysis without Normative Policy Analysis: The Case of the Living Wage," *Public Integrity* 4 (2002): 101–14.

2. Russell Hardin, *Morality within the Limit of Reason* (Chicago: University of Chicago Press, 1988).

3. See Martin E. Marty, *The One and the Many: America's Struggle for the Common Good* (Cambridge, Mass.: Harvard University Press, 1997).

4. Victor Grassian, *Moral Reasoning* (Englewood Cliffs, N.J.: Prentice Hall, 1981).

5. Arnold Meltsner, *Policy Analysts in the Bureaucracy* (Berkeley: University of California Press, 1976), 3–25.

6. Abraham Kaplan, "Social Ethics and the Sanctity of Life," in *Life or Death: Ethics and Options*, ed. D. H. Labby (London: Macmillan, 1968), 58–71.

7. Guido Calabresi and Phillip Bobbitt, *Tragic Choices* (New York: Norton, 1978), 21. See also B. Guy Peters, "Tragic Choices: Administrative Rulemaking and Policy Choice," in *Ethics in Public Service*, ed. Richard A. Chapman (Edinburgh: University of Edinburgh Press, 1993).

8. Sheryl Gay Stolberg, "Live and Let Die over Transplants," *New York Times,* 5 April 1998.

9. As a part of its rationing program, the State of Oregon made this determination. The justification was primarily utilitarian, assuming that the treatments would be less beneficial for people with substance abuse problems.

10. Dave Davis, Ted Wendling, and Joan Mazzolini, "U.S. Order Revisions in Rules on Transplants: Current System's Range of Waits is Called Unfair," *Cleveland Plain Dealer*, 27 March 1998.

11. Bonnie Steinbock, *Life before Birth: The Moral and Legal Status of Embryos and Fetuses* (New York: Oxford University Press, 1992).

12. Ronald Dworkin, *Life's Dominion: An Argument about Abortion, Euthanasia and Individual Freedom* (New York: Knopf, 1993).

13. Steven H. Miles, "Doctors and Their Patients' Suicides," *Journal of the American Medical Association* 271 (8 June 1994): 1786–88; and Daniel Avila, "Medical Treatment Rights of Older Persons and Persons with Disabilities," *Issues in Law and Medicine* 9 (1994): 345–60.

14. Jonathan Glover, *Causing Deaths and Saving Lives* (Harmondsworth, England: Penguin, 1977).

15. Robert Nozick, *Anarchy, The State, and Utopia* (New York: Basic Books, 1974).

16. This individualistic and conservative interpretation of the law was common during the late nineteenth and early twentieth centuries. See, for example, *Lochner v. New York* (1905).

17. Robert E. Goodin, *Reasons for Welfare* (Princeton: Princeton University Press, 1988), 312–31; and Christian Bay, *The Structure of Freedom* (New York: Atheneum, 1965).

18. John Kultgen, *Autonomy and Intervention: Paternalism in the Caring Life* (New York: Oxford University Press, 1994).

19. Desmond King, *Illiberal Policies in Liberal States* (Oxford: Oxford University Press, 1999).

20. See Dennis A. Robbins, *Ethical and Legal Issues in Home Health and Long-term Care: Challenges and Solutions* (Gaithersburg, Md.: Aspen, 1996); and Bonnie Steinbock and Alastair Norcross, *Killing and Letting Die*, 2d. ed. (New York: Fordham University Press, 1994).

21. Some conservatives have argued, for example, that even professional licensure of

doctors and lawyers should be abandoned in the name of free choice. In the long run, it is argued, the market would take care of the problem.

22. Jerome S. Legge, *Traffic Safety Reform in the United States and Great Britain* (Pittsburgh: University of Pittsburgh Press, 1991); and Kenneth E. Warner, "Bags, Buckles and Belts: The Debate over Mandatory Passive Restraints in Automobiles," *Journal of Health Politics, Policy and Law* 8 (1983): 44–75.

23. Howard M. Leichter, *Free to be Foolish* (Princeton: Princeton University Press, 1991).

24. The FDA has to some extent relaxed its usual guidelines for drugs that may help victims of AIDS and a few other extremely deadly diseases, for example, "Lou Gehrig's Disease." See Harold Edgar and David J. Rothman, "New Rules for New Drugs: The Challenge of AIDS to the Regulatory Process," in *A Disease of Society*, ed. Dorothy Nelkin, David P. Willis, and Scott V. Parris (Cambridge: Cambridge University Press, 1991). See also Peter Davis, *Contested Ground: Public Purpose and Private Interest in the Regulation of Prescription Drugs* (New York: Oxford University Press, 1996).

25. Sissela Bok, *Lying: Moral Choice in Public and Private Life* (New York: Vintage, 1979).

26. Loch K. Johnson, *Secret Agencies: U.S. Intelligence in a Hostile World* (New Haven: Yale University Press, 1996).

27. See Raymond L. Goldstein and John K. Schoor, *Demanding Democracy after Three Mile Island* (Gainesville: University of Florida Press, 1991).

28. James C. Petersen, *Whistleblowing: Ethical and Legal Issues in Expressing Dissent* (Dubuque, Iowa: Kendall/Hunt, 1986); Daniel P. Westman, *Whistleblowing: The Law of Retaliatory Discharge* (Washington, D.C.: Bureau of National Affairs, 1991); and U.S. Merit Systems Protection Board, *Whistleblowing in the Federal Government* (Washington, D.C.: USMSPB, 1993).

29. See, respectively, Edward Weisband and Thomas M. Franck, *Resignation in Protest* (New York: Penguin, 1975); and David Burnham, "Paper Chase of a Whistleblower," *New York Times*, 16 October 1982.

30. William T. Gormley, *Taming the Bureaucracy: Muscles, Prayers and Other Strategies* (Princeton: Princeton University Press, 1989). In addition to the academic literature on the freedom of information, the novel *So Now You Know* by Michael Frayn (London: Penguin, 1992) provides interesting insights into the question.

31. See Joseph S. Nye, Philip D. Zelikow, and David C. King, eds., *Why People Don't Trust Government* (Cambridge, Mass.: Harvard University Press, 1997).

32. Michael Walzer, "Political Action: The Problem of Dirty Hands," *Philosophy and Public Affairs* (1973): 160–80; and Thomas Nagel, "Ruthlessness in Public Life," in *Public and Private Life*, ed. Stuart Hampshire (Cambridge: Cambridge University Press, 1978).

33. Jan-Erik Lane, *The Public Sector: Concepts, Models and Approaches* (Newbury Park, Calif.: Sage, 1993).

34. See Robert E. Goodin, *Protecting the Vulnerable: A Re-Analysis of Our Social Responsibilities* (Chicago: University of Chicago Press, 1985). Even such a committed conservative as Charles Murray could argue that "there is no such thing as an undeserving five-year-old"; see his *Losing Ground* (New York: Basic Books, 1984).

35. Richard Allen Epstein, *Takings: Private Property and the Power of Eminent Domain*

(Cambridge, Mass.: Harvard University Press, 1985); and William A. Fischel, *Regulatory Takings: Law, Economics and Politics* (Cambridge, Mass.: Harvard University Press, 1995).

36. Karl Marx, *Criticism of the Gotha Program* (New York: International Universities Press, 1938), vol. 929, 14.

37. For an important attempt to provide such a justification, see Goodin, *Reasons for Welfare,* 287–305. See also Bo Rothstein, *Just Institutions Matter: The Moral and Political Logic of the Universal Welfare State* (Cambridge: Cambridge University Press, 1998).

38. Edith Brown Weiss, *In Fairness to Future Generations: International Law, Common Patrimony, and Intergenerational Equity* (Tokyo: United Nations University, 1988).

39. Peter S. Burton, "Intertemporal Preferences and Intergenerational Equity Considerations in Optimal Resource Harvesting," *Journal of Environmental Economics and Management* 24 (1993): 119–32; and Laurence J. Kotlikoff, *Generational Accounting* (New York: Free Press, 1992).

40. John Rawls, "Justice as Fairness," *Philosophical Review* (1958): 164–94, esp. 166.

41. John Rawls, *A Theory of Justice* (Cambridge, Mass.: Harvard University Press, 1971).

42. Ibid., 19.

43. For an earlier literary treatment of this view of fairness, see L. P. Hartley, *Facial Justice* (London: Hamish Hamilton, 1960). On desert, see George Bernard Shaw, *Doctor's Dilemma.*

44. Epstein, *Takings.*

45. This is obviously related to the utilitarian logic that undergirds cost-benefit analysis.

46. Roberto Alejandro, *The Limits of Rawlsian Justice* (Baltimore: Johns Hopkins University Press, 1998).

47. Richard A. Epstein, *Forbidden Grounds: The Case against Employment Discrimination Laws* (Cambridge, Mass.: Harvard University Press, 1992); and Russell Nieli, ed., *Racial Preference and Racial Justice: The New Affirmative Action Controversy* (Washington, D.C.: Ethics and Public Policy Center, 1991).

48. Douglas E. Ashford, *The Emergence of the Welfare State* (Oxford: Basil Blackwell, 1986). But see T. H. Marshall, *Class, Citizenship, and Social Development* (New York: Doubleday, 1965).

49. See Gareth Davies, *From Opportunity to Entitlement* (Lawrence: University Press of Kansas, 1996).

50. W.E. Leuchtenberg, *Franklin D. Roosevelt and the New Deal, 1932–1940* (New York: Harper & Row, 1963), 133.

51. In a few places, e.g., City University of New York, there was once free higher education as well, but budget constraints have since forced the imposition of fees in those institutions.

52. See also Kimberly J. Cook, *Divided Passions: Public Opinions on Abortion and the Death Penalty* (Boston: Northeastern University Press, 1997).

53. Frances Fox Piven and Richard A. Cloward, *Regulating the Poor,* 2d. ed. (New York: Viking, 1993).

54. Amitai Etzioni, ed., *New Communitarian Thinking: Virtues, Institutions, and Communities* (Charlottesville: University Press of Virginia, 1995).

Index